THE NATIONAL UNDERWRITER COMPANY
a division of ALM Media, LLC

2019 HEALTHCARE REFORM FACTS

Michael D. Thomas, J.D.

The *2020 Healthcare Reform Facts* is the comprehensive, go-to source for information regarding the impact of the Patient Protection and Affordable Care Act (PPACA). Uniquely organized in a convenient and easy-to-understand Question and Answer format, *2020 Healthcare Reform Facts* helps you quickly and confidently find the answers you need to the most frequently asked questions on the PPACA.

This publication helps you ensure that you and your clients are in compliance with the Affordable Care Act by clearly explaining:

- "Medicare for All" and the future of healthcare reform

- Types of health insurance affected by healthcare reform

- Reasons employers should or should not continue to offer health insurance

- Tax incentives for offering health insurance and required coverages

- Tax and other benefits of a grandfathered or grandmothered plan

- How the health insurance exchanges work as well as a host of other valuable information

With *2020 Healthcare Reform Facts,* professionals will be able to provide accurate and authoritative answers to questions related to healthcare reform changes, as well as understand the continuing implementation of the ACA and related legislation, rules, regulations and requirements.

The 2020 edition of *Healthcare Reform Facts* for has been completely revised, featuring:

- 165 newly added questions and answers, including 20 new questions on Short-Term Limited Duration policies and 76 new questions on the future of health care reform

- Update on the continuing legal challenges to the Affordable Care Act

- Updates on the status of Grandfathered Plans and Grandmothered Plans

- New developments with Cafeteria Plans and SIMPLE Cafeteria Plans

- Changes to Medical Loss Ratio and limited wrap around coverage

- Changes in Qualified Health Plan (QHP) certifications

- Changes in how Individual Health Insurance Tax Credits are calculated

- Changes in participation of Health Exchanges from state to federal sites

- Medicaid Expansion update and analysis

- Update in reporting requirements

- Effect of HRAs and QSEHRAs

- Updated deductible values, cost sharing limits, Wellness program information, and Federal Poverty Guidelines

- Changes in Employer Mandate to offer coverage and the penalty for not meeting affordability requirements

- Effect of the repeal of Individual Mandate

- 2020 update on related taxes, such as tanning bed tax, the additional Medicare tax, medical device tax, and Medicare tax on investment income of 3.8%, and the continuing delay in the implementation of the Cadillac Tax

2020 Healthcare Reform Facts brings together the guidance, rules, and regulations from all the governing bodies into one resource, making it easy to find authoritative, insightful, and current answers to healthcare reform questions.

Related Titles Also Available:

- *Social Security & Medicare Facts*

- *Tax Facts on Insurance & Employee Benefits*

- *Tax Facts on Individuals & Small Business*

- *The Advisor's Guide to Long-Term Care*

For customer service questions or to place orders for any of our products, please call 1-800-543-0874.

2020 HEALTHCARE REFORM FACTS

- Employer & Individual Provisions • Financial & Tax Decisions • Compliance, Penalties & Safe Harbors • Employer Mandates • Required Coverages • Required Disclosures & Reporting • Taxes, Fees & Revenue Provisions • Exchanges/Marketplace Rules • Affordability & Cost of Coverage • Eligibility, Enrollment, & Subsidies • Grandfathered and Grandmothered Plans • Status of SHOP • Continuing Legal Challenges • Elimination of Individual Mandate Penalty • TrumpCare: Short-Term Limited Duration Policies • "Medicare For All" and the Future of Healthcare Reform

Michael D. Thomas, J.D.

ISBN 978-1-949506-66-2

THE NATIONAL UNDERWRITER COMPANY

ABOUT THE NATIONAL UNDERWRITER COMPANY
a division of ALM Media, LLC

For over 110 years, The National Underwriter Company, *a division of ALM Media, LLC* has been the first in line with the targeted tax, insurance, and financial planning information you need to make critical business decisions. Boasting nearly a century of expert experience, our reputable Editors are dedicated to putting accurate and relevant information right at your fingertips. With *Tax Facts*, *Tools & Techniques*, *National Underwriter Advanced Markets*, *Field Guide*, *FC&S®*, *FC&S Legal* and other resources available in print, eBook, and online, you can be assured that as the industry evolves National Underwriter will be at the forefront with the thorough and easy-to-use resources you rely on for success.

Update Service Notification

This National Underwriter Company publication is regularly updated to include coverage of developments and changes that affect the content. If you did not purchase this publication directly from The National Underwriter Company, *a division of ALM Media, LLC* and you want to receive these important updates sent on a 30-day review basis and billed separately, please contact us at (800) 543-0874. Or you can mail your request with your name, company, address, and the title of the book to:

The National Underwriter Company
a division of ALM Media, LLC
4157 Olympic Boulevard
Suite 225
Erlanger, KY 41018

If you purchased this publication from The National Underwriter Company, *a division of ALM Media, LLC,* directly, you have already been registered for the update service.

Contact Information

To order any National Underwriter Company title, please

- call 1-800-543-0874, 8-6 ET Monday – Thursday and 8 to 5 ET Friday

- online bookstore at www.nationalunderwriter.com, or

- mail to Orders Department, The National Underwriter Company, *a division of ALM Media, LLC*, 4157 Olympic Blvd., Ste. 225, Erlanger, KY 41018

PREFACE TO THE 2020 EDITION

2020 Healthcare Reform Facts is written for employers and advisors in many specialties including Insurance, Human Resources, Benefits, Finance, Staffing, Law as well as others. Healthcare reform has now been part of the American experience for nearly a decade, leaving an indelible mark on healthcare in the United States. Some healthcare reform changes were incremental, but the cumulative effect has had dramatic effects on all Americans. Changes include creation of the marketplaces, small business tax credits, tax credits for low-income Americans to acquire health insurance coverage, as well as making Medicaid more available to the neediest of our citizens. In the past decade, twenty million have joined the healthcare rolls. The Affordable Care Act has changed the very complexion of health insurance itself by eliminating pre-existing conditions and annual and lifetime dollar limits on coverages, extending the ability of adult children to remain on parents' policies until age 26, and establishing the ten Essential Health Benefits.

The Affordable Care Act remains one of the most contentious and volatile issues on the political and public policy stage, but it continues to survive. The ACA has weathered both minor and substantial adjustments made through regulations, guidance, statutes, operation of law and judicial review. The law has survived over 50 attempts at repeal, with the bill nearly repealed in 2017, saved only by the vote of the late Senator John McCain. The past year has offered perhaps the greatest legal challenge through the Texas federal district court ruling that the reduction of the Individual mandate penalty to zero is unconstitutional and that the individual mandate is not severable from the rest of the law. In the past year, continued change is evidenced by shorter enrollment periods, new CMS guidelines allowing states to implement work requirements for Medicaid, and regulations allowing companies to apply for exemptions from offering or paying for contraceptives because of moral or religious objections. The 2020 election portends more potential change with Democratic legislators proposing new healthcare initiatives including "Medicare for All", Medicare and Medicaid buy-in options, and several public plans. Each is covered in detail in this edition.

This 2020 version continues to be important by incorporating the original provisions of healthcare reform as well as substantially updating the 2019 edition to reflect the many recent developments over the past year. This book continues to offer a thorough and practical discussion of the tax and non-tax rules relating to United States healthcare reform, and the volumes of regulations interpreting the law as well as other guidance issued by the Internal Revenue Service and the Departments of Labor and Health and Human Services.

2020 Healthcare Reform Facts is intended to help employers and their advisors understand, plan for, and comply with the many requirements of federal healthcare reform. To assist readers, important statutes, cases, and regulations are cited throughout the book. The book discusses the federal law's objectives and discusses the factors that have influenced whether the law has worked as intended. Also discussed are some of the loopholes and unintended consequences of the law. The book also discusses several provisions of the original law that did not go into effect, as well as repeals and delays that have occurred in the past year as well as discussion of the changes that have occurred during the Trump administration and how proposed plans could change healthcare reform.

As the reader is no doubt aware, the comprehensive federal changes concerning healthcare have required that employers rethink past practices and choices about whether and how to offer healthcare benefits to employees. As in prior editions, updated forms and sample required notices are provided along with a detailed timeline of when each important provision of the rules goes into effect. I hope that you will find this book useful, both as a resource with answers for your questions as well as a starting point for some of the required notices documentation. Of course, this book does not provide legal advice for specific situations, which should be sought from a competent professional.

Michael D. Thomas
September 2019

ABOUT THE AUTHOR

Michael D. Thomas, J.D.

Michael D. Thomas, is an author and consultant and has served as the Manager of Online Product Development and as a Senior Editor with the National Underwriter Company, a division of ALM Media. In addition, Mike has served as a consultant to the State of Ohio Department of Medicaid and as a writer for "The Digital Broker Podcast", which focuses on insurance technology and operations. Mike currently works with a major commercial healthcare insurance company and provider of Medicare and Medicaid services. In addition to co-authoring *2020 Healthcare Reform Facts*, Mike has been responsible for the editorial process and development of other healthcare and insurance publications including *Advisor's Guide to Long Term Care 2nd Edition, Social Security & Medicare Facts, ERISA Facts, and Health Savings Accounts Facts* for The National Underwriter Company as well as designing, implementing, and managing the *NUPro Healthcare Reform* online service. Mike has also authored numerous articles on healthcare reform, Social Security, Medicare and Insurance issues. In addition, he has developed, hosted, and taught webinars on Healthcare Reform and Social Security, including *"The Affordable Care Act and the Employer Mandate"*, *"The Affordable Care Act and the Cadillac Tax — Use the Delay for Your Advantage!"*, *"How to Successfully Navigate the Latest Changes to the Affordable Care Act"*, and *"The Impact of Social Security on Retirement Plans"*.

Prior to joining National Underwriter, Mike spent over twenty-five years with LexisNexis®, where he was responsible for the editorial content and new product development of new online and traditional legal products, including *Health Law, Insurance Law, Social Security Law, Labor & Employment Law, Family Law*, as well as other legal research tools. In addition, he worked as a Field Agent for Knights of Columbus Insurance specializing in life, health, disability income, long-term care insurance as well as annuity sales.

Mike has a Bachelor of Arts from Tufts University and a Juris Doctorate from the University of Dayton.

ABOUT THE EDITOR

Jason Gilbert, J.D., M.A., is a senior editor with the Practical Insights Division of The National Underwriter Company, a division of ALM Media, LLC. He edits and develops publications related to tax and insurance products, including titles in the *Advisor's Guide* and the *Tools & Techniques* series of investment and planning products. He also develops content for National Underwriter's other financial services publications and online products. He has worked on insurance and tax publications for more than nine years.

Jason has been a practicing attorney for more than a dozen years in the areas of criminal defense, products liability, and regulatory enforcement actions. Prior to joining National Underwriter, his experience in the insurance and tax fields has included work as a Westlaw contributor for Thomson Reuters and a tax advisor and social media contributor for Intuit.

He is an honors graduate from Wright State University and holds a J.D. from the University of Cincinnati College of Law as well as a master's degree in Economics from Miami University in Ohio.

EDITORIAL SERVICES

Connie L. Jump, Senior Manager, Editorial Operations

Patti O'Leary, Senior Editorial Assistant

TABLE OF CONTENTS

List of Questions .... Page xi
Part I: Goals and Major Components of Healthcare Reform .... Q 1 – Q 123
Part II: Impact of Healthcare Reform on Employer Fringe Benefits .... Q 124 – Q 139
Part III: Timeline for Implementation of Provisions:
     What Needs to Be Done and When .... Q 140 – Q 141
Part IV: Health Reform Provisions That Have Been Repealed, Expired,
     or Not Implemented... Q 142 – Q 152
Part V: Small Business Provisions .... Q 153 – Q 192
Part VI: Grandfathered Health Plans .... Q 193 – Q 235
Part VII: PHSA Coverage Mandates and Enforcement .... Q 236 – Q 402
Part VIII: Required Disclosures and Information Reporting .... Q 403 – Q 514
Part IX: Tax Increases and Revenue Raisers .... Q 515 – Q 613
Part X: State Insurance Exchanges (Marketplaces) .... Q 614 – Q 655
Part XI: The Employer Mandate .... Q 656 – Q 725
Part XII: Short-term Limited Duration Health Insurance .... Q 726 – Q 749
Part XIII: "Medicare for All" and the Future of Healthcare Reform.............. Q 750 – Q 825

APPENDICES

Model SBC and Uniform Glossary ....Appendix A

U.S. Department of Labor Model Notices ....Appendix B
     Model Notice of Final Internal Adverse Benefit Determination
     Model Notice of Adverse Benefit Determination
     Model Notice of Final External Revision Decision
     Employer Coverage Tool
     FLSA with Plans
     FLSA without Plans

Health Reimbursement Arrangement... Appendix C

Index..Page 661

Keep Up with Critical Healthcare Reform Changes

Critical legislative changes that affect the subject matter in these books will be posted at http://pro.nuco.com/booksupplements/healthcarereform. Bookmark the site so that you can easily access new critical information that affects our clients and your business.

COMPLETE LIST OF QUESTIONS
PART I: GOALS AND MAJOR COMPONENTS OF HEALTHCARE REFORM

Overview

1. What is healthcare reform?

2. What terms and acronyms will be used repeatedly in this book?

3. What does health reform do?

4. Has the Affordable Care Act actually worked to reduce health care costs?

5. What is the focus of this book?

6. What benefits are regulated by health reform?

7. What health benefits are not affected by health reform?

8. Do the provisions of healthcare reform only apply to businesses and residents in the United States?

9. Do the provisions of healthcare reform only apply international students living in the United States?

10. Where are the provisions of the health reform law found?

11. How does healthcare reform provide for expanded coverage?

12. Has healthcare reform been revised since it was enacted?

Health Coverage Not Affected by Healthcare Reform: "Excepted Benefits" and Retiree-Only Plans

13. What benefits are not governed by the Patient Protection and Affordable Care Act?

14. What are the "excepted benefits" that are not covered by the health reform law?

15. What are the retiree-only health plans that are not governed by PPACA?

16. Is the retiree-only exemption available for self-funded and insured plans?

17. From which PPACA mandates are retiree-only plans exempt?

18. Does the 2022 "Cadillac Tax" apply to retiree-only health plans?

19. Who are "current employees" for purposes of the retiree-only exemption?

20. What should plan sponsors do to demonstrate that they have established a retiree-only plan that satisfies the exemption?

21. What will happen if a plan sponsor does not amend its group health plan to carve out retirees into a separate retiree-only ERISA plan?

22. Can a plan sponsor amend its plan to carve out retirees into a retiree-only plan and preserve the grandfather status of the plan for current (i.e., active) employees?

23. Is a retiree with an option to receive retiree health coverage from a former employer eligible to buy insurance on an exchange (marketplace) and receive, if qualified, a subsidy?

24. How does the retiree-only exemption relate to the Retiree Drug Subsidy Program (RDS) and Early Retiree Reinsurance Program (ERRP)?

Employer and Individual Mandates

See Part XI for a Complete Discussion of the Employer Mandate Provisions and Appendix B Copies of Several Mandatory Notices

25. What mandates were delayed by the IRS in July 2015?

26. What final regulations have been issued regarding employer information reporting for healthcare reform for employers subject to the employer mandate?

27. What did Notice 2013-45 specify regarding information reporting?

28. What is the Employer Mandate?

29. How do the State Exchanges obtain information on affordability for an individual?

30. How do the two Employer Mandate penalties work?

31. Is the employer mandate penalty tax-deductible?

32. How is the 95 percent threshold of the employer's employees calculated?

33. Does the employer have to offer coverage for all days of the month in order to avoid the penalty?

34. How are full-time and full-time-equivalent employees (FTEs) calculated?

35. What are some examples of the Employer Mandate tax penalties?

36. What reporting is required by employers, other than the W-2 requirements?

37. How do the information reporting requirements and the Employer Mandate penalties interact?

38. Were employees still able to receive premium tax credits in 2014?

39. Does a state health insurance exchange notify the employer if an individual is determined to be eligible for the income tax credit?

40. Under what circumstances may employers otherwise subject to the tax qualify for exemption?

41. What effect will a state's decision whether to expand Medicaid under the ACA have on the employer mandate penalty?

42. How does an employer appeal the tax penalties?

43. What other issues must be considered by employers in planning for the employer mandate tax penalties?

44. Is there any employer relief for misclassified independent contractors in the final employer mandate regulations?

45. What is (or was) the Individual Mandate?

46. What is the effect of the Executive Order signed by President Trump in regard to the Affordable Care Act?

47. Have there been clarifications as to when health insurance needs to be obtained to avoid penalties under the Affordable Care Act?

48. Has the individual mandate worked to induce individuals to purchase health insurance?

Controlled Group and Affiliated Service Group Issues

49. Are there special issues for controlled groups and affiliated service groups?

50. What are the types of Controlled Groups and how are they treated under the Employer Mandate?

51. Have applicable employers terminated their health plans so that employees must purchase health insurance on a state exchange because the penalties are much less than the costs of a group health plan?

PEO (Staffing Industry) Compliance with Employer Mandate

52. Will the employee mandate and related penalties apply to Professional Employer Organizations (PEO), also known as the staffing industry?

53. How does the nature of a PEO's clients affect how the PEO may handle the employer mandate?

54. What specific issues will PEOs likely need to consider in regard to the employer mandate?

Impact of the Repeal of the Individual Mandate Penalty on Health Care

55. What is the expected impact of the repeal of the individual mandate penalty on healthcare?

Individual Health Insurance Premium Tax Credits

56. Who is entitled to a subsidy in the form of a tax credit for purchasing health insurance from a state exchange?

57. How is income determined for defining who is eligible for a subsidy for health insurance purchased on an exchange?

58. What is the effect of same-sex marriage recognition rules for exchange determinations of premium tax credits and for Medicaid and CHIP?

59. Can the federal government subsidize health insurance premiums for people in states that use an exchange run by the federal government rather than the state?

60. Who are "qualified individuals" for purposes of the final regulation for the Code section 36B credit?

61. What is the purpose of the Code section 36B credit regulation?

62. How did the October 2013 "No Subsidies without Verification Act" change the rules for verification of individuals, financial information on the healthcare exchanges (marketplaces)?

63. How can a qualified individual receive a Code section 36B credit?

64. How does the Code section 36B credit work for related individuals?

65. How can employers use the Code section 36B in its health-insurance planning?

66. May an employer establish an employee contribution schedule and allow employees to be eligible for reduced contributions if they provide evidence that their required contributions would otherwise be in excess of the affordability limits?

67. Can Applicable Large Employers (ALEs) with fifty or more full-time and Full-Time Equivalent (FTE) employees avoid the employer mandate penalty by offering an actuarially equivalent contribution to an HSA, HRA, or FSA so that employees can buy health care coverage on the exchange or in the private non-group market?

68. What is Minimum Essential Coverage (MEC)?

69. What individuals are not subject to the Individual Mandate?

70. Which persons are not subject to the individual mandate because they are not "applicable individuals"?

71. What are the requirements to obtain a hardship exemption?

72. How long do hardship exemptions last?

73. Is there a hardship exemption for being unemployed?

74. Can a person with a hardship exemption enroll in a catastrophic plan?

75. What do catastrophic plans cover and what do they cost?

76. Is the individual mandate tax penalty being enforced even though it has been repealed?

Health Plan and Insurance Changes: Coverage Mandates

77. What are the ten Essential Health Benefits (EHBs) required by the Affordable Care Act? How do state health insurance mandates relate to them?

78. Do the FAQs relax the fixed indemnity standards and allow per-service payments as excepted benefits if the insured has other minimal essential coverage?

79. How has the Essential Health Benefits (EHB) mandate been implemented?

80. What is required to become a state selected EHB-benchmark plan?

81. What new requirements are there for grandfathered and grandmothered health plans?

82. What new requirements are there for new and nongrandfathered health plans?

83. What are grandmothered plans?

84. Which states still have grandmothered plans?

85. Have the number of grandfathered and grandmothered plans declined?

State Health Insurance Exchanges

86. What are the state health insurance exchanges?

87. How do employers use exchanges?

88. What factors should be considered when enrolling in SHOP?

89. Are there any issues with state exchanges?

90. How do individuals apply for health insurance from an exchange?

91. What is the loophole in the law as it applies to exchange purchased insurance and its impact on insureds and providers?

92. What are the functions of the state health insurance exchanges?

93. What are the areas over which HHS has responsibility for the state health insurance exchanges?

94. What are the primary federal requirements for state exchanges?

95. What is a Qualified Health Plan (QHP)?

96. How are state health insurance exchanges regulated?

97. What was the process used by states to set up health insurance exchanges?

98. What types of exchanges are operated by each of the states?

99. What is the Navigator program and what are the positions?

100. Are there any prohibitions for Agents and Brokers who want to apply for Navigator funds under this Funding Opportunity?

101. Are tribal entities eligible to apply to be a Navigator?

102. Are individuals eligible to apply to be a Navigator?

103. Is an entity that sells Medicaid or Medicare managed care plans eligible to apply to be a Navigator?

104. Is there anyone who is ineligible to be a Navigator?

105. Do Navigators have to maintain a physical presence in the FFE service area it is approved to serve?

106. What is the status of federal SHOP exchanges for small employers?

107. What are the requirements for small employers to get employer tax credits through the Small Business Health Options Program (SHOP)?

108. What are the rules for the small business health insurance tax credit?

109. What are the small business insurance exchange revisions, and SHOP enrollment periods?

110. What is the Employer Exchange Notice requirement?

111. What is the role of health insurance brokers or agents in the state health insurance exchanges?

Employer Funds for Insurance Purchased on State Exchange and ERISA

112. Are individual health or other policies purchased in whole or part with employer funds an ERISA plan and subject to COBRA?

113. How does ERISA define a group health plan? How does the IRS define a group plan?

114. What is the DOL safe harbor on ERISA plan status?

115. What is the three-part test to determine whether an ERISA plan exists?

116. What other factors have been used to determine whether a plan does fall under ERISA?

117. Which courts have ruled that plans are not employee welfare benefits plans under ERISA despite employee contributions to them?

118. What are examples of cases with rulings that plans with employer financial involvement do fall under ERISA?

The U.S. Supreme Court Decisions on Health Reform

119. What is the impact of the U.S. Supreme Court decisions on the constitutionality of the health reform law?

120. What is the potential impact of the lawsuit filed by the group of states attorneys-general (Texas v. U.S. Dept. of HHS)?

Health Reform's Medicaid Expansion

121. What is the current status of Medicaid Expansion in the fifty states?

122. What is the Medicaid expansion in the Affordable Care Act?

123. Can a state later change its decision as to whether to participate in the Medicaid expansion and withdrawl?

PART II: IMPACT OF HEALTHCARE REFORM ON EMPLOYER FRINGE BENEFITS

Fringe Benefit Tax Planning

124. Why should employers verify whether they have a grandfathered health plan?

125. Why should an eligible employer consider a SIMPLE cafeteria plan?

126. What are the limits on health FSAs in cafeteria plans (also called flex plans)?

127. Is a MERP, HRA, FSA, HSA, employer payment plan or cafeteria plan subject to the prohibition on annual and lifetime dollar limits or the preventive care requirements?

128. Are strategies promoting employers reimbursing employees for the purchase of individual health insurance approved by the IRS?

129. Are executive physical and executive diagnostic reimbursement plans still available under Healthcare reform?

130. Will student health insurance payments or reimbursement by the educational institution violate IRS Notice 2013-54 and IRS Notice 2016-17 regarding impermissible payments for individual health insurance?

131. Can an employer with employees in different states with different employer health insurance plans in each state integrate these plans with an employer funded Health Reimbursement Account (HRA)?

132. Can a HSA be combined with exchange-purchased High Deductible Health Insurance Plans (HDHP)?

133. Must preventive services be provided by nongrandfathered HSA-eligible HDHPs?

134. May an employer reimburse the cost of Medigap insurance for those employees enrolled in Medicare?

135. Are there any differences in treatment of same-sex spouses in regard to HSAs, cafeteria plans, health FSAs and DCAPs?

136. Are third-party payors permitted to make premium payments to health insurance issuers for Qualified Health Plans on behalf of enrolled individuals?

137. Could cafeteria plan elections to purchase health insurance be changed midyear to purchase insurance on an exchange or in the employer-offered plan?

138. How can employers use a state healthcare insurance exchange (marketplace) and other rules to their advantage?

139. What is limited wrap-around healthcare coverage and how can it be used by employers with at least some employees purchasing subsidized exchange health insurance?

PART III: TIMELINE FOR IMPLEMENTATION OF PROVISIONS: WHAT NEEDS TO BE DONE AND WHEN

140. What are the major components of healthcare reform and when are they effective?

141. If an employer offers an HRA and a group health plan but there is limited participation, will the HRA pass Code section 105(h)?

PART IV: HEALTH REFORM PROVISIONS THAT HAVE BEEN REPEALED, EXPIRED, OR NOT IMPLEMENTED

Free Choice Vouchers – Repealed

142. What were free choice vouchers and what were they intended to do?

143. When was the provision for free choice vouchers repealed?

144. What was the impact of the repeal of free choice vouchers?

Expanded 1099 Requirements – Repealed

145. What were the repealed 1099 requirements?

146. When and how were the expanded 1099 requirements repealed?

147. Did the repeal of the expanded 1099 reporting repeal the penalties for 1099 failures that were increased in 2010?

148. Why were the expanded 1099 requirements repealed?

Early Retiree Reinsurance Program (ERRP) – Expired

149. How was the Early Retiree Reinsurance Program (ERRP) intended to work?

Federal Long-Term Care Benefit – Not Implemented

150. What was the federal long-term care benefit for which employees could have elected to pay?

151. Why was the federal long-term care program cancelled by HHS?

Automatic Enrollment Repealed

152. Why was the automatic enrollment provision repealed?

PART V: SMALL BUSINESS PROVISIONS

Employer Income Tax Credit for Health Insurance

153. Which employers are eligible for the tax credit for the purchase of health insurance available in 2010 and thereafter?

154. Can more than one employer be treated as a single employer for determining the credit available, the number of employers, and the average compensation?

155. Can an employer use the credit to offset its alternative minimum tax liability?

156. Can an employer reduce employment tax payments such as withholding for income taxes, Social Security taxes or Medicare taxes in advance anticipation of receiving the credit?

157. Can the credit be used in determining estimated tax payments for the year?

158. How are FTEs determined for the health care tax credit?

159. How is the employer 50 percent payment requirement applied?

160. Which persons are not counted in determining the number of employees or their average compensation?

161. Is a household employer eligible for the small employer tax credit?

162. How does an employer claim the health care tax credit?

163. How much is the employer tax credit for employer purchase of health insurance?

164. Are employers outside of the United States eligible for the small business tax credit?

165. Can a farmers' cooperative be eligible for the small business tax credit?

166. How is the small employer tax credit for the purchase of health insurance calculated?

167. Can an employer that has already claimed the small employer health insurance tax credit prior to 2014 still be eligible for the credit after 2014?

168. Are there exceptions to the rule that the small business health insurance tax credit is available only through purchases of Qualified Health Plans from a SHOP exchange during 2014 and later?

169. How is the average annual wage calculated?

170. How did the employer health insurance tax credit change beginning in 2014?

Simple Cafeteria Plan

171. How do existing cafeteria plans work?

172. What is the simple cafeteria plan created through the Affordable Care Act?

173. Are simple cafeteria plans subject to any of the regular cafeteria plan tax rules?

174. What is the benefit of the simple cafeteria plan?

175. What is a Premium Conversion Cafeteria Plan (POP)?

176. How does a Premium Conversion Cafeteria Plan work?

177. What are the special rules for Premium Conversion Cafeteria Plans (POP)?

178. Can business owners participate in a simple cafeteria plan?

179. Which employers are "eligible employers" who can sponsor a simple cafeteria plan?

180. What happens when an employer with a simple cafeteria plan ceases to qualify to sponsor such a plan?

181. What aggregation rules apply in defining an employer?

182. Who are "qualified employees" that must be eligible to participate in a simple cafeteria plan?

183. What are the definitions of a Highly Compensated Employee (HCE) and "key employee"?

184. Which employees are excludable employees?

185. What is the benefit nondiscrimination requirement?

186. What is the employer minimum contribution requirement?

187. Does the Matching Contribution Method require a 100 percent or 200 percent employer match?

188. What happens when an employer has all HCEs, all key employees and no qualified employees?

189. How does an employer test a Simple Cafeteria Plan for non-discrimination?

190. What are the consequences if a plan fails the discrimination test?

No Employer Mandate for Small Employers

191. Is there an employer mandate for small employers?

W-2 Reporting Exemption

192. Which employers are exempt from the W-2 reporting requirement?

PART VI: GRANDFATHERED HEALTH PLANS

193. What is a grandfathered health plan?

194. If I have a grandfathered plan, am I considered covered?

195. What events can cause a plan to lose grandfathered status?

196. Are there different types of grandfathered plans?

197. What are the differences in coverage requirements between grandfathered policies and ACA-compliant policies?

198. Administrative extension until October 31, 2019, of Non-ACA compliant individual & small group health insurance policies.

199. How does an employer or other plan sponsor decide whether to maintain grandfathered status?

200. Has the DOL provided any tools to assist in determining grandfathered status?

201. What are the details for the DOL self-help healthcare reform tool and grandfathered plan checklist?

202. What health reform requirements apply to grandfathered plans?

203. What health reform requirements do not apply to grandfathered plans and apply only to new plans or plans that lose grandfathered status?

204. What changes to a plan will not result in loss of grandfather status?

205. What happens is a grandfathered plan is cancelled?

206. What happens is a grandfathered plan is changed to meet ACA standards?

207. Can an insured plan change insurance companies?

208. What documentation is required for an insured grandfathered plan to change insurance companies?

209. Can a grandfathered insured group plan change to become self-insured or a self-insured plan change to an insured plan without losing grandfathered status?

210. What other changes can be made to a grandfathered self-insured plan without losing grandfather status?

211. May enhancements or additions to a grandfathered health plan be made without loss of grandfathered status?

212. What special rules apply to collectively bargained plans in determining grandfathered plan status?

213. Can new enrollees, including new hires and family members, enroll in a grandfathered health plan?

214. Can employees transfer from one grandfathered plan to another?

215. Are there limits on employees moving from one plan to another?

216. What happens to a grandfathered plan after a merger or acquisition?

217. If grandfather status is lost, when does the loss of status become effective?

218. What changes to a health plan will result in a loss of grandfather status?

219. What is an impermissible elimination of benefits that terminates grandfathered status?

220. What is an increase in percentage cost-sharing (coinsurance) that terminates grandfather status?

221. What is an increase in fixed-amount cost-sharing (coinsurance) that terminates grandfather status?

222. How do the fixed-amount cost-sharing limitations apply to HRAs and QSE-HRAs paired with HDHPs?

223. How much can a fixed-amount cost-sharing (coinsurance) payment be increased without losing grandfather status?

224. What is Value-Based Insurance Design (VBID)?

225. Are there special rules for Value-Based Insurance Design (VBID) copayments?

226. When will a decrease in the rate of plan sponsor contributions terminate grandfather status?

227. How is this greater than 5 percent reduction test applied if there are multiple health packages offered by the plan sponsor?

228. How is the grandfathered status affected if the employer plan offers several tiers of coverage, such as employee, employee and spouse, and employee and family?

229. How do the grandfathered plan rules relate to wellness programs?

230. How do plan sponsor fixed dollar amount contributions work for grandfathered plans?

231. How do insurers know if the 5 percent sponsor contribution reduction test has been violated?

232. How does the 5 percent reduction rule work for collectively bargained plans?

233. What if a grandfathered plan imposes an annual or lifetime limit on benefits, or increases an existing limit?

234. What type of notice is required for grandfathered plans?

235. What are the recordkeeping requirements for grandfathered plans?

PART VII: PHSA COVERAGE MANDATES AND ENFORCEMENT

Coverage Mandates and Enforcement

236. What coverage mandates imposed by health reform and incorporated into the Public Health Services Act (PHSA) applied to all plans including grandfathered plans?

237. What health reform coverage mandates apply to new plans or plans that lose grandfathered status?

238. How are these coverage mandates enforced?

239. What is the status of transitional policies not compliant with healthcare reform?

Status of Individual Mandate and Penalties

240. Does the hardship exemption which was available under the Individual Mandate still exist?

Catastrophic Health Plans

241. What are the qualifications for the hardship exemption?

No Annual Limits on Essential Health Benefits Beginning in 2014

242. What changes has health reform imposed on annual limits in health plans?

243. How does the Affordable Care Act apply to self-insured (self-funded) health plans?

244. What are the essential health benefits?

245. What exceptions to the annual limit rules are there?

246. Were any waivers to the annual limit rule available?

Lifetime Limits on Essential Health Benefits Eliminated

247. When did the rules against lifetime limits become effective?

Dependent Coverage Extended to Children until Age Twenty-six

248. What are the rules that require extending coverage to children of the insured until the child reaches age twenty-six?

249. When was the until age twenty-six coverage requirement effective?

250. What about adult children who were previously ineligible for coverage who became eligible for the first plan year beginning on or after September 23, 2010?

251. What is the definition of a child for this purpose?

252. Must all health plans now offer the until age twenty-six coverage?

253. If adult child coverage is provided, was it required that prohibitions against preexisting conditions for adult children be eliminated before 2014?

254. Does this rule require the elimination of preexisting condition exclusions for all Code section 152(f)(1) children up to age twenty-six?

255. May a plan exclude, for the up to age twenty-six rule, children based on tax-dependent status, residency, age, income, employment, marital, or tax-filing status?

256. What is the definition of "child" and how should the employer define child in its health plan?

257. May a plan allow a choice of coverage as an employee or dependent coverage as a child, but not both?

258. What about the children of a person's same-sex partner (stepchildren)?

259. What if a plan covers grandchildren? Does the until age twenty-six requirement apply to them?

260. Who is a child for income tax purposes and what is the tax treatment of the until age twenty-six coverage?

261. Do the Internal Revenue Code's dependency tests apply in determining qualifying adult child status?

262. What is a "taxable year" for employees?

263. How does a plan sponsor know the age of adult children?

264. Will the employer's payments to a health plan for adult children also be given favorable tax treatment?

265. Can mid-year election changes be made to cafeteria plans due to the new adult child until age twenty-six rules?

266. What other changes were made for HRAs, QSE-HRAs, FICA, FUTA, VEBAs, and Section 401(h) accounts?

267. Does the "until age twenty-six" adult child rules apply to Health Savings Accounts (HSAs)?

268. Does the "until age twenty-six" adult child rules apply to Health Reimbursement Arrangements (HRAs) or Qualified Small Employer Health Reimbursement Arrangements (QSE-HRAs)?

269. May an employee purchase health care coverage for their adult childing using pre-tax dollars through an employer's cafeteria plan?

270. What options do adults have that "age out" of a parents' plan at age twenty-six?

Civil Rights Discrimination by Health Programs Prohibited

271. What existing antidiscrimination laws were affected by health reform?

272. What guidance has been issued on these rules?

Preventive Health Services Required

273. What does health reform do to encourage preventive care?

274. What guidance has been issued by the agencies regarding the preventive care coverage requirements?

275. What preventive services are covered?

276. What specific preventive care is offered for adults under the Affordable Care Act for 2019?

277. What specific preventive care is offered for women under the Affordable Care Act for 2019?

278. What specific preventive care is offered for children under the Affordable Care Act for 2019?

279. Are there any limits on the frequency, method, treatment, or setting for preventive services to prevent patients from abusing this rule?

280. What are the requirements as to the prohibition on patient payment, i.e., cost-sharing requirements?

281. How do these rules deal with in-network and out-of-network providers?

Contraception and Sterilization Services

282. How have the ACA rules relating to contraception and sterilization services for employees of religious organizations and social organizations sponsored by religious groups changed under the Trump Administration?

Historical Background

283. What specific changes have been made under the Trump Administration versus the Obama Administration's contraception rules?

284. How did the Zubik v. Burwell case affect the Affordable Care Act?

285. Are there any other options for religious organizations that object to these rules?

286. How did the Supreme Court Hobby Lobby decision affect the ACA contraception mandate for profit businesses?

287. How did the Hobby Lobby decision affect disclosure and notice requirements for employers who cease providing contraceptive services?

Rescissions Limited

288. How does health reform limit insurers' ability to terminate coverage?

289. What is a rescission?

290. When is an insurer allowed to rescind or terminate an individual or group policy retroactively?

291. If an employer with an insured group plan covering employees who work thirty hours or more per week forgets to advise the insurer that a covered employee's hours have been reduced below thirty, can this individual's policy be rescinded?

292. What should the sponsor of an insured group plan do if the plan wants to be able to rescind coverage retroactively?

293. Has the government declared any coverage terminations not to be rescissions?

New Claims and Appeals Procedures

294. What are health reform's required claims and appeals procedures?

295. Were any of the requirements postponed?

296. Which state insurance departments offer claims assistance?

297. Is there a minimum claim (de minimis claim) threshold under these new claim and appeal rules?

298. How are health reimbursement account claims handled?

299. How do these claims and appeal rules relate to the ERISA claims and appeal rules?

300. Can state versus federal standards apply?

301. Which external review process (state or federal) applies to plans?

302. What are the requirements of the new claims and appeals rules?

303. What if a plan fails to follow these claims and external review rules?

304. What are the requirements for Summary Plan Descriptions (SPDs) to incorporate the new claims and appeals rules?

Wellness Program Rules

305. What are wellness programs?

306. How are stand-alone wellness programs treated?

307. How are wellness programs that relate to group health plans regulated?

308. How does the Genetic Information Nondiscrimination Act (GINA) affect wellness programs?

309. What effect did the case of AARP vs. EEOC have on wellness programs?

Bringing Down the Cost of Coverage

Medical Loss Ratio (MLR) Rules; PHSA, ERISA and Tax Ramifications

310. What are the health reform provisions relating to reducing the cost of health insurance?

311. When were the final Medical Loss Ratio (MLR) regulations issued?

312. How may the insurance company rebates be paid to persons ("enrollees") purchasing individual policies in the individual market?

313. How much in rebates have been paid out thus far under the Medical Loss Ratio (MLR)?

314. How are insurers to pay Medical Loss Ratio (MLR) rebates in connection with employer health insurance plans?

315. What if the plan has been terminated when the Medical Loss Ratio (MLR) rebate is due?

316. What if the Medical Loss Ratio (MLR) limits on insurers cause financial problems for insurers?

317. Do the Medical Loss Ratio (MLR) rules limit commissions paid to brokers and agents?

318. How is the Medical Loss Ratio (MLR) computed?

319. How are Medical Loss Ratios (MLRs) calculated if an insurer has several entities licensed in a state?

320. What are the rules for Medical Loss Ratio (MLR) rebates for state and local government (non-federal) group health plans?

321. What are the rules for group insured health plans sponsored by employers and subject to ERISA?

322. How does an employer comply with the three-month rule?

323. How does an employer decide whether a Medical Loss Ratio (MLR) belongs to the employer or the employees when the health plan is not funded through a trust?

324. How does an employer decide how amounts belonging to employees are used?

325. What are the special considerations when an employer has a plan with several insurance options?

326. What are the special issues if insurance is paid in part by employee pre-tax cafeteria plan payments?

327. How do the Medical Loss Ratio (MLR) rebate rules differ for non-ERISA plans?

328. What is the income tax treatment for Medical Loss Ratio (MLR) rebates paid to owners of individual health insurance policies issued in the individual market?

329. What are the income tax rules for Medical Loss Ratio (MLR) rebates paid to employees in employer-sponsored group health insurance plans?

330. Are self-funded plans subject to the MLR reporting and rebating requirements?

331. Are health insurance benefits provided through a Medicaid Managed Care Organization (MCO) though a state Medicaid agency subject to the MLR reporting and rebate requirements?

332. Are health insurance benefits provided through CMS through Medicare, such as Medicare Advantage or Medicare Part D prescription coverage subject to the MLR reporting and rebate requirements?

Summary of Benefits and Coverage (SBC) Requirement for Insurers and Employers

333. Are insurance companies and health plans required to prepare and distribute to participants/insureds a Summary of Benefits and Coverage (SBC)?

334. What guidance has been provided for the SBC requirement?

335. What is new in the updated SBC template?

336. Are there any changes to the glossary, instructions, or coverage examples?

337. What impact do the SBC changes have on annual limits?

338. What if there is more than one benefit package for essential health benefits?

339. Does the SBC/Uniform Glossary requirement apply to grandfathered plans?

340. What plans are exempt from the SBC and Uniform Glossary requirements? What about HSAs, HRAs, QSE-HRAs, MERPs, health FSAs, EAPs, and wellness programs?

341. What is the reason for the SBC requirement?

342. Who must distribute the SBC and Glossary, and what happens if they fail to do so?

343. When is the SBC required to be distributed?

344. To whom must an SBC be provided?

345. May the SBC be distributed electronically?

346. What is the required format for the SBC?

347. Can a state impose its own requirements on the SBC or Uniform Glossary?

348. Is the SBC used in connection with COBRA continuation coverage?

Exchange Notice Required

349. What is the Exchange Notice Requirement for employers?

350. When must employers give employees this Exchange Notice?

351. Which employers are subject to the Exchange Notice requirement?

352. Is there a penalty for failing to give the Exchange Notice?

HIPAA Electronic Transactions and Operating Rules

353. How has health reform expanded HIPAA's electronic transaction requirements?

354. What are the HIPAA's adopted standards and operating rules?

355. What is a covered entity under HIPAA?

356. What is a business associate under HIPAA?

357. What is a transaction under HIPAA?

358. When is compliance required with these expanded requirements?

359. When Must Self-Insured Group Health Plans Certify Compliance with HIPAA's Transaction Standards?

360. What should group health plan sponsors do to comply with these expanded requirements?

361. What requirements are there for electronic funds transfer and health claims attachment transactions?

362. What new development has occurred relating to HPIDs and OEIDs?

363. What are the HPID rules for a Controlling Health Plan (CHP) and a Subhealth Plan (SHP)?

364. How are HPIDs and OEIDs used?

365. What are the penalties for failure to comply with the requirements and operating rules?

Automatic Enrollment – Repealed

366. What is the status of the requirement that employers automatically enroll employees in their health benefits plan?

New Health Insurance Nondiscrimination Provisions

367. What are the health insurance income tax nondiscrimination rules?

368. How do the health insurance income tax nondiscrimination rules apply to retiree medical coverage?

369. Will the income tax nondiscrimination rules for nongrandfathered group health insurance plans ever become effective?

370. What is the consequence of violating the new health insurance nondiscrimination rules?

371. What is the small employer exception to the application of the excise tax, and does it apply to avoid the nondiscrimination tax penalty?

372. What are the issues involved in applying the nondiscrimination excise tax?

373. What are the limits or exceptions to the application of the nondiscrimination excise tax on nongrandfathered insured plans?

374. Who is liable to pay the excise tax?

375. Who must file to pay the excise tax?

376. How is the liability for the excise tax reported?

377. What is the penalty if an insured plan incorrectly believes that it is grandfathered, but it is not?

378. What if the failure to meet the nondiscrimination rules is due to reasonable cause and not willful neglect?

Waiting Period Limits and Eligibility Requirements

379. What is a waiting period?

380. What is the definition of eligibility or "being otherwise eligible"?

381. Are conditions for eligibility permitted?

382. What is the maximum waiting period for essential health benefits?

383. When does a waiting period begin?

384. Is the ninety-day limit extended if employees take additional time to elect coverage?

385. What other eligibility requirements can an employer have?

386. What other prohibitions apply to the eligibility requirements?

387. How are permissible eligibility requirements applied to part-time and variable hour employees?

Guaranteed Coverage

No Preexisting Conditions or Health Status Discrimination for Essential Health Benefits

388. How does health reform affect the ability of a health insurance policy or plan covering essential health conditions not to deny coverage or reimbursement for preexisting condition exclusions (PECs)?

389. What is a Pre-existing Condition Exclusion (PCE)?

390. Are certificates of creditable coverage still required?

Cost-Sharing Limits

391. What are the cost-sharing limits on out-of-pocket expenses and annual deductibles?

392. What are the limits for annual deductibles?

Clinical Trials and Coverage

393. What patient protections does the law create for persons participating in clinical trials?

Fair Insurance Premiums

Health Insurance Rating Rules

394. What are the health insurance rating rules imposed by health reform?

Health Insurance Coverage Transparency Reporting and Cost-Sharing Disclosure

395. What are the "transparency in coverage" reporting and cost-sharing disclosures?

396. What information must be provided for transparency in coverage reporting and made available to the public?

397. What cost-sharing disclosures to individuals must be made?

No Discrimination against Providers

398. How does health reform prohibit discrimination against healthcare providers, such as physicians?

399. What are some examples of prohibited discrimination against providers?

400. What is the effective date of the provider nondiscrimination requirements?

401. How will the nondiscrimination requirement be enforced?

402. To what products or programs do these provider nondiscrimination rules not apply?

PART VIII: REQUIRED DISCLOSURES AND INFORMATION REPORTING

W-2 Reporting Beginning 2013 and Subsequent Years

403. What is the W-2 reporting requirement and when did it become effective?

404. What is the income tax impact of this requirement to employers and employees?

405. Which employers must comply with the expanded W-2 reporting?

406. Do third-party sick pay providers have to report costs of coverage?

407. Is the amount reported on the W-2 the amount for health coverage paid by the employer?

408. Which employers are exempt from the W-2 reporting requirement?

409. What about related employers that each employ and pay the same person?

410. Is the cost of coverage under a multiemployer plan required to be included in the aggregate reportable cost reported on Form W-2?

411. In the case of an individual who transfers to a new employer that qualifies as a successor employer must both the predecessor and successor employers report the aggregate reportable cost of coverage each provided?

412. How is the amount of reportable cost determined?

413. How do employers with self-insured health plans calculate the aggregate cost of applicable employer-sponsored coverage?

414. How is the cost for EAPs, wellness programs, and on-site medical clinics reported?

415. What is the penalty for failure to follow the W-2 reporting requirements?

416. What about health costs paid for retirees not entitled to a W-2?

417. Has the IRS provided a chart summarizing the W-2 health cost reporting requirements?

Exchange Notice Required Beginning October 1, 2013

418. What is the Exchange Notice that employers must give and when was the requirement effective?

419. Who is an employer for this purpose?

420. What is the purpose and content of the Exchange Notice?

421. Which employees must receive the notice?

422. What are the penalties for failure to give the Exchange Notice to employees?

423. What information should the Exchange Notice provide to employees?

Reporting of Health Insurance Coverage (Insurers and Employers that Self-Insure)

424. In addition to the W-2 reporting, what other reporting must employers make to the IRS and covered individuals?

425. When did this reporting requirement go into effect?

426. Who is required to report under Section 6055?

427. Is an employer required to report under section 6055 if it sponsors a health plan that provides coverage by purchasing insurance from a health insurance issuer?

428. For self-insured group health plan coverage, who is the plan sponsor that must report under section 6055?

429. How do the reporting requirements under section 6055 apply to reporting entities that are part of a controlled group?

430. Must a government employer report under section 6055 if it maintains a self-insured health plan?

431. For a government-sponsored program, who must report under section 6055?

432. Should a health insurance issuer report under section 6055 for coverage in a qualified health plan in the individual market enrolled in through a Marketplace?

433. Must a health coverage provider report under section 6055 for arrangements that provide benefits in addition or as a supplement to an arrangement that is minimum essential coverage?

434. Must a health coverage provider report under section 6055 if some or all of its covered individuals may be exempt from the individual shared responsibility provision?

435. What type of information must be reported to the IRS?

436. Did the IRS Notice 2013-45 postpone all elements of the PPACA reporting requirements?

437. Did Notice 2016-70 affect the rules under sections 6721(b) and 6722(b) concerning the reduction of penalty amounts for reporting under section 6055 or 6056?

438. What were the filing deadlines for Forms 1094-C and 1095-C for 2019?

439. What are the filing deadlines for Forms 1094-C and 1095-C for 2020?

440. What relief is available from penalties for incomplete or incorrect returns either filed with the IRS or for statements furnished to employees for coverage offered or not offered?

441. Are nonprofit and government entities required to report under section 6056?

442. Why were the reporting requirements postponed until 2015?

443. Do the employer shared responsibility provisions apply if an employer that is not otherwise an ALE offers coverage through an Association Health Plan (AHP)?

444. What do the final regulations on employer information reporting require?

445. Is an employees' ability to receive premium tax credits affected by the reporting requirement delay?

446. Were any 2014 requirements of the PPACA affected by the extension of the effective date of these reporting requirements?

447. What are the reporting requirements that were not affected by the postponement of these three reporting requirements?

448. What is the "Minimum Essential Coverage" that must be reported?

449. When did the reporting requirement become effective?

450. What information must be reported to the IRS?

451. What statement must be furnished to covered individuals?

452. What is the sanction for noncompliance with this reporting requirement?

Health Insurance Coverage Reporting by Large Employers and Offering Employers for 2015 and Thereafter

453. In addition to the requirements described above in Q 418 to Q 452, for employers to report to the IRS and employees, what other similar reporting requirements exist?

454. Who is required to report under section 6056?

455. If two or more related employers together are an Aggregated ALE Group under section 4980H (so that each related employer is an ALE Member), how do they comply with the information reporting requirements?

456. Are nonprofit organizations and government entities required to report under section 6056?

457. What information is reported by the Applicable Large Employers and offering employers?

458. Which statements must be furnished to employees by "applicable large employers" and "offering employers?"

459. What are the consequences for failure to comply with the Internal Revenue Code section 6056 reporting requirements?

460. How do ALE Group members under Section 4980H comply with information reporting requirements?

461. Does an Applicable Large Employer under section 6056 if the ALE has no full-time employees?

462. Do ALEs that sponsor self-insured health plans need to file Form 1094-C and Form 1095-C if the ALE has no full-time employees?

463. Is an employer that is not an ALE Member required to report under section 6056 or to file Form 1094-C or Form 1095-C?

464. Is an employer that sponsors a self-insured health care plan but is not an ALE required to report under section 6056 or to file Form 1094-C or Form 1095-C?

465. Is an ALE required to report under section 6056 for a full-time employee who is not offered coverage during the year?

466. Are different reporting methods available to ALEs for reporting required information statements?

467. What is the general method of reporting?

468. What are the alternative methods of reporting?

469. How does an ALE report under the Qualifying Offer method?

470. What is a Qualifying Offer in relation to the Form 1095-C?

471. How does an ALE report under the 98 percent Offer Method?

472. When must an ALE file the required information return?

473. When must an ALE furnish the statements to full-time employees?

474. Must an ALE file returns with the IRS electronically?

475. Must an ALE furnish the employee statements to full-time employees electronically?

476. May an ALE furnish a Form 1095-C to an employee by hand delivery?

477. Must an ALE furnish a Form 1095-C within 30 days of the employee's written request if the employee terminates employment and requests the statement?

478. May an ALE file more than one Form 1094-C?

479. May an ALE satisfy reporting requirements for an employee by filing and furnishing more than one Form 1095-C that together provide the necessary information?

480. May an ALE hire a third-party administrator or service provider to file the return with the IRS and furnish the statements to employees required under section 6056?

481. May an ALE that is a governmental unit designate a third party to file the return and furnish the statements under section 6056 on its behalf?

482. May an ALE that is a governmental unit that sponsors a self-insured health plan designate a third party to file the return and furnish the statements under section 6055 on its behalf?

483. May an ALE that is a governmental unit that sponsors a self-insured health plan designate a DGE for its reporting obligations under section 6055 but not for its reporting obligations under section 6056?

484. How does the delegation of the reporting responsibility to a DGE affect the requirement that one Form 1094-C be designated as the Authoritative Transmittal containing aggregate employer-level data?

Annual Report by DOL about Self-Insured Plans (Using Form 5500 Information)

485. What information must the DOL report to Congress regarding self-insured health plans?

486. What types of self-insured plans exist?

487. How many participants are there in self-insured plans?

488. What types of benefits are offered though the self-insured health plans?

Insured Health Plan Transparency in Coverage and Cost-Sharing Reporting

489. What are the transparency in coverage and cost-sharing reporting requirements?

490. What information must be reported under these rules?

491. Must any of this information be disclosed to individuals?

SPD Content Requirements for ERISA Group Health Plans

492. What is covered in the Summary Plan Description?

493. When must a Summary Plan Description be provided?

494. Are there any exceptions to the Summary Plan Description?

495. How often must a Summary Plan Description be updated?

496. What are common errors found in Summary Plan Descriptions that can result in litigation under ERISA?

Quality of Care Reporting by Group Health Plans and Insurers

497. What reporting is required by group health plans and insurers that is designed to improve the quality of care?

498. What information must be reported and when?

Cadillac Plan Excise Tax Determination

499. What is the "Cadillac Tax" and what reporting is required?

List of Required Disclosures and Notices to Health Plan Participants

500. What are the various notices required to be made to health plan participants?

501. What notices are required for Grandfathered and Grandmothered plans?

502. What notice is required for Rescission Prohibition?

503. What notice is required for a Primary Care Designation Notice?

504. What notice is required for the PPACA Prohibition on Lifetime Dollar Limits and Re-enrollment rights?

505. What notice is required for Adult Child Coverage through age twenty-six?

506. What notice is required for Claims and Appeals Processes?

507. What is the notice required for Summary of Benefits and Coverage (SBC)?

508. What notice is required for the Explanation of the Exchange and the Exchange Notice?

509. What notice was required for the Automatic Enrollment provision?

510. What notice is required for the Model Wellness Program Disclosure?

511. What notice is required for the Model Newborns' Act Disclosure?

512. What notice is required for the Model WHCRA Enrollment Disclosure?

513. What notice is required for the Model Special Enrollment Notice?

514. What notice is required for Disclosure of Plan Data and Financials?

PART IX: TAX INCREASES AND REVENUE RAISERS

Additional Requirements for Nonprofit Hospitals

515. When was the Affordable Care Act's additional requirements for Internal Revenue Code section 501(c)(3) hospitals effective?

516. Why were these additional requirements enacted?

517. What are the requirements under Section 501(r)(4) for the establishment of a Financial Assistance Policy (FAP) and emergency medical care policies?

518. What are the specific eligibility criteria for financial assistance and the basis for determining charges?

519. What are the methods to apply for financial assistance?

520. What actions can be taken for non-payment?

521. What procedures must be used to publicize the hospital FAP?

522. What are the Community Health Needs Assessment requirements under Section 501 (r)(3)?

523. How does Community Health Needs Assessment define the community served?

524. How does a hospital assess community health needs?

525. How is community input solicited?

526. What other sources of input must be solicited?

527. How must a CHNA be documented?

Penalty for Lack of Economic Substance

528. What is the "economic substance" doctrine?

529. When did the economic substance penalties become effective?

Tanning Bed Tax

530. What is the tanning bed tax?

531. Which tanning services are covered and which are exempt from the indoor tanning services tax?

Limits on Reimbursement of Nonprescription Over-the-Counter Drugs

532. How have the rules changed on the ability to reimburse for Over-the-Counter (OTC) drugs?

Doubled HSA and MSA Penalty for Spending for Nonhealth Care and Nonprescription Over-the-Counter Items

533. How has health reform changed the penalty for a Health Savings Account (HSA) or an Archer Medical Savings Account (MSA) regarding payment for nonmedical items?

534. When were the new HSA and Archer MSA rules effective?

535. What is a prescription for purposes of these rules?

536. How are purchases of over-the-counter medical devices and supplies affected by healthcare reform?

Annual Fee on Manufacturers and Importers of Branded Drugs

537. What is the annual fee on manufacturers and importers of branded drugs?

538. What is a covered entity?

539. What is a designated entity?

540. What is the definition of specified government programs?

541. What is a Controlled Group?

542. What are Branded Prescription Drugs and Orphan Drugs?

543. When is the annual fee on manufacturers and importers of branded drugs effective?

544. How is reporting done for Branded Prescription Drug?

Repeal of Employer-Paid Retiree Prescription Drug Rebate Income Tax Exclusion

545. What was the employer-paid retiree prescription drug rebate income tax exclusion?

Tax on Sale of Medical Devices – Moratorium Extended to 2019

546. What is the new tax on the sale of taxable medical devices?

547. When is the Form 720 due?

548. What is a taxable medical device?

549. Are there any exemptions to the medical device tax?

550. Are there instances where medical devices can be sold tax-free?

551. How is the medical device tax computed and who must report it?

552. Who constitutes the manufacturer or the importer for purposes of the medical excise tax?

553. How are "convenience kits" treated under the terms of the medical excise tax?

554. When does the moratorium on the medical device excise tax end?

Expanded Medicare Tax on Wages

555. How does the Expanded Medicare Tax on Wages work?

556. When is liability incurred for the Additional Medicare Tax?

557. What wages are subject to the Additional Medicare Tax?

558. Is Railroad Retirement Tax Act compensation subject to the Additional Medicare Tax?

559. Is income subject to the Additional Medicare Tax subject to the Medicare Tax on Investment Income?

560. Are nonresident aliens and expatriate U.S. citizens subject to the Additional Medicare Tax?

561. Are non-cash wages or tips subject to the Additional Medicare Tax?

562. How is the Additional Medicare Tax reported?

563. When must an employer withhold Additional Medicare Tax and what are the ramifications for failing to withhold?

3.8 Percent Medicare Tax on Investment Income (Net Investment Income Tax)

564. What is the 3.8 percent Medicare tax on investment?

565. Who is subject to the Net Investment Income Tax?

566. Will someone have to pay the 3.8 percent Net Investment Income Tax AND the additional 0.9 percent Medicare Tax?

567. How does the Medicare tax on investment income apply to estates and trusts?

568. How does the Medicare tax on investment income apply to S corporations electing small business trusts?

569. What is "net investment income?"

570. What types of gains are included in Net Investment Income?

571. How does the Medicare tax on investment income apply to pass-through entities?

572. What items are not subject to the Medicare tax on net investment income?

573. What are some examples of the calculations of the Net Investment Income Tax?

Cafeteria Plan Changes
$2,700 Cap on Employee FSA Contributions

574. What are the cafeteria plan changes enacted in health reform?

575. To what does the new FSA limit apply?

576. What clarifications has the IRS made regarding issues relating to the health FSA employee dollar deferral limit?

577. What was the deadline to amend a cafeteria plan to limit employee deferrals into health FSAs?

578. What is the penalty if a cafeteria plan is not timely amended or does not comply with the $2,700 employee deferral limit?

Health Insurers Executive Compensation

579. How has the Trump tax reform affected taxes on executive compensation for health insurance companies?

580. What is a covered health insurance provider?

581. What is the applicable individual remuneration for purposes of the $500,000 annual limit?

582. How is the $500,000 cap applied? Does it make any difference if compensation is earned and paid later as deferred compensation?

583. What rules applied to a covered health insurance provider for compensation earned in 2010 through 2012?

584. What is the current status of executive physical/executive diagnostic reimbursement plans under the Affordable Care Act?

Increase Threshold for Personal Deduction for Medical Expenses

585. How does health reform limit individual income tax deductions for health care?

The Individual Mandate

586. What is the status of the Individual Mandate?

587. What was the intended purpose of the Individual Mandate?

The Employer Mandate

588. How does the employer mandate improve health care?

589. What are the incentives created by health reform for employers, including but not limited to the employer mandate?

Health Insurance Premium Tax – Moratorium Status

590. What is the health insurance premium "tax" that began in 2014?

Tax on "Cadillac" Policies

591. Why did Congress decide to tax generous high-cost health plans?

592. What type of plans are intended to be taxed?

593. How does the Cadillac tax work on expensive health plans work?

594. What is the effect on the excise tax if the employee pays for all or part of the coverage?

595. What coverage is not subject to the excise tax on high-cost employer-sponsored coverage?

596. Is there any relief in the Cadillac tax rules for people whose health coverage is expensive because their occupation is dangerous?

597. How is the excise tax calculated and paid?

598. Who pays the excise tax and how it is allocated?

599. What is the sanction on the employer for underreporting liability for the tax?

Patient Centered Outcomes Research Institute (PCORI) and PCORI Fees

600. What is the Patient Centered Outcomes Research Institute?

601. What are PCORI fees?

602. How are PCORI fees to be paid?

603. When are PCORI fees due?

604. Who pays the PCORI fees?

605. Can plan sponsors delegate the PCORI filing and fee payment to third parties?

606. Are any plans excluded from being subject to the PCORI fees?

607. How are the average number of lives determined and the fees calculated?

608. How the lives covered under a health insurance policy or self-insured health plan determined?

609. If an employer provides coverage under COBRA or coverage to retirees, do those employees count as "lives covered" for purposes of PCORI?

610. How are multiple self-funded plans counted for purposes of the fee?

611. How were the number of covered lives determined in the first year?

612. Are there special rules for health FSAs, QSE-HRAs, and HRAs?

613. Are health insurance policies for self-insured plans for tax-exempt organizations or government entities subject to the PCORI fee?

PART X: STATE INSURANCE EXCHANGES (MARKETPLACES)

State, State-Federal Partnerships, and Federally Facilitated Exchanges (FFEs)

614. What are the state health insurance exchanges or marketplaces?

615. What issues have there been with the marketplaces/exchanges and health insurance coverage?

616. What is the status of the exchanges and healthcare reform in the five US territories?

617. What is the status of SHOP exchanges and small business insurance purchases?

618. What is the status of the SHOP program on Healthcare.gov?

619. What individuals and employers are eligible to purchase health insurance on an exchange?

620. May individuals with Medicare enroll for coverage through the exchange?

621. How do exchanges determine which individuals are eligible to purchase on an exchange?

622. What is the Federal Data Services Hub?

623. What are the specific standards to determine if an individual is eligible to purchase health insurance on an exchange?

624. How are eligibility determinations for premium tax credit and cost-sharing reductions made?

625. What rules apply for spouses?

626. What rules apply for determination of household income for eligibility for Exchange tax credits and subsidies?

627. How does an Exchange obtain IRS Tax Return Information to help verify income?

628. What happens when the Exchange determines an applicant is eligible to receive advance payment of the premium tax credits or cost-sharing reductions based in part on a finding that his or her employer does not provide minimum essential coverage, or provides coverage that is not affordable, or does not meet the minimum value standard?

629. How do Exchanges verify whether an employee is enrolled in employer-sponsored health coverage or are eligible for employer-sponsored health coverage that meets affordability and minimum value standards?

630. Can employers appeal a determination that an employee is eligible for an Exchange tax credit or subsidy?

631. What are the procedures for Exchanges to determine eligibility for coverage?

632. How do Exchanges report information about premium tax credits and subsidies?

633. What is the biggest loophole in the law as to exchange purchased health insurance?

634. What if a state did not create its own exchange?

635. When can individuals and businesses purchase insurance on the exchanges' open enrollment and special enrollment periods?

636. What levels of health insurance are available on the exchanges?

637. What subsidies are available for individuals purchasing health insurance on an exchange?

638. If my spouse receives affordable insurance through his/her workplace, but family coverage is too expensive and my spouse does not elect to have it, can family members access health insurance subsidies through a health insurance exchange?

639. What is the Effect of the Supreme Court Upholding Exchange Health Insurance Subsidies in King v. Burwell?

640. What is the current status of lawsuits against the Affordable Care Act—Texas v. United States?

641. Can pharmaceutical companies help pay for copays and deductibles for prescription drugs for exchange-purchased insurance; can hospitals and other healthcare providers make premium payments for individuals with exchange health insurance?

642. What consumer-assistance tools must exchanges provide?

643. Which decisions of the healthcare marketplace can be appealed?

644. Which states do not use the healthcare.gov site?

645. How are health care plans on the exchanges rated?

646. What changes have been effected on the exchanges for American Indians and Alaska Natives?

Exchange Navigators

647. What is the role of the exchange navigators?

648. What standards must navigators and non-navigator assistance personnel meet?

Agent and Broker Roles

649. What is the role of health insurance agents and brokers on the exchanges?

650. What assistance is available for agents and brokers on the Exchange?

651. What additional guidance has HHS issued about health insurance agents and brokers as to their role vis-à-vis the exchanges?

652. What special rules apply to insurance agents and brokers assisting taxpayers on the Exchanges?

653. What are the rules regarding insurance broker and agent compensation?

654. Are there special rules for brokers operating on-line, i.e., web-brokers?

655. What other existing organizations will assist individuals on the exchanges?

PART XI: THE EMPLOYER MANDATE

(a/k/a Shared Responsibility or Play or Pay Rules)

Overview

656. What are the Shared Responsibility Provisions under the Internal Revenue Code and regulations?

657. What topics are covered in the employer mandate regulations?

Definitions

658. What employers are subject to the employer mandate penalty?

659. Do the employer shared responsibility rules apply to government units, and non-profit businesses?

660. What transition relief existed for the employer mandate penalty during 2014, 2015, and 2016?

661. Which workers qualify as employees?

662. If the employer hires additional employees, including some part-time employees, how is it determined when ALE status is achieved?

663. How are non-traditional employees such as contingent workers (leased employees and independent contractors), seasonal employees, temporary employee, rehired employees, volunteers, education employees, student workers and adjunct faculty defined under the regulations?

664. Which workers are not considered employees?

665. Who are dependents for purposes of the employer mandate?

Applicable Large Employers

666. Which "Applicable Large Employers" are potentially subject to the employer mandate penalties?

667. Are related employers treated as one employer?

668. Does the employer mandate shared responsibility rules apply if an employer that is not an ALE offers coverage through an Association Health Plan?

669. How is a new employer's status as an ALE determined if they were not in existence during the prior year?

Two Alternate Employer Mandate Penalties

670. In general, what are the two alternative employer mandate penalties?

671. What qualifies as an employer offer of health coverage?

672. How does the IRC section 4980H(a) penalty work?

673. How does the IRC section 4980H(b) alternative penalty work?

674. What does "affordable value" for a plan mean?

675. When does an employer health plan provide minimum value?

676. Can an inexpensive health plan that fails to cover inpatient hospitalization services provide minimum value and allow employers to avoid employer mandate penalties?

677. Does a health plan with no hospitalization option qualify as meeting the Minimum Value standard?

678. When is employer coverage unaffordable?

679. What safe harbors are available for an employer to determine if its health coverage is affordable?

680. What are the limited nonassessment periods when the employer mandate penalty will not be assessed?

HRA Reimbursement Arrangements and the Employer Penalty

681. Can an employer Health Reimbursement Account (HRA) that pays or reimburses employees for exchange or individual health insurance qualify as employer-provided minimum essential coverage to avoid the 4980H(a) penalty?

Separate Assessment of Shared Responsibility Penalties within Controlled Group

682. Where there is an applicable large employer comprised of related employers, how is the employer mandate penalty, if applicable, calculated?

683. Will the insured plan nondiscrimination requirements, when effective, impact health insurance offered by related employers?

Determining Applicable Large Employer Status

684. How are those "applicable large employers" potentially subject to the employer mandate penalty determined?

685. What if payroll periods begin after the calendar year starts or end after the calendar year ends?

686. What if the employer only has fifty or more full time and full-time equivalent employees for four or fewer months?

687. How are total U.S. employees for the preceding calendar year determined using the look-back method?

688. What if an employer's workforce exceeds fifty full-time employees for no more than 120 days?

689. How is an employer with fewer than fifty employees not counting seasonal employees treated?

Counting U.S. Employees
Full-time and Part-time

690. How are employees' U.S. hours of service counted and determined?

691. How are hours of service counted for hourly workers?

692. How are salaried employees' hours of service counted?

693. Are there rules for employees with special work patterns?

694. Can different counting methods be used by different controlled or affiliated group members?

695. What is the definition of a full-time employee under the application of the Affordable Care Act?

696. What is the optional method for counting full-time employees in a prior year that eliminates the need to count for the current month?

697. What are part-time employees and variable hour employees and how does one determine how part-time employees are converted into full-time equivalent employees?

698. Is there a difference between full-time employees and full-time equivalent employees?

Calculating the Employer Mandate Penalty

699. How are employees counted in the current year for the "applicable large employer" penalty calculation?

700. How does the look-back method work?

701. What are the rules for stability periods that are longer than the associated measurement period?

702. How are measurement and stability periods implemented?

703. How are new nonseasonal full-time employees treated?

704. How are ongoing employees tested during the safe harbor standard measurement period?

705. Can payroll periods be used in lieu of calendar months?

706. What happens after an employee has completed an initial measurement period and has been employed for a full standard measurement period?

707. How does the optional administrative period work?

708. Can an employer change its measurement and stability periods?

709. May different measurement and stability periods be used for different types of employees?

710. What is the latest update from the IRS regarding changes in employer mandate measurement periods and changes in testing methods?

711. What is a new employee for purposes of the look-back rule?

712. How does the optional lookback method apply to new variable hour, part-time and new seasonal employees?

713. How are new variable hour employees treated for an applicable large employer using the look-back method?

714. What happens if there is a change in status to full-time for new variable hour or seasonal employees?

715. What happens after variable-hour and seasonal employees have been employed for at least one standard measurement period?

716. What are some examples of how these rules work?

Anti-abuse Rules and Staffing (Employee Leasing or Professional Employment Organization) Firms

717. Are any anti-abuse rules contemplated for employers who shift employees to staffing companies?

Planning to Minimize Impact of Employer Mandate Penalties

718. Can an employer reduce or minimize the impact of the employer mandate by reducing employee's hours to less than thirty hours per week to avoid having full-time employees?

719. Is outsourcing work a solution to reduce the employee count?

720. How can an applicable large employer offer low cost health benefits and still avoid or reduce the impact of the employer mandate penalty?

721. How does an employer avoid the section 4980H(a) employer mandate penalty?

722. How does an employer avoid or reduce the 4980H(b) employer mandate penalty?

723. Does this dual option comprehensive insurance or catastrophic insurance employer mandate strategy work?

724. How does an applicable large employer utilize the 95 percent rule in planning for the employer mandate penalties?

Employer Mandate Traps for Employers to Avoid

725. What are the traps regarding employer mandate rules that employers should avoid?

PART XII: SHORT-TERM LIMITED DURATION HEALTH INSURANCE

(a/k/a "TrumpCare")

Overview

726. What is Short-Term Limited Duration Health Insurance?

727. How do short-term plans compare with ACA policies in terms of premiums and coverage?

Implementation

728. What are the limits on covered benefits on STLD policies?

729. What are the cost-sharing limits for covered benefits?

730. What notice must Short-Term Limited Duration Health Insurance display for consumers?

731. Can eligibility for short-term health insurance be based on health status?

732. What rules apply regarding length of coverage and renewability?

733. Can STLD policies be sold on the marketplace sites?

734. Does loss of coverage under a short-term limited duration policy enable you for a special enrollment period (SEP)?

735. How does State Regulation impact STLD policies?

736. Can Short-Term Limited Duration policies be sold as Student Health Insurance?

737. Are federal subsidies available for purchase of STLD policies?

738. How do STLD policies compare with the ACA requirement of Minimum Essential Coverage?

739. What are the typical characteristics of short-term policies?

740. Do any States ban short-term plans?

History

741. How were Short-Term Limited Duration policies managed in the past?

742. How did the Obama Administration treat Short-Term Limited Duration Coverage?

Proposed and Final Rules

743. What changes did the February 2018 proposed rule contain?

744. How has the final rule issued in August 2018 affected length of STLD policies?

745. What are the notice requirements in the final rule?

746. Does Section 1557, the non-discrimination rule of the Affordable Care Act apply to STLD policies?

747. What is the effective date of the regulation on STLD policies?

748. When did the new STLD policies become effective?

749. What is the final rule's Severability Provision?

PART XIII: "MEDICARE FOR ALL" AND THE FUTURE OF HEALTHCARE REFORM

The Future of Healthcare Reform in the United States

750. What does the future hold for healthcare reform?

"Medicare for All" Single Payer Program

751. What does the proposed "Medicare for All" single payer program entail?

752. Would the proposed "Medicare for All" eliminate private health insurance?

753. Who would be eligible to participate in the Medicare for All plan?

754. How would the enrollment process for Medicare for all work?

755. What benefits are offered under the Medicare for All Proposals?

756. What cost-sharing provisions are imposed?

757. Are there premiums or tax subsidies for Medicare for All?

758. What are the rules for providers to participate in Medicare for All?

759. How will providers be paid under Medicare for All?

760. How are prescription drug prices set under Medicare for All?

761. How does Medicare for All change the current Medicare program?

762. How does Medicare for All change the current Medigap and Supplemental Insurance?

763. How does Medicare for All change the current Marketplace plans and private plans?

764. How does Medicare for All change existing Medicaid?

765. Are there changes to VA and Indian Health Services under Medicare for All?

766. How would the Sanders Medicare for All plan handle coverage during the four-year transition period?

767. How would the Jayapal Medicare for All plan handle coverage during the two-year transition period?

Public Plan Option with Ability to Opt Out

768. What does the proposed "Medicare for America" payer program entail?

769. Who would be eligible to participate in the Medicare for America plan?

770. How would the enrollment process work?

771. What benefits are offered under Medicare for America?

772. What cost-sharing provisions are imposed?

773. What are the premiums for the Medicare for All plans?

774. What are the rules for providers to participate in Medicare for America?

775. How will providers be paid under Medicare for All?

776. How does Medicare for America change the current Medicare program?

777. How does Medicare for America change the current Medigap and Supplemental Insurance?

778. How does Medicare for America change the current Marketplace plans and private plans?

779. How does Medicare for All change existing Medicaid?

780. Are there changes to VA and Indian Health Services under Medicare for All?

781. How would the Medicare for America plan handle coverage during the transition period?

782. How is the Medicare for America Plan financed?

Public Plan Options

783. What does the proposed Public Plan Options entail?

784. What are the rules of participation in the public option plans?

785. How would the enrollment process work for the public option plans?

786. What benefits are offered under the public option plans?

787. What cost-sharing provisions are imposed on the public option plans?

788. What are the premiums for the public option plans?

789. What are the rules for providers to participate in the public option plans?

790. How will providers be paid under the public option plans?

791. How do the public option plans change the current Medicare program?

792. How do the public option plans change the current Medigap and Supplemental Insurance?

793. How do the public option plans change the current Marketplace plans and private plans?

794. How do the public option plans change existing Medicaid?

795. Are there changes to VA and Indian Health Services under the public option plans?

796. How would the public option plan handle coverage during the transition period?

797. How are the public option plans financed?

Medicare Buy-In Plans for Over 50 Adults

798. What do the proposed Medicare for Over 50 Adults entail?

799. What are the rules of participation in the Medicare for Over 50 Adult plans?

800. How would the enrollment process work for the Over 50 plans?

801. What benefits are offered under the public option plans?

802. What cost-sharing provisions are imposed on the public option plans?

803. What are the premiums for the public option plans?

804. What are the rules for providers to participate in the public option plans?

805. How will providers be paid under the public option plans?

806. How do the Over 50 plans change the current Medicare program?

807. How do the Over 50 plans change the current Medigap and Supplemental Insurance?

808. How do the Over 50 plans change the current Marketplace plans and private plans?

809. How do the Over 50 plans change existing Medicaid?

810. Are there changes to VA and Indian Health Services under the Over 50 plans?

811. How would the Over 50 plans handle coverage during the transition period?

812. How are the public option plans financed?

Medicaid Buy-In Plan

813. What does the State Public Option Act entail?

814. What are the rules of participation in the State Public Option Act plans?

815. How would the enrollment process work for the State Public Option Act plans?

816. What benefits are offered under the State Public Option Act?

817. What cost-sharing provisions are imposed on the State Public Option Act?

818. What are the premiums for the State Public Option Act?

819. What are the rules for providers to participate in the State Public Option Act?

820. How will providers be paid under the State Public Option Act?

821. How does the State Public Option Act change current Medicare, Medigap/Supplemental Insurance, and Marketplace plans?

822. How does the State Public Option Act change existing Medicaid?

823. Are there changes to VA and Indian Health Services under the State Public Option Act?

824. How would the State Public Option Act handle coverage during the transition period?

825. How is the State Public Option Act financed?

PART I: GOALS AND MAJOR COMPONENTS OF HEALTHCARE REFORM

Overview

1. What is healthcare reform?

The term "healthcare reform" refers to the healthcare laws passed in March 2010, known as the Affordable Care Act (ACA) or the Patient Protection and Affordable Care Act (PPACA),[1] as well as subsequent regulations and other guidance implementing that law. The effective date of the law was March 23, 2010, although various provisions have their own effective dates from January 1, 2010, (the small business income tax credit) through 2020. Since the advent of the Trump Administration, significant changes (most notably the elimination of the Individual Mandate penalty) have occurred to the Affordable Care Act, but most of the legislation remains in place.

The intent of the Affordable Care Act is as follows:

- To provide easy and universal access to healthcare for all Americans

- To improve the overall quality of healthcare in the United States

- To educate consumers as to healthcare choices available and make choices more user-friendly

- To help control the costs of healthcare

- To establish regulations for the private insurance industry by implementing state-based private exchanges

- To encourage employers to offer health insurance

- To help expand Medicaid to enable more individuals with low income to obtain coverage

- To provide credits to moderate and low-income Americans who do not qualify for Medicaid

- To require most Americans to obtain health insurance, although some of this requirements has been diluted by the elimination of the penalties imposed by the Individual Mandate.

---

1. See H.R. 3590, the Patient Protection and Affordable Care Act, Pub. L. No. 111-148 (PPACA), signed on March 23, 2010; and H.R. 4872, the Health Care and Education Reconciliation Act of 2010, Pub. L. No. 111-152 (HCERA), signed on March 30, 2010.

2. What terms and acronyms will be used repeatedly in this book?

The following are the most common terms and acronyms that will be used throughout this book.

- **Applicable Large Employer (ALE).** An employer with fifty or more full-time employees.

- **Cafeteria Plan (Section 125 Plan).** An employee benefit plan that is offered under the auspices of Section 125 of the Internal Revenue Code. A cafeteria plan must allow employees to choose from two or more benefits, including one taxable benefit such as cash and at least one qualified benefit plans. A Section 125 Plan is the only vehicle by which an employer offer employees choices between taxable and non-taxable benefits.

- **Code.** Internal Revenue Code, as amended. Also referred to as "IRC" or "Title 26, United States Code".

- **DOL.** The United States Department of Labor.

- **EAP.** Employee Assistance Program.

- **Employer Mandate.** A tax penalty on certain employers not offering a group health plan or offering one that does not meet specified requirements.

- **ERISA.** The Employee Retirement Income Security Act of 1974, as amended, which governs employer-sponsored, qualified retirement plans and welfare benefit plans, including group health plans.

- **Essential Health Benefits.** The ten benefits that are considered absolutely necessary and must be offered in non-grandfathered plans sold in the small group market on or outside of an exchange beginning in 2015. Grand-fathered plans, self-insured group health plans, and health insurance coverage offered in the large group market are not required to offer essential health benefits. *Minimum essential coverage* is a separate concept. It is the term used to describe the coverage required to fulfill the individual mandate and coverage that employers must offer to avoid the employer mandate tax.

- **Exchange, State Exchange, or Health Insurance Exchange.** State or multi-state exchanges where health insurance options may be compared and purchased.

- **Grandfathered Health Plan.** A group health plan in existence on March 23, 2010, that meets specified requirements and is exempt from certain health reform requirements.

- **Group Health Plans.** Plans provided by employers or employee organizations (unions) providing comprehensive health benefits. The term does not include "excepted benefits" or retiree-only plans.

- **Health FSA.** Flexible savings accounts (FSAs), often found in cafeteria plans (sometimes called "flex plans"), for health care, but not dependent care.

- **Health Savings Accounts (HSAs).** A HSA is a tax-favored account used to pay for qualified medical expenses. HSA contributions are tax-deductible, or potentially pretax if made by an employer. It is always used in conjunction with a qualified High-Deductible Health Plan (HDHP).

- **Health Reform or Healthcare Reform.** Healthcare reform under the 2010 federal law known as the Affordable Care Act (ACA) or the Patient Protection and Affordable Care Act (PPACA), including regulations and other guidance implementing that law. Health reform amended the Code, ERISA, and the Public Health Service Act (PHSA).

- **HHS.** The United States. Department of Health and Human Services.

- **High Deductible Health Plan (HDHP).** A HDHP is a legally defined term for a health insurance plan with a higher deductible than traditional insurance. Key requirements that must be met are federal limits for annual deductible and for maximum out-of-pocket expenses.

- **HIPAA.** The Health Insurance Portability and Accountability Act of 1996.

- **HRA.** Health Reimbursement Arrangements.

- **Individual Mandate.** The tax penalty originally imposed on individuals (currently reduced to $0) (unless they are exempt) who do not have health coverage from an employer or individual health insurance.

- **MEC.** Minimum essential coverage.

- **MLR.** Medical Loss Ratio, a concept limiting how much insurers can pay for administrative expense for health insurance governed by health reform.

- **MSA.** Medical Savings Account.

- **PCE.** Pre-exisiting conditions exclusion, a pre-existing condition exclusion is a medical condition that started before a person›s health benefits went into effect. Before 2014 some insurance policies would not cover expenses due to pre-existing conditions.

- **PCORI.** Patient-Centered Outcomes Research Institute – a non-governmental 501(c)(3) institute created as part of a modification of the Social Security Act by the Affordable Care Act. The main purpose is to determine the effectiveness of certain medical treatments.

- **PEO.** Professional Employer Organizations are companies that provide services to employers allowing them to outsource tasks traditionally done by the employer such as employee benefits, payroll, workers' compensation, training, recruiting, etc.

- **PHSA or PHS Act.** Public Health Service Act.

- **Qualified Benefit.** A benefit that does not defer compensation and is excludable from an employee's gross income.

- **QSEHRA.** Qualified Small Employer Health Reimbursement Arrangement. Commonly referred to as a Small Business HRA (see HRA above). These can be offered by employers that are not Applicable Large Employers (ALE) meaning they employ less than fifty full-time or full-time equivalent employees and are not subject to ACA coverage requirements. These eligible employers also do not offer group health insurance to any of their employees.

- **QHP.** A qualified health plan offered on a state health insurance exchange.

- **SBC.** A summary of benefits and coverage summarizing health plan or health insurance benefits that must meet specified requirements.

- **SHOP.** Small Business Health Options Program Marketplace is a marketplace for small employers that what to provide healthcare and dental insurance to their employees.

3. What does health reform do?

The Affordable Care Act has materially changed and unless ultimately repealed or replaced, will continue to affect healthcare law in the United States. Healthcare reform introduced an array of new requirements for individuals, employers, health plans, and healthcare providers. The purpose of this law is to:[1]

- improve the overall quality of healthcare in the United States,

- make insurance companies more accountable,

- lower healthcare costs,

- guarantee greater choices of providers and plans,

- provide credits to moderate and low-income Americans who do not qualify for Medicaid,

- make health care more available and easier to obtain (including but not limited to eliminating exclusions for pre-existing conditions as well as Medicare and Medicaid expansions),

- educate consumers as to healthcare choices available and make choices more user-friendly,

---

1.   See http://www.nejm.org/doi/full/10.1056/NEJMp1014722; John K. Iglehart, "Implementing Health Care Reform — An Interview with HHS Secretary Kathleen Sebelius" 364 N Engl. J. Med. pp. 297-99 (Jan. 27, 2011). (Last accessed July 1, 2019).

- establish regulations for the private insurance industry by implementing state-based private exchanges,

- encourage employers to offer health insurance,

- require most Americans to obtain health insurance,

- expand preventive services, and

- promote the use of health information technology through electronic medical records, and generally to enhance the quality, safety, and coordination of health.

4. Has the Affordable Care Act actually worked to reduce health care costs?

March 2019 marked the tenth anniversary of the passage of the Affordable Care Act. It would seem that a decade of existence be a great assessment point to judge the effectiveness of the healthcare reform effort especially in regard to cost control.

In April 2009, one month after passage, the Office of the Actuary of the Department of Health and Human Services projected the expected financial impact in their report "Estimated Financial Effects of the 'Patient Protections and Affordable Care Act', as Amended." In 2009, the Actuary estimated that health care costs under the Affordable Care Act would be $4.14 trillion per year by 2017 and encompass 20.2 percent of the Gross Domestic Product (GDP).[1]

In December 2018, the Office of the Actuary of the Department of Health and Human Services released the government's official report on health-care spending during 2017. According to this report, the ACA reduced healthcare spending from 2010 to 2017 by a total of $2.3 trillion. During 2017 alone, healthcare expenditures were $650 billion under projections, and health care spending was under 18 percent of GDP only slightly higher than during 2010 when the ACA was passed while expanding health coverage to more than 20 million previously uninsured American.[2] In addition, the cost of Medicare for 2017 declined by $70 billion or 10 percent. Spending for Medicaid and the Children's Health Insurance Program (CHIP) was $250 billion less than projected. (Part of this is partially due to the states which did not expand the Medicaid program) The Office of the Actuary projected during 2010 that employer-sponsored insurance would cost $1.21 trillion in 2017, however actual costs were actually $1.04 trillion, $170 billion under projections.

On a per capita comparison, healthcare spending for 2017 was $2,000 less than projected or approximately $4,000 per family, significantly more than the $2,500 per family savings estimated by then-candidate Barack Obama.

The Affordable Care Act uses a "carrot and stick" approach. One big "carrot" is the subsidies individuals can receive for purchasing insurance on an exchange if their income is less than 400 percent of Federal Poverty Level. Two of the original sticks included the Employer Mandate

---

1.   https://www.cms.gov/research-statistics-data-and-systems/research/actuarialstudies/downloads/ppaca_2010-04-22.pdf.
2.   https://www.healthaffairs.org/doi/10.1377/hlthaff.2018.05085.

and the Individual Mandate (officially known as the Individual Shared Responsibility Provision) penalties. One stick has been effectively fed into the chipper – the Tax Cuts and Jobs Act (TCJA)[1] signed into law on December 22, 2017, by President Donald Trump repealed the Individual Mandate, with the repeal taking effect in January 2019. However, the Employer Mandate continues and essentially has been and remains "the bigger stick".

It would seem that the Individual Mandate killed by the Trump Administration was not the primary motivation for obtaining healthcare. It would seem that price and value are the primary motivators. Prior to the passage of the ACA, there were low participation rates in many company-sponsored health insurance plans, even in many companies that offered health coverage and especially those with lower wage workers. Prior to the implementation of the Affordable Care Act, one CEO asked employees why they didn't participate in the employer provided coverage.[2] The answers he received were typical:

- Younger workers were unconcerned about illness or injury.

- Others already had insurance through a spouse or parent.

- A significant number said they declined coverage because they could get medical treatment "for free at the emergency room." This fact remains true as the federal law known as the Emergency Medical Treatment and Labor Act (EMTALA) requires hospitals to provide emergency services, even to those who cannot pay.

- Among those who had signed up, many said it was because they were concerned about developing a medical condition and then being unable to get affordable coverage due to this pre-existing condition. Significantly, beginning in 2014, these people were able to obtain health insurance on exchanges despite any pre-existing conditions, which can further cause disincentive to enrollment in both employer offered health insurance especially by lower paid employees who are not offered affordable coverage by their employer and who can qualify for subsidized health insurance on a state health insurance exchange.

Other cost-containment provisions, such as the "Cadillac Tax" have not yet become effective. The Cadillac Tax implementation has been delayed once again by Congress until 2022.[3] In addition, the Independent Payment Advisory Board (IPAB) – while still unstaffed, was not triggered because costs did not increase enough in the first three years of the Affordable Care Act to the trigger the IPAB. With the passage of the Bipartisan Budget Act of 2018, the IPAB was repealed on February 9, 2018.[4] While potentially significant as potential cost-control devices, both IPAB and the Cadillac tax were never popular on either side of the political fence.

---

1.   Pub. L. 115-97.
2.   CEO's-Eye View of ObamaCare, Wall Street Journal p. A-17 (July 22, 2013), available at http://online.wsj.com/article/SB10001424127887323309404578613653344566068.html?mod=hp_opinion. (Last accessed July 1, 2019).
3.   https://www.congress.gov/115/bills/hr195/BILLS-115hr195enr.pdf (Last accessed July 15, 2018).
4.   Pub. L. 115-123.

5. What is the focus of this book?

This book focuses on the health reform requirements for employers and individuals. It does not discuss in any detail the rules that relate to healthcare providers, such as physicians, hospitals, or accountable care organizations, etc., except in their capacity as employers. For the purposes of this book, healthcare reform primarily relates to the requirements for major medical coverage offered by employers, both insured and self-insured, and purchased by individuals from insurance companies.

The book is written in several parts, and each part covers specific provisions of healthcare reform as it pertains to employers and individuals.

Many healthcare reform provisions (such as the individual and employer mandates, healthcare exchanges, and the ban on pre-existing conditions) went into effect beginning in 2014 or 2015. However, many of the group health plan and individual health insurance requirements for content, design, and administration were effective sooner, and many have been in effect. In addition, a number of changes and adjustments have been made over the years with significant changes occurring during the first year of the Presidency of Donald Trump. The law closely avoided an attempt to repeal it during 2017 and other attempts to nullify or change it during 2018 and 2019.

Part III of this book contains a timeline as to when the various requirements become effective.

Part IV discusses financial and tax decisions that employers face.

6. What benefits are regulated by health reform?

The Affordable Care Act has imposed many requirements on individual health insurance policies and group health plans, both insured and self-insured. The new requirements on group health plans are in addition to those previously imposed by HIPAA in 1996.

A group health plan is defined as an insured or self-insured plan of, or contributed to by, an employer (including a self-employed person) or employee organization to provide health care (directly or otherwise) to the employees, former employees, the employer, others associated or formerly associated with the employer in a business relationship, or their families.[1] The definition of a group health plan does not include any group health plan that has fewer than two participants who are current employees—one subset of which is retiree-only plans.[2] While this is an important exclusion, there are a number of open issues regarding the scope of retiree-only plans. In addition, a group health plan does not include a plan offering "excepted benefits."[3]

---

1.   IRC Secs. 9832(a) and 5000(b)(1).
2.   ERISA Sec. 701(a); IRC Sec. 9801(a).
3.   See Preamble to Grandfathered Health Plan Regulations, 75 Fed. Reg. 34537, 34539 (June 17, 2010) (confirming that the exceptions in the IRC and ERISA still exist, and announcing an HHS nonenforcement policy with respect to the PHSA provisions).

The Health Insurance Portability and Accountability Act of 1996 (HIPAA) imposed several new requirements for group health coverage that are designed to provide protection to health plan participants. These protections include:

- limitations on exclusions from coverage based on pre-existing conditions;

- the prohibition of discrimination on the basis of health status;[1]

- guaranteed renewability in multiemployer plans and certain employer welfare arrangements;[2]

- standards relating to benefits for mothers and newborns;[3]

- mental health benefits parity;[4] and

- coverage of dependent students on medically necessary leaves of absence.[5] [These requirements are located in HIPAA Chapter 100 of Subtitle K, Group Health Plan requirements].

Internal Revenue Code Section 9834 makes it explicit that the tax imposed by Code section 4980D applies to any failure to satisfy the requirements of Code Sections 9801 through 9812. The excise tax is $100 for each day in the noncompliance period with respect to each individual to whom such failure relates. Civil suits may be brought for violation of certain HIPAA requirements under ERISA section 701.[6]

7. What health benefits are not affected by health reform?

Health reform does not change the rules for "excepted benefits" or retiree-only plans. These items will be discussed later, in Q 13 through Q 24.

8. Do the provisions of healthcare reform only apply to businesses and residents in the United States?

In general, the answer is yes. By letter dated July 16, 2014,[7] HHS has reversed its position that healthcare reform required insurers in five US territories to comply with the law's major market reforms, i.e., guaranteed coverage, mandated benefits, and limits on insurers' profits. Healthcare reform does not require residents in Puerto Rico, the U.S. Virgin Islands, American Samoa, Guam and the Northern Mariana Islands to get coverage nor does it provide subsidies like those on the states' exchanges to help lower income persons afford coverage. The HHS has

---

1. ERISA Sec. 702 and IRC Sec. 9802.
2. ERISA Sec. 703; IRC Sec. 9803(a).
3. ERISA Sec. 711 and IRC Sec. 9811.
4. ERISA Sec. 712 and IRC Sec. 9812.
5. ERISA Sec. 714 and IRC Sec. 9813.
6. ERISA Sec. 502. Group health plans of governmental employers and churches that are exempt from ERISA by virtue of ERISA Sec. 4(b) are not subject to ERISA Sec. 701. Instead, plans of nonconforming, nonfederal governmental employers and church plans generally are subject to the parallel provisions under the PHSA.
7. See letter from HHS to US territory insurance commissioners at http://www.cms.gov/CCIIO/Resources/Letters/Downloads/letter-to-Ilagan.pdf. (Last accessed July 1, 2019).

determined, contrary to its prior position, that the definition of "state" in the Public Health Service Act (PHSA), which is the law that imposes the insurance mandates, indicates that the ACA market rules don't apply to the territories, reversing its prior position. The territories will be exempted from guaranteed coverage, community rating, single risk pools, rate review, the medical loss ratio, and essential health benefits. However, group health plans in the territories must still comply with other requirements, such as the prohibition on lifetime and annual limits (PHSA section 2711), the prohibition on rescissions (PHSA section 2712), coverage of preventive health services (PHSA section 2713), and the internal and external appeals process (PHSA section 2719).

All bona fide residents of United States territories are exempt from the individual shared responsibility provision. Individuals who qualify for this exemption should file Form 8965, Health Coverage Exemptions, when filing their tax returns.[1]

9. Do the provisions of healthcare reform only apply international students living in the United States?

Generally, no.

Resident Aliens ARE required to comply with the Affordable Care Act or pay a fine with their tax return. However, all international students holding an F, J, Q or M visa are exempt from the ACA as "Non-Resident Aliens" for their first five calendar years in the United States, therefore, there is no obligation to maintain ACA coverage.

International students are exempt from the requirement to carry such coverage. However, when they transition from a "Non-Resident Alien" to a "Resident Alien", usually between the end of their fifth year and the middle of their calendar year in the United States.

The Department of State does requires international students (and their dependents) in the J visa category to purchase insurance coverage that meets a list of requirements, and to maintain that policy for the full duration of their J program. During the initial appointment at their local Embassy, these students will need to provide proof of insurance before their visa is granted. However, these requirements are considerably different than the requirements imposed by the Affordable Care Act.

10. Where are the provisions of the health reform law found?

The Patient Protection and Affordable Care Act or PPACA, the health reform law, is contained in three places:

- The Internal Revenue Code

- The Employee Retirement Income Security Act (ERISA)

- The Public Health Service Act (PHS Act or PHSA)

---

1.   See 2018 Form 8965, https://www.irs.gov/pub/irs-access/f8965_accessible.pdf.

For health reform, the IRS, Department of Labor (DOL), and Department of Health and Human Services (HHS) respectively administer the laws. Many of the regulations are co-authored by all three federal agencies. The states have the primary authority to enforce the PHSA provisions with respect to group and individual market health insurance issuers, and HHS will only step in to the extent HHS believes the state has failed to substantially enforce these provisions. HHS, IRS and DOL have issued one volume of PPACA regulations, and more regulations are expected. In many cases, the law is vague, and regulations are needed to know what it means in practice.

11. How does healthcare reform provide for expanded coverage?

The law does this in several ways. Healthcare reform provides incentives for:

1. individuals without health coverage to buy insurance; and

2. employers to provide group health benefits. It also requires employer-provided group health plans and insurers to meet certain standards, with some exceptions for plans and coverage existing on March 23, 2010, referred to as "grandfathered health plans." New rules contain requirements for health plans and health insurance, including coverage requirements and administration. Provisions exist, for example, for eliminating pre-existing condition exclusions, limiting waiting periods, eliminating annual and lifetime limits, expanded adult child coverage, and claims appeals.

Expanded health coverage is encouraged with a "carrot-and-stick" approach. The carrots include mechanisms to expand coverage through state health insurance exchanges and tax subsidies for specified individuals and small employers. The sticks included a tax penalty for individuals, with several exceptions, who do not have health insurance (called the individual mandate – although the individual mandate penalties have been repealed effective 2019), as well as penalties for certain employers with fifty or more full-time equivalent employees who provide:

1. no healthcare benefits; or

2. coverage that does not meet several tests, including affordability, minimum essential health benefits, and a minimum employer contribution.

The penalties are known as the Employer Mandate.

12. Has healthcare reform been revised since it was enacted?

Yes.

Part II of this book discusses the provisions that have already expired, been repealed, or will not be implemented.

Part III provides a timeline of implementation dates, many of which have been revised since 2010.

Since the initial ratification of the Affordable Care Act there have been a number of legislative changes to the law including the following changes listed below.

2019

2018 Tax Cuts and Jobs Act (TCJA)

- Effective January 1, 2019, lowers the penalty for non-compliance with the Individual Mandate of the Affordable Care Act to $0.

State-imposed Penalties for Not Carrying Insurance

- New Jersey, the District of Columbia, Rhode Island, and Massachusetts impose penalties for not carrying health insurance, in spite of the elimination of the federal fine.

Changes in the Premium Tax Credit

- "TrumpCare"–Longer Terms for Short-Term Limited Duration Insurance (non-ACA compliant)

- Expanded availability of Association Health Plans

- Shorter open enrollment periods on the Healthcare Exchanges

- Modification of Medical Loss Ratios (MLRs)

- Increased income verification for tax subsidies

- Changes in Open Enrollment periods

- Changes in the Premium Tax Credit

2018

February 9, 2018: Bipartisan Budget Act, P.L.115-123

- Repeal of the Independent Payment Advisory Board (IPAB)

January 22, 2018: Federal Register Printing Savings Act P.L. 115-120

- Delayed implementation of the "Cadillac Tax" until 2022

- Moratorium on assessment and collection of Health Insurers Tax delayed until 2019

- Moratorium on assessment of 2.3 percent tax on medical devices continued through 2019

2017

December 2017: Tax Cuts and Jobs Act of 2017, P.L. 115-97

- Repealed the Individual Mandate effective 2019

2015

December 18, 2015: Consolidated Appropriations Act, 2016. P.L. 114-113

- Two-year delay of the Cadillac tax

- One-year moratorium on the Affordable Care Act annual fee on certain health insurance providers

- Two-year moratorium on the Affordable Care Act medical device excise tax

December 11, 2015: Improving Access to Emergency Psychiatric Care Act. P.L. 114-97

- Extends the Medicaid Emergency Psychiatric Demonstration program implemented under Affordable Care Act section 2707, through September 30, 2016, Gives the Secretary of Health and Human Services the power to extend and expand the demonstration program through December 31, 2019. Requires the Secretary to submit recommendations to Congress on whether to make the program permanent by April 1, 2019

November 2, 2015: Bipartisan Budget Act of 2015. P.L. 114-74

- Repealed the Affordable Care Act requirement that employers with more than 200 employees automatically enroll new full-time employees in health insurance and continue coverage for current employees

October 7, 2015: Protecting Affordable Coverage for Employees (PACE) Act. P.L. 114-60

- Amended the Affordable Care Act definition of "small employer" to include employers that have up to fifty employees, while giving states the option to expand the definition to include employers with up to 100 employees

    - Originally, the Affordable Care Act designated employers with 100 or fewer employees as small employers as of January 1, 2016

    - Employers with 51 to 100 employees are now defined under the Affordable Care Act as large employers

    - Is significant because a number of Affordable Care Act reforms apply only to individual and small group/small employer plans

July 31, 2015: Surface Transportation and Veterans Health Care Choice Improvement Act of 2015. P.L. 114-41

- Incorporated the Hire More Heroes Act excluding employees from the employer's full time equivalent employee calculation who are provided health care through the Department of Veterans Affairs or TRICARE

April 16, 2015: Medicare Access and CHIP Reauthorization Act of 2015. P.L. 114-10

- Amended section 1848(p) of the Social Security Act (SSA), (added by Affordable Care Act section 3007)

    - Terminates application of the physician Value-Based payment Modifier (VBM) at the end of 2018

- The VBM will be used as one of the components of the composite score under the new Merit-Based Incentive Payment System (MIPS) starting in 2019

- Monetary authorizations:

  - Affordable Care Act section 5508(c): Designated $60 million for each of Fiscal Years 2016 and 2017 for graduate medical education payments to teaching health centers

  - Affordable Care Act section 2951: Designated $400 million for each for Fiscal Years 2015, 2016, and 2017 for the Maternal, Infant, and Early Childhood Home Visiting program

  - Appropriated $75 million for Fiscal Years 2016 and 2017 for the Personal Responsibility Education Program (PREP), (established by Affordable Care Act section 2953)

  - Affordable Care Act 5507(a): Appropriated $85 million for each of FY2016 and FY2017 for the Health Profession Opportunity Grant (HPOG) program (established by Affordable Care Act section 5507(a))

  - Affordable Care Act section 2701: Appropriated $20 million for the two-year period FY2016 through FY2017 to develop Medicaid adult quality measures

2014

April 1, 2014: Protecting Access to Medicare Act of 2014. P.L. 113-93

- Affordable Care Act section 1302(c): Deleted paragraph (2) of section 1302(c) which limited the deductibles for small group health plans at $2,000 for singles and $4,000 for families

- Affordable Care Act section 2951: Authorized $400 million for the first half of Fiscal Year 2015 for the Maternal, Infant, and Early Childhood Home Visiting program

- Affordable Care Act section 5507(a): Authorized $85 million for Fiscal Year 2015 for HPOG program

- Affordable Care Act section 2953: Authorized $75 million for Fiscal Year 2015 for the PREP

2013

January 2, 2013: American Taxpayer Relief Act of 2012. P.L. 112-240

- Repeal of the CLASS ACT: Title VIII of the Affordable Care Act , the Community Living Assistance Services and Supports (CLASS) Act

- Repealed of appropriations for the National Clearinghouse for Long-Term Care Information and rescinding of all unspent funds

- Nonrefundable Adoption Tax Credit was made permanent

2012

February 22, 2012 Middle Class Tax Relief and Job Creation Act of 2012. P.L. 112-96

- Amended Affordable Care Act section 4002 to reduce the PPHF annual appropriations over the period FY2013-FY2021 by a total of $6.25 billion to help offset the cost of extending the payroll tax cut and other programs in P.L. 112-96

- Amended section 1923(f) of the Social Security Act to extend for a year the Disproportionate Share Hospital (DSH) allotment reduction required under Affordable Care Act section 3203

- Amended section 1905(aa) of the Social Security Act (added by Affordable Care Act section 2006) to make a technical correction to the formula to phase down the Medicaid disaster-recovery Federal Medical Assistance Percentage (FMAP) adjustment as originally intended

2011

November 21, 2011 3 Percent Withholding Repeal and Job Creation Act. P.L. 112-56

- Amended IRC section 36B (added by Affordable Care Act section 1401(a))

  - The amendment modified the calculation of Modified Adjusted Gross Income (MAGI) to include Social Security benefits. MAGI is used to determine eligibility for exchange subsidies and Medicaid since 2014.

April 14, 2011 Comprehensive 1099 Taxpayer Protection and Repayment of Exchange Subsidy Overpayments Act of 2011. P.L. 112-9

- Amended IRC section 6041, (amended by Affordable Care Act section 9006) revoking the requirement that businesses file a Form 1099 information report when they pay a vendor more than $600 for goods within a single taxable year

- Amended section 36B of the Internal Revenue Code (IRC) (added by Affordable Care Act section 1401(a)) by adjusting the scale that determines the amount of excess premium tax credits that individuals have to repay based on household income

January 7, 2011 Ike Skelton National Defense Authorization Act for Fiscal Year 2011. P.L. 111-383

- Expanded TRICARE coverage to dependent adult children up to age twenty-six to match private health insurance requirements under the Affordable Care Act

2010

December 17, 2010 Tax Relief, Unemployment Insurance Reauthorization, and Job Creation Act of 2010. P.I. 111-312

- Amended Affordable Care Act section 10909 extending the nonrefundable adoption tax credit through tax year 2012

Health Coverage Not Affected by Healthcare Reform: "Excepted Benefits" and Retiree-Only Plans

13. What benefits are not governed by the Patient Protection and Affordable Care Act?

The law does not apply to "excepted benefits" and retiree-only health plans.

14. What are the "excepted benefits" that are not covered by the health reform law?

The Internal Revenue Service, Department of Labor and Public Health Service Act (PHSA) regulations identically define excepted benefits.[1]

Excepted benefits are:

(1) Accident, or disability income insurance, or any combination thereof; a supplement to liability insurance; liability insurance, including general liability insurance and automobile liability insurance; workers' compensation or similar insurance; automobile medical payment insurance; credit-only insurance; coverage for on-site medical clinics; or other similar insurance coverage, specified in regulations;[2]

(2) Benefits not subject to requirements if offered separately and not part of a health plan:

   o   limited scope dental or vision benefits;

   o   long-term care, nursing home care, home healthcare, community-based care, or any combination thereof; and

   o   similar benefits specified in regulations;[3]

(3) Benefits not subject to requirements if offered as independent, noncoordinated benefits. (Coverage only for a specified disease or illness; or hospital indemnity or other fixed indemnity insurance;[4] and

(4) Medicare supplemental health insurance (so-called "Medigap insurance") offered by a separate policy.[5]

PPACA inadvertently removed the exemption for retiree-only plans and "excepted benefits" from the PHSA, but left those exemptions intact in the Internal Revenue Code and ERISA. The preamble to the interim final grandfathered plan regulations clarifies the issue by stating that

---

1. Treas. Reg. §26, CFR §54.9831–1(c), Labor Reg. 29 CFR §2590.732(c), PHSA Reg. §45, CFR §146.145(c). (Effective December 30, 2016).
2. IRC Sec. 9832(c)(1).
3. IRC Sec. 9832(c)(2).
4. IRC Sec. 9832(c)(3).
5. IRC Sec. 9832(c)(4).

the exemption for retiree-only plans and excepted benefit plans still applies for those plans subject to the Code and ERISA. Thus, with respect to retiree-only and excepted benefits, the regulators have decided that they will read the PHSA as if an exemption for retiree-only and excepted benefit plans is still in effect, and they have encouraged state insurance regulators to do the same.

On June 10, 2016, the Departments of Labor, Health and Human Services and the Internal Revenue Service proposed joint regulations to address excepted benefits which were finalized on November 21, 2016 and effective on December 30, 2016.[1]

The regulations provide new guidance on some excepted benefits, which are exempt from most of the ACA's market reform requirements:

(1)   SUPPLEMENTAL HEALTH INSURANCE

- Health services NOT covered by the primary coverage can be an excepted benefit as long as none of the benefits are an Essential Health Benefit (EHB) in the state in which the policy is issued.

    - The regulations confirm that a supplemental health policy that covers cost sharing (such as deductibles and copays) and additional categories of nonessential benefits may also be an excepted benefit.

(2)   DENTAL AND VISION COVERAGE

- Is deemed to be excepted benefits if the benefits are limited and either part of a policy separate from the health insurance or not considered part of the medical plan.

    - This can also include self-funded plans where the claims administration is done separately from the medical plan.

(3)   WRAPAROUND COVERAGE

- Coverage that "wraps around" a primary coverage can be excepted benefits.

    - An example might include coverage offered to part time employees who are not eligible for the coverage offered to full time employees

(4)   EMPLOYEE ASSISTANCE PROGRAMS

- EAPs can still be an excepted benefit yet offer limited medical benefits. The key seems to be that they do not require payment of premiums and do not coordinate with other plans.

---

1.   Expatriate Health Plans, Expatriate Health Plan Issuers, and Qualified Expatriates; Excepted Benefits; Lifetime and Annual Limits; and Short-Term, Limited-Duration Insurance, 26 CFR Parts 1, 46, 54, 57, and 301; 29 CFR Part 2590; 45 CFR Parts 144, 146, 147, 148, and 158, 81 Fed. Reg. 38019 (June 10, 2016) https://www.gpo.gov/fdsys/pkg/FR-2016-06-10/pdf/2016-13583.pdf (Last accessed July 10, 20189).

(5)   TRAVEL INSURANCE

- Travel insurance products with limited health benefits may also qualify as excepted benefits, provided that they are not offered on a stand-alone basis and are incidental to other coverage.

    o   The regulations define "travel insurance" as coverage for personal risks such as cancellations and interruptions; lost baggage; damages to accommodations or rented vehicles; and sickness, accident, disability or death during travel. Travel insurance cannot include major medical plans that provide major medical coverage for trips lasting six months or more.

(6)   HOSPITAL INDEMNITY AND OTHER FIXED-INDEMNITY COVERAGE

- May be "noncoordinated" excepted benefits.

- These can be hospitalization indemnity as well as contracts for coverage for specific diseases.

    o   An example of this type of policy would be a "cancer" policy. To ensure that enrollees don't mistake these policies for minimum essential coverage, the departments add additional requirements for hospital indemnity and other fixed-indemnity insurance to be excepted benefits:

- Requirements include

    o   The benefits must be provided under a separate coverage of insurance.

    o   The coverage cannot coordinate with benefits of another group plan of the same sponsor.

    o   Enrollment materials must include a notice with the following language (in at least 14-point font):

    o   This is a supplement to health insurance and is not a substitute for major medical coverage. This is not qualifying health coverage ("minimum essential coverage") that satisfies the health coverage requirement of the Affordable Care Act. If you don't have minimum essential coverage, you may owe an additional payment with your taxes.

    o   The benefit amount may not be linked to the item or service provided and must be paid regardless of whether benefits are provided under a group plan.

    o   Benefits must be provided on a per diem (or per other time period, such as per week) basis. For example, policies that provide benefits for doctors' visits at a fixed amount per visit would not be excepted benefits.

(7)   *MULTIPLE DISEASE OR ILLNESS POLICIES* (e.g., cancer-only policies)

- *These* may constitute "noncoordinated" excepted benefits, as long as the coverage meets the conditions for independent, noncoordinated benefits. There has been concern as to whether such policies might be mistaken for comprehensive medical coverage.

- The regulations change the required length of short-term, limited-duration insurance from less than twelve to less than three months. Such insurance may be offered to help people who lose their coverage transition to new coverage. The regulations also require the prominent display of the following notice in contract and enrollment materials (in at least fourteen-point font):

- This is not qualifying health coverage ("minimum essential coverage") that satisfies the health coverage requirement of the Affordable Care Act. If you don't have minimum essential coverage, you may owe an additional payment with your taxes.

15. What are the retiree-only health plans that are not governed by PPACA?

A "retiree-only" plan that is exempt from PPACA's mandates for a particular plan year is defined as any group health plan (and group health insurance coverage offered in connection with a group health plan) with less than two participants who are current employees. Exempt retiree plans covering dependents need not follow the adult child to age twenty-six rule but they must follow any applicable state rule unless the plan is self-insured, in which case state insurance law does not apply.

When the Affordable Care Act was enacted, the retiree-only exception was deleted from the Public Health Services Act (PHSA), but the exception remains in place in both ERISA and the IRC. The agencies take the position that the deletion of the retiree-only exception does not conflict with ERISA and the IRC unless they "cannot be read consistently with an incorporated provision" of the PHSA.

In *King v. Blue Cross and Blue Shield of Illinois*, a participant in a retiree-only plan challenged the plan's lifetime dollar limits on benefits. The court decided in favor of the plan, stating the even though the retiree-only exception is no longer in the PHSA, it did not mean that Congress intended to actually eliminate the exception.[1]

In addition, a retiree-only plan that also covers individuals with long-term disability insurance can meet the requirements for exemption from compliance with HIPAA portability and health care reform requirements.

In another development, the IRS issued a final rule providing that a retiree may decline retiree coverage and qualify for a subsidy if otherwise eligible based on his or her income.[2]

---

1.   BLUE CROSS AND BLUE SHIELD OF ILLINOIS et al., Defendants, 104 F.Supp.3d 1062 (U.S.D.C., S.D. Cal.), May 13, 2015.
2.   See Federal Register, Vol. 80, No. 243, December 18, 2015, https://www.gpo.gov/fdsys/pkg/FR-2015-12-18/pdf/2015-31866.pdf (Last accessed July 5, 2019).

16. Is the retiree-only exemption available for self-funded and insured plans?

Yes, the retiree-only exemption applies to both self-funded and insured plans. PPACA technically eliminates the exemption in the Public Health Services Act for "plans with less than two participants who are current employees" but preserves the exemption under the parallel provisions in ERISA and the Internal Revenue Code.

The PHSA is applicable to governmental plans and to issuers of insured plans. The preamble to the PPACA grandfathering Interim Final Regulation, however, confirms that the retiree-only plan exemption under ERISA and the Internal Revenue Code has been preserved, and also provides that, even though the exemption was technically eliminated from the PHSA:[1] (See Q 15.)

- HHS will not enforce the requirements of HIPAA or PPACA with regard to nonfederal governmental retiree-only plans.

- States are encouraged not to apply the provisions of PPACA to issuers of retiree-only plans (i.e., insured plans).

17. From which PPACA mandates are retiree-only plans exempt?

Retiree-only plans are exempt from the PPACA-mandated "insurance market reforms" listed below (referring to PPACA sections):

- Section 2711 – No lifetime or annual limits.

- Section 2712 – Prohibition on rescission.

- Section 2713 – Coverage of preventive health services.

- Section 2714 – Extension of dependent coverage.

- Section 2715 – Development and utilization of uniform explanation of coverage documents and standardized definitions.

- Section 2715A – Provision of additional information.

- Section 2716 – Prohibition on discrimination in favor of highly compensated individuals for insured plans.

- Section 2717 – Ensuring the quality of care reporting.

- Section 2718 – Medical loss ratio restrictions.

---

1.   75 Fed. Reg. 34538, 34540.

- Section 2719 – Required appeals process.

- Section 2719A – Patient protections (selecting providers and emergency room services).

- Section 2794 – Rate review.

- Section 2704 – Prohibition of pre-existing condition exclusions or other discrimination based on health status.

- Section 2701 – Restrictions on what criteria can be used in rating and rate band limits.

- Section 2702 – Guaranteed issue.

- Section 2703 – Guaranteed renewability.

- Section 2705 – Prohibiting discrimination against individual participants and beneficiaries based on health status.

- Section 2706 – Non-discrimination towards healthcare providers.

- Section 2707 – Cost-sharing requirements and essential benefit requirements.

- Section 2708 – Prohibition on waiting periods of more than ninety days.

- Section 2709 – Coverage for individuals participating in approved clinical trials.

18. Does the 2022 "Cadillac Tax" apply to retiree-only health plans?

For retirees under the age of sixty-five, the Cadillac excise tax is a 40 percent tax that applies to coverage in excess of $10,200 ($11,850 for qualified retirees and those in certain high-risk professions) for self-only coverage and $27,500 for family coverage ($30,900 for qualified retirees and those in certain high-risk professions). In determining the applicable cost of employer-sponsored coverage to retired employees, the plan may elect to treat retirees under age sixty-five and retirees aged sixty-five and older as being "similarly-situated beneficiaries," meaning that the costs for both groups can be blended together. Since the cost of retiree coverage for Medicare-eligible retirees is considerably less than for retirees under the age of sixty-five, such blending would usually lower the average cost of the retiree plan for purposes of determining whether there is any taxable excess.

The Cadillac Tax was scheduled to take effect in 2018 but was delayed until 2020 by the Consolidated Appropriations Act of 2016. On July 27, 2017, "Heller Amendment 502", introduced by Senator Dean Heller (R-Nevada), which would repeal the "Cadillac Tax" was passed by the United States Senate by a vote of 52-48. The vote was split on partisan lines with the exception of Democrats Catherine Cortez Mastro (D-Nevada) and Martin Heinreich (D-New Mexico) adding support. The repeal was not taken up by the United States House of Representatives.

On January 22, 2018, Congress passed and President Trump signed the same day, the Federal Register Printing Savings Act, which included another delay (to 2022) in implementation of the Cadillac Tax.

On July 17, 2019, the United States House of Representatives voted to repeal the Cadillac Tax. As of publication time of the 2020 edition of this book, the United States Senate has not yet scored or voted on a repeal bill, however, at least one repeal bill has forty-two co-sponsors.

The Cadillac Tax is discussed in more detail in Part VIII of this book.

19. Who are "current employees" for purposes of the retiree-only exemption?

The HIPAA regulations do not provide any guidance defining who is a current employee for purposes of the retiree-only plan exemption. However, a retiree who is rehired as an employee (and receives either a Form W-2 or Form 1099 for the year) should be treated as a <u>current</u> (i.e., active) employee that counts against retiree-only plan status and should be covered under the ERISA plan maintained for purposes of current employees immediately upon rehire.

HHS issued an FAQ indicating that the retiree-only exemption may be available for plans that cover both retirees and persons on long-term disability.[1] Until further guidance has been issued, HHS will treat such plans as satisfying the retiree-only exemption. To the extent, future guidance on this issue is more restrictive with respect to the availability of the retiree-only exemption; the guidance will be prospective, applying to plan years that begin sometime after its issuance.

20. What should plan sponsors do to demonstrate that they have established a retiree-only plan that satisfies the exemption?

For ERISA welfare plans, the plan sponsor should maintain a separate plan document and Summary Plan Description (SPD) and file a separate Form 5500[2] (if it has more than 100 participants at the beginning of the plan year). Plan sponsors that do not currently maintain a separate retiree-only plan but intend to establish one on a prospective basis for the following plan year should also follow these steps.

For non-ERISA retiree-only plans (for example, government plans), the plan should be a separate document and cover fewer than two current employees, other than dependents, who are beneficiaries for this purpose. Because non-ERISA plans do not file a Form 5500 or maintain SPDs as required by ERISA, as part of the certification process some insurance companies will require formal documentation describing the plan's eligibility rules.

---

1.   FAQs About the Affordable Care Act Implementation Part III, Q&A 2, at https://www.dol.gov/sites/default/files/ebsa/about-ebsa/our-activities/resource-center/faqs/aca-part-iii.pdf. (Last accessed July 15, 2019).

2.   Form 5500 Series information: https://www.dol.gov/agencies/ebsa/employers-and-advisers/plan-administration-and-compliance/reporting-and-filing/form-5500 (Last accessed July 1, 2019).

21. What will happen if a plan sponsor does not amend its group health plan to carve out retirees into a separate retiree-only ERISA plan?

If a plan sponsor continues covering current employees and retirees under the same ERISA plan, the retiree-only plan exemption will most likely not be met. This means that PPACA's requirements will apply. Plans that are not exempt from PPACA still may be "grandfathered" if they were in effect on March 23, 2010 and meet the criteria in PPACA for grandfathered status. Grandfathered plans are subject to some but not all of the PPACA mandates.

22. Can a plan sponsor amend its plan to carve out retirees into a retiree-only plan and preserve the grandfather status of the plan for current (i.e., active) employees?

Yes. Regulators have informally confirmed that amending a plan to carve out retirees into a separate retiree-only plan will not impact the grandfathered status of the plan for current employees under the following conditions:

- No changes may be made to the benefits or cost sharing for current employees.

- The new separate retiree-only plan must be created as the new plan in the sequence.

The grandfathered plan Final Regulations[1] contain complex anti-abuse rules for changes in plan eligibility, but these rules apply only when the individuals transferred into another plan are employees, not retirees.[2]

23. Is a retiree with an option to receive retiree health coverage from a former employer eligible to buy insurance on an exchange (marketplace) and receive, if qualified, a subsidy?

Yes, if the retiree is not enrolled in the retiree coverage. If the retiree can opt out of the retiree coverage, the retiree may qualify for the credit, even if the retiree coverage is otherwise affordable and provides minimum value. Current employees don't have that flexibility – if the offered coverage is affordable and provides minimum value they are precluded from the credit whether they take the employer coverage or not.

The rule for former employees depends on whether they are actually covered. If a retiree declines coverage, then the retiree may qualify of an exchange subsidy. Treas. Reg. 1.36B-2(c)(3)(iv) states:

> **(iv) Post-employment coverage.** A former employee (including a retiree), or an individual related (within the meaning of paragraph (c)(3)(i) of this section) to a former employee, who may enroll in eligible employer-sponsored coverage or in continuation coverage required under Federal law or a State law that provides comparable continuation

---

1.   80 Fed. Reg. 72274, 80 Fed. Reg. 72298 (November 18, 2015).
2.   45 CFR §147.140(b)(2)(ii).

coverage is eligible for minimum essential coverage under this coverage only for months that the former employee or related individual is enrolled in the coverage.[1]

24. How does the retiree-only exemption relate to the Retiree Drug Subsidy Program (RDS) and Early Retiree Reinsurance Program (ERRP)?

A plan may receive reimbursements under the ERRP or subsidies under the RDS regardless of whether it meets the retiree-only plan exemption for HIPAA (and PPACA) purposes.[2] Prior to January 1, 2014, when guaranteed issue of insurance coverage, elimination of pre-existing condition exclusions, and several other critical ACA protections took effect for individual health insurance coverage, early retirees between ages fifty-five and sixty-four often faced difficulties obtaining insurance in the individual market because of age or chronic conditions that made coverage unaffordable or inaccessible. These early retirees were often charged more for health coverage based on their health status or denied coverage altogether in the individual market. Early retiree health coverage through employment-based plans provides a valuable bridge from employment coverage, for active workers, to Medicare coverage, for eligible retirees. The Early Retiree Reinsurance Program subsidized these programs with $5 billion to nearly three thousand employers and other sponsors of retiree plans, which was expended within eighteen months after healthcare reform was enacted in March 2010. The median total amount paid per plan was approximately $190,000. Upwards of 2.6 million early retirees were assisted by this plan.

Employer and Individual Mandates

See Part XI for a Complete Discussion of the Employer Mandate Provisions and Appendix B Copies of Several Mandatory Notices

25. What mandates were delayed by the IRS in July 2015?

IRS Notice 2013-45 provided a one-year delay to three requirements under the healthcare reform law:

- The annual obligation under section 6055 of the Internal Revenue Code for insurers, self-insuring employers and other parties that provide "minimum essential coverage" to provide certain information to the IRS.

- The annual obligation under Internal Revenue Code section 6056 for applicable large employers to report to the IRS and to the employer's full-time employees as to whether and what healthcare coverage is offered to such employees.

- The requirement under Internal Revenue Code section 4980H for applicable large employers to offer healthcare coverage to full-time employees or pay penalties, commonly known as the "Play-or-Pay" penalties (POP) or employer mandate. A second delay for certain employers was later announced. In 2015, the ACA's employer shared responsibility provisions generally applied to larger

---

1. 26 C.F.R. §1.36B–2, Treas. Reg. §1.36B–2. (As amended through July 26, 2017).
2. See Successful Support of Early Retiree Health Coverage at https://www.cms.gov/CCIIO/Programs-and-Initiatives/Insurance-Programs/Early-Retiree-Reinsurance-Program.html (Last accessed July 18, 2019).

firms (Applicable Large Employers or ALEs) with one-hundred or more full-time employees. Employers with fifty to ninety-nine full-time employees will have to comply starting in 2016.

- Under additional transition relief, an employer was able to determine its status as an ALE for 2015 by reference to a period of at least six consecutive calendar months, chosen by the employer, during the 2014 calendar year, rather than the entire 2014 calendar year. This period had to begin no later than July 1, 2014, and to end no earlier than ninety days before the first day of the plan year beginning on or after January 1, 2015, (ninety days being the maximum permissible administrative period).

- To have avoided a payment for failing to offer health coverage in 2015, ALEs needed to offer coverage to 70 percent of their full-time employees.

- To avoid a payment in 2016 and years subsequent, ALE must offer coverage to 95 percent of their full-time employees.

- Employers who are new ALEs (employers that were not in existence in 2014) will not be subject to penalties for January through March of their first year of applicability, as long as they offer employee coverage that provides minimum value on or before April 1.

Other aspects of PPACA that were scheduled to become effective in 2014 went into effect as planned.

26. What final regulations have been issued regarding employer information reporting for healthcare reform for employers subject to the employer mandate?

Sections 6055 and 6056 of the Internal Revenue Code ("Code") prescribe reporting of healthcare coverage and became effective for 2015, with the first forms required to be filed in 2016, an administratively delayed effective date.[1] The employer mandate generally requires employers with fifty or more full-time employees (Applicable Large Employers or "ALEs") to offer coverage to their full-time employees that meets minimum value and affordability standards under the ACA or pay a penalty. Employers that have fewer than fifty full-time and full-time equivalent employees are exempt from the ACA employer shared responsibility provisions and therefore from the employer reporting requirements. The final March 2014 regulations on this reporting provide for a single, combined form for information reporting under both Code sections 6055[2] and 6056[3] as well as a simplified option for employer reporting of "qualified offers" of coverage to employees.

---

1.   IRS Notice 2013-45 delayed that law's 2014 effective date until 2015.
2.   Treas. Reg. §1.6055-1 and 1.6055-2.
3.   Treas. Reg. §301.6056-1 and -2.

Employers that were subject to a delayed employer mandate, i.e., those with at least fifty full-time employees but fewer than one-hundred full-time employees (including full-time equivalent employees), in transitioning into compliance with section 4980H, the final regulations provided transition relief from Code section 4980H for 2015 (plus, in the case of any non-calendar plan year that begins in 2015, the portion of the 2015 plan year that falls in 2016).[1]

Code section 6055 describes reporting requirements to the IRS and individuals for self-insuring employers, insurers, government entities, and certain other providers of minimum essential coverage ("MEC"). Wellness programs that are an element of other minimum essential coverage (such as wellness programs offering reduced premiums or cost sharing under a group health plan) do not require separate Code section 6055 reporting. Code section 6056 describes reporting requirements for applicable large employers to provide employees with information so that they can determine whether they can receive a premium tax credit if they purchase insurance from a health care exchange. Code section 6056 also requires such employers to report to the IRS information concerning health care coverage. Reporting under these new requirements will be similar to the reporting of W-2 information where individual statements are provided to each employee on form W-2 and the W-2s are accumulated and summarized on Form W-3. Employers who sponsor self-insured health care plans and who are therefore required to report under both sections 6055 and 6056 may file a combined report for the IRS and employees. Electronic reporting is required for employers who have more than 250 employees for whom individual reports are required. Large employers that self-insure (employers that pay their employees' medical costs directly, instead of joining a traditional plan) will fill out both sections of the form. Large employers that do not self-insure will only fill out the top half of the form, for reporting under Code section 6056.

The final regulations under Code section 6055 require an employer to report information about the employer, the employees insured, and information on the minimum essential coverage provided, including employee and dependent social security numbers or a date of birth if the SSN is not available after reasonable efforts to obtain it. Code section 6056 requires applicable large employers to report information about themselves, such as the number of full-time employees for each month during the calendar year, certify whether they offered coverage to their full-time employees, and provide certain information about the plan offered, including the monthly premium for the plan.

The regulations provide that a qualifying offer of coverage is "an offer of minimum value coverage that provides employee-only coverage at a cost to the employee of no more than about $1,100 (9.5 percent of the estimated federal poverty level in 2015) in 2015" combined with an offer of coverage to the employee's family, which does not need to meet the cost threshold. An employer makes a qualifying offer if it offered the employee coverage that provides 60 percent minimum value at an employee cost for employee-only coverage of no more than 9.5 percent of the federal poverty line, and also offered minimum essential coverage to employees' spouses and dependents. For 2015, refer to Revenue Procedure 2014-37,[2] for 2016

---

1.   See section XV.D.6 of the preamble to the final regulations under section 4980H for a description of eligibility conditions for transition relief.
2.   Revenue Procedure 2014-37 https://www.irs.gov/pub/irs-drop/rp-14-37.pdf. (Last accessed September 16, 2018)

refer to Revenue Procedure 2014-62,[1] which set the affordability coverage at 9.56 percent to 2015 and at 9.66 percent for 2016. For 2017, Revenue Procedure 2016-24[2] increased the affordability percentage to 9.69 in 2017 and Revenue Procedure 2017-36 established 9.56 percent of the Federal Poverty Level for 2018. For 2019, Revenue Procedure 2018-34 sets the affordability coverage at 9.86 percent. For 2020, Revenue Procedure 2019-29, sets the affordability coverage at 9.78 percent.[3]

For employees receiving a qualified offer for all twelve months, employers will need to report only the names, addresses, and taxpayer identification numbers of such employees. For employees receiving a qualifying offer in fewer than twelve months in the year, employers will be able to report such employees for each of those months by simply entering a code.

Employers need not report their health plan waiting periods nor the employer's share of costs paid under the health plan.

27. What did Notice 2013-45 specify regarding information reporting?

The IRS encouraged employers, insurers and other reporting entities to voluntarily comply with the proposed rules for information reporting for 2014, but no penalties for failure to comply with these reporting provisions existed for not reporting for 2014.

The Notice made clear that the 2014 transition relief is limited solely to these three items and has no effect on the effective date or application of other provisions under the Act, many of which went into effect during 2014. For example, the transition relief has no effect on the provisions which took effect in 2014 as to premium tax credits for those purchasing subsidized health insurance on an exchange marketplace or the individual mandate requirements under Internal Revenue Code section 5000A for individuals to maintain healthcare coverage for themselves or pay penalties.

28. What is the Employer Mandate?

Health reform and its "Employer Mandate" do not require employers to provide health coverage for their employees. However, beginning in 2015, any applicable large employer (one with fifty or more full-time employees) became liable for a substantial "assessable payment"[4] if it "fails to offer its full-time employees (and their dependents) the opportunity to enroll in minimum essential coverage under an eligible employer-sponsored plan."[5] As discussed above, however, employers with at least fifty full-time employees but fewer than one-hundred full-time employees (including full-time equivalent employees), enjoyed transition relief from Internal Revenue Code section 4980H for 2015 (plus, in the case of any non-calendar plan year that begins in 2015, the portion of the 2015 plan year that falls in 2016).

---

1.   Revenue Procedure 2014-62 https://www.irs.gov/pub/irs-drop/rp-14-62.pdf.
2.   Revenue Procedure 2016-24 https://www.irs.gov/pub/irs-drop/rp-16-24.pdf. (Last accessed September 16, 2018)
3.   Revenue Procedure 2019-29 https://www.irs.gov/pub/irs-drop/rp-19-29.pdf.
4.   In contrast, the amount that individuals are required to pay for failure to comply with the Individual Mandate is called a "penalty."
5.   IRC Sec. 4980H(a)(1), (2).

Understanding the Penalties

There are two alternative penalties for the Employer Mandate. The ANNUAL amounts for 2019 are $2,500 or $3,750, but the actual amount is calculated on a monthly basis. Although the penalties began at $2,000 and $3,000, they have been adjusted for inflation.[1] Neither penalty is triggered unless an employee receives a tax credit for the purchase of health insurance on a state exchange. Employer Mandate penalties for 2020 are $2,570 and $3,860.

Generally, if an employee is offered affordable Minimum Essential Coverage (MEC) under an employer-sponsored plan, then the individual is ineligible for a premium tax credit and cost-sharing reductions for health insurance purchased through a state exchange. However, an employee may be offered minimum essential coverage by the employer that is either "unaffordable" or that consists of a plan under which the plan's share of the total allowed cost of benefits is less than 60 percent. In that situation, the employee is eligible for a premium tax credit and cost-sharing reductions if the employee declines to enroll in the coverage and purchases coverage through an exchange.

"Unaffordable" is defined by PPACA as coverage with a premium required to be paid by the employee that is more than 9.69 percent in 2017, 9.56 in 2018, 9.86 in 2019, and 9.78 in 2020 of the employee's household income (as defined for purposes of the premium tax credit[2] for individuals, discussed in Q 30). Although this percentage began at 9.5 percent of the employee's household income in 2014, it was increased to 9.56 percent in 2015 and to 9.66 percent for 2016.[3] This percentage of the employee's income is indexed to the per capita growth in premiums for the insured market as determined by the Secretary of Health and Human Services. The employee must seek an affordability waiver from the state exchange and provide information as to family income and the lowest cost employer option offered to the employee. The state exchange then provides the waiver to the employee. The employer penalty generally applies for employees receiving an affordability waiver.

For purposes of determining whether coverage is unaffordable, required salary reduction contributions are treated as payments required to be made by the employee. However, if an employee is reimbursed by the employer for any portion of the premium for health insurance coverage purchased through the exchange, including any reimbursement through salary reduction contributions under a cafeteria plan, the coverage is employer-provided, and the employee is not eligible for premium tax credits or cost-sharing reductions. Thus, an individual is not permitted to purchase coverage through the exchange, apply for the premium tax credit, and pay for the individual's portion of the premium using salary reduction contributions under the cafeteria plan of the individual's employer.[4]

---

1.   IRC Sec. 4980H(c)(5).
2.   IRC Sec. 36B, as discussed in more detail hereafter.
3.   IRS Notice 2015-87, December 16, 2015.
4.   Joint Comm. Staff, Tech Explanation of the Revenue Provisions of the Reconciliation Act of 2010, as amended, in combination with the Patient Protection and Affordable Care Act (JCX-18-10), 3/21/2010, p.37.

29. How do the State Exchanges obtain information on affordability for an individual?

The Internal Revenue Code[1] (section 6103) permits the disclosure of taxpayer return information to assist exchanges and state agencies, but not employers, in performing certain functions for which income verification is required. IRS regulations permit the IRS to disclose income and other specified information about an individual taxpayer to Health & Human Services (HHS)[2] for purposes of making eligibility determinations for advance payments of the premium tax credit or the cost-sharing reductions.[3] HHS could then disclose the information to the Exchange or the state agency processing the individual's application. As a condition for receiving return information, each receiving entity (i.e., HHS, the Exchanges, and state agencies as well as their respective contractors) is required to adhere to the privacy safeguards established under Internal Revenue Code section 6103(p)(4).

30. How do the two Employer Mandate penalties work?

Employers can be penalized for not providing minimum essential coverage or for having an inadequate health plan.

<u>No Minimum Essential Coverage – $2,570 Per Full Time Employee minus the first 30 employee Penalty</u>. Employers with at least fifty full-time equivalent employees and with at least thirty-one full-time employees must offer minimum essential health coverage meeting specified requirements. If the employers offer no health plan, they must pay a $2,570 per full-time employee penalty if any of the full-time employees receive a federal premium subsidy through a health care exchange. 2019 penalties were $2,500.

The calculation of "a large employer" includes part-time workers. However, the $2,570 per Full-Time Employee minus the first 30 Penalty is only calculated based on full-time workers therefore, not all large employers who have a full-time employee receiving a credit would actually pay a penalty. This could occur because the first thirty workers are not counted.

For example, an employer with one-hundred part-time workers (fifteen hours per week) and thirty full-time workers (thirty-plus hours per week) would be considered a large employer with eighty full-time equivalent workers. Even if one or more workers received a premium credit, the penalty would only be assessed against the number of full-time workers: $(30 - 30) \times $2,570 = 0$. Thus, read literally, if only one employee purchases insurance on an exchange and receives a premium tax credit, the penalty applies to all full-time employees minus thirty full-time employees times $2,570.

The IRS has indicated that "it is contemplated that the proposed regulations will make clear that an employer offering [minimum essential] coverage to all, or substantially all, of its full-time

---

1.   IRC Sec. 6103(l)(21).
2.   T.D. 9628, Internal Revenue Bulletin 2013-36 https://www.irs.gov/irb/2013-49_IRB/ar09.html. (Last accessed July 1, 2019).
3.   77 Fed. Reg. 25378 (Apr. 30, 2012).

employees would not be subject to the Internal Revenue Code section 4980H(a) 'all-full-time employees minus 30' assessable payment provisions."[1]

To avoid the $2,570 penalty, the employer must offer "minimum essential coverage" to its full-time employees and their dependents.[2] Dependents can include not only children, but also parents, siblings, uncles, aunts, nieces, nephews, grandchildren, and various in-laws.[3] Any person who has the same principal place of abode and is a member of the same household as the taxpayer is eligible to become a dependent.[4]

The minimum essential coverage that an employer must offer in order to avoid the "all full-time employees minus 30" penalty calculation is defined in the statutory provisions imposing the individual mandate. It includes only:

- government-sponsored programs (such as Medicare, etc.);

- eligible employer-sponsored plans;

- plans offered in the "individual market";

- grandfathered health plans; and

- other coverage that "the Secretary of Health and Human Services, in coordination with the Secretary [of the Treasury], recognizes" for purposes of this determination.[5]

There are some fundamental unresolved issues with respect to this definition. First, an "eligible employer-sponsored plan" is defined as a "group health plan or group health insurance coverage" that is either a governmental plan or another "plan or coverage offered in the small or large group market within a State."[6] Even though the language of that definition specifically seems to contemplate a "group health plan," as opposed to "group health insurance coverage," there was a question as to whether a private self-insured plan would qualify as "any other plan or coverage offered in the small or large group market within a State." However, the IRS has indicated that self-insured plans qualify.[7]

---

1.   IRS Notice 2011-36.

2.   IRC Sec. 4980H(a)(1), (b)(1)(A); IRC Sec. 5000A(b)(3)(A). Several comments submitted in response to Notice 2011-36 argue that employers should not be obligated to provide coverage to dependents of full-time employees. These comments contend that employers should not be mandated to provide family or other types of coverage beyond self-only coverage and that such dependents will often either have minimum essential coverage available elsewhere or will not be required to carry minimum essential coverage under the exceptions contained in Code section 5000A . *See, e.g.,* Business Round Table Comments on IRS Notice 2011-36 (submitted June 17, 2011); Society for Human Resource Management Comments on IRS Notice 2011-36 (submitted June 17, 2011); American Benefits Council Comments on IRS Notice 2011-36 (submitted June 15, 2011).

3.   IRC Secs. 152(d)(2)(A)-(C), (E)–(G).

4.   IRC Sec. 152(d)(2).

5.   IRC Sec. 5000A(f)(1).

6.   IRC Sec. 5000A(f)(2).

7.   *See* IRC §5000A(f)(5); 42 USC §18024(a)(1) (PPACA §1304(a)(1)) (defining "group market" as "the health insurance market under which individuals obtain health insurance coverage (directly or through any arrangement) on behalf of themselves (and their dependents) through a group health plan maintained by an employer" (emphasis added)). However, the preamble to the proposed regulations under Code section 36B, states that regulations under Code section 5000A will "provide that an employer-sponsored plan will not fail to be minimum essential coverage solely because it is a plan to reimburse employees for medical care for which reimbursement is not provided under a policy of accident and health insurance (a self-insured plan)."

Second, the grandfathered health plan exception may not be applicable because of the ease with which a plan can lose grandfathered status. The actions that can destroy grandfathered status include:

- the elimination of all or substantially all benefits to diagnose or treat a particular condition;

- any increase in a percentage cost-sharing requirement;

- a decrease in the employer contribution rate by more than 5 percent; and

- certain changes to annual limits on benefits.[1]

In addition, it seems that failure annually to give plan participants a notice that the plan is grandfathered causes a loss of grandfathered status.[2]

Third, minimum essential coverage is treated as being provided only if "the plan's share of the total allowed costs of benefits provided under the plan is at least 60 percent of such costs."[3] However, if the employee nevertheless participates in the plan, this rule does not apply.[4] Determining whether this requirement is satisfied is easy only for fully insured plans with no deductibles, co-pays or coinsurance. When the employer pays 60 percent or more of the premium, such a plan would be treated as providing "minimum essential coverage."

How deductibles, co-pays, and coinsurance should be handled is not clear. The plan's 60 percent share is measured against "the total allowed costs of benefits provided under the plan." To the extent that an employee pays deductibles, co-pays, and coinsurance, those benefits are not provided under the plan. If deductibles, co-pays, and coinsurance are to be counted, then, application of the 60 percent test is much more difficult.

<u>Inadequate Health Plan – $3,860 Per Full-Time Employee Penalty</u>. A different penalty applies for employers of at least fifty full-time equivalent employees that offer minimum essential coverage that does not meet the federal requirements. Employers that offer health coverage will not meet the requirements if:

- at least one full-time employee obtains a premium credit in an exchange plan; and

- the plan does not provide

---

1. Treas. Reg. §54.9815-1251T(g)(1)(i), (ii), (v). When the interim final regulations were first issued, an employer's entrance into a new policy, certificate or contract of insurance after March 23, 2010 (*e.g.*, because the previous policy, certificate or contract was not being renewed), would trigger loss of grandfathered status. Treas. Reg. §54.9815-1251T(a)(1)(ii). However, this was subsequently changed in Treasury Decision 9506. This decision amended the interim final regulations to allow employers to change insurance providers, so long as the new policy, certificate or contract did not otherwise make changes triggering loss of grandfathered status under the regulations. It should be noted that this amendment does not apply retroactively; therefore, plans undergoing carrier changes prior to November 17, 2010 still lost grandfathered status (subject to a special exception for collectively bargained plans). T.D. 9506 (amending Treas. Reg. §54.9815-1251T(a)(1)).

2. This issue is discussed in more detail later in this book.

3. IRC Sec. 36B(c)(2)(C)(ii). This special rule does not apply if the employee, or dependent, does in fact procure coverage under the eligible employer-sponsored plan or grandfathered health plan. IRC Sec. 36B(c)(2)(C)(iii).

4. IRC Sec. 36B(c)(2)(C)(iii).

    o   minimum essential benefits;

    o   the employee's required contribution for self-only coverage exceeds 9.69 percent in 2017, 9.56 in 2018, 9.86 in 2019, and 9.78 in 2020 of the employee's household income; or

    o   the employer pays for less than 60 percent of the benefits.

In 2020, the monthly penalty assessed to the employer for each full-time employee who receives a premium credit will be one-twelfth of $3,860 for any applicable month. However, the total penalty is limited to the total number of the firm's full-time employees minus thirty, multiplied by one-twelfth of $2,570 for any applicable month. After 2020, the penalty amounts will be indexed by the premium adjustment percentage for the calendar year. The 2019 penalties were $2,500 and $3,750.

This penalty is imposed for any month in which "at least one full-time employee of the applicable large employer has been certified to the employer under section 1411 of the Patient Protection and Affordable Care Act as having enrolled for such month in a qualified health plan through a state health insurance exchange for which a tax credit is allowed or paid."[1] As explained in Q 29, this individual tax credit is available to most low- and middle-income individuals that are not offered affordable, minimum essential coverage by their employers and are not covered by Medicaid.[2]

31. Is the employer mandate penalty tax-deductible?

No. Because the employer mandate penalty is an excise tax, it is NOT deductible. The IRS will calculate and assess the tax proactively without self-reporting by employers. To avoid the tax, proper health coverage must be offered to at least 95 percent of an employer's employees. Independent contractors who should be treated as full-time employees under the common law standards must be considered in the 95 percent threshold test.

32. How is the 95 percent threshold of the employer's employees calculated?

The 95 percent threshold must be calculated monthly, because the excise tax is assessed monthly, at a rate of $214.17 ($2,570/12). Therefore, each month, an employer must identify its full-time employees based on weekly average hours of service during the month and determine whether they have been offered coverage for the month. For hourly employees, actual hours must be counted. For salaried employees, actual hours may be counted, or hours-equivalency rules may be used to eliminate the administrative burden of counting actual hours.

To make the full-time employee determination more predictable, an employer can take advantage of rules that allow an employee's status as a full-time employee in future periods to be

---

1.   IRC Sec. 4980H(a)(2).
2.   IRC Sec. 36B(c)(1), (2)(C); 42 USC §18071(b) (PPACA §1402(b)).

based on hours of service in prior periods. While these rules are helpful, they, too, are complex and have exacting standards.

As a historical note, please remember that for ALEs subject to the employer mandate during 2015, the threshold was set at 70 percent.

33. Does the employer have to offer coverage for all days of the month in order to avoid the penalty?

Yes. If an employer fails to offer coverage to a full-time employee for ANY day of the month, the employee is treated as not having been offered coverage for the <u>ENTIRE</u> month.

34. How are full-time and full-time-equivalent employees (FTEs) calculated?

An employer that is potentially subject to the employer mandate penalty is an employer with at least fifty full-time-equivalent employees (Applicable Large Employer) during the preceding calendar year. Additionally, an employer who is part of a group of employers treated as a single employer under Internal Revenue Code sections 414 (b), (c), (m), or (o) (including employees of a controlled group of corporations, employees of partnerships, proprietorships, etc., which are under common control, and employees of an affiliated service group) is treated as a single employer.[1] When a mandate penalty applies, it is to be paid ratably by members of the group.[2] For employers not in existence throughout the preceding calendar year, the determination of large employer is based on the average number of employees a firm is reasonably expected to employ on business days in the current calendar year.[3] Any reference to an employer includes a reference to any predecessor of that employer.[4]

The statutes use the term "full-time employee" and "full-time equivalent employee" in the definition of Applicable Large Employer, but then expand on the definition to include both full- and part-time workers.[5] Full-time employees are those working thirty or more hours per week.[6] The number of full-time employees excludes any full-time seasonal employees[7] who work for less than 120 days during the year.[8] The hours worked by part-time employees (i.e., those working less than thirty hours per week) are included in the calculation of a large employer, on a monthly basis, by taking their total number of monthly hours worked divided by 120.[9] In addition, an employer will not be considered a large employer if its number of full-time-equivalent employees constituted fifty for 120 days or less or the employees in excess of fifty employed during the 120 day period were seasonal workers.[10]

---

1. IRC Sec. 4980H(c)(2)(C)(i).
2. IRC Sec. 4980H(c)(2)(D)(ii).
3. IRC Sec. 4980H(c)(2)(C)(ii).
4. IRC Sec. 4980H(c)(2)(C)(iii).
5. IRC Sec. 4980H(c)(2).
6. IRC Sec. 4980H(c)(4).
7. The term "seasonal worker" means a worker who performs labor or services on a seasonal basis as defined by the Secretary of Labor, including workers covered by section 500.20(s)(1) of Title 29, Code of Federal Regulations and retail workers employed exclusively during holiday seasons. IRC Sec. 4980H(c)(2)(B)(ii).
8. IRC Sec. 4980H(c)(2)(B).
9. IRC Sec. 4980H(c)(2)(E).
10. IRC Sec. 4980H(c)(2)(B).

Example: A firm has thirty-five full-time employees who work thirty or more hours per week. In addition, the firm has twenty part-time employees who all work twenty-four hours per week (ninety-six hours per month). These part-time employees' hours would be treated as equivalent to sixteen full-time employees, based on the following calculation:

20 employees × 96 hours = 1920

1920 / 120 = 16

35. What are some examples of the Employer Mandate tax penalties?

Example A: The large employer does not offer coverage, but no full-time employees receive credits for exchange coverage. *No penalty would be assessed.*

Example B: The large employer offers coverage and no full-time employees receive credits for exchange coverage. *No penalty would be assessed.*

Example C: The large employer does not offer coverage, and one or more full-time employees receive credits for exchange $2,570. The penalty does not vary if only one employee or all fifty employees received the credit; *the employer's annual penalty in 2020 would be $51,400 calculated as follows:*

50 − 30 = 20

20 × $2,570 = $51,400.

Example D: The employer offers health plan coverage, but one or more full-time employees receive credits for exchange coverage. The number of full-time employees receiving the credit is used in the penalty calculation for an employer that offers coverage. *The annual penalty is the <u>lesser</u> of the following:*

- The number of full-time employees minus the first thirty, multiplied by $2,570, or $51,400 for the employer with fifty full-time employees, as shown in Example C, or

- The number of full-time employees who receive credits for exchange coverage, multiplied by $3,860. If, for example, twenty-five employees purchased coverage on the exchanges and received a federal premium subsidy, the formula would be:

25 × $3,860 = $96,500

Therefore, this employer would be subject to the lesser amount of $51,400.

Thus, for an employer that hires only full-time employees, hiring that fiftieth employee could trigger a penalty of $51,400 if the employer does not offer health coverage to its employees. This will possibly affect hiring for small employers close to the "applicable large employer" fifty full-time-equivalent employee limit.

Although the penalties are assessed on a monthly basis (with the dollar amounts above then divided by twelve), this example uses annual amounts, assuming the number of affected employees is the same throughout the year.

Example E: However, if the employer with fifty full-time employees had ten full-time employees who received premium credits, then the potential annual penalty on the employer for those individuals would be $38,600. Because this is less than the overall limitation for this employer of $51,400, the employer penalty in this example would be $38,600.

However, if the employer with fifty full-time employees had thirty full-time employees who received premium credits, then the potential annual penalty on the employer for those individuals would be $115,800. Because $115,800 exceeds this employer's overall limitation of $51,400, the employer penalty in this example would be limited to $51,400.

36. What reporting is required by employers, other than the W-2 requirements?

Beginning in 2015 and continuing through today,[1] large employers with fifty or more full-time-equivalent employees and "offering employers"[2] have had certain reporting requirements with respect to their full-time employees.[3] Employers must file a return including:

- the employer's name, address, and employer identification number;

- a certification as to whether the employer offers its full-time employees (and dependents) the opportunity to enroll in minimum essential overage under an eligible employer-sponsored plan;

- the length of any waiting period;

- the months that coverage was available;

- monthly premiums for the lowest-cost option;

- the employer plan's share of covered healthcare expenses;

- the number of full-time employees; and

- the name, address, and tax identification number of each full-time employee.

Additionally, an offering employer will have to provide information about the plan for which the employer pays the largest portion of the costs (and the amount for each enrollment category).

Insurers must also report certain information to the IRS[4] as discussed subsequently in this book.

Additionally, the employer must also provide each full-time employee with a written statement showing contact information for the person preparing the required return, and the specific information included in the return, for that individual employee. An employer may enter into an agreement with a health insurance issuer to provide necessary returns and statements.

37. How do the information reporting requirements and the Employer Mandate penalties interact?

The information reporting required by Internal Revenue Code sections 6055 and 6056 must occur for the IRS to enforce and administer the employer mandate requirements under

---

1. IRS Notice 2013-45.
2. An offering employer is one that offers minimum essential coverage through an employer plan and pays for some of the costs. Reporting requirements apply to these employers, regardless of size, only if the required contribution for self-only coverage by any employee exceeds 8 percent of wages. This is required because individuals whose household income exceeds 8 percent of wages are exempt from the individual mandate and may be eligible for free-choice vouchers. However, an employer would only have knowledge of the individual's wages, not his or her household income. Because this reporting requirement is linked to wages (and not household income), it is a first step in determining whether an individual is exempt from the individual mandate.
3. PPACA §1502.
4. PPACA §§1501, 1502, and 10106 adding IRC Secs. 5000A and 6055.

Internal Revenue Code section 4980H. Additionally, this information is needed by the employee and the IRS for the administration of the premium tax credit for the purchase of health insurance on an exchange.

The employer mandate penalties are triggered if one or more of an applicable large employer's full-time employees are entitled to premium tax credits for the purchase of insurance on a state exchange marketplace under Internal Revenue Code section 36B AND

(1)   the employer fails to offer 95 percent of full-time employees and their dependents the opportunity to enroll in minimum essential coverage OR

(2)   the employer offers full-time employees and dependents the opportunity to enroll in minimum essential coverage but the coverage is not affordable or does not provide minimum value. The second penalty can never exceed the first penalty.

An employer typically will not know whether a full-time employee has received such a tax credit, and the employer will not have all the information needed to determine whether it owes an employer mandate penalty. Therefore, IRS Notice 2013-45 provides that applicable large employers do not have to calculate employer mandate penalties or file returns submitting payment for such penalties. Instead, the IRS, after receiving the information returns filed by applicable large employers under Internal Revenue Code section 6056 and the information about employees claiming the premium tax credit for any given calendar year, will determine whether any of the employer's full-time employees received the premium tax credit and, if so, whether any employer mandate penalty is due. The IRS will thus contact any applicable large employer if the employer owes a penalty, and the employer will have an opportunity to respond to the information provided by IRS before any penalty is assessed.

38. Were employees still able to receive premium tax credits in 2014?

Yes. IRS Notice 2013-45 stated that the transition relief does not affect an individual's eligibility for a premium tax credit if he or she purchased health insurance through one of the health insurance exchange marketplaces established under the Act.[1] Participants in the exchanges continued to qualify for premium tax credits if their household income was within the specified range and they were not eligible for other minimum essential coverage. Such other minimum essential coverage includes eligible employer-sponsored group health plans that are affordable and provide minimum value.

39. Does a state health insurance exchange notify the employer if an individual is determined to be eligible for the income tax credit?

HHS regulations require that the Exchange must notify the employer that an employee has been determined to be eligible for advance payments of the premium tax credit and cost-sharing reductions in accordance with 45 CFR 155.305 (g) or 45 CFR 350(a) and has enrolled in a Qualified Health Plan through the Exchange.[2]

---

1.   IRS Notice 2013-45, Q-3 and A-3.
2.   45 CFR §155.310(h), as amended by 81 Fed. Reg. 12341 (March 8, 2016).

The notice provided must do the following:

- Identify the employee

- Indicate that the employee has been determined to be eligible for advance payments of the premium tax credit and cost-sharing reductions

- Indicate that the employee has enrolled in a Qualified Health Plan through the Exchange

- Indicate that the employer may be liable for the assessed payment under section 4980H of the Internal Revenue Code, if the employer has fifty or more employees

- Notify the employer the right to appeal[1]

The details such as the employee's tax return information or the exact reason the employee is eligible for assistance are not included.[2]

40. Under what circumstances may employers otherwise subject to the tax qualify for exemption?

Employers otherwise subject to the tax are exempt if:

(1)   no full-time employee decides to purchase health insurance through a state or federal exchange or

(2)   no full-time employee's household income is low enough to qualify for a premium tax credit or subsidy.

Income below these levels below qualifies for the subsidy. The premium credits will be provided as advanceable, refundable federal tax credits ultimately calculated through individual tax returns (although the credit payments will go directly to insurers). The credits can only be obtained by qualifying individuals (among others, lawful state residents) who file tax returns and are not eligible for other acceptable minimum essential coverage, such as an employer plan (that is affordable [IRS and HHS will issue guidance and provide an on-line calculator for this] and pays for at least 60 percent of projected health costs), Medicare, Medicaid, the Children's Health Insurance Program (CHIP), coverage related to military service, a grandfathered plan. The federal poverty level that applies is that of the preceding year, i.e., for determining the Federal Poverty Level (FPL).

---

1.   45 CFR §155.310(h), as amended by 81 Fed. Reg. 12341 (March 8, 2016).
2.   PPACA; Establishment of Exchanges and Qualified Health Plans; Exchange Standards for Employers, 77 Fed. Reg. 18310, 18357 (Mar. 27, 2012).

2019 POVERTY GUIDELINES FOR THE 48 CONTIGUOUS STATES AND THE DISTRICT OF COLUMBIA

Persons in family/household   Poverty guideline

For families/households with more than 8 persons, add $4,420 for each additional person.

1	$12,490
2	16,910
3	21,330
4	25,750
5	30,170
6	34,590
7	39,010
8	43,430

2019 POVERTY GUIDELINES FOR ALASKA

Persons in family/household   Poverty guideline

For families/households with more than 8 persons, add $5,530 for each additional person.

1	$15,600
2	21,130
3	26,660
4	32,190
5	37,720
6	43,250
7	48,780
8	55,310

2017 POVERTY GUIDELINES FOR HAWAII

Persons in family/household   Poverty guideline

For families/households with more than 8 persons, add $5,080 for each additional person.

1	$14,380
2	19,460
3	24,540
4	29,620
5	34,700
6	39,780
7	44,860
8	49,940

Alaska and Hawaii have had separate poverty guidelines as reflected by Office of Economic Opportunity administrative practice beginning in 1966. The poverty guidelines are not defined for Puerto Rico, the U.S. Virgin Islands, American Samoa, Guam, the Republic of the Marshall Islands, the Federated States of Micronesia, the Commonwealth of the Northern Mariana Islands, and Palau. In cases where a Federal program using the poverty guidelines serves those jurisdictions, the Federal office which administers the program is responsible for deciding whether to use the contiguous states and Washington, D.C. guidelines for those jurisdictions or to follow a different procedure.

41. What effect will a state's decision whether to expand Medicaid under the ACA have on the employer mandate penalty?

Yes. If a state elects to expand Medicaid under healthcare reform, a person earning less than 138 percent[1] of the Federal Poverty Level (FPL) ($17,236.20 for an individual in 2020) can qualify even if not a parent or not disabled. If a state does not elect the healthcare reform Medicaid expansion, additional penalty exposure is created for employees whose household income is between 100 percent and 138 percent of FPL because they could be eligible for exchange purchased health insurance premium subsidies.

42. How does an employer appeal the tax penalties?

Employers have an appeals mechanism to contest a determination that it is liable for the new employer mandate penalties imposed under Internal Revenue Code section 4980H because:

- the employee was not eligible for an individual tax credit due to the employee's household income; or

- the employer had provided minimum essential coverage that was affordable.

As part of the appeals process, the employer will "have access to the data used to make the determination to the extent allowable by law," but it is still subject to the nondisclosure provision.[2] This appeals mechanism would be in addition to the employer's appeals rights under the Internal Revenue Code.[3]

The appeal process cannot begin until after the submission of the Forms 1094-C and 1095-C to the Internal Revenue Service which begins the penalty portion. Penalties under sections 4980H(a) and 4980H(b) will be levied against employers based on, among other things, the information that the Applicable Large Employer (ALE) provided on the Forms 1094-C and 1095-C.

If an employer is assessed a penalty, there are actually TWO appeal processes available. One appeal is to the Department of Health and Human Services (HHS) and the other is to the Department of Internal Revenue (IRS).

---

1.   In fact, eligibility is not 133 percent but is 138 percent of FPL because §1004(e) of P.L. 111-152 requires income equivalent to 5 percent FPL to be disregarded.
2.   42 USC §18081(f)(2) (PPACA §1411(f)(2)).
3.   *Id.*

Appeal to the HHS

It is important to understand an appeal to HHS will not be the final determination on whether an employer will be assessed a penalty under section 4980H. The HHS appeal is entirely separate from the IRS appeal. The Exchange is required by ACA section 1411(e)(4) (B)(iii) to notify an employer that an employee has received a premium tax credit and that the employer may be liable for penalties under section 4980H. These marketplace notices are only going to be provided to "certain employers" whose employees enrolled in an Exchange with advance premium tax credits and that these "certain employers" would only be receiving the marketplace notice <u>if the Exchange has the address of the employer</u>. The plan from CMS is to increase the number of employers getting the notices.

Appeals to HHS must occur within ninety days of when the marketplace notice is dated. There is a form on healthcare.gov that can be used by employers that get notices from either a Federally-facility Exchange or from a state exchange in California, Colorado, Kentucky, Maryland, Massachusetts, New York, Vermont, or Washington D.C. If appealing from other states, the employer must use the procedures established by that state.[1]

It is critical for employers to remember the ACA added Fair Labor Standards Act (FLSA) section 18C. This provision prevents any employer from discharging or discriminating against any employee who receives a premium tax credit. In an ever increasingly litigious world even an employee who is terminated or has his/her circumstances change for valid reasons may claim section 18C of the FLSA was violated. To protect against a frivolous claim it may be prudent for an employer to be unaware of which particular employees received a premium tax credit. This can be done by ignoring the marketplace notices all together or having a third-party handle all of an employer's marketplace appeals. As a result of the FAQ, which says not every employer with an employee receiving a premium tax credit will receive a marketplace notice, it is possible for an employer to not receive a marketplace notice and still be assessed an employer mandate penalty. The FAQ may take away one of the possible appeal options for an employer. To the contrary, just because an employer receives a marketplace notice does not mean the IRS will assess an employer mandate penalty.

Appeal to the IRS

The other option of appeal is a direct appeal to the IRS regarding the assessment of a section 4980H(a) or a section 4980H(b) penalty. The IRS details how an employer will know if they have been assessed liability:

"The IRS will adopt procedures that ensure employers receive certification that one or more employees have received a premium tax credit. The IRS will contact employers to inform them of their potential liability and provide them an opportunity to respond before any liability is assessed or notice and demand for payment is made. The contact for a given calendar year will not occur until after the due date for employees to file individual tax returns for that year claiming premium tax credits and after the due date for applicable large

---

1.   Employer Appeal Request Form https://www.healthcare.gov/downloads/marketplace-employer-appeal-form.pdf (Last updated April 2018).

employers to file the information returns identifying their full-time employees and describing the coverage that was offered (if any)."[1]

The IRS began enforcement of the employer mandate penalty and assessments during 2017.

The IRS appeal procedures have been detailed in IRS Publication 556.[2] An employer can appeal an employer mandate penalty within the IRS or to the United States Tax Court, the United States Court of Federal Claims, or a United States District Court. At this point, no special appeals process for the IRS has been released. Receipt of a marketplace notice is not a conclusive presumption that the IRS will assess an employer mandate penalty under IRC section 4980H.

Again, two types of appeals are possible – the IRS appeal is completely separate from the HHS appeal. A successful appeal made through the HHS appeal would presumably be successful in an appeal to the IRS, which would be more critical since monetary penalties can be levied.

43. What other issues must be considered by employers in planning for the employer mandate tax penalties?

Applicable large employers (those with fifty or more full time equivalent employees) that may be subject to an employer mandate penalty will need to consider taking action, if possible:

(1)   to avoid the employer mandate versus,

(2)   minimizing its effect or,

(3)   embracing it strategically.

Certain industries and business sectors will be hit hard while others will gain relief. In addition, the competitive balance regarding costs will be impacted. For example, consider regional and national restaurants operating as one employer versus franchised operations where the small franchisees will not be subject to the employer mandate tax penalty. Issues to be considered include workforce size and composition.

- Workforce size determines whether the mandate applies and potential cost/penalty exposure.

- Workforce composition will trigger other issues, such as:

   ○   part-time vs. full-time employees;

   ○   independent contractors and/or leased employees;

   ○   lower-income vs. higher-income;

   ○   bargaining-unit employees.

---

1.   Questions and Answers on Employer Shared Responsibility Provisions Under the Affordable Care Act, Question 27 https://www.irs.gov/affordable-care-act/employers/questions-and-answers-on-employer-shared-responsibility-provisions-under-the-affordable-care-act (Last updated May 24, 2018).

2.   IRS Publication 556, Examination of Returns, Appeal Rights and Claims for Refund https://www.irs.gov/pub/irs-pdf/p556.pdf (as revised 2013).

<u>Risk of Independent Contractor Reclassification</u>. An employer may have one or more independent contractors that are reclassified as employees. As a result, that employer with fewer than fifty full-time employees could find itself with fifty or more after the reclassification. Additionally, such persons could trigger one of the employer mandate penalties if they receive a tax credit for purchasing health insurance on an exchange.

<u>Changing Status of Full-Time Employees</u>. Employers with group health plans that consider converting full-time employees to part-time status or independent contractors, or terminating employees to avoid the employer mandate penalties, could face ERISA claims by these employees.

A group health plan is an employee welfare plan governed by ERISA. Under ERISA section 510, it is unlawful to hire, suspend, fine, discipline, expel, or discriminate against a participant or beneficiary for the purpose of interfering with the attainment of any right to which such a participant may become entitled under the plan or ERISA. A plaintiff in such a case typically has the burden of proving there was an adverse action against the participant or beneficiary for the purpose of interfering with the attainment of an ERISA benefit. However, employers should be cautious as to the reasons and documentation for any such employee changes.

<u>Employers Slightly Below 50 Full-Time Equivalent Employee Limit</u>. Thus, for an employer that hires only full-time employees, hiring that fiftieth employee could trigger a penalty of $51,400 if the employer does not offer health coverage to its employees. This will likely affect hiring for small employers close to the "applicable large employer" fifty full-time-equivalent employee limit.

44. Is there any employer relief for misclassified independent contractors in the final employer mandate regulations?

The final employer mandate (a/k/a/ "shared responsibility" or "play or pay") regulations[1] offer no relief for an applicable large employer's failure to offer that coverage due to employee misclassification. Counting employees is important for determining whether an employer is an applicable large employer potentially subject to the Internal Revenue Code section 4980H(a) or 4980H(b) employer mandate penalties, and if so, if an offer of health coverage has been made to enough employees to avoid the Internal Revenue Code section 4980H(a) $2,570 (as of 2020) per employee per year penalty. The final regulations, like the proposed regulations, take the position that an "employee" is defined by reference to a common law standard, which means an employment relationship where the entity controls how and what the employee does in the scope of his or her provision of services to the employer. This definition excludes individuals who are correctly classified as independent contractors; as such, employers are not required to count independent contractors for purposes of determining whether the coverage mandate applies or which individuals must be offered coverage under the employer's plans. The employee definition also excludes a leased employee (a technical term[2]), a sole proprietor, a partner in a partnership, or a more than 2 percent S corporation shareholder.

---

1.   IRC Sec. 4980H; Reg. §54.4980H-1 et seq.
2.   IRC Sec. 414(n). Note however if a worker is in fact the common law employee of the recipient employer, the worker is not a leased employee.

No relief is provided for reasonable but wrong decisions classifying employees as independent contractors. The final regulations preamble specifically provides that there is no "Section 530 Relief," which allows employers to cut off liability for failing to withhold federal income tax, FICA and FUTA taxes due to worker misclassification if certain requirements are met.[1] Thus, there is no avenue for the employer mandate penalty to ameliorate the impact of a misclassification error on compliance with the employer mandate provisions. Thus, employers should review their arrangements with independent contractors, consultants, and other non-employee workers to ensure that they have been properly classified.

To avoid penalties, applicable large employers are required to offer coverage to 95 percent of their "common law" full-time employees. An individual is a common law employee of a company if the company has the right to "control and direct the individual who performs the work, not only as the result is to be accomplished by the work but also as to the details and means by which that result is accomplished." If paying with a Form 1099, the employer has cause to worry. If workers paid with a Form 1099 should actually be employees and are classified incorrectly as independent contracts, the employer could be on the hook for an offer of coverage.

When it comes to temporary staffer, an individual might be issued a W-2 by one company, but another company has the right to control and direct that individual as to what job needs to be done and how to do it. Here, the company has the right to control and direct that individual has the obligation to offer coverage, even though it might not be the employer for payroll purposes. There are rules that allow the client employer to take credit for an offer of coverage made by a staffing agency, but the arrangement between the client employer and the staffing agency must meet certain criteria.

45. What is (or was) the Individual Mandate?

In 2012, the U.S. Supreme Court ruled that the individual mandate is constitutional.[2] Beginning January 1, 2014, health reform required most individuals to have some form of health coverage. If an applicable individual does not have minimum essential coverage for that individual or his or her dependents who also meet the definition of applicable individual, a tax "penalty" will be imposed on the individual.[3] The penalty is equal to the greater of:

(i)   the "applicable dollar amount" for the individual and all such dependents (up to a maximum of three applicable dollar amounts); or

(ii)   a specified percentage of the applicable individual's household income.

       ○   Only the part of the household income that is above the yearly tax filing threshold is counted.

       ○   Only people in the household that don't have insurance are paid for.

---

1.   "In response to the limitation on the relief under section 530, commenters requested that the Treasury Department and the IRS formulate a similar provision in these final regulations applicable to potential liabilities under section 4980H. The Treasury Department and the IRS are concerned that the relief requested would serve to increase the potential for worker misclassification by significantly increasing the benefit of having an employee treated as an independent contractor. Accordingly, the final regulations do not adopt this suggestion." See Explanation and Summary of Comments, Final Regulations, XII (Worker Classification and section 4980H) at https://www.federalregister.gov/articles/2014/02/12/2014-03082/shared-responsibility-for-employers-regarding-health-coverage#h-17. (Last accessed July 4, 2019).

2.   *NFIB v. Sebelius* (June 28, 2012).

3.   IRC Sec. 5000A(f).

Taxpayers who didn't have health insurance in 2014 and didn't qualify for one of the many exemptions were required to pay a specified penalty or a percentage of their Modified Adjusted Gross Income (MAGI) — whichever was greater.

The minimum penalty ranged from $95 in calendar year 2014 to $325 per adult and $162.50 per child under age eighteen in 2015 up to $695 per adult and $347.50 per child under age eighteen in calendar year 2016, and will be inflation-adjusted thereafter.[1]

The applicable percentage of income increased from 1 percent in calendar year 2014, to 2 percent in calendar year 2015, and to 2½ percent for calendar year 2016 and thereafter.[2] For low-income employees, the minimum penalty is small in comparison to the actual cost of coverage, thereby increasing the likelihood that an individual without minimum essential coverage will not purchase health insurance, although the tax credit subsidies will make the insurance less expensive. The maximum for a family during 2018 tops out at $2,085 (unchanged from 2017). The maximum for 2015 was $975 and the maximum for 2014 was the total yearly premium for the average national price of a Bronze plan sold through the Marketplace.[3]

Revenue Procedure 2017-48 sets forth the monthly national average premium for bronze level coverage for an individual is $272, i.e., $3,264 for twelve months. For a family of five or more members, it is $1,360 per month or five times the individual coverage premium, $16,320 for twelve months.

On January 20, 2017, President Donald J. Trump signed Executive Order Minimizing the Economic Burden Patient Protection and Affordable Care Act Pending Repeal. In an evident conformance with this Executive Order, the Internal Revenue Service is no longer requiring individual filers to indicate whether they maintained health insurance or paid the penalty required by the individual mandate. The Affordable Care Act requires the payment of the "shared responsibility payment". Taxpayers either had to complete line 61 on their form 1040 or claim that they were exempt by filing Form 8965. Prior to the Executive Order, the IRS would reject any "silent returns" that did not either have a completed line 61 or a Form 8965. It should also be noted that the IRS did not reject silent returns filed in 2016, but had intended to do so for 2017 until the Executive Order. The IRS is maintaining that they can still "follow up" on silent returns but what situations would cause that are currently unclear.

On December 22, 2017, the Tax Cut and Jobs Act of 2017 was passed, repealing the Individual Mandate penalty effective in 2019. It can be argued that the legislation did not repeal the actual Individual Mandate, but effectively it is repealed, as without the "teeth" of the penalty, it has no force.

---

1. IRC Secs. 5000A(c)(3)(A), (B), (D).
2. IRC Sec. 5000A(c)(2)(B). The net effect of these percentage increases for taxpayers who do not procure minimum essential coverage and whose income is sufficient to be above the minimum penalty is an increase in their marginal tax rate by 1 percent in calendar year 2014 rising to a 2.5 percent marginal tax rate increase for subsequent years.
3. IRC Secs. 5000A(b)(1), (c)(1), (2). Use of the national average for bronze coverage means that the calculation might not bear much relationship to the actual cost of coverage available in a specific location. However, the premium amounts likely will not be lower than the penalty.

On December 14, 2018, a Federal District Court in Texas ruled that the entire ACA is invalid because Congress reduced to $0 the tax penalty tied to its individual mandate.[1] The Fifth Circuit Court of Appeals began oral arguments in July 2019 and it is expected that this case — and the future of the entire ACA will go to the United States Supreme Court.

46. What is the effect of the Executive Order signed by President Trump in regard to the Affordable Care Act?

On January 20, 2017, President Donald J. Trump signed Executive Order Minimizing the Economic Burden Patient Protection and Affordable Care Act Pending Repeal.

In response to this, the Internal Revenue Service is no longer requiring individual filers to indicate whether they maintained health insurance or paid the penalty required by the individual mandate. The law requires taxpayers to either complete line 61 on their form 1040 or claim that they were exempt by filing Form 8965. The IRS had intended to reject any "silent returns" that did not either have a completed line 61 or a Form 8965.

According to the statement issued by the IRS, "Processing silent returns means that taxpayer returns are not systemically rejected, allowing them to be processed and minimizing burden on taxpayers, including those expecting a refund."

US law gives the administration authority to provide exemptions from the mandate. However, it is uncertain and unlikely that it allows the administration to not enforce the mandate. Arguably, since the U.S. Supreme Court has upheld the mandate as constitutional, enforcement seems to mandatory.

The IRS notes that taxpayers are still required to pay the mandate penalty, if applicable. "Legislative provisions of the ACA law are still in force until changed by the Congress, and taxpayers remain required to follow the law and pay what they may owe," according to the IRS statement.

47. Have there been clarifications as to when health insurance needs to be obtained to avoid penalties under the Affordable Care Act?

Internal Revenue Code section 5000A requires most U.S. citizens and legal residents for tax years ending after December 31, 2013, to maintain minimum essential health insurance coverage or pay a penalty. "Health insurance coverage" includes government sponsored programs such as Medicare, Medicaid, The Children's Health Insurance Program; eligible employer-sponsored plans; plans in the individual market; certain grandfathered group health plans; and other coverage as recognized by the Department of Health and Human Services. This requirement is referred to as the "individual mandate," and the penalty is often referred to as the "shared responsibility payment." The individual mandate was highly controversial and challenged soon after the ACA was enacted. The mandate was upheld by the Supreme Court as a valid exercise of Congress's taxing power.

---

1.   *Texas, et. al., vs. United States of America*, Civil Action No. 4:18-cv-00167-O, https://affordablecareactlitigation.files.wordpress.com/2018/12/Texas-v.-US-partial-summary-judgment-decision.pdf

Applicable individuals have a choice of either maintaining minimum essential coverage for themselves and any nonexempt family members or including an additional payment with the Federal income tax return. The amount of the shared responsibility payment for any tax year is generally the sum of monthly penalty amounts for all months in the tax year in which any nonexempt individual for whom the taxpayer is liable under Internal Revenue Code section 5000A(b) did not have minimum essential coverage, computed based on either a flat dollar amount or a percentage of the taxpayer's income over established thresholds.[1]

A number of situations can apply in which an individual is exempt from the penalty imposed by Internal Revenue Code section 5000A(a), including "short coverage gaps," i.e., when the individual isn't covered by minimum essential coverage for a continuous period (beginning no earlier than January 1, 2014) of less than three months.

There has been confusion about the "short coverage gaps" provision as it applies to the operative dates for the individual mandate. Things to remember:

- You are considered covered any month you had coverage for even one day.

- If you had more than one coverage gap during the year, the short coverage gap extension only applies to the FIRST gap. For example, if you lacked coverage in January and February, then had coverage March through November, but lost coverage in December. The short coverage gap exemption would only apply to January and February. You would not be eligible for an exemption to the penalty for the month of December.

- If you have a coverage gap that begins in one year and ends in another year, the short coverage gap exemption applies only to the first year. For example, if you lacked coverage from November 2015 until February 2016, you could apply for the short coverage gap on your 2015 tax return for the months of November 2015 and December 2015. You would not be eligible for the short coverage gap in 2016. This is because the two months that you did not have coverage in 2015 are counted in 2016 since you didn't have coverage for three consecutive months –November 2015 through January 2016.

- Application for the short coverage gap exemption is done when filing the return for federal income tax, using Form 8965, Health Coverage Exemptions and filing it with Form 1040, Form 1040A, or Form 1040EZ.

The individual mandate went into effect on January 1, 2014. Open Enrollment for 2019 coverage starts November 1, 2019, and ends December 15. 2019. After that, you can still get 2020 coverage only:

- if you qualify for a Special Enrollment Period due to a life change like marriage, losing your job, having a baby, or losing other coverage;

---

1.   IRC Sec. 5000A(c).

- through Medicaid and the Children's Health Insurance Program, which provide coverage to families and individuals with limited income or other reasons.

The Administration has clarified the deadline, stating that individuals who sign up for insurance on the Exchange within the open enrollment period won't face a penalty. The Administration, as well as the Department of Health and Human Services (HHS), have emphasized that this "clarification" isn't a substantive modification and that the start date for benefits and overall deadline for enrolling remain unchanged. This clarification is viewed by many as welcome news as it effectively gives individuals more time than originally thought to obtain coverage and not face a penalty. On the other hand, a number of politicians are calling for even more change such as extending the open enrollment period or delaying the individual mandate penalty for a year.

See also Q 652.

48. Has the individual mandate worked to induce individuals to purchase health insurance?

There are low participation rates in health insurance, even in many companies that offer health coverage. One CEO asked employees why they do not participate in the employer provided coverage.[1] The answers he received are typical:

- Younger workers were unconcerned about illness or injury.

- Others already had insurance through a spouse or parent.

- A significant number said they declined coverage because they could get medical treatment "for free at the emergency room." This fact remains true in and after 2014, as the federal law known as EMTALA (Emergency Medical Treatment and Labor Act) requires hospitals to provide emergency services, even to those who cannot pay.

- Among those who had signed up, many said it was because they were concerned about developing a medical condition and then being unable to get affordable coverage due to this pre-existing condition. Starting in 2014, these people were able to obtain health insurance on exchanges despite any pre-existing conditions, which will further disincentive to enrollment in both employer and exchange offered health insurance.

One of the law's answers to those that do not want insurance is the individual mandate penalty tax on uninsured individuals that went into effect in 2014. The penalty in 2014 was $95 or 1 percent of household income, whichever is greater. It increased in 2016 and 2017 to $695 or 2½ percent of household income, whichever is greater. The individual mandate is not sufficient to change the behavior of many persons who are not otherwise inclined to buy

---

1. A CEO's-Eye View of ObamaCare, Wall Street Journal p. A-17 (July 22, 2013), available at: http://online.wsj.com/article/SB10001424127887323309404578613653344566068.html?mod=hp_opinion. (Last accessed July 1, 2019).

health insurance. A person making $50,000 per year with no health coverage will be subject to an initial individual mandate penalty of $500 and a maximum penalty of $1,250 in 2016. The typical share of employee cost for company sponsored health coverage will often exceed this amount, often by a significant amount. Low paid employees who earned, for example, $11,500 per year, would have been subject to an initial penalty of $115 in 2014 and a maximum penalty of $695 in 2019. Such workers' share of health insurance premiums will again often be more than any potential penalty.

Thus, the individual mandate will likely neither raise as much money as projected nor induce as many uninsured to purchase insurance as hoped. In addition, if more individuals move from employer to subsidized state exchange provided insurance than projected, this too will make healthcare reform much more expensive than projected.

However, the Affordable Care Act does seem to be enjoying success. According to the Department of Health and Human Services in 2013, over 10,200,000 people had paid their premiums and had active insurance through the Marketplace.[1] According to the Kaiser Family Foundation, over 12.2 million people have signed up for health insurance through the Affordable Care Act during 2017.[2] During 2018, 11.8 million signed up, a decline of about 3.8 percent, which was less than expected. Other interesting statistics include an additional 2.3 million African American adults and 4.2 million additional Latinos obtaining coverage during 2017. During 2019, 11.45 million people signed up for healthcare coverage on the exchanges even though the Individual Mandate penalty had been eliminated by the Trump Administration, indicating interest in healthcare coverage is not forced but of interest by the populace.

Controlled Group and Affiliated Service Group Issues

49. Are there special issues for controlled groups and affiliated service groups?

If there is more than one such business involved, the thirty-employee base amount must be allocated among all such businesses "ratably" on the basis of the number of full-time employees in each business. However, there are still some unanswered questions, for example:

- What if one employer within a controlled group of corporations provides coverage for all of its employees? Will it be exempt from the penalties, even though another employer within the same controlled group is not?

- Will the exempt employer's employees serve to increase the penalty on a related taxable employer?

Example: A married couple owns two businesses: a financial planning business (with fourteen full-time (FT) employees and six part-time employees), plus a franchise (with eighteen FT employees and fifty part-time employees). The businesses are treated as a single employer because they are commonly owned (80 percent or more by same five or fewer people) by the husband and wife. Assuming the part-time

---

1.   http://www.hhs.gov/about/news/2015/06/02/march-effectuated-enrollment-consistent-with-departments-2015-goal.html.
2.   http://www.kff.org/health-reform/state-indicator/total-marketplace-enrollment/?currentTimeframe=0&sortModel=%7B%22colId%22:%22Location%22,%22sort%22:%22asc%22%7D.

employees each work an average of eighty hours per month, they collectively count as thirty-seven full-time-equivalent employees.

FTE status is calculated by taking the average number of hours worked per month times the number of part-time employees [those regularly scheduled to work less than thirty hours per week] divided by 120, rounded down to the whole number). Thus, the combined business will be subject to the employer mandate in 2019 (because thirty-two FT employees and thirty-seven FTEs is a total of sixty-nine FTEs).

First, if the businesses do not provide all of the full-time employees of both businesses with coverage that meets the new standards, the combined businesses will be subject to a $4,000 per year nondeductible excise tax. While the businesses are subject to the employer mandate, the penalty is calculated on the basis of full-time employees only (a total of thirty-two) and there is an exemption for the first thirty full-time employees.

$$32 - 30 = 2$$

$$2 \times \$2,570 = \$5,140.$$

Second, even if the businesses do not provide affordable minimum essential coverage, the penalty will not exceed $4,000 per year even if one or more full-time employees:

- opt out of the coverage;

- purchase their own coverage on an exchange; and

- qualify for taxpayer-subsidized coverage (because their family incomes fall below the applicable federal thresholds).

The overall penalty is limited to what it would be if the employers provided no coverage at all.

50. What are the types of Controlled Groups and how are they treated under the Employer Mandate?

Employees of companies within the same controlled group must be aggregated to determine whether the commonly owned companies are subject to the employer mandate. Internal Revenue Code section 4980H(c)(2)(C)(i) states that all persons treated as a single employer under Code subsections 414 (b), (c), (m), or (o) shall be treated as one employer. Thus, the employer-controlled group definition is the same as for pension purposes, and the common ownership requirement is 80 percent.

Three Types of Controlled Groups

There are three types of controlled groups that are considered one employer for the purposes of the ACA employer mandate. The IRS defines, and provides example of, these three controlled groups in Internal Revenue Code sections 414 (b) and 414 (c).

1. **Parent-Subsidy Group:** When one or more businesses are connected through stock ownership with a common parent corporation (such as a chain); and

    o   80 percent of the stock of each corporation (except the common parent) is owned by one or more corporations in the group; and

    o   Parent Corporation must own 80 percent of at least one other corporation.

2. **Brother-Sister Group:** A group of two or more corporations, where five or fewer common owners own directly or indirectly a "controlling interest" of each group and have "effective control." A common owner must be an individual, a trust, or an estate.

    o   *Controlling interest*: Generally, means 80 percent or more of the stock of each corporation (but only if such common owner own stock in each corporation).

    o   *Effective control*: More than 50 percent of the stock of each corporation, but only to the extent such stock ownership is identical with respect to such corporation.

Example: Individuals A and B own 100 percent of corps X and Y as follows:

Individuals	Corps		Identical Ownership
	X	Y	
A	30%	70%	30%
B	70%	30%	30%
Total	100%	100%	60%

As A and B own all of the stock of both corporations, the 80 percent ownership of the vote or value, has been satisfied.

Reviewing the identical ownership in the two corporations, A's identical ownership in respect of X and Y is 30 percent, and likewise, B's identical ownership in the two corporations is 30 percent. For purposes of the test it is the combined identical ownership of the five or fewer shareholders that must exceed 50 percent. Since A and B together have identical ownership in X and Y of 60 percent that aspect of the test is satisfied. Accordingly, X and Y are members of a brother-sister controlled group.

As A and B own all of the stock of both corporations, the 80 percent ownership of the vote or value has been satisfied.

Reviewing the identical ownership in the two corporations, A's identical ownership in respect of X and Y is 30 percent, and, likewise, B's identical ownership in the two corporations is 30 percent. For purposes of the test it is the combined identical ownership of the five or fewer shareholders that must exceed 50 percent. Since A and B together have identical ownership in X and Y of 60 percent that aspect of the test is satisfied. Accordingly, X and Y are members of a brother-sister controlled group.

3.   **Combined Group:** A group consisting of three or more organizations that are organized as follows:

- ○ Each organization is a member of either a parent-subsidiary or brother-sister group.

- ○ At least one corporation is the common parent of a parent-subsidiary and is also a member of a brother-sister group.

51. Have applicable employers terminated their health plans so that employees must purchase health insurance on a state exchange because the penalties are much less than the costs of a group health plan?

No. Fears of employers deciding to cease offering healthcare coverage and choosing to pay the $2,570 "all-full-time employees minus 30" penalty is likely to substantially affect the ultimate impact of health reform. In many instances, employer's annual healthcare costs is much greater than the penalty but employers are realizing that good employees expect and demand health benefits.[1] Even though the penalty is nondeductible, and amounts paid for employee healthcare coverage should continue to be deductible, some employers considered ceasing to offer a group health plan in 2015 or thereafter, especially those with low-paid workforces whose employees receive income tax subsidies for health insurance purchased on a state exchange. The tax credit discussed in Q 56 for low- and middle-income persons (with incomes below 400 percent of the federal poverty level), buying insurance through the exchanges will be substantial. Therefore, as described in more detail in Q 56, although health coverage is an important part of many employers' benefit packages, discontinuing such coverage would allow some employers with lower wage employees, as well as the employees themselves, to both come out ahead economically. For example, the employer could terminate health coverage and pass some of the net savings (after taking the penalty into account) on to its employees in the form of additional cash compensation.

However, it could be more expensive for many employers to discontinue coverage and increase employee compensation up to the amount saved in health costs less the penalty paid. Depending on workforce demographics, offering coverage may save money.

Exchanges and Individual Tax Subsidies Change Calculations[2]

Today about 155 million workers and their families received health insurance coverage from their employers during 2016 according to the Congressional Budget Office analysis of March 2016[3]. In 2019, Kaiser Family Foundation (KFF) reported that 156,199,800 Americans received employer-sponsored healthcare. In addition, approximately 70 million receive healthcare through Medicaid, 50 million are on Medicare. Proponents of PPACA insisted that a key

---

1.   https://www.nytimes.com/2016/04/05/business/employers-keep-health-insurance-despite-affordable-care-act.html. (Last accessed July 29, 2019).

2.   See KFF, Estimated Total Premium Tax Credits, https://www.kff.org/health-reform/state-indicator/average-monthly-advance-premium-tax-credit-aptc/?currentTimeframe=0&selectedDistributions=average-monthly-advanced-premium-tax-credit&sortModel=%7B%22colId%22:%22Location%22,%22sort%22:%22asc%22%7D.

3.   Federal Subsidies for Health Insurance for People Under Age 65: 2016 to 2026, March 2016.

tenet was to build on this system of employer-sponsored coverage. Importantly then President Obama himself repeatedly promised during the creation of the Affordable Care Act that individuals would get to keep their own health insurance if they liked it. The average monthly advanced tax credit for 2019 was $519.[1]

Roughly half of the $900 billion of spending in PPACA is devoted to subsidies for individuals who do not receive health insurance from their employers. These subsidies are remarkably generous, even for those with relatively high incomes. For example, in 2014:

- a family earning about $59,000 a year would receive a premium subsidy of about $7,200;

- a family earning about $71,000 would receive a premium subsidy of about $5,200;

- a family earning about $95,000 would receive a premium subsidy of almost $3,000.

By 2019, subsidy amounts and the income levels to qualify for those subsidies would grow substantially:

- A family earning about $65,000 would receive a subsidy of approximately $10,254.

- A family earning $78,000 would receive a subsidy of $8,164.

- Families earning $100,000 would receive a subsidy of almost $5,995.

- For families of four earning over $100,000, subsidies are unlikely.

An obvious question is how employers will react to the presence of an alternative – a subsidized source of insurance for their workers – that can be accessed if companies drop coverage for their employees. The simplest calculation focuses on the tradeoff between employer savings and the $2,570 penalty (per employee) imposed by the PPACA on employers whose employees move to an exchange for subsidized health insurance.

If an employer were to decide to drop healthcare, it would likely be a purely economic decision. The answer frequently depends on the size of the federal tax credit subsidy. It is possible with subsidies being cut under the current administration, we will see an increase in companies dropping health care plans.

The Congressional Budget Office (CBO) estimated that only nineteen million residents would receive subsidies, at a cost of about $450 billion over the first ten years. This analysis suggests that the number could easily triple (nineteen million plus an additional thirty-eight million in 2014). The gross price tag would be roughly $1.4 trillion, which would be partially offset by employer mandate tax penalties.

---

1.   https://www.kff.org/health-reform/state-indicator/marketplace-enrollment/?currentTimeframe=0&sortModel=%7B%22colId%22:%22Location%22,%22sort%22:%22asc%22%7D.

PEO (Staffing Industry) Compliance with Employer Mandate

52. Will the employee mandate and related penalties apply to Professional Employer Organizations (PEO), also known as the staffing industry?

The healthcare reform employer mandate tax penalty (also called "Play or Pay" or "Shared Responsibility") rules apply to "Applicable Large Employers (ALE)," which include employers with fifty or more full-time and full-time equivalent employees. Many, if not most Professional Employer Organizations (PEOs) (also known as staffing firms and employee leasing companies) are Applicable Large Employers.

There is no right answer for how employers will comply with the employer mandate penalty. Some will continue to offer health insurance or not offer it if they do not now. Others may adopt a different program or cease to offer health coverage.

See Q 25 through Q 43 for information on the employer mandate and the employer mandate penalty.

See also Part XI for a detailed discussion of the employer mandate penalties.

53. How does the nature of a PEO's clients affect how the PEO may handle the employer mandate?

The complexity in complying with the employer mandate rules differ based on the nature of the recipient, i.e., the client of the PEO. Industries with large, stable workforces consisting mostly of full-time employees who are provided with major medical benefits will likely continue these benefits and will be able to comply with the employer mandate rules without significant difficulty. However, businesses that rely on variable hour, contingent, or low-paid workers will face difficulties. Many PEOs, along with hospitality, retail, and restaurant businesses, are in this latter group and face significant issues in dealing with the employer mandate rules.

PEOs specializing in IT or professional employees routinely offer comprehensive health care coverage to employees placed on long-term assignments. PEO firms often provide several services and benefits, including permanent placement, temp-to-permanent, and payroll for the recipient employer in addition to the placement of temporary workers on short-term assignments to supplement a client company's core workforce.

Another change is the Small Business Efficiency Act (SBEA), signed in December 2014 and effective on January 1, 2016. This law provides statutory recognition of Professional Employer Organizations. Under the law, the created a voluntary certification process – a PEO that completes this process gains the authority to act as a "co-employer" of sorts and has the authority to collect and remit taxes. As of July 2017, dozens of companies have been certified as CPEOs. The law is just now going into effect and the IRS only began accepting applications for certification on July 1, 2016. It is expected that small and middle-sized employers may reach out to PEOs for assistance with ACA compliance as well as gaining access to large-group health benefits as PEOs can leverage their larger size to gain more favorable rates with health insurers.

It is uncertain whether the PEO can take over the liability for the ACA employer mandate as provided by Section 4980H. It seems to turn on whether the PEO is the common law employer or not which generally turns on who has the "right to control and direct" the employee. The SBEA avoids addressing this issue by stating that "nothing in this section shall be construed to affect the determination of who is an employee or employer."

IRS PEO certification is important because it:

- Confirms the certified PEO (CPEO) can pay federal employment taxes under its EIN.

- Protects customers through the CPEO's sole liability on wages paid to worksite employees by the CPEO.

- Provides certainty with respect to when a wage base restart is not necessary for new customers.

- Confirms the CPEO's FUTA credit for all SUTA paid by CPEO or customer.

- Offers clear guidance for the CPEO and the customer on pass-through of tax credits and employment tax exclusions.

- Gives increased comfort for potential client with use of an IRS-certified PEO.

- Lends credibility to PEO business model, especially with investor community and federal regulators.

More information on CPEOs[1] and a list of those certified can be found at the IRS website.[2]

54. What specific issues will PEOs likely need to consider in regard to the employer mandate?

Issues for PEOs from Employer Mandate

Most PEOs employ internal staff who run the company and recruit the temporary employees and workers to perform temporary work for the PEO firms' clients (recipients). The latter often consist of lower-wage employees, sometimes with high rates of turnover.

Temporary employees have, at least in the past, shown little interest in obtaining health insurance coverage. Thus, many PEO firms have not provided health benefits to those workers. They are more likely to have arrangements under which the internal employees are provided major medical benefits, and the temporary employees are offered no plan or perhaps a limited benefit plan. The employer mandate rules encourage broad-based offers of major medical health coverage to all full-time employees and dependents. Thus, many PEO firms that do not offer affordable minimum value coverage to at least 95 percent of their full-time employees will

---

1.   https://www.irs.gov/tax-professionals/certified-professional-employer-organizations-what-you-need-to-know (Current through July 14, 2019).

2.   https://www.irs.gov/businesses/small-businesses-self-employed/certified-professional-employer-organizations-what-you-need-to-know., Current though July 14, 2019. (Last accessed July 21, 2019).

be subject to an annual nondeductible employer mandate penalty of $2,570 multiplied by the number of all full-time employees, including full-time temporary employees, less thirty.

Additionally, nondiscrimination rules, presently delayed, will apply to health insurance plans. Those rules are to be based on IRS regulations, not yet issued, and modeled on the nondiscrimination rules that apply to self-insured plans. There are exclusions in the self-insured nondiscrimination rules that allow exclusion of high-turnover employers or part-time employees.

Employer Mandate and PEO Employees Working for Recipient Employers

For the employer mandate, employee status is determined under the common law standard. A worker is a common law employee if the employer has the right to control and direct the individual who performs the services, not only as to the result to be accomplished by the work but also as to the details and means by which that result is accomplished. It is not necessary that the employer actually direct or control the manner in which the services are performed; it is sufficient if the employer has the right to do so. It is uncertain whether the PEO can take over the liability for the ACA employer mandate as provided by Section 4980H. The SBEA avoids addressing this issue by stating that "nothing in this section shall be construed to affect the determination of who is an employee or employer."

Historically, many temporary employees assigned by PEO firms to client firms have been treated as common law employees of the PEO firm. There is no reason to believe this will change, at least with respect to traditional temporary PEO services. PEO employees performing services for many clients, such as payroll services, likely will continue to be PEO employees unless the PEO leases back employees performing payroll solely for one recipient employer. However, where the PEO employee is assigned to one recipient employer, it is likely that the worker will be the common law employee of the recipient if the recipient determines the services to be performed and has a right to determine the details and means used by the employee to perform those services.

Additionally, the employer mandate regulations preamble states that if the primary purpose of the PEO arrangement is to avoid the employer mandate provisions of the Act, the client may be the responsible employer.

Obtaining Minimum Value Coverage to Satisfy Employer Mandate

Healthcare reform's insurance market reforms require that insurers guarantee the availability and renewability of health insurance products in the individual and group markets with no exclusions for pre-existing health problems. Thus, PEO firms that want to offer coverage should be able to obtain coverage that provides 60 percent of minimum value, the required minimum threshold for adequate coverage. Prior to 2014, health insurers have often required employers to meet minimum participation requirements to meet their underwriting requirements and avoid adverse selection. This practice is no longer permitted. In the past, many health plans also imposed annual and lifetime payment limits to contain health care coverage costs. Beginning in 2014, this practice was no longer allowed. The Act also imposes maximum limits on out-of-pocket costs. Large PEO firms may also elect to self-insure their own health plan, administered by an insurance company or a third-party administrator.

The requirement of guaranteed availability means that carriers cannot apply traditional underwriting practices. This could result in adverse selection with greater numbers of people needing health care to elect it, which would increase the cost of health coverage. Final HHS regulations acknowledge that adverse selection may present a significant economic exposure to insurance companies. As a result, HHS allows insurance companies to limit open enrollment periods in the individual and small group markets to once a year to reduce the risk that those needing health care would wait to purchase it when they needed the coverage.

However, HHS did not extend that provision to the large group market. Despite measures to limit adverse selection, insurance costs could still increase substantially due to these insurance reform rules, thereby making affordable, minimum value coverage impracticable for many PEOs. However, nonminimum value health plans may provide a solution, as discussed hereafter.

PEOs and Other Employers May Offer Nonminimum Value Group Health Plans

Penalties under the Internal Revenue Code section 4980H(b) apply where an employer offers health coverage that is not affordable or does not provide minimum essential coverage. The term "minimum essential coverage" refers to the source and not the scope of the coverage. Medicare, Medicaid, and VA health benefits provide minimum essential coverage, as does coverage under an eligible employer-sponsored health plan. An "eligible employer-sponsored plan" means a "group health plan" that provides for medical care other than just a HIPAA excepted benefit (e.g., stand-alone vision and/or dental, fixed indemnity, and single disease plans).[1]

Internal Revenue Code section 5000A, the individual mandate, requires U.S. citizens and green card holders to maintain minimum essential coverage for themselves and any nonexempt family members or pay a penalty with their federal income tax return. Employer-sponsored minimum essential coverage need not provide for essential health benefits. Nevertheless, it avoids the employee mandate penalty if it is affordable, in which the cost does not exceed 9.78 percent of the individual's household income for self-only Bronze coverage or individual and family Bronze coverage where the individual has nonexempt family members. Essential health benefits are ten types of health coverage[2] that must be included in fully-insured products sold in the individual and small group markets as part of an "essential health benefits package." These rules don't apply, however, to large group and self-funded plans.

Minimum essential coverage need not offer minimum value, which requires that the coverage pay for 60 percent or more of expected health costs. As discussed, if an employer plan does not provide minimum value coverage, an employee may apply for subsidized coverage through a public exchange, which could trigger a $3,750 employer penalty per full-time employee per year. If an employer is not concerned with meeting the minimum value standard, it may sponsor a

---

1. Medical care is amounts paid for the diagnosis, cure, mitigation, treatment, or prevention of disease, or amounts paid for the purpose of affecting any structure or function of the body; it includes amounts paid for transportation primarily for and essential to such care, as well as amounts paid for insurance covering such care.

2. Essential health benefits are ambulatory patient services, emergency services, hospitalization, maternity and newborn care, mental health and substance use disorder services (including behavioral health treatment), prescription drugs, rehabilitative and habilitative services and devices, laboratory services, preventive and wellness services and chronic disease management, and pediatric services, including oral and vision care.

group plan that covers "medical care" and that complies with the Act's insurance market reforms. Thus, a plan that covers only preventative care and clinical trials covers medical care and qualifies as an eligible employer-sponsored plan. Indeed, excepted benefits included dental or vision insurance offered under a separate policy, certificate, or contract of insurance, so theoretically it is possible that a self-insured vision plan could be minimum essential coverage.

Nonminimum value plans will generally be much less expensive and may not require underwriting. Such plans allow the employer to satisfy the coverage option and avoid the $2,570 per full-time employee less thirty no-coverage penalty. Admittedly, the employer can be liable for the Internal Revenue Code section 4980H(b) penalty. In many cases, however, the plan's cost plus any penalty will be much lower than the cost of providing affordable coverage that provides minimum value.

Plans that fail to provide minimum value means that low-income employees in firms sponsoring such plans can still obtain subsidized coverage under a plan that provides an essential health benefits package from a public exchange, and the applicable large employer can be subject to the employer mandate penalties. Moreover, for low-income employees, the cost of subsidized coverage will in most cases be less than 9.69 percent of household income, which is what an "affordable" employer plan would cost. If the employee decides to forgo exchange coverage and buys the employer's nonminimum value product, he or she will not be subject to the individual tax penalty for failing to have minimum essential coverage, and the employer will not be subject to the employer mandate for such employees.

Impact of the Repeal of the Individual Mandate Penalty on Health Care

55. What is the expected impact of the repeal of the individual mandate penalty on healthcare?

In a November 2017 study prepared by the Congressional Budget Office and the Joint Committee on Taxation,[1] the recent repeal of the Individual Mandate penalty will have major effects on health care and the economy. The analysis includes revised projections of health insurance enrollment, premium costs and other factors. Although based on a repeal of the Individual Mandate, the analysis recognized that the repeal of the individual mandate penalty would have essentially the same effect. The predicted effects seem to have been borne out by the lack of effect on subscription to healthcare services through the Marketplace. The predicted effects include the following:

- there would be a reduction in the Federal budget deficits by approximately $338 billion between 2018 and 2027;

- the increases in health care coverage will be reversed, showing decreases of covered individuals by approximately 4 million in 2019 increasing to 13 million by 2027;

---

1.   Repealing the Individual Health Insurance Mandate: An Updated Estimate, November 2017, https://www.cbo.gov/system/files?file=115th-congress-2017-2018/reports/53300-individualmandate.pdf.

- nongroup insurance markets remain stable over the next ten years;

- average healthcare premiums in the nongroup market would increase by about 10 percent for most years of the decade;

- there would be little change in the relative ages of individuals purchasing insurance;

- healthier people would be less likely to purchase insurance;

- the increases in premiums would cause more people to decide not to purchase insurance; and

- only a small percentage of those that purchase insurance simply to comply with the law would continue to do so without the penalty.

Individual Health Insurance Premium Tax Credits

56. Who is entitled to a subsidy in the form of a tax credit for purchasing health insurance from a state exchange?

The premium tax credit (cost-sharing reduction) for individuals who purchase in insurance on a state exchange is what triggers both the $2,570 all-full-time employees minus 30 and $3,860 per-employee penalties for violating the employer mandate, employee eligibility for either of these subsidies is likely to be a matter of significant concern for many employers. Both subsidies are available to lower and middle-income taxpayers with "household incomes" up to 400 percent of the "poverty level."[1] The following chart reflects the Federal Poverty Level (FPL) and multiples of income. The FPL that applies for determining premium credits and subsidies for a year is that in effect for the preceding calendar year, i.e., for 2020 the 2019 FPL applies.

2020 Federal Poverty Level Percentage of Gross Yearly Income

Family Size	50%	75%	100%	133%	138%	175%	200%	250%	300%	400%
1	$6,245	$9,368	$12,490	$16,612	$17,236	$21,858	$24,980	$31,225	$37,470	$49,960
2	$8,455	$12,683	$16,910	$22,490	$23,336	$29,593	$33,820	$42,275	$50,730	$67,640
3	$10,665	$15,998	$21,330	$28,369	$29,435	$37,328	$42,660	$53,325	$63,990	$85,320
4	$12,875	$19,313	$25,750	$34,248	$35,535	$45,063	$51,500	$64,375	$77,250	$103,000
5	$15,085	$22,628	$30,170	$40,126	$41,635	$52,798	$60,340	$75,425	$90,510	$120,680
6	$17,295	$25,943	$34,590	$46,005	$47,734	$60,533	$69,180	$86,475	$103,770	$138,360
7	$19,505	$29,258	$39,010	$51,883	$53,834	$68,268	$78,020	$97,525	$117,030	$156,040
8	$21,710	$32,565	$43,420	$57,749	$59,920	$75,985	$86,840	$108,550	$130,260	$173,680
Source: The information is compiled from the 2020 HHS Poverty Guidelines, U.S. Dept. of Health and Human Services										

---

1.   42 USC §18071(b) (PPACA §1402(b)); IRC Secs. 36B(b)(2)(B)(ii), (3)(A).

Under the current poverty-line income levels and the household income multiples thereof triggering eligibility for the premium tax credit and cost-sharing, a large part of the population will be eligible for these subsidies. [1] As the chart above shows, an individual with annual income below $49,960 and a family of four with a household income of $103,000 would qualify for the tax credit based on 400 percent of the calendar year 2020 poverty-level numbers, which are adjusted each year for inflation. The median household income in the United States was $49,445 in 2010. [2]

The applicable poverty level for any given employee is dependent upon the number of dependents for which he or she is entitled to personal exemption deductions. Generally, employers typically do not have this information, even though they may be obligated to provide coverage for all such dependents.

A large number of Americans purchasing insurance on a state exchange will be eligible for the individual premium subsidies and cost-sharing reductions. The following chart shows the percent of household income that an individual is required to spend on his insurance premiums. The federal government will provide the rest of the health insurance premium cost with a tax subsidy.

Income Level*	Premium/Percent of Income
• 100-133% of FPL	2% of income
• 133-150% of FPL	3-4% of income
• 150-200% of FPL	4-6.3% of income
• 200-250% of FPL	6.3-8.05% of income
• 250-300% of FPL	8.05-9.5% of income
• 300-400% of FPL	9.5% of income

   * Note: In 2018, 100 percent of FPL for a family of 4 was $25,750; 400 percent was $103,000. The actual numbers that will apply will be based on the 2020 federal poverty level tables.

<u>Household Income Defined</u>. Household income is defined as the modified adjusted gross income of the taxpayer and all other individuals for whom the taxpayer is allowed a dependency exemption. [3] Moreover, proposed regulations would limit this to include only dependents who actually file their own income tax returns. [4] Modified adjusted gross income is adjusted gross income increased by the foreign earned income exclusion, tax-exempt interest, and the tax-exempt portion of Social Security benefits. [5]

---

1. There is a single uniform poverty line for the forty-eight contiguous states and the District of Columbia, and separate ones for Alaska and Hawaii, respectively. The Secretary of HHS is to conduct a study to determine the feasibility and implications of adjusting the poverty line for different geographic locations. PPACA §1416, as added by PPACA §10105.
2. Health Insurance in the United States: 2016, Report P60-260, Jessica C. Barnett and Edward R. Berchick, https://www.census.gov/library/publications/2017/demo/p60-260.html.
3. IRC Secs. 36B(d)(1), (2)(A).
4. Prop. Treas. Reg. §1.36B-1(e).
5. IRC Sec. 36B(d)(2)(B) (as amended by the Three Percent Withholding Repeal and Job Creation Act, Pub. L. No. 112-56, §401). This is in contrast to the definition of "modified adjusted gross income" for purposes of the new Medicare tax on "net investment income", which does not adjust for tax-exempt interest.

Knowing employees' household income is important to an employer for several reasons. First, the employee will only be entitled to a premium tax credit or cost-sharing reduction if his or her household income is below 400 percent of the poverty level.[1] The required contribution for the employer mandate affordability test is based on the cost of self-only coverage to the employee. Employer-sponsored coverage is affordable for an employee (and his or her dependents) if the cost of employer-sponsored self-only coverage is less than 9.69 percent in 2017, 9.56 in 2018, 9.86 in 2019, or 9.78 in 2020 of household income, even if the employee selects employer-sponsored family coverage at a cost greater than 9.69 percent of household income in 2017, 9.56 percent in 2018, 9.86 in 2019, and 9.78 in 2020.[2]

Second, even if an employer offers minimum essential coverage, an employee is eligible for the premium tax credit or cost-sharing reduction if that employee's required contribution to obtain employer coverage exceeds 9.69 percent[3] in 2017, 9.56 in 2018, 9.86 in 2019, and 9.78 in 2020 of "household income."[4] An employee who is offered such affordable minimum essential coverage by the employer cannot claim the premium tax credit or cost-sharing reduction, even though he or she would otherwise be eligible.[5]

The determination of affordability is made at the time that the employee enrolls in the exchange, and the determination lasts the entire plan year.[6] Thus, if the exchange initially determined that the employer-sponsored plan was not affordable, then it is treated as such, regardless of whether the employee's household income ultimately proves high enough to make it affordable in hindsight. On the other hand, the employer will not be responsible for the penalty if the exchange determines that the coverage is not affordable but in fact it is.

<u>W-2 Safe Harbor</u>. The regulations will provide an affordability safe harbor for employers. An employer that meets certain requirements, including offering its full-time employees (and their dependents) the opportunity to enroll in eligible employer-sponsored coverage, will not be subject to an assessable payment under Internal Revenue Code section 4980H(b) (the $3,860 "per-employee" penalty) with respect to an employee who receives a premium tax credit or cost-sharing reduction for a taxable year if the employee portion of the self-only premium for the employer's lowest cost plan that provides minimum value does not in fact exceed 9.78 percent in 2020, 9.86 percent in 2019 of the employee's current wages from the employer, as shown in Box 1 of Form W-2.[7]

For employers who are interested in providing coverage only to the extent necessary to avoid penalties, these household income and poverty level tests are problematic. It will be difficult,

---

1.   IRC Sec. 36B(c)(1)(A); 42 USC §18071(b) (PPACA §1402(b)).
2.   See Treas. Reg. §1.36B-2(c)(3)(v)(A)(*l*) and preamble thereto.
3.   This 9.5 percent cap may be adjusted for the excess of premium growth inflation over income growth and/or the consumer price index. *See* IRC Sec. 36B(c)(2)(C)(iv), (b)(3)(A)(ii).
4.   IRC Sec. 36B(c)(2)(C); 42 USC §18071(f)(2) (PPACA §1402(f)(2)).
5.   IRC Sec. 36B(c)(2)(C).
6.   Treas. Reg. §1.36B-2(c)(3)(v).
7.   See IRS Notice 2011-73, which states that it believes this would be a "workable and predictable method" based on information that "employers know." The Notice states that employers may be able to use the safe harbor prospectively to structure its plan and operations to set the employee contribution at a level so that the employee contribution for each employee would not exceed 9.5 percent of that employee's W-2 wages for the upcoming year.

if not impossible, for an employer to reliably know what an employee's household income is.[1] Even if the employer pays an employee compensation in excess of 400 percent of the poverty level, it is still possible for the employee or his or her spouse to have a net loss from partnership, S corporation, or even sole proprietorship activities that will bring their joint household income down below that level.

Employees eligible for Medicaid are treated as being "eligible for minimum essential coverage other than eligibility for coverage described in Internal Revenue Code section 5000A(f)(1)(C) (relating to coverage in the individual market)," and therefore not eligible for the premium tax credit or cost sharing reduction.[2] Such eligibility is typically based, at least in part, on an individual's income in relation to the poverty level or a related statistic.

Additionally, it could be difficult or impossible for an employer to procure such household income information for an employee and his or her dependents. The employee can refuse to provide it. Section 1411(f)(2)(B) of PPACA provides as follows:

Notwithstanding any provision of this title (or the amendments made by this title) or section 6103 of the Internal Revenue Code of 1986, an employer shall not be entitled to any taxpayer return information with respect to an employee for purposes of determining whether the employer is subject to the penalty under Internal Revenue Code section 4980H with respect to the employee, except that:

(i)   the employer may be notified as to the name of an employee and whether or not the employee's income is above or below the threshold by which the affordability of an employer's health insurance coverage is measured; and

(ii)   this subparagraph shall not apply to an employee who provides a waiver (at such time and in such manner as the Secretary may prescribe) authorizing an employer to have access to the employee's taxpayer return information.

There is a question as to whether this provision only restricts the federal government from disclosing this information, or whether it precludes an employer from asking the employee for such information. To avoid penalties, an employer potentially subject to the penalty may have to provide minimum essential coverage to each of its employees if it does not know whether their respective household incomes are or were above or below 400 percent of the poverty level (or low enough to trigger Medicaid). Under the above provision, the employer would only be entitled to know "whether or not the employee's income is above or below the threshold by which the affordability of an employee's health insurance coverage is measured."[3] Presumably, the employer would have to inform the Secretary of HHS of what the actual employee contribution was and then the Secretary would be able to tell the employer whether the employee is eligible

---

1.   The safe harbor noted above based on an employee's actual W-2 wages from the employer would apply only for purposes of the affordability test.

2.   IRC Secs. 36B(c)(2)(B)(i); 5000A(f)(1)(A)(ii); Treas. Reg. §1.36B-2(c)(2).

3.   42 USC §18081(f)(2)(B) (PPACA §1411(f)(2)(B)). Presumably, this language is intended to allow the employer to find out whether its required employee contribution is above or below the 9.5 percent household income affordability threshold for the employee in question, although the language is not clear.

for reduced cost-sharing or the premium tax credit (and the employer was therefore subject to the penalty). It could be too late for the employer to avoid substantial penalty(ies) for prior years.

The affordability tests are for employee-only coverage. It must cost no more than the household income or one of several safe harbors, such as the employee's current Box 1, W-2 income: 9.78 percent of the employee's rate of pay, or 9.78 percent of the FPL for a single person. The insurance offered in 2020 must be for employees and dependents (including children under twenty-six but not their spouses), but only the employee coverage needs to meet the affordability test. Uninsured spouses are eligible for exchange subsidies if they qualify, based on household income being under 400 percent of FPL and dependents (where employer dependent coverage is offered but not selected) may be eligible for coverage in a state sponsored plan. Remember that the percentage changed from 9.86 in 2019 to 9.78 in 2020.

57. How is income determined for defining who is eligible for a subsidy for health insurance purchased on an exchange?

The Internal Revenue Code section 36B tax credits and subsidies for health insurance purchased on an exchange where the employer does not offer affordable minimum value coverage are based on household income under Code section 36B(b)(3)(A) between 100 percent and 400 percent of federal poverty level ("FPL"), using the FPL for the preceding calendar year. Household income is defined as Modified Adjusted Gross Income (MAGI). See Q 720 for discussion of "affordable value."

Internal Revenue Code section 36B(d)(3) defines "modified adjusted gross income" as adjusted gross income increased by:

(1)   any amount excluded from gross income under section 911;

(2)   any amount of interest received or accrued by the taxpayer during the taxable year which is exempt from tax; and

(3)   any social security benefits not included in gross income.

Internal Revenue Code section 36B(d)(2) defines household income as the sum of the:

(1)   modified adjusted gross income of the taxpayer;

(2)   the aggregate modified adjusted gross incomes of all other individuals who determine the taxpayer's family size; and

(3)   the portion of the taxpayer's social security not included in gross income.

Family size is determined under Internal Revenue Code section 36B(d)(1) as the number of individuals for whom the taxpayer is allowed a dependent deduction under Internal Revenue Code section 151.

Thus, an individual not eligible for Medicare or Medicaid would include in income taxable income from an employer: interest from tax exempt bonds, trust payments, untaxed social security payments, and taxable retirement plan and annuity payments, but not the value of gifts.

58. What is the effect of same-sex marriage recognition rules for exchange determinations of premium tax credits and for Medicaid and CHIP?

In 2015, the U.S. Supreme Court in the case of *King v. Burwell* ruled that individuals purchasing insurance on exchanges run by the federal government qualify for subsidies. It also ruled that same-sex marriage was a right granted by the Constitution in *Obergefell v. Hodges*. Thus, same sex couples in all states may now qualify for subsidies for exchange purchased health insurance if they otherwise qualify. Same-sex married couples are now treated as married for both federal and state tax purposes. All benefits that were available only to opposite-sex married couples are now available to same-sex married couples nationwide, including eligibility for healthcare insurance provided by the same-sex spouse's insurer. In addition, COBRA law applies to same-sex couples as well. It must be remembered however, that married couples are ineligible for ACA tax credits and subsidies if their combined income exceeds the threshold.

Additionally, married couples must file a joint tax return to qualify for premium tax credits. Rev. Rul. 2013-17 recognizes same-sex marriages for federal tax purposes. Prior to the 2015 Supreme Court decisions, CMS required Exchanges to evaluate marital status based on the law of the state or country where the marriage had been entered, even if the state of residence did not recognize same-sex marriages. Federally-Facilitated Exchanges recognize same-sex marriages for this purpose with respect to married couples who have filed joint tax returns for the 2014 tax year and thereafter.

In separate, contemporaneous guidance,[1] CMS explains eligibility for Medicaid and the Children's Health Insurance Program (CHIP), which are joint federal-state, needs-based programs. For income-based eligibility determinations under these programs, CMS, prior to 2015, permitted states to apply their own choice-of-law rules in deciding whether a couple is lawfully married. That is no longer a consideration after the Supreme Court decided that same-sex couples have the right to marry in all states. Additional information is available at the CMS website.[2]

59. Can the federal government subsidize health insurance premiums for people in states that use an exchange run by the federal government rather than the state?

Yes. The Supreme Court so held in the case of *King v. Burwell* in 2015, ruling that regardless of whether a state exchange is run by the state or the federal government, the same subsidy rules apply. Prior to the Supreme Court's decision, two United States Circuit Courts issued conflicting rulings on whether the federal government can subsidize health insurance premiums for people in thirty-six states that use an insurance exchange run by the federal government. Due to this split in the Circuits and the importance of the issue, the U.S. Supreme Court decided this issue in 2015.

The Fourth Circuit in *King v. Burwell*,[3] unanimously upheld the subsidies saying that the regulations issued by the IRS saying that the eligible (by income below set thresholds) residents

---

1.   See http://www.medicaid.gov/Federal-Policy-Guidance/Downloads/SHO-13-006.pdf. (Last accessed July 1, 2019).
2.   https://www.ssa.gov/people/same-sexcouples/.
3.   No. 14-1158 (4th Cir. July 22, 2014).

of all states are eligible for the subsidies was "a permissible exercise of the agency's discretion." The DC Circuit ruled 2 to 1 in *Halbig v. Burwell*[1] that the federal government could not subsidize insurance for people in states whose exchanges were established by HHS and vacated the IRS regulations under Internal Revenue Code section 36B. The IRS interpreted Internal Revenue Code section 36B broadly to authorize the subsidy also for insurance purchased on one of the thirty-six exchanges established by the federal government.[2] For some of those exchanges, the states in question assisted the federal government in creating the exchange for that state. Initially, fourteen states and the District of Columbia established their own exchanges.

The key language in dispute was the provision that the tax subsidies are available to eligible taxpayers "enrolled in through an Exchange established by the State."[3] In essence, those who argued that all exchanges qualify, argue that all exchanges are state exchanges, including those states where the exchange was established for that state by HHS or by HHS in cooperation with that state and that purpose of the law would be frustrated if those only in state created state exchanges would qualify for the tax subsidies. Those arguing that the tax subsidies should only be given to lower income taxpayers in states in which the state itself established the exchange, pointed to the literal language of the law, arguing that the purpose was to encourage states to create their own exchanges so that their residents could enjoy the tax subsidies.

Historical Background

A group of small business owners (and individuals) in six states filed a lawsuit on May 2, 2013, against the federal government over an IRS regulation making available the Exchange-provided tax credits and subsidies to all Exchanges, including those state exchanges run by HHS. The plaintiffs claimed that the law would force the plaintiffs to pay exorbitant fines, cut back employees' hours, or severely burden their businesses due to the employer mandate penalty on employers with fifty or more full-time and full-time equivalent employees.

Plaintiffs stated that employers would, but for their employees' eligibility for subsidies, be exempt from the potential employer mandate tax penalty. Plaintiffs also alleged that individuals would, but for their eligibility for federal subsidies, be exempt from the Act's individual mandate penalty under an exemption applicable to low- or moderate-income individuals for whom insurance is "unaffordable." For these people, the Subsidy Expansion Rule, by making insurance less "unaffordable," subjects them to the individual mandate's requirement to purchase costly, comprehensive health insurance that they otherwise would forgo.

The Internal Revenue Code section 36B credit is designed to make health insurance purchased on a state Exchange (marketplace) affordable for taxpayers whose income is less than 400 percent of the federal poverty level and who do not have affordable, minimum value health insurance from their employer. Healthcare reform required each state to establish a health insurance Exchange by January 1, 2014. If a state decided not to do so, HHS established an Exchange. Most state Exchanges are run by HHS. The Exchange makes subsidy payments on the

---

1.   No. 14-5018 (D.C. Cir. July 22, 2014).
2.   Treas. Reg. §1.36B-2(a)(1).
3.   IRC Sec. 36B(2)(A).

individual's behalf to the health plan, based on information available at the time of enrollment, then that person's income tax return for the year reconciles the actual credit that he is due with the amount of the subsidy payments that were made.[1]

In describing the premium assistance amount, Internal Revenue Code section 36B(b)(2)(A)[2] refers to "the monthly premiums for…qualified health plans offered in the individual market… which were enrolled in through an Exchange *established by the State*" (*emphasis added*). However, the regulations under Internal Revenue Code section 36B provide that the premium tax credit is not limited to state-created Exchanges, but also includes federally facilitated Exchanges.[3] The plaintiffs in *Halbig v. Sebelius* contend that the Internal Revenue Code section 36B regulations contradict the express text of the law that provides for tax credits and subsidies for state-established Exchanges.

The U.S. District Court for the District of Columbus in the case of *Halbig v. Sebelius* (D.C.D.C. January 15, 2014) had ruled in favor of the federal government in a lawsuit contending that the IRS did not have the authority under healthcare reform to write rules that provide tax credits provided by Internal Revenue Code section 36B to individuals purchasing health insurance on the thirty-four state health insurance exchanges (a/k/a marketplaces) set up and run in whole or part by the federal government.

The IRS issued a final regulation in May 2012 implementing the premium tax credit provision of the Affordable Care Act, in which it interpreted the ACA as authorizing the agency to grant tax credits to individuals who purchase insurance on either a state-run health insurance exchange or a federally run exchange. An eligible taxpayer receives a tax credit if he or she, or a member of his or her family, "[i]s enrolled in one or more qualified health plans through an Exchange."[4] The law defines "Exchange" as follows:

> Exchange means a governmental agency or non-profit entity that meets the applicable standards of this part and makes [Qualified Health Plans] available to qualified individuals and/or qualified employers. Unless otherwise identified, this term includes an Exchange serving the individual market for qualified individuals and a [Small Business Health Options Program] serving the small group market for qualified employers, ***regardless of whether the Exchange is established and operated by a State (including a regional Exchange or subsidiary Exchange) or by HHS.***[5]

The plaintiffs, who included the conservative Competitive Enterprise Institute, contended that the IRS's interpretation was contrary to the statute, which, they asserted, authorizes tax credits only for individuals who purchase insurance on state-run exchanges, but not on federal exchanges. The plaintiffs in the case claimed that the rule promulgated by the IRS exceeded the agency's statutory authority and was arbitrary, capricious, and contrary to law, in violation of the Administrative Procedure Act.

1.	IRC Sec. 36B(b).
2.	Enacted by PPACA §1311.
3.	Treas. Reg. §1.36B-1(k).
4.	Treas. Reg. §1.36B-2(a)(1).
5.	45 CFR §155.20. Treas. Reg. §1.36B-1(k) provides that the term Exchange "has the same meaning as in 45 CFR §155.20."

The court ruled that the statute, the statutory structure, and the statutory purpose make clear that Congress intended to make premium tax credits available on both state-run and federally-facilitated exchanges. The court stated that the scant legislative history that exists supports this conclusion.

As of July 2019, management of the exchanges is as follows:

- Twelve state-based marketplaces

- Five state-based marketplaces that utilize the Federal platform

- Six state-federal partnership marketplaces

- Twenty-eight federal exchanges

However, Arkansas and Kentucky have switched to federally-supposed, state-based exchanges and Hawaii has changed to a federally-facilitated exchange. Kentucky changed from kynect to healthcare.gov, but the other states will continue to use healthcare.gov.

A breakout of states and marketplace types is available at kff.org.[1]

See Q 56 and Q 60.

60. Who are "qualified individuals" for purposes of the final regulation for the Code section 36B credit?

Technical Decision 9611, 01/30/2013, Regulation section 1.36B explains the Internal Revenue Code section 36B health insurance premium tax credit enacted by healthcare reform. The regulation applies to tax years ending after December 31, 2013 and provides guidance to individuals related to employees who may enroll in eligible employer-sponsored coverage and who wish to enroll in qualified health plans through Affordable Insurance Exchanges and claim the premium tax credit. The regulations extend these tax credits and subsidies to the purchase of health insurance on state created exchanges and federal exchanges created in states without exchanges of their own. As noted earlier, the U.S. Supreme Court upheld these regulations in 2015, in the *King. v. Burwell* decision.

61. What is the purpose of the Code section 36B credit regulation?

The Internal Revenue Code section 36B credit is designed to make health insurance affordable to individuals with modest incomes (i.e., between 100 percent and 400 percent of the federal poverty level, or FPL) who are not eligible for other qualifying coverage, such as Medicare, or "affordable" employer-sponsored health insurance plans. Eligibility for other coverage is determined on a month-by-month basis. The credit applied beginning in 2014.

---

1.   http://www.kff.org/health-reform/state-indicator/state-health-insurance-marketplace-types/?activeTab=map¤tTimeframe=0&selec
      tedDistributions=marketplace-type&sortModel=%7B%22colId%22:%22Location%22,%22sort%22:%22asc%22%7D.

Internal Revenue Code section 5000A(e) provides an employer-sponsored plan is not affordable if the employee's required contribution for single (self-only) coverage exceeds 9.69 percent of household income for the tax year. The percentage may be adjusted after 2014. The employee's cost for self-only coverage is used even if the employee has family coverage, which is more expensive. For an individual other than an employee who is eligible to enroll in the plan because of a relationship the individual bears to the employee, affordability is also measured by the employee's cost of self-only coverage.

Thus, the statutory language specifies that for both employees and others (such as spouses or dependents) who are eligible to enroll in employer-sponsored coverage because of their relationship to an employee (related individuals), the coverage is unaffordable only if the required contribution for "self-only" coverage exceeds 9.5 percent of household income (increased to 9.86 percent in 2019 and decreased to 9.78 in 2020).

In May of 2012, final Internal Revenue Code section 36B regulations were issued. However, Regulation section 1.36B-2(c)(3)(v)(A)(2) reserved the question of determining affordability of employer-sponsored coverage for related individuals. Consistent with these statutory provisions, the proposed regulation would provide that an employer-sponsored plan also is affordable for a related individual if the employee's required contribution for self-only coverage under the plan does not exceed 9.66 percent for 2016, 9.69 percent for 2017, 9.56 in 2018, 9.86 in 2019 and 9.78 in 2020 of the applicable taxpayer's household income for the tax year, even if the taxpayer's required contribution for the family coverage exceeds 9.86 (increasing to 9.78 percent in 2020) percent of household income for the year.

62. How did the October 2013 "No Subsidies without Verification Act" change the rules for verification of individuals, financial information on the healthcare exchanges (marketplaces)?

Healthcare reform provides premium tax credits to make health insurance affordable to individuals with modest incomes between 100 percent and 400 percent of the federal poverty level. These credits are available to those who are not eligible for other qualifying coverage, such as Medicare, or "affordable" employer-sponsored health insurance plans that provide "minimum value." They are refundable tax credits, applicable for tax years ending after December 31, 2013, available to individuals who purchase coverage through "Affordable Insurance Exchanges," also known as Marketplaces.[1]

In July 2013, the Department of Health and Human Services (HHS) issued a final rule for the exchange's income verification process, which the *Washington Post* reported would "significantly scale back" the law's verification requirement for those receiving federally subsidized coverage.[2] Note however, that the Exchange subsidies are not paid to individuals but, rather, to insurers.

---

1.   IRC Sec. 36B.
2.   PPACA §1411 establishes requirements whether someone meets the income and coverage qualifications for such premium tax credits and cost-sharing subsidies for those whose incomes are below 400 percent of federal poverty level.

These July 2013 regulations,[1] which were delayed for one year from 2014 until 2015, included two reporting requirements for certain large employers and health insurance coverage providers. Under the final July 2013 HHS regulation, applicants' income is to be verified against their IRS and Social Security records. When that cannot be achieved, income will be checked against employer records submitted to Equifax. If the IRS, the Social Security Administration, and Equifax cannot provide data to substantiate the income information a consumer has supplied, the consumer will have to provide an explanation or additional documentation of income.[2]

The July 2013 regulation also allows state exchanges to check a statistically valid sample of applicants in cases where an applicant claims income more than 10 percent below what IRS and Social Security records show and there is no Equifax data.

In the summer of 2013, shortly after announcing the one-year delay of the ACA's employer mandate and its associated reporting requirements, the Administration delayed a requirement that state-run Marketplaces verify an ACA subsidy applicant's claim that he does not receive employer health insurance. The Administration also relaxed the verification requirements with respect to individuals who reported a significant decrease in income.

H.R. 2775, the 2014 Continuing Appropriations Act containing the bill entitled the No Subsidies without Verification Act, passed in October 2013. In addition to continuing U.S. appropriations, it requires that HHS ensure that the Exchanges verify that individuals applying for coverage in the Marketplace and seeking premium tax credits and cost-sharing reductions are, in fact, eligible for these subsidies. The HHS Secretary was required to submit a report to Congress by January 1, 2014, detailing the verification procedures, and the Inspector General for HHS was required to submit a report to Congress by July 1, 2014, on the procedures' effectiveness.

Section 1001 of the Act requires HHS on the exchanges it runs to:

(1)   ensure that American Health Benefit Exchanges (healthcare reform's health care exchanges, also called marketplaces) verify that individuals applying for premium tax credits and reductions in cost-sharing for the purchase of qualified health benefit plans are eligible for such credits and cost sharing reductions consistent with healthcare reform's requirements; and

(2)   prior to making such credits and reductions available in January 2014, certify to Congress that the Exchanges have a program to verify such eligibility.

63. How can a qualified individual receive a Code section 36B credit?

The eligible individual purchases affordable coverage through "Affordable Insurance Exchanges" that will make qualified health insurance plans available to individuals as well as small businesses.

---

1.   79 Fed. Reg. No. 135 at p. 42160 et seq., Medicaid and Children's Health Insurance Programs (CHIPs): Essential Health Benefits (EHBs) in Alternative Benefit Plans, Eligibility Notices, Fair Hearings and Appeals Processes, and Premiums and Cost Sharing; Exchanges: Eligibility and Enrollment http://www.gpo.gov/fdsys/pkg/FR-2013-07-15/pdf/2013-16271.pdf. (Last accessed July 1, 2019).
2.   45 CFR §155.315.

The Exchange makes subsidy payments to the qualified health plan on behalf of the individual. The subsidy payments take the form of an advance credit payment ("monthly premium assistance amount") under Internal Revenue Code section 36B. Using information available at the time of enrollment, the Exchange determines:

(1)   whether the individual meets the income and other requirements for advance credit payments; and

(2)   the amount of the advance payments.

Advance payments are made monthly to the issuer of the qualified health plan in which the individual enrolls. The monthly premium assistance amount is the lesser of the premium for the qualified health plan in which a taxpayer or family member enrolls, or the excess of the premium for the benchmark plan (the second-lowest "silver plan") over the applicable percentage of the taxpayer's household income. The applicable percentage of the premium assistance increases as the percentage of the FPL for the taxpayer's family size increases.

The eligible individual reconciles the actual credit for the tax year computed on the taxpayer's tax return for the prior year with the amount of advance payments paid on the taxpayer's behalf. If a taxpayer's credit amount exceeds the amount of advance payments paid on the taxpayer's behalf for the tax year, the taxpayer may receive the excess as an income tax refund. If advance payments made on the taxpayer's behalf exceed the taxpayer's credit amount, the taxpayer owes the excess as an additional income tax liability. However, Internal Revenue Code section 36B(f)(2)(B) caps the additional tax liability for taxpayers with household income under 400 percent of the FPL. The repayment limitation amounts for 2019 are unchanged from 2018 and range from $600 to $2,550 (one half that amount for single taxpayers) depending on FPL, and is adjusted to reflect the cost of living each year. The cost-of-living figures for 2020 have not yet been published but will be made available on the IRS website.[1]

64. How does the Code section 36B credit work for related individuals?

The final regulation provides guidance to individuals related to employees who may enroll in eligible employer-sponsored coverage and who wish to enroll in qualified health plans through Affordable Insurance Exchanges and claim the premium tax credit.

> *Example:* H is married to W, and Employer X's plan requires H to contribute $5,300 for coverage for H and W for 2020, which reflects 11.3 percent of H's household income. However, the contribution attributable to self-only coverage of $3,750 does not exceed 9.78 percent of household income as required by Reg. section 1.36B-2(c)(3)(v)(A)(2). Therefore, X's plan is affordable for both H and W. Reg. section 1.36B-2(c)(3)(v)(D), Example 2.

By contrast, Internal Revenue Code section 5000A, which establishes the shared responsibility payment applicable to individuals (the individual mandate) for failure to maintain minimum essential coverage addresses affordability for employees in Code section 5000A(e)(1)(B) and for related individuals in Internal Revenue Code section 5000A(e)(1)(H). The proposed regulations

---

1.   https://www.irs.gov/affordable-care-act/individuals-and-families/premium-tax-credit-claiming-the-credit-and-reconciling-advance-credit-payments.

under Code section 5000A provide that, for purposes of applying the affordability exemption from the shared responsibility payment in the case of related individuals, the required contribution is based on the premium the employee would pay for employer-sponsored family coverage.[1]

65. How can employers use the Code section 36B in its health-insurance planning?

If an employer limits every employee's premium for self-only coverage at 9.78 percent (9.86 in 2019) of pay, it will never pay the $3,860 employer mandate penalty for failure to provide affordable coverage. It is perfectly legal to set lower premiums for lower-paid employees. An employer can set the employee's premium for family coverage as high as it wishes.

66. May an employer establish an employee contribution schedule and allow employees to be eligible for reduced contributions if they provide evidence that their required contributions would otherwise be in excess of the affordability limits?

An employee's information for as many as three taxable years could be relevant in making all of these various determinations.

First, eligibility for the premium tax credit is dependent upon an employee's household income for the current taxable year.[2]

Second, the determination as to whether an employee is eligible for reduced cost-sharing is apparently going to be based on the employee's income for the preceding taxable year.[3]

Third, any advance payment of the credit or cost-reduction, which can also trigger an employer penalty, must be made "on the basis of the individual's household income for the most recent taxable year for which the Secretary of HHS, after consultation with the Secretary of the Treasury, determines information is available," which could easily be the employee's second preceding taxable year.[4]

67. Can Applicable Large Employers (ALEs) with fifty or more full-time and Full-Time Equivalent (FTE) employees avoid the employer mandate penalty by offering an actuarially equivalent contribution to an HSA, HRA, or FSA so that employees can buy health care coverage on the exchange or in the private non-group market?

No, not if that coverage is the <u>only</u> coverage offered by the employer.

To avoid the employer penalties, coverage must offer "minimum essential coverage". Health Savings Accounts (HSAs) do not offer "minimum essential coverage" because they are not group

---

1.   See T.D. 9611, 01/30/2013.
2.   IRC Sec. 36B(b)(2)(B)(ii).
3.   42 USC §18071(f)(3); 18082(b)(1)(B) (PPACA §§1402(f)(3); 1412(b)(1)(B)).
4.   IRC Sec. 4980H(c)(3)(C); 42 USC §18082(b)(1)(B) (PPACA §1412(b)(1)(B)).

health plans under ERISA.[1] Stand-alone Health Reimbursement Accounts (HRAs) that are not integrated with another employer group health plan do not meet the PPACA's annual dollar maximums and preventive benefits requirements.[2] However, HRAs that reimburse only excepted benefits, such as dental or vision, may be offered without being integrated with another group health plan because they are excepted benefits.[3] Likewise, stand-alone FSAs not integrated with another group health plan are not minimum essential coverage. FSAs cannot be used to pay premiums for other coverage (other than COBRA coverage, if the plan allows).

Health FSAs <u>are</u> group health plans and will be considered to provide only excepted benefits as long as two conditions are met:

(1)   The employer also offers a group health plan that is not limited to excepted benefits.

(2)   The health FSA is structured so a participant's maximum benefit cannot exceed twice his or her salary reduction election for the year (or, if greater, cannot exceed $500 plus the amount of the salary reduction election).

Otherwise, health FSAs are generally subject to the market reforms of the Public Health Services Act (PHSA), discussed in more detail in Part VII of this book.

68. What is Minimum Essential Coverage (MEC)?

The individual mandate requires individuals to be responsible for ensuring that they, and any of their dependents, are covered under Minimum Essential Coverage (MEC). Minimum Essential Coverage (MEC) includes the following:

- **Government sponsored programs**

    o   Medicare Part A

    o   Medicare Advantage plans

    o   Most Medicaid coverage

    o   Children's Health Insurance Program coverage (CHIP)

    o   Most TRICARE coverage

    o   Comprehensive health care coverages through the Department of Veterans Affairs

    o   Health Care for Peace Corps volunteers

    o   Department of Defense Nonappropriated Fund Health Benefits Program

---

1.   DOL FAB 2004-1.
2.   IRS Notice 2013-54.
3.   Amendments to Excepted Benefits, 26 CFR Part 54, 29 CFR Part 2590, 45 CFR Part 146, 79 Fed. Reg. 59130 (Oct. 1, 2014).

- o   Refugee Medical Assistance

- o   Basic Health Program (BHP) standard health plan

- **Employer-sponsored plans**

  - o   Governmental plans (such as the Federal Employees Health Benefit Program)

  - o   Grandfathered plans

  - o   Plans offered in the small or large group market

  - o   Self-insured group health plan for employees

  - o   COBRA coverage

  - o   Retiree coverage

  - o   Coverage under an expatriate health plan for employees

- **Individual health coverage**

  - o   Health insurance purchased directly from an insurance company

  - o   Health insurance purchased through the Health Insurance marketplace

  - o   Health insurance provided through a student health plan

  - o   Catastrophic plans

  - o   Coverage under an expatriate health plan for non-employees such as students, missionaries, etc.

  - o   Certain foreign coverages

  - o   Certain coverages for business owners

  - o   Other coverage designated as Minimum Essential Coverage (MEC) by HHS and/or the Dept. of the Treasury.[1] There is more detail on this in the following section.

69. What individuals are not subject to the Individual Mandate?

Beginning January 1, 2014, all U.S. residents have been required to maintain Minimum Essential Coverage (MEC) unless the individual falls into one of the following exceptions:

- Individuals with a religious conscience exemption (applies only to certain faiths — see Internal Revenue Code section 1402(g)(l)).

---

1.   PPACA §1501, adding IRC Sec. 5000A(f).

- There are no specific list of religious groups which qualify other than the religion must have been in continuous existence since December 31, 1950.

- Incarcerated individuals (except those pending the disposition of charges).

- Undocumented aliens.

- Nonresident aliens.

- Dual-status aliens in their first year of residency.

- Nonresident aliens or dual-status aliens that elect to file a joint return with a U.S. spouse.

- Individuals who cannot afford coverage (i.e. required contribution exceeds 8.30 percent of household income in 2019).

  - Threshold was set at 8.0 percent in 2014 and is indexed by amount of premium growth from previous year over income growth from previous year.

  - Threshold for 2015 was 8.05 percent

  - Threshold for 2016 was 8.13 percent

  - Threshold for 2017 was 8.17 percent

  - Threshold for 2018 was 8.05 percent

  - Threshold for 2019 was 8.30 percent

  - Threshold for 2020 has not been set due to reduction of Individual Mandate penalty to $0.

- Health care sharing ministry membership.

  - Section 501(c) defines this as an organization (including corporations and any community chest, fund, or foundation organized and operated exclusively for religious, charitable, scientific, or testing for public safety) that is exempt from taxation under Section 501(a). Members share a common set of ethical or religious beliefs and share medical expenses, and retain membership even after they develop a medical condition.

- American citizen living abroad at least 330 days within a twelve month period as well as bona fide residents of any U.S. possession.

- Individuals with a coverage gap of less than three months.

- Individuals in a hardship situation (as defined by HHS).

- Hardship exemptions can obtain catastrophic plans.

- Individuals with income below the tax filing threshold.

    o Threshold for tax filings in 2014 was $10,150 for single filers and $20,300 for married filing jointly.

    o Threshold for tax filings in 2015 was $10,300 for single filers and $20,600 for married filing jointly.

    o Threshold for tax filings in 2016 was $10,350 for single filers and $20,700 for married filing jointly and $13,350 for heads of households.

    o Threshold for tax filings in 2017 was $10,400 for single filers and $20,800 for married filing jointly and $13,400 for heads of households.

    o Threshold is linked to the inflation adjustment for the CPI for All Urban Consumers. Figures are not yet available for 2018.

- Members of Indian tribes.[1]

70. Which persons are not subject to the individual mandate because they are not "applicable individuals"?

Note: This question is retained in the 2020 Edition for historical and prior year applicability. The Individual Mandate penalty has been lowered to $0 for 2019 and subsequent years, therefore the discussion of being exempt from the Individual Mandate is moot for 2019 and 2020.

Applicable Individual. The individual mandate tax penalty (which is repealed effective in 2019 but still applies to prior years) applies only to applicable individuals, and the definition of that term excludes designated categories of individuals. These excluded categories include members of certain religious faiths already exempt from self-employment tax, members of healthcare-sharing ministries which, among other things, share medical expenses among members and have been in continuous existence since December 31, 1999, aliens not legally present, and incarcerated individuals after they have been convicted.[2]

There are also exemptions for members of Indian tribes, short-term coverage gaps of one or two months, hardships (as determined by the Secretary of HHS) and persons residing outside of the United States or within U.S. possessions.[3] There are no corresponding exceptions for employers under the employer mandate. Thus, it appears that both the "all full-time employees minus 30" and per-employee penalties under the employer mandate would take such employees into account.[4]

Affordability. Another major exemption is the one for applicable individuals whose "required contribution (determined on an annual basis) for coverage for the month exceeds

---

1. PPACA §1501 and 10106 adding IRC Sec. 5000A(d) and (e).
2. IRC Sec. 5000A(d)(2), (3), (4).
3. IRC Sec. 5000A(e)(3), (4), (5), (f)(4).
4. *See generally* IRC Sec. 4980H(c).

8.30 percent of such individual's household income for the taxable year."[1] For this exemption, the required contribution for an individual eligible to participate in an employer-sponsored plan is equal to "the portion of the annual premium which would be paid by the individual (without regard to whether paid through salary reduction or otherwise) for self-only coverage."[2] For individuals whose sole option is to purchase insurance through an exchange, the required contribution is equal to the annual premium for the lowest cost bronze plan available in the individual market through the exchange in the state in the rating area in which the individual resides reduced by the amount of the credit allowable under Internal Revenue Code section 36B for the taxable year (determined as if the individual was covered by a qualified plan offered through the exchange for the entire taxable year).[3] The tax code provision does not define required contribution for other types of plans. For example, the Medicare Part A premium should be the required contribution for individuals over sixty-five who are not eligible to participate in employer-sponsored plans.

While an individual's current "required contribution" is "determined on an annual basis," the 8.30 percent affordability amount is determined "on the basis of the individual's household income for the most recent taxable year for which the Secretary of Health and Human Services, after consultation with the Secretary of the Treasury, determines information is available."[4] Thus, the household income for affordability is likely to be determined on the basis of the income tax return filed for the preceding, and possibly the second preceding, taxable year of the applicable individual. Finally, the 8.30 percent affordability factor is to be adjusted to reflect "the excess of the rate of premium growth between the preceding calendar year and 2013 over the rate of income growth for such period."[5]

Income below Filing Threshold. Taxpayers whose household income for a taxable year is less than the gross income necessary to trigger an income tax return filing requirement[6] are not applicable individuals and are not subject to the employee mandate. These gross income levels are unlikely to exempt many applicable individuals who are not already exempt under the 8.30 percent affordability exemption discussed above. However, many such individuals are also likely to be eligible for Medicaid and thus exempt from the penalty as long as they apply to procure such coverage.

Dependents. The individual mandate Code provisions' use of the dependency deduction for triggering and calculating the penalty creates conflicting planning considerations for individuals who may be subject to the penalty. Claiming someone as a dependent is favorable under the Code. For example, in addition to the dependency exemption itself, and possible

---

1. IRC Sec. 5000A(e)(1)(A). It is not clear why the affordability test for employers is 9.5 percent whereas this individual "affordability test" is 8.05 percent.
2. IRC Sec. 5000A(e)(1)(B)(i). This affordability test based on the premium for self-only coverage will be integrated into the penalty calculation under which an individual may also be responsible for providing coverage for a spouse and/or dependents. *See* Preamble to Proposed Regulations for Code section 36B.
3. IRC Sec. 5000A(e)(1)(B)(ii).
4. IRC Sec. 5000A(e)(1)(A); 42 USC §18082(b)(1)(B) (PPACA §1412(b)(1)(B)).
5. IRC Sec. 5000A(e)(1)(D).
6. IRC Sec. 5000A(e)(2).

qualification for head-of-household tax rates,[1] there is the benefit of having a higher applicable poverty-level threshold for purposes of the premium tax credit discussed above. On the other hand, the $95/$325/$695 (inflation adjusted) 2014/2015/2016/2017/2018 minimum penalty is increased with each additional dependent, although at a rate of only one-half of the applicable dollar amount for children under the age of 18.[2] Thus, a parent getting divorced may be less willing to be allocated the dependency deduction for children of the marriage if it means being obligated to procure health coverage for such children.[3] Parents will be less inclined to provide over one-half of the individual's support for the calendar year (the requirement to be a dependent) if it means that the taxpayer will end up owing a penalty for failure to procure health coverage for such individual.[4]

It seems that the household income of a young child with no income would be zero, and therefore such a child would not trigger additional penalty obligations for his or her parents under the individual mandate provisions as a result of the affordability and filing threshold exemptions.

Spouses. The individual mandate creates issues for certain spouses. Both spouses are jointly liable for whatever penalty is due on a joint return.[5] However, the individual mandate only requires that an applicable individual ensure that minimum essential coverage is procured both for the individual and any dependent of the individual who is an applicable individual.[6] Additionally, the definition of "family-size" for determining household income is "the number of individuals for whom the taxpayer is allowed a deduction under Internal Revenue Code section 151."[7] Neither spouse is a dependent of the other. Rather, they are each entitled to the deduction on a joint return.[8] There is a provision that entitles a taxpayer to take an additional exemption for his or her spouse when the spouse has no gross income and is not a dependent of another taxpayer. However, this provision only applies when a joint return is *not* filed.[9]

As for dependents, there is an issue of how the penalty is calculated for a nonearning spouse. Such spouse should be entitled to an exemption based on the 8.16 percent affordability test or the low-income filing threshold test. Both are based on household income, but, again, that in turn is defined by reference to the modified adjusted gross income of the taxpayer and all other "individuals for whom the taxpayer is allowed a deduction under Internal Revenue Code section 151 (relating to allowance of deduction for personal exemptions)."[10] Thus, it seems that the income of the earning spouse and dependent should not be included in a nonearning spouse's household income. Therefore, a nonearning spouse might not be considered in calculating the penalty for the earning spouse because the Code provides that "[n]o penalty

---

1. IRC Sec. 2(b)(1)(A)(i) (being entitled to the dependency exemption for a child is a precondition to qualifying for head of household status).
2. IRC Sec. 5000A(c)(3)(C).
3. *See* IRC Sec. 152(e).
4. *See* IRC Sec. 152(b)(1)(C).
5. IRC Sec. 5000A(b)(3)(B).
6. IRC Sec. 5000A(a).
7. IRC Sec. 5000A(c)(4)(A).
8. *See* IRC Sec. 151, 152.
9. *See* IRC Sec. 151(b).
10. IRC Sec. 5000A(e)(1), (2), (c)(4)(b), (a).

shall be imposed . . . with respect to" exempted individuals. Although there is no penalty with respect to a nonearning spouse, that spouse is still jointly and severally liable for the individual mandate penalty with respect to his or her spouse and the dependents of his or her spouse. The nonearning spouse could refuse to sign a joint return. However, in addition to the tax bracket, deduction, and other ramifications of that decision, the earning spouse would also then not be eligible for the premium tax credit.[1]

71. What are the requirements to obtain a hardship exemption?

The hardship exemption was first utilized by the Obama administration on December 19, 2013, when it was announced that individuals whose insurance plans were cancelled were eligible for "hardship exemptions" from the individual mandate requirement to have coverage in 2014 or pay a penalty. HHS Secretary Kathleen Sebelius outlined the policy in a letter[2] to Sen. Mark Warner and five other senators who had raised concerns about the issue. "I agree with you that these consumers should qualify for this temporary hardship exemption, and I can assure that the exemption will be available to them," Sebelius said. However, she made it clear that the exemption is limited to persons who have difficulty purchasing exchange coverage.

Sebelius also announced that individuals with canceled policies will be allowed to purchase catastrophic coverage. Previously, only individuals under the age of thirty could avoid incurring a financial penalty after March 31, 2014, by purchasing such plans. However, there are no federal subsidies available for those buying catastrophic coverage.

2018 and Prior Years

There are fourteen categories of hardship exemptions in 2018 and prior:[3]

1. Homelessness.

2. Eviction or facing eviction or foreclosure.

3. Shutoff notice from a utility company.

4. Recent experience with domestic violence.

5. Death of a close family member.

6. Experienced a fire, flood, or other disaster that caused substantial damage to your property.

7. Bankruptcy.

8. Medical expenses that couldn't be paid.

---

1. IRC Sec. 36B(c)(1)(C).
2. At http://www.scribd.com/doc/192619675/Sec-Sebelius-Response-to-Senator-Warner?wpisrc=nl_wonk. (Last accessed August 21, 2017).
3. https://www.healthcare.gov/health-coverage-exemptions/hardship-exemptions/ (Last accessed July 21, 2018).

9. Unexpected increases in necessary expenses due to caring for an ill, disabled or aging family member.

10. Dependent child has been denied coverage in Medicaid and CHIP and another person is required by court order to give medical support for the child.

11. Eligibility for — as a result of a Health Insurance Marketplace appeal decision.

   a. Enrolment in a Qualified Health Plan (QHP) through the Marketplace.

   b. Lower costs on monthly premiums.

   c. Cost-sharing reductions for a time period when not enrolled in a QHP marketplace.

12. An adult in the household was determined ineligible for Medicaid because the state did not expand Medicaid eligibility under the ACA.

13. Current health insurance purchased on the individual market is being cancelled because it does not meet ACA requirements and other plans are unaffordable.

14. Other hardships.

In fact, some argued that the hardship definition is so broad that it undermines the individual mandate.

2019 and Subsequent Years

Starting with the 2019 plan year the penalty no longer applies. (The fee is sometimes called the "Shared Responsibility Payment" or "mandate.") If you don't have coverage during 2019, you don't need an exemption in order to avoid the penalty. However, if you are thirty or older and want to buy a catastrophic health plan, you must apply for a hardship exemption to qualify.

See also Q 69 and Q 70.

72. How long do hardship exemptions last?

A hardship exemption generally only covers the month before the hardship, the months of the hardship, and the month after the hardship ends.

- In some cases, the marketplace may provide the exemption for additional months, up to a full calendar year.

- For individuals ineligible for Medicaid because a state hasn't expanded Medicaid coverage, the hardship exemption will be granted for the whole calendar year.

- For individuals eligible for Indian Health Services, the hardship exemption lasts as long as the person remains eligible.

- For individual under the age of twenty-one who are eligible for an exemption due to religious conscience, they will need to reapply if you remain a member when turning age twenty-one.

73. Is there a hardship exemption for being unemployed?

There is no hardship exemption for being unemployed, however, a number of the hardship exemptions mentioned in the prior questions may apply. Also, remember that the hardship exemption is unnecessary for 2019 and subsequent years.

74. Can a person with a hardship exemption enroll in a catastrophic plan?

Yes, if an individual is granted a hardship exemption, they CAN enroll in a catastrophic health plan.

- Catastrophic Health Plan: this is a plan that meets all of the requirements applicable to other Qualified Health Plans (QHPs) but that doesn't cover any benefits other than three primary care visits per year before the plan's deductible is met.
  - Premiums are generally lower than for other QHPs, but the out-of-pocket costs for deductibles, copayments, and coinsurance are generally higher.
  - To qualify, an individual must be
    - under thirty years old OR
    - qualify for a "hardship exemption" because of inability to afford health coverage.
  - It is not required to purchase a catastrophic plan – it is an option

To purchase catastrophic coverage with a hardship exemption it is required to provide the ECN (Exemption Certificate Number). This is provided on the exemption notice.

75. What do catastrophic plans cover and what do they cost?

Premiums: Premiums for these plans are usually low but premium tax credit is not available. In many cases, the Bronze or Silver plan might be a better value.

Deductibles: The deductible for catastrophic plans for 2019 is $7,900. As of the printing date, the 2020 deductible is not available.

Coverage: These plans cover the same Essential Health Benefits (EHBs) as the other plans and cover preventive services without cost and include three primary care visits per year before meeting deductible.

76. Is the individual mandate tax penalty being enforced even though it has been repealed?

The law limits the IRS ability to collect this tax penalty from individuals. Although the individual mandate tax penalty is supposed to be assessed and collected in the same manner as other penalties assessable under the Code, there can be no criminal prosecution or penalty for failure to pay the penalty,[1] though presumably civil penalties could be applicable. Moreover, the Service "shall not . . . file notice of lien with respect to any property of a taxpayer by reason of any failure to pay the [Individual Mandate] penalty . . . or levy on any such property with respect to such failure."[2]

Thus, the IRS's collection tools are limited, although it could send a notice of demand, but it appears that the only enforcement method available is to offset any unpaid penalty from tax refunds. In addition, with the signing of the Executive Order Minimizing the Economic Burden of the Patient Protection and Affordable Care Act Pending Repeal by President Trump,[3] the IRS was not officially not rejecting "silent returns" that don't include the Form 8965 exemption or the completion of line 61 on the Form 1040. Enforcement ceased with the repeal of the Individual Mandate penalty effective in 2019 by the Tax Cut and Jobs Act of 2017.

It should also be noted that twenty states have filed suit in the U.S. District Court for the Northern District of Texas arguing that the repeal of the Individual Mandate penalties causes the entire Affordable Care Act to be unconstitutional because the mandate penalties are not severable from the remainder of the Act. The District Court has held that the Affordable Care Act is unconstitutional. The case is currently in oral arguments at the United States Court of Appeals for the Fifth Circuit. The case will most certain find resolution ultimately with the United States Supreme Court.

Health Plan and Insurance Changes: Coverage Mandates

77. What are the ten Essential Health Benefits (EHBs) required by the Affordable Care Act? How do state health insurance mandates relate to them?

The 2010 Patient Protection and Affordable Care Act[4] requires the Secretary of HHS to define the EHBs through regulation. It also requires that at least some items and services within specific categories of benefits be included in the definition. The term "essential health benefits" means the benefits that non-grandfathered plans sold in the small group market on or outside of a state exchange must have, beginning in 2014. Grandfathered plans, self-insured group health plans, and health insurance coverage offered in the large group market are not required to offer essential health benefits. Minimum essential coverage is a separate concept and the phrase used to describe the coverage required to fulfill the individual and employer mandates.

---

1. IRC Sec. 5000A(g)(2)(A). This leaves open the question of whether or not there could be a criminal penalty, for example under section 7203 of the Code, with respect to the failure "to make a return, keep any records or supply any information" as required by the Code for purposes of calculating and imposing the penalty.
2. IRC Sec. 5000A(g)(2)(B).
3. Executive Order of President Donald J. Trump. https://www.whitehouse.gov/the-press-office/2017/01/2/executive-order-minimizing-economic-burden-patient-protection-and.
4. PPACA §1302(b).

The ten EHB categories are:

- ambulatory patient services;

- emergency services;

- hospitalization;

- maternity, pregnancy and newborn care;

- mental health and substance use disorder services, including behavioral health treatment (including counseling and psychotherapy);[1]

- prescription drugs;

- rehabilitative and habilitative services and devices;

- laboratory services;

- preventive and wellness services and chronic disease management; and

- pediatric services, including oral and vision care.

* Note that adult dental and vision care are NOT essential health benefits.

The scope of essential health benefits is intended to equal the scope of benefits provided under a "typical employer plan" and establish an appropriate balance among the ten benefit categories.[2] Each state's essential health benefits are based on that state's base-benchmark plan.[3] After the application of any adjustments, the plan is known as the "EHB-benchmark plan."[4] The EHB-benchmark plan contains the scope of services and limits offered by a typical employer plan in that state.[5]

HHS is required to take into account:

- the need for balance between the ten federal EHB categories;

- the needs of diverse segments of the population; and

- the need to not discriminate against individuals because of age, disability, or expected length of life.

1.	In general, the plans and products studied cover inpatient and outpatient mental health and substance use disorder services; however, coverage in the small group market often has limits. ASPE Research Brief, "Actuarial Value and Employer Sponsored Insurance," November 2011. Available at: http://aspe.hhs.gov/health/reports/2011/AV-ESI/rb.pdf. (Last accessed July 1, 2018).
2.	PPACA §1302(b).
3.	45 CFR §156.100.
4.	45 CFR §156.20.
5.	PPACA; Standards Related to Essential Health Benefits, Actuarial Value, and Accreditation; 45 Parts 147, 155, and 156, 78 Fed. Reg. 12841 (Feb. 25, 2013).

EHB Requirements by Market Segment[1]		
Market Segment	**Subject to EHB Requirement**	**Not Subject to EHB Requirement**
Large Group Market	Effective 2017, states may allow large group purchasing through the exchange, which would subject large group plans and policies to EHB requirements[2]	**Outside the Exchange:** • State regulated plans and policies
Small Group Market	**Outside the Exchange:** • State regulated plans and policies **Inside the Exchange:** • QHPs and COOP plans[3] • Multistate Plans offered by the federal Office of Personnel Management (OPM)[4]	**Outside the Exchange:** • Grandfathered plans • Grandfathered policies

Individual Market	**Outside the Exchange:**
	• State regulated plans and policies
	Inside the Exchange:
	• State regulated QHPs, including:
	  - Catastrophic plans[5]
	  - CO-OP plans[6]
	  - Interstate healthcare choice compacts
	• Multistate Plans, offered by the federal Office of Personnel Management (OPM)
		Outside the Exchange:
		• Grandfathered plans
		• Grandfathered policies

78. Do the FAQs relax the fixed indemnity standards and allow per-service payments as excepted benefits if the insured has other minimal essential coverage?

The Labor Department, Department of Health and Human Services, and the Treasury Department on January 9, 2014, issued FAQ Part XVIII[7] regarding implementation of the market reform provisions of the ACA. FAQs are so-called "subregulatory guidance" intended to provide quick guidance in response to issues affecting group health plans. FAQ Part XVIII includes new relaxed rules for fixed indemnity plans that meet certain requirements. A fixed indemnity plan generally pays a fixed dollar amount upon the occurrence of a covered illness or injury, rather than an amount based on expenses actually incurred by the individual. For example, it might pay $100 upon admission to a hospital for particular treatments. These fixed indemnity plans can be designed to fit within the category of "excepted benefits" that are exempt from healthcare reform.

---

1.   There are other sources of health insurance, including self-insured plans, the Veterans Administration, and Medicare, that are not addressed in this table. These coverages are not subject to the EHB coverage requirements.

2.   PPACA §1312(f)(2)(B).

3.   PPACA §1322 provides for nonprofit, member-run health insurance issuers offering qualified health plans (QHPs) in the individual and small group markets.

4.   PPACA §1334 directs OPM to offer at least two multistate qualified health plans in each state exchange.

5.   PPACA §1302(e).

6.   PPACA §1322 provides for nonprofit, member-run health insurance issuers offering qualified health plans in the individual and small group markets.

7.   FAQs about Affordable Care Act Implementation (Part XVIII) https://www.dol.gov/sites/default/files/ebsa/about-ebsa/our-activities/resource-center/faqs/aca-part-xviii.pdf (Last accessed July 1, 2019).

"Noncoordinated excepted benefits," includes specific (dread) disease coverage, such as cancer policies, and fixed dollar indemnity coverage. In the group market these benefits are excepted only if:

1) they are provided under a separate policy, certificate, or contract of insurance;

2) there is no coordination between the benefits offered by the plan and exclusions under a group health plan offered by the same plan sponsor, and

3) benefits are paid regardless of any benefits provided under a group health plan.[1]

In an earlier and now obsolete FAQ, FAQ Part XI, the Departments had indicated that a fixed indemnity plan could not pay on a "per-service basis," even if it was a fixed amount. Instead, it would have to pay benefits on a "per-period basis." For example, if an individual was injured, the preferred way to pay the benefit was to pay a certain amount per day regardless of the services provided as opposed to reimbursing different amounts for different services. By contrast, a plan that covers doctors' visits at $50 per visit, surgical procedures at $75 per procedure, or prescription drugs at $15 per prescription would not be considered to be a fixed indemnity plan under FAQ Part XI (and would not be an excepted benefit) because the payments would be provided on a per-service basis.

In FAQ Part XVIII, the Departments have changed position and permit a fixed indemnity plan to reimburse on a per-service basis and still be considered excepted benefits if the plan:[2]

- is sold only to individuals who have other health coverage that is minimum essential coverage;

- does not coordinate between the provision of benefits and an exclusion of benefits under any other health coverage;

- pays benefits in a fixed dollar amount regardless of the amount of expenses incurred and without regard to the amount of benefits provided with respect to an event or service under any other health coverage; and

- includes a prominently displayed notice informing policyholders that the coverage does not meet the definition of minimum essential coverage and will not satisfy the individual mandate.

79. How has the Essential Health Benefits (EHB) mandate been implemented?

Federal health reform requires coverage of Essential Health Benefits (EHBs) for most major medical health plans and policies sold in the individual and small group markets, both inside and outside the state's health insurance exchange. Broadly, inside the state's health insurance exchange, Qualified Health Plans (QHPs) are subject to state and federal mandates. See Q 95.

---

1. 26 CFR 54.9831–1(c)(4); 29 CFR 2590.732(c)(4); 45 CFR 146.145(b)(4).
2. Q&A 11, FAQs about Affordable Care Act Implementation (Part XVIII).

Self-insured group health plans, health insurance offered in the large group market (generally companies with more than 100 employees), and grandfathered health plans are not required to cover essential health benefits or provide minimum essential coverage. Additionally, outside of a state's health insurance exchange, non-grandfathered plans and policies in the individual and small group markets will be required to cover essential health benefits. Effective beginning in 2017, states can allow large group purchasing through the exchange, which would subject large group plans and policies to the EHB requirements.[1]

The Affordable Care Act requires that certain items and services within ten specific categories of benefits must be included in the essential health benefits, which must be defined by HHS through regulation.[2] The law distinguishes between a plan's covered services and the plan's cost-sharing features, such as deductibles, copayments, and coinsurance. The cost-sharing features will determine the level of actuarial value of the plan, expressed as a "metal level" as specified in the statute:

- Bronze at 60 percent of actuarial value

- Silver at 70 percent of actuarial value

- Gold at 80 percent of actuarial value

- Platinum at 90 percent of actuarial value

In December 2011, HHS released initial guidance on essential health benefits. HHS's approach to defining the essential health benefits allows states to select a benchmark plan from four options that reflect the scope of services offered by a "typical employer plan."[3] The general categories to be considered in defining a typical employer plan (which is undefined by the statute or regulations) include large employer, small employer, and government health plans.

HHS states that the following four benchmark plan types best reflect the statutory standards for EHB in the Affordable Care Act:[4]

A state may select its base-benchmark plan from four types of health plans:

- one of the three largest by enrollment small group plans in the state;

- one of the three largest by enrollment state employee health plans;

- one of the three largest by enrollment federal employee health plan options; or

- the largest by enrollment insured commercial HMO operating in the state.[5]

---

1.   PPACA §1312(f)(2)(B).
2.   PPACA §1302(b).
3.   CCIIO, Essential Health Benefits Bulletin (December 16, 2011). Available at https://www.cms.gov/CCIIO/Resources/Files/Downloads/essential_health_benefits_bulletin.pdf. (Last accessed July 1, 2019).
4.   CCIIO, Essential Health Benefits Bulletin (December 16, 2011). Available at https://www.cms.gov/CCIIO/Resources/Files/Downloads/essential_health_benefits_bulletin.pdf. (Last accessed July 1, 2019).
5.   45 CFR §156.100(a).

A plan's enrollment is determined from that of the first quarter two years prior to the coverage year.[1] If a state fails to select, the benchmark plan will be the largest plan by enrollment in the largest product in the state's small group market.[2]

80. What is required to become a state selected EHB-benchmark plan?

In order to become a state selected EHB-benchmark plan, a base-benchmark plan must include coverage of the ten categories listed previously.[3] A state's benchmark selection in 2012 was applicable for the 2014, 2015 and 2016 benefit years, and be based on plan benefits offered by the selected benchmark at the time of selection, including any applicable state-required benefits enacted prior to December 21, 2011.[4] For plan years of 2017 and later, the EHB benchmark plan is one that was sold in 2014.

The state's EHB-benchmark plan standard covers the benefits, limits on coverage (including limits on the amount, duration, and scope of covered benefits), and prescription drug benefits.[5] Mental health and substance use disorder services must be provided in a manner that complies with the parity standards under the Mental Health Parity and Addiction Equity Act of 2008.[6] Insurers may substitute benefits, or sets of benefits, that are actuarially equivalent to the benefits in the state's EHB benchmark plan within each of the ten categories[7] but not between different benefit categories.[8] Additionally, benefit substitution cannot occur for prescription drug benefits.[9] For prescription drug benefits, a plan must cover at least the *greater of* one drug in every category or class; or the same number of drugs in each category and class as the EHB-benchmark plan.[10] Thus, if the EHB benchmark plan's drug list offers more than one drug in a category or class, then plans covering essential health benefits must offer at least the number of drugs in the EHB-benchmark plan for that class.

The benefits and services included in the benchmark plan option selected by the state are considered the essential health benefits. State benefit mandates that fall within the benchmark plan selected by the state would be included in the defined essential health benefits. A requirement in the law that states must defray the costs of state benefit mandates that fall outside the essential health benefits would be waived. However, for any mandates that fall outside the selected benchmark plan, the state would be required to cover the cost of those mandates. If a state's benchmark plan does not cover one or more of the required benefit categories, a state must identify supplemental benchmark plans for those benefits.

---

1.   PPACA; Standards Related to Essential Health Benefits, Actuarial Value, and Accreditation; 45 Parts 147, 155, and 156, 78 Fed. Reg. 12841 (Feb. 25, 2013).
2.   45 CFR §156.100(c).
3.   45 CFR §156.100(a); PPACA; Standards Related to Essential Health Benefits, Actuarial Value, and Accreditation; 45 Parts 147, 155, and 156, 78 Fed. Reg. 12841 (Feb. 25, 2013).
4.   PPACA; Standards Related to Essential Health Benefits, Actuarial Value, and Accreditation; 45 Parts 147, 155, and 156, 78 Fed. Reg. 12841 (Feb. 25, 2013).
5.   45 CFR §156.115(a)(1).
6.   45 CFR §156.115(a)(2).
7.   45 CFR §156.115(b)(1)(i).
8.   45 CFR §156.115(b)(1)(ii).
9.   45 CFR §156.115(b)(1)(iii).
10.   45 CFR §156.120(a)(1).

Whether the coverage for an existing state benefit mandate will be included in the essential health benefits will depend on the benchmark plan the state selects. State laws regarding required coverage of benefits vary widely in number, scope, and topic, so that generalizing about mandates and their impact on typical employer plans is difficult. All states have adopted at least one health insurance mandate, and there are more than 1,600 specific service and provider coverage requirements across the fifty states and the District of Columbia.[1] Each of the benchmark plan options will include a differing set of state benefit mandates.

The 2017-2020 Final List of Benchmark Plans by State is available at the CMS site.[2]

81. What new requirements are there for grandfathered and grandmothered health plans?

It is estimated that there are still over one million people in the United States with coverage under a grandfathered or grandmothered health care plan. Grandfathered plans can continue in force indefinitely, at the discretion of the health care carrier as long as substantial changes are not made to the coverage. While attempts have been made to end grandmothered plans, they have been allowed to stay in effect.

Grandmothered Plans

Originally it was intended that grandmothered plans terminate at the end of 2013, or at their renewal in 2014 and be replaced by ACA compliant policies. In March of 2014, HHS extended the transitional relief, allowing renewals as late as October 1, 2016, with plans allowed to remain in force until September 30, 2017.[3] An additional extension was issued in February 2016, allowing plans to continue to renew up to October 1, 2017 but requiring a termination date by December 31, 2017.[4] Another extension was issued by CMS on February 23, 2017 extending the permission for grandmothered plans to stay in effect until December 31, 2018.[5] Yet another extension allowing grandmothered plans to stay in effect until December 31, 2020 was issued by CMS on March 25, 2019.[6]

Grandfathered Plans

Grandfathered health plans are those continuously in existence since March 23, 2010, and with no prohibited changes subsequently described in this book. Grandfathered health plans are subject to certain health reform requirements, as follows:

---

1.   Information on Essential Health Benefits (EHB) Benchmark Plans https://www.cms.gov/CCIIO/Resources/Data-Resources/ehb.html#Alabama.

2.   https://www.cms.gov/CCIIO/Resources/Data-Resources/Downloads/Final-List-of-BMPs_4816.pdf.

3.   https://www.cms.gov/Newsroom/MediaReleaseDatabase/Fact-sheets/2014-Fact-sheets-items/2014-03-05-2.html.

4.   Industry Standards Bulletin Service – INFORMATION – Extension of Transitional Policy through Calendar Year 2017, Kevin Counihan, Director, Center for Consumer Information and Insurance Oversight, February 29, 2016 https://www.cms.gov/CCIIO/Resources/Regulations-and-Guidance/Downloads/final-transition-bulletin-2-29-16.pdf.

5.   Insurance Standards Bulletin Services – Information – Extension of Transitional Policy through Calendar Year 2018, Jeff Wu, Acting Director, Center for Consumer Information and Insurance Oversight, February 23, 2017. https://www.cms.gov/CCIIO/Resources/Regulations-and-Guidance/Downloads/Extension-Transitional-Policy-CY2018.pdf.

6.   https://www.cms.gov/CCIIO/Resources/Regulations-and-Guidance/Downloads/Limited-Non-Enforcement-Policy-Extension-Through-CY2020.pdf.

- Prohibition of annual and lifetime benefit limits (except that provisions annual limit prohibitions not applicable for individual health insurance coverage but not group coverage).[1]

- No rescission except for fraud or intentional misrepresentation.[2]

- For plan years beginning before January 1, 2014, children who are not eligible for employer-sponsored coverage must be covered up to age twenty-six on an employee's family policy.[3]

- Pre-existing condition exclusions for covered individuals younger than age nineteen are prohibited.[4]

- Pre-existing condition exclusions prohibited for all persons in 2014.[5]

- Plans may not require a waiting period of more than ninety days.[6]

- Plans must provide a Summary of Benefits and Coverage (SBC).[7]

- Medical Loss Ratio (MLR) provisions.[8]

82. What new requirements are there for new and nongrandfathered health plans?

New and nongrandfathered plans are subject to the requirements for grandfathered plans (described in Q 81) plus the following requirements:

- The plan must guarantee that coverage is renewable regardless of health status, utilization of health services, or any other related factor. Coverage can only be cancelled under specific, enumerated circumstances.[9]

- The plan may not require cost-sharing for preventive services, immunizations, and screenings.[10]

- Discrimination based on salary is prohibited (the effective date has been postponed until regulations are issued).[11]

---

1. PHSA §2711.
2. PHSA §2703.
3. PHSA §2714.
4. PHSA §2704.
5. PHSA §2704.
6. PHSA §2708.
7. PHSA §2709.
8. PHSA §2718.
9. PHSA §2703.
10. PHSA §2713.
11. See IRC Sec. 9815, incorporating by reference Public Health Service Act §2716, which in turn incorporates by reference the principles of IRC Sec. 105(h).

- Children must be covered up to age twenty-six on a family policy, regardless of whether they are eligible for coverage with their employer.[1]

- The plan must provide internal appeal and external review processes to ensure independent review.[2]

- Emergency services must be available at the in-network cost-sharing level with no prior authorization.[3]

- Parents must be allowed to select a pediatrician as a primary care physician for children and women must be allowed to select an OB-GYN as their primary care physician.[4]

- Health insurance issuers may not charge discriminatory premium rates. The rate may vary only by whether such plan or coverage covers an individual or family, the rating area, the actuarial value of the plan, the age of the plan participant, and tobacco use.[5]

- Health insurance companies in the small group and individual markets (and large group markets to the extent of purchasing insurance through state exchanges) must include coverage that incorporates defined essential benefits, provides a specified actuarial value, and requires all group health plans to comply with limitations on allowable cost sharing.[6]

- Health insurance issuers are prohibited from dropping coverage because an individual (who requires treatment for cancer or another life-threatening condition) chooses to participate in a clinical trial. Issuers also may not deny coverage for routine care that they would otherwise provide because an individual is enrolled in a clinical trial.[7]

- HIPAA nondiscrimination requirements are continued and no discrimination due to health status is permitted for wellness programs and individual insurance.[8]

- Group health plans and health insurance issuers offering group or individual health insurance coverage must disclose certain enrollee information, such as claims payment policies and practices and enrollee rights, to the federal government and the state insurance commissioner. Such plans and issuers also must provide information to enrollees on the amount of cost-sharing for a specific item or service.[9]

---

1.   PHSA §2714.
2.   PHSA §2719.
3.   PHSA §2719A.
4.   PHSA §2719A.
5.   PHSA §2701.
6.   PHSA §2707.
7.   PHSA §2709.
8.   PHSA §2705.
9.   PHSA §2715A.

- Health insurance issuers must report information on initiatives and programs that improve health outcomes. A wellness program may not require the disclosure or collection of any information relating to the presence or storage of a lawfully possessed firearm or ammunition in the residence or the lawful use, possession, or storage of a firearm or ammunition by an individual.[1]

83. What are grandmothered plans?

A part of the basis of the federal healthcare reform was that when individuals are required to have health insurance (or pay a penalty), the insurance must be worth buying, meaning:

(1)   Important benefits must be covered; and

(2)   Older and unhealthier people should not be charged amounts dramatically larger than young, healthy individuals.

When the Affordable Care Act was originally passed, there were no provisions for grandmothered plans. These are plans that were purchased AFTER the Affordable Care Act was signed into law but before the Exchanges opened on October 1, 2013. On November 14, 2013,[2] HHS announced a one year retreat and allowed policies that did not comply with certain healthcare reform requirements to continue to be sold if the insurance companies wish to do so and if the state insurance regulators allow them to do so. Such policies could be renewed for one policy year between January 1, 2014 through October 1, 2014, if insurers decided to do so and if the state insurance regulators permit. The intent was that they terminate at the end of 2013, or at their renewal in 2014 and be replaced by ACA compliant policies. This HHS action was in response to the complaints that millions of individuals that received notices that the insurance they had in 2013 would be cancelled, thus meaning that those people would not be able to keep their insurance, even if they liked it. The ultimate decision was left up to the states and the insurance companies. Some states and carriers mandated that grandmothered plans terminate as originally planned while other states accepted the new guidelines.

However, in March of 2014, HHS extended the transitional relief, allowing renewals as late as October 1, 2016, with plans allowed to remain in force until September 30, 2017.[3] An additional extension was issued in February 2016, allowing plans to continue to renew up to October 1, 2017 but requiring a termination date by December 31, 2017.[4] These extensions are also subject to approval by states and the carriers. As of 2017, there are thirty-five states where grandmothered plans are still in place. Most of these states have agreed to carry the plans until the end of 2017.

---

1.   PHSA §2717.

2.   See HHS, CMS, Center for Consumer Information & Insurance Oversight (CCIIO) letter from CCIIO Director Gary Cohen to state insurance commissioners at http://www.cms.gov/CCIIO/Resources/Letters/Downloads/commissioner-letter-11-14-2013.PDF. Footnote 2 of this letter indicates that the IRS and Department of Labor concur with this program. Insurers who use this new option must notify policyholders. (Last accessed July 30, 2019).

3.   https://www.cms.gov/Newsroom/MediaReleaseDatabase/Fact-sheets/2014-Fact-sheets-items/2014-03-05-2.html. No longer available on CMS site.

4.   https://www.cms.gov/CCIIO/Resources/Regulations-and-Guidance/Downloads/final-transition-bulletin-2-29-16.pdf. No longer available on CMS site.

Grandmothered plans are not the same as grandfathered plans. There are different requirements that must be met – and although they've been extended in lifetime, they arguably will not be allowed to remain active indefinitely. Grandmothered plans need to meet more ACA regulations than grandfathered plans. These requirements include covering preventive care without cost-sharing, and eliminating annual benefit limits for any Essential Health Benefit (EHBs) covered by the plan. Grandmothered plans do not have to cover EHBs other than preventive care, but if they DO cover them, they cannot place an annual dollar limit on them. Some states opted not to allow grandmothered plans and others have already terminated them. In some states, even where allowed, a number of carriers terminated the plans and replaced them with plans that complied with the Affordable Care Act. By 2016, 15 of the 50 states plus the District of Columbia had eliminated grandmothered plans. It should also be noted that grandmothered plans can no longer be sold. These plans needed to be in effect no later than either October 1, 2013 or December 31, 2013 but dependents can still be added to a grandmothered plan in effect.

Tax Credits: These plans are not (and never were) eligible for subsidies from the Exchanges or eligible for Small Business Tax Credits, therefore anyone using them is paying the full premium.

Special Enrollment Period: When the grandmother plan is ended (or at a renewal), subscribers will have access to the "special enrollment period" on the Exchange.

84. Which states still have grandmothered plans?

Grandmothered plans still exist as of 2019 in the following states but continue to decline in number and availability:

- Alabama

- Alaska

- Arizona

- Arkansas

- Florida

- Georgia

- Hawaii

- Idaho

- Illinois

- Indiana

- Iowa

- Kansas

- Kentucky
- Louisiana
- Michigan
- Mississippi
- Missouri
- Nebraska
- New Hampshire
- New Jersey
- North Carolina
- North Dakota
- Ohio
- Oklahoma
- Pennsylvania
- South Carolina
- South Dakota
- Texas
- Utah
- Virginia
- Wisconsin and
- Wyoming.

Fifteen states plus the District of Columbia have eliminated renewals of non-ACA compliant plans

- California – allowed through end of 2015.
- Colorado – allowed through end of 2015.
- Connecticut – ended in 2014.
- Delaware – ended in 2014.
- District of Columbia – ended in 2014.

- Maine – discontinued all plans in January 2017 (Anthem)

- Maryland – ended in 2014.

- Massachusetts – ended in 2014.

- Minnesota – needed to be compliant as of January 1, 2014.

- Montana – had no grandmothered plans.

- Nevada – ended in 2014.

- New Mexico – ended in 2015.

- New York – ended in 2014.

- Oregon – ended in 2015.

- Tennessee – no grandmothered plans available after 2017

- Rhode Island – ended in 2014.

- Washington – ended in 2014.

- West Virginia – no grandmothered plans available after 2017

- Vermont – ended all plans on March 31, 2014.

85. Have the number of grandfathered and grandmothered plans declined?

Yes. In 2013, according to the Kaiser Family Foundation (kff.org) there were nearly 10.7 million non-ACA compliant plans. It is difficult to get an accurate assessment of those remaining but most estimates seem to indicate that the number of non-compliant plans is between 1.5 million and 1.75 million at this point.

With the possible expiration of the grandmother plan authority on December 31, 2020, it is likely that that number will decline further. The grandfathered plans have no hard expiration, so it is possible they could remain active for a long time.

State Health Insurance Exchanges[1]

86. What are the state health insurance exchanges?

The law refers to state health insurance exchanges, a major component of the federal health reform, as "American Health Benefit Exchanges."[2] The rules for the state exchanges or marketplaces are discussed in detail in Part X of this book. In theory, insurance companies will compete for business on a transparent, level playing field, which should reduce costs and give

---

1.   For more detailed information see Part X of this publication, which discusses state health insurance exchanges (marketplaces) in detail.
2.   PPACA §1311(b).

individuals and small businesses the purchasing power enjoyed by big businesses. However, health reform does many things to increase costs by covering those who are now uninsurable and by increasing mandated benefits. Many predict these factors will far outweigh any efficiencies created by the exchanges and that health insurance prices will increase. If exchanges succeed, they will create the first viable alternative to the group markets for the younger than age sixty-five population.

Beginning in 2014:

- Each state was required to create an exchange (a governmental agency or nonprofit organization, established by the state[1]) to facilitate the sale of qualified health plans (QHPs), including federally administered multistate plans and nonprofit cooperative plans.[2] The law requires HHS to create an exchange in states that do not set up their own exchanges. However, the health reform law does not provide the federal government with adequate funding to set up or operate federal health insurance exchanges.

  - States could create either one exchange to serve both small group and individual markets[3] or separate exchanges for these pools.

  - One goal is to facilitate a comparison of available health insurance options by purchasers.

- Standards for qualified coverage must include:

  - Mandated essential coverage.

  - Cost-sharing requirements (deductibles, copayments, and coinsurance).

  - Out-of-pocket limitations

  - Minimum actuarial value of 60 percent, which means that the policy, on average, pays 60 percent of the costs for essential health benefits and the insured pays the remaining 40 percent. The coverage levels are Bronze (60 percent), Silver (70 percent), Gold (80 percent), and Platinum (90 percent).

  - Catastrophic coverage for purchasers aged thirty and younger in the individual market.

  - States must also create Small Business Health Option Programs, or "SHOP Exchanges,"[4] for small employers to purchase coverage. See Q 96. The states can expand the programs to include large employers beginning in 2017.

---

1.   PPACA §1311(d)(1).
2.   PPACA §1311(f).
3.   PPACA §1311(b)(1)(C).
4.   PPACA §1311(b)(1)(B).

States can offer employers certain options:

- Employers can choose any QHP offered in the SHOP in any tier.

- Employers can select specific tiers from which an employee may choose a QHP.

- Employers can select specific QHPs from different tiers of coverage from which an employee may choose a QHP.

- Employers can select a single QHP to offer employees.

87. How do employers use exchanges?

Employers can enroll in a group health plan through a state SHOP exchange, but, upon enrollment, the employer is locked into the plan for one-year periods. The plan premiums are also locked in for the same period of time. Once the employer enrolls in a state exchange:

- the employer must offer Exchange coverage to all full-time employees;

- the Exchange must provide an aggregate bill to the employer for all covered employees;

- employers must notify the Exchange about any employee change of status, for example, adding dependents or terminating employment;

- employers with multiple worksites can offer access either to a single Exchange or to state Exchanges where employees are located.

Participation in a SHOP is strictly voluntary for small employers. Purchasing employer-provided health coverage for employees through a SHOP is intended to be the only way for qualified employers to obtain a small business health care tax credit from 2014 forward.[1] To qualify for the tax credit, all of the following must apply to an employer:

- The employer must have fewer than twenty-five Full-Time Equivalent (FTE) employees (excluding owners and relatives whose insurance is not eligible for the credit).

- The average employee salary is about $50,000 per year or less (excluding owners and relatives whose insurance is not eligible for the credit).

- The employer pays at least 50 percent of full-time employees' premium costs.

- The employer offers coverage to full-time employees through the SHOP Marketplace.

The tax credit, which began in 2014, is worth up to 50 percent of the employer's contribution toward the employees' premium costs (up to 35 percent for tax-exempt employers), and may only be claimed for two years.

---

1. *See* SHOP FAQs at https://www.cms.gov/CCIIO/Resources/Fact-Sheets-and-FAQs/Downloads/SBM-SHOP-Transitional-Flexibility-FAQ-Rev-5-29-2015.pdf. (Last access August 21, 2017).

To qualify for this credit, an employer need NOT offer coverage to part-time employees (those working fewer than thirty hours per week) or to dependents to qualify for the tax credit.[1] The tax credit is greatest for those companies with fewer than 10 employees and who are paid an average of $25,000 per year. Essentially the smaller the company, the larger the tax credit.

Major Change in Enrollment Process for 2018, 2019 and 2020

At the completion of the 2017 plan, HealthCare.gov no longer was used to renew coverage. Instead of using the website, renewals are handled through the insurance company or SHOP-registered agent or broker. There are two options for signing up for a SHOP health plan and/or a dental plan.

- Contact the insurance company and enroll through them - Identify plan, apply, enroll and pay premiums

- Work with a SHOP agent/broker

88. What factors should be considered when enrolling in SHOP?

1. Deciding whether to offer employees one plan or a choice of several plans.

2. Deciding whether to offer medical coverage, dental coverage, or both.

3. Deciding how much of employees' premiums to pay.

4. Deciding whether to offer coverage to dependents and part-time employees.

5. Deciding when coverage starts.

6. Deciding how long new employees must wait before eligible for coverage.

89. Are there any issues with state exchanges?

There are several issues that may affect a state's exchange. For example, states do not have full authority over their own exchanges. HHS has final approval authority for each exchange.

Another issue is the interaction with cafeteria plans regulated by Internal Revenue Code section 125. Coverage offered through an exchange is not a permitted benefit under Code section 125 and cannot be offered under a cafeteria plan[2] unless the employer offers its employees the opportunity to enroll through an exchange in a group market.[3]

Although the law does not provide the federal government with adequate funding to set up or operate federal health insurance exchanges, exchange costs must be funded by HHS until January 1, 2015. Thereafter, all exchanges must be self-funded.

---

1.   IRC §45R.
2.   PPACA §1515(a); IRC 125(f)(3)(A).
3.   PPACA §1515(a); IRC 125(f)(3)(B).

90. How do individuals apply for health insurance from an exchange?

Open enrollment for the Affordable Care Act began on November 1, 2017 and ended on January 31, 2018. For 2019, the Open Enrollment Period will be November 1, 2018 through January 31, 2019.

Under the Affordable Care Act, you only have a set amount of time to sign up for health insurance in order to avoid paying a penalty fee for non-compliance unless you qualify for an exemption or meet other circumstances. These are the times that an individual can sign up for coverage unless they qualify for an exception – and can sign up through a "Special Enrollment Period". Special Enrollment Periods include certain life events such as losing health coverage, losing a job, getting married, having a baby, adoption of a child, etc. Ordinarily there is a sixty-day window from the event to enroll in a plan.

Enrolling on the Exchanges

There are four ways to enroll on the exchanges:

- Online

- Telephonically

- Mail

- With in-person assistance

Online Applications

The online process is likely to be much simpler than other methods. The federal and state marketplaces are designed to streamline the enrollment process. An online account is opened and an application completed and the user is presented with immediate results based on eligibility. The marketplace will inform the user if they qualify for cost assistance or federal programs like Medicaid and CHIP. The user can browse through the available plans and select one.

Phone Applications

Customer service representatives are available twenty-four hours a day, seven days a week to answer questions and help you fill out and apply for coverage. This method is similar to the online process - you fill out an application over the phone with the assistance of a representative are presented with your available options. The representative can help you choose and apply for a policy.

Mail Applications

You cannot actually enroll in a plan through the mail, but application process can begin in that manner. Paper applications and instructions for filling them out appear at the HealthCare. gov website and are mailed directly to the Department of Health and Human Services. The mailing address is on the instructions. Eligibility results should be expected within two weeks. When results are received, at that point the applicant will need to create an online account or call the customer service center to enroll.

In-person Assistance

There are organizations that been created to help people sign up for health insurance on the exchanges. Assistance is also available at brokers and insurance agencies, or by making contact with an agent who specializes in the Affordable Care Act. The HealthCare.gov site, allows users to find locations of in person assistance by entering a ZIP code or state. The same enrollment process works for the federal exchanges as well as the state-run marketplaces. Individual exchanges may have slightly different application processes, but generally they are quite similar to the federal site.

Online Application Options

1.   Healthcare.gov

2.   State Health Exchange

3.   Private Insurance Company

Healthcare.gov – https://www.healthcare.gov/

Healthcare.gov is the official website of the federal government for the Marketplace, which is place where Americans can create an account, sign up for insurance as well as receive subsidy assistance to pay for the costs of the insurance.

There are a number of steps involved in starting and completing the application process as detailed below. The website is fairly intuitive and will walk the user through the process.

Account Creation: The user is prompted to fill out name, email address, select a password and complete three security questions. After submitting the information an e-mailed link is provided to finalize the login process.

Providing Contact Information: After logging in, the site will ask for profile information such as name, date of birth, social security number which is optional, address and phone number.

Accepting Privacy Policy: The privacy policy must be checked that the user agrees and understand the terms of the privacy policy.

Additional Contact Information: The site will ask for more contact information, such as your mailing address and information regarding how you would like to receive notices and alerts.

Inquiry Regarding Application Assistance: The site will ask if help for the application is being provided and by whom.

Inquiry Regarding Cost Assistance: Users that make between 100 percent and 400 percent of the Federal Poverty Level (income between $11,670 and $46,680 for an individual and between $23,850 and $95,400 for a family of four) may qualify for a subsidy. This step can be skipped if the user knows they don't qualify.

Individuals to be Covered: User will need to provide name, date of birth and other information for all individuals to be covered.

Household and Dependent Information: This step needs to be completed during one session or will be lost. Questions include details of each person to be covered including gender, social security number and citizenship, disability, needing assistance with daily living, pregnancy, Native American or Native Alaskan status, etc.

Review: Review and accept information input.

Inquiry Regarding Income Information: The site recommends having the latest tax return or W-2 forms and recent pay stubs available from which to obtain financial data. If no subsidy is requested, then this area can be skipped. This area inquires in facts such as employment, collection of social security benefits, pensions, unemployment, retirement, capital gains, investment income, rental income, alimony, etc. Other questions include expenses such as alimony, student loan interest or other payments.

Additional Information: Questions include inquiries as to whether insurance has recently been lost or is anticipated to be lost in the next sixty days. Other questions ask about recent marriages, adoptions, immigration status, recent moves or possible incarcerations.

Final Review and Submission: The application will summarize everything the submission and ask for confirmation. It will then again ask about incarcerations, as for agreement to allow the Marketplace to use data from your tax returns for the next five years to determine information and whether you agree or disagree to update your application and/or insurance company of any changes to your circumstances in the future (i.e. you make less money and can get a subsidy, you have insurance through your employer, etc.).

Subsidy Results: If a subsidy was requested, the results will be provided.

Selection of Insurance: Plans are offered in levels, equating to price and coverage. The levels in order of least expensive and least coverage to most are: catastrophic, bronze, silver, gold, platinum.

There are two types of subsidies: Premium subsidy which offsets insurance cost and tax credit that is reimbursed when taxes are filed.

State Exchanges

In states that manage their own state-funded insurance marketplace, the application and shopping is done on their websites. If you are unsure whether your state has opted to run its own state exchange you can either refer to the list in this article or you can go to Healthcare.gov and indicate the state that you reside in and it will inform you whether you should stay on Healthcare.gov or whether you should go to a different website to shop for insurance.

There are also states that are partnering with the federal government to implement the requirements of the Affordable Care Act. These states use Healthcare.gov to provide insurance policies but are responsible for managing components of the program.

The following states have their own state exchanges:

California – http://www.coveredca.com

Colorado – http://www.connectforhealthco.com

Connecticut – https://www.accesshealthct.com

Washington D.C. – https://dchealthlink.com/

Idaho – http://www.yourhealthidaho.org/

Maryland – http://www.marylandhealthconnection.gov/

Massachusetts – https://www.mahealthconnector.org/

Minnesota – http://www.mnsure.org/

Nevada – https://www.nevadahealthlink.com/

New Mexico – https://bewellnm.com/

New York – https://nystateofhealth.ny.gov/

Oregon – https://www.coveroregon.com/

Washington – https://www.wahealthplanfinder.org

The application required to sign up for health insurance through a state exchange is very similar to the application used on Healthcare.gov described above.

91. What is the loophole in the law as it applies to exchange purchased insurance and its impact on insureds and providers?

Doctors and hospitals who contract with insurers selling policies on state health insurance exchanges may find themselves liable for treatment costs due to the healthcare reform law. Under the ACA,[1] families who obtain subsidized health plan coverage through an exchange and who fail pay their premiums have a three-month grace period for premium payment[2] before the policy is cancelled.[3]

However, insurers are responsible only for paying claims during the first month of this three-month grace period. During months two and three, families are asked to pay their hospital and doctor's bills or their insurance premium if they seek health care services. However, if they do not pay either bill, providers will not be paid for the cost of the treatment. Such families would face a tax penalty for the advance payment of the premium tax credit paid on their behalf when

---

1.   PPACA §1412(c)(2)(B)(iv)(II).

2.   45 CFR §§155.430(b)(2)(ii)(A) and (B) and 156.270(d).

3.   76 Fed. Reg. 41866; 45 CFR §§155.430 & 156.270 available at https://www.federalregister.gov/articles/2012/03/27/2012-6125/patient-protection-and-affordable-care-act-establishment-of-exchanges-and-qualified-health-plans#h-165. (Last accessed July 30, 2019).

the initial coverage was purchased, but they would not receive a fine, a premium rate increase, or a repayment order. They could also purchase another subsidized exchange policy the next year.

The three-month grace period was meant to ensure continuity of care for low-income families who might be between jobs and cannot afford to pay their premiums for a few weeks. However, it is not the provider's job to manage this risk.

Health plans are supposed to give providers fifteen days' notice of the termination of payment by the policy, in which case providers might be unable to avoid treating exchange patients. However, contracts by providers with large health insurers often include an "all-products" clause, which requires that doctors treat any patients covered under the health plan. Additionally, doctors have legal and ethical obligations not to abandon their patients during course of treatment. A round of chemotherapy can cost tens of thousands of dollars or more.

In a notice published in the Federal Register,[1] HHS acknowledged that nonpayment of premiums for subsidized exchange policies would "increase uncertainty for providers and increase the burden of uncompensated care." HHS officials said that the agency will "monitor this issue moving forward and will continue to work on the development of policies to prevent misuse of the grace period."

Here is how this three-month grace period works per examples in the regulations:

Example 1: Individual misses $50 payment that is due February 28 for March coverage and misses $50 payment that is due March 31st for April coverage. Individual Pays $150 on April 30 for March, April, and May coverage.

- Issuer adjudicates claims for March.

- Coverage continues for April and May (2nd and 3rd months of the grace period), but:

    1) providers are notified of the potential for a denied claim;

    2) issuer pends claims for services performed in April and May until individual pays outstanding premiums;

    3) individual has paid full premium for March, April, and May and is eligible for premium tax credit for March, April, and May.

Example 2: Same facts as Example #1 except that the individual does not pay enrollee's share of premium for March, April, or May.

- Coverage terminated retroactively to March 31.

- Issuer can deny claims for services rendered during April and May. Provider could then seek payment directly from the individual for any services provided during that time.

- Individual may have additional tax liability attributable to the $450 for the advance payment of the premium tax credit paid on his or her behalf for March's coverage. The exact amount of additional tax liability would be determined in accordance with the rules for tax credit reconciliation under section 36B of the Code.

---

1.   *Id.*

92. What are the functions of the state health insurance exchanges?

The exchange functions and responsibilities[1] include the following:

- Certification, recertification, and decertification of health insurance options as qualified.

- Operation of a toll-free hotline.

- Maintenance of a website for providing information on plans to current and prospective enrollees.

- Assignment of a price and quality rating to plans.

- Presentation of plan benefit options in a standardized format.

- Provision of information on Medicaid and CHIP eligibility and determination of eligibility for individuals in these programs, as well as eligibility for the refundable income tax credit.[2]

- Provision of an electronic calculator to determine the actual cost of coverage, considering eligibility for premium tax credits and cost sharing reductions.

- Certification of individuals exempt from the individual responsibility requirement.

- Provision of information on certain individuals and to employers.

- Establishment of a "navigator" program that provides grants to entities assisting consumers.

93. What are the areas over which HHS has responsibility for the state health insurance exchanges?

HHS is responsible for regulatory standards in five areas that insurers must meet in order to be certified as Qualified Health Plans (QHPs) by an exchange:

- Marketing

- Network adequacy

- Accreditation for performance measures

- Quality improvement and reporting

- Uniform enrollment procedures[3]

---

1.   PPACA §1311(d)(4)(A)-(K).
2.   45 CFR §155.300.
3.   PPACA §1311(c).

94. What are the primary federal requirements for state exchanges?

Only lawful U.S. residents may obtain coverage in an exchange.[1] Exchanges must comply with federal regulatory standards in the following areas:

- Information on the availability of in-network and out-of-network providers, including provider directories and availability of essential community providers.

- Consideration of plan patterns and practices with respect to past premium increases and a submission of the plan justifications for current premium increases.

- Public disclosure of specific plan data, including claims-handling policies, financial disclosures, enrollment and disenrollment data, claims denials, rating practices, cost sharing for out-of-network coverage, and other information identified by HHS.

- Timely information for consumers requesting their amount of cost sharing for specific services from specified providers.

- Establishment of "navigators" to assist consumers in selecting their health insurance.[2]

- Information for participants in group health plans.

- Information on plan quality-improvement activities.

- Presentation of enrollee satisfaction-survey results.

- Publication of data on the Exchange's administrative costs.[3]

Additionally, exchanges must meet detailed requirements for call centers and an Internet website.[4]

95. What is a Qualified Health Plan (QHP)?

A Qualified Health Plan (QHP) is health insurance certified by a state Exchange that offers "essential health benefits."[5] A QHP must be offered by an insurer that:

(1)   is licensed and in good standing to offer health insurance coverage in each state in which it offers health coverage;

(2)   agrees to offer at least one QHP in the silver level and at least one QHP in the gold level in each Exchange;

(3)   agrees to charge the same premium rate for each QHP, whether offered through an Exchange or offered directly from the insurer or through an agent; and

---

1.   PPACA §1312(f).
2.   45 CFR §155.210.
3.   PPACA §1311.
4.   45 CFR §155.205.
5.   PPACA §1301(a).

(4)   complies with regulations to be issued by HHS and any requirements established by an applicable Exchange.[1]

However, a QHP may vary premiums by rating area.[2]

For QHP purposes, the term health plan includes "health insurance coverage" and a "group health plan."[3] Health insurance coverage means benefits consisting of medical care (provided directly, through insurance or reimbursement, or otherwise, and including items and services paid for as medical care) under any hospital or medical service policy or certificate, hospital or medical service plan contract, or health maintenance organization contract offered by a health insurer.[4]

A "group health plan" is an ERISA welfare benefit plan that provides medical care.[5] Health plans must be subject to state regulation; therefore, the term "health plan" does not include a group health plan or multiple employer welfare arrangement (MEWA) not subject to state insurance regulation under ERISA section 514. Thus, self-insured group health plans cannot qualify as QHPs.[6]

Health insurance plans must:

- meet certain marketing requirements;

- ensure a sufficient provider choice and include, where available, providers that serve low-income and medically underserved individuals;

- be accredited (see Q 25) for clinical quality, patient experience, consumer access, and quality assurances, and implement a quality improvement strategy;

- use a uniform enrollment form and a standard format for presenting plan options; and

- provide information on quality standards used to measure plan performance.[7]

The U.S. Office of Personnel Management (OPM) must enter into contracts with health insurers to offer at least two multistate QHPs through each Exchange in each state.[8]

96. How are state health insurance exchanges regulated?

The Patient Protection and Affordable Care Act includes two federal requirements for state health insurance exchanges:[9]

---

1.   PPACA §1301(a)(1).
2.   PPACA §1301(a)(4).
3.   PPACA §1301(b)(1(A)).
4.   PPACA §1301(b)(2); PHSA §2791(b)(1).
5.   PPACA §1301(b)(3); PHSA §2791(a)(1).
6.   PPACA §1301(b)(1)(B).
7.   PPACA §1311(c).
8.   PPACA §1334(a).
9.   PPACA §1311.

- Minimum functions that Exchanges must perform directly or by contract

- Oversight responsibilities Exchanges must exercise in certifying and monitoring the performance of Health Plans[1]

Plans participating in the exchanges also must comply with state insurance laws and federal requirements in the Public Health Service Act.

The final regulations set "standards for establishing exchanges, setting up a Small Business Health Options Program (SHOP), performing the basic functions of an exchange, certifying health plans for participation in the exchange," and establishing "a streamlined, web-based system for consumers to apply for and enroll in qualified health plans and insurance affordability programs." HHS has also issued questions and answers on federally facilitated Exchanges, including for instance, how the Exchanges will interact with state departments of insurance.[2]

State exchanges became operational in 2014. A change in the final rule gave more flexibility to states that were not able to show "complete readiness" to operate an exchange on January 1, 2013. HHS could conditionally approve a state-based exchange upon demonstration that it was likely to be fully operationally ready by October 1, 2013. Applications of a state's Exchange Blueprint had to be submitted thirty business days before January 1, 2013, or by November 16, 2012.

Exchanges are intended to:

- facilitate the comparison by individuals and small businesses of health plans;

- provide answers to questions;

- determine eligibility for tax credits for private insurance or health programs like the Children's Health Insurance Program (CHIP); and

- allow enrollment by individuals and small employers in a Qualified Health Plan (QHP).

97. What was the process used by states to set up health insurance exchanges?

The U.S. Department of Health and Human Services (HHS) issued final regulations[3] that provided a framework to assist states in building health insurance exchanges, state-based competitive marketplaces authorized by the Affordable Care Act.[4] These rules set minimum standards for

---

1.   PPACA §1301.
2.   See https://www.cms.gov/CCIIO/Resources/Fact-Sheets-and-FAQs/ . (Last accessed July 21, 2019).
3.   Federal Register Volume 77, Number 59 (March 27, 2012), 45 CFR Parts 155 and 157 (March 27, 2012) (superseding two sets of proposed regulations, namely, Establishment of Exchanges and Qualified Health Plans, 45 CFR Parts 155 and 156, 76 Fed. Reg. 41866 (July 15, 2011); PPACA; Standards Related to Reinsurance, Risk Corridors, and Risk Adjustment, 45 CFR Part 153, 76 Fed. Reg. 41930 (July 15, 2011)).
4.   Federal Register Volume 77, Number 59 (March 27, 2012), 45 CFR Parts 155 and 157 (March 27, 2012).

exchanges and gave states some flexibility to design the exchanges to fit their insurance markets, subject to HHS approval. The regulations propose rules and guidance on how to structure the exchanges in two areas:

- Setting standards for establishing exchanges, setting up a Small Business Health Options Program (SHOP) , performing the basic functions of an exchange, and certifying health plans for participation in an exchange

- Ensuring premium stability for the exchanges, especially in the first three years

According to HHS, forty-eight states and the District of Columbia were awarded grants to help plan and operate exchanges.[1]

By mid-August 2016, thirteen states and the District of Columbia were operating state-based exchanges, four were operating federally-supported state-based exchanges; seven were operating state partnership exchanges, and twenty-seven declined to establish a state-based exchange and defaulted to a Federally-Facilitated Exchange (FFE). All of the twenty-four states working toward state-based or state partnership exchanges have been conditionally approved by HHS.[2]

The rules allow states to decide:

- whether their exchanges should be local, regional, or operated by a nonprofit organization;

- how to select plans to participate; and

- whether to collaborate with HHS for the work.

However, HHS must approve each exchange and the criteria for its insurance policies.

Exchanges were initially available only to individuals and small employers, but states were allowed to expand them in 2017 to be available to large employers as well.

Using the standards and processes in the regulations to approve exchanges, HHS had to determine by January 1, 2013, whether an exchange would be operational by 2014, which meant it had to begin open enrollment on October 1, 2013. In states that did not obtain this HHS approval (or decided not to establish an Exchange), a federally facilitated exchange was implemented for 2014.

<u>Open Enrollment Periods</u>. The initial open-enrollment period began on October 1, 2013 and ran though through March 31, 2014.[3] Only those enrolling in a Qualified Health Plan (QHP) on or before December 23, 2013, were ensured of coverage effective on January 1, 2014.

---

1.   Kansas governor Sam Brownback returned the state's $30 million grant as did Alaska.
2.   http://kff.org/health-reform/state-indicator/state-health-insurance-marketplace-types/. State Health Insurance Marketplace Types, 2019. (Last accessed July 30, 2019).
3.   45 CFR §155.410(b).

As mentioned elsewhere in this book, special enrollment periods are also provided in the regulations.[1]

The annual enrollment period for 2015 began on November 15, 2014 and ran through February 15, 2015.[2] In addition, there was a special enrollment period (in most states) that extended enrollment to April 30, 2015.

The open enrollment for 2016 began on November 1, 2015 and ran through January 31, 2016.

The open enrollment for 2017 began on November 1, 2016 and ran through January 31, 2017.

The open enrollment for 2018 began on November 1, 2017 and ran through January 31, 2018.

The open enrollment for 2019 begins on November 1, 2018 and runs through December 15, 2018.

The open enrollment for 2020 begins on November 1, 2019 and runs through December 15, 2019.

Eligibility and Consumer Assistance. Exchanges make eligibility determinations and provide consumer assistance tools, including a toll-free call center, a website with comparative information about available Qualified Health Plans (QHPs), and a "navigator" program that facilitates enrollment and provides other information and services. Navigators cannot be insurers but can be agents or brokers. They cannot receive direct or indirect compensation from an insurer for enrolling eligible individuals, employers, or employees in a QHP.

Each exchange must provide the following:

- A toll-free call center to address the needs of those seeking assistance

- An website providing a variety of features, including comparative information on available QHPs, certain financial information, and information about the Navigator and call center

- An Exchange calculator to facilitate comparisons of QHPs that takes into consideration the premium tax credit and any cost-sharing reductions

- A consumer-assistance function, including the Navigator program discussed below

- Outreach and education activities[3]

Small Business Health Options Program (SHOP). Each state will establish insurance options for qualifying small businesses through a SHOP, and participation by small employers will be

---

1.   PPACA §1311(c)(6) (2010). Special enrollment periods include those specified in Code section 9801, other special enrollments under circumstances similar to such periods under part D of title XVIII of the Social Security Act, and special monthly enrollment periods for Indians pursuant to section 4 of the Indian Health Care Improvement Act).
2.   45 CFR §155.410(e).
3.   45 CFR §155.205.

voluntary. SHOP is intended to give small employers the same purchasing power that large employers have and to allow them to offer employees a choice of plans for a single monthly payment. For 2014 through 2016, only employers with fewer than 100 employees or fewer than fifty employees (states have the option of choosing either) were granted access to the SHOP exchange. As discussed in Q 27, certain small employers will be eligible to receive a small business tax credit for up to 50 percent of the contributions they make toward employees' premiums for two consecutive years if certain tax rules are met. See Q 106 for additional information on SHOPs.

<u>QHP Certification</u>. Exchanges needed to establish procedures, approved by HHS, for certification, recertification, and decertification of Qualified Health Plans (QHPs). The regulations do not require exchanges to accept all eligible QHPs, although that is allowed. Alternatively, exchanges can limit QHP participation to those plans that meet the state's selection criteria. The regulations include minimum standards for QHPs and QHP issuers. States may impose additional requirements, if approved by HHS.

An Exchange is required to allow the insurer of a plan that provides certain limited-scope dental benefits to offer the plan through the Exchange (either separately or in conjunction with a QHP) if the plan provides pediatric dental benefits.[1]

<u>Reinsurance, Three-Year Risk Corridor Program, and Risk Adjustment</u>. The HHS regulations outline standards for various programs required by healthcare reform that are intended, to mitigate the impact of adverse selection and stabilize premiums in the individual and small group markets. Standards were established for the transitional reinsurance program, which is a required state-based program that reduces uncertainty for insurers during the first three years the exchange is in operation by making payments for high-cost cases. CMS announced that the reinsurance program would pay $7.9 billion in reinsurance claims for 2014.

A temporary risk corridor program from 2014 through 2016 protected against uncertainty in setting rates within the exchanges by limiting the extent of insurer losses and gains. Payment is based on how closely the premiums cover their insured medical expenses. The program is modeled somewhat like the Medicare Part D prescription drug program. The risk corridor program has become controversial because the federal government will cover only a portion of the promised payments. The program was structured so that if a health plan exceeded anticipated by 3 percent, the federal government would reimburse 50 percent of the loss. If the loss exceeded expectations by over 8 percent, the government would reimburse 80 percent. It also works the opposite way — companies whose profits exceeded expectations would have to pay back half of the profits. CMS will pay out $362 million for 2014, although insurers have requested $2.87 billion — resulting in a payment of 12.6 percent on the dollar. This is the first year of payments of the three-year program.

The risk adjustment program, which is an optional program that a state may establish inside or outside of an exchange, after 2014. The program is intended to provide stability in the individual and small group markets by transferring funds from insurers of lower-risk enrollees to insurers of higher-risk enrollees. The intent is to protect consumer access to a variety of coverage options by

---

1.   PPACA §1311(d)(2) (2010). The limited-scope dental benefits must meet the requirements of IRC Sec. 9832(c)(2)(A). The pediatric dental benefits must meet the requirements of PPACA §1302(b)(1)(J).

minimizing the incentive for insurance companies to seek out only very healthy applicants. This program, according to CMS, will distribute approximately $4.6 billion to insurance companies.

An additional complication was imposed when Republicans in Congress passed appropriations riders making the program "budget-neutral", allowing risk-corridor payments only from the funds it collected from insurers as part of the program resulting in a shortfall of funding. The United States Court of Appeals for the Federal Circuit had determined that the government was required to pay the full amount of risk-corridor payments, but Congress eliminated that obligation.

98. What types of exchanges are operated by each of the states?

The following types of exchanges are currently in operation:

Federally-Facilitated Exchanges: The Department of Health and Human Services manages and handles all of the exchange functions. Application and enrollment is done through healthcare.gov.

State-Based Exchanges: The state is responsible for running all exchange functions. Application and enrollment is done through state websites.

Federally-Supported State-Based Exchanges: This sort of a hybrid, considered to be a State-Based Exchange where the state is responsible for performing all exchange functions, except that the state will rely on the FFE platform. Application and enrollment is done through healthcare.gov.

State-Partnership Exchanges: These states administer in-person customer service and assistance functions and HHS perform the other exchange functions. Application and enrollment is done through healthcare.gov.

FEDERALLY-FACILITATED EXCHANGES

Alabama	New Jersey
Alaska	North Carolina
Arizona	North Dakota
Florida	Ohio
Georgia	Oklahoma
Hawaii	Pennsylvania
Indiana	South Carolina
Kansas	South Dakota
Kentucky (former state exchange)	Tennessee
Louisiana	Texas
Maine	Utah (State administers SHOP)
Mississippi (State administers SHOP)	Virginia
Missouri	Wisconsin
Montana	Wyoming
Nebraska	

STATE-BASED EXCHANGES

California	Nevada (Federally Supported)
Colorado	New Mexico (Federally Supported but State operates the SHOP)
Connecticut	New York
District of Columbia	Oregon (Federally Supported)
Idaho	Rhode Island
Maryland	Vermont
Massachusetts	Washington
Minnesota	

STATE PARTNERSHIP EXCHANGE

Arkansas (State administers the SHOP)	Michigan
Delaware	New Hampshire
Illinois	West Virginia
Iowa	

99. What is the Navigator program and what are the positions?

Centers for Medicare & Medicaid Services (CMS) created programs to advise and help consumers make health insurance purchase decisions. Funding has been diminished over the years for this program. In 2016, CMS awarded $67 million in ACA funding to provide assistance for 2016. During 2017, CMS awarded $63 million in ACA funding to provide assistance. During 2018, funding was reduced to $36.8 million. For 2019, funding was further reduced to $10 million dollars. Funding for 2020 and 2021 is being maintained at $10 million. Positions include Navigators, Assisters, and Certified Application Counselors. These funding cuts have had an impact. For 2019, the number of navigator organizations dropped by about half—from more than eighty organizations for 2018 to only thirty-nine grantees for 2019. Three states (Iowa, Montana, and New Hampshire) had no navigators at all, and entire areas of some states (such as Cleveland and Dallas) are not served by the navigator program.

Section 1311(i) of the Affordable Care Act (ACA) requires health insurance marketplaces to establish a navigator program. Navigators are organizations that must have (or can readily build) relationships with employers, employees, uninsured and underinsured consumers, or self-employed individuals who likely qualify to enroll in qualified health plans (QHPs). The navigator program was modeled after other successful outreach efforts for public coverage programs, such as Medicaid, CHIP, and the State Health Insurance Assistance Programs (for Medicare).

Among other duties, navigators must:

1.   conduct public education activities to raise awareness of the availability of QHPs;

2.   distribute fair and impartial information concerning enrollment in QHPs and the availability of premium tax credits and cost-sharing reductions;

3.   facilitate enrollment in QHPs; and

4.   provide information in a manner that is culturally and linguistically appropriate to the needs of the population being served by the marketplace.

Navigators may be organizations such as trade, industry, and professional associations; chambers of commerce; ranching and farming organizations; and community and consumer-focused nonprofit organizations.

Historically, navigator organizations have been organizations such as United Way affiliates, universities, health systems, legal aid societies, and patient advocacy organizations.

For 2019 and subsequent years, CMS scaled back the navigator program by eliminating the requirement that each marketplace have at least two navigator entities and that one of these entities be a community and consumer-focused nonprofit group. The rule also eliminated the requirement that navigators maintain a physical presence in a marketplace service area. CMS made additional changes to the navigator program in the payment rule for 2020 by eliminating a requirement that navigators provide post-enrollment assistance and scaling back explicit training requirements.

CMS has determined that independent agents and brokers are a more cost-effective way to enroll new consumers. CMS reports that 42 percent of enrollees at a cost of $2.40 per enrollee. In comparison, Navigators enrolled fewer than one percent of enrollees.

Navigator

The position was created to provide assistance and advice to people to enable them to enroll in coverage through the exchange. They can also assist with Medicaid enrollment. Funding is through the exchanges. HHS regulations bar anyone who gets payments from insurance companies from being a Navigator. Navigators also must meet cultural competency standards and go through training and certification. Beginning in 2018, Navigators will provide ongoing assistance to consumers after the enrollment process is complete as well. Currently Navigators must complete fourteen online courses which take approximately twenty hours to complete. They must pass the assessment with a score of 80 percent or higher.

Assisters

This is an In-Person assister. Assisters must meet training and conflict-of-interest standards. They perform duties that need more enrollment assistance, and provide education about the ACA to individuals who have not traditionally had access to health insurance coverage. Assisters must complete the same training as Navigators.

Certified Application Counselors

The CAC also aid individuals to apply and enroll in the exchanges. Each state exchange must have a Certified Application Counselor program, offering comparable training and privacy standards as Navigators and Assisters. The training and certification requirements for CACs is not as rigorous as for Navigators and Assisters. The CAC's role is to help people understand and choose the appropriate health plan, provide information and services in a fair, impartial and culturally competent manner; and facilitate selection of a QHP. CACs are not required to begin providing additional post-enrollment assistance in 2018, although they can if properly trained.

100. Are there any prohibitions for agents and brokers who want to apply for Navigator funds under this Funding Opportunity?

Yes. Although licensed agents and brokers are eligible to apply, PPACA 1311(i)(4) prohibits a Navigator from being "a health insurance issuer" and from "receiving any consideration directly or indirectly from any health insurance issuer in connection with the enrollment of any qualified individuals or employees of a qualified employer in a [QHP]." CMS regulations at 45 C.F.R §§155.210(d)(1)-(4) and 155.215(a)(1) implement this statutory provision. In guidance, CMS has explained that agents and brokers who sell lines of insurance other than health insurance or stop loss insurance (for example, auto, life, and homeowners' policies) would not be prohibited from receiving consideration from the sale of those other lines of insurance while serving as a Navigator. However, agents and brokers that sell lines of insurance other than health insurance or stop loss insurance, and that opt to become Navigators, would have to disclose these non-prohibited lines of business to the FFE and (in plain language) to each consumer assisted, per 155.215(a)(1)(i)(iv)(A).

101. Are tribal entities eligible to apply to be a Navigator?

Yes, Indian Tribes, tribal organizations, and urban Indian organizations are eligible to apply. Tribal Applicants should include the federally recognized Indian Tribal lands of their target Tribal population, the county(ies) it includes, and how they plan to serve the different geographic areas of their target population in their application as noted in the Funding Opportunity.

102. Are individuals eligible to apply to be a Navigator?

Yes. However, all applicants, including those applying as individuals, must apply using a valid Employer Identification Number (EIN), or other Taxpayer Identification Number (TIN) assigned by the Internal Revenue Service. Individuals may choose to provide their personal Social Security Numbers (SSNs) to apply via Grants.gov.

103. Is an entity that sells Medicaid or Medicare managed care plans eligible to apply to be a Navigator?

It depends. If an applying entity or one of its corporate affiliates is required to be licensed to engage in the business of insurance in a state and is subject to state law that regulates insurance, it might be a health insurance issuer or have a relationship with a health insurance issuer that would make it ineligible for a Navigator cooperative agreement. See definition of "health insurance issuer" at 45 C.F.R. §§155.20 and 144.103. CMS will evaluate specific corporate structures on a case-by-case basis. The Funding Opportunity requires applicants to submit a brief statement attesting that they are not an ineligible entity. Please keep the foregoing guidance in mind when drafting that statement (for example, by disclosing any corporate relationships with an entity that is required to be licensed to engage in the business of insurance in a state and that is subject to state law that regulates insurance).

104. Is there anyone who is ineligible to be a Navigator?

Yes, health insurance issuers; subsidiaries of health insurance issuers; issuers of stop loss insurance and their subsidiaries; associations that include members of, or lobby on behalf of, the insurance industry; or recipients of any direct or indirect consideration from any health insurance or stop loss insurance issuer in connection with the enrollment of any individuals or employees in a qualified health plan (QHP) or non-QHP. CMS has clarified in regulation that no health care provider shall be ineligible to operate as a Navigator in an FFE solely because it receives consideration from a health insurance issuer for health care services provided.

105. Do Navigators have to maintain a physical presence in the FFE service area it is approved to serve?

No. The PPACA, HHS Notice of Benefit and Payment Parameters for 2019 Final Rule, effective June 18, 2018, eliminated the requirement for Navigators to maintain a physical presence in the Exchange service area it is approved to serve.

106. What is the status of federal SHOP exchanges for small employers?

The FF-SHOP program has had a troubled and difficult history. The winding down of the online SHOP program is continuing.

Historical background: Each state Exchange was required to create a Small Business Health Options Program (SHOP).[1] HHS also provided for a Federally Facilitated SHOP (FF-SHOP) in states that did not establish a state-based Exchange.[2] Participation in a SHOP is strictly voluntary for small employers.

Beginning in 2014, however, purchasing employer-provided health coverage for employees through a SHOP was the only way for qualified employers to obtain a small business health care tax credit.[3] Both state operated SHOPs and Federally-Facilitated SHOPs (FFSHOPs) are to allow employees to have a choice among all QHPs at the metal level chosen by the employer (bronze, silver, gold, or platinum). However, SHOP regulations delayed the effective date for this "employee-choice" model for FFSHOPS until 2015, so that, for plan years beginning before January 1, 2015, FF-SHOPS only offered one option and state-operated SHOPs may choose but are not be required to offer an employee choice option.[4]

---

1. PPACA §1311(b)(1)(B).
2. General Guidance on Federally-facilitated Exchanges (May 16, 2012); Fact Sheet: Affordable Insurance Exchanges (May 16, 2012) at https://www.cms.gov/CCIIO/Resources/Fact-Sheets-and-FAQs/Downloads/ffe-guidance-05-16-2012.pdf. (Last accessed August 21, 2017).
3. 45 CFR §§155.705(b)(2) and (3).
4. Patient Protection and Affordable Care Act; Establishment of Exchanges and Qualified Health Plans; Small Business Health Options Program, 45 CFR Parts 155 and 156, 78 Fed. Reg. 15553 (Mar. 11, 2013).

This will allow employers who prefer to offer employees a single Qualified Health Plan (QHP) to participate in an FF-SHOP and retain potential eligibility for the small business tax credit is only available through a SHOP Exchange.

For SHOP eligibility, a "small employer" is an employer that employed an average of at least one but not more than 100 employees on business days during the preceding calendar year and that employs at least one employee on the first day of the plan year.[1] A qualified employee is an individual employed by a qualified employer who has been offered health insurance coverage by such qualified employer through the SHOP.[2]

For counting employees to determine whether an employer is a small employer that is SHOP eligible, the regulations use the Internal Revenue Code section 4980H(c)(2) employer mandate counting method, which counts not only full-time employees, i.e., those averaging thirty hours of service per week, but also part-time employees as full-time equivalents under Code section 4980H(c)(4)). However, a transitional rule allows state-operated SHOPS to rely on state count-ing methods, which in some states may not include part-time employees, for determining group size and status as a full-time employee until 2016.[3] A qualified employer participating in a SHOP must provide information to its employees about the methods for selecting and enrolling in a QHP through the SHOP.[4] This requirement is in addition to the Notice of Exchange.

On May 15, 2017, CMS announced that it was essentially ending the Federally Facilitated SHOP exchange as of the end of 2017.[5] The SHOP program covers thirty-three states. CMS decided that as of January 1, 2018, healthcare.gov would make decisions regarding eligibility for FF-SHOP participation for small employers (determining eligibility for the small employer tax credit) however, it would not handle enrollment for employers or employees, process premium payments, or handle other SHOP functions. For coverage starting January 1, 2018, employers can enroll in SHOP through private insurance companies, or with the help of a SHOP-registered agent or broker. SHOP plans are generally the only way to qualify for the Small Business Health Care Tax Credit to lower premium costs. State-based SHOP marketplaces would continue to provide enrollment online, or if they wished, could take the federal approach and direct small employers to insurance companies or to SHOP registered agents and brokers to enroll.

CMS Administrator Seema Verma states that the plan is to reduce the burden of the Afford-able Care Act on small businesses and to allow an easier method to purchase coverage by help-ing "employers find affordable healthcare coverage for their employees and make their SHOP exchanges function more effectively."

The FF-SHOP was only mildly successful. As of the start of 2017, approximately 7500 employers were covering 39,000 employees. The state-based SHOPs have coverage of nearly

---

1.   PPACA §§1304(b), 1312(f); HHS Reg. §155.20.
2.   45 CFR §155.20.
3.   45 CFR §155.20.
4.   45 CFR §157.205(c).
5.   https://www.cms.gov/CCIIO/Resources/Regulations-and-Guidance/Downloads/The-Future-of-the-SHOP-CMS-Intends-to-Allow-Small-Businesses-in-SHOPs-Using-HealthCaregov-More-Flexibility-when-Enrolling-in-Healthcare-Coverage.pdf.

20,000 employers and nearly 200,000 individuals. Nearly half of SHOP enrollments are from Vermont and Washington, DC where small employers MUST purchase through SHOP.

107. What are the requirements for small employers to get employer tax credits through the Small Business Health Options Program (SHOP)?

In order to get employer tax credits for health insurance,[1] eligible small employers must enroll online for 2015. SHOP enrollment using paper applications was permitted in 2014. Small employers who enrolled in the SHOP with paper applications (including those who worked with an agent or broker) were permitted to claim a small business health care tax credit for 2014, if they were eligible. For qualifying small employers to get the tax credit in 2015, they will need to enroll online, either on their own or with agent/broker assistance.

CMS initially announced[2] that online enrollment will be available for coverage through the Small Business Health Options Program (SHOP—the Exchange for small businesses) beginning November 15, 2014. The initial rollout of the SHOP program had its problems, and online enrollment was delayed in 2013, and employers worked with an agent, broker, or insurer to complete and submit paper applications for 2014 on exchanges where the small employer SHOP option was available.

Employers using SHOP for employee health insurance will be able to choose coverage, complete an application, and enroll entirely online. Employers can also work with a registered agent or broker, who may obtain online capabilities. Employers are also reminded that a SHOP full-time equivalent employee calculator[3] and a tax credit estimator[4] are available. The website links indicates a 2014 plan but it does correctly link out to 2016 plans and prices.[5] As indicated in the prior question, the FF-SHOP program was essentially eliminated at the end of 2017.

108. What are the rules for the small business health insurance tax credit?

Prior Law: For tax years 2010 through 2013, eligible small employers were entitled to a 35 percent tax credit for health insurance premiums they pay for employees. Tax-exempt entities have been eligible for a 25 percent credit. Employers with ten or fewer Full-Time Equivalent employees (FTEs) and average annual wages of $25,000 or less were eligible for the maximum tax credit.

There was a phase-out of the credit for employers that have eleven through twenty-four FTEs or average annual wages from $25,001 to $49,999.99. Employees who are owners and family members do not count for the number of employees or the average compensation. To qualify for the credit, an employer must pay at least 50 percent of the premium for qualifying employee only (not spouses' or dependents') health insurance.

---

1.   IRC §45R.

2.   CMS Bulletin: Get Health Care for Your Small Business (Oct. 8, 2014) at http://content.govdelivery.com/accounts/USCMSHIM/bulletins/ d3f753. (Last access July 30, 2019.

3.   Full-time Equivalent (FTE) Employee Calculator at https://www.healthcare.gov/shop-calculators-fte. (Last accessed July 30, 2019).

4.   See https://www.healthcare.gov/small-businesses/choose-and-enroll/tools-and-calculators./ . (Last accessed July 30, 2019).

5.   https://www.healthcare.gov/see-plans/?utm_medium=email&utm_source=govdelivery&utm_campaign=getready&utm_content=10_08_14. (Last accessed July 30, 2019).

Employers claimed the credit using IRS Form 8941. Taxable employers claim the credit on their federal tax return and can apply the credit to both regular and alternative minimum tax. Tax-exempt employers claim the credit by filing Form 990-T, and can receive a refundable credit up to the amount of the employer's payroll taxes.

<u>Current law</u>: Employers will only be eligible for the credit if they purchase health insurance through the new Small Business Health Options Program (SHOP). The SHOP is one component of the state based health insurance exchanges, also known as marketplaces. In addition:

- the maximum credit is 50 percent (35 percent for tax-exempt organizations);

- employer has fewer than twenty-five full-time or full-time equivalent employees;

- the employee average sales are $50,000 or less;

- does not have to be offered to dependents or employees working fewer than 30 hours per week to qualify for the tax credit;

- the $50,000 and $25,000 average annual dollar amounts will be indexed for inflation;

- the credit is based on the lesser of the employer's actual premium payments or the average premiums in the small group market in its employees' rating area;

- the credit is only available for two consecutive tax years after 2013, but it can be carried back or carried forward.

109. What are the small business insurance exchange revisions, and SHOP enrollment periods?

Regulations finalized in March 2016 make the following changes in the operation of the Small Business Health Options Program (SHOP) program.

SHOP Enrollment Period

The annual open enrollment periods for qualified employers and qualified employees in all SHOPs, both state based or federally facilitated, are the same as the open enrollment in the corresponding individual marketplace exchanges.[1]

SHOP Insurance Choices

For plan years beginning on and after January 1, 2015, all SHOPs must make available to qualified employers the option of selecting an actuarial value level of coverage (bronze, silver, gold and platinum[2]) and making all qualified health plans at that level available to qualified employees (employee choice).[3]

---

1.   45 CFR §155.725(c) and (e) (March 21, 2014).
2.   PPACA §1302(d)(1).
3.   45 CFR §155.705(b)(2) and (3) (March 21, 2014).

Note: 2015 Insurance Choice Exception: However, HHS and state insurance commissioners were concerned that, in some circumstances, implementing employee choice in 2015 might significantly disrupt some small group markets and negatively affect the ability of small business employees to access coverage. The concern is that employee choice might lead to sicker people enrolling in disproportionate numbers in certain plans, which could have the effect of discouraging issuers from participating in the SHOP or causing adverse selection that cannot be fully addressed by the single risk pool provisions of the statute or the premium stabilization programs. Thus, there was a one year transition under which a SHOP would be permitted to not implement employee choice in 2015 under specific circumstances:

(1)   If employee choice would result in significant adverse selection in the State's small group market that could not be fully remediated by the single risk pool or premium stabilization programs

(2)   If there is an insufficient number of issuers offering qualified health plans or qualified stand-alone dental plans to allow for meaningful plan choice among qualified health plans or qualified stand-alone dental plans for all actuarial value levels in the State's SHOP

During this first year, a state regulatory agency, such as the state department of insurance, could submit a recommendation to the state SHOP[1] or HHS in the case of an FF-SHOP.

110. What is the Employer Exchange Notice requirement?

The Affordable Care Act amends the Fair Labor Standards Act (FLSA)[2] to require that employers provide all new hires and current employees with a written notice (Employer Exchange Notice) about the exchange and some of the consequences if an employee decides to purchase a qualified health plan through the exchange in lieu of employer-sponsored coverage.[3] Regulations implementing the Employer Exchange Notice requirement will be issued and enforced by the Department of Labor.[4]

The Employer Exchange Notice requirement was effective on March 1, 2013. Employees hired on or after the effective date must be provided with the notice when they are hired. The Employer Exchange Notice rule applies to employers that are subject to the FLSA. The FLSA's minimum wage and maximum hour provisions apply to entities that are engaged in interstate commerce and have a gross annual volume of sales that is not less than $500,000 (enterprises engaged in commerce or in the production of goods for commerce).[5] However, the Employer Exchange Notice requirement does not have the same limitation. As a result, it seemingly applies to "any person acting directly or indirectly in the interest of an employer in relation to an employee."[6]

---

1.   45 CFR §155.705(b)(2) and (3) (March 21, 2014).
2.   29 USC §201 et seq.
3.   FLSA §18B.
4.   DOL delegated responsibility for regulations under FLSA §18B, to its Employee Benefits Security Administration (EBSA). See FAQs About the Affordable Care Act Implementation Part V, Q/A-2, at https://www.dol.gov/sites/default/files/ebsa/about-ebsa/our-activities/resource-center/faqs/aca-part-v.pdf. (Last accessed July 15, 2019).
5.   29 USC §§206 and 207.
6.   29 USC §203(d).

The Employer Exchange Notice must include the following information:[1]

- Employees must be informed of the existence of an Exchange, given a description of the services provided by the Exchange, and told how to contact the Exchange to request assistance.

- Employees must be informed that they may be eligible for a premium tax credit (under Internal Revenue Code section 36B) or a cost-sharing reduction (under PPACA section 1402) through the Exchange if the employer's plan share of the total cost of benefits under the plan is less than 60 percent.

- Employees must be informed that:

  - if they purchase a qualified health plan through the Exchange, they may lose any employer contribution toward the cost of employer-provided coverage; and

  - all or a portion of the employer's contributions to employer-provided coverage may be excludable for federal income tax purposes.

111. What is the role of health insurance brokers or agents in the state health insurance exchanges?

The final regulation contains welcome news for agents and brokers of health insurance.[2] HHS, in the final regulation, permits states to allow an agent or broker to enroll individuals, employers or employees in Qualified Health Plans (QHPs), in a manner that constitutes "enrollment through the exchange," on their own website. It is up to each state to determine whether its exchange can list approved insurance agents and brokers.[3] However, navigators need not be agents or brokers.[4] An individual can be enrolled in a QHP through an exchange with the assistance of an agent or broker only if the agent or broker ensures that the individual receives an eligibility determination through the state's Exchange website.[5]

If the consumer would be eligible for a refundable federal income tax credit (See Q 56) for a QHP purchased on the exchange's website, the consumer may access the tax credit for purchases through the broker or agent's private Web portal.

The regulation sets out a series of requirements brokers or agents must meet in order for their clients to be able to access the tax credits for purchases through their websites. For consumers to do this, brokers and agents must be registered with the Exchange. This means that the state (or the federal government in the case of a Federally Facilitated Exchange (FFE)), controls whether their exchange remains the exclusive market for the tax credit or whether brokers and agents can assist eligible individuals and families in obtaining the subsidies.

---

1.   FLSA §18B.
2.   45 CFR §155.220(a)(3).
3.   45 CFR §155.205(b)(3).
4.   45 CFR §155.210(c)(2).
5.   45 CFR §155.220(c)(1).

Additionally, all QHPs must be available for purchase through the website, and the agents and brokers assisting the customer must be trained on all QHP options. Thus, a single-carrier exchange will not meet the qualifications for a purchaser to access the tax credit. The private websites must present all QHPs and all QHP data in a manner that meets HHS standards and must not use financial incentives, such as rebates or free prizes, to lure customers to one QHP instead of another. Consumers may withdraw from this process at any time and use the exchange website. Any private web portal must be compliant with exchange privacy and security standards. Of course, state laws related to the qualifications and conduct of agents and brokers continue to apply.

Interestingly, the private web portals, unlike the state or federally facilitated exchanges, do not have restrictions on selling products other than QHPs. Thus, brokers and agents can use their existing web portals to sell other products as well as QHPs, as long as the requirements noted previously in this section are met.

Thus, if permitted to use an agent or broker, consumers never have to go to the state exchange website to buy a product and access the refundable tax credit. All of the information transfers between the private broker site, the exchange, and the insurance carriers can be invisible to the consumer.

This aspect of the final regulation indicates that HHS believes that private distribution of exchange health insurance will help to stimulate the use of exchanges. For agents, brokers, and private exchanges, the shift presents a new opportunity to access the exchange population. For consumers, it is likely that more will look into whether or not they qualify for a tax credit while shopping for insurance, which could increase QHP sales.

Employer Funds for Insurance Purchased on State Exchange and ERISA

112. Are individual health or other policies purchased in whole or part with employer funds an ERISA plan and subject to COBRA?

This will be an important issue if employers provide funds for employees to purchase policies at a state health insurance exchanges. While the policies purchased by individual employees are not necessarily ERISA plans, a program where the employer systematically pays all or a portion of the premium may become an ERISA plan. Consider whether an HRA or cafeteria plan funded at least in part by the employer that allows reimbursement for individual health insurance purchased by employees creates an ERISA plan for the policies themselves. Clearly, there is a plan as to the HRA or cafeteria plan.

As discussed in this section, there are several court decisions finding that where an employer pays for or contributes to an individual policy for one or more employees, there is an ERISA plan. There are also cases to the contrary. The employer's payment of all or part of the premiums on behalf of the employee is an important factor when courts determine whether an individual policy is part of an ERISA welfare plan.

113. How does ERISA define a group health plan? How does the IRS define a group plan?

Group Health Plan – ERISA Definitions

ERISA defines a group health plan as one "established or maintained by an employer" (rather than "of, or contributed to by, an employer").[1] Seemingly, while the HRA or 125 plan with employer funding is an ERISA plan, the individual policies purchased by employees with no employer involvement in their selection may mean that the policies themselves are not part of an ERISA plan. See *Waks v. Empire Blue Cross/Blue Shield*,[2] where the issue arose as to whether an individual policy arising out of a conversion from a group health plan is covered by ERISA preemption. There, the Ninth Circuit ruled no, that the conversion policy was not an ERISA plan, and stated:

> We conclude that claims arising under a converted individual policy are not "related to" an ERISA plan for purposes of ERISA preemption. This conclusion is consistent not only with the words but also the purposes of the statute. A converted policy is created when an ERISA plan participant leaves the plan and obtains a new, separate, individual policy based on conversion rights contained in the ERISA plan. The contract under the converted policy is directly between the insurer and insured. It is independent of the ERISA plan and does not place any burdens on the plan administrator or the plan. There are also no relevant administrative actions by the employer.

Arguably, the same analysis applies and the fact that the employer funds are in an ERISA plan does not mean that the policies purchased with those funds by employees without any employer involvement in the purchase are part of an ERISA plan. However, the conclusion is not clear. Additionally, *Brooks v. Blue Cross & Blue Shield of Florida*,[3] held that individual health insurance policies purchased through payroll deduction do not constitute a group health plan for purposes of the Medicare Secondary Payor rule, despite the fact that Medicare regulations include an "employee-pay-all plan." See Q 238 for additional information on ERISA and the ACA requirements.

Group Health Plan – Internal Revenue Code Definitions

Internal Revenue Code section 5000(b)(1) (Tax on nonconforming health plans) – "The term "group health plan" means a *plan* (including a self-insured plan) *of, or contributed to by, an employer* (including a self-employed person) or employee organization to provide health care (directly or otherwise) to the employees, former employees, the employer, others associated or formerly associated with the employer in a business relationship, or their families." Employer does not include a federal or any other government entity. Under *Fort Halifax Packing Co. v. Coyne*,[4] a plan requires a commitment to systematically pay benefits, including ongoing administrative

---

1.   29 USC §1002(1).
2.   263 F3d 872 (9th Cir. 2001).
3.   116 F.3d 1364 (11th Cir. 1997).
4.   482 U.S. 1 (1987).

responsibilities to determine eligibility and calculate benefits. It would be an unusual situation where an arrangement providing health benefits to employees will not qualify as a plan, fund, or program.

The regulations at Regulation section 1.5000A-1(d)(7) state that group health plan has the same meaning as in section 2791(a)(1) of the Public Health Service Act,[1] Regulation section 54.9831-1(a)(1) provides special rules for group health plans and defines group health plan as "a plan (including a self-insured plan) of, or contributed to by, an employer (including a self-employed person) or employee organization to provide health care (directly or otherwise) to the employees, former employees, the employer, others associated or formerly associated with the employer in a business relationship, or their families."[2]

114. What is the DOL safe harbor on ERISA plan status?

DOL regulations establish a safe harbor that provides no ERISA plan exists where several conditions are met:

(1)   The employer does not contribute any funds.

(2)   Employee participation is voluntary.

(3)   The employer does not endorse the arrangement (interpreted from employee's point of view, not that of insurance company).

(4)   The employer does nothing more than allow uninsured to publicize the arrangement to employees and to collect premiums through payroll deductions.

(5)   The employer receives no consideration beyond reasonable compensation for administrative services.[3]

In addition, ERISA does not apply to government and church plans.[4]

115. What is the three-part test to determine whether an ERISA plan exists?

Determining whether an ERISA plan exists involves a three-part test, which was established in *Thompson v. American Home Assurance Co.*[5] This case provides for a detailed analysis of whether a plan is an ERISA plan. The existence of an ERISA plan is a question of fact, to be answered in light of all the surrounding circumstances and facts from the point of view of a reasonable person.[6]

---

1.   42 U.S.C. 300gg-91(a)(1).

2.   Code sections 4980D (Tax For Failure to Meet PHSA Mandates), 4980B(g)(2) (Tax for COBRA failures), and 9832(a)(definitions) all cross reference the Code section 5000(b)(1) definition.

3.   29 CFR §2510.3-1(j). See *New England Mut. Life Ins. Co. v. Baig,* 166 F.3d 1 (1st Cir. 1999); *O'Brien v. Mutual of Omaha Ins. Co.,* 99 F.Supp. 2d 744 (E.D. La. 1999).

4.   See ERISA Secs. 4(b)(1), (3) and (32) and 4(b)(2) and 3(33), respectively.

5.   95 F.3d 429, 434-35 (6th Cir. 1996).

6.   See *Credit Managers Ass'n of So. Calif. v. Kennesaw Life and Acc. Ins. Co.,* 809 F.2d 617, 625 (9th Cir.1987), citing *Donovan v. Dillingham,* 688 F.2d 1367, 1373 (11th Cir.1982) (en banc). Accord *Gahn v. Allstate Life Ins. Co.,* 926 F.2d 1449, 1451 (5th Cir.1991); *Wickman v. Northwestern Nat'l Ins. Co.,* 908 F.2d 1077, 1082 (1st Cir.), *cert. denied,* 498 U.S. 1013 (1990).

Part I - Does a Plan Exist?

First, the court must look to see if there was a "plan" by inquiring whether "from the surrounding circumstances a reasonable person [could] ascertain the intended benefits, the class of beneficiaries, the source of financing, and procedures for receiving benefits."[1]

Part II - Does the Plan Fall Within the DOL "Safe Harbor" Provision?

Second, the court must apply the so-called "safe harbor" regulations established by the Department of Labor to determine whether the program was exempt from ERISA.[2] See Q 114.

Part III - Was the Plan Established or Maintained to Benefit Employees?

Third and finally, the court must ask whether the employer "established or maintained" the plan with the intent of providing benefits to its employees.[3]

Some courts collapse the first and third prongs of this analysis by interpreting the Department of Labor regulations as the indicia for determining whether a plan is established and maintained by the employer.[4] However, those courts agree that even if a plan is not within the safe harbor, there must be an additional finding that the employer intended to establish or maintain a plan in order to find that an ERISA plan exists.

A policy will be exempted under ERISA only if all the "safe harbor" criteria of 29 CFR 2510.3-1(j) are satisfied.[5]

Often, the third part of the test, whether the employer "endorsed the policy," is argued by insurers to establish ERISA preemption. In *Thompson*, the Sixth Circuit adopted the test set out previously by the First Circuit in *Johnson v. Watts Regulator Co.*[6] In *Johnson*, the First Circuit clarified the standards that govern a finding of endorsement, including its belief that "endorsement of a program requires more than merely recommending it."[7] According to the *Johnson* court, "[a]s long as the employer merely advises employees of the availability of group insurance, accepts payroll deductions, passes them on to the insurer, and performs other ministerial tasks that assist the insurer in publicizing the program, it will not be deemed to have endorsed the program under 29 CFR 2510.3-1(j) It is only when an employer purposes to do more, and takes substantial steps in that direction, that it offends the ideal of employer neutrality and brings ERISA into the picture."[8] The First Circuit further found that, while the

---

1. *Int'l Resources, Inc. v. New York Life Ins. Co.*, 950 F.2d 294, 297 (6th Cir.1991) (citing *Donovan*, 688 F.2d at 1373), *cert. denied*, 504 U.S. 973 (1992).
2. *Fugarino v. Hartford Life and Accident Ins. Co.*, 969 F.2d 178, 183 (6th Cir. 1992) (abrogated on other grounds in *Yates v. Hendon*, 541 U.S. 1 (2004)).
3. See *McDonald v. Provident Indem. Life Ins. Co.*, 60 F.3d 234, 236 (5th Cir.1995), *cert. denied*, 516 U.S. 1174 (1996); *Hansen v. Continental Ins. Co.*, 940 F.2d 971, 977 (5th Cir.1991).
4. See, e.g., *Gahn*, 926 F.2d at 1451.
5. *Fugarino*, 969 F.2d at 184, citing *Hansen*, 940 F.2d at 977. Accord *Grimo*, 34 F.3d at 150; *Gahn*, 926 F.2d at 1451; *Kanne v. Connecticut General Life Ins. Co.*, 867 F.2d 489, 492 (9th Cir.1988) (per curiam), *cert. denied*, 492 U.S. 906 (1989).
6. 63 F.3d 1129 (1st Cir.1995).
7. 63 F.3d at 1136.
8. *Id.* at 1133.

Hansen court had relied on the employer's intent in determining endorsement, the proper focus was on whether employees could reasonably conclude that the employer had endorsed the policy based on their observation of the employer's activities in connection with the plan.[1]

The Sixth Circuit ruled that the First Circuit's approach in *Johnson* was consistent with Congress' intent in enacting ERISA. According to the Department of Labor, "employer neutrality is the key to the rationale for not treating such a program as an employee benefit plan".[2] As Johnson noted, therefore, where the employer "offends the ideal of employer neutrality" because of its level of involvement, ERISA is properly invoked.[3] "Where, however, the employer separates itself from the program, making it reasonably clear that the program is a third party's offering, not subject to the employer's control, then the safe harbor may be accessible."[4]

Thus, the Sixth Circuit explained that the key element whether an employer endorsed a plan, is whether the employer acted neutrally. A finding of endorsement is appropriate if, upon examining all the relevant circumstances, there is some factual showing on the record of substantial employer involvement in the creation or administration of the plan.[5] For example, where the employer plays an active role in either determining which employees will be eligible for coverage or in negotiating the terms of the policy or the benefits provided thereunder, the extent of employer involvement is inconsistent with "employer neutrality" and a finding of endorsement may be appropriate.[6] Similarly, where the employer is named as the plan administrator, a finding of endorsement may be appropriate.[7]

The test of whether the employer "endorsed" the plan is not measured from the point of view of the insurance company, but from the point of view of the employee viewing the conduct of the employer.[8] In *Thompson,* the Court found that the employer did not endorse the plan. While the insurance policy here included an introductory letter encouraging employees to obtain accident insurance, that letter was not printed on Burns' letterhead, nor did it refer to the accident insurance policy as Burns' plan. Further, while Burns' name was featured on the cover of the policy description, this fact may be as consistent with identification as endorsement, depending on what the evidence on remand shows concerning the circumstances of its placement. The policy documentation nowhere mentions that the policy is subject to ERISA, nor does it set out a description of an employee's rights under ERISA. It is unclear from the record whether Burns acts as an administrator, nor is it clear whether Burns participated in either devising the terms of the policy or in processing claims, although the record does indicate that Thompson submitted her claim directly to American Home. The court finds that such evidence presents a

---

1.   63 F.3d at 1134 and 1137 n. 6.
2.   40 Fed. Reg. 34,526 (1975).
3.   63 F.3d at 1133.
4.   *Id.* at 1137.
5.   See *Hansen,* 940 F.2d at 977 (requiring "some meaningful degree of participation by the employer in the creation or administration of the plan").
6.   See, e.g., *Custer v. Pan American Life Ins. Co.,* 12 F.3d 410, 417 (4th Cir.1993) (considering, inter alia, employer's role in negotiating terms and benefits of the policy in determining whether a plan should fall out of the safe harbor); *Wickman,* 908 F.2d at 1083 (considering, inter alia, employer's role in devising eligibility requirements when determining the applicability of the safe harbor regulations).
7.   See, e.g., *Kanne,* 867 F.2d at 493; *Shiffler v. Equitable Life Assur. Soc. of U.S.,* 838 F.2d 78, 82 n. 4 (3d Cir.1988) (both considering, inter alia, the employer's role in administering the plan when determining whether to allow the policy to come under the safe harbor provision of the DOL regulation).
8.   *Johnson,* 63 F.3d at 1134 & 1137 n. 6; *Thompson,* 95 F.3d at 436-7.

material question of fact as to whether Burns endorsed the policy under the DOL regulation.[1] ("The question of endorsement *vel non* is a mixed question of fact and law. In some cases, the evidence will point unerringly in one direction so that a rational fact finder can reach but one conclusion. In those cases, endorsement is a question of law, in other cases, the legal significance of the facts is less certain and the outcome will depend on inferences that the fact finder chooses to draw. In those cases, endorsement becomes a question of fact. This case is of the latter type.")[2]

In remanding the claim, the Sixth Circuit gave specific instructions as to what factors a trial court should consider:

The district court's further consideration of this issue, whether in the context of a renewed summary judgment motion based on a more complete factual record or at trial, should take into account, but is not limited to, Burns' role in administering benefits under the plan, whether the policy language itself contemplates the application of ERISA, and Burns' role in determining eligibility and coverage. The crucial question is whether Burns was substantially involved in the creation and administration of the plan to such an extent that employees could reasonably conclude that Burns had endorsed the plan. Further, if the district court determines that the policy is not excluded from ERISA coverage under the safe harbor regulations, the court on remand must also determine that a "plan" exists under the standards set forth in *Int'l Resources, Inc.*[3] Furthermore, the district court must conclude that Burns "established or maintained" the plan with an intent to provide benefits to its employees.[4] ("In addition to some meaningful degree of participation by the employer in the creation or administration of the plan, the statute requires that the employer have had a purpose to provide health insurance, accident insurance or other specified types of benefits to its employees.[5] Thus, the evidence must show that the employer had an intent to provide its employees with a welfare benefit program through the purchase and maintenance of [the] group insurance policy.") Only upon completing a three-step factual inquiry can a district court ascertain that an ERISA plan exists, thus requiring the application of the federal common law of ERISA to the underlying insurance claim.[6]

116. What other factors have been used to determine whether a plan does fall under ERISA?

ERISA applies if the employer intends to establish or maintain a plan to provide benefits as part of the employment relationship, regardless of whether the employer intended the plan to be governed by ERISA.[7] However, as noted in the following, if there is a plan document and it says it is governed by ERISA that is a factor counting toward ERISA plan status in some court decisions.

---

1.   See *Johnson*, 63 F.3d at 1135 n. 3.

2.   See 95 F.3d at 437.

3.   950 F.2d at 297 (a "plan" exists if "from the surrounding circumstances a reasonable person [could] ascertain the intended benefits, the class of beneficiaries, the source of financing, and procedures for receiving benefits"). See also *Dist. of Columbia v. Greater Wash. Bd. of Trade*, 506 U.S. 125, 131 n. 2 (1992); *Fort Halifax Packing Co. v. Coyne*, 482 U.S. 1, 12, (1987); *Belanger v. Wyman–Gordon Co.*, 71 F.3d 451, 454 (1st Cir.1995) (all defining "plan").

4.   See *McDonald*, 60 F.3d at 236; Hansen, 940 F.2d at 977.

5.   29 USC 1002(1).

6.   95 F.3d at 437-8.

7.   *Anderson v. Unum Provident Corporation*, 369 F.3d 1257, 1262 (11th Cir. 2004).

In determining whether an ERISA "plan, fund or program" exists when individual policies are purchased, courts must "determine whether from the surrounding circumstances a reasonable person could ascertain the intended benefits, beneficiaries, source of financing, and procedures for receiving benefits." *Donovan v. Dillingham,*[1] is the seminal case followed in all circuits and holds that the purchase of a group policy or multiple individual policies covering a class of employees was substantial evidence that a plan, fund, or program had been established under ERISA if a reasonable person could ascertain the intended benefits, a class of beneficiaries, the source of financing, and procedures for receiving benefits.

Additionally, courts will look at facts surrounding:

- representations made by employers in internal documents;

- representations made orally by the employer;

- the employer's intent;

- whether a fund has been established to pay benefits;

- how any benefits are paid; and

- the employee's reasonable understanding of the program.

The courts have gone both ways on the issue of whether individual policies can constitute an ERISA plan.

117. Which courts have ruled that plans are not employee welfare benefits plans under ERISA despite employee contributions to them?

In *McCall v. Focus Worldwide Television Network Inc.,*[2] the court ruled that an employer's employment contract agreement to pay premiums for an employee's life insurance policy of $10,000 per year "funded in her name and on her behalf" was not an employee welfare benefit plan under ERISA. In *New Eng. Mut. Life Ins. Co., Inc. v. Baig,*[3] the court stated that no ERISA plan had been established from an employer's reimbursement of premiums paid directly by an employee. The policy was not initially established by a contractual arrangement between Cardiology Associates and New England Mutual, and Baig made the initial purchase and paid the premiums directly.

118. What are examples of cases with rulings that plans with employer financial involvement do fall under ERISA?

In *O'Leary v. Provident Life and Accident Ins. Co.*[4] the court reasoned that an ERISA plan existed where an employer agreed to provide disability insurance to one employee, when the employee applied for the individual policy and the employer paid the premiums. *O'Leary* noted that, while an ERISA plan can be established through the purchase of insurance, the purchase of insurance

---

1.   688 F.2d 1367 (11th Cir. 1982).
2.   2009 WL 1046791 (E.D. La. 2009).
3.   166 F.3d 1 (1st Cir. 1999).
4.   456 F. Supp. 2d 285 (D. Mass. 2006).

does not mean that an ERISA plan always exists. *O'Leary* stated that to prove an ERISA plan, the employer must have paid the premiums and intended to provide benefits on a regular and long-term basis.

Another example is *Pierson v. Cont'l Cas. Co.*[1] In this case, an ERISA plan existed where the employee was insured under two individual income protection policies issued by CNA that were individual policies not issued pursuant to a master policy and the employee paid 100 percent of the premiums for the policy. In *Peterson v. American Life & Health Ins. Co.*,[2] the court held that an individual insurance policy was part of an ERISA plan where the employer "not only paid its partners' and employees' insurance premiums but also played an active role in the administration of the coverage, including choosing the insurance, adding and deleting employees and partners from various policies, contacting insurance companies for employees and partners, and distributing information relevant to the coverage.

Other examples are:

Heidelberg v. National Foundation Life Ins. Co.,[3] in which the court held that the employer's purchase of two individual health insurance policies constituted an ERISA plan where there was evidence of employer intent to provide health insurance coverage for its white-collar employees and there was testimony that, had it been economically feasible, the employer would have purchased a group policy rather than two individual policies).

Burrill v. Leco Corp.,[4] a case in which the court ruled that several individual insurance policies purchased by the employer constituted a group health plan for COBRA purposes where such plans were "an integral part of a broader scheme to provide health coverage to LECO employees.

Strange v. Plaza Excavating, Inc.,[5] where individual health policies were provided to provide benefits on a regular and long term basis and COBRA applied.

Madonia v. Blue Cross & Blue Shield,[6] which involved an individual health insurance policy of sole shareholder who is thus not an "'employee" but nevertheless was part of an ERISA plan. The court reasoned that payment of premiums on behalf of employees is substantial evidence that a plan, fund, or program was established.

Other Examples

When the employer selects the insurance and pays the premiums, an ERISA plan almost universally is found. This is shown in *Fugarino v. Hartford Life and Acc. Ins. Co.*[7] and *Randol v. Mid-West Nat. Life Ins. Co. of Tennessee.*[8]

---

1.   2000 U.S. Dist. LEXIS 21380, 4-5 (C.D. Cal. Nov. 22, 2000).
2.   48 F.3d 404 (9th Cir. 1995).
3.   2000 WL 1693635 (E.D. La. 2000).
4.   1998 WL 34078144 (W.D. Mich. 1998).
5.   2001 WL 114407 (N.D. Ill. 2001).
6.   11 F.3d 444(4th Cir. 1993).
7.   969 F.2d 178, 183 (6th Cir. 1992) (abrogated on other grounds in *Yates v. Hendon*, 541 U.S. 1 (2004)).
8.   987 F.2d 1547, 1551-2 (11th Cir. 1993).

The court ruled in *Heral v. Unum Life Ins. Co. of Am.*,[1] that individual disability policies purchased by the employer for two or more employees was an ERISA plan, but a separate policy that the employer purchased for an owner from another insurer was not a plan. That program did not cover at least one employee.

In *Burrill v. Leco Corp.*,[2] the court held that a short-term individual health insurance policy purchased by the employer for employees before they became eligible for the employer's group health plan is an ERISA employee welfare benefit plan.

The court, in *Nicholas v. Standard Ins. Co.*,[3] ruled that ERISA applied where the insurance agent who sold the policy testified that he helped procure employee benefits for the employer, the employer was named as the plan administrator, and the documents specifically referred to ERISA.

The court, in *Libbey-Owens Ford v. Blue Cross & Blue Shield*,[4] reasoned that an employer may establish an ERISA plan very easily, through the mere purchase of a group health insurance policy – even though it does not retain control, administrative power, or responsibility for benefits. Likewise, in *Int'l Resources v. New York Life Ins. Co.*,[5] the court held that, where the employer obtained insurance coverage for employees and paid the premiums, an ERISA plan was established.

The U.S. Supreme Court Decisions on Health Reform

119. What is the impact of the U.S. Supreme Court decisions on the constitutionality of the health reform law?

There are two major cases that have *NFIB v. Sebelius* (June 28, 2012 and *King v. Burwell*, June 25, 2015.

The U.S. Supreme Court in *NFIB v. Sebelius* (June 28, 2012)[6] upheld the health reform law (PPACA), except for the federal government's power to terminate existing federal Medicaid funds for states not agreeing to participate in the law's Medicaid expansion that begins in 2014. Several decisions were five to four, with different combinations of justices for different issues. Chief Justice Roberts proved to be the critical swing vote.

The threshold issue was whether the Supreme Court could rule on the constitutionality of the individual mandate, which is effective in 2014, before any taxpayer is required to pay the tax. Beginning in 2014, individuals who fail to have minimum essential coverage will be subject to a penalty,[7] which is known as the individual mandate. The Anti-Injunction Act applies to suits "for the purpose of restraining the assessment or collection of any tax."[8] Under the Anti-Injunction Act, a court cannot rule on the validity of a tax until it has been assessed by the IRS on a taxpayer. The Supreme Court,

---

1. 2008 U.S. Dist. LEXIS 94418, 6-8 (E.D. Ark. Nov. 18, 2008).
2. 1998 U.S. Dist. LEXIS 8178 (W.D. Mich. May 11, 1998).
3. 48 Fed.Appx. 557, 564 (6th Cir. 2002).
4. 982 F.2d 1031, 1034 (6th Cir. 1993).
5. 950 F.2d 294, 297-98 (6th Cir. 1991), cert. denied, 504 U.S. 973, 119 L. Ed. 2d 565, 112 S. Ct. 2941 (1992).
6. *National Federation of Independent Business v. Sebelius*, 567 U.S. ___, 132 S. Ct. 2566, 183 L. Ed. 2d 450, 2012 U.S. LEXIS 4876, 2012 WL 2427810, 80 U.S.L.W. 4579; 2012-2 U.S. Tax Cas. (CCH) P50,423; 109 A.F.T.R.2d (RIA) 2563; 53 Employee Benefits Cas. (BNA) 1513.
7. IRC Sec. 5000A.
8. IRC Sec. 7421(a).

by a vote of nine justices to none, stated that its decision on the validity of the individual mandate was not precluded by the Anti-Injunction Act, because the law calls the mandate a penalty, not a tax.

The Court ruled, in a five to four decision, that the individual mandate is not authorized by the Constitution's Commerce Clause or the Necessary and Proper Clause, but it is valid because the federal taxing power allows it. For purposes of determining its constitutionality, the Court ruled that the individual mandate is a tax on individuals (despite being a penalty for purposes of the Anti-Injunction Act):

> Our precedent demonstrates that Congress had the power to impose the exaction in section 5000A under the taxing power, and that section 5000A need not be read to do more than impose a tax. This is sufficient to sustain it.

> The only effect of not complying with the mandate is that one must pay the tax.

Why did the Supreme Court rule that the individual mandate penalty is really a tax for this purpose? There were four reasons:

- A person who is subject to the "tax" has not violated the law.

- The "tax" is low enough so that a person can make a "reasonable financial decision" to pay the tax instead of doing whatever is being taxed. The tax is not at a "prohibitory" level.

- The "tax" is collected by the Internal Revenue Service in the same manner as other taxes.

- The individual mandate has no intent requirement. Intent ("scienter") is required for crimes or other unlawful acts.

The third issue before the Court of whether the entire law is invalid if the individual mandate is invalid became moot when the individual mandate was upheld.

Finally, while the law's Medicaid expansion was ruled constitutional by a seven to two vote, seven justices agreed that the law's sanction[1] for not participating in the Medicaid expansion is unconstitutional. The Court held that it is unconstitutional for the federal government to withhold existing Medicaid funds for noncompliance with the Medicaid expansion provisions.[2]

King v. Burwell[3] was a challenge to a key component of the Patient Protection and Affordable Care Act – tax credits.

---

1.   42 USC §1396c.
2.   Chief Justice Roberts' opinion, joined by Justices Breyer and Kagan, contains the narrowest rationale and is controlling. [When Congress threatens to terminate other grants as a means of pressuring the States to accept a Spending Clause program, the legislation runs counter to this Nation's system of federalism.] Justice Ginsburg, joined by Justice Sotomayor, upheld the expansion on a broader ground. [Construing the Commerce Clause to permit Congress to regulate individuals precisely because they are doing nothing would open a new and potentially vast domain to congressional authority.]
3.   David KING, et al., Petitioners v. Sylvia BURWELL, Secretary of Health and Human Services, et al., June 25, 2015, 135 S.Ct. 2480, 192 L.Ed.2d 483, 115 A.F.T.R.2d 2015-2203, 83 USLW 4541.

The ACA provides that individuals can purchase health insurance on exchanges that are run either the States or the federal government. The Affordable Care Act provides a federal tax credit for low-income and middle-income individuals who purchase insurance on the exchanges. The Internal Revenue Service issued a regulation that the federal tax credit is available to all financially eligible Americans, regardless of whether insurance is purchased on a state-run or federally-facilitated.

Exchange

The plaintiffs in King filed suit in the United States District Court for the Eastern District of Virginia, challenging the IRS rule on the ground that the ACA authorizes tax credits only for individuals who purchase insurance on state-established exchanges. A similar action, *Halbig v. Burwell*, was filed in the United States District Court for the District of Columbia. On January 15, 2014, the district court in *Halbig* ruled in favor of the IRS and was subsequently appealed to the United States Court of Appeals for the District of Columbia Circuit. On February 18, 2014, the district court in *King*, like the district court in Halbig, rejected the plaintiffs' arguments and granted the government's motion to dismiss the case. King was appealed to the United States Court of Appeals for the Fourth Circuit.

On July 22, 2014 the Fourth Circuit held that the IRS regulation holding that tax credits and subsidies are available to individuals purchasing health insurance through the federal as well as state exchanges was a "permissible exercise of the agency's discretion." The same day the D.C. Circuit, by a 2-1 vote, issued a contrary ruling in *Halbig*. The D.C. Circuit's opinion in Halbig was subsequently vacated when the full D.C. Circuit agreed to re-hear the case *en banc*.

On July 31, 2014, the plaintiffs in *King* filed a petition for certiorari asking the Supreme Court to hear the case. The petition was granted on November 7, 2014. In light of the Court's decision to review *King*, the D.C. Circuit issued an order holding *Halbig* in abeyance pending the Court's disposition of *King*. The Supreme Court heard oral argument on March 4, 2015.

On June 25, 2015, in a 6-3 ruling, the Court rejected the ACA's challengers' arguments. In an opinion authored by Chief Justice Roberts, the Court held that tax credits are available to individuals in states that utilize a federally-facilitated Exchange. According to Roberts, because the phrase "an Exchange stablished by the State" is ambiguous as it relates to tax credits, the Court needs to look to the broader text and structure of the Act to determine the meaning of that phrase. The Court ruled that when the text of the ACA is considered as a whole, tax credits must be available to all qualifying citizens in every state. To hold otherwise would disrupt the reforms Congress intended to foster the law's goal of affordable health care for all Americans. With this ruling, the Court affirmed that tax credits are available to eligible citizens for insurance purchased on any Exchange created under the ACA, be it state-run or federally-facilitated.

Had the Court ruled the other way, the Affordable Care Act would have been severely damaged if not left moribund.

Although not yet in front of the U.S. Supreme Court, the case of *Texas v. United States*, currently in oral argument at the Fifth Circuit Court of Appeals, has the potential of leaving the entire Affordable Care Act rendered unconstitutional. By way of background, in April 2018, Texas and nineteen other states, as well as two individual plaintiffs, filed a complaint in the U.S. District Court for the Northern District of Texas, arguing that the law's individual mandate provision (Section 5000A) was unconstitutional, and that the rest of the law is inseverable from that provision and therefore must also fall. The district court agreed with the plaintiffs, holding that the individual mandate is unconstitutional, that the mandate is inseverable from the rest of the ACA, and that the entire ACA therefore cannot stand. California and other states that had previously intervened in the case appealed to the U.S. Court of Appeals for the Fifth Circuit. Regardless of the decision at the Fifth Circuit, this case will certainly go to the U.S. Supreme Court, possibly as early as mid-2020.

120. What is the potential impact of the lawsuit filed by the group of states attorneys-general (Texas v. U.S. Dept. of HHS)?

Background

The Affordable Care Act, since its inception has faced legal and legislative challenges. One of the most significant came in 2012, with Supreme Court decision in *NFIB v. Sebelius*. Part of the ACA's operational components was the "Individual Mandate" which requires that individuals without health insurance (who could afford it) must purchase a private plan or face a financial penalty for failing to do so. In a 5-4 decision, the Court held the Individual Mandate penalty to be constitutional because it was a tax and thus not an overreach of power by Congress. Moving forward five years, as part of the Republican-led tax reform plan, the monetary penalties included in the Individual Mandate were reduced to zero effective beginning in 2019, while the mandate itself technically remains.

The Lawsuit and Rationale – "The House That Jack Built"

On February 26, 2018, twenty state attorneys-general joined a lawsuit, styled as *Texas, et. al. v. United States Department of Health and Human Services, et. al.*[1] The suit alleges that the changes made to the Affordable Care Act by Congress, namely the repeal of the Individual Mandate penalty, has caused the <u>entire</u> Affordable Care Act to become unconstitutional. The individual mandate penalty levies a penalty, (a "tax") on those who do not purchase health insurance as required by law. The position of the attorneys-general is that since the 2012 NFIB decision found the Affordable Care Act to be constitutional was predicated upon the fact that Congress has the power to levy and collect taxes, and that the penalty was in fact a tax - if there is no Individual Mandate tax penalty, the "Court should hold that the ACA is unlawful and enjoin its operation."

The Attorneys-General further reason that if the Individual Mandate was constitutional only because it contained a tax – and that tax has now been repealed, *ergo*, the remainder of the mandate is unconstitutional. The AGs go on to reason, echoing the words of the NFIB dissent, that the rest of the law could not stand because upturning the Individual Mandate would create an "inability of the other major provisions to operate as Congress intended."

---

1.   *Texas, et. al. v. United States Department of Health and Human Services, et. al.*, Case No. 4:18-cv-00167-O, United States District Court for the Northern District of Texas, filed February 26, 2018.

Removing the tax penalty from the Individual Mandate essentially invalidates the mandate, and in a "house that Jack built" argument, causes the rest of the law to tumble down like a house of cards.

Time will tell regarding the outcome of this argument. The position of the AGs is clearly not a universal one. There is a great deal of disagreement on the theory that an eviscerated Individual Mandate actually rises to the level of "unconstitutional". Additionally, it is safe to reason that even if the Individual Mandate does fail constitutional muster, it is fallacious logic on the part of the Attorneys-General to conclude that the law cannot "operate as Congress intended". It can be counter-argued that the ONLY part of the law that has actually been changed is the Individual Mandate itself. The other provisions – provisions that Congress clearly intended, such as elimination of pre-existing conditions, the ability to retain dependents on a plan until age twenty-six and other major components of the law remain unchanged and would survive the constitutional failure of the Individual Mandate.

Implications if the Suit Prevails

If the Texas lawsuit and the Attorneys-General succeeds, who will be most affected? The most likely affected include:

- Individual health insurance consumers: Approximately 20 million individuals that purchase their own insurance from the Exchanges

- Individuals with pre-existing conditions: This number is difficult to ascertain because there is no universally accepted definition of "pre-existing condition". In the past, it was not uncommon for health insurers to reject non-group applications from individuals with cancer, diabetes, heart disease and even arthritis and other conditions. The Kaiser Family Foundations estimates that 27 percent of individuals under the age of sixty-five (non-Medicare eligible) have a pre-existing condition. Most of those individuals, if working or a dependent will be covered under an employer's group policy. The remaining people could face challenges in securing insurance.

- Dependents covered under the extension of the Affordable Care Act to age twenty-six: Assessing this number is also difficult. Generally, before the ACA, dependents could stay on a policy until their 19th birthday or until age twenty-three if a full-time student. Much would depend on how policies were structured after the ACA.

Immediate changes are unlikely. Although the Trump Administration has stated that they will not oppose this lawsuit, it will likely be heard by the U.S. Supreme Court. Even though the Trump Administration is not defending the Affordable Care Act in the courts, the District Court has certified a number of Democratic state attorneys-general as well as the United States House of Representatives to intervene in the case. In the meantime, the Act stays in place. The major effect has been on premiums for 2019 and 2020. The lawsuit brings uncertainty and accountants and actuaries dislike risk. Premiums certainly could rise in light of insurers not knowing what the future will bring.

Health Reform's Medicaid Expansion

121. What is the current status of Medicaid Expansion in the fifty states?

Medicaid Expansion has not Been Fully Implemented but Continues Expansion

Some, perhaps many, states may decide not to participate in the Medicaid expansion due to political opposition to the federal health reform law or because the new federal funds provided will be 10 percent less than the extra costs to the state (which will be the case in 2020 and thereafter). In that situation, the burden for the care of those persons who would have been covered by Medicaid will be shifted from federal and state governments to free care provided by hospitals and physicians, as is now the case.

The following states have adopted the Medicaid Expansion at this time – Coverage was effective January 1, 2014 unless noted. There has been some movement – both for expansion and against – see the footnotes below for specific details.

Currently thirty-seven states have adopted the Medicaid expansion (including DC).

In the past year some of the significant developments include:

- The states of Arizona, Arkansas, Iowa, Indiana, Michigan, Montana and New Hampshire have approved Section 1115 waivers

- The District of Columbia Federal District Court has invalidated the Kentucky expansion waiver and sent it to the Department of HHS for reconsideration

- Idaho, and Nebraska, and Utah have approved ballot measures seeking to expand Medicaid to 138 percent of FPL

- Maine implemented Medicaid expansion in 2019

- Virginia began implementation

- of Medicaid expansion in January 2019 with enrollment beginning in November 2018

- Utah has passed a law in November 2018 seeking to expand Medicaid to 138 percent of FPL beginning in April 2019 and financed by the state's sales tax.

The following states have NOT adopted the Medicaid Expansion at this time:

Alabama	Oklahoma
Florida	South Carolina
Georgia	South Dakota
Kansas	Tennessee
Mississippi	Texas
Missouri	Wyoming
North Carolina	Wisconsin

122. What is the Medicaid expansion in the Affordable Care Act?

Medicaid provides healthcare and long-term care services for lower-income individuals. It is administered by the states and jointly funded by state and federal governments. The current Medicaid program offers federal funding to states to pay for healthcare for pregnant women, children, needy families, the blind, the elderly, and the disabled.[1] Many states now cover adults with children but only if their income is considerably lower than 133 percent of the Federal Poverty Level (FPL) and they meet certain asset tests. Most states do not cover childless adults at all.

Beginning in 2014, the Affordable Care Act allowed expansion of Medicaid coverage to everyone whose income is at or below 133 percent of the Federal Poverty Level (FPL).[2] If all states ultimately participate, this would add about fifteen million individuals to the Medicaid program, nearly twenty-six million by 2020.[3] For the first three years of the expansion (2014 through 2016), the federal government paid the entire extra cost of a state participating in the expansion.

For the states who have not accepted the Medicaid expansion due to political opposition to the federal health reform law or because the new federal funds for the expansion will be 10 percent less than the extra cost to the state in 2020 and thereafter, the Supreme Court decision, by making participation in the Medicaid expansion optional for each state, will remove part of the law's safety net for people in states who decide not to participate in Medicaid expansion. However, many individuals, as they do now, likely will be able to get free care from hospitals and physicians.

Other reasons that a state may not, at least initially, participate in the Medicaid expansion include:

- operational challenges that could affect their ability to meet Medicaid expansion and system development deadlines, such as time-consuming state procurement processes;

- the need to modify existing systems or develop new systems;

- coordination of multiple programs and systems; and

- resource limitations.

State eligibility determination systems must interface with a Federal Data Services Hub—an electronic service states will use to verify certain information with other federal agencies, such as an applicant's citizenship, immigration status, and income data.[4]

---

1. 42 U.S.C. §1396d(a).
2. PPACA §2001(a)(1).
3. Office of the Actuary, Centers for Medicare and Medicaid Services, U.S. Department of Health and Human Services: 2011 Actuarial Report on the Financial Outlook for Medicaid (Mar. 16, 2012).
4. GAO letter to Sen. Charles Grassley (Aug. 1, 2012) at http://gao.gov/assets/600/593210.pdf. (Last accessed July 1, 2018).

Despite the initial funding of the extra benefits at the rate of 100 percent by the federal government, participating states' costs could be increased by three aspects of Medicaid expansion:

- The administration for managing Medicaid enrollment

- The acquisition or modification of information technology systems to support Medicaid (although federal assistance is available)

- Enrolling previously eligible but not enrolled individuals in Medicaid

Another complicating factor for those in states not participating in the expansion is that most individuals with incomes less than 100 percent of the federal poverty level will not eligible in 2014 for income tax subsidies to purchase insurance at the state insurance exchanges.[1] These individuals still may end up without affordable access to insurance.

For states participating in the Medicaid expansion, states with low coverage levels and high uninsured rates will see the largest increases in coverage and federal funding.

Studies show that Medicaid expansion resulted in: [2]

- significant coverage gains and reductions in uninsured rates, both among the low-income population broadly and within specific vulnerable populations;

- increased access to health care;

- increased utilization of health care and more positive health outcomes;

- increased affordability

- reduction in uninsured rates

- reduction of uncompensated care costs; and

- either positive or neutral effects on employment.

The state exchanges will determine eligibility for Medicaid. HHS regulations implement rules on Medicaid and Children's Health Insurance Program (CHIP) eligibility, enrollment simplification, and coordination by the state exchange.[3]

---

1.   IRC Sec. 36B(c)(1)(A).
2.   Kaiser, The Effects of Medicaid Expansion on the ACA. https://www.kff.org/health-reform/state-indicator/state-activity-around-expanding-medicaid-under-the-affordable-care-.act/?currentTimeframe=0&sortModel=%7B%22colId%22:%22Location%22,%22sort%22:%22asc%22%7D Current though May 13, 2019 (Last accessed on July 1, 2019).
3.   Medicaid Program; Eligibility Changes Under the Affordable Care Act of 2010, 77 Fed. Reg. 17144 (Mar. 23, 2012).

123. Can a state later change its decision as to whether to participate in the Medicaid expansion and withdraw?

There is no clear answer to this question in the law.

The GAO has stated that in "the Supreme Court's June 28, 2012, decision that states can make their own decisions about whether to expand Medicaid, HHS reiterated that:

(1)   there is no deadline for a state to decide to undertake the expansion;

(2)   a state can receive an enhanced administrative federal match for information technology costs, even if it has not yet decided whether to expand Medicaid, as long as it is modernizing its eligibility systems; and

(3)   a state will not have to pay back the extra funding if it ultimately decides not to expand Medicaid."[1]

In addition, a spokesperson for CMS – Cindy Mann, deputy director for CMS, during the National Conference of State Legislatures in Chicago in 2012 – commented that a state could initially expand coverage and then later choose to reduce it.[2] While no further legislation has been advanced, it seems generally accepted, especially in light of the attempts to repeal the Affordable Care Act since the start of the Trump Administration that states could withdraw from the expansion if desired.[3]

Currently thirty-seven states have adopted it (including DC) and fourteen states have not.

---

1.   GAO letter to Sen. Charles Grassley (Aug. 1, 2012) at http://gao.gov/assets/600/593210.pdf. (Last accessed August 17, 2015).

2.   Governing, CMS: States Could Adopt Medicaid Expansion, then Drop It. http://www.governing.com/news/federal/gov-cms-no-deadline-for-state-decisions-on-medicaid-expansion.html August 6, 2012. (Last accessed August 16, 2016).

3.   http://www.modernhealthcare.com/article/20170504/NEWS/170509923. (Last accessed August 31, 2017).

PART II: IMPACT OF HEALTHCARE REFORM ON EMPLOYER FRINGE BENEFITS

Fringe Benefit Tax Planning

124. Why should employers verify whether they have a grandfathered health plan?

Grandfathered health plans are discussed in detail in Part VI of this book. They offer a way to avoid the health insurance nondiscrimination rules. An employer is eligible to implement a simple cafeteria plan if, during either of the preceding two years, the business employed 100 or fewer employees on average (based on business days). For a new business, eligibility is based on the number of employees the business is reasonably expected to employ on average (based on business days). Businesses maintaining a simple cafeteria plan that grow beyond 100 employees can maintain the simple arrangement until they have exceeded an average of 200 or more employees during a preceding year.

For many employers, the most important benefit is that an employer's grandfathered health insurance plan will not be subject to the new health insurance nondiscrimination rules, discussed in detail in Part VII of this book. Under these rules, if an insured plan discriminates in favor of the top 25 percent of Highly Compensated Employees (HCEs), for example, by paying more of the premiums, then there will be a $100 per day per employee penalty for the employer based on the number of Non-Highly Compensated Employees (NHCEs). For an employer with twenty-eight employees, violation of the nondiscrimination rules could result in a penalty of $766,500!

> *Example:* The employer's grandfathered plan is in effect for the entire year, and twenty-one participants are not highly compensated employees.
>
> 21 NHCEs × $100 = $2,100 penalty per day
>
> $2,100 × 365 days = $766,500

Thus, for employers that have had their plan since March 23, 2010, have made few if any changes, and provide better benefits or pay more for HCEs, a careful review of the grandfathered plan requirements should be done before any changes are made to the plan.[1]

125. Why should an eligible employer consider a SIMPLE cafeteria plan?

The SIMPLE cafeteria plan is discussed in detail in Part V of this book. The Affordable Care Act includes a provision creating "simple cafeteria plans" for small businesses beginning in 2011.

<u>Meets Nondiscrimination Requirements</u>: Simple cafeteria plans will be treated as meeting nondiscrimination requirements applicable to cafeteria plans if they meet minimum eligibility, participation, and contribution requirements. This safe harbor covers the regular cafeteria plan nondiscrimination requirement of Internal Revenue Code section 125(b) (the provision that limits benefits to key employees to 25 percent of the plan's benefits) and also the nondiscrimination

---

1.   See IRC Section 105(c).

requirements of Internal Revenue Code sections 79(d), 105(h), and 129(d), which are applicable to group term life insurance, a self-insured health or medical reimbursement plan, and dependent care assistance benefits (child care), respectively.

<u>Payroll Taxes</u>: Incentive to employers is the savings on payroll taxes.

<u>Document Costs</u>: Employers will save on plan document costs as well.

<u>Maximize Benefits For Highly Placed Employees</u>: In a company with a greater number of highly paid employees, such as a physicians' practice or a law firm, a SIMPLE Cafeteria Plan can allow key employees and executives to maximize their benefits by freeing them from discrimination testing.

One of the changes proposed in the original legislation drafted by the Small Business Council of America was not adopted. When a business wants to avoid the 25 percent concentration test and contribute for owner-employees, only a regular C corporation can do so. The provisions for simple cafeteria plans apply to "employees," but the term excludes proprietors, partners, LLC members in LLCs taxed as partnerships, and more than 2 percent shareholders in S corporations, all of whom are self-employed individuals and not employees for income tax purposes.

Simple cafeteria plans offer a work-around to the new health insurance nondiscrimination rules applicable to all employer-sponsored plans other than grandfathered plans. In addition, these plans allow shareholder-employees and other key employees to benefit under the plan and be exempt from the regular cafeteria plan rule that limits benefits for such individuals to 25 percent of the total nontaxable plan benefits (the so-called "concentration test"). Additionally, a simple cafeteria may allow key employees to have greater dependent care reimbursement than otherwise available in a regular cafeteria plan.

It would seem safe for the employer to proceed on the basis that the health insurance non-discrimination rules are met when the plan provides the same eligibility and offers the same benefit options for all participants. Even if all HCEs take family coverage (and it was available on an equal basis and equal contribution level for NHCEs) and all NHCEs took single or none, then the employer should still pass.

126. What are the limits on health FSAs in cafeteria plans (also called flex plans)?

A health FSA is a Flexible Spending Account (FSA), typically part of a cafeteria plan that reimburses participants from their pretax salary deferrals for medical and dental expenses. The deferrals are not reported as taxable income and the reimbursement is not taxable. In effect, the expenses are paid with pretax dollars.

Prior to 2013, there was no limit on such accounts except those the employer imposed on the plan. It has not been unusual for such health FSAs to be available in amounts of $5,000, $10,000, and sometimes more. The health reform law limits the annual reimbursement from health FSAs to $2,700 for 2019, indexed for inflation,[1] as a revenue raiser to help pay for the law's new costs. The details of this rule are discussed in Part VIII of this book. Figures for 2019 are not expected to be released until October or November of 2018.

Plans must be amended to provide for this new limit. The $2,700 limit does not apply to dependent care (child care) FSAs, adoption assistance FSAs, or health insurance premium conversion plan elections, where salary deferrals can be used to pay an employee's share of health insurance with pretax dollars.

127. Is a MERP, HRA, FSA, HSA, employer payment plan or cafeteria plan subject to the prohibition on annual and lifetime dollar limits or the preventive care requirements?

PHSA section 2711, effective in 2014 and discussed in Part VII, prohibits annual and lifetime dollar limits by group health plans on essential health benefits by group health plans and individual insurance policies, including grandfathered plans and policies.[2] Annual or lifetime dollar limits can be imposed on benefits that are not essential health benefits.[3] PHSA section 2713 requires that group health plans pay or reimburse preventive care with no out of pocket costs by the group health plan participant. Healthcare reform also adds new ERISA section 715 and new Internal Revenue Code section 9815, which impose the PHSA mandates not only on group health plans but also on health insurance issuers. The penalty for violating PHSA section 2711 is an excise tax under Internal Revenue Code section 4980D of $100 per day ($36,500 per year) per affected individual (per participant) for violating the Chapter 100 requirements, including Internal Revenue Code section 9815, which incorporates the PHSA mandates. The first government guidance concerned whether these plans are group health plans and whether they must comply with the no annual dollar limit rule.

<u>Group Health Plan</u>. ERISA and the PHSA define "group health plan" in virtually identical language, providing that the term means an employee welfare benefit plan to the extent that the plan provides medical care (including items and services paid for as medical care) to employees or their dependents directly or through insurance, reimbursement, or otherwise.[4] The Tax Code's definition is broader. Under the Internal Revenue Code, a group health plan is "a plan (including a self-insured plan) of, or contributed to by, an employer (including a self-employed person) or employee organization to provide health care (directly or otherwise) to the employees, former employees, the employer, others associated or formerly associated with the employer in a business relationship, or their families.[5] The Code's definition, unlike the ERISA definition, does not depend on the arrangement being an ERISA welfare benefit plan, and explicitly includes a plan contributed to by a self-employed person if there are at least two plan participants. Which includes either common law employees or self-employed individuals (partners, proprietors, 2 percent or more S corporation shareholders, etc.)

---

1.   The $2500 was increased to $2550 for 2015 and 2016.
2.   PHSA §2711(a)(1).
3.   PHSA §2711(b).
4.   ERISA Sec. 733(a)(1); PHSA §2791(a)(1). Under ERISA, group health plans are welfare benefit plans.
5.   IRC Sec. 9832(a), incorporating by reference IRC Sec. 5000(b)(1). See also Treas. Reg. §54.9831-1(a)(1) (providing a definition of "group health plan " that mirrors the statute's definition.

An HRA or MERP that is a group health plan is subject to the ninety-day waiting period maximum requirement of PHSA section 2708 beginning in 2014.

<u>HRA/MERP.</u> IRS guidance specifically confirms that, generally, health reimbursement accounts (HRAs) and their cousin, Medical Expense Reimbursement Accounts (MERPs), both of which are funded with employer contributions, are generally group health plans.[1] Group health plans generally are subject to the PHSA section 2711 prohibition on annual/lifetime dollar limits in 2014 and thereafter.[2] This means that if an employer has one without also having a major medical plan that is properly integrated with the HRA or MERP (as discussed hereafter), the employer is subject to a $100 per day per participant penalty. However, for small employers and S corporation shareholders, the IRS postponed the application of this rule until July 1, 2015.[3] However, the initial guidance indicated that five types of HRAs are exempt from PHSA and can continue in 2014 and thereafter:

- A stand-alone HRA or MERP that is limited to one participant or retiree is not subject to the PHSA section 2711 annual/lifetime dollar limit restrictions.[4] Such HRAs are not group health plans because they do not cover two or more employees.[5]

- A plan with no annual dollar limits.

- A plan is not an ERISA welfare benefit plan if it covers only individuals who own, or whose spouses own, an interest in an unincorporated business (as partner or proprietor). It is not a plan subject to federal regulation, but ERISA does apply if one or more common law employees is a participant.[6] If a corporation is wholly owned by an individual (or by an individual and his or her spouse), a plan that does not cover any other employee is also exempt from ERISA.[7] Accordingly, the incorporation of a sole proprietorship does not affect ERISA's coverage, but the incorporation of a partnership usually does because there will be shareholders who are not spouses of one another. However, these plans are rare, as there is no income tax benefit to them for the partners. In addition, while not ERISA group health care plans, they are group health plans for the Code, so in effect this exception is no exception at all.

- HRAs that are or provide for excepted benefits (vision and dental coverage) are exempt from the annual/lifetime dollar limit prohibition.[8] The regulators have con-

---

1. Rev. Rul. 2002-41; IRS Notice 2002-45.
2. IRS Notice 2013-54.
3. IRS Notice 2015-17.
4. Preamble to TD 9491, 6/22/2010.
5. PHSA section 2719(d)(6) provides "employer" has the meaning given such term under section 3(5) of the Employee Retirement Income Security Act of 1974 [29 U.S.C. 1002 (5)], except that such term shall include only employers of two or more employees. PHSA section 2719(d)(5) provides that "employee" has the meaning given such term under section 3(6) of the Employee Retirement Income Security Act of 1974 [29 U.S.C. 1002 (6)]. Additionally, 45 CFR 155.20 applies the controlled group and affiliated service group rules to these requirements.
6. 29 CFR §2510.3-3(b), (c) (1997). To trigger ERISA the program must cover a common law employee who is not an owner's spouse.
7. Id. This rule applies even if the shareholder or spouse is also a common law employee of the corporation. It does not extend to cases where the corporation is closely held but not wholly owned by an individual or a married couple.
8. To be excepted benefits, limited-scope dental or vision benefits must be provided either under a separate policy, certificate, or contract of insurance, a condition generally not met by an HRA or must satisfy the conditions necessary for the benefits to be considered "not an integral part" of the employer's other group health plan(s).

firmed that the HIPAA excepted benefits provisions apply for the PHSA mandates, including those in the PHSA itself (applicable to insurers and governmental employers) and as incorporated into ERISA and the Code.[1]

- Finally, HRAs that are integrated with other major medical coverage as part of a group health plan will not violate the annual limit rules so long as the other coverage on its own would comply "because the combined benefit satisfies the requirements."[2]

Later agency guidance[3] also explains how the ban on annual dollar limits in health plans and, in addition, the first-dollar preventive care coverage mandate applies to the following arrangements:

- HRAs that are group health plans, including those integrated with a group health plan

- Group health plans under which an employer reimburses an employee for health insurance premiums, or arrangements where the employer pays an employee's premium for an individual health policy (collectively, an employer payment plan)

- Certain FSAs

- Employee Assistance Programs (EAPs)

The guidance generally applies for plan years beginning on and after January 1, 2014.

Stand-alone HRAs/MERPs that do not satisfy the definition of "integrated" cannot continue beyond 2014 (or July 1, 2015 for employers not subject to the employer mandate and S corporations as to their shareholders) unless they cover only retirees or only one employee (an owner for this purpose is an employee), are limited to excepted benefits, or have no annual or lifetime dollar limit and cover all preventive care with no copays or deductibles (which could expose an employer to substantial, perhaps devastating, liability). The agencies have provided limited transition relief for HRAs in existence prior to January 1, 2013, for amounts accrued prior to January 1, 2014. To qualify for the transition relief, the accrued amounts must be made pursuant to a formula established prior to January 1, 2013, or, if there is no formula, must be less than the amounts accrued in 2012.[4]

The later agency guidance[5] provides two ways of integrating HRAs (including MERPs) with group health plans so that these requirements are met. Neither method requires that the HRA

---

1. Treas. Reg. §54.9831-1(c)(3)(ii); DOL Reg. §2590.732(c)(3)(ii); HHS Reg. §146.145(b)(3)(ii); . Preamble to Grandfathered Health Plan Regulations, 75 Fed. Reg. 34537, 34539 (June 17, 2010) (confirming that the exceptions in the Code and ERISA still exist, and announcing an HHS nonenforcement policy with respect to the PHSA provisions); FAQs About the Affordable Care Act Implementation Part II, Q/A-6.
2. Preamble to Interim Final Rules Relating to Preexisting Condition Exclusions, Lifetime and Annual Limits, Rescissions, and Patient Protections Under PPACA, 75 Fed. Reg. 37188, 37190 (June 28, 2010).
3. Department of Labor Technical Release 2013-03 and Internal Revenue Service Notice 2013-54.
4. See FAQs About the Affordable Care Act Implementation Part XI, Q/A-3.
5. Department of Labor Technical Release 2013-03 and Internal Revenue Service Notice 2013-54.

and associated coverage share the same plan sponsor, plan document or governing instruments, or that they file a single Form 5500.

Integration Method 1: Minimum Value Not Required

To integrate an HRA with another group health plan for both the annual dollar limit prohibition and preventive services rule, the following requirements must be satisfied:

- The employer's group health plan provides more than excepted benefits.

- The HRA participant is actually enrolled in the group health plan that is integrated with the HRA or a spouse's employer's group health plan.

- The HRA is available only to employees also enrolled in non-HRA group coverage (which might be a group health plan offered by another employer, such as a spouse's employer).

- The HRA is limited to reimbursing one or more of the following: copayments, coinsurance, deductibles and premiums under the non-HRA group coverage, as well as medical care that does not constitute essential health benefits.

- Under the HRA, employees (or former employees) may permanently opt out of and waive future reimbursements from the HRA at least annually and, upon terminating employment, either forfeit the HRA balance or opt out of and waive future HRA reimbursements. By opting out of HRA coverage, individuals may preserve their eligibility for a federal premium tax credit.

Example: Employer A sponsors a group health plan and an HRA, which meets the above conditions. Employer A employs Employee X, who enrolls in non-HRA group coverage sponsored by Employer B, his spouse's employer. Employer A and Employer B are not treated as a single employer, and Employee X informs Employer A that he is covered by Employer B's non-HRA group coverage.

When seeking reimbursement under Employer A's HRA, Employee X attests that the expense is a copayment, coinsurance, deductible or premium under Employer B's group health plan or medical care that is not an essential health benefit.

Employer A's HRA is "integrated" with Employer B's group health plan for purposes of the annual dollar limit prohibition and the preventive services requirements, so the HRA does not violate those mandates.

Integration Method 2: Minimum Value Required

An HRA that does not limit reimbursements may be integrated with a group health plan for purposes of the annual dollar limit prohibition and the preventive services requirements if the following conditions are met:

- The employer offers a group health plan that provides minimum value under the PPACA.

- The HRA participant is enrolled in a group health plan that provides minimum value, whether or not it is an employer-sponsored plan.

- The HRA is available only to employees who are enrolled in non-HRA minimum value group coverage (whether or not it is an employer-sponsored plan).

- Under the HRA, the employee (or former employee) may permanently opt out of and waive future HRA reimbursements at least annually, and, upon termination of employment, the employee may either forfeit the remaining balance or opt out of the HRA and waive future reimbursements.

Example: Employer A sponsors a group health plan that provides minimum value and also sponsors an HRA, which meets the conditions above. Employer A employs Employee X. Employee X enrolls in a non-HRA group health plan sponsored by Employer B, his spouse's employer.

Employer A and Employer B are not treated as a single employer, and Employee X attests to Employer A that he is covered by Employer B's group plan that provides minimum value coverage. Employer A's HRA is integrated with Employer B's group health plan for purposes of the annual dollar limit prohibition and the preventive services requirements.

<u>Unused HRA Amounts</u>. If the plan permits, unused HRA amounts that were credited while the HRA was integrated with other group health plan coverage may be used to reimburse medical expenses incurred even after the employee is no longer covered by the other integrated group health plan. Unless the coverage consists entirely of excepted benefits, coverage provided through an HRA constitutes an eligible employer-sponsored plan and thus minimum essential coverage under the individual mandate.

<u>Group Health Plans and Essential Health Benefits</u>. An HRA integrated with a group health plan will generally violate the prohibition on annual dollar limits if the HRA covers a category of essential health benefits not covered by the group health plan and limits the coverage to the HRA's maximum benefit. Under the minimum value required integration method, however, as long as a group health plan provides minimum value, the integrated HRA will not violate the prohibition on annual limits.

Health Savings Accounts (HSAs) are not subject to the PHSA rule prohibiting annual and lifetime dollar limits or the preventive care rules.

A health savings account (HSA) is a tax-favored individual account vehicle for paying medical expenses.[1] An HSA may be used only in conjunction with a high-deductible health plan (HDHP). An HSA may be established by an employee (with or without employer involvement), and contributions may be made by the employee, the employer, or both. The DOL has stated that HSAs are not ERISA employee welfare benefit plans even if funded by the employer.[2] Similarly, the preamble to the DOL/HHS/IRS) HIPAA portability regulations notes that "the HIPAA portability requirements generally are not relevant for purposes of HSAs."[3] Therefore, HSAs will not be group health plans for the PHSA mandate.

---

1.   IRC Sec. 213(d).
2.   DOL Field Assistance Bulletins 2004-1 and 2006-02. However, too much employer control over an HSA could make the HSA subject to ERISA. Id.
3.   69 Fed. Reg. 78719, 78734 (December 30, 2004).

<u>Health Flexible Spending Accounts</u>. Health FSAs meeting two conditions, which most of them meet, are excepted benefits and thus not required to comply with the PHSA mandates.[1] First, the maximum benefit payable under the health FSA to any participant in the class for a year cannot exceed two times the participant's salary reduction election under the health FSA for the year (or, if greater, the amount of the participant's salary reduction election for the health FSA for the year, plus $500).[2] Thus, the maximum health FSA annual benefit where the participant makes the maximum annual $2,650[3] salary reduction contribution means that the employer can contribute up to $500 per year to the health FSA.[4] IRS officials have informally indicated that for purposes of the maximum benefit condition, benefits provided during a grace period from the prior year's contributions are attributed to the prior year. Second, other nonexcepted group health plan coverage (major medical coverage) must be made available for the year to the class of participants by reason of their employment.[5] Finally, interim final regulations jointly issued by the IRS, DOL, and HHS on the annual and lifetime limits (the "joint regulations") appear to go further, exempting any plan that is a health FSA within the meaning of Code section 106(c)(2), even if it does not satisfy the two additional conditions for the HIPAA exception, so long as the amount of available reimbursement is less than 500 percent of the value of such coverage.[6]

Notwithstanding the foregoing, health FSAs cannot be used to reimburse the costs of health insurance.[7] A health FSA is a plan that reimburses medical costs that the health plan does not pay, whether due to co-pays, deductibles or otherwise. As a practical matter, beginning in 2014, an employer cannot offer a stand-alone FSA. It can only be offered to employees who are offered qualifying group medical coverage, whether or not they elect to take it.[8]

<u>Employee Assistance Plans</u>. EAPs generally are considered to provide excepted benefits as long as they do not provide significant medical or treatment benefits; thus, in most cases they do not constitute minimum essential coverage and will not need to meet the prohibition on an annual limit or preventive care requirements.

<u>Employer Payment of Individual Insurance Premiums; Employer Payment Plan</u>. Notice 2013-54 coins the term employer payment plan and states that pretax dollar reimbursement plans for individual health insurance are not permitted, commencing in 2014 (extended to July 1, 2015 for small employers not subject to the employer mandate and S corporation

---

1.   Treas. Reg. §54.9831-1(c)(3)(v); DOL Reg. §2590.732(c)(3)(v); HHS Reg. §146.145(c)(3)(v).

2.   Treas. Reg. §54.9831-1(c)(3)(v)(B); DOL Reg. §2590.732(c)(3)(v)(B); HHS Reg. §146.145(c)(3)(v)(B).

3.   As indexed for inflation, which was $2,550 beginning in 2015 and for 2017.

4.   Other examples of health FSA funding that meet the maximum benefit condition are:

  •   Any one-for-one employer match (employer $600, employee $600).
  •   Any employer contribution of $500 or less (employer $500, employee $200).

5.   Treas. Reg. §54.9831-1(c)(3)(v)(A); DOL Reg. §2590.732(c)(3)(v)(A); HHS Reg. §146.145(c)(3)(v)(A).

6.   Treas. Reg. §54.9815-2711T(a)(2)(ii); DOL Reg. §2590.715-2711(a)(2)(ii); HHS Reg. §147.126(a)(2)(ii). IRC Sec. 106(c)(2) defines the term "flexible spending arrangement" as a benefit program providing coverage under two conditions, one of which is that "the maximum amount of reimbursement which is reasonably available to a participant for such coverage is less than 500 percent of the value of such coverage."

7.   2007 Prop. Reg. §1.125-5(k)(2).

8.   IRS Notice 2013-54, Q&A-7 states: "If an employer provides a health FSA that does not qualify as excepted benefits, the health FSA generally is subject to the market reforms, including the preventive services requirements. Because a health FSA that is not excepted benefits is not integrated with a group health plan, it will fail to meet the preventive services requirements." Q&A-7 says, in effect, that a health FSA that is not an excepted benefit cannot meet the preventive care mandate because the FSA is not integrated with a group health plan.

shareholders).[1] There is no explanation as to why the tax status of the reimbursement is relevant, but perhaps it is because an after-tax reimbursement is the equivalent of a compensation increase, something that is clearly permitted to replace employer health benefits that are eliminated. There was language in Notice 2013-54 that could be interpreted to mean that after tax reimbursements for individual health insurance are permitted, but Notice 2015-17 states that such reimbursements are prohibited, whether after-tax or pretax. However, an across the board compensation increase is permitted.

Cafeteria Plans. There is no question that either employer or employee elective deferral contributions can be used to purchase or reimburse employee payments for group health insurance if the cafeteria plan requirements are met. However, while there is an argument that a cafeteria plan can be used to reimburse individual health insurance, other than exchange purchased insurance, the issue not entirely clear. Read literally the requirements indicate that it cannot be so used. As noted above, the Tax Code defines a group health plan as a plan "of, or contributed to by, an employer." Even if the premiums for individual policies are reimbursed solely by employee elective deferrals, for tax purposes, they are employer contributions and are used to reimburse health insurance costs and thus are a group health plan. An argument, based on statutory interpretation, can be made that elective deferrals can be used to pay for individual nonexchange purchased policies because healthcare reform amended section 125 of the Internal Revenue Code to prohibit the use of cafeteria plans to fund individual, exchange-based coverage. This suggests that purchases of individual insurance policies is otherwise permitted through a cafeteria plan. If it was impermissible to pay for such individual policies through a cafeteria plan, there would be no need to amend section 125 for individual, exchange-based policies. Healthcare reform amends section 125 of the Internal Revenue Code to provide that insurance purchased through a state exchange may not be funded through a cafeteria plan unless the individual's employer is eligible to participate in the SHOP exchange and elects to make group coverage available to employees through the exchange. An employer is exchange-eligible if it averages fewer than 100 full-time employees during the year, or fewer than fifty full-time employees at the state's election.[2] Nevertheless, if the cafeteria plan is found to be a "group health plan" because it reimburses health insurance, it will fail both the preventive care and annual limit prohibition rules even if, illogical as it may be, the plan funds are used to purchase insurance that does comply.

128. Are strategies promoting employers reimbursing employees for the purchase of individual health insurance approved by the IRS?

No. As discussed above, in IRS Notice 2013-54 and confirmed in May 2014[3] and IRS Notice 2015-17, the Internal Revenue Service issued a warning that employer health reimbursement arrangements that attempt to reimburse employees for the purchase of individual health insurance with "pretax dollars," i.e., payments deductible to the employer and nontaxable to the

---

1.   IRS Notice 2015-17.
2.   PPACA §1515; IRC Sec. 125(f)(3).
3.   Employer Health Care Arrangements at https://www.irs.gov/affordable-care-act/employer-health-care-arrangements, Current through June 20, 2018 (Last accessed July 30, 2019).

employee are not permitted. Nevertheless, it has been reported that several organizations are promoting such employer pretax health insurance reimbursement plans.[1]

The IRS has reaffirmed the guidance of Notice 2013-54:

"Under IRS Notice 2013-54, such arrangements are described as employer payment plans. An employer payment plan, as the term is used in this notice, generally does not include an arrangement under which an employee may have an after-tax amount applied toward health coverage or take that amount in cash compensation. As explained in Notice 2013-54, these employer payment plans are considered to be group health plans subject to the market reforms, including the prohibition on annual limits for essential health benefits and the requirement to provide certain preventive care without cost sharing. Notice 2013-54 clarifies that such arrangements cannot be integrated with individual policies to satisfy the market reforms. Consequently, such an arrangement fails to satisfy the market reforms and may be subject to a $100/day excise tax per applicable employee (which is $36,500 per year, per employee) under section 4980D of the Internal Revenue Code."[2]

The issue involves the healthcare law requirement effective in 2014 that there be no annual dollar limits[3] on the coverage for a person's basic medical needs, which the law calls essential health benefits. As noted above, the IRS clearly has stated that a plan reimbursing employees on a pretax basis for insurance they buy on their own cannot comply with this ACA prohibition on annual limits because the company's contribution is by definition limited, even if the health insurance the employee purchases has no annual limits. This rule was postponed until July 1, 2015 for small employers not subject to the employer mandate and S corporation shareholders.[4] Second, the technical argument that insurance premiums are not Essential Health Benefits ("EHBs") and therefore are not subject to the annual limit rule only addresses one issue. These pretax reimbursement plans also violate the preventive care mandate (the obligation to provide unlimited, no-cost coverage for specified preventive-care benefits),[5] which mandate does not depend on whether the plan otherwise covers EHBs. The penalty for violating either the no annual limit or preventive care rule is $36,500 per participant per year,[6] not to exceed $500,000 per year or, if less, 10 percent of the cost of the employer's group health plan for the year if the employer can demonstrate that noncompliance was due to reasonable cause.[7]

---

1.   "Taking a Chance on a Health Insurance Strategy the I.R.S. May Not Approve" at http://www.nytimes.com/2014/06/05/business/smallbusiness/taking-a-chance-on-a-health-insurance-strategy-the-irs-may-not-approve.html?emc=edit_sb_20140604&nl=business&nlid=4896825&_r=0. (Last accessed July 30, 2019).

2.   Employer Health Care Arrangements at https://www.irs.gov/affordable-care-act/employer-health-care-arrangements, Current through June 20, 2018 (Last accessed July 30, 2019).

3.   PHSA §2711.

4.   IRS Notice 2015-17.

5.   PHSA §2713.

6.   IRC Sec. 4980D(b)(1).

7.   IRC Sec. 4980D(c)(3(A).

129. Are executive physical and executive diagnostic reimbursement plans still available under Healthcare reform?

Internal Revenue Notice 2013-54 does not alter Revenue Ruling 61-146, which allows the income tax-free payment of medical expenses to employees with employer deductible dollars. Additionally, the logic of Notice 2013-54 is helpful because it provides that Employee Assistance Plans are not subject to healthcare reform as long as they do not provide significant benefits in the nature of medical care or treatment. Excluding executive diagnostic and physical programs from healthcare reform requirements is therefore consistent with the treatment of EAPs under Notice 2013-54.

So-called executive diagnostic reimbursement plans have existed for decades under the tax law and provide employers with the ability to reimburse employees for expenses not paid by their health plans. However, such plans, even if in place on March 23, 2010, and grandfathered from certain healthcare reform requirements, must still comply with certain healthcare reforms. Newer plans that are not grandfathered must comply with more reforms or face a fine of $36,500 per year per participant. All such plans, including grandfather plans, must cover preventive care without any deductible or annual or lifetime limit. Thus, grandfathered executive reimbursement plans should be amended to so provide.

Preventive care must be offered without charge and without dollar limit and is defined as care provided to a person when healthy, such as routine physicals, check-ups, screenings, and immunizations. Certain so-called self-funded "executive medical reimbursement plans" can be offered by employers on a discriminatory basis. While the tax regulations regarding permissible discriminatory employer medical reimbursement plans use the term "diagnostic reimbursement plans", they actually describe preventative care, not diagnostic care, as those terms are defined by healthcare reform. It is not totally free from doubt whether covering all of the items required by PHSA section 2713 would fall within the definition of a "plan for medical diagnostic procedures" under IRS regulation section 1.105-11(g)(1) for these plans. However, that regulation describes the same things as what healthcare reform describes as preventive care but not diagnostic care. Preventive care is not for treatment, cure, diagnosis, or testing of a known condition, complaint, or symptom, but preventive care is medical care under Internal Revenue Code section 213, as opposed to items merely beneficial to general health.

A discriminatory executive reimbursement plan intended to provide pretax dollar benefits (deductible to the employer and not taxed to the employee) is limited solely to employees and cannot include dependents or spouses. This benefit is deductible to the employer and not taxed to the employee under the regular tax rules governing employer paid health plans. However, it is available solely for "employees" under the tax law. Thus, it is available to employees who are not owners or owners who are shareholders and employees of a regular "C" corporation but not partners, proprietors, more than 2 percent S corporation shareholders, or other self-employed individuals.

The prohibition of an annual dollar-limit on essential benefits and the requirement to cover preventive care without cost sharing affects arrangements that constitute "group health plans" and do not apply to "excepted benefits." A discriminatory preventive care reimbursement plan would be a group health plan and not an excepted benefit. Thus, it is subject to the expanded healthcare reform requirements, including the claims procedures requirements. It would need annually to distribute a summary of benefits and coverage. It cannot be limited to physicals but must cover all preventive care services because it would be subject to the no annual dollar limit requirement. From a drafting perspective, the plan should state that it is not limited to the procedures specifically described in Regulation section 1.105-11(g) but covers all PHSA preventive care requirements. Notice 2013-54 states that if a group health plan is not an excepted benefit, then it is required to comply with all the PHSA mandates. Failure to do so exposes the employer to the $100/day/participant excise tax.

Seemingly, but again not completely free from doubt, the executive reimbursement plan is not subject to the tax rules governing HRAs, i.e., self-insured health reimbursement accounts, also called medical expense reimbursement plans. While an HRA cannot be available to employees unless they are covered by the employer or spouse's comprehensive medical plan, it would seem that the so-called diagnostic reimbursement plan under Regulation section 1.105-11(g) could be offered on a stand-alone basis because it is not an HRA. Unlike the normal HRA, there is no account for an employee or maximum annual dollar limit because the preventive care benefit cannot have an annual dollar limit.

The so-called discriminatory executive reimbursement plan does not cause an employer's high deductible health plan to cease to be a high deductible plan, which is a requirement for maintaining a health savings account. There is a specific exception in the Tax Code's definition of a high deductible plan for preventive care services. Additionally, Notice 2013-57 provides that the preventive care required under PHSA section 2713 without any deductible does not cause a plan to fail to be an HDHP. While this type of a plan is an employer funded stand-alone plan, and not part of a HDHP), the same rationale of Notice 2013-57 applies.

<u>Preventive Care, Diagnosis & Treatment</u>. Under healthcare reform, diagnosis and treatment are different from preventive care and need not be provided free of charge. They involve testing or treatment for a symptom or health issue, such as an existing illness or injury. Services are diagnostic care when:

- services are ordered due to current issues or symptoms(s) that require further diagnosis;

- abnormal test results on a previous preventive or diagnostic screening test requires further diagnostic testing or services;

- abnormal test results found on a previous preventive or diagnostic service requires the same test be repeated sooner than the normal age and gender guideline recommendations would require.

If preventive care is offered free of charge by in-network providers, cost sharing can be imposed if the participant elects more expensive in-network options, or seeks services which are out of network.

Preventive services and tests are as follows:

<u>Adults and Children</u>

- Routine physical examinations

- Alcohol misuse screening and counseling (primary care visits only, beginning at age eleven)

- Cholesterol screening

- Depression screening (adults, children ages twelve-eighteen, primary care visits only)

- Diet behavioral counseling (included as part of annual visit and intensive counseling by primary care clinicians or by nutritionists and dieticians)

- Hemoglobin A1c

- Hepatitis B testing

- Immunizations, including flu shots (flu shots at age nineteen and above at a doctor's office or pharmacy; under age nineteen at a doctor's office)

- Obesity screening and counseling (adults and children, in primary care settings)

- Sexually transmitted diseases (STDs) – screenings and counseling (adolescents, adults, and pregnant women)

- Tobacco use screening and counseling, including smoking cessation counseling and FDA-approved nicotine replacement therapy (primary care visits only)

- Total cholesterol tests

<u>Adults Only</u>

- Aspirin for the prevention of heart disease when prescribed by a health care provider

- Blood pressure screening (adults without known hypertension)

- Colorectal cancer screening, including colonoscopy, sigmoidoscopy, and fecal occult blood test

- Diabetes screenings

- HIV screening and counseling

- Vitamin D supplements for the prevention of falls when prescribed by a health care provider to community-dwelling members beginning at age sixty-five

<u>Women Only</u>

- BRCA 1 or 2 genetic counseling, evaluation and testing for women with a family history associated with increased risk of mutation

- Breast cancer chemoprevention (counseling only for women at high risk for breast cancer and low risk for adverse effects of chemoprevention)

- Breast cancer screening, including mammograms and counseling for genetic susceptibility screening

- Breastfeeding primary care interventions (applicable to pregnant women and new mothers), including electric and manual breast pumps, lactation classes and support at prenatal and post-partum visits, and newborn visits

- Cervical cancer screening, including pap smears

- Comprehensive lactation support, counseling, and costs of renting breastfeeding equipment

- Contraceptive methods approved by the FDA, sterilization procedures and contraceptive patient education and counseling (contraceptives covered with no member cost sharing include generics and brand name drugs with no generic alternative, including emergency contraceptives.)

- Folic acid supplements (women planning or capable of pregnancy only)

- Gestational diabetes screening

- HPV (human papillomavirus) testing

- Interpersonal and domestic violence counseling and screenings

- Iron deficiency anemia (pregnant women at prenatal visits)

- Microalbuminuria test (pregnant women)

- Osteoporosis screening (screening to begin at age fifty for women at increased risk)

- Ovarian cancer susceptibility screening

- Over the counter contraceptive items such as sponges and spermicides, when prescribed by a health care provider

- Rh (D) incompatibility, screening (pregnant women)

- Routine OB/GYN examinations

- Routine outpatient prenatal and postpartum visits

<u>Children Only</u>

- Autism screening (for children between eighteen and twenty-four months of age; primary care settings)

- Behavioral assessments (children of all ages; developmental surveillance, in primary care settings)

- Congenital hypothyroidism (screening for newborns only)

- Dental prevention – oral fluoride (for children to age five only) Note: Coverage for fluoride is only provided if your plan includes outpatient pharmacy coverage

- Dyslipidemia screening (for children at high risk for higher lipid levels)

- Hearing screening (screening for newborn only, primary care settings)

- Iron deficiency prevention (primary care counseling for children ages six to twelve months only)

- Lead screening (children at risk)

- Phenylketonuria screening (newborns before seven days old)

- Sickle cell disease, screening (screening at birth and first newborn visit)

- Tuberculosis skin testing

- Vision screening (children to age five only)

<u>Men Only</u>

- Abdominal aortic aneurysm screening (for males sixty-five to seventy-five one time only, if a history of smoking)

130. Will student health insurance payments or reimbursement by the educational institution violate IRS Notice 2013-54 and IRS Notice 2016-17 regarding impermissible payments for individual health insurance?

Yes, if paid for a student that is also an:

(1)   employee of the educational institution; and

(2)   if paid to the student in the student's capacity of employment. Student health insurance coverage is defined by HHS as a type of individual health insurance coverage.[1]

---

1.   45 CFR §147.145.

Notice 2013-54 prohibits an educational institution from paying all or part of student health insurance premiums on behalf of its employees; however, subsidies provided to non-employees are not prohibited.

If a graduate student's financial aid package includes loans, scholarships, a paid graduate assistantship, and a subsidy to help pay the student health insurance premiums, the student is both an employee (paid graduate assistantship) and a student.

On February 5, 2016, the Internal Revenue Service issued Notice 2016-17 which provides temporary transition relief for employers that offer premium reduction arrangements in connection with student health coverage. These "Premium reduction arrangements" are arrangements designed to reduce the cost of student health insurance to students through a credit, offset, reimbursement, stipend, or similar arrangement. Colleges and universities tend to use these types of arrangements to pay for some or all of the cost of student health coverage for their graduate students. Notice 2016-17 states that the IRS, the Department of Labor, and the Department of Health and Human Services will not assert that these premium reduction arrangements fail to satisfy the requirements of the Affordable Care Act for plan years or policy years that begin before January 1, 2017.

Notice 2016-17 is intended as a supplement to Notice 2013-54 and Notice 2015-17 which deal with the effect of the ACA on employer payment plans. An "employer payment plan" is an arrangement where an employer either reimburses its employees or directly pays on behalf of its employees, on a pretax or post-tax basis, some or all of the cost of purchasing individual insurance coverage.

Notice 2013-54 stated that employer payment plans are group health plans which are subject to the ACA, including the prohibition on annual dollar limits on essential health benefits. An employer payment plan cannot be integrated with individual insurance coverage in order to satisfy the ACA group market reforms. Notice 2013-54 was effective for policy years after January 1, 2014. An employer sponsoring an employer payment plan after that date can be subject to a potential excise tax of $100 a day for each affected employee. Notice 2016-17 is recognition that institutions may not have realized that Notice 2013-54 viewed premium reduction arrangements as impermissible employer payment plans. Notice 2016-17 is intended to give institutions additional time to determine whether their arrangements comply with Notice 2013-54, and to make alternative arrangements where needed. During this time, enforcement action will not be taken against premium reduction arrangements offered in connection with student health coverage for plan or policy years that began before January 1, 2017.

The clean solution is the payment award of taxable cash. Student workers can always be given a taxable cash stipend that is not conditioned on the purchase of health insurance.[1] The cash payment may be the best solution for many schools because student health insurance coverage will not help the educational institution meet the employer mandate.

---

1.   See IRS Notice 2015-17.

131. Can an employer with employees in different states with different employer health insurance plans in each state integrate these plans with an employer funded Health Reimbursement Account (HRA)?

Assume that an employer has in-state employees and will soon have one out-of-state employee in Hawaii. The local medical insurance provider cannot cover this employee as it does not sell health insurance in Hawaii. The employee and employer have identified reasonable-cost coverage for the employee in Hawaii, offered by the Hawaii Medical Service Association. It is a small business plan for companies with less than fifty employees.

Can this employee and dependents be covered by the employer's HRA or Medical Expense Reimbursement Plan (MERP) with annual dollar limits via integration with the Hawaii insurance plan?

Assume further that this employee will be the only employee of the employer covered by the Hawaii insurance plan. Question 4 and the answer found in IRS Notice 2013-54 states that the employer's HRA can be continued with the annual limit on benefits under PHSA section 2711 as long as the HRA is integrated with a "group health plan" and is not integrated "with individual policies" or with "individual market coverage."[1]

Assuming the HRA is properly integrated with both insured health plans, this arrangement should be acceptable because it is part of an employer's group plan with two sources for the employees' medical insurance coverage.

132. Can a HSA be combined with exchange-purchased High Deductible Health Insurance Plans (HDHP)?

Yes. A tax-deductible HSA may be established by an employer for an "eligible individual" who, for any month:

(1)   Is covered under a High-Deductible Health Plan (HDHP) on the first day of the month;

(2)   Is not also covered by any other non-HDHP health plan (with certain exceptions), including an FSA (except for dental. vision, preventive care, and general medical benefits only after the HDHP deductible is reached);

(3)   Is not entitled to benefits under Medicare (has not yet reached age sixty-five); and

(4)   Is not claimed as a dependent on another person's tax return.

IRS Notice 2013-54 prohibits pretax employer dollar payments to be integrated with exchange purchased insurance. HRAs and MERPs (employer funded cash medical reimbursement) thus violate the rule prohibiting annual dollar limits (with an annual per participant penalty of

---

1.   IRS Notice 2013-54.

$36,500) unless employees are not limited to the annual or lifetime reimbursement they may claim from the employer under the employer's plan, a risk most employers will not want to take.

Fortunately, neither Health Savings Accounts (HSAs) nor most Health Flexible Spending Accounts (Health FSAs), which cover medical reimbursement as part of a cafeteria or flex plan, are subject to the healthcare reform PHSA rule prohibiting annual nor lifetime dollar limits. An employer could therefore contribute to an HSA for those employees who have a high deductible plan for the month of the employer contribution. Those eligible for an exchange purchased insurance subsidy will want to purchase their health insurance on an exchange. The question is whether one can get a high deductible plan on an exchange which will be an exchange-by-exchange determination. For anyone under age thirty, they can buy a "young invincible" catastrophic policy, which will likely not meet the high deductible definition because maximum out-of-pocket costs to qualify for an HSA cannot exceed stated amounts.

Anecdotal evidence suggests that the cost-sharing features of many exchange offered QHPs would allow them to qualify as HSA-eligible High Deductible Health Plans. For example, there are platinum plans on the Kansas exchange with $1,500 individual deductibles, and the deductibles generally go higher in the gold, silver and bronze plans. Notice 2013-57 confirms that first-dollar preventive care under PHSA section 2713 won't cause a plan to fail to be an HDHP. Thus, many exchange QHPs would be HSA-qualified.

There is nothing at the present moment that suggests that employers who provide HSA contributions for employees directly or through a cafeteria plan would be treated as providing coverage under an eligible employer-sponsored plan which would in turn render the employees ineligible for the Internal Revenue Code section 36B tax credit.

Two features of HDHPs that will be applied to all insurance plans include:

(1)   first-dollar coverage of preventive care (no copays or deductibles can apply); and

(2)   Annual limits on out-of-pocket expenses.

These two features have been a part of the HSA design since their inception. The most significant change brought by the ACA requires all insurance plan designs to cover, on average, 60 percent of the cost of benefits covered by the plan. Fortunately, even the highest deductible HSA-qualified plans can meet this standard. This means that HSA plans may be offered in each state health insurance exchange.

Of course, individuals can purchase high deductible health insurance on the individual market and not through an exchange, but if they do so they cannot qualify for a subsidy.

An additional and more worrisome concern with High Deductible Health Plans on the marketplace is what the effect of the "Cadillac Tax" will be on their viability — assuming that the Cadillac Tax ever takes effect. At this point, the Cadillac Tax will not activate until at least 2022 if ever — as there are currently bills proposed for the complete repeal.

133. Must preventive services be provided by nongrandfathered HSA-eligible HDHPs?

IRS Notice 2013-57 states that High-Deductible Health Plans (HDHPs) eligible to be linked with Health Savings Accounts (HSAs) must cover all preventive services mandated under health-care reform without imposing a deductible. Grandfathered HDHPs may elect to do the same.

Notice 2013-57 clarifies that, for purposes of the HDHP/HSA rules, preventive care not subject to deductibles may include all preventive services and benefits previously defined by the IRS as well as those required under the PPACA and will not jeopardize the HDHP's health savings account (HSA) qualified status.

For HSA contributions to be tax favored, the employee must be covered under an HSA-qualifying HDHP and generally may not have other health coverage, although there are exceptions, such as stand-alone vision, dental, and long-term care coverage. For 2018 and 2019, annual deductibles in HSA-eligible HDHPs must be at least $1,350 for self-only coverage or $2,700 for family coverage Also, first-dollar and low-deductible coverage is allowed for preventive care. For 2019, the HDHP Out of pocket maximums are $6,750 for self-only HDHP coverage (an increase of $100 from 2018) and $13,500 for family HDHP coverage (an increase of $200 from 2018).[1]

The IRS considers some drugs and medications as excepted preventive care, and health care reform added others. IRS Notice 2004-23 lists the types of preventive care that need not be subject to the high deductible. Its nonexclusive list of safe-harbor preventive care services includes things not intended to treat an existing illness, injury, or condition:

- Periodic health evaluations, including tests and diagnostic procedures ordered in conjunction with a routine exam, such as an annual physical.

- Routine prenatal and well-child care.

- Child and adult immunizations.

- Tobacco-cessation programs, including prescription drugs.

- Obesity weight-loss programs, including prescription drugs.

- Screening services, such as for cancer, heart and vascular diseases, infectious diseases, mental health conditions and substance abuse, metabolic/nutritional/endocrine conditions, musculoskeletal disorders, obstetric/gynecological conditions, pediatric conditions, and vision and hearing disorders.

All nongrandfathered group health plans, including HDHPs, must provide in-network coverage for mandated PPACA preventive services without participant cost sharing, namely:

- evidence-based items or services that are rated "A" or "B" by the U.S. Preventive Services Task Force;

---

1.   Revenue Procedure 2018-30.

- routine immunizations recommended by the Advisory Committee on Immunization Practices of the Centers for Disease Control and Prevention;

- for infants, children and adolescents, evidence-informed preventive care and screenings in the comprehensive guidelines supported by the Health Resources and Services Administration (HRSA);

- for women, preventive care and screenings provided in HRSA's Women's Preventive Services.

134. May an employer reimburse the cost of Medigap insurance for those employees enrolled in Medicare?

No, if the employer has twenty or more participants in its health plan, it may not offer an economic incentive for employees to drop out of the health plan and elect to be covered by Medicare.[1] Further, such an employer cannot exclude those eligible for Medicare from its group health plan.[2]

If the employer has fewer than twenty participants in its health plan, that reimbursement would not be a group health plan and thus is an excepted benefit.

135. Are there any differences in treatment of same-sex spouses in regard to HSAs, cafeteria plans, health FSAs and DCAPs?

No. By way of historical background, IRS Notice 2014-1 provided guidance as a result of the U.S. Supreme Court's *Windsor* decision for same-sex spouse benefits and addresses issues arising under cafeteria plans, health FSAs, DCAPs, and HSAs. With the advent of the landmark decision of *Obergefell v. Hodges* which extended the right to marry to same-sex couples in ALL states – and by virtue of that decision, simplifies and equalizes the rules relating to married couples. The *Obergefell* decision decided that a spouse is a spouse, regardless of gender.

Health Insurance. It must be remembered that neither IRS Notice 2014-1 nor the *Obergefell* decision changed the Affordable Care Act regarding providing health care to spouses – that is, there is no requirement to provide employee spousal benefits. However, *Obergefell* mandates that if an employer chooses to insure the spouses of employees, they cannot choose WHICH spouses to insure. The exclusion of spouses from favorable benefits by virtue of gender is a violation of the 14th Amendment of the United States Constitution.

HSA Limits. Same-sex married couples are subject to the joint deduction limit for HSA contributions ($7,000 in 2019 if either spouse has family HDHP coverage). If the spouses previously elected to make contributions to separate HSAs that will exceed the joint limit, contributions may be reduced as necessary for the remainder of the year. Any excess contributions may be

---

1. If an employer offers a Medicare beneficiary an incentive, financial or otherwise, not to enroll in the plan, the group health plan is subject to a civil money penalty of up to $5,000 for each violation. In addition, an excise tax could be applied that would equal 25 percent of the plan's expenses incurred during the calendar year. 42 USC §1395y (3)(C).
2. 42 USC §1395y (b)(1)(A)(1).

distributed from the HSAs no later than the spouses' tax return due date. Excess contributions not distributed by that date will be subject to excise taxes.

<u>Cafeteria Plan Election Changes</u>. Cafeteria plan election change rules allow participants to change plan elections midyear—e.g., to add health coverage for a spouse—if specified events occur, and if the change is consistent with the event. This election change guidance appears to apply to all cafeteria plan benefits, including health FSAs and DCAPs, so long as the consistency rules are met.

- *Change in marital status.* The guidance allows participants who were married to a same-sex spouse on June 26, 2013, (the date of the *Windsor* decision) to be treated as if they experienced a change in legal marital status for purposes of the cafeteria plan election change rules. Employees wishing to make election changes due to *Windsor* may do so at any time during the cafeteria plan year that includes either June 26, 2013, or December 16, 2013. Participants marrying a same-sex spouse after June 26, 2013, may also make election changes due to a change in marital status.

- *Significant change in cost of coverage.* According to the guidance, a change in a cafeteria plan benefit's tax treatment generally does not constitute a significant change in the cost of coverage (and thus would not ordinarily be a proper basis for allowing an election change with respect to a same-sex spouse). However, given the legal uncertainty created by the *Windsor* decision, plans will not be treated as having failed to comply with the election change rules solely because they permitted midyear election changes on this basis between June 26 and December 31, 2013.

- *Effective date.* Election changes made under a cafeteria plan because of *Windsor* generally take effect when other changes become effective under the plan. However, for *Windsor*-related elections made between June 26 and December 16, 2013, a plan may provide that the change becomes effective no later than the later of (1) the date that the change would become effective under the plan's usual procedures, or (2) a reasonable period of time after December 16, 2013.

- *FSA reimbursements.* Participants in health FSAs, DCAPs, or adoption assistance FSAs may be reimbursed for a same-sex spouse's covered expenses that were incurred on or after the first day of the plan year that includes June 26, 2013, or, if later, the date of marriage. The guidance does not apply to 2012 or earlier years. Same-sex spouses may be treated as covered even if the employee initially elected self-only coverage.

- *Pre-tax health coverage.* Employers receiving notice of the existence of a same-sex marriage before the end of the plan year that includes December 16, 2013, must begin treating amounts paid for spousal coverage as pre-tax salary reductions by the date that a change in marital status is required to be reflected for federal tax withholding purposes following the filing of IRS Form W-4, or, if later, a reasonable period of time after December 16, 2013. Employee payments for spousal coverage are excluded from the employee's gross income even if the employer reports the amount as taxable income, and participants may seek a refund of any related federal income and employment taxes on their tax return.

- *DCAP limits.* Same-sex spouses are subject to the DCAP exclusion limits for married couples ($5,000 for married couples filing jointly and $2,500 for married individuals filing separately). If the combined DCAP contributions previously elected by the spouses will exceed the applicable limit for the year, contributions for one or both spouses may be reduced for the rest of the tax year so that the limit will not be exceeded. Calendar-year plans are unlikely to be able to make adjustments so late in the plan year. If adjustments are not made, same-sex couples must treat any reimbursements in excess of the applicable limit as taxable income on their tax returns.

- *Plan amendments.* Cafeteria plans that permit election changes due to changes in legal marital status need not be amended to permit *Windsor*-related election changes. However, if an employer chooses to permit election changes not already provided for in the written plan document, **the plan must be amended to permit the changes by the end of the first plan year beginning on or after December 16, 2013.** The amendment may be effective retroactively to the first day of the plan year that includes December 16, 2013, so long as the plan operates in accordance with the guidance.

- Family and Medical Leave Act (FMLA). The Family and Medical Leave Act (FMLA) requires covered employers to provide up to twelve weeks of unpaid, job-protected leave per year for employees who are dealing with their own serious health condition or that of a close family member (including a spouse). These benefits, along with leave for a spouse's military service, are now inclusive of same-sex spouses. (This is not a ruling from the Notice but from the *Obergerfell* case).

- COBRA. All employees and their legally married spouses are eligible to continue their health coverage at group rates for up to thirty-six months. (This is not a ruling from the Notice but from the *Obergerfell* case).

Employers and administrators should quickly communicate relevant information to participants and to those responsible for day-to-day plan operations. For example, this could include informing participants of their ability to submit spousal expenses for health FSA reimbursement, health insurance reimbursement, and making human resources staff aware of any changes affecting Form W-2.

See also Q 58, Q 127 to Q 140, and Q 622 to Q 624.

136. Are third-party payors permitted to make premium payments to health insurance issuers for Qualified Health Plans on behalf of enrolled individuals?

Yes. The Department of Health and Human Services (HHS) has broad authority to regulate the Federal and State Marketplaces (e.g., section 1321(a) of the Affordable Care Act). Although

HHS had concerns about this practice skewing the insurance risk pool and creating an unlevel playing field, the following guidance has been issued:

1.   §156.1250 Acceptance of certain third-party payments.

2.   Issuers offering individual market QHPs, including stand-alone dental plans, and their downstream entities, must accept premium and cost-sharing payments for the QHPs from the following third-party entities from plan enrollees (in the case of a downstream entity, to the extent the entity routinely collects premiums or cost sharing):

   (a) A Ryan White HIV/AIDS Program under title XXVI of the Public Health Service Act;

   (b) An Indian tribe, tribal organization, or urban Indian organization; and

   (c) A local, State, or Federal government program, including a grantee directed by a government program to make payments on its behalf.[1]

137. Could cafeteria plan elections to purchase health insurance be changed midyear to purchase insurance on an exchange or in the employer-offered plan?

Yes, if the plan is amended, despite the fact that this is not a change in status, which is a normal prerequisite to change a cafeteria plan election.

Employees may want to terminate their election to purchase health insurance through the employer's cafeteria plan and go to the exchange if they are eligible for health insurance exchange tax credits. Other employees may want to elect to purchase health insurance from the employer plan effective January 1, 2014, to avoid the individual mandate penalty. If the cafeteria plan year is a fiscal year, employees wanting exchange insurance on January 1, 2014, would have to terminate or change their elections midyear. However, under current cafeteria plan regulations, these two elections are not a change in status allowing an election change midyear.

The regulations allow an Applicable Large Employer with a fiscal year cafeteria plan, at its election, to amend the plan any time during the year on a retroactive basis to permit either or both of the following changes in salary reduction elections:[2]

   (1)   An employee who elected to salary reduce through the fiscal year cafeteria plan for accident and health plan coverage is allowed to prospectively revoke or change his or her election with respect to the accident and health plan once, during that plan year, without regard to whether the employee experienced a change in status event described in Regulation section 1.125-4.

---

1.   45 C,F,R, Section 156.1250, Acceptance of certain third-party payments, effective March 8. 2016.
2.   Preamble to Proposed Rules on Shared Responsibility for Employers Regarding Health Coverage, 78 Fed. Reg. 217, 237 (January 2, 2013).

(2)   An employee who failed to make a salary reduction election through his or her employer's fiscal year cafeteria plan for accident and health plan coverage before the deadline in proposed section 1.125-2 is allowed to make a prospective salary reduction election for accident and health coverage on or after the first day of plan year of the cafeteria plan without regard to whether the employee experienced a change in status event as described in Regulation section 1.125-4.

138. How can employers use a state healthcare insurance exchange (marketplace) and other rules to their advantage?

There are positive planning opportunities for businesses buying health insurance for employees on these state exchanges. Some incentives are gone now that the individual mandate penalty has been lowered to $0, but other opportunities remain.

Employers with fifty or more full-time and full-time equivalent employees will pay penalties if they do not offer health plans that provide "minimum value" for all ten "essential health benefits" to at least 95 percent of their employees or the coverage is not affordable for the employee, and one or more employees purchase health insurance on an exchange and obtains a subsidy.

<u>Dropping Employer Provided Insurance and Giving Raises</u>. Proponents of healthcare reform state that exchange purchased health insurance coverage will be available for many, especially those with lower incomes at a very low monthly premium after tax credits are applied. The net cost of health insurance purchased on an exchange could be dramatically lower than what is otherwise available for lower income individuals after the subsidies are factored in.

Thus, an employer should look at the aggregate amount the employer pays for health-related coverage and see if it is more cost effective to stop providing insurance coverage and have all of its employees, including management, obtain coverage through the exchange. If an employer has thirty or fewer full-time employees, it will not pay any employer mandate penalty regardless of how the employer handles its health insurance program or if it has none. On the other hand, if an employer's competitors provide good healthcare coverage, it may be difficult for the employer to retain and attract new employees unless it can show that, with the level of its pay scale and the net cost of health insurance bought by an employee on the exchange, the employee comes out ahead financially.

Thus, if an employer terminates coverage but provides a pay increase, it is possible that the lower income employee (generally under 250 percent of federal poverty income) and the employer could both come out ahead due to the employer's savings in what it was paying for health benefits and the employee's increased pay, net after income taxes and subsidized health insurance.

<u>Not Providing Spousal Coverage</u>. The employer mandate penalty is triggered for Applicable Large Employers if the employer does not make an offer of qualifying health coverage to at least 95 percent of its employees and dependents. For this purpose, spouses are not dependents. Thus, some employers are excluding spousal coverage from their health plans. If an employer has high insurance rates because of health liabilities associated with employees' spouses and terminates

spousal coverage, the spouses can obtain insurance coverage through the Exchange regardless of any preexisting conditions. The employer may be better off giving its employee a bonus that he or she can use to pay for spousal coverage through the Exchange than paying the cost to provide insurance coverage for that spouse.

<u>Providing Employee Health Benefits Not Costing Employee More than 9.66 Percent of Any Employee's Income</u>. If employer coverage provides minimum value, is affordable, and is offered to at least 95 percent of employees and dependents, the employer, even if an "applicable large employer," will not face an employer mandate penalty. Affordability is determined by whether the coverage offered to the employee (but not the dependents) costs an employee more than 9.78 percent of his or her annual household income. Because employers may not know employees' household incomes, three affordability safe harbors may be used.[1]

Thus, an employer can provide enough of the payment toward lower income employees' insurance so that no employee's coverage costs more than 9.78 percent of the employee's pay. An employer can pay a larger amount of a lower paid worker's health benefits than of a higher paid employee. The employer can charge as much as it wants for dependent coverage (or work with the insurer to do so), as that is not counted in the affordability determination. Remember, it is unaffordable coverage for the <u>employee</u> that can trigger the employer mandate penalty if the employee purchases coverage on an Exchange and obtains a subsidy.

<u>Conclusion</u>. Financial analysis of health benefits is critical for a successful business. Be careful, however, because changing or eliminating health benefits could create employee recruitment and retention issues more significant than the savings.

139. What is limited wrap-around healthcare coverage and how can it be used by employers with at least some employees purchasing subsidized exchange health insurance?

Limited Wraparound Coverage was a new pilot project concept effective for plan years beginning in 2015. In late 2017, CMS issued a notice seeking comments on the possible extension of the pilot program. The program is spelled out in regulations[2] from the Departments of the Treasury, Labor, and Health and Human Services (the "Departments"). The Departments amended the excepted benefit regulations under the Employer Retirement Income Security Act of 1974 (ERISA), the Internal Revenue Code, and the Public Health Service Act (PHSA). Excepted benefits are generally exempt from the market reforms added to these laws by the Patient Protection and Affordable Care Act (PPACA or ACA). Employers are allowed to provide

---

1.   Form W-2: An employee's monthly contribution for self-only coverage is affordable if it does not exceed 9.78 percent of their W-2 wages for that calendar year.

    <u>Rate of pay</u>: An employee's monthly contribution for self-only coverage is affordable if it is no more than 9.78 percent of their monthly wages (hourly rate of pay × 130 hours, or, for salaried employees, their monthly salary figure).
    <u>Federal Poverty Line (FPL)</u>: An employee's monthly contribution for self-only coverage is affordable if it does not exceed 9.78 percent of the FPL for a single individual.

2.   Treas. Reg. 26 C.F.R. §54.9831–1(c)(3)(i), DOL Reg. 29 C.F.R. §2590.732(c)(3)(i), HHS Reg. 45 C.F.R. §146.145(c) (3) (i), (effective October 31, 2016).

the wraparound benefits under this program with a sunset date. The coverage needed to begin between January 1, 2016 and December 31, 2018 and must ultimately end either

- Three years after the date that wraparound coverage is initially offered

- The date the last collective bargaining agreement relating to the plan terminates

Wraparound coverage is limited coverage that is an excepted benefit and used as a supplement when at least some of an employer's employees are purchasing subsidized exchange health insurance. For an applicable large employer subject to the employer mandate, it will be paying an employer mandate penalty due to employees receiving subsidized coverage on an exchange. In addition, the employer would be paying for the cost of the coverage in the wrap around plan.

These regulations assume that employer-sponsored major medical plans are better than any plan an individual can purchase through an exchange (marketplace). The regulations then assume that some employees will not be able to afford the employer-sponsored plan and will waive the coverage and instead purchase exchange coverage. The employer could then offer wraparound coverage to those employees who purchase exchange coverage comparable to the employer-sponsored plan, taking into account the exchange coverage. The wraparound coverage, subject to certain requirements, is an excepted benefit and thus not subject to the healthcare reform insurance market reform requirements. Thus, an employee enrolled in this limited wraparound coverage would not be disqualified from eligibility for premium tax credits or cost sharing subsidies through the exchange.

In order for wraparound coverage to be an excepted benefit, it must meet seven conditions:

- It can be combined only with individual coverage purchased in the individual market that is not solely excepted benefits.

- It must provide "meaningful benefits" beyond the essential health benefits (EHBs) provided by the individual plan or reimburse the cost of care from out-of-network providers, or both. The wraparound coverage cannot merely provide benefits pursuant to a coordination-of-benefits provision (i.e., just pay for benefits when the individual plan does not cover all or part of an expense).

- The employer's "primary plan" must offer group coverage that meets minimum value. The primary plan must be affordable for a majority of the eligible employees. Only employees eligible for the primary plan are eligible for the wraparound plan.

- Total annual cost of coverage per employees and any covered dependent under the wraparound must not exceed the greater of 15 percent of the cost of coverage under the primary plan or the maximum annual salary-reduction contribution toward a health Flexible Spending Arrangement (FSA), which is 2,700 for 2019.

- The wraparound coverage must not discriminate as to eligibility, benefits, or premiums based on a health factor; it must not contain any preexisting condition exclusions; and neither the wraparound coverage nor the primary coverage can discriminate in favor of highly compensated individuals. These limits prevent employers from using wraparound coverage to send "excessive numbers" of low wage workers to the exchange or to shift employees with high medical costs to the exchange.

- The wraparound coverage cannot replace group coverage for employers that drop coverage altogether or offer coverage that is not of minimum value (i.e., a skinny plan). Individuals cannot be enrolled in an FSA

- The wraparound coverage cannot be structured so that low-income workers receive fewer primary benefits than high-income workers. Furthermore, enrolling an employee in limited wraparound coverage does not satisfy the large employer's obligation to offer minimum essential coverage (MEC) under Internal Revenue Code section 4980H that is affordable.

A large employer sponsoring limited wraparound coverage will be paying for that coverage and the tax penalty associated with the employee for whom the primary plan was unaffordable. The preamble to these regulations states that "[s]ome group health plan sponsors have asked whether wraparound coverage could be provided for employees for whom the employer premium is unaffordable and who obtain coverage through [the exchange]." The Departments claim that the availability of limited wraparound coverage "promot[es] equity in coverage" by allowing a plan sponsor "to maintain a comparable level of benefits for all potential enrollees."

Reporting Requirements Form

CMS has released a form for use by plan sponsors offering limited wraparound coverage to satisfy the reporting required for the coverage to qualify as an excepted benefit. The form, as finalized, largely mirrors the proposed version.

The form requires the plan sponsor to provide information such as:

- Identification information including the formal name of the plan, plan identification number, plan sponsor, EIN, phone number.

- Background information including if the plan is part of a collective bargaining agreement, type of coverage the limited wraparound coverage is designed to supplement (i.e., eligible individual health insurance, a multi-state plan, or basic health program coverage), first day of the first plan year and plant year start and end date. Individual who are eligible to enroll

- Number of individuals enrolled, full time employees and part time employees participating, retired or separated participant, description of the additional benefits that the limited wraparound coverage is designed to provide (e.g., expanded in-network medical clinics or providers, home health coverage). A glossary is provided with definitions of terms.

- Plan sponsors must file a form for each type of limited wraparound coverage that they offer.

- The form must be filed on a one-time basis within the later of sixty days after publication of the form or sixty days after the first day of the first plan year that the coverage is first offered.[1]

---

1. https://www.cms.gov/CCIIO/Resources/Forms-Reports-and-Other-Resources/Downloads/Limited-Wraparound-Coverage-Qs-Instructions.pdf.

PART III: TIMELINE FOR IMPLEMENTATION OF PROVISIONS: WHAT NEEDS TO BE DONE AND WHEN

140. What are the major components of healthcare reform and when are they effective?

2010

- January 1, 2010

  - ➤ <u>Tax Credit</u>. Beginning in 2010, small employers with low-paid employees are eligible for a tax credit for purchasing health care for their employees. The full credit applies to a business with no more than ten Full-Time Equivalent (FTE) employees who have average wages not exceeding $25,000. The credit is phased out entirely if the business has twenty-five or more FTE employees or if the average wages of its employees is $50,000 or more. For 2010 through 2013, the credit is 35 percent (25 percent for tax-exempt employers) of the employer's nonelective premium for qualified health insurance policies. Starting in 2014, the credit increased to 50 percent (35 percent for tax-exempt employers) but it is available only if the health insurance policy is purchased on a state health insurance exchange. Related employers are treated as a single employer.

  - ➤ <u>ERRP (Early Retiree Reinsurance Program</u>.) Temporary large claim reinsurance assistance was available for employers providing early retirement benefits to retirees ages fifty-five to sixty-four under a retiree group health plan. The reinsurance reimbursement, up to a $60,000 annual maximum per eligible retiree, is 80 percent of the costs incurred by the plan for eligible retirees (and their dependents) in excess of the first $15,000 of such costs. The costs that may be reimbursed include the portion paid by the retiree for deductibles, copayments, and coinsurance. Medical expenses incurred after June 1, 2010, were eligible for reimbursement under this program. Up to $5 billion was allocated for the program, but the money was spent quickly, and HHS stopped taking claims on Dec. 31, 2011.[1]

- March 23, 2010

  - ➤ <u>Grandfather Provision</u>. Group plans in existence and with actual membership on and after March 23, 2010, have the right to maintain their existing coverage, except as otherwise provided.[2] Family members of individuals enrolled in grandfathered plans and new employees can enroll in the plan if its provisions allow such enrollment without jeopardizing the plan's "grandfathered" status.[3]

---

1. PPACA §§1102, 10102.
2. PPACA §1251.
3. PPACA §1251(b) & (c).

➢ <u>Reasonable Break Time for Nursing Mothers</u>. Employers must provide reasonable break times to allow nursing mothers to express breast milk for a child up to age one.[1]

➢ <u>Nondiscrimination Rules for Health Program or Activity</u>. An individual generally cannot be excluded from participation in, denied benefits of, or subjected to discrimination due to race, color, national origin, sex, age, or disability under any health program or activity that is receiving federal financial assistance on a ground that is prohibited under the following laws:

  ○ Title VI of the Civil Rights Act of 1964

  ○ Education Amendments of 1972

  ○ Age Discrimination Act of 1975

  ○ Section 504 of the Rehabilitation Act of 1973[2]

➢ <u>Employee Whistleblower Protections</u>. PPACA added the FLSA "Protections for Employees", which prohibits employers from taking adverse action against any employee because the employee:

  ○ received a premium tax credit or subsidy for a health plan;

  ○ provided information to the employer or the federal or state government concerning a violation, act or omission the employee reasonably believes to be a violation relating to Title I of the Act. (Title I of the Act, among other things, provides rules for the establishment and operation of the Exchange and imposes certain mandates on employers, including the provision of certain standards of benefits for health coverage, the automatic enrollment requirements described above and the elimination of certain restrictions in health coverage, such as pre-existing condition exclusions and lifetime and annual dollar limitations in coverage);

  ○ testified or is about to testify in a proceeding concerning such violation;

  ○ assisted or participated, or is about to assist or participate, in such a proceeding; or

  ○ objected to, or refused to perform, any activity or assigned task the employee reasonably believes to be such a violation.[3]

The procedures for handling retaliation complaints are at 29 CFR 1984.102 et seq.

---

1.   PPACA §4207; FLSA §(r).
2.   PPACA §1557.
3.   PPACA §1558; FLSA §18C.

- March 30, 2010

    ➢ Tax-free coverage to children under age twenty-seven.[1]

- June 21, 2010

    ➢ <u>Temporary High-Risk Health Insurance Pool</u>. Adults with pre-existing conditions can participate in a temporary high-risk pool, the Pre-Existing Condition Insurance Plan (PCIP) program. The program can be run by the states or by HHS, if a state so elects. It was superseded by the state healthcare exchanges in 2014. To qualify for coverage, applicants must have a pre-existing health condition and have been uninsured for at least the six months prior to enrolling in coverage. There is no age requirement to enroll. The program sets premiums as if for a standard population, and it allows premiums to vary by age, geographic area, and family composition. It also limits out-of-pocket spending to $5,950 for individuals and $11,900 for families, excluding premiums.[2]

- Plan Years Beginning on or after September 23, 2010

    ➢ <u>Annual and Lifetime Limits</u>. Use of lifetime dollar limits on health benefits is prohibited. A group health plan may impose lifetime limits on nonessential health benefits for beneficiaries, but not participants. This applies to grandfathered plans. Use of unreasonable annual dollar limits for "essential health benefits" is prohibited. Starting in 2014, all annual dollar limits for nonessential health benefits are prohibited. Grandfathered plans are exempt from this rule.

    ➢ <u>Pre-Existing Condition Exclusion for Children under Age Nineteen</u>. Any pre-existing condition exclusion for children less than nineteen years of age is prohibited. This provision also applies to grandfathered plans.[3]

    ➢ <u>Adult Dependent Coverage</u>. Group health plans that provide dependent coverage must provide coverage to their employees' adult children (including those who are married) until age twenty-six, provided that, with respect to grandfathered plans, the child is not otherwise eligible for coverage under another employer-sponsored health plan.[4]

    ➢ <u>Preventive Care</u>. Group health plans must provide first-dollar coverage for preventive care. Grandfathered plans are exempt from this requirement.[5]

    ➢ <u>Primary Care Physicians for Children and Women</u>. Group health plans that use primary care provider gatekeepers must give participants the right to select any available primary care provider, including pediatricians for children. Women must

---

1.   IRC §105(b); IRS Notice 2010-38.
2.   PPACA §1201: PHSA §2704.
3.   PHSA §2704; PPACA §§1201 1255, 10103.
4.   PHSA §2714.
5.   PPACA §§1001, 10101; PHSA §2713.

have the right to see any participating OB/GYN physician without a primary care provider referral.[1]

> <u>Emergency Care</u>. Group health plans must cover emergency care without a requirement for a primary care provider referral or imposition of any "out-of-network" penalty. Grandfathered plans are exempt.[2]

> <u>Policy Rescission Limited</u>. Group health plans and health insurance issuers may not rescind coverage for reasons other than fraud or material misrepresentation by the plan participant or beneficiary. This provision also applies to grandfathered plans.[3]

> <u>Claims and Appeals Procedures</u>. All plans, including grandfathered plans, must implement an "effective appeals process." Church and government plans without ERISA-compliant claims procedures are required to adopt such procedures. External review must be conducted by one of the approved Independent Review Organizations (IROs) with which the plan has contracted. Nongrandfathered, self-insured plans had an enforcement safe harbor that allowed them to contract with as few as two IROs. As of July 1, 2012, that was increased to at least three IROs for the safe harbor to apply. A grace period extended some of these requirements to July 1, 2011. The Employee Benefits Security Administration (EBSA) Technical Release 2011-01 extended the grace period for some of these rules to plan years beginning on or after January 1, 2012.[4]

> <u>Income Tax Nondiscrimination Requirements for Employer Provided Insured Health Plans Postponed</u>. Originally to be effective for plan years beginning on or after September 23, 2010 but postponed by IRS Notice 2011-1 until regulations are issued. These nondiscrimination rules do not apply to grandfathered insured plans.[5]

- January 1, 2011

  > <u>New SIMPLE Cafeteria Plan</u>. For employers with 100 or fewer employees during either of the two prior years, and employers can increase the number of employees to 200. Simple cafeteria plans are exempt from the 25 percent concentration tests and deemed nondiscriminatory for purposes of the nondiscrimination requirements applicable to life insurance, dependent care plans, and other benefits if the employer provides:

    - at least a 2 percent of pay contribution for participants; or

    - a matching contribution for participants, which is the lesser of 6 percent of pay, or two times each qualified employee's pretax contribution.

---

1.   PPACA §§1001, 10101; PHSA §2719A(c) & (d).
2.   PPACA §§1001, 10101, PHSA §2719A.
3.   PPACA §1001; PHSA §2712.
4.   PPACA §10101; PHSA §2719.
5.   PHSA §2716.

A "qualified employee" is any employee who is not an HCE (as defined in Internal Revenue Code section 414(q)) or a key employee (as defined in Internal Revenue Code section 415(i)). Simple cafeteria plans must still comply with Internal Revenue Code section 125 nondiscrimination requirements regarding eligibility and benefits. Simple Cafeteria Plans are discussed in more detail in Part V of this book.[1]

➤ <u>Reimbursement for Over-the-Counter Drugs</u>. Reimbursement under Flexible Spending Accounts (FSAs), Health Saving Accounts (HSAs), Medical Savings Accounts (MSAs), and Health Reimbursement Accounts (HRAs) for over-the-counter drugs (except insulin) is no longer allowed unless the patient has a prescription for the drug.[2]

➤ <u>HSA/MSA Excise Tax</u>. The excise tax for distributions from HSAs and MSAs for expenses that are not Internal Revenue Code section 213 medical expenses increased to 20 percent from the current 10 and 15 percent respectively.[3]

➤ <u>Employer W-2 Reporting</u>. Postponed.

➤ <u>Federal Long-Term Care</u>. The Community Living Assistance Services and Support (CLASS) Act authorized a voluntary federal insurance program for employees to purchase long-term care insurance. Employers could elect to automatically enroll employees in the program, allowing employees to opt-out. The provision was intended to be effective January 1, 2011; however, HHS has announced that it will not implement this program because it could not function cost effectively.

➤ <u>Medical Loss Ratio (MLR) Requirements</u>. The required MLRs are 85 percent in the large group health insurance market and 80 percent in the small group and individual markets (or higher, based on state regulations). The remaining percentage of health insurance premiums can be spent by insurers on administrative costs. Insurers' reports to policy holders for calendar year due by June 1 of following year; rebates by August 1 of following year. Health insurance companies must comply with medical loss ratio standards and are required to submit reports to HHS for each plan year relating to an accounting for costs and are also required to provide rebates to policyholders under certain circumstances. Although the obligations to calculate the MLR and make rebates fall on insurers, in many cases the rebates will be paid to group health plans, and the plans will be required to determine how to use the rebates or refund them to plan participants.[4]

2012

- January 1, 2012

    ➤ <u>Expanded 1099 Reporting</u>. Repealed.

---

1. IRC Sec. 125(j).
2. IRC Secs. 106(f), 223(d)(2), 220(d)(2).
3. IRC Secs. 223(f)(4)(A), 220(f)(4)(A).
4. PHSA §2718.

- February 13, 2012

  - ➢ Co-ops permitted.[1]

- March 23, 2012

  - ➢ Quality of Care Reporting. Health care reform requires group health plans and health insurance issuers to submit an annual report to the Secretary of HHS addressing plan or coverage benefits and provider "reimbursement structures" that may affect the quality of care in certain specified ways. The reporting requirements are to be developed in consultation with health care quality experts and "stakeholders" (e.g., representatives of care providers, care recipients, insurers, and employers) and may be enforced by "appropriate penalties" developed by the Secretary. Copies of the report must be made available to enrollees during each open enrollment period. HHS was required to "develop" the reporting requirements no later than March 23, 2012, and to issue regulations that provide criteria for determining whether a "reimbursement structure" is subject to the reporting rule. HHS guidance under this provision remains outstanding.[2]

- August 1, 2012

  - ➢ Medical Loss Ratio Reports and Rebates. Health plans must have procedures in place to handle any rebates received from the insurer in accordance with the rules for distribution, including the rules requiring ERISA plans to determine the extent to which rebates are plan assets. Rebates need to be apportioned if premiums are paid with both employer and employee contributions. (Effective Aug. 1, 2012.)[3]

  - ➢ Preventive Health Services for Women. Nongrandfathered group health plans must provide recommended preventive health services without cost sharing and must adjust the services covered in accordance with changes to recommended preventive services guidelines.

- September 23, 2012

  - ➢ SBC Disclosures. HHS prescribed uniform summary of benefits that a group health plan sponsor or insurance issuer will need to distribute to plan participants and potential enrollees. This disclosure is in addition to the ERISA summary plan description. If any material modification is made after such summary is provided, then a notice of material modifications must be provided to participants at least sixty days prior to the modification's (Effective date: Must be distributed during open enrollment periods for plan years beginning or after September 23, 2012, or, for other enrollments (such as new hires), beginning on the first day of the first plan year that

---

1.   PPACA §§1322 and 10104.
2.   PPACA §1251, adopting PHSA §2717.
3.   PHSA §2718.

begins on or after September 23, 2012. (Effective Sept. 23, 2012; originally to be effective March 23, 2012.)[1]

2013

- January 1, 2013

  > **W-2 Reporting.** W-2s must be issued showing employer and employee payments for certain health care items in 2012. This does not change the employer's deduction or cause employees to be taxed. IRS announced an exemption for employers that did not file at least 250 W-2s in preceding year, but this exemption can be eliminated in the future by IRS notice.[2]

  > **Health FSAs.** A $2,500 annual limit was imposed on health FSA deferrals in 2013; previously, there was no such limit. Dependent care and adoption FSAs are not to be limited.[3] Health FSAs are subject to annual cost of living adjustments. The limit for 2019 is currently $2,700.

  > **Individual Deduction Threshold Increased.** The current 7.5 percent of Adjusted Gross Income (AGI) floor on income-tax deductions for healthcare expenses is raised to 10 percent of AGI. However, the floor was waived during 2013, 2014, 2015, and 2016 for individuals who turned age sixty-five before the end of those years.[4]

  > **Employer Deduction for Government-Subsidized Employer Drug Benefits Eliminated.** The employer deduction for the portion of healthcare expenses that are reimbursed to the employer through the Medicare Part D subsidy program is eliminated.

  > **Administrative Simplification.** The health reform law will affect relationships between payers and providers (hospitals, physicians, and allied care practitioners), as well as claims clearinghouses and banks that perform intermediary functions. HHS prescribes new "operating rules" that will govern the exchange of health data transactions, including eligibility, claim status, electronic funds transfers, electronic remittance advices, and other transactions. Group health plans must comply with "administrative simplification" rules for electronic exchange health information and electronic fund transfers, and they also must file a certification with the federal government that the plans are in compliance. This provision also applies to grandfathered plans. Systems must be compliant, and employers must certify compliance by December 31, 2013.[5]

---

1. PHSA §2715.
2. IRC Sec. 6051(a).
3. IRC Sec. 125(i).
4. IRC Sec. 213(a).
5. PPACA §1104.

> ➤ <u>Medicare Tax Increases</u>. The FICA Medicare tax rate will be increased by 0.9 percent for wages/earnings over $200,000 for individuals ($250,000 for married couples filing jointly). This will result in a combined 2.35 percent on wages over $200,000 ($250,000 for joint filers). The employer is required to collect the employee's share in the case of wages. The employer's share of FICA Medicare tax remains 1.45 percent. A new Medicare tax on investment income of 3.8 percent will apply to individuals who earn more than $200,000 a year ($250,000 for married couples filing jointly). Effective for tax years beginning January 1, 2013.

- July 31, 2013

> ➤ <u>Comparative Clinical Effectiveness Research Fee</u>. First temporary fees imposed on self-insured health plan sponsors[1] and insurers for insured plans.[2] (Effective July 21, 2013, for plan years ending prior to that date.)

> ➤ <u>Patient Centered Outcomes Research Institute (PCORI) Health Plan Fees</u>. Health insurance issuers and self-funded health plans were required to pay an annual fee of $2.00, ($1.00 during the first year) indexed for inflation starting in 2014, times the average number of covered lives under the health insurance policy or self-insured health plan. (Effective for plan years ending after September 3, 2012; scheduled to end for plan years ending after September 3, 2019.) The first payments are required July 31, 2013, and each July 31 thereafter through 2020.[3] The tax and return is due July 31 following the calendar year in which the plan year ends. For calendar year plans, the first return is due July 31, 2013. For a PYE 3/31/13, the calendar year ends in 2013 and the tax and return would be due 7/31/14. (See Q 646 through Q 658.) The PCORI fee for 2019 is $2.39.

- October 1, 2013

> ➤ <u>Employer Health Insurance Exchange Notice.</u> Employers, regardless of size and whether or not they have a health plan, must provide notice to employees of the upcoming existence of state insurance exchanges, which are to be established by all the states in 2014 or by HHS if a state fails to do so. Notice must be in the form specified in DOL guidance. (Original effective date of March 1, 2013 delayed until October 1, 2013.)

- December 31, 2013

> ➤ <u>Plan Communications with Providers</u>. Health plans must certify and document compliance with HHS rules for electronic transactions between providers and health plans.

---

1.   IRC Sec. 4376.
2.   IRC Sec. 4375.
3.   PPACA §6301; IRC Secs. 4375, 4376.

2014

- January 1, 2014

  ➤ <u>Cafeteria Plans with Fiscal Plan Year Beginning in 2013 Can Be Amended to Allow Employees to Change Election to Purchase Health Insurance or to Terminate Election to Purchase Insurance</u>. Employees may want to terminate their election to purchase health insurance through the employer's cafeteria plan and go to the exchange if they are eligible for health insurance exchange tax credits. Other employees may want to elect to purchase health insurance effective January 1, 2014, to avoid the individual mandate penalty. If the cafeteria plan year is a fiscal year, employees wanting exchange insurance on January 1, 2014, would have to terminate or change their elections midyear. However, under current cafeteria plan regulations, these two elections are not a change in status allowing an election change midyear. The proposed regulations allow an applicable large employer with a fiscal year cafeteria plan, at its election, to amend the plan any time during the year on a retroactive basis (by December 31, 2014, retroactive to beginning of 2013 plan year) to permit either or both of the following changes in salary reduction elections:[1]

    (1) An employee who elected to salary reduce through the fiscal year cafeteria plan for accident and health plan coverage beginning in 2013 is allowed to prospectively revoke or change his or her election with respect to the accident and health plan once, during that plan year, without regard to whether the employee experienced a change in status event described in Reg. section 1.125-4.

    (2) An employee who failed to make a salary reduction election through his or her employer's fiscal year cafeteria plan beginning in 2013 for accident and health plan coverage before the deadline in proposed section 1.125-2 for making elections is allowed to make a prospective salary reduction election for accident and health coverage on or after the first day of the 2013 plan year of the cafeteria plan without regard to whether the employee experienced a change in status event described in Reg. section 1.125-4.

    Some provisions of the transition relief refer to "applicable large employer members" (i.e., employers that are subject to healthcare reform's employer mandate), raising questions as to whether the relief is available for all noncalendar-year cafeteria plans or only those that are sponsored by applicable large employer members.

  ➤ <u>State Health Insurance Exchanges</u>. Each state must establish a health insurance exchange (or HHS will do so) for use by the uninsured and small employers with 100 or fewer employees (although states may set the cap at fifty employees). The exchanges will offer fully insured insurance contracts that provide essential health

---

1.   Preamble to Proposed Rules on Shared Responsibility for Employers Regarding Health Coverage, 78 Fed. Reg. 217, 237 (Jan. 2, 2013).

benefits at different levels of coverage (bronze, silver, gold, and platinum).[1] Employees of small employers who offer health insurance coverage through an exchange may pay their employee premiums for such coverage on a pretax basis through the employer's cafeteria plan.[2]

➤ <u>Health Insurance Exchange Tax Subsidies</u>. Individuals who do not have affordable minimum essential coverage from their employer will be eligible for tax credit subsidies for their health insurance purchase on a state exchange if their income is below 400 percent of federal poverty level. The US Supreme Court held in 2015 in *King v. Burwell* that these subsidies are available on exchanges run by a state as well as a state exchange run by HHS.

➤ <u>Individual Mandate Tax Penalty</u>. Individuals are required to obtain minimum essential health coverage for themselves and their dependents or pay a monthly penalty tax for each month without coverage. The monthly penalty tax is one-twelfth of the greater of the dollar penalty or gross income penalty amounts. The dollar penalty is an amount per individual of:

   o $95 for 2014 (capped at $285 per family);

   o $325 for 2015 (capped at $975 per family); and

   o $695 for 2016 and beyond (capped at $2085 per family).

These dollar penalties will be indexed for inflation starting in 2017. The gross income penalty established was a percentage of household income in excess of a specified filing threshold of:

   o   1 percent for 2014;

   o   2 percent for 2015; and

   o   2.5 percent for 2016 and later years.

In no event will the maximum penalty amount exceed the national average premium for bronze-level exchange plans for families of the same size.

For 2017, the penalties are the HIGHER of 2.5 percent of household income (with the maximum being the yearly premium for a Bronze healthcare plan on the Marketplace) or $695 per adult/$347.50 per child under 18 with a maximum of $2,085.

Minimum essential coverage includes Medicare, Medicaid, CHIP, TRICARE, individual insurance, grandfathered plans, and eligible employer-sponsored plans.

---

1.   See Q 79, Part 1, for more information about the levels.
2.   PPACA §1557.

Workers compensation and limited-scope dental or vision benefits are not considered minimum essential health coverage.[1]

> ➤ <u>Employer Free Choice Vouchers</u>. Repealed.

> ➤ <u>Health Reform' Out-Of-Pocket Limits – Generally Effective In 2014 – One Delayed Effective Date</u>.

Healthcare reform's requirement that health insurance individual and small group plans cap how much consumers must pay out-of-pocket each year for medical care will take effect as scheduled in 2014 for some and 2015 for others.

For 2014 and thereafter, the health reform law requires that private insurance plans offered in the individual and small group markets[2] limit how much in cost-sharing charges—deductibles, copayments, and coinsurance—that people enrolled in a plan must pay each year for covered benefits provided by the plan's network of health care providers. The requirement does not apply to "grandfathered" plans or to self-insured employer plans, large group employer plans, or large group market insurers.[3] In 2019, the maximum out-of-pocket limit will be $7,900 for an individual and $15,800 for a family (the same as for HSA compatible high deductible plans), and will apply in 2014 to health insurance offered in the individual, non-group, market.[4] The deductible cannot exceed $2,000 for a plan covering a single individual or $4,000 for any other plan.[5]

The agencies interpret the annual deductible limit as applying only to employers and insurers in the individual and small group markets for nongrandfathered plans.[6] In the case of a plan using a network of providers, cost sharing paid by, or on behalf of, an individual for benefits provided outside of such network does not count toward the annual limitation on cost sharing or the annual limitation on deductibles.[7]

> ➤ *One Delay until 2015*. However, employer plans that have "separately administered" benefits, such as a primary package of health benefits and a different insurer or administrator for other benefits, such as prescription drugs, need not comply until 2015.[8] Employer plans with separately administered benefits that qualify for the delay must apply some out-of-pocket limits in 2014. These plans, for 2019, must

---

1. PPACA §§1501, 10106; IRC Sec. 5000A.

2. A group health plan shall ensure that any annual cost sharing imposed under the plan does not exceed the limitations provided for under paragraphs (1) and (2) of section PPACA §1302(c).

3. Standards Related to Essential Health Benefits, Actuarial Value, and Accreditation, 45 CFR Parts 147, 155, and 156, 78 Fed. Reg. 12834, 12837 (Feb. 25, 2013); FAQs About the Affordable Care Act Implementation Part XII, Q/A-1 https://www.dol.gov/sites/default/files/ebsa/about-ebsa/our-activities/resource-center/faqs/aca-part-xii.pdf. (Last accessed July 18, 2018).

4. PPACA §1302(c)(1)(A) IRC Sec. 223(c)(2)(A)(ii).

5. PPACA §1302(c)(2)(A).

6. HHS Reg. §156.130(b); Standards Related to Essential Health Benefits, Actuarial Value, and Accreditation, 45 CFR Parts 147, 155, and 156, 78 Fed. Reg. 12834, 12837 (February 27, 2015).

7. HHS Reg. §156.130(c).

8. FAQs About the Affordable Care Act Implementation Part XII, Q/A-2 at https://www.dol.gov/sites/default/files/ebsa/about-ebsa/our-activities/resource-center/faqs/aca-part-xii.pdf. (Last accessed1July 14, 2018).

ensure that their primary package of health benefits has an out-of-pocket limit of no more than $7,900 for individuals and $15,800 for families. A separately administered benefit, such as prescription drugs, that already has an existing limit on out-of-pocket costs must also comply with the limits of $7,900 for individuals and $15,800 for families in 2019.[1]

➤ <u>Pre-Existing Condition Exclusion Practices Eliminated</u>. Pre-existing condition exclusions no longer will be allowed in group health plans or individual insurance policies, not even the limited exclusions previously allowed under HIPAA. This also applies to grandfathered plans.[2] Effective for plan years beginning on or after January 1, 2014.

➤ <u>Ninety-Day Maximum Waiting Period</u>. Group health plans and health insurance issuers may not impose waiting periods of more than ninety days before coverage becomes effective. This also applies to grandfathered plans.[3]

➤ <u>Cost-Sharing Limits</u>. Group health plans, including grandfathered plans, may not impose cost-sharing amounts (i.e., copays or deductibles) that are more than the maximum allowed for high-deductible health plans (currently these limits are $6,750 for an individual and $13,500 for a family coverage). After 2014, these amounts will be adjusted for health insurance premium inflation.[4]

➤ <u>Annual or Lifetime Limits</u>. Group health plans, including grandfathered plans, may no longer include more than restricted annual or any lifetime dollar limits on essential health benefits for participants. Limits may exist in and after 2014 for nonessential benefits.[5]

➤ <u>Wellness Program Health Plan Discount</u>. The maximum premium discount an employer can offer under its health plan for participation in a wellness program is 30 percent. This is an increase from the prior 20 percent maximum premium discount. Regulatory agencies can increase this maximum discount to 50 percent in the future.

➤ <u>Coverage for Those in Clinical Trials</u>. Insurers and health plans, unless grandfathered, may not discriminate against an individual for participating in a clinical trial. If a plan covers a qualified individual, it may not deny or impose additional conditions for participation in a clinical trial.[6]

➤ <u>Medicaid Expansion</u>. The Supreme Court in 2012 in effect ruled that the requirement for states to offer Medicaid benefits to all persons with incomes at or below

---

1.   *Id.*
2.   PHSA §2704 & §2705.
3.   PHSA §2708.
4.   PPACA §1302(c); PHSA §2707(b).
5.   PHSA §2711.
6.   PHSA §2709.

133 percent of federal poverty level is optional with each state. States that participate will receive full reimbursement of additional costs from federal government until 2017, at which point reimbursement will gradually decline to 90 percent of extra costs in 2020 and thereafter.

2015

➤ <u>Health Insurance Income Tax Nondiscrimination Requirements</u>. Internal Revenue Code section 105(h) currently taxes the benefits received by highly compensated employees (HCEs) under discriminatory self-funded health plans. Healthcare reformed extends these nondiscrimination rules to insured plans, but only after the IRS issues regulations, which has not yet occurred. Employers with discriminatory insured arrangements, however, will need to consider changing them or face a $100 per day ($36,500 per year) per affected participant penalty once the rules go into effect. Grandfathered insured plans, however, are exempt from this rule. (This new requirement for insured plans was postponed in 2010 until IRS publishes regulations, which have not yet been issued; originally to be effective for plan years beginning on or after September 23, 2010.)[1]

➤ <u>Automatic Enrollment</u>. Employers with more than 200 employees who maintain one or more health plans must automatically enroll new full-time employees in a health plan. The employer must give affected employees notice of this automatic enrollment procedure and an opportunity to opt out. State wage withholding laws are preempted to the extent that they prevent an employer from instituting this automatic enrollment program. DOL Technical Release No. 2012-01 delayed the implementation of the automatic enrollment requirements contained in the Affordable Care Act (ACA). The final effective date will be established by DOL regulations, which have not yet been released.[2]

➤ <u>Employer Mandate (Play or Pay) Tax Penalties</u>. Employers with one hundred or more full-time equivalent (FTE) employees will be required to offer their full-time employees (FTEs) minimum essential health coverage or pay a fine of up to $2,320 per year for each FTE in excess of thirty FTEs if any employee receives a premium tax credit on a state health insurance exchange. If an employer provides minimum essential health coverage to its FTEs but fails to pay at least 60 percent of its actuarial value or the coverage is considered unaffordable (costs more than 9.86 percent of household income in 2019), then the employer must pay a penalty of up to $3,480 per year for each FTE who receives the premium credit on an exchange, but not more than would be owed for the $2,320 per year penalty. An FTE is defined as an employee who is employed for thirty or more hours per week, calculated on a forty-hour work week. This provision also applies to grandfathered plans.[3] (Originally effective January 1, 2014 but delayed until January 1, 2015.)

---

1.   PPACA §1201; PHSA §2716.
2.   PPACA §1511; FLSA §18A.
3.   IRC Sec. 4980H. See Q 29, Part 1, for an explanation of how the penalties are calculated.

> ➤ <u>If employer has on average 100 or more Full-Time (including full-time equivalents) Employees</u>:

  - o If an employer fails to offer coverage to a full-time employee for any day of a calendar month, that employee is treated as not having been offered coverage during the entire month. For January 2015, if an employer offers coverage to a full-time employee no later than the first day of the first payroll period that begins in January 2015, the employee will be treated as having been offered coverage for January 2015.

> ➤ <u>Employers with Fiscal Year Health Plans</u>. The employer mandate retains it's effective of January 1, 2015. However, employers with noncalendar (fiscal) year plans can be subject to the mandate based on the start of their 2015 plan year rather than on January 1, 2015, and other transition relief where certain conditions are met, as follows:

  (a) Pre-2015 Fiscal Year Plan Eligibility Transition Relief. Pre-2015 eligibility transition relief applies to employees, whenever hired, who are:

  - o eligible for coverage on the first day of the 2015 plan year under the eligibility terms of the plan as of February 9, 2014 (whether or not they elected coverage); and

  - o offered affordable coverage that provides minimum value effective no later than the first day of the 2015 plan year.

  Where these two conditions are satisfied, the employer will not be subject to a potential employer shared responsibility payment until the first day of the 2015 plan year. This relief applies only to employees to whom coverage was previously offered by the employer. Thus, penalties may still be imposed for the months in 2015 that are part of the plan year commencing in 2014 for employees to whom coverage was not previously offered.

  (b) <u>Significant Percentage Fiscal Year Plan Transition Relief (All Employees)</u>. No employer mandate penalty applies for any month before the first day of the plan year beginning in 2015 for employees who are offered affordable coverage that provides minimum value by the first day of the 2015 plan year if as of any date in the twelve months ending on February 9, 2014, an employer:

  - o covers at least one-quarter of its employees (full-time and part-time) under its noncalendar year plan; or

  - o offered coverage under the plan to one-third or more of its employees during the open enrollment period that ended most recently before February 9, 2014.

To qualify for this relief, the employee must not have been eligible for coverage as of February 9, 2014 under any group health plan maintained by his or her employer that has a calendar year plan year.

Unlike the pre-2015 eligibility transition relief discussed above, an employer that qualifies for this relief and who offers affordable, minimum value coverage commencing with the 2015 plan year has no Internal Revenue Code section 4980H exposure for periods before the 2015 plan year. Relief under this and the next transition rule applies for the period before the first day of the first noncalendar year plan year beginning in 2015 but only for employers that maintained noncalendar year plans as of December 27, 2012, and only if the plan year was not modified after December 27, 2012, to begin at a later calendar date.

➢ <u>70 percent Offer In 2015</u>. For 2015 (and for any calendar months during a noncalendar year plan year beginning in 2015 that fall in 2016), the 95 percent offer of coverage threshold is lowered to 70 percent. Thus, in 2015, an employer will be in compliance if employer offers coverage to at least 70 percent of full-time employees and dependents in 2015 (unless the employer qualifies for the 2015 dependent coverage transition relief, discussed below), although an employer will owe penalty if at least one of the full-time employees receives a premium tax credit for coverage in the public marketplace, which may occur because the employer did not offer coverage to that employee or because the coverage the employer offered was either unaffordable or did not provide minimum value.

➢ <u>Dependent Coverage</u>. In order to avoid exposure for the employer mandate penalty, an employer must offer coverage not only to full-time employees but also their dependents (but not spouses). The final regulations provide transition relief to plan years that begin in 2015 if the employer takes steps during the 2015 plan year toward satisfying this requirement.in 2016. The transition relief applies to employers for the 2015 plan year for plans under which (i) dependent coverage is not offered, (ii) dependent coverage that does not constitute minimum essential coverage is offered, or (iii) dependent coverage is offered for some, but not all, dependents. This relief is not available, however, if the employer had offered dependent coverage during either the plan year that begins in 2013 or the 2014 plan year and subsequently eliminated that offer of coverage.

➢ <u>Employer Minimum Essential Coverage Reporting</u>. All employers providing minimum essential coverage must file information with the IRS and plan participants.[1] (Effective for calendar years beginning on and after Jan. 1, 2015, after one-year delay.)

---

1.   PPACA §1502; IRC Sec. 6055.

> ➤ <u>Large Employer Health Information Reporting</u>. Large employers and employers with at least fifty full-time equivalent employees must submit annual health insurance coverage returns to the FTEs and the IRS. The returns must certify whether the employer offers healthcare insurance to its employees and, if so, describe the details regarding plan participation, applicable waiting periods, coverage availability, the lowest cost premium option under the plan in each enrollment category, and other information.[1] (Effective January 1, 2015, after one-year delay.)

- December 31, 2015

  > ➤ Group health plans must use electronic systems for processing health claims, enrollment, and premium payments and certify to the federal government that their systems comply. This also applies to grandfathered plans (plans must certify compliance by December 31, 2015).

2016

- January 1, 2016

  > ➤ <u>If employer has on average between fifty and ninety-nine Full-Time (including full-time equivalents) Employees</u>

    - ○ Employer has a one-year delay in the employer mandate, until January 1, 2016, (and for noncalendar-year plans, any calendar months during the plan year beginning in 2015 that fall in 2016) if:

    - — employer certifies it did not lay off employees during the period beginning on February 9, 2014, and ending on Dec. 31, 2014, to fall below the 100 employee threshold and that employer did not reduce any coverage you were already offering; and

    - — during the period beginning on February 9, 2014 and ending on Dec. 31, 2014, employer does not eliminate or materially reduce the health coverage, if any, offered as of February 9, 2014. An employer will not be treated as eliminating or materially reducing health coverage if, for each employee who is eligible for coverage on February 9, 2014:

    - (a) the employer offers to contribute toward the cost of employee-only coverage that is either (i) at least 95 percent of the dollar amount of the contribution the employer was making toward the coverage in effect as of February 9, 2014, or (ii) at least the same percentage of the cost of coverage that the employer offered to contribute toward coverage in effect as of February 9, 2014;

---

1.   PPACA §§1311(e)(3), 10104; PHSA §2715A; IRC Sec. 5056.

(b) benefits offered as of February 9, 2014 at the employee-only coverage level does not change, or, if it does, the coverage after the change provides minimum value; and

(c) eligibility under the employer's group health plans is not amended to narrow or reduce the class or classes of employees (or the employees' dependents) to whom coverage under those plans was offered as of February 9, 2014.

○ Such employer must report coverage of employer's employees for 2015.

2017

- January 1, 2017

  ➢ <u>Employers Purchasing Insurance on Exchange Can Be Increased</u>. States can allow larger employers (those with more than 100 employees) to purchase health insurance for their employees on the state health insurance exchanges.

  ➢ <u>Employer Mandate (Play or Pay) Tax Penalties</u>. Employers with fifty or more full-time equivalent (FTE) employees will be required to offer their full-time employees (FTEs) minimum essential health coverage or pay a fine of up to $2,320 per year for each FTE in excess of thirty FTEs if any employee receives a premium tax credit on a state health insurance exchange. If an employer provides minimum essential health coverage to its FTEs, but fails to pay at least 60 percent of its actuarial value or the coverage is considered unaffordable (costs more than 9.56 percent (9.86 in 2019) of household income), then the employer must pay a penalty of up to $3,390 per year for each FTE who receives the premium credit on an exchange, but not more than would be owed for the $2,320 per year penalty. An FTE is defined as an employee who is employed for thirty or more hours per week, calculated on a forty-hour work week. This provision also applies to grandfathered plans.[1]

2019

- January 1, 2019

  ➢ Elimination of the individual mandate penalty for non-compliance with having mandatory coverage of health insurance.

2022

- January 1, 2020

  ➢ <u>Cadillac Health Plan Tax</u>. Delayed from 2018 to 2020, and now again to 2022 - an excise tax of 40 percent, called the "Cadillac health plan" tax, will be imposed on "coverage providers" (i.e., health insurer for fully insured plans, the employer

---

1.   IRC Sec. 4980H. See Q 29, Part 1, for an explanation of how the penalties are calculated.

with respect to HSA or MSA contributions, and in all other cases, the "person that administers the plan") that provide high-cost healthcare coverage to the employer's employees. The excise tax will be imposed on the "excess benefit" provided to the employees.[1] There is a strong likelihood the Cadillac Tax will never be implemented. On July 27, 2017, the United States Senate passed a bill by a vote of 52-48, based solely on party lines, which would permanently repeal the "Cadillac Tax". To become effective, the House of Representatives would need to pass it as well. The bill was introduced by Nevada Senator Dean Heller but was never passed. On January 22, Congress passed, and President Trump signed another delay in the tax, postponing it until 2022.

141. If an employer offers an HRA and a group health plan but there is limited participation, will the HRA pass Code section 105(h)?

Probably yes. An employer offers a group health plan and an HRA to those employees participating in the group health plan (or a spouse's employer's group health plan). The employer has ten eligible employees, but only two employees participate in the group health plan and thus in the HRA, and one of them is the employer's only highly compensated employee. Is there any way that the HRA can pass the nondiscrimination rules of Internal Revenue Code section 105(h), which apply to self-funded (uninsured) employer health plans?

The answer is not definitive but is probably yes. In order to avoid "excess reimbursements," which are not excludible from taxable income, a plan must meet either:

(a)   one of two numerical tests; or

(b)   a general nondiscriminatory classification test set forth in Internal Revenue Code section 105(h)(3).

The numerical test is satisfied if the plan covers either:

(a)   at least 70 percent of all employees; or

(b)   at least 80 percent of all employees who are eligible to benefit under the plan if at least 70 percent of all employees are eligible to benefit.

If these tests are not met, section 105(h) is nevertheless met if such employees qualify under a classification established by the employer and found by the IRS not to discriminate in favor of highly compensated employees.[2] The nondiscriminatory classification test is met if the plan benefits a classification of employees set up by the employer which is found by the IRS not to be discriminatory in favor of highly compensated employees. In general, this determination is made based upon the facts and circumstances of each case.[3] It seems reasonable to assume that while the Code uses the word "cover," since the Code has a separate coverage nondiscrimination

---

1.   See Part VIII of this book for more information on Cadillac plans. IRC Sec. 4980I.
2.   IRC Sec. 105(h)(3)(A).
3.   Reg. §1.105-11(c)(2)(ii).

test, if the general nondiscriminatory classification test is used, it is passed if the employee classification is reasonable and the plan, as here, is offered to all eligible employees.

On this basis, the employer could treat the group health plan and the HRA as a single plan (even if they have separate plan documents) and test them on eligibility, not actual participation. An employer may "designate" two or more plans as one plan for purposes of the nondiscrimination requirements.[1]

Additionally, a determination that the combination of plans so designated does not satisfy such requirements does not preclude a determination that one or more of such plans, considered separately, satisfies such requirements. A single plan document may be utilized by an employer for two or more separate plans provided that the employer designates the plans that are to be considered separately and the applicable provisions of each separate plan.[2]

See also Q 95.

---

1.   Reg. §1.105-11(c)(4)(i).
2.   Reg. §1.105-11(c)(4)(i).

PART IV: HEALTH REFORM PROVISIONS THAT HAVE BEEN REPEALED, EXPIRED, OR NOT IMPLEMENTED

Free Choice Vouchers – Repealed

142. What were free choice vouchers and what were they intended to do?

As originally enacted in 2010, the health reform law required certain employers to provide free choice vouchers to qualified employees to allow those employees to purchase a health plan through a state health insurance exchange, beginning in 2014.[1] The original provision, advanced by Senator Ron Wyden (D., Ore.), would have allowed approximately 300,000 employees to "opt out" of their employer-sponsored plans and choose their own coverage using employer-financed vouchers. Due to concerns that it would result in the younger and healthier workers to "opt out" and result in higher costs for others, it was eliminated as part of the budget agreement on August 11, 2011. In the original law, employers offering health coverage and paying a portion of the costs of the plan were to provide vouchers to certain employees with a value equal to the contribution that the employer would have made to its own plan. If multiple plans were offered, the amount of the voucher would have been equal to the most generous employer contribution. The employer was to provide its share of self-only or dependent coverage at the worker's choice. Employers providing these vouchers would not have been subject to the employer mandate tax penalty as to such employees.

Originally, employers that offered minimum essential coverage were required to offer vouchers beginning in 2014 to certain employees whose cost of coverage was more than 8 percent but less than 9.8 percent of household income. Those lower-income workers could then opt out of their employer's health insurance and purchase more affordable coverage on the insurance exchange, where they would have received a premium subsidy through an income tax credit if their income was below 400 percent of the federal poverty level.

The voucher would have permitted the employee to take the employer's contribution toward health coverage and use it for a potentially cheaper exchange plan when the tax subsidy was taken into account. If the amount of the voucher exceeded the cost of the premium for the plan the worker bought through the exchange, the excess was to be paid to the employee. The money spent on health insurance would have been income-tax free, and any cash payment to the employee would have been taxed.

143. When was the provision for free choice vouchers repealed?

In 2011, appropriations legislation[2] repealed the free choice voucher provisions. It is not clear why, but the motive may have been, at least in part, to save money because some of the individuals who would have received vouchers were not eligible for the premium subsidy.

---

1. PPACA §10108(a); IRC Sec. 4980H(b)(3).
2. Department of Defense and Full-Year Continuing Appropriations Act, 2011, Pub. L. No. 112-10 (2011).

Additionally, it has been reported that certain groups, such as employers and unions, did not want workers to be able to buy health insurance on their own.

144. What was the impact of the repeal of free choice vouchers?

With free choice vouchers, Americans whose income fell below 400 percent of the federal poverty level and whose employer-sponsored health insurance premiums were between 8 and 9.8 percent of their total income would have been allowed to access the state insurance exchange and qualify for government assistance to buy insurance.

In 2014, if employees' share of their employer-sponsored health insurance premiums rose to 9.9 percent of their total income, they would be allowed to shop for more affordable health insurance in the new health insurance exchanges, with a taxpayer-funded subsidy. But again, at 9.8 percent and below, their only options would be to pay for their employer-sponsored coverage or to go without health coverage.

Had free choice vouchers survived, fewer Americans would have had to go without health insurance. Through the use of private subsidy dollars versus relying solely on taxpayer funded subsidies, arguably money would have been saved for taxpayers. If employer premiums continue to rise, more and more Americans would have become eligible for this option. More choice, and perhaps competition, would have been present in the health insurance market.

Some employers, especially small employers, had expressed interest in expanding the free choice voucher provision so that they would no longer need to pick their employees' health insurance. They liked the idea of giving their employees access to a health insurance system, much like the Federal Employee Health Benefits Plan, in which employers can essentially subsidize their employees' ability to shop on the new health insurance exchanges.

Vouchers could have proven to be good for employees because they would have been able to pick the plans that worked best for them versus the plans that worked best for their employer. Additionally, vouchers would likely have resulted in more Americans using the exchanges' risk pools, which could have assisted in holding down costs for everyone. As of 2019, however, the issue of free choice vouchers seems to have left the public stage which no interest by lawmakers in reviving.

Expanded 1099 Requirements – Repealed

145. What were the repealed 1099 requirements?

Under current tax law, a business making payments to a service provider (the "payee"), other than a corporation, aggregating $600 or more for services in the course of a trade or business in a year is required to send an information return (IRS Form 1099) to the IRS (and to the service provider-payee) setting forth the amount, as well as name and address of the recipient of the payment (generally on IRS Form 1099).[1]

---

1.   Internal Revenue Service https://www.irs.gov/forms-pubs/about-form-1099misc. Current though January 28, 2019 (Last accessed July 31, 2019).

<u>Expanded 1099 Requirements to Have Been Effective in 2012</u>. The Affordable Care Act made two changes to Internal Revenue Code section 6041.

First, businesses would have to issue the Forms 1099 to all persons and businesses, including corporations, for which aggregate annual payments are $600 or more.

Second, the forms would have to be issued for payments made to "property" providers as well as service providers. The new law adds the phrase "amounts in consideration of property" as payments made to a provider that must be reported, but the law does not define the term "property." Regulations will need to define this term, but it probably means all property, including the goods a business purchases for resale.[1]

<u>Exceptions</u>. The report of the Joint Committee on Taxation, beginning at page 113, provided for exceptions to the expanded 1099 requirement for a payee that is a tax-exempt corporation under Code section 501 and other specific provisions in the Code that except certain payments from reporting, such as securities or broker transactions as defined under Internal Revenue Code section 6045(a). This includes items reported under Internal Revenue Code sections 6042(a)(1), 6044(a)(1), 6047(e), 6049(a), or 6050N(a), other than payments with respect to which a statement is required under the authority of Internal Revenue Code sections 6042(a)(2), 6044(a)(2), or 6045.[2]

146. When and how were the expanded 1099 requirements repealed?

The Comprehensive 1099 Taxpayer Protection and Repayment of Exchange Subsidy Overpayments Act of 2011[3] repealed both the expanded Form 1099 information reporting requirements mandated by the 2010 health reform law and also the new 1099 reporting requirements imposed on taxpayers with rental income enacted by the 2010 Small Business Jobs Act.[4]

The Small Business Jobs Act enacted a requirement that individuals who receive rental income issue Forms 1099 to service providers for payments of $600 or more. It did this by specifying that "a person receiving rental income from real estate shall be considered to be engaged in a trade or business of renting property." The 1099 Act strikes Code section 6041(h), retroactively and effective for payments made after December 31, 2010, the original effective date of Code section 6041(h).

As a result of the repeal, the 1099 reporting rules continue unchanged. "All persons engaged in a trade or business and making payment in the course of such trade or business to another person" of $600 or more must report the amount and the name and address of the recipient to the IRS and to the recipient.[5] The Internal Revenue Code applies this requirement to payments of "rent, salaries, wages, premiums, annuities, compensations, remunerations, emoluments, or other fixed or determinable gains, profits, and income." Treasury regulations add "commissions,

---

1.   Internal Revenue Service https://www.irs.gov/forms-pubs/about-form-1099misc. Current though January 28, 2019 (Last accessed July 31, 2019).
2.   PPACA §9006, amending IRC Sec. 6041(a) and adding IRC Secs. 6041(h) and (i).
3.   P.L. 112-9.
4.   P.L. 111-240.
5.   IRC Sec. 6041(a).

fees, and other forms of compensation for services rendered aggregating $600 or more," as well as interest (including original issue discount), royalties, and pensions.[1]

147. Did the repeal of the expanded 1099 reporting repeal the penalties for 1099 failures that were increased in 2010?

No. The 2011 repeal did not repeal the expanded penalties for 1099 reporting failures enacted by the 2010 Small Business Jobs Act.

As of 2019, the penalty amounts are as follows:

- $50 per information return if correctly filed within thirty days (by March 30 if the due date is February 28); maximum penalty $545,500 per year ($191,000 for small businesses).

- $100 per information return if correctly filed more than thirty days after the due date but by August 1; maximum penalty $1,637,500 per year ($545,500 for small businesses).

- $270 per information return if correctly filed after August 1 or required information returns are not filed; maximum penalty $3,275,500 per year ($1,091,500 for small businesses).

Section 6724 provides for a waiver of these penalties due to reasonable cause. The regulations provide that the penalty will be waived only if the filer establishes that either:

(1)   there are significant mitigating factors with respect to the failure; or

(2)   the failure arose from events beyond the filer's control (an impediment). In addition, the filer must establish that the filer acted in a responsible manner; both before and after the failure occurred.[2]

148. Why were the expanded 1099 requirements repealed?

The expanded 1099 reporting requirements would have created significant burdens for businesses and many property owners by dramatically increasing the number of 1099 filings. Payments by any method were included, such as check, credit card, etc. Consider the airlines, hotels, rental cars, and restaurants that appear on a proprietor's or business credit card bill. Under the repealed law, 1099s would have been required if annual payments were more than $600. Additionally, any business that pays a person – for example, a plumber – more than $600 would be sending that person a Form 1099.

In addition, affected businesses and property owners would have been responsible for obtaining Taxpayer Identification Numbers from every payee that required a Form 1099. If a business

---

1.   Treas. Reg. §1.6041-1(a)(1)(i).
2.   See §301.6724-1 (a)(2).

was unable to obtain this information, it would have been required to withhold federal income taxes from payments to that payee ("backup withholding") and forward them to the government.

Absent the repeal, a huge increase in the paperwork burden would have ensued. It was not simply a matter of completing the forms, but also the work and time involved in obtaining the proper tax identification numbers and dealing with backup withholding requirements. Businesses are on different tax years, and some use cash-basis tax reporting while others use accrual accounting. As a result, the IRS would not have been able to match 1099s and tax returns in any meaningful way. Congress understood this, and both the House and Senate passed the repeal by very small bipartisan margins. President Obama also supported the repeal.[1]

Early Retiree Reinsurance Program (ERRP) – Expired

149. How was the Early Retiree Reinsurance Program (ERRP) intended to work?

Health reform provided for the Early Retiree Reinsurance Program (ERRP).[2] The statute and regulations required that reimbursements be used to lower plan sponsor and employee costs for the medical plan in various ways. Plan sponsors, including employers, unions, and other organizations, participating in health reform's ERRP were required to explain how they would use funds received under the program. HHS has stated that this program will be a major audit target over the next six years. Thus, plan sponsors must decide on how the funds will be used and develop a sustainable plan. Plan sponsors that deviate from their stated use run the risk of having their funds reclaimed after an HHS audit.

ERRP was a temporary program for sponsors of employment-based health plans to provide retiree health benefits to retirees who were over age fifty-five and not yet eligible for the Medicare program. The program provided an 80 percent subsidy for retiree claims of between $15,000 and $90,000 for plan sponsors that applied to and were accepted by HHS. Congress appropriated $5 billion for the program, which was effective June 1, 2010. The subsidy was to be available through the earlier of January 1, 2014, or the date when the funds were exhausted, which was at the end of 2011.[3] An HHS report stated that almost 5,500 plan sponsors have been approved to participate in the ERRP and that $535 million in ERRP reimbursement payments were made by December 31, 2010.[4] On December 9, 2011, the Centers for Medicare & Medicaid Services (CMS) and HHS announced that ERRP would not reimburse any claims incurred after December 31, 2011. As of December 2, 2011, HHS had reimbursed $4.5 billion of the program's total funds.

---

1.   See the White House Blog at https://www.irs.gov/forms-pubs/about-form-1099misc. Current through January 28, 2019 (Last accessed July 31, 2019). Note: This was from the White House website from the Obama Administration and is maintained as historical but not updated.

2.   PPACA §1102; 45 C.F.R. Part 149. See also 75 Fed. Reg. 24,450 (May 5, 2010).

3.   Employee Benefit Research Institute – see http://www.ebri.org/pdf/notespdf/EBRI_Notes_07-July10.Reins-Early.pdf. (No longer available online).

4.   HHS, "Report on Implementation and Operation of the Early Retiree Reinsurance Program During Calendar Year 2010" (Mar. 2, 2011), available at http://nasuad.org/documentation/ship/HHS%20REPORTS%20ON%20ERRP%20IMPLEMENTATION%20AND%20 OPERATION.pdf. (Last accessed July 31, 2019). The largest share of 2010 reimbursements went to state and local governments, including school districts and other local agencies, for their early retirees, but approved sponsors also included for-profit companies, unions, religious organizations, and other nonprofits.

Funds Use Requirements. Plan sponsors had to explain how they would meet the two primary requirements and then follow-through and continue to use the funds in that prescribed fashion.

Reduce Overall Costs. Plan sponsors were required to use reimbursements to reduce overall costs to the Plan. This could include:

- using the funds to pay any increases in health benefit (or health benefit premium) costs for the plan sponsor (i.e. to offset increases in those costs);

- reducing individuals' premium contributions, copayments, deductibles, coinsurance, or other out-of-pocket costs (or some combination of these costs); or

- providing a combination of these two options.

An "employment-based plan" qualifying for ERRP reimbursements also was required to implement programs and procedures to generate cost-savings with respect to participants with chronic and high-cost conditions. Health benefit claims that qualified for ERRP reimbursement were only those for medical services that would be covered by the Medicare program.[1] The HHS guidance also described specific items and services that would not be covered. HHS issued a document providing a list of Current Procedural Terminology (CPT) and Healthcare Common Procedure Coding System (HCPCS) codes excluded under Medicare, which could not be credited toward the ERRP cost threshold or reimbursed as part of the ERRP claims submission process.[2] Further, the HHS guidance stated that sponsors must comply with applicable state and federal requirements regarding benefits. Even though an item or service would not be reimbursed under the ERRP, a sponsor could cover the item or service in its health benefits plan.

Offset Future Increases. Plan sponsors that elected to use the reimbursements (or a portion of the reimbursements) to offset future increases to the plan sponsor would have to summarize how the reimbursements would relieve the organization of using its own funds to subsidize the increases and instead use its own funds to maintain current contributions. A plan sponsor had to explain how long it would continue to maintain its current level of financial support to the plan.

Federal Long-Term Care Benefit – Not Implemented

150. What was the federal long-term care benefit for which employees could have elected to pay?

The Affordable Care Act contained a provision whereby individuals could elect to purchase long-term care coverage from the federal government.[3] By January 1, 2012, the Department

---

1. This requirement is not specified in the law or regulations. See "Common Questions, Costs and Reimbursement," available at http://www.errp.gov/faq_costs.shtml. A question, originally posted on August 31, 2010, and updated on December 2, 2010, asked, "For what types of health benefit items and services can a sponsor receive reimbursement?" The answer states: "A sponsor can receive reimbursement for health benefit items and services for which Medicare would reimburse under Parts A, B, and D. For general reference as to what items and services are covered by Medicare Parts A and B, please refer to the Centers for Medicare & Medicaid Services' (CMS) Medicare & You 2010 and Your Medicare Benefits publications, which are available on the Medicare.gov website." (Last accessed July 31, 2019).

2. HHS, "Claims Ineligible for Reimbursement under the Early Retiree Reinsurance Program, Coding Details for Ineligible Services under Medicare which will apply to ERRP" (Oct. 18, 2010), Previous available at (no longer available) http://www.errp.gov/download/cpt/ProcedureCodesIneligibleForReimbursement.pdf.

3. PPACA §8002.

of Health and Human Services (HHS) was to determine eligibility requirements for a federal long-term care program. By October 1, 2012, plan design and development was to have been completed. However, HHS asked Congress to de-fund the program, although its provisions remain in the law. These provisions provide that employees of companies that choose to participate will be automatically enrolled in the long-term care program, and they may elect to opt out. This part of the health reform law was called the Community Living Assistance Services and Support (CLASS) Act. The employee, not the employer, who does not opt out would pay for this coverage through payroll deductions. Other workers and the self-employed would have been able to enroll on their own. Retirees were not eligible.

After paying premiums for five years, the employee would be eligible for a cash benefit of about $50 per day if he or she would have been unable to perform two or three Activities of Daily Living (ADLs), such as walking, bathing or dressing, or if he or she would have been cognitively impaired. In order to qualify for benefits, the employee was required to work for three of the five years during which he or she paid the premiums.

Under the CLASS Act, a person could not have been rejected for coverage because of health problems. It would have helped people with medical conditions that do not qualify for private long-term-care insurance or are subject to very high rates for the coverage. Additionally, it would have covered services that are not eligible for benefits under some long-term-care plans, including homemaker services, home modifications, and transportation, which could help a person stay out of a nursing home.

With the 2020 election looming, the possibility of long-term care as a federal benefit occasionally surfaces, with long-term care proposals being offered,

One proposal being offered by U.S. Representative Frank Pallone (D-NJ) would provide a daily cash benefit of about $100 after a two-year waiting period. As an alternative to the waiting period, Pallone also proposed a cash deductible that would increase with a beneficiary's income

In the current Congress, the new House Medicare for All bill from Reps. Pramila Jayapal (D-Wash.) and Debbie Dingell (D-Mich.) offers the most generous benefit. Under their bill, people of any age could qualify if illness, injury or age limit their ability to perform at least one "activity of daily living," such as bathing or dressing, or one or more "instrumental activities of daily living," such as managing money or taking prescribed medications. There would be no income or assets tests to qualify, and no copays or deductibles. The House bill—known as H.R. 1384—emphasizes home- and community-based care in the "least restrictive setting." But it would also pay for nursing home care. The earlier version of the House bill included a few mentions of long-term care but did not specify benefits. In addition, Senator Bernie Sanders (I-VT) is supporting long-term care as part of his Medicare For All program.

Costs have not been fully scored but estimates include costs of several hundred billion dollars a year to approximately $25 to $36 trillion over tem years.

151. Why was the federal long-term care program cancelled by HHS?

On September 21, 2011, the Senate Appropriations Committee deleted the $120 million that was earmarked for the annual design and marketing of CLASS policies from the 2012 HHS budget, and HHS disbanded the CLASS program. On October 14, 2011, HHS Secretary Kathleen Sebelius told Congress by letter[1] that HHS did not see a viable fiscal future for the CLASS program.[2] (Implementation of the program was contingent on HHS determining that the program was fiscally sustainable and on not using any other funds to pay benefits. The administration determined that the program would be too costly over the long run.)

Certain Republicans and Democrats had claimed that the program would eventually become a source of federal deficits. Senator Kent Conrad (D-N.D.) derided the program as a "Ponzi scheme of the first order". The nonpartisan Congressional Budget Office found the long-term care program would generate tens of billions of dollars between 2012 and 2021, when it was taking in premiums and paying out little in claims. However, the federal actuary for Medicare and Medicaid warned that, in subsequent years, the program would pay out more than it received.

The CLASS Act was ultimately repealed as part of the American Taxpayer Relief Act of 2012, signed by President Obama on January 2, 2013.

Automatic Enrollment Repealed

152. Why was the automatic enrollment provision repealed?

Under the Affordable Care Act as originally enacted, Section 18A of the Fair Labor Standards Act (FSLA) (as added by section 1511) required an employer with more than 200 full-time employees to automatically enroll new full-time employees in one of the employer's health-care benefits plans. Employers with 200 or fewer full-time employees were exempt from the automatic enrollment requirement.

On November 2, 2015, the Bipartisan Budget Act of 2015 was enacted, which repealed the automatic enrollment requirement. By virtue of this action, IRS Technical Release 2012-01 was superseded as well.

This requirement was very unpopular with employers who had concerns about how it would be administered. Because the Department of Labor advised in a Frequently Asked Questions (FAQ) document issued on December 22, 2010 that because the statute required implementation of the requirement "[i]n accordance with regulations promulgated by the Secretary [of Labor]," and no regulations had yet been issued, employers were not required to comply with 18A until the rules were completed and issued.

---

1.   U.S. Department of Health and Human Services. Secretary Sebelius' Letter to Congress about CLASS. (October 14, 2011) at http://www.ltcconsultants.com/articles/2011/class-dismissed/Sebelius-CLASS-Letter.pdf. (Last accessed July 31, 2019).

2.   In September 2011, HHS foreshadowed the administration's decision by terminating the CLASS program's chief actuary and reassigning other staff.

Employers under Internal Revenue Code Section 125[1] could use what is referred to as "default" or a "negative" election to enroll employees into a health care plan. In this scenario, the employee is deemed to have elected coverage unless they return a waiver in a timely manner. In this situation, the employer would have to provide adequate notice regarding the coverages and the costs, as well as allowing the employee to waive or drop out of the coverage.[2] Employers employing this method would probably want to be certain that state laws regarding withholding of wages would not be raised (even though probably pre-empted by ERISA).

1.   https://www.irs.gov/irb/2007-39_IRB/ar14.html. (Last Accessed July 31, 2019).
2.   IRS Revenue Bulletin 2002-20, May 20, 2002.

PART V: SMALL BUSINESS PROVISIONS

Employer Income Tax Credit for Health Insurance

153. Which employers are eligible for the tax credit for the purchase of health insurance available in 2010 and thereafter?

The new health insurance tax credit[1] is designed to help small for-profit businesses and tax-exempt organizations (estimated to be four million in number) that primarily employ low- and moderate-income workers.[2] This credit is available to employers that:

- have twenty-four or fewer eligible Full-Time Equivalent (FTE) employees with wages averaging less than $53,000 per employee per year (last indexed for inflation in 2017)[3] and pay at least 50 percent of health insurance costs;[4] or

- purchase Qualified Health Plans (QHP) from a Small Business Health Options Program (SHOP) Marketplace and offer coverage to all full-time employees. (Coverage does not have to be offered to dependents or employees working fewer than thirty hours per week to qualify for the tax credit).

Eligible employees do not include seasonal workers who work for an employer for 120 days a year or less,[5] owners, and owners' family members with average annual compensation of less than $53,000. Such employees are also not eligible if the business pays 50 percent or more of employee-only (single person) health insurance costs. Thus, compensation for seasonal workers, specified owners, and their family members and dependents are not counted in determining average compensation, nor is the health insurance cost for these people eligible for the health insurance tax credit.[6]

The credit is a general business credit is only available for two consecutive years after 2013 but can be carried back for one year and forward for twenty years.[7] The credit, which can be applied to tax liability under the alternative minimum tax, is 50 percent (35 percent for a tax-exempt employer).[8] A tax-exempt employer can use the credit against payroll taxes.

154. Can more than one employer be treated as a single employer for determining the credit available, the number of employers, and the average compensation?

Yes. All employers treated as a single employer under the controlled group rules or the affiliated service group rules are treated as a single employer for purposes of the tax credit.[9]

---

1. IRC Sec. 45R.
2. https://www.healthcare.gov/small-businesses/provide-shop-coverage/small-business-tax-credits/.
3. https://www.irs.gov/affordable-care-act/employers/small-business-health-care-tax-credit-and-the-shop-marketplace.
4. IRC Sec. 45R(d)(2).
5. IRC Sec. 45R(d)(5).
6. https://www.healthcare.gov/small-businesses/provide-shop-coverage/small-business-tax-credits/.
7. IRC Sec. 38(b) & 39(A).
8. IRC Sec. 38(c)(4)(B)(vi).
9. IRC Sec. 45R(e)(5), incorporating the controlled group rules of IRC Sec. 414(b) and (c), the affiliated service group rules of IRC Sec. 414(m), and the anti-abuse rules of IRC Sec. 414(o).

155. Can an employer use the credit to offset its alternative minimum tax liability?

Yes. The credit can be used in conjunction with section 38(c)(1) of the Internal Revenue Code (Code).[1]

156. Can an employer reduce employment tax payments such as withholding for income taxes, Social Security taxes or Medicare taxes in advance anticipation of receiving the credit?

No. The credit is for income taxes not employment taxes.

157. Can the credit be used in determining estimated tax payments for the year?

Yes.

158. How are FTEs determined for the health care tax credit?

Generally, the employer must consider all employees who perform services for the small employer during the tax year when determining the number of full-time equivalent employees, as well as average annual wages and premiums paid.

In the FTE calculation, do not include the wages and hours worked of the certain types of employees mentioned below:

- Owner of a sole proprietorship

- Partner in a partnership

- Shareholder of S Corporation owning more than 2 percent

- Owner of more than 5 percent of the business or other businesses

- Family members of the above

Premiums paid on behalf these employees cannot be included to determine the amount of the health care tax credit.

For purposes of the health care tax credit, one FTE generally equals 2,080 hours per year. This is different from other provisions of the Affordable Care Act that count thirty hours per week as one FTE. Any number of part-time employees that work a combined number of hours equal to that of a full-time employee equals one FTE. For example, two half-time employees count as one FTE; twenty half-time employees are equivalent to ten FTEs. Exclude from the calculation the hours that exceed 2,080. Also exclude seasonal employees who work 120 or fewer days per year from the calculation of the number of FTEs and average annual wages; however, the

---

1.   As modified by section 38(c)(4)(B)(vi).IRC section 38.

health insurance premiums paid by the employer on behalf of these employees may be counted in determining the amount of the credit.

159. How is the employer 50 percent payment requirement applied?

Originally, in 2010, the employer would qualify if it paid at least 50 percent of the cost of employee-only coverage, regardless of the actual coverage elected by an employee. For example, at Company A, where employee-only coverage costs $500 per month and family coverage costs $1,500 per month, the employer paid at least $250 per month (50 percent of employee-only coverage) per covered employee. Even if an employee selected family coverage, Company A would meet the contribution requirement to qualify for the tax credit during 2010.

Beginning in 2011, however, the percentage paid by the employer for each enrolled employee needed to be a uniform percentage for that coverage level. If the employee received coverage that is more expensive than single coverage (such as family or self-plus-one coverage), the employer must pay at least 50 percent of the premium for each employee's coverage in 2011 and there-after. Each part-time employee counts as a fraction of a full-time employee – for example, two employees working half-time would count as one employee.

Thus, grandfathered health insurance plans that, for instance, provide for 100 percent of family coverage for executives and 100 percent of employee-only coverage for staff will qualify for the tax credit in 2010 but not in 2011 or beyond.[1]

160. Which persons are not counted in determining the number of employees or their average compensation?

Owners are all self-employed individuals (proprietors, partners, members of LLCs taxed as partnerships), (more than) 2 percent shareholders of an S corporation,[2] (more than) 5 percent or more owners of a small business,[3] and family members[4] and dependents of the self-employer, (more than) 2 percent S corporation shareholders, or (more than) 5 percent or more owners.[5] Leased employees are eligible employees for the credit.[6]

Leased employees are considered eligible employees for purposes of the credit.[7]

161. Is a household employer eligible for the small employer tax credit?

Yes. A household employer can be eligible for the credit even if they have employees that are not performing services in a trade or business.

---

1.   *See* http://www.irs.gov/newsroom/article/0,,id=220839, 00.html (No longer available on IRS.gov). See also, Part VI for more information on grandfathered health plans.
2.   IRC Sec. 1372(b).
3.   Defined by IRC Sec. 416(i)(1)(B)(i), which contains the top-heavy retirement plan rules.
4.   Any individual who bears any of the relationships described in IRC Sec. 152(d)(2)(A) through (G).
5.   IRC Sec. 152(d)(2)(H).
6.   IRC Sec. 45R(e).
7.   IRC Sec. 45R(e).

162. How does an employer claim the health care tax credit?

The proper form is Form 8941, "Credit for Small Employer Health Insurance Premiums," to calculate the credit.[1] Detailed instructions are available on the IRS website.[2]

Small businesses must include the amount as part of the general business credit on your income tax return. Tax-exempt organizations must include the amount on line 44f of the Form 990-T, *Exempt Organization Business Income Tax Return*. The form 990-T[3] must be filed to claim the credit as a tax-exempt.

Small business employers may be able to carry the credit back or forward and may be eligible for a refundable credit.

163. How much is the employer tax credit for employer purchase of health insurance?

The new tax credit applies to for-profit and nonprofit employers meeting certain requirements. From 2010 through 2013, the amount of the credit for for-profit employers was 35 percent, and 25 percent for nonprofit employers, of qualifying health insurance costs. The credit is increased for any two consecutive years beginning in 2014 to 50 percent of a for-profit employer's qualifying expenses and 35 percent for nonprofit employers.[4]

164. Are employers outside of the United States eligible for the small business tax credit?

Yes. An employer located outside of the United States may be eligible for the tax credit if the employer has income that is considered to be effectively connected with the conduct of a trade or business in the United States. Businesses in U.S. territories would be eligible as well. In addition, they would have to meet the other requirements to claim the credit.

165. Can a farmers' cooperative be eligible for the small business tax credit?

Yes. A farmers' cooperative, as defined under IRC section 521, and subject to tax under IRC section 1381 can be eligible for the credit as long as it otherwise meets the definition of an eligible small employer.

---

1. https://www.irs.gov/forms-pubs/about-form-8941.
2. https://www.irs.gov/pub/irs-pdf/i8941.pdf.
3. https://www.irs.gov/pub/irs-pdf/f990t.pdf.
4. See https://www.irs.gov/uac/small-business-health-care-tax-credit-questions-and-answers-who-gets-the-tax-credit (Last accessed August 18, 2018). See Q 3.

166. How is the small employer tax credit for the purchase of health insurance calculated?

The credit is available to small employers, as determined by including all employers in the controlled group or affiliated service group.[1] The credit is largest if there are ten or fewer employees and their average wages do not exceed $25,000.[2] The amount of the credit is phased out for businesses with more than ten eligible employees (but less than twenty-five) and average compensation of more than $25,800 (but less than $51,600). For the average compensation and number of employees, owners and owners' family members are excluded.[3] Employers must contribute at least 50 percent of the cost of the health insurance premiums to qualify for the credit. The amount of an employer's premium payments that counts for purposes of the credit is capped by the average premium for the small group market in the employer's geographic location, as determined by HHS.[4]

For nonprofit employers, the credit is taken against the employer's income tax and Medicare withholding obligations and the employer's Medicare payment obligation, but not against Social Security taxes.[5]

Until 2014, the credit applies to any accident and health insurance (major medical) coverage purchased by an employer.

Beginning in 2014, the credit is only:

- available for coverage offered through the SHOP Exchange;[6]

- available for two consecutive years but can be taken any time in 2014 or thereafter;[7]

- 50 percent for for-profit employers and 35 percent for nonprofit employers.

After January 1, 2018, for SHOP insurance employers have two options for enrolling:

- Through an insurance company

- With the assistance of a SHOP-registered agent or broker

---

1.   IRC §45R(e)(5).
2.   IRC §45R(c).
3.   IRC §45R(e).
4.   https://www.irs.gov/uac/small-business-health-care-tax-credit-questions-and-answers (Last accessed July 31, 2019).
5.   IRC Sec. 45R(f)(1)(B).
6.   An exception was made in 2014 for employers in designated counties of the states of Washington and Wisconsin. See IRS Notice 2014-6. An exception was made for businesses in Iowa for 2015. See IRS Notice 2015-08.
7.   IRC §45R(e)(2).

Tax Credit Calculations – Examples using 2010 and 2014 and subsequent years	
Example: For-Profit Employer with Ten Employees	
Number of Employees:	10
Wages:	$250,000 total, or $25,000 per worker
Employee Health Care Costs:	$70,000
2010 Tax Credit:	35% × $70,000 = $24,500
2014 and later Tax Credit:	50% × $70,000 = $35,000
Example: For-Profit Employer with Forty Part-Time Employees	
Number of Employees:	40 half-time employees (the equivalent of 20 full-time workers)
Wages:	$500,000 total, or $25,000 per full-time equivalent worker
Employee Health Care Costs:	$240,000
2010 Tax Credit:	$28,000 (35% credit with phase-out)
2014 and later Tax Credit:	$40,000 (50% credit with phase-out)
Example: Nonprofit Employer with Nine Employees	
Employees:	9
Wages:	$198,000 total, or $22,000 per worker
Employee Health Care Costs:	$72,000
2010 Tax Credit:	25% × $72000 = $18,000
2014 and later Tax Credit:	35% × $72,000 = $25,200[1]

167. Can an employer that has already claimed the small employer health insurance tax credit prior to 2014 still be eligible for the credit after 2014?

Yes. Even if an eligible small employer has taken the credit for tax years beginning in 2010 through 2013, those years <u>do not count</u> toward the two-consecutive taxable year period.

Starting in 2014, that employer may claim the credit for two-consecutive taxable years, beginning with the first taxable year in or after 2014.

168. Are there exceptions to the rule that the small business health insurance tax credit is available only through purchases of Qualified Health Plans from a SHOP exchange during 2014 and later?

Yes, there are instances where the IRS has offered an exception to that rule because Qualified Health Care Plans were not available during the SHOP Marketplace. Also remember that after January 1, 2018, SHOP coverage is purchased only through insurance companies or SHOP-registered agents or brokers.

---

1.   For additional guidance, see IRS Notices 2010-44 and 2010-82.

Exception 1 – Counties in Washington and Wisconsin

IRS Notice 2014-06[1] provides that Small employers that have principal business addresses in one of the following counties – because QHPs were not available through the SHOP Marketplace in 2014, can claim the credit under the pre-tax year 2014 rules.

The credit will be calculated at the maximum rate for the entire 2014 taxable year:

- 50 percent rate and 35 percent rate for tax-exempt eligible.

- The 2014 taxable year will be the first year of the two consecutive taxable year credit period. For a detailed description of this transition relief, see Notice 2014-6.

Washington counties affected:

Adams, Asotin, Benton, Chelan, Clallam, Columbia, Douglas, Ferry, Franklin, Garfield, Grant, Grays Harbor, Island, Jefferson, King, Kitsap, Kittitas, Klickitat, Lewis, Lincoln, Mason, Okanogan, Pacific, Pend Oreille, Pierce, San Juan, Skagit, Skamania, Snohomish, Spokane, Stevens, Thurston, Wahkiakum, Walla Walla, Whatcom, Whitman, and Yakima counties.

Wisconsin:

Green Lake, Lafayette, Marquette, Florence, and Menominee counties.

Exception 2 – Counties in Iowa

IRS Notice 2015-08[2] provides that small employers with a principal business addresses in one of the listed counties where QHPs are not available through the SHOP Marketplace for all or part of 2015, may claim the credit under the pre-tax year 2014 rules.

The credit will be calculated at the maximum rate for the entire 2015 taxable year:

- 50 percent rate.

- 35 percent rate for tax-exempt eligible small employers.

- If the eligible small employer does not claim the credit for the 2014 taxable year, but claims the credit for the 2015 taxable year, then the 2015 taxable year will be the first year of the two consecutive taxable year credit period. If the eligible small employer first claims the section 45R credit for the 2014 taxable year, then the 2015 taxable year is the second year of the two-consecutive taxable year credit period, regardless of whether the eligible small employer takes advantage of the relief described in this paragraph.

---

1.   See IRS Notice 2014-06.
2.   See IRS Notice 2015-08 and IRS Notice 2016-75.

Iowa counties affected:

Adair, Adams, Appanoose, Audubon, Benton, Black Hawk, Boone, Bremer, Buchanan, Buena Vista, Butler, Calhoun, Carroll, Cass, Cedar, Cerro Gordo, Cherokee, Chickasaw, Clarke, Clinton, Crawford, Dallas, Davis, Decatur, Delaware, Des Moines, Dubuque, Floyd, Franklin, Fremont, Greene, Grundy, Guthrie, Hamilton, Hancock, Hardin, Harrison, Henry, Humboldt, Iowa, Jackson, Jasper, Jefferson, Johnson, Jones, Keokuk, Kossuth, Lee, Linn, Louisa, Lucas, Madison, Mahaska, Marion, Marshall, Mills, Mitchell, Monona, Monroe, Montgomery, Muscatine, Page, Palo Alto, Pocahontas, Polk, Pottawattamie, Poweshiek, Ringgold, Sac, Scott, Shelby, Story, Tama, Taylor, Union, Van Buren, Wapello, Warren, Washington, Wayne, Webster, Winnebago, Worth, and Wright counties.

169. How is the average annual wage calculated?

Average annual wages are calculated by dividing the aggregate amount of wages paid by the employer by the number of Full-Time-Equivalent (FTE) employees, for the taxable year.[1] Full-time employees would be calculated by dividing the total hours worked by all employees during the tax year by 2,080 (with a maximum of 2,080 hours for any one employee).

Seasonal workers are generally disregarded and are counted as FTE equivalents only if they work for the employer for more than 120 days per year.[2] In addition, the owner of a business is not counted as an employee for purposes of the tax credit if he or she is a sole proprietor, a partner in a partnership, a shareholder owning more than 2 percent of an S corporation or an owner of more than 5 percent of other businesses. Family members are not counted if they are children or grandchildren; siblings or step-siblings; parents or grandparents; step-parents; nieces or nephews; aunts or uncles; sons- or daughters-in-law; fathers- or mothers-in-law; or brothers- or sisters-in-law.

Average annual wages are determined by dividing the aggregate amount of wages paid by the employer by the number of FTE employees, for the taxable year.[3] The result is rounded down to the nearest $1,000.

Example:

An employer pays $288,000 in wages to thirteen Full Time Employees.

The employer's annual wage would be $22,000 — $288,000 divided by 13 equals $22,153.85 = $22,000 (rounded down to nearest thousand)

The average wage threshold for determining the phase-out of credits is adjusted for inflation after 2013.

---

1.   IRC Sec. 45R(c) and (d).
2.   IRC Sec. 45R(d)(5).
3.   IRC Sec. 45R(c) and (d).

170. How did the employer health insurance tax credit change beginning in 2014?

Beginning in 2014, the following changes were implemented to the small business health care tax credit.

- The amount of the credit increased from 35 percent to 50 percent (25 percent to 35 percent in the case of a tax-exempt eligible small employer) of the lesser of:

  - the aggregate amount of employer contributions for premiums for qualified health plans offered by the employer (nonelective contributions excluding employee compensation deferrals) to its employees through an exchange; or

  - the average employer contributions (nonelective contributions excluding employee compensation deferrals) which the employer would have made to a qualified health plan for the small group market in the rating area in which the employee enrolls for coverage.[1]

Firms could claim the credit for 2010 through 2013 and for any two consecutive years after that.[2] [This includes regulations to prevent avoiding the two-year limit on the credit period through the use of successor or multiple entities.][3]

The self-employed are eligible for individual premium assistance (the individual tax credit) for health insurance purchased through an exchange available if they met the income requirements (less than 400 percent of the federal poverty level).

To continue receiving a tax credit for 2014 and afterward, a small employer must have dropped its existing coverage and purchase group coverage in the newly created exchanges.[4]

The average annual wage thresholds are indexed for inflation.[5]

Simple Cafeteria Plan

171. How do existing cafeteria plans work?

In general, employer and employee contributions to any cafeteria plan are deductible to the employer, not subject to Social Security tax, and not taxable income to the participant. Thus, available benefits, which can be purchased with "pre-tax dollars," include:

- health and dental insurance;

- accidental death and dismemberment policies;

- vision coverage

---

1. IRC Sec. 45R(e).
2. IRC Sec. 45R(e)(2).
3. IRC Sec. 45R(i).
4. IRC Sec. 45R(e)(2).
5. IRC Sec. 45R(d)(3).

- reimbursement for health and dental expenses not covered by insurance;

- dependent care;

- adoption assistance;[1]

- group term life insurance;

- COBRA premiums;

- Health Savings Accounts (Health FSA and dependent care FSA);

- 401(k) deferrals;

- adoption assistance; and

- disability insurance.

Benefits not available through cafeteria plans are:

- Archer Medical Savings Accounts (MSAs);

- athletic facilities;

- employee discounts;

- lodging on business premises;

- meals;

- moving expense reimbursements;

- tuition reduction;

- transportation and commuting benefits;

- scholarships or fellowships;

- educational assistance;

- Section 132 fringe benefits;[2]

- long-term care insurance and LTC services,[3] (though may be paid from an HSA funded through a cafeteria plan);

---

1. See Notice 97–9 Sec. II; Reg. §601.601(d)(2)(ii)(b); 2007 Prop. Reg. §1.125-5(h) (adding adoption assistance as a permissible FSA benefit to health and dependent care FSAs.
2. IRC Sec. 125(f)(1).
3. IRC Sec. 125(f)(2).

- health insurance purchased on an exchange that is not purchased pursuant to an employer's exchange-purchased group health insurance plan;[1]

- group term insurance for a spouse or dependent; and

- 403(b) elective deferrals.

A plan offering any nonqualified benefit is not a cafeteria plan.[2] If a cafeteria plan fails to operate in compliance with Internal Revenue Code section 125 or fails to satisfy any of the written plan requirements for health FSAs, the plan is not considered an Internal Revenue Code section 125 cafeteria plan, and employees' election of nontaxable benefits results in gross income to all employees.[3]

172. What is the simple cafeteria plan created through the Affordable Care Act?

Simple cafeteria plans were created through the Affordable Care Act in 2011 in order to make it easier for small businesses to be able to qualify under the tax requirements for this type of benefit. The simple cafeteria plan became effective in 2011.[4]

In order to qualify for a simple cafeteria plan the following requirements must be met:

- Qualify as an Eligible Employer

- Employees must meet eligibility requirements

- Employer must make contributions on behalf of any qualified employees

Each of these requirements is further discussed in subsequent Questions and Answers.

The concept of the simple cafeteria plan is similar to 401(k) retirement plan safe harbors, SIMPLE 401(k)s, and SIMPLE-IRAs, whereby most nondiscrimination requirements can be met by plan design and the use of either nonelective employer contributions for all eligible employees or employer-matching contributions for participating employees making salary reduction contributions.

Simple cafeteria plans will be of interest to eligible employers that might otherwise have difficulty passing one or more of the applicable income tax nondiscrimination tests. For example, small employers may have difficulty passing the 25 percent key employee concentration test[5] for cafeteria plans or the 55 percent average benefits test for dependent care.[6] In the past, these

---

1.   IRC Sec. 125(f)(3).
2.   IRC Sec. 125(d)(1)(B); Treas. Reg. §1.125-1(q).
3.   Treas. Reg. §1.125-1(c)(1), (c)(6) and (c)(7). However, benefits that fail discrimination tests under the various IRC sections do not fail to be qualified benefits. Rather, the discriminatory amounts are included in gross income, not the entire amount of the benefit(s).
4.   IRC Sec. 125 (j).
5.   IRC Sec. 125(b).
6.   IRC Sec. 129(d).

employers might have decided not to sponsor a cafeteria plan or designed their plans to exclude Highly Compensated Employees (HCEs).

173. Are simple cafeteria plans subject to any of the regular cafeteria plan tax rules?

Yes. A simple cafeteria plan is a cafeteria plan adopted by an eligible employer that meets specified contribution, eligibility, and participation requirements.[1] Except for the special rules that apply to the simple cafeteria plan, the plan also must meet the other cafeteria plan rules.[2] Thus, it must be a written plan[3] administered in accordance with the written plan terms. The cafeteria plan must, among other things:

- be maintained by an employer for employees; and

- operate in compliance with the Internal Revenue Code and regulation requirements as well as the requirements of other applicable laws.

In part, the written plan requirements include the following:

- Describe all benefits

- Provide rules for eligibility to participate

- Indicate how employer and employer contributions are made under the plan

- State the maximum amount of employer and employee elective contributions

- Describe the procedure for making elections

- Provide that all elections are irrevocable (except to the extent that the plan includes the "change in status" rules)

- List additional requirements if one of the offerings is a health, dependent care, or adoption assistance FSA

- State the plan year

- Provide rules for substantiation of expenses

- If the plan provides a grace period, it must include required language applicable to the two-and-a-half-month grace period

- Coverage during Family and Medical Leave Act (FMLA) leave

- Describe the regulations' "use it or lose it" rule

---

1.   IRC Sec. 125(j)(2).
2.   IRC Sec. 125(j)(2), stating that a "simple cafeteria plan" means a **cafeteria plan** .... [Emphasis added.]
3.   IRC Sec. 125(d)(1).

An employer maintaining a cafeteria plan in which any highly compensated employee participates must make sure that both the cafeteria plan and each qualified benefit satisfies the cafeteria plan and benefit-specific nondiscrimination requirements. A failure to satisfy the non-discrimination rules results in additional taxable income to all employees.

174. What is the benefit of the simple cafeteria plan?

Simple cafeteria plans automatically meet all "applicable nondiscrimination requirements,"[1] which are the nondiscrimination requirements of Internal Revenue Code section 125(b) (the 25 percent concentration test) and the nondiscrimination requirements of Internal Revenue Code sections 79(d), 105(h), and 129(d) applicable to group term life insurance, self-insured health benefits (medical expense reimbursement), and dependent care assistance benefits (child care), respectively.

Through an apparent oversight, Internal Revenue Code section 125(j) does not provide an express exception for the Affordable Care Act's health insurance nondiscrimination rules of new Internal Revenue Code section 9815. However, it is likely that if the same insurance options are available to all participants, regardless of their use, the health insurance nondiscrimination rules will be met.[2] The health insurance nondiscrimination regulations, when they are issued, will provide the definitive answer.

Certain benefit-specific nondiscrimination rules continue to apply, such as those for adoption assistance plans because Internal Revenue Code section 137 is not listed in the exemptions from the nondiscrimination rules.

175. What is a Premium Conversion Cafeteria Plan (POP)?

A Premium Conversion Cafeteria Plan (POP) – but not a health FSA – is a form of cafeteria plan specifically authorized by Section 125 of the IRC that offers an election between cash and payment of the employee share of the premium for employer-provided health insurance. Section 125 of the Internal Revenue Code permits employers to sponsor a plan that enables their employees to pay premiums for certain types of benefits on a pre-tax basis. Section 125 also permits employers to sponsor health and dependent care flexible spending account plans. These types of plans are referred to as "cafeteria plans." A plan that does not offer flexible spending accounts is often referred to as a "premium conversion," "premium only," or "POP" cafeteria plan.

Health insurance premium conversion cafeteria plans meet the regular cafeteria plan eligibility nondiscrimination rules if they meet a "safe harbor" test[3] and pass a safe harbor/unsafe harbor facts-and-circumstances test.[4]

---

1.   IRC Sec. 125(j)(6).
2.   Kevin Knopf, Attorney-Advisor, Office of Tax Policy of the Treasury Department, ECFC Annual Symposium (Aug. 6, 2010) stated that the safe harbor for simple cafeteria plans does extend to the nondiscrimination requirements of IRC Sec. 9815 that apply to employer-provided health insurance plans.
3.   Reg. §1.125-7.
4.   Reg. §1.125-7(b)(3).

Examples of situations that meet or fail this test include the following:[1]

Example 1. Same qualified benefit for same salary reduction amount. Employer A has one employer-provided accident and health insurance plan. The cost to participants electing the accident and health plan is $10,000 per year for single coverage. All employees have the same opportunity to purchase the plan and reduce their salaries by $10,000. The cafeteria plan <u>satisfies</u> the eligibility test.

Example 2. Same qualified benefit for unequal salary reduction amounts. Same facts as Example 1 except the cafeteria plan offers Non-Highly Compensated Employees (NHCEs) the election to reduce their salaries by $10,000 to pay premiums for single coverage. The cafeteria plan provides an $8,000 employer flex-credit to Highly Compensated Employees (HCEs) to pay a portion of the premium, and it provides an election to reduce their salaries by $2,000 to pay the balance of the premium. The cafeteria plan <u>fails</u> the eligibility test because the employer contribution – the flex credit – is given solely to HCEs.

Example 3. Accident and health plans of unequal value. Employer B's cafeteria plan offers two employer-provided accident and health insurance plans: Plan X, available only to HCEs, is a low-deductible plan. Plan Y, available only to NHCEs, is a high-deductible plan (as defined in Internal Revenue Code section 223(c)(2)). The annual premium for single coverage under Plan X is $15,000 per year, and it is $8,000 per year for Plan Y. Employer B's cafeteria plan provides that HCEs may elect salary reduction of $15,000 for coverage under Plan X, and that NHCEs may elect salary reduction of $8,000 for coverage under Plan Y. The cafeteria plan <u>fails</u> the eligibility test.

Example 4. Accident and health plans of unequal value for unequal salary reduction amounts. Same facts as Example 3, except that the amount of salary reduction for HCEs to elect Plan X is $8,000. The cafeteria plan also <u>fails</u> the eligibility test.

176. How does a Premium Conversion Cafeteria Plan work?

The employer's group health insurance program requires an employee to pay a portion of the premium. A Premium Conversion Plan allows you to make these payments on pre-tax rather than on an after-tax basis. These premium payments are considered salary redirections, or reductions. Therefore, the employee will not owe Federal income tax, FICA, state or local tax on the premium amounts. Employees walk away with more dollars in their paychecks. Because the money is not included as income for FICA, employers also enjoy the benefit of lower payroll taxes.

177. What are the special rules for Premium Conversion Cafeteria Plans (POP)?

Premium Conversion Cafeteria Plans are a tax benefit under IRC Section 125. It allows employees to save both FICA and Federal Income Tax on their portion of insurance premiums that are deducted from their paychecks. When employees decrease their gross pay, the employer pays less in matching FICA taxes, which amounts to employer savings. The Premium Conversion Cafeteria plan requires a written plan that the administrator should keep on file. In addition, the administrator should have a written enrollment form that evidences that employees have elected to contribute a portion of their pay on a pre-tax basis.

---

1.   Reg. §1.125-7(b)(3)(iv).

178. Can business owners participate in a simple cafeteria plan?

When a business wants to avoid the 25 percent concentration test and contribute for owner-employees, it is likely that only a regular C corporation can do so because only these shareholder-employees are "employees" for income tax purposes. Sole proprietors, more-than-2-percent S corporation shareholders, and partners (including members of LLCs taxed as partnerships) are not employees for income tax purposes. Rather, they are "self-employed" individuals.

179. Which employers are "eligible employers" who can sponsor a simple cafeteria plan?

In order to establish and maintain a simple cafeteria plan, an employer must qualify as an "eligible employer". An "eligible employer" is one that employed an average of 100 or fewer employees during business days during either of the two preceding years.

- A year may only be taken into account if the employer was in existence throughout that year.[1]

    - The Internal Revenue Code's simple cafeteria plan provisions do not define the term "year" for the eligible employer definition. Pending IRS guidance, it seems reasonable to use the plan year selected by the employer as the plan's measuring period. If an employer was not in existence throughout the preceding year, the eligible employer determination is based on the average number of employees that it is reasonably expected such employer will employ on business days in the current year.[2]

There are special rules for "growing employers". If an eligible employer's workforce continues to grow, it can remain eligible in subsequent years until the employer employs an average of 200 or more employees on business days during any year preceding any such subsequent year.[3] In the year following a year in which an employer employs more than two hundred employees on business days, the plan must be converted to a classic cafeteria plan.

If an employer has 100 or fewer employees in the current year but more than 100 employees in either of the two preceding years, the employer cannot adopt a simple cafeteria plan for the current year but will be able to do so in the succeeding year.

Special Rules:

Leased employees: Leased employees within the meaning of Internal Revenue Code sections 414(n) and (o) are counted as employees.[4] However, the Internal Revenue Code is silent as to whether an employer can disregard (or count on a full-time equivalent basis) part-time, temporary, or seasonal employees when determining whether it is an eligible employer.

---

1.   IRC Secs. 125(j)(5)(A) and (B).
2.   IRC Sec. 125(j)(5)(B).
3.   IRC Sec. 125(j)(5)(C)(ii).
4.   IRC Sec. 125(j)(5)(D)(ii).

Pending guidance, the conservative approach is to count all employees when making an eligible employer determination.

Aggregation: Controlled corporations and other entities under common control as defined in IRC section 52(a) or IRC section 52(b) must be combined to calculate employer size.[1]

There is no lower limit on the size of the employer. Additionally, an employer whose only employees are prohibited group members (key employees or HCEs), or with only one owner-employee, could qualify as an eligible employer. However, the prohibition against sole proprietors, partners, and more-than-2 percent shareholders in a Subchapter S Corporation participating in a cafeteria plan applies, so, in general, only owner (shareholder)-employees of C corporations can participate in a simple cafeteria plan. Moreover, it is not clear whether such an employer could meet the required employer contributions test discussed below in Q 186.

180. What happens when an employer with a simple cafeteria plan ceases to qualify to sponsor such a plan?

Employers with simple cafeteria plans will cease to qualify as eligible employers as their workforces expand beyond 200 employees. Thus, employers that maintain simple cafeteria plans must monitor their status as eligible employers. If an employer ceases to be an eligible employer, the regular concentration and nondiscrimination tests will apply. Employers that cease to qualify as eligible employers will need to determine whether to amend or discontinue their cafeteria plan.

181. What aggregation rules apply in defining an employer?

The employer aggregation rules under Internal Revenue Code sections 52 and 414 (controlled and affiliated service groups) generally apply for purposes of determining an eligible employer.[2] Additionally, an employer includes a "predecessor employer," but the term is undefined.[3]

182. Who are "qualified employees" that must be eligible to participate in a simple cafeteria plan?

For purposes of a simple cafeteria plan, "qualified employees" are all nonexcludable employees who:

- had at least 1,000 hours of service during the preceding plan year (except a Highly Compensated Employee[4] or a "key employee"[5]) and who is eligible to participate in the plan;[6]

- are at least twenty-one years old;

- have more than one year of service as of any day in the plan year;

---

1.   IRC Sec. 52(a), IRC Sec. 52(b).
2.   IRC Sec. 125(j)(5)(D)(ii).
3.   IRC Sec. 125(j)(5)(D)(i).
4.   As defined by IRC Sec. 414(q). See IRC Sec. 125(j)(3)(D)(iii).
5.   As defined by IRC Sec. 416(i).
6.   IRC Sec. 125(j)(3)(D)(iv).

- are not covered under a collective bargaining agreement; and

- are U.S. citizens or resident aliens working within the United States.

Qualified employees must be able to elect any benefit under the plan.

This definition of qualified employee is relevant only to the two alternative minimum contribution requirements, discussed below in Q 186, and to Highly Compensated Employees (HCEs) and key employees. HCEs and key employees may participate like everyone else so long as they are "employees" and do not receive disproportionate employer nonelective or matching contributions. Comparable contributions must be made for all eligible employees.

183. What are the definitions of a Highly Compensated Employee (HCE) and "key employee"?

Internal Revenue Code section 414(q) defines a Highly Compensated Employee (HCE) as an employee who:

- was a more-than-five-percent owner of the employer at any time during the current or preceding plan year regardless of salary; or

- was for the preceding plan year, had compensation in excess of a specified dollar threshold ($125,000 for 2019).

If elected by the employer, an HCE may also be an employee in the "top-paid group" (generally constituting the top 20 percent ranked by compensation) of employees.

Internal Revenue Code section 416 defines a key employee as an employee who, during the plan year, was:

- an officer of the employer with annual compensation in excess of a specified dollar threshold ($180,000 2019);

- a more-than-five-percent owner of the employer; or

- a more-than-one-percent owner of the employer with annual compensation in excess of $150,000.

184. Which employees are excludable employees?

Excludable employees (employees who need not be allowed to participate) are those who:

- have not attained age twenty-one (or a younger age provided in the plan) before the end of the plan year;

- have less than 1,000 hours of service in the prior plan year;

- have less than one year of service as of any day during the plan year;

- are covered under a collective bargaining agreement; or

- are nonresident aliens working outside the United States.[1]

An employer may have a shorter age and service requirement but only if such shorter service or younger age applies to all employees.[2]

Employees who worked 1,000 hours in a previous plan year but who do not have a year of service in the current plan year can be excluded for the current year.[3] However, since the rule is that they can be excluded if they do not have a year of service on any day in the year, they may have 1,000 hours if they go from full-time to part-time during the current plan year. This is an important point when the employee's salary is less than the health benefits. Employees should be entitled to the entire maximum benefit if elected, even if greater than their compensation in order to safeguard simple status for the cafeteria plan.

185. What is the benefit nondiscrimination requirement?

Each participating employee must be able to elect any benefit under the plan under the same terms and conditions as all other participants.[4] Again, if the special requirements of a specific benefit apply, such as adoption assistance, they must be met as well.

186. What is the employer minimum contribution requirement?

The employer must make contributions to provide qualified benefits on behalf of any qualified employees. As stated, these are non-Highly Compensated Employees and non-key employees. There are two alternative employer contribution requirements. Employer contributions to a simple cafeteria plan must be sufficient to provide benefits to qualified employees of at least either:

- Non-Elective Contribution

  - A uniform percentage of at least 2 percent of compensation (defined as it is under Internal Revenue Code section 414(s) for retirement plan purposes, whether or not the employee makes salary reduction contributions to the plan).[5]

- Matching Contribution

  - An amount that meets or exceeds the lesser of twice the employee's contribution through reduction of salary (200 percent matching contribution) or more, if specified by the plan or 6 percent of the employee's compensation for the plan year.[6]

---

1.   IRC Sec. 125(j)(4)(B).
2.   IRC Sec. 125(j)(4)(B)(iv).
3.   IRC Sec. 125(j)(4)(B)(ii).
4.   IRC Sec. 125(j)(4)(A)(ii).
5.   IRC Sec. 125(j)(3)(A)(i).
6.   IRC Sec. 125(j)(3)(A)(ii).

Additional contributions can be made, but the rate of any matching contribution for HCEs or key employees cannot be greater than the rate of the match for the qualified employees (the participating employees other than key and highly compensated employees).[1] The compensation method must be the same for all qualified employees.

The minimum contribution must be available for application toward the cost of any qualified benefit (any permitted benefit other than a taxable benefit) offered under the plan.[2]

187. Does the Matching Contribution Method require a 100 percent or 200 percent employer match?

The 200 percent matching requirement may be only a 100 percent requirement. An argument may be made for counting an employee's salary reduction contributions when determining whether an employer has contributed "twice the amount of the [employee's] salary reduction contributions." Arguably, the law calls for the employer to contribute the employee's salary reductions (which are employer contributions for tax purposes[3]) plus a 100 percent match, for a total contribution equal to twice the employee's salary reductions. Another reading is that the employer must contribute twice the amount of the employee's salary reductions as matching contributions. The 6 percent of compensation limit applies under either interpretation. The report on health reform by the Joint Committee on Taxation supports the 100 percent view and states that the minimum matching contribution is the lesser of 100 percent of the employee's salary reduction contribution, or 6 percent of the employee's compensation for the plan year.[4]

Compensation for purposes of the minimum contribution requirement is compensation within the meaning of Internal Revenue Code section 414(s).[5]

188. What happens when an employer has all HCEs, all key employees and no qualified employees?

An employer whose workforce consists of only one or more HCEs or Key Employees would not have any qualified employees. The Internal Revenue Code's simple cafeteria plan provisions require a contribution for each qualified employee. Thus, if the plan provides for that contribution but there is no qualified employee, it is not clear whether such an employer would be exempt from this requirement (in which case the plan could be funded entirely with salary reductions) or would be disqualified from having a simple cafeteria plan.[6]

---

1.   IRC Sec. 125(j)(3)(B).
2.   IRC Sec. 125(j)(3)(A).
3.   Treas. Reg. §1.125-1(r).
4.   Technical Explanation of the Revenue Provisions of the "Reconciliation Act of 2010," as amended, in Combination With the "Patient Protection and Affordable Care Act," p. 119 (JCX-18-10) (Mar. 21, 2010) at https://www.jct.gov/publications.html?func=startdown&id=3673. Kevin Knopf, Attorney-Advisor, Office of Tax Policy of the Treasury Department, ECFC Annual Conference (Mar. 4, 2011), has also unofficially expressed this view. (Last accessed July 15, 2018).
5.   IRC Sec. 125(j)(7).
6.   IRC section 125.

189. How does an employer test a Simple Cafeteria Plan for non-discrimination?

Testing for non-discrimination of a Section 125 plan is a three-pronged approach:

1. **Eligibility Test**: If too many Highly Compensated Employees (HCEs) are excluded from the plan, it will be deemed by the IRS to be discriminatory

2. **Contribution and Benefits Test**: The plan will be found to be discriminatory if the HCEs and other key employees can obtain more or better benefits than employers.

3. **Concentration Test**: The plan will be found to be discriminatory if HCEs and key employees actually select more benefits under the plan.

    a. Under this test, No more than 25 percent of total nontaxable benefits may be elected by key employees

If the plan is properly created and implemented, meeting items one and two above should not be a problem because all benefits are equally available to all employees. However, with the third test, compliance review is necessary to ensure that the utilization of the plan is not skewed.

190. What are the consequences if a plan fails the discrimination test?

In the event of a failure, HCEs and key employees must include the highest aggregate value of taxable benefits that could have been chosen for that table in their taxable income. This penalty applies, regardless of actual elections. Note that the entire plan does not fail for all participants just because it is discriminatory. Employees who are not in the prohibited group (non-HCE or non-Key) can still exclude the benefits from income.

No Employer Mandate for Small Employers

191. Is there an employer mandate for small employers?

No. As discussed in Part VIII, the Employer Mandate ("play or pay") tax penalty on employers failing to provide specified health coverage for employees only applies to employers with fifty or more full-time equivalent employees. Thus, small employers have no tax penalty for not offering health insurance. Instead, certain small employers who would otherwise be eligible for the tax credit for health insurance will not obtain that benefit if they provide no health insurance or if they provide health insurance that does not meet the requirements to obtain the tax credit.

W-2 Reporting Exemption

192. Which employers are exempt from the W-2 reporting requirement?

The Affordable Care Act requires employers to report the cost of coverage under an employer-sponsored healthcare plan. This does not mean that the coverage is taxable. The value of the employer's excludable contribution to health coverage continues to be excluded from an employee's income and is not taxable. This reporting is for informational purposes only and will provide employees useful and comparable consumer information on the cost of their health care coverage.

Transition relief was in place for the reporting requirement beginning in 2012 and continues to apply until the IRS publishes additional guidance.

Employers filing fewer than 250 Forms W-2 for the preceding calendar year are exempt from the W-2 reporting requirement until further notice. Otherwise, employers must comply with the W-2 requirements for the W-2 forms.[1]

Employers that provide "applicable employer-sponsored coverage" under a group health plan are subject to a W-2 reporting requirement. This includes businesses, tax-exempt organizations, and federal, state, and local government entities (except with respect to plans maintained primarily for members of the military and their families).

The health reform law requires the value of the health care coverage to be reported in Box 12 of Form W-2, with Code DD to identify the amount. There is no reporting on the Form W-3 of the total of these amounts for all the employer's employees. In general, the amount reported should include both the portion paid by the employer and the portion paid by the employee.

---

1.   IRS Notice 2012-9, Q&A-3.

PART VI: GRANDFATHERED HEALTH PLANS

193. What is a grandfathered health plan?

A grandfathered plan is:

- one continuously in existence since March 23, 2010;

- with at least one person (need not be the same person) covered at all times;

- not changed except as permitted, as discussed hereafter;

- plans that lose their grandfathered status cannot regain that status;

- grandfathered status is determined separately for each benefit package; and

- employers can offer both grandfathered coverage and new (or non-grandfathered) coverage.

Grandfathered plans are exempt from many, but not all, health reform rules,[1] described in more detail below, as long as grandfather status is maintained, which can last indefinitely. A self-insured group plan, an insured group plan, and an individual insurance policy may each be grandfathered. As of 2017, 23 percent of firms offering health care plans offer at least one grandfathered plan and 17 percent of covered workers are actually covered by a grandfathered plan.[2]

A plan that is grandfathered may permit employees to re-enroll and their family members to enroll after March 23, 2010.[3] While new employees can join the plan, there are restrictions on whether new groups of employees can be transferred to the plan without tainting grandfathered status.[4]

For plan or insurance changes made before March 23, 2010, the changes will be considered to be part of the coverage on March 23, 2010, though they were not in effect on such date, and will not cause the plan to lose grandfathered status, if:

- the changes were effective after March 23, 2010, pursuant to a legally binding contract entered into on or before March 23, 2010;

- the changes were effective pursuant to a filing with the state insurance department that was filed on or before March 23, 2010; or

---

1.   PHSA §§2701, 2702, 2703, 2705, 2706, 2707, 2709, 2713, 2715A, 2716, 2717, 2719, and 2719A. See also https://www.federalregister.gov/articles/2015/11/18/2015-29294/final-rules-for-grandfathered-plans-preexisting-condition-exclusions-lifetime-and-annual-limits. (Last accessed July 31, 2019).
2.   KFF, Section 13 Grandfathered Health Plans, https://www.kff.org/report-section/ehbs-2017-section-13-grandfathered-health-plans/.
3.   https://www.federalregister.gov/articles/2015/11/18/2015-29294/final-rules-for-grandfathered-plans-preexisting-condition-exclusions-lifetime-and-annual-limits. (Last accessed July 31, 2019).
4.   https://www.federalregister.gov/articles/2015/11/18/2015-29294/final-rules-for-grandfathered-plans-preexisting-condition-exclusions-lifetime-and-annual-limits. (Last accessed July 31, 2019).

- the changes were effective after March 23, 2010, pursuant to written amendments to the plan that were adopted on or before March 23, 2010.[1]

Changes that would cause a plan to lose grandfathered status adopted after March 23, 2010, but before June 14, 2010, had to be undone for the first year beginning on or after September 23, 2010, for grandfather status to be maintained.[2]

It should be noted that after September 23, 2010, all plans, whether grandfathered or not, need to include:

- no lifetime dollar limits to key health benefits;

- plan cannot be canceled solely because of an honest mistake made by you or your employer on your insurance application; and

- plans must extend dependent coverage to adult children until they turn twenty-six.

Job-based plans and grandfathered plans are not required to:

- provide preventive services at no cost;

- provide claim appeals and coverage denials;

- provide protection of choice of health care providers and access to emergency room care.

194. If I have a grandfathered plan, am I considered covered?

Yes. For plan years through 2020, grandfathered plans count as qualifying health coverage. Another consideration is that since the penalty of non-compliance has been reduced to zero, even if the plan didn't count as covered, there is no fine.

195. What events can cause a plan to lose grandfathered status?

Plans can lose their grandfathered status if they:

- reduce or lower coverage;

- raise coinsurance, copayments, or deductibles by significant amounts;

- significantly low employer contributions to the plan; or

- change the yearly limit of what the plan pays.

196. Are there different types of grandfathered plans?

Yes. Essentially grandfathered plans can have originated from either a person's employment or have been acquired from an insurance company, agent, or broker.

---

1. https://www.federalregister.gov/articles/2015/11/18/2015-29294/final-rules-for-grandfathered-plans-preexisting-condition-exclusions-lifetime-and-annual-limits. (Last accessed July 31, 2019).
2. Treas. Reg. §54.9815-1251T(g)(2)(ii); DOL Reg. §2590.715-1251(g)(2)(ii); HHS Reg. §147.140(g)(2)(ii).

Employment-based grandfathered plans could enroll people after March 23, 2010, and still maintain their grandfathered status if the plans:

- haven't been changed to substantially cut benefits or increase costs for plan holders;

- notify plan holders they have a grandfathered plan; and

- have continuously covered at least one person since March 23, 2010.

Individual grandfathered plans COULD NOT enroll people after March 23, 2010 and have those new enrollments considered a grandfathered policy. But insurance companies can continue to offer the grandfathered plans to people <u>who were enrolled before</u> that date. If an insurance company decides to stop offering a grandfathered plan, it must provide notice ninety days before the plan ends and offer other coverage options.

197. What are the differences in coverage requirements between grandfathered policies and ACA-compliant policies?

The table below is a thumbnail comparison of major the differences between grandfathered and marketplace plans:

REQUIRED COVERAGE	GRANDFATHERED PLAN	MARKETPLACE PLAN
1. No lifetime limits on coverage	Yes	Yes
2. Ban on arbitrary cancellations of policy	Yes	Yes
3. Cover adult children until age 26	Yes	Yes
4. Provide a Summary of Benefits and Coverage	Yes	Yes
5. Spend majority of premium dollars on health care vs. administrative cost	Yes	Yes
6. Free preventive care	No	Yes
7. Guaranteed right of appeal of decision	No	Yes
8. Held accountable through Rate Review	No	Yes
9. No yearly limits on coverage	No	Yes
10. Cover pre-existing conditions	No	Yes

198. Administrative extension until October 31, 2019 of Non-ACA compliant individual and small group health insurance policies.

The administration announced on March 5, 2014 that noncompliant individual health and small group policies can be extended an additional two years for policy years beginning on or before Oct. 1, 2016.[1] As with the original extension, the state insurance regulator needed to agree to approve such policies, and the health insurance companies must decide to continue offering such policies. However, the extension has in fact been further extended multiple times.

In February 2016, an additional extension was issued, allowing plans to be renewed up to October 1, 2017 but required a termination date by December 31, 2017.[2] On April 9, 2018, the Department of Health and Human Services further allowed plans to be renewed up to October 31, 2019, but require a termination date of these policies by December 31, 2019.[3] On March 25, 2019, the Centers for Medicare & Medicaid Services (CMS) announced a one-year extension to the transition policy for individual and small group health plans that allows issuers to continue policies that do not meet ACA standards. The transition policy has been extended to policy years beginning on or before October 1, 2020, provided that all policies end by December 31, 2020. This means individuals and small businesses may be able to keep their non-ACA compliant coverage through the end of 2020, depending on the policy year. Carriers may have the option to implement policy years that are shorter than twelve months or allow early renewals with a January 1, 2020 start date in order to take full advantage of the extension.[4]

The following states are allowing renewals of 2013 policies.

Insurance departments in thirty-five states now allow insurers to renew 2013 policies, while fifteen states and the District of Columbia prohibited renewals, as shown by the list below.

ALLOW RENEWALS

Alabama	Nebraska
Alaska	New Hampshire
Arizona	New Jersey
Arkansas	North Carolina
Florida	North Dakota
Georgia	Ohio
Hawaii	Oklahoma
Idaho	Pennsylvania
Illinois	South Carolina
Indiana	South Dakota
Iowa	Tennessee
Kansas	Texas

---

1.   See CMS memo at http://www.cms.gov/CCIIO/Resources/Regulations-and-Guidance/Downloads/transition-to-compliant-poli-cies-03-06-2015.pdf and http://www.cms.gov/Newsroom/MediaReleaseDatabase/Fact-sheets/2014-Fact-sheets-items/2014-03-05-2.html. (Last accessed August 12, 2018).

2.   https://www.cms.gov/CCIIO/Resources/Regulations-and-Guidance/Downloads/final-transition-bulletin-2-29-16.pdf. (Last accessed August 12, 2018).

3.   Insurance Standards Bulletin Series – INFORMATION – Extension of Transitional Policy through 2019, https://www.cms.gov/CCIIO/Resources/Regulations-and-Guidance/Downloads/Extension-Transitional-Policy-Through-CY2019.pdf.

4.   https://www.cms.gov/newsroom/press-releases/cms-issues-2019-exchange-open-enrollment-period-final-report.

Kentucky   Utah

Louisiana   Virginia

Maine (until December 2019)[1]   West Virginia (allowed until October 2016)

Michigan   Wyoming

Mississippi   Wisconsin

Missouri

ELIMINATED RENEWALS

California (2015)   Montana

Colorado (2015)   Nevada (2014)

Connecticut (2014)   New Mexico (2015)

Delaware (2014)   New York (2014)

District of Columbia (2014)   Oregon (2015)

Maryland (2014)   Rhode Island (2014)

Massachusetts (2014)   Vermont (March 31, 2014)

Minnesota (2014)   Washington (2014)

199. How does an employer or other plan sponsor decide whether to maintain grandfathered status?

The sponsor should review the benefits obtained by grandfathered status, i.e., the rules that would otherwise apply that do not apply to grandfathered plans. A plan sponsor should evaluate the relative cost versus the benefit of preserving grandfathered status, including business objectives, such as employee recruitment and retention. In cases in which a collective bargaining agreement or other contract restricts changes that can be made to coverage or contributions, the decision to retain grandfathered status will be relatively easy. Otherwise, the new mandates' increased costs will need to be evaluated. For instance, an employer that already provides rich preventive care benefits should experience less of a cost increase from the preventive care requirements than an employer that provides little or no preventive care coverage. Additionally, an employer that pays the same amount for individual and family coverage for all employees would not be impacted by the new rules preventing discrimination in insured group plans in favor of highly compensated individuals. This analysis will need to be repeated in a year in which changes are contemplated.

200. Has the DOL provided any tools to assist in determining grandfathered status?

Yes. The Department of Labor's Employee Benefits Security Administration (EBSA) has published an online self-help tool to enable group health plans, plan sponsors, plan administrators, and health insurance issuers comply with the healthcare reform's group

---

1. Bulletin 428, Extension of Transitional Authorization to Renew Small Group Health Plans, https://www.maine.gov/pfr/insurance/legal/bulletins/pdf/428.pdf.

health plan requirements, namely, the "Self-Compliance Tool for Part 7 of ERISA: Affordable Care Act Provisions."[1]

It provides a detailed and cumulative list of ninety-three self-compliance questions and answers in a checklist addressing the various Affordable Care Act (ACA) provisions applicable to group health plans and health insurance issuers. Various questions allow users to assess their plan's compliance with ACA provisions addressing grandfather plan status, extension of dependent coverage to adult children, prohibitions on lifetime limits and restrictions on annual limits, prohibition on preexisting condition exclusions for individuals under age nineteen, Summary of Benefits and Coverage (SBC) and uniform glossary, preventive services, internal claims and appeals, and external review.

201. What are the details for the DOL self-help healthcare reform tool and grandfathered plan checklist?

Section A. Determining Grandfather Status[2]

Grandfather status is intended to allow people to keep their coverage as it existed on March 23, 2010, while giving plans some flexibility to make "normal" changes while retaining grandfather status. Grandfathered health plan coverage provides individuals' protection from significant reductions in coverage, provides for coverage to include numerous protections implemented through the Affordable Care Act, and allows employers the flexibility to manage costs.

The analysis for determining grandfather status applies separately to each benefit package or option. Accordingly, grandfather status might be retained for some benefit packages or options and relinquished for others. By contrast, if an employer relinquished grandfather status for self-only, family, or any other tier within a benefits package, it would relinquish grandfather status for the entire package.[3]

There are transitional rules regarding grandfather status as related to recent changes to plan terms.

- Specifically, a plan will not relinquish grandfather status for changes effective after March 23, 2010, pursuant to a legally binding contract entered into on or before March 23, 2010; changes effective after March 23, 2010, pursuant to a filing on or before March 23, 2010, with a State insurance department; or changes effective after March 23, 2010, pursuant to written amendments to a plan that were adopted on or before March 23, 2010.

- If after March 23, 2010, a group health plan or issuer made changes to the terms of the plan or coverage and the changes were adopted prior to June 14, 2010, the

---

1.   See https://www.dol.gov/sites/default/files/ebsa/about-ebsa/our-activities/resource-center/publications/compliance-assistance-guide-appendix-a.pdf. (Last accessed July 31, 2019).

2.   See https://www.dol.gov/sites/default/files/ebsa/about-ebsa/our-activities/resource-center/publications/compliance-assistance-guide-appendix-a.pdf. (Last accessed August 12, 2018).

3.   See 29 CFR 2590.715-1251(a)(1)(i).

changes will not cause the plan or coverage to relinquish grandfather status, if the changes were revoked or modified effective as of the first day of the first plan year beginning on or after September 23, 2010, and the terms of the plan or health insurance coverage on that date, as modified, would not cause the plan or coverage to otherwise cease to be a grandfathered health plan.[1]

If the answer is "yes" to questions 1 and 2 below the group health plan may be a grandfathered health plan.

Question 1 – Did the plan exist with at least one individual enrolled on March 23, 2010? A grandfathered group health plan must have been in existence with an enrolled individual on March 23, 2010. Any plan that does not meet this requirement is not in grandfathered status.[2]

Question 2 – Has the plan continuously covered someone (not necessarily the same person) since March 23, 2010? A group health plan will not relinquish its grandfather status merely because one or more (or all) individuals enrolled on March 23, 2010, cease to be covered. However, a grandfathered health plan must continuously cover someone (not necessarily the same person) since March 23, 2010, to maintain its status.[3]

Question 3 – Has the plan eliminated all or substantially all benefits to diagnose or treat a particular condition? For the purpose of determining grandfather status, the elimination of benefits for any necessary element to diagnose or treat a condition is considered the elimination of all or substantially all benefits to diagnose or treat a particular condition.[4]

Question 4 – Has the plan increased a percentage cost-sharing requirement (such as an individual's coinsurance)? Any increase measured from March 23, 2010, in a percentage cost-sharing requirement causes a plan to relinquish grandfather status.[5]

Question 5 – Has the plan increased a fixed-amount cost-sharing requirement other than a copayment (such as a deductible or out-of-pocket limit) such that the total percentage increase measured from March 23, 2010, exceeds the maximum percentage increase? The maximum percentage increase is medical inflation, expressed as a percentage, plus 15 percentage points.[6] Medical inflation is the increase since March 2010, in the overall medical care component of the Consumer Price Index for All Urban Consumers (CPI-U) (unadjusted) published by the Department of Labor using the 1982-1984 base of 100.[7]

Question 6 – Has the plan increased a fixed-amount copayment such that the increase measured from March 23, 2010 exceeds the greater of: the maximum percentage increase, or an amount equal to $5 plus medical inflation? The maximum percentage increase is medical

---

1.   See 29 CFR 2590.715-1251(g)(2).
2.   See 29 CFR 2590.715-1251(a)(1)(i).
3.   See 29 CFR 2590.715-1251(a)(1)(i).
4.   See 29 CFR 2590.715- 1251(g)(1)(i).
5.   See 29 CFR 2590.715-1251(g)(1)(ii).
6.   See 29 CFR 2590.715-1251(g)(3)(ii).
7.   See 29 CFR 2590.715-1251(g)(3)(i).

inflation, expressed as a percentage, plus 15 percentage points.[1] Medical inflation is the increase since March 2010 in the overall medical care component of the Consumer Price Index for All Urban Consumers (CPI-U) (unadjusted) published by the Department of Labor using the 1982-1984 base of 100.[2]

Question 7 – Has there been a decrease in the contribution rate by the employer (or employee organization) towards the cost of any tier of coverage for any class of similarly situated individuals by more than 5 percentage points below the contribution rate for the coverage period that includes March 23, 2010? If the contribution rate is based on a formula, was the decrease in the contribution rate based on a formula by more than 5 percent below the contribution rate for the coverage period that includes March 23, 2010?[3]

If a group health plan modifies the tiers of coverage it had on March 23, 2010, (for example, from self-only and family to a multitiered structure of self-only, self-plus-one, self-plus-two, and self-plus-three-or-more), the employer contribution for any new tier would be tested by comparison to the contribution rate for the corresponding tier on March 23, 2010. If the plan adds one or more new coverage tiers without eliminating or modifying any previous tiers and those new coverage tiers cover classes of individuals that were not covered previously under the plan, the new tiers would not be analyzed under the standards of paragraph (g)(1).[4]

In cases of a multiemployer plan that has either a fixed-dollar employee contribution or no employee contribution towards the cost of coverage, if the employer's contribution rate changes, provided any changes in the coverage terms would not otherwise cause the plan to cease to be grandfathered and there continues to be no employee contribution or no increase in the fixed-dollar employee contribution towards the cost of coverage, the change of the employer's contribution rate will not, in and of itself, cause a plan that is otherwise a grandfathered health plan to relinquish grandfather status.[5]

Question 8 – Has the plan added or decreased an overall annual limit on benefits? A plan will relinquish its grandfathered status if it:

- adds an overall annual limit on the dollar value of all benefits when it did not previously impose an overall annual limit;[6]

- previously imposed an overall lifetime limit on the dollar value of benefits (but no overall annual limit) and adopts an overall annual limit at a dollar value that is lower than the dollar value of the lifetime limit on March 23, 2010;[7] or

---

1.   See 29 CFR 2590.715-1251(g)(3)(ii).
2.   See 29 CFR 2590.715-1251(g)(3)(i).
3.   See 29 CFR 2590.715-1251(g)(1)(v)(B).
4.   See Part II, question 3 at https://www.dol.gov/sites/default/files/ebsa/about-ebsa/our-activities/resource-center/faqs/aca-part-ii.pdf. (Last accessed August 12, 2018).
5.   See DOL FAQs About the Affordable Care Act Implementation Part I, question 4 at https://www.dol.gov/sites/default/files/ebsa/about-ebsa/our-activities/resource-center/faqs/aca-part-i.pdf (Last accessed August 12, 2018).
6.   See 29 CFR 2590.715-1251(g)(1)(vi)(A).
7.   See 29 CFR 2590.715-1251(g)(1)(vi)(B).

- decreases the dollar value of the overall annual limit that was in place on March 23, 2010.[1]

If the answer to any of questions 3-8 was "yes", the plan is NOT a grandfathered plan.

Question 9 – Did the plan change issuers after March 23, 2010? If the answer to question 9 is "yes", if the group health plan changed issuers after March 23, 2010, and the change in issuer was effective on or after November 15, 2010, the plan will continue to be a grandfathered plan provided no other changes that would relinquish grandfather status are made.[2]

If a group health plan changed issuers after March 23, 2010, and the change was effective prior to November 15, 2010, the plan will have relinquished grandfather status. The operative date is the effective date of the new contract, not the date the new contract was entered into. Special rules apply for collectively bargained plans.[3]

Question 10 – Did the plan change from self-insured to fully-insured after March 23, 2010? If the group health plan was self-insured and changed to fully insured after March 23, 2010, and the change was effective on or after November 15, 2010, the plan will continue to be a grandfathered plan provided no other changes are made that would relinquish grandfather status.[4] Proceed to question 11. If a group health plan was self-insured and changed to fully-insured after March 23, 2010, and the change was effective prior to November 15, 2010, the plan will have relinquished grandfather status.

Question 11 – If the group health plan changed issuers (including a plan that was self-insured and changed to fully insured) and has maintained grandfather status did the plan provide documentation to the new issuer of the plan terms under the prior health coverage sufficient to determine whether any other change was made that would relinquish grandfather status? To maintain status as a grandfathered health plan, the plan must provide to the new issuer (and the new issuer must require) documentation of plan terms (including benefits, cost sharing, employer contributions, and annual limits) under the prior health coverage sufficient to determine whether any other change is being made that would relinquish grandfathered status.[5]

Question 12 – Does the plan include a statement that it believes it is a grandfathered health plan in any plan materials provided to participants and beneficiaries that describe the benefits provided under the plan? To maintain status as a grandfathered group health plan, the plan must include a statement, in any plan materials provided to a participant or beneficiary describing the benefits under the plan, that the plan believes it is a grandfathered health plan within the meaning of section 1251 of the Affordable Care Act and must provide contact information for questions and complaints. Model language is available.[6]

---

1.   See 29 CFR 2590.715-1251(g)(1)(vi)(C)).
2.   See 29 CFR 2590.715-1251(a)(1)(ii), as amended.
3.   See 29 CFR 2590.715-1251(f) for collectively bargained plans.
4.   See 29 CFR 2590.715-1251(a)(1)(ii), as amended.
5.   See 29 CFR 2590.715-1251(a)(3)(ii), as amended.
6.   See 29 CFR 2590.715-1251(a)(2).

Question 13 – Is the plan maintaining records documenting the terms of the plan in connection with the coverage in effect on March 23, 2010, and are these records made available upon request? To maintain status as a grandfathered group health plan the plan must maintain records documenting the terms of the plan in connection with the coverage that was in effect on March 23, 2010, and any other documents necessary to verify, explain, or clarify its status as a grandfathered health plan. These records must be maintained for as long as the plan takes the position that it is grandfathered and must be available for examination upon request.[1]

202. What health reform requirements apply to grandfathered plans?

These seven requirements apply to all health plans, including grandfathered plans.

Health Reform Rules That Apply to All Plans, Including Grandfathered Plans

1. Pre-existing Condition Exclusions (PCE) prohibited.[2] Grandfathered individual coverage can continue to apply these exclusions, but group health plans and group health insurance issuers cannot impose PCEs for plan years beginning on or after January 1, 2014. This prohibition took effect for plan years beginning on or after September 23, 2010, (i.e., January 1, 2011, for calendar-year plans) with respect to individuals enrolled in the plan who are younger than nineteen years of age.

2. Excessive waiting periods of more than ninety days have been prohibited for plan years beginning in 2014.[3]

3. Annual/lifetime limits have been prohibited for plan years beginning in 2014.[4] These rules apply to grandfathered plans, but the annual limit prohibition does not apply to grandfathered individual coverage. For benefits that are not "essential health benefits," both lifetime and annual limits are allowed if not prohibited by other federal and state laws.[5] Failure to provide any services for a condition is allowed, but if any benefits are provided for a condition, these prohibitions apply.[6] While grandfathered health plans are not required to offer essential health benefits, they cannot impose either annual or lifetime dollar limits on the essential health benefits they do offer. Individual grandfathered policies may continue annual limits but not lifetime limits.

4. Rescission of policies is prohibited except for fraud or misrepresentation beginning in 2014.[7]

---

1.   See 29 CFR 2590.715-1251(a)(3)(i)(A) & (i)(B), as amended.
2.   PHSA §2704(a), IRC Sec. 9815 & ERISA Sec. 715.
3.   PHSA §2708.
4.   PHSA §2711.
5.   https://www.federalregister.gov/articles/2015/11/18/2015-29294/final-rules-for-grandfathered-plans-preexisting-condition-exclusions-lifetime-and-annual-limits. (Last accessed August 1, 2019).
6.   https://www.federalregister.gov/articles/2015/11/18/2015-29294/final-rules-for-grandfathered-plans-preexisting-condition-exclusions-lifetime-and-annual-limits. (Last accessed August 1, 2019).
7.   PHSA §2712.

5.   <u>Dependent coverage</u> for children under age twenty-six must be offered until 2014, except for adults eligible for coverage through their own employer.[1]

6.   <u>SBC Requirement</u>. The requirement to provide at least a four-page summary of benefits and coverage to plan participants applies to grandfathered plans.[2] This is discussed in more detail in Part VII of this publication.

7.   <u>Medical Loss Ratio (MLR)</u> reporting and rebates, designed to lower health insurance costs apply to grandfathered plans.[3]

203. What health reform requirements do not apply to grandfathered plans and apply only to new plans or plans that lose grandfathered status?

These thirteen requirements apply only to new plans or plans that lose grandfathered status, not to grandfathered plans:

Additional Rules Applicable to New and Nongrandfathered Health Plans

1.   <u>Fair health insurance premiums</u>.[4] These are the rules that limit insurers in the individual or small group market as to allowable factors to alter premiums:

   * coverage category (e.g., whether the coverage is individual versus family coverage);

   * rating area (as established by states);

   * age (may not vary by more than 3 to 1 for adults); and

   * tobacco use (may not vary more than 1.5 to 1).[5]

2.   <u>Guaranteed-Availability Rules Applicable to Small and Large Group Markets</u>.[6] Healthcare reform makes changes to these requirements.

   Through December 31, 2013, the guaranteed-availability rules apply to health insurance issuers in the small group market, but not to issuers in the large group market. These rules require a health insurance issuer that actively markets coverage in the small group market to accept every small employer that applies for coverage and to make all products that it actively markets in the small group market available to all small employers. The issuer also must accept for enrollment every eligible individual who applies for coverage when first eligible. Insurers are permitted to impose employer contribution and minimum participation requirements (to the extent consistent with applicable state law), within certain limitations.

---

1.   PHSA §2714.
2.   PHSA §2715.
3.   PHSA §2718.
4.   PHSA §2701.
5.   PHSA §2701(a)(1)(A).
6.   PHSA §2702.

As of January 1, 2014, the guaranteed-availability rules are significantly expanded. The statutory changes amended and restructured the guaranteed-availability provisions, making these rules applicable to health insurance issuers in the large and small group markets and effecting certain other changes.[1] Each health insurance issuer that offers health insurance coverage in the individual or group market (regardless of whether the coverage is offered in the large or small group market) is required to accept every employer and individual in the state that applies for such coverage. Enrollment may, however, be restricted to open or special enrollment periods.[2]

3. Guaranteed renewability, which means that an insurer must renew coverage if requested by the plan sponsor.[3] Prior to January 1, 2014, these rules apply to both the small and large group market. They require group insurance issuers in both the small and large group market to renew coverage at the option of the plan sponsor subject to specified exceptions and restrictions (such as nonpayment of premiums, fraud, or violation of certain employer contribution or group participation requirements).

4. Nondiscrimination based on health status. Group health plans and health insurance issuers offering health insurance coverage are prohibited from discriminating against an individual with regard to eligibility or coverage based on a health status factor.[4] Health reform extended these rules, effective January 1, 2014, to health insurance issuers offering individual health insurance coverage.[5]

5. Nondiscrimination against healthcare providers, beginning in 2014 if they act within the scope of their license or certification.[6]

6. Comprehensive health insurance coverage. Effective for plan years beginning on or after January 1, 2014, health insurance issuers offering coverage in the individual or small group market must ensure that such coverage includes the "essential health benefits package."[7] A plan must provide essential health benefits,[8] limit cost-sharing,[9] and provide either bronze, silver, gold, or platinum level coverage (benefits that are actuarially equivalent to 60 percent, 70 percent, 80 percent, or 90 percent of the full actuarial benefits provided under the plan), or a catastrophic plan (also known as "young invincibles" coverage).[10] An insurer that offers bronze, silver,

---

1.   PPACA renumbered PHSA §2711as PHSA §2731; PPACA §1105 included new PHSA §2702(a); and PPACA §1563(c)(8) made changes to PHSA §2731 and renumbered it as PHSA §2702.
2.   PHSA §2702(b).
3.   PHSA §2703.
4.   Health status factors are health status; medical condition (including both physical and mental illnesses); claims experience; receipt of health care; medical history; genetic information; evidence of insurability (EOI) (including conditions arising out of acts of domestic violence); disability; and any other health status-related factor determined appropriate by the Secretary of HHS. IRC Sec. 9802(a)(1); ERISA Sec. 702(a)(1); PHSA §2705(a). The last category was added by health reform. PHSA §2705(a).
5.   PHSA §2705.
6.   PHSA §2706.
7.   PHSA §2707(a).
8.   PPACA §1302(b).
9.   PPACA §1302(c).
10. PPACA §1302(e).

gold, or platinum coverage must offer the same level of coverage in a "child-only plan" designed for persons under age twenty-one.[1]

7. No denial of coverage for individuals participating in approved clinical trials.[2]

8. No cost-sharing (copayments) for preventive and wellness services.[3]

9. <u>Transparency in coverage</u>.[4] A health plan seeking Qualified Health Plan (QHP) certification from an exchange must disclose certain information to the exchange, HHS, and the state insurance commissioner, and make the information available to the public as well as cost-sharing disclosures to participants.

10. Nondiscrimination is prohibited in favor of highly compensated employees by nongrandfathered insured group plans.[5] Those rules are discussed in detail in Part VII of this book.

11. <u>Quality of care reporting</u> requires group health plans and health insurance issuers annually to report to HHS about plan or coverage benefits and provider "reimbursement structures" that may affect the quality of care.[6]

12. <u>Claims appeals</u>[7] and <u>external review</u>[8] rules.[9] These rules apply in addition to the ERISA claims procedures. Insurers will handle this duty for insured plans. Plan documents, summary plan descriptions (SPDs), existing claims procedures, any forms and notices used to communicate benefit determinations, and service contracts with TPAs and insurers will need to be updated. Non-ERISA self-insured plans not previously subject to the ERISA claims procedure requirement must adopt the existing DOL claims procedures and comply with these new requirements, such as governmental and church plans that have not elected to be subject to ERISA. In March 2011, a grace period for some requirements was extended until plan years beginning on or after January 1, 2012, (with one exception).[10]

13. <u>Patient protections</u>.[11] for women to select an OB-GYN and parents to select a pediatrician as their child's primary care provider. Additionally, for group health plans providing for emergency services, the plan:

  • may not require preauthorization, including for emergency services provided out-of-network;

---

1. PHSA §2707(c).
2. PHSA §2709.
3. PHSA §2713.
4. PHSA §2715A.
5. PHSA §2716, IRC Sec. 9815 & ERISA Sec. 715.
6. PHSA §2717.
7. DOL Reg. §2590.715-2719(b)(2).
8. DOL Reg. §2590.715-2719(a).
9. PHSA §2719.
10. DOL Technical Release 2011-02.
11. PHSA §2719A.

- must provide coverage regardless of whether the provider is in- or out-of-network;

- may not impose any administrative requirement or coverage limitation that is more restrictive than would be imposed on in-network emergency services; and

- must comply with cost-sharing requirements.[1]

204. What changes to a plan will not result in loss of grandfather status?

Any change that does not result in loss of grandfathered status will not affect grandfathered status. Changes that are not prohibited do not cause a loss of grandfathered status.[2] Changes to premiums, changes to comply with the law, changes voluntarily to implement healthcare reform changes, and changes by third-party administrators are allowed if they are made without exceeding the standards for changes that terminate grandfather status.[3]

205. What happens if a grandfathered plan is cancelled?

Essentially there are three options:

- Option One: Buy another plan from the same company: A person is allowed to buy any other plan available to you. The new plan will include the rights and protections.

- Option Two: Buy a plan through the marketplace: All marketplace plans include ACA rights and protections. When applying it will be determined if qualification for credits based on income exist.

  - Losing health coverage qualifies a person for a special enrollment period, allowing enrollment even outside the yearly open enrollment period.

  - If a plan is cancelled and a person cannot afford a new plan, a Catastrophic plan may be an option. These plans meet all of the requirements applicable to other Qualified Health Plans (QHPs) but that don't cover any benefits other than three primary care visits per year before the plan's deductible is met. The premium amount for health care is generally lower than for other QHPs, but the out-of-pocket costs for deductibles, copayments, and coinsurance are generally higher. To qualify for a Catastrophic plan, a person must be under thirty years old OR get a "hardship exemption" because the marketplace determined that you're unable to afford health coverage.

---

1. Treas. Reg. §54.9815-2719AT(b)(3)(i); DOL Reg. §2590.715-2719A(b)(3)(i); HHS Reg. §147.138(b)(3)(i).
2. Preamble to Grandfathered Health Plan Regulations, 75 Fed. Reg. 34537 (June 17, 2010); FAQs About the Affordable Care Act Implementation Part II, Q/A-1, available at https://www.dol.gov/sites/default/files/ebsa/about-ebsa/our-activities/resource-center/faqs/aca-part-i.pdf (Last accessed August 1, 2019).
3. Preamble to Grandfathered Health Plan Regulations, 75 Fed. Reg. 34537 (June 17, 2010).

- <u>Option Three</u>: Buy a plan outside of the marketplace. This may be a good option if the person doesn't qualify for credits based on income. Most plans outside the marketplace include the ACA rights and protections.

206. What happens if a grandfathered plan is changed to meet ACA standards?

Essentially there are three options:

- <u>Option One</u>: Accept the plan and renew it. The prices may go up and benefits may change.

- <u>Option Two</u>: Buy a plan through the marketplace. Losing health coverage qualifies for the special enrollment period, so enrollment can occur even outside the yearly open enrollment period. All marketplace plans include the ACA rights and protections.

- <u>Option Three</u>: Purchase a plan outside of the marketplace. This may be a good option if there are no savings available based on income credits. Most plans outside the marketplace include the rights and protections.

207. Can an insured plan change insurance companies?

The initial regulations provided that if an employer entered into a new policy, certificate, or contract of insurance after March 23, 2010, the new policy, certificate, or contract would not be grandfathered health coverage.[1] This provoked a firestorm of protest because plan sponsors could not improve their plans or decrease costs (in permitted ways) by changing insurers without losing grandfather status. Revised regulations changed this result, but only for changes on or after November 15, 2010.[2] A change entered into prior to November 15, 2010, that is effective thereafter is permitted.[3]

For changes of insurer between March 23, 2010, and June 14, 2010, (when the initial grandfather regulations were issued), changes to group health insurance coverage on or after March 23, 2010, but before June 14, 2010, (the date the regulations were made publicly available), the agencies' enforcement safe harbor remains in effect for good faith efforts to comply with a reasonable interpretation of the statute.[4] If no prohibited change in costs or coverage was made, such a plan should retain its grandfather status because the regulations, as amended, allow such a change.

The amendment to the regulations applies only to group health plans, not to insurers in the individual market.[5]

---

1. Treas. Reg. §54.9815-1251T(a)(1)(i) (November 8, 2015); DOL Reg. §2590.715-1251(a)(1)(i) (November 8, 2015); HHS Reg. §147.140(a)(1)(i) (November 8, 2015).
2. https://www.federalregister.gov/articles/2015/11/18/2015-29294/final-rules-for-grandfathered-plans-preexisting-condition-exclusions-lifetime-and-annual-limits. (Last accessed August 1, 2019).
3. Preamble to the Amendment to the Grandfathered Health Plan Regulations, 75 Fed. Reg. 70114, 70116 (November 17, 2010).
4. Preamble to the Amendment to the Grandfathered Health Plan Regulations, 75 Fed. Reg. 70114, 70116 (November 17, 2010).
5. Preamble to the Amendment to the Grandfathered Health Plan Regulations, 75 Fed. Reg. 70114, 70116 (November 17, 2010).

208. What documentation is required for an insured grandfathered plan to change insurance companies?

An insurance contract or policy must provide to the new insurer (and the new insurer must require) documentation of plan terms (including benefits, cost-sharing, employer contributions, and annual limits) under the prior health coverage sufficient to determine whether any change is being made that would cause a loss of grandfather status. This documentation may include a copy of the policy and any summary plan description.[1]

209. Can a grandfathered insured group plan change to become self-insured or a self-insured plan change to an insured plan without losing grandfathered status?

The regulations do not address the scenario of an insured grandfathered plan becoming self-insured. However, they allow a self-insured grandfathered plan to move to an insured plan but only after November 15, 2010.[2] However, the reasonable good faith compliance standard went into effect between March 23, 2010, and June 14, 2010.[3]

210. What other changes can be made to a grandfathered self-insured plan without losing grandfather status?

A self-insured plan can change its third-party administrator without losing grandfather status.[4]

A self-insured plan also should be able to change its stop-loss insurance without losing grandfather status because it is not health insurance when maintained by a self-insured plan.[5]

211. May enhancements or additions to a grandfathered health plan be made without loss of grandfathered status?

Yes. Additions to a grandfathered plan generally will not result in loss of grandfathered status. They are not prohibited changes. Thus, adding domestic partner benefits or a new health coverage option (such as an HMO where employer now only offers a PPO), is allowed, as these are two "benefit packages" and each is analyzed on its own to determine whether it is grandfathered.[6] Thus, the existing PPO option would remain grandfathered.

212. What special rules apply to collectively bargained plans in determining grandfathered plan status?

For insured plans, i.e., health insurance coverage maintained under one or more collective bargaining agreements ratified before March 23, 2010, the coverage will be treated as

---

1.   https://www.federalregister.gov/articles/2015/11/18/2015-29294/final-rules-for-grandfathered-plans-preexisting-condition-exclusions-lifetime-and-annual-limits. (Last accessed August 1, 2019).

2.   https://www.federalregister.gov/articles/2015/11/18/2015-29294/final-rules-for-grandfathered-plans-preexisting-condition-exclusions-lifetime-and-annual-limits. (Last accessed July 15, 2019).

3.   https://www.cms.gov/CCIIO/Resources/Fact-Sheets-and-FAQs/aca_implementation_faqs4.html (Last accessed July 15, 2019).

4.   Preamble to Grandfathered Health Plan Regulations, 75 Fed. Reg. 34537 (June 17, 2010).

5.   Nonbinding comments of Amy Turner, Senior Health Law Specialist, Office of Health Plan Standards and Compliance Assistance of the DOL, Department of Labor Affordable Care Act Compliance Assistance Webcast (September 7, 2010).

6.   https://www.federalregister.gov/articles/2015/11/18/2015-29294/final-rules-for-grandfathered-plans-preexisting-condition-exclusions-lifetime-and-annual-limits. (Last accessed July 15, 2019).

grandfathered until the last collective bargaining agreement terminates, regardless of whether there is a change that would otherwise destroy grandfathered status.[1] Self-funded collectively bargained plans will be treated the same as non-bargained plans and will need to comply with the grandfathering rules, including the new mandates and the limitations on plan changes, if this date is before the relevant collective bargaining agreement expires.[2]

This collectively bargained plan rule does not provide a delayed effective date for changes required by health reform for collectively bargained plans. Although the grandfather rule allows collectively bargained insured plans to maintain grandfathered plan status during the term of the agreement, they must comply with the rules that apply to grandfathered health plans. Therefore, collectively bargained plans (both insured and self-insured) that are grandfathered plans must comply with all the provisions that apply to grandfathered plans with no extension of any effective dates.[3]

Once the collective bargaining agreement expires, the plan may or may not be a grandfathered health plan. Such status will be determined under the otherwise applicable rules, by comparing the plan in existence at the end of the collective bargaining period with the plan in existence on March 23, 2010.[4] If the plan has made changes that, absent the special collectively bargained rule, would take it out of grandfathered status, then the plan is not a grandfathered plan once the collective bargaining agreement expires.

213. Can new enrollees, including new hires and family members, enroll in a grandfathered health plan?

Yes. An individual who was enrolled in a grandfathered health plan on March 23, 2010, may enroll his or her family members in the grandfathered health plan after March 23, 2010.[5] Additionally, new and existing employees and family members may enroll in a grandfathered health plan.[6] Employees not covered in a grandfathered plan option may move into a grandfathered option at open enrollment without jeopardizing its grandfathered status.[7]

214. Can employees transfer from one grandfathered plan to another?

Yes, and when this is voluntary, there is no change in the grandfathered status.[8] This is similar to a newly hired employee enrolling in a grandfathered plan.

1.   https://www.federalregister.gov/articles/2015/11/18/2015-29294/final-rules-for-grandfathered-plans-preexisting-condition-exclusions-lifetime-and-annual-limits. (Last accessed July 15, 2019).
2.   https://www.federalregister.gov/articles/2015/11/18/2015-29294/final-rules-for-grandfathered-plans-preexisting-condition-exclusions-lifetime-and-annual-limits); Preamble to Grandfathered Health Plan Regulations, 75 Fed. Reg. 34537 (June 17, 2010). (Last accessed July 15, 2019).
3.   Preamble to Grandfathered Health Plan Regulations, 75 Fed. Reg. 34537 (June 17, 2010).
4.   https://www.federalregister.gov/articles/2015/11/18/2015-29294/final-rules-for-grandfathered-plans-preexisting-condition-exclusions-lifetime-and-annual-limits. (Last accessed July 15, 2019).
5.   https://www.federalregister.gov/articles/2015/11/18/2015-29294/final-rules-for-grandfathered-plans-preexisting-condition-exclusions-lifetime-and-annual-limits. (Last accessed July 15, 2019).
6.   https://www.federalregister.gov/articles/2015/11/18/2015-29294/final-rules-for-grandfathered-plans-preexisting-condition-exclusions-lifetime-and-annual-limits. (Last accessed July 15, 2019).
7.   https://www.federalregister.gov/articles/2015/11/18/2015-29294/final-rules-for-grandfathered-plans-preexisting-condition-exclusions-lifetime-and-annual-limits. (Last accessed July 15, 2019).
8.   https://www.federalregister.gov/articles/2015/11/18/2015-29294/final-rules-for-grandfathered-plans-preexisting-condition-exclusions-lifetime-and-annual-limits. (Last accessed July 15, 2019).

215. Are there limits on employees moving from one plan to another?

Yes. The regulations state that transferring employees from one grandfathered plan or benefit package (transferor plan) to a transferee plan will cause the transferee plan to relinquish grandfather status if amending the transferor plan to replicate the terms of the transferee plan would have caused the transferor plan to relinquish grandfather status and there was no bona fide employment-based reason to transfer the employees.[1] There may be many other circumstances in which a benefit package can be eliminated for a bona fide employment-based reason. The term "bona fide employment-based reason" includes a variety of circumstances, such as the following, which is not intended to be an exhaustive list:

- A benefit package is eliminated because the issuer is exiting the market.

- A benefit package is eliminated because the issuer no longer offers the product to the employer (for example, because the employer no longer satisfies the issuer's minimum participation requirement).

- Low or declining participation by plan participants in the benefit package makes it impractical for the plan sponsor to continue to offer the benefit package.

- A benefit package is eliminated from a multiemployer plan as agreed upon as part of the collective bargaining process.

- A benefit package is eliminated for any reason and multiple benefit packages covering a significant portion of other employees remain available to the employees being transferred.[2]

- After a plant closing, the employer transfers employees to a new location, eliminating the option offered only at the closed plant, and the employees enroll in another option.[3]

However, there is no bona fide employment-based reason when there are two or more health plan options and a higher priced option is eliminated to save money, if that amendment would have resulted in a loss of grandfather status. For example, a group health plan may offer two benefit packages, a more generous PPO and a less generous HMO. The employer eliminates the PPO due to its high cost and transfers the employees to the HMO. There is no bona fide employment-based reason for this transfer, and the PPO would have lost its grandfathered status if, instead of being eliminated, its terms had been modified to match the terms of the HMO. Thus, the HMO will lose its grandfathered status. This loss of grandfathered status applies to

---

1. https://www.federalregister.gov/articles/2015/11/18/2015-29294/final-rules-for-grandfathered-plans-preexisting-condition-exclusions-lifetime-and-annual-limits. (Last accessed July 15, 2019).

2. HHS, DOL, and the Treasury, Frequently Asked Questions (FAQs), Part VI (April 2011) at https://www.dol.gov/sites/default/files/ebsa/about-ebsa/our-activities/resource-center/faqs/aca-part-vi.pdf. (Last accessed July 15, 2019).

3. https://www.federalregister.gov/articles/2015/11/18/2015-29294/final-rules-for-grandfathered-plans-preexisting-condition-exclusions-lifetime-and-annual-limits. (Last accessed July 15, 2019).

all enrollees in the HMO, including those in the plan before the employees were transferred from the PPO.[1]

216. What happens to a grandfathered plan after a merger or acquisition?

An anti-abuse rule provides that a plan will lose grandfathered status if it engages in a transaction, such as a merger, acquisition, purchase of assets, etc., for the principal purpose of covering new individuals under a grandfathered health plan.[2]

217. If grandfather status is lost, when does the loss of status become effective?

The status is lost on the date a prohibited change becomes effective, rather than the date it is adopted. Thus, if a plan amendment is effective at the beginning of the next plan year, the status is lost for that next plan year.[3]

218. What changes to a health plan will result in a loss of grandfather status?

A change to a health plan effective after March 23, 2010 (unless legally binding prior to that date, as discussed above), can result in loss of grandfathered status. The regulations provide detailed rules for determining if design changes cause a loss of grandfather status. However, only specified changes result in loss of grandfather status.

Any of the six changes discussed in the following section can result in loss of grandfathered plan status:

- Violation of Anti-Abuse Rules (described in Q 216)

- Elimination of benefits

- Any increase in Percentage Cost-Sharing

- Increase in Fixed-Amount Cost-Sharing

- Decrease in Rate of Employer (or Employee Organization) Contributions

- Certain changes to Annual Limits

In addition, as discussed after the questions about these impermissible changes, either of the following failures will cause loss of grandfather status:

- Failure to provide the Annual Grandfather Notice to Participants

- Failure to retain Records of the Plan in Effect on March 23, 2010

---

1. https://www.federalregister.gov/articles/2015/11/18/2015-29294/final-rules-for-grandfathered-plans-preexisting-condition-exclusions-lifetime-and-annual-limits. (Last accessed July 15, 2019).
2. https://www.federalregister.gov/articles/2015/11/18/2015-29294/final-rules-for-grandfathered-plans-preexisting-condition-exclusions-lifetime-and-annual-limits. (Last accessed July 15, 2019).
3. HHS, DOL & Treasury, FAQs About the Affordable Care Act Implementation Part VI (April 1, 2011) at https://www.dol.gov/sites/default/files/ebsa/about-ebsa/our-activities/resource-center/faqs/aca-part-vi.pdf. (Last accessed August 1, 2019).

Other changes may be made without loss of grandfather status.[1] Thus, a grandfathered plan can adopt one or more of the requirements that apply to nongrandfathered plans, as listed above in Q 203, and discussed in more detail in Part VII, without losing grandfathered status.

219. What is an impermissible elimination of benefits that terminates grandfathered status?

The elimination of all or substantially all benefits to diagnose or treat a particular condition will cause a group health plan or insurance to lose its grandfathered status. For this purpose, elimination of any element necessary to diagnose or treat the condition is considered elimination of all or substantially all of the benefits for that condition.[2] For example, if a plan decides to no longer cover care for a particular condition, e.g., diabetes, cystic fibrosis, or HIV/AIDS, grandfathered status will be lost when that change is effective. Termination will also occur if one of two necessary treatments needed for a condition is deleted, such as elimination of drugs or counseling for a mental disorder when both are required.[3]

It is not clear whether certain changes in prescription drug benefits will result in loss of grandfathered status. For example, before March 23, 2010, a plan covered a specific brand-name drug that is effective for a medical condition. If the plan changes its prescription drug provider and that specific drug is no longer covered, grandfather status may be jeopardized. However, if another drug that treats the condition is available, then arguably there has not been an elimination of the benefits to treat that condition. Similarly, if elimination of one treatment for a condition is made, but another treatment is substituted, that may not terminate grandfather status.

220. What is an increase in percentage cost-sharing (coinsurance) that terminates grandfather status?

Coinsurance requires a patient to pay a fixed percentage of a charge, such as 20 percent of a hospital bill. Grandfathered plans cannot increase this percentage. An increase after March 23, 2010, in participant percentage cost sharing terminates grandfather status for a group health plan.[4] Thus, an increase in the amount that the insured pays for hospitalization from 10 to 15 percent causes the plan to lose its grandfathered status.[5]

If a plan has multiple grandfathered options, and the insured's coinsurance percentage is increased in only one option, the other options remain grandfathered.[6]

1.   Preamble to Grandfathered Health Plan Regulations, 75 Fed. Reg. 34537 (June 17, 2010).
2.   https://www.federalregister.gov/articles/2015/11/18/2015-29294/final-rules-for-grandfathered-plans-preexisting-condition-exclusions-lifetime-and-annual-limits. (Last accessed July 15, 2019).
3.   https://www.federalregister.gov/articles/2015/11/18/2015-29294/final-rules-for-grandfathered-plans-preexisting-condition-exclusions-lifetime-and-annual-limits. (Last accessed July 15, 2019).
4.   https://www.federalregister.gov/articles/2015/11/18/2015-29294/final-rules-for-grandfathered-plans-preexisting-condition-exclusions-lifetime-and-annual-limits. (Last accessed July 15, 2019).
5.   https://www.federalregister.gov/articles/2015/11/18/2015-29294/final-rules-for-grandfathered-plans-preexisting-condition-exclusions-lifetime-and-annual-limits. (Last accessed July 15, 2019).
6.   https://www.federalregister.gov/articles/2015/11/18/2015-29294/final-rules-for-grandfathered-plans-preexisting-condition-exclusions-lifetime-and-annual-limits. (Last accessed July 15, 2019).

If the owner of an individual policy may elect an option to pay reduced premiums in exchange for higher cost sharing, such an election can be made without affecting the individual policy's grandfather status.[1]

Example 1. A grandfathered plan includes prescription drug benefits with different cost sharing divided into tiers as follows:

- Tier 1 includes generic drugs only.

- Tier 2 includes brand-name drugs with no generic available.

- Tier 3 includes brand-name drugs with a generic available in Tier 1.

- Tier 4 includes IV chemotherapy drugs.

A drug was previously classified in Tier 2 as a brand-name drug with no generic available. However, a generic alternative for the drug has just been released and is added to the formulary. The plan moves the brand-name drug into Tier 3 and adds the generic to Tier 1. Does this change terminate the plan's grandfathered status?

No. The increase in the cost sharing for a brand-name drug where it is replaced by a generic drug with the same or less cost sharing does not terminate grandfathered status.[2]

Example 2. A grandfathered plan covers treatment at 80 percent without any precertification requirement. In 2013, the plan is amended so that it will pay for treatment at 70 percent if an out-of-network provider is used unless the individual obtains precertification, but otherwise will pay 80 percent. Does this change terminate grandfather status? This issue has not been addressed as yet.

221. What is an increase in fixed-amount cost-sharing (coinsurance) that terminates grandfather status?

Frequently, plans require patients to pay a fixed dollar amount for doctor's office visits and other services. Compared with the required payments in effect on March 23, 2010, grandfathered plans will be able to increase those copays by no more than a percentage equal to percentage medical inflation since 2010 plus 15 percent.[3]

Medical inflation is defined by reference to the Overall Medical Care Component (OMCC) of the Consumer Price Index for All Urban Consumers (CPI-U) (unadjusted) published by the Department of Labor.[4] The change in medical inflation is measured from March 2010 by taking the greatest value of the unadjusted medical index of the CPI-U within twelve months of the date the increase is effective and subtracting the March 2010 medical component of the unadjusted CPI-U. The difference is divided by the March 2010 medical care component of the CPI-U (387.142), which is then added to 15 percent.

1.   HHS, DOL & Treasury FAQs About the Affordable Care Act Implementation Part IV, Q/A-2 at https://www.dol.gov/sites/default/files/ebsa/about-ebsa/our-activities/resource-center/faqs/aca-part-iv.pdf. (Last accessed July 15, 2019).

2.   HHS, DOL & Treasury, FAQs About the Affordable Care Act Implementation Part VI, Q/A-2, at https://www.dol.gov/sites/default/files/ebsa/about-ebsa/our-activities/resource-center/faqs/aca-part-vi.pdf. (Last accessed July 15, 2019).

3.   https://www.federalregister.gov/articles/2015/11/18/2015-29294/final-rules-for-grandfathered-plans-preexisting-condition-exclusions-lifetime-and-annual-limits. (Last accessed July 15, 2019).

4.   https://www.federalregister.gov/articles/2015/11/18/2015-29294/final-rules-for-grandfathered-plans-preexisting-condition-exclusions-lifetime-and-annual-limits. (Last accessed July 15, 2019).

While the increase in fixed-amount cost sharing is determined as of the effective date of the increase, the OMCC is computed using any month in the twelve months before the new change is to take effect.[1] Thus, if a change became effective on July 15, 2011, this was evaluated on the OMCC using the month between July 2010 and June 2011 with the "greatest value," not the OMCC for July 2011.[2]

A plan is allowed a 15 percent cumulative increase, measured from March 23, 2010. Thus, smaller increases may be made annually, but the overall limitation over time is 15 percent.[3]

> *Example*: If medical inflation is 4 percent for 2010 and the copay for 2010 is $30, 4 percent plus 15 percent equals 19 percent. The copay cannot increase more than 19 percent or to a maximum of $35 in 2011.

Beginning in 2012, only medical inflation is added, so assuming medical inflation is again 4 percent, then the 2012 percentage allowed is 23 percent (19 percent plus 4 percent) above the 2010 copay for a maximum copay of $37. The medical inflation rate as predicted by the Health Research Institute for 2020 is expected to be approximately 6 percent, which shows something of an increase from the 5.7 percent inflation rate of 2018 and 2019.

222. How do the fixed-amount cost-sharing limitations apply to HRAs and QSE-HRAs paired with HDHPs?

A Health Reimbursement Arrangement (HRA) is an employer-funded medical expense reimbursement plan, reimbursing specified items not paid by insurance. An HRA may allow unused amounts to carry over into future years. An HRA is sometimes paired with an employer-provided High Deductible Health Plan (HDHP) so that HRA amounts can pay medical expenses not covered by the high deductible plan. The employer HRA contributions likely would be viewed as lowering an otherwise applicable deductible, so long as the HRA balance is available for all expenses subject to the deductible. Similarly, if an employer decreased HRA contributions, this could be treated as an increase in the deductible and subject to the 15 percent limit. This would apply in the instance of a QSE-HRA as well.

223. How much can a fixed-amount cost-sharing (coinsurance) payment be increased without losing grandfather status?

Some plans have a feature with a fixed-amount cost-sharing requirement, such as a deductible or an out-of-pocket limit, which is based on a percentage-of-compensation. This cost-sharing arrangement will not cause the plan or coverage to cease to be a grandfathered health plan so long as the formula for determining an out-of-pocket limit remains the same as on March 23,

---

1. https://www.federalregister.gov/articles/2015/11/18/2015-29294/final-rules-for-grandfathered-plans-preexisting-condition-exclusions-lifetime-and-annual-limits. (Last accessed July 15, 2019).
2. https://www.federalregister.gov/articles/2015/11/18/2015-29294/final-rules-for-grandfathered-plans-preexisting-condition-exclusions-lifetime-and-annual-limits. (Last accessed July 15, 2019).
3. Nonbinding comments of Amy Turner, Senior Health Law Specialist, Office of Health Plan Standards and Compliance Assistance of the DOL, Department of Labor Affordable Care Act Compliance Assistance Webcast (September 7, 2010) at http://www.dol.gov/ebsa/newsroom/webcasts.html. No longer available on DOL website as of August 28, 2016.

2010.[1] Thus, even if an employee's compensation increases and the employee faces a higher out-of-pocket limit as a result, that change will not cause the plan to relinquish grandfather status.

Any increase after March 23, 2010, in fixed-amount co-payments above the <u>greater of</u>:

- $5, increased by medical inflation; or

- 15 percent above medical inflation, will cause a group health plan or insurer to lose its grandfathered status.[2] This limit applies even to copayments that are for a single category of service.[3]

Example: On March 23, 2010, a grandfathered health plan has a copayment of $30 per office visit for specialists. The plan is later amended to increase the copay requirement to $40. Within the twelve-month period before the $40 copay takes effect, the greatest value of the OMCC is 475. The percentage increase in the copayment from $30 to $40 is 33.33 percent.

$40 - 30 = 10$

$10/30 = 0.3333$ or 33.33%

Medical inflation from March 2010 is 0.2269, calculated as follows:

$475 - 387.142 = 87.858$

$87.858 \div 387.142 = 0.2269$ or 22.69%

The maximum percentage increase permitted is 37.69 percent, calculated as follows:

$22.69\% + 15\% = 37.69\%$

Because 33.33 percent does not exceed 37.69 percent, the change in the copayment does not cause the plan to cease to be a grandfathered health plan.[4]

224. What is Value-Based Insurance Design (VBID)?

The Affordable Care Act focuses on increasing both the efficiency and the quality of health care. Part of this is due to the focus on preventative services, a component required in all health care plans. Value-based insurance design" aims to increase health care quality and decrease costs by using financial incentives to promote cost-efficient health care services and consumer choices. It promotes a patient's use of high value care approaches by changing cost sharing amounts that must be paid for different care options, rather than using the same deductible for all services. Using a VBID model, treatments that offer high value will have reduced or even no out of pocket costs (cost-sharing), promoting affordability.

---

1. HHS, DOL & TREASURY FAQs About the Affordable Care Act Implementation Part V, Q/A-7 at https://www.dol.gov/sites/default/files/ebsa/about-ebsa/our-activities/resource-center/faqs/aca-part-v.pdfe. (Last accessed July 28, 2019).

2. https://www.federalregister.gov/articles/2015/11/18/2015-29294/final-rules-for-grandfathered-plans-preexisting-condition-exclusions-lifetime-and-annual-limits (Last accessed July 28, 2019).

3. HHS, DOL & TREASURY FAQs About the Affordable Care Act Implementation, Part II, Q/A-4, at https://www.dol.gov/sites/default/files/ebsa/about-ebsa/our-activities/resource-center/faqs/aca-part-ii.pdf. (Last accessed July 28, 2019).

4. https://www.federalregister.gov/articles/2015/11/18/2015-29294/final-rules-for-grandfathered-plans-preexisting-condition-exclusions-lifetime-and-annual-limits. (Last accessed July 28, 2019).

Health benefit plans can be designed to reduce barriers to maintaining and improving health. By covering preventive care, wellness visits and treatments that control health problems early on, health plans may ultimately save money by reducing potentially more invasive and more expensive medical procedures in the future. In deciding which procedures are the most effective and cost efficient, insurance companies are seeking to use evidence-based data to design their plans, which thus far has been somewhat limited.

Some approaches that have been proposed include:

- <u>Elimination or reduction of cost-sharing amount for care considered to be high-value</u>. This includes care that would produce the best results for the particular patient at the most effective price. Additionally, use of better rated providers could be encouraged over ineffective or inefficient ones. The strategy is to rely on evidence-based data. Some actual policies could use

  - No-cost sharing imposed on medications to control chronic conditions such as high-blood pressure, diabetes, cholesterol, etc. could prevent the need for far more costly procedures down the road.

- <u>Increasing the cost sharing amount for care considered to be of lower value</u>. This would be based on evidence showing the procedures not to be particularly effective or not more effective than less expensive options. In addition, providers could be rated as well and less effective providers could be discouraged.

- <u>Elimination of cost-sharing for doctor visits</u> focused on preventative care or managing chronic conditions.

- <u>Creating of an exceptions process</u> to ensure that patient can get care that fits their particular situation.

The development is continuing and data is still somewhat limited but results appear promising. There is increasing interesting in the approach evidenced by growing adoption or study of VBID in the marketplace. Some instances where it is being used include:

- Michigan Medicaid Expansion includes the Healthy Michigan Plan, which relies on VBID.

- Medicare Advantage is starting a seven-state test in 2017 to run for five years.

  - Beginning in January 2017, the VBID model began testing the impact of providing eligible Medicare Advantage plans the flexibility to offer reduced cost sharing or additional supplemental benefits to enrollees with select chronic conditions, focusing on the services that are of highest clinical value to them. The model tested whether providing this flexibility could improve health outcomes and reduce expenditures for Medicare Advantage enrollees.

  - In 2017, CMS tested the VBID model in seven states, Arizona, Indiana, Iowa, Massachusetts, Oregon, Pennsylvania, and Tennessee, and allowed testing of VBID interventions for the following disease states: diabetes, congestive heart failure, chronic obstructive pulmonary disease (COPD), past stroke, hypertension, coronary artery disease, mood disorders, and combinations of these categories.

- In 2018, CMS updated the model to include Alabama, Michigan, and Texas and also allowed for VBID interventions for dementia and rheumatoid arthritis.

- For 2019, CMS updated the model to include organizations in fifteen additional states, California, Colorado, Florida, Georgia, Hawaii, Maine, Minnesota, Montana, New Jersey, New Mexico, North Carolina, North Dakota, South Dakota, Virginia, and West Virginia to apply and allowed participants to propose a methodology that either 1) identifies enrollees with different chronic conditions than those previously established by CMS or 2) revises the existing approved CMS chronic condition category to focus on a broader or smaller subset of the existing chronic condition.

- The Bipartisan Budget Act of 2018 required that the model be revised to include all fifty states and territories by 2020. Consistent with these requirements, eligible Medicare Advantage health plans in all fifty states and territories may apply for the health plan innovations being tested under the VBID model for CY 2020.

- Connecticut Health Enhancement Program is a voluntary program for state employees which has been in effect since 2011.

- Vermont and Oregon are working on VBID plans.

- Private companies such as Blue Cross/Blue Shield, CVS Caremark, Caterpiller. Marriott, Pitney Bowes, Novartis and the Mayo Clinic have been implementing VBID programs.

- On December 27, 2016, President Obama signed the 2017 Defense Bill which included authorization for a TRCARE VBID project.

- For CY 2020 and subsequent years, CMS is testing the following health plan innovations in Medicare Advantage through the VBID model. The new interventions described below represent a broad array of value-based approaches to service delivery in MA.

  - *Value-Based Insurance Design by Condition and/or Socioeconomic Status*

  - *Rewards and Incentives*

  - *Telehealth Networks*

  - *Wellness and Health Care Planning*

225. Are there special rules for Value-Based Insurance Design (VBID) copayments?

Yes. A copayment may be imposed for an inpatient treatment for preventive services as a part of value-based insurance design, when there is:

- no increase in copayment for the outpatient treatment for the same condition; and

- a waiver process allowing a waiver of the new hospital inpatient copayment for individuals for whom the outpatient services are medically inappropriate.

Example 1: One healthcare reform FAQ addressed the interaction of Value-Based Insurance Design (VBID) and the no cost-sharing preventive care services requirements.[1] In that example, a group health plan did not impose a copayment for colorectal cancer preventive services when performed in an in-network ambulatory surgery center. However, the same preventive service provided at an in-network outpatient hospital setting generally required a $250 copayment, although the copayment was waived for individuals for whom it would be medically inappropriate to have the preventive service provided in the ambulatory setting. The FAQ indicated that this VBID did not cause the plan to fail to comply with the no cost-sharing preventive care requirements.

Example 2: Under another group health plan, since March 23, 2010, similar preventive services are available both at an in-network ambulatory surgery center and at an in-network outpatient hospital setting without a copayment in either setting. If this plan wished to adopt the VBID approach described in Example 1 by imposing a $250 copayment for these preventive services only when performed in the in-network outpatient hospital setting (i.e., not an in-network ambulatory surgery center), and with the same waiver of the copayment for any individuals for whom it would be medically inappropriate to have these preventive services provided in the ambulatory setting, would implementation of that new design now cause the plan to relinquish grandfather status?

No. This increase in the copayment for these preventive services solely in the in-network outpatient hospital setting (subject to the waiver arrangement described above) without any change in the copayment in the in-network ambulatory surgery center setting would not be considered to exceed the thresholds described in the interim final regulations on grandfather status and thus would not cause the plan to relinquish grandfather status.

226. When will a decrease in the rate of plan sponsor contributions terminate grandfather status?

<u>More Than 5 Percentage Point Decrease in Plan Sponsor Contributions</u>. A grandfathered plan will lose its grandfather status if the employer or an employee organization, such as a union, decreases its contribution rate (whether based on a formula or on cost of coverage) for any tier of similarly situated individuals by more than 5 percent below the contribution rate that was in place on March 23, 2010.[2] The regulations indicate that a change from, for instance, 90 percent to 85 percent is permitted, because that is a 5 percent reduction, even though the actual number is 4.5 percent ($.90 \times .05 = 0.45$).

---

1.   HHS, DOL & TREASURY FAQs About Affordable Care Act Implementation, Part V Q/A 1 at https://www.dol.gov/sites/default/files/ebsa/about-ebsa/our-activities/resource-center/faqs/aca-part-v.pdf. (Last accessed August 1, 2019).

2.   Treas. Reg. §54.9815-1251(g)(1)(v); DOL Reg. §2590.715-1251(g)(1)(v); HHS Reg. §147.140(g)(1)(v).

For a self-insured plan, the cost of coverage is determined by using the COBRA rate of coverage.[1] Contributions by an employer or employee organization to a self-insured plan are equal to the total cost of coverage minus the employee contributions toward the total cost of coverage.[2] Employee salary reduction deferrals through a cafeteria or premium conversion plan are treated as employee contributions for this purpose.[3]

> *Example: Self-Insured Plan COBRA Cost of Coverage:* On March 23, 2010, a self-insured grandfathered health plan has a COBRA premium for the 2010 plan year of $5,000 for self-only coverage and $12,000 for family coverage. The required employee contribution for the coverage is $1,000 for self-only coverage and $4,000 for family coverage. Thus, the contribution rate based on cost of coverage for 2010 is 80 percent for self-only coverage, calculated as follows:
>
> 5,000 – 1,000 = 4,000
>
> 4,000/5,000 = 80%
>
> The contribution rate based on cost of coverage for 2010 is 67 percent for family coverage calculated as follows:
>
> 12,000 – 4,000 = 8,000
>
> 8,000/12,000 = 67%
>
> For a subsequent plan year, the COBRA premium is $6,000 for self-only coverage and $15,000 for family coverage. The employee contributions for that plan year are $1,200 for self-only coverage and $5,000 for family coverage. The contribution rate based on cost of coverage remains 80 percent for self-only coverage calculated as follows:
>
> 6,000 – 1,200 = 4,800
>
> 4,800/6,000 = 80%
>
> The contribution rate based on cost of coverage remains 67 percent for family coverage, calculated as follows:
>
> 15,000 – 5,000 = 10,000
>
> (10,000/15,000) = 67%
>
> There is no change in the employer's contribution rate based on the COBRA cost of coverage. Therefore, the plan retains its status as a grandfathered health plan.[4]

227. How is this greater than 5 percent reduction test applied if there are multiple health packages offered by the plan sponsor?

The test for loss of grandfather status is applied separately to each health package offered by the plan sponsor. It is possible for one package to lose its grandfathering and the others to remain grandfathered.[5]

---

1. Treas. Reg. §54.9815-1251(g)(3)(iii)(A); DOL Reg. §2590.715-1251(g)(3)(iii)(A); HHS Reg. §147.140(g)(3)(iii)(A).
2. Treas. Reg. §54.9815-1251(g)(3)(iii)(A); DOL Reg. §2590.715-1251(g)(3)(iii)(A); HHS Reg. §147.140(g)(3)(iii)(A).
3. Treas. Reg. §54.9815-1251(g)(4), Example (8); DOL Reg. §2590.715-1251(g)(4), Example (8); HHS Reg. §147.140(g)(4), Example (8).
4. https://www.federalregister.gov/articles/2015/11/18/2015-29294/final-rules-for-grandfathered-plans-preexisting-condition-exclusions-lifetime-and-annual-limits. (Last accessed August 1, 2019).
5. HHS, DOL & TREASURY, FAQs About the Affordable Care Act Implementation Part II, Q/A 2 at https://www.dol.gov/sites/default/files/ebsa/about-ebsa/our-activities/resource-center/faqs/aca-part-ii.pdf l. (Last accessed August 1, 2019).

Example: Multiple Packages (Options): ABC, Inc. maintains a group health plan that is not maintained pursuant to a collective bargaining agreement. It offered three benefit packages on March 23, 2010.

- • Option F is a self-insured option.

- • Options G and H are insured options.

Beginning July 1, 2019, the plan increases employee coinsurance under Option H from 10 percent to 15 percent, which is a reduction in the employer contribution of 5.56 percent. The coverage under Option H loses its grandfather status on the effective date of this change, July 1, 2018. Assuming no other changes to options F and G, they remain grandfathered.[1]

228. How is the grandfathered status affected if the employer plan offers several tiers of coverage, such as employee, employee and spouse, and employee and family?

The standards for employer contributions apply on a tier-by-tier basis. The results differ depending on whether tiers are simply modified or a new tier is added. If a plan modifies its tiers of coverage, such as by changing employee and family to employee, employee and spouse, and employee and family, the employer contribution for any new tier would be tested by comparison to the contribution rate for the corresponding tier on March 23, 2010.[2] All of the tiers for a benefit package must pass the 5 percent test to remain grandfathered.

On the other hand, if the plan merely adds a new tier and does not reduce the sponsor contribution percentage to the existing tier by more than 5 percent, then the existing tier remains grandfathered. The new tier not in existence on March 23, 2010, is not grandfathered, regardless of the contribution rate for the new tier.

Example – One Coverage Option; Several Tiers (Combinations) of Insureds: Prior to March 23, 2010, ABC, Inc. contributed 80 percent of the cost of single and family coverage. Due to premium increases, ABC, Inc. reduces its payment for family coverage from 80 percent to 50 percent, a reduction of 30 percent. The employer payment for single coverage remains at 80 percent. This reduction in employer payments for family coverage is more than 5 percent and causes the entire plan to lose grandfather status.[3]

If ABC, Inc. alters its options to employee coverage, employee-plus-spouse coverage, and family coverage, and the employer payment for any category is less than 75 percent, the grandfather status would be lost.

229. How do the grandfathered plan rules relate to wellness programs?

The final wellness plan rules[4] apply to both grandfathered and nongrandfathered plans. An employer can add a wellness program without losing grandfathered status, but needs to take care to make sure it maintains employer contributions and benefits at the needed levels. Grandfathered plans may continue to provide wellness incentives through, for instance, premium discounts or

---

1.   https://www.federalregister.gov/articles/2015/11/18/2015-29294/final-rules-for-grandfathered-plans-preexisting-condition-exclusions-lifetime-and-annual-limits; HHS, DOL & TREASURY, FAQs About the Affordable Care Act Implementation Part II, Q/A-2 at https://www.dol.gov/sites/default/files/ebsa/about-ebsa/our-activities/resource-center/faqs/aca-part-ii.pdf. (Last accessed August 1, 2019).

2.   HHS, DOL & TREASURY, FAQs About the Affordable Care Act Implementation Part II, Q/A-3 at https://www.dol.gov/sites/default/files/ebsa/about-ebsa/our-activities/resource-center/faqs/aca-part-ii.pdf. (Last accessed August 1, 2019).

3.   https://www.federalregister.gov/articles/2015/11/18/2015-29294/final-rules-for-grandfathered-plans-preexisting-condition-exclusions-lifetime-and-annual-limits. (Last accessed August 1, 2019).

4.   Incentives for Nondiscriminatory Wellness Programs in Group Health Plans, 26 CFR Part 54, 29 CFR Part 2590, 45 CFR Parts 146 and 147, 78 Fed. Reg. 33158 (June 3, 2013).

additional benefits to reward healthy behaviors. But penalties (e.g., increasing the surcharge on premiums for smokers) may implicate the types of changes that defeat grandfather status and may violate other nondiscrimination rules, so they should be implemented carefully.[1]

230. How do plan sponsor fixed dollar amount contributions work for grandfathered plans?

If an employer's contribution toward the cost of coverage for retirees that is covered by the law is not an excepted benefit (because active employees participate in the same plan) and is a fixed dollar amount multiplied by years of service, subject to a flat dollar cap per retiree, how is the 5 percent threshold for decreases in the rate of employer contributions calculated?

The 5 percent threshold for decreases in employer contributions is not violated so long as the formula for calculating the employer's contribution remains the same.[2]

231. How do insurers know if the 5 percent sponsor contribution reduction test has been violated?

If insurers follow certain requirements, a plan is treated as a grandfathered plan until the first date the insurer knows that the employer has decreased its contribution rate by more than five percent or until grandfathering is lost for another reason. The steps are as follows:

- Upon renewal, the insurer must require the plan sponsor to make a representation regarding its contribution rate for the plan year covered by the renewal, as well as its contribution rate on March 23, 2010 (if the issuer does not already have it).

- The issuer's policies, certificates, or contracts of insurance must disclose in a prominent and effective manner that plan sponsors are required to notify the issuer if the contribution rate changes at any point during the plan year.[3]

An insurer may request additional advance notice of a decrease in contribution rate.[4] The impact of this rule is to avoid penalties that might be imposed, for example, if the plan thought to be grandfathered in fact is not and does not adhere to the new nondiscrimination rules for insured plans.

232. How does the 5 percent reduction rule work for collectively bargained plans?

Multiemployer plans and contributing employers will be provided the same relief as insurers if they follow steps similar to those provided for insurers, described in Q 231. In addition,

---

1.   See FAQs About the Affordable Care Act Implementation Part II, Q/A-5 at https://www.dol.gov/sites/default/files/ebsa/about-ebsa/our-activities/resource-center/faqs/aca-part-ii.pdf. (Last accessed August 1, 2019).
2.   See HHS, DOL & TREASURY, FAQs About the Affordable Care Act Implementation Part VI, Q/A-6 at https://www.dol.gov/sites/default/files/ebsa/about-ebsa/our-activities/resource-center/faqs/aca-part-vi.pdf (Last accessed August 1, 2019).
3.   HHS, DOL & TREASURY, FAQs About the Affordable Care Act Implementation Part I, Q/A-2 at https://www.dol.gov/sites/default/files/ebsa/about-ebsa/our-activities/resource-center/faqs/aca-part-i.pdf. (Last accessed August 1, 2019).
4.   HHS, DOL & TREASURY, FAQs About the Affordable Care Act Implementation Part I, Q/A-2 at https://www.dol.gov/sites/default/files/ebsa/about-ebsa/our-activities/resource-center/faqs/aca-part-i.pdf l. (Last accessed August 1, 2019).

a decrease in an employer's rate of contribution does not necessarily mean that the employee's rate has increased. The test is contingent upon an actual increase in the employee contribution rate, rather than the rate of employer contribution. Therefore, an employer's decrease will not, in itself, cause a plan to lose its grandfathered status.[1]

233. What if a grandfathered plan imposes an annual or lifetime limit on benefits, or increases an existing limit?

Plans that do not have an annual dollar limit cannot add a new one unless they are replacing a lifetime dollar limit with an annual dollar limit that is at least as high as the lifetime limit, as this change benefits the participants. However, the regulations prohibit three other changes regarding annual or lifetime limits:

- A grandfathered plan that did not impose an overall annual or lifetime limit on the value of all benefits on March 23, 2010, will lose its grandfathered status if it imposes an annual limit.[2]

- A plan that had an overall lifetime limit on the value of all benefits but no overall annual limit will lose its grandfathered status if it imposes an overall annual limit on the value of all benefits that is lower than the lifetime limit in place on March 23, 2010.[3]

- For plans with an overall annual limit on the value of all benefits on March 23, 2010, grandfathering is lost if that annual limit is lowered, regardless of whether the plan had a lifetime limit).[4]

The regulations address an "overall limit on the value of all benefits." It remains unclear whether a limit on nonessential benefits would violate this requirement.

234. What type of notice is required for grandfathered plans?

Section 1251 of the Affordable Care Act has no explicit notice provision requiring notice by the plan, the employer or other entity sponsoring the health plan. The regulations do impose a notice requirement that is not well known, which in effect could negate the law for most employers and eliminate grandfathered plans for all but that handful of employers who have sophisticated, specialized healthcare reform legal and benefits advisors and were aware of and in fact issued the grandfathered plan notice each year.

1.   HHS, DOL & TREASURY, FAQs About the Affordable Care Act Implementation Part I, Q/A-3 available at https://www.dol.gov/sites/default/files/ebsa/about-ebsa/our-activities/resource-center/faqs/aca-part-i.pdf, stating: "If multiemployer plans and contributing employers follow steps similar to those outlined in Q/A-2 [for insurers], above, the same relief will apply to the multiemployer plan unless or until the multiemployer plan knows that the contribution rate has changed." (Last accessed August 1, 2019).

2.   https://www.federalregister.gov/articles/2015/11/18/2015-29294/final-rules-for-grandfathered-plans-preexisting-condition-exclusions-lifetime-and-annual-limits. (Last accessed August 1, 2019).

3.   https://www.federalregister.gov/articles/2015/11/18/2015-29294/final-rules-for-grandfathered-plans-preexisting-condition-exclusions-lifetime-and-annual-limits. (Last accessed August 1, 2019).

4.   https://www.federalregister.gov/articles/2015/11/18/2015-29294/final-rules-for-grandfathered-plans-preexisting-condition-exclusions-lifetime-and-annual-limits. (Last accessed August 1, 2019).

The loss of this important statutory provision far outweighs the Department of Labor "goal that the notice encourages plan sponsors and issuers to identify other communications in which disclosure of grandfather status would be appropriate and consistent with the goal of providing participants and beneficiaries' information necessary to understand and make informed choices regarding health coverage."

The Final Regulations issued in November 2015[1] require notices to plan participants beginning in the fall of 2010. Failing to distribute the required grandfathered notice will cause a plan to lose its grandfathered status. A plan that intends to maintain grandfathered status must provide, in any plan materials describing benefits for participants or beneficiaries:

1.   A statement that the plan or coverage is believed to be a grandfathered plan; and

2.   Contact information for questions or complaints.

A plan or individual grandfathered policy must provide, in any plan materials describing benefits for participants or beneficiaries, (a) a statement that the plan or coverage is believed to be a grandfathered plan, and (b) contact information for questions or complaints. To maintain grandfather status,[2] group health plans should assume that this requirement applies to enrollment materials, summary plan descriptions, summary of material modifications to an SPD, and perhaps when the SBC (Summary of Benefits & Coverage) is distributed. A grandfathered plan need not provide a disclosure statement regarding its grandfather status every time it sends out a communication, such as an explanation of benefits to participants.[3]

It is not clear when this notice requirement applies. There are a number of possibilities: the first plan year on or after March 23, 2010, or perhaps for the first plan year beginning after June 17, 2010, when the regulations were published in the federal register, or preferably after the regulations are finalized. The latter seems most fair because the law[4] requires no notice of grandfathering and likely most US employers have no knowledge of this notice requirement. Additionally, a plan sponsor may not make the decision on grandfathering until well after March 23, 2010, and perhaps not until subsequent years.

However, the statute has no notice requirement.

PPACA Sec. 1251, Preservation of Right to Maintain Existing Coverage, provides as follows:

(a) No Changes to Existing Coverage—

(1)   In general. Nothing in this Act (or an amendment made by this Act) shall be construed to require that an individual terminate coverage under a group health plan

---

1.   https://www.federalregister.gov/articles/2015/11/18/2015-29294/final-rules-for-grandfathered-plans-preexisting-condition-exclusions-lifetime-and-annual-limits. (Last accessed August 1, 2019).

2.   https://www.federalregister.gov/articles/2015/11/18/2015-29294/final-rules-for-grandfathered-plans-preexisting-condition-exclusions-lifetime-and-annual-limits. (Last accessed August 1, 2019).

3.   HHS, DOL & TREASURY, FAQs About the Affordable Care Act Implementation Part IV, Q https://www.dol.gov/sites/default/files/ebsa/about-ebsa/our-activities/resource-center/faqs/aca-part-iv.pdf. (Last accessed August 1, 2019).

4.   PPACA §1251.

or health insurance coverage in which such individual was enrolled on the date of enactment of this Act.

   (2)   CONTINUATION OF COVERAGE. With respect to a group health plan or health insurance coverage in which an individual was enrolled on the date of enactment of this Act, this subtitle and subtitle A (and the amendments made by such subtitles) shall not apply to such plan or coverage, regardless of whether the individual renews such coverage after such date of enactment.

(b) Allowance for Family Members to Join Current Coverage. With respect to a group health plan or health insurance coverage in which an individual was enrolled on the date of enactment of this Act and which is renewed after such date, family members of such individual shall be permitted to enroll in such plan or coverage if such enrollment is permitted under the terms of the plan in effect as of such date of enactment.

(c) Allowance for New Employees to Join Current Plan. A group health plan that provides coverage on the date of enactment of this Act may provide for the enrolling of new employees (and their families) in such plan, and this subtitle and subtitle A (and the amendments made by such subtitles) shall not apply with respect to such plan and such new employees (and their families).

(d) Effect on Collective Bargaining Agreements. In the case of health insurance coverage maintained pursuant to one or more collective bargaining agreements between employee representatives and one or more employers that was ratified before the date of enactment of this Act, the provisions of this subtitle and subtitle A (and the amendments made by such subtitles) shall not apply until the date on which the last of the collective bargaining agreements relating to the coverage terminates. Any coverage amendment made pursuant to a collective bargaining agreement relating to the coverage which amends the coverage solely to conform to any requirement added by this subtitle or subtitle A (or amendments) shall not be treated as a termination of such collective bargaining agreement.

(e) Definition. In this title, the term 'grandfathered health plan' means any group health plan or health insurance coverage to which this section applies.

235. What are the recordkeeping requirements for grandfathered plans?

The plan and coverage terms in effect on March 23, 2010, must be documented.[1] Such documentation, plus any additional documentation needed to verify, explain, or clarify grandfathered health plan status must be retained for so long as the plan or coverage takes the position that it is a grandfathered plan.[2] Such documentation may include intervening and current plan

---

1.   https://www.federalregister.gov/articles/2015/11/18/2015-29294/final-rules-for-grandfathered-plans-preexisting-condition-exclusions-lifetime-and-annual-limits. (Last accessed August 1, 2019).
2.   https://www.federalregister.gov/articles/2015/11/18/2015-29294/final-rules-for-grandfathered-plans-preexisting-condition-exclusions-lifetime-and-annual-limits. (Last accessed August 1, 2019).

documents, health insurance policies, certificate or contracts of insurance, SPDs, and other cost and cost-sharing documentation.[1]

In addition, the plan or coverage must make those records available for examination upon request.[2] The regulations indicate that a participant, beneficiary, individual policy subscriber, or state or federal agency official may inspect the grandfathered plan documentation.[3]

---

1. Preamble to Grandfathered Health Plan Regulations, 75 Fed. Reg. 34537 (June 17, 2010).
2. https://www.federalregister.gov/articles/2015/11/18/2015-29294/final-rules-for-grandfathered-plans-preexisting-condition-exclusions-lifetime-and-annual-limits. (Last accessed August 1, 2019).
3. Preamble to Grandfathered Health Plan Regulations, 75 Fed. Reg. 34537 (June 17, 2010).

PART VII: PHSA COVERAGE MANDATES AND ENFORCEMENT

Coverage Mandates and Enforcement

236. What coverage mandates imposed by health reform and incorporated into the Public Health Services Act (PHSA) applied to all plans including grandfathered plans?

As discussed earlier in connection with grandfathered plans, health reform's revision of the Public Health Services Act imposes numerous coverage mandates for policies and plans covering essential health benefits. These do not include "excepted benefits."[1] In addition to their inclusion in the PHSA, these provisions are incorporated by reference into section 715 of the Employee Retirement Income Security Act of 1974 (ERISA) and section 9815 of the Internal Revenue Code (Code). The mandates for Essential Health Benefits (EHB) for grandfathered plans are as follows:

Health Reform Rules That Apply to All Plans, Including Grandfathered Plans
<u>Pre-existing condition exclusions (PCE) prohibited</u>.[2] Grandfathered individual coverage can continue to apply these exclusions, but group health plans and group health insurance issuers cannot impose PCEs for plan years beginning on or after January 1, 2014. This prohibition took effect for plan years beginning on or after September 23, 2010, (i.e., January 1, 2011, for calendar-year plans) with respect to individuals enrolled in the plan who are younger than nineteen years of age.
<u>Excessive waiting periods</u> of more than ninety days are prohibited for plan years beginning in 2014 and thereafter.[3]
<u>Annual/lifetime limits are prohibited</u> for plan years beginning in 2014 and thereafter.[4] These rules apply to grandfathered plans, but the annual limit prohibition does not apply to grandfathered individual coverage. For benefits that are not "essential health benefits," both lifetime and annual limits are allowed if not prohibited by other federal and state laws.[5] Failure to provide any services for a condition is allowed, but if any benefits are provided for a condition, these prohibitions apply.[6] While grandfathered health plans are not required to offer essential health benefits, they cannot impose either annual or lifetime dollar limits on the essential health benefits they do offer. Individual grandfathered policies may continue annual limits but not lifetime limits.
<u>Rescission of policies</u> is prohibited except for fraud or misrepresentation beginning in 2014.[7]

<ol>
<li>Preamble to Grandfathered Health Plan Regulations, 75 Fed. Reg. 34537 (June 17, 2010) and HHS, DOL & TREASURY, FAQs About the Affordable Care Act Implementation Part II, Q&A-6, at https://www.dol.gov/sites/default/files/ebsa/about-ebsa/our-activities/resource-center/faqs/aca-part-ii.pdf. (Last accessed August 17, 2019).</li>
<li>PHSA §2704(a), IRC Sec. 9815 and ERISA Sec. 715.</li>
<li>PHSA §2708.</li>
<li>PHSA §2711.</li>
<li>https://www.federalregister.gov/articles/2015/11/18/2015-29294/final-rules-for-grandfathered-plans-preexisting-condition-exclusions-lifetime-and-annual-limits. (Last accessed August 17, 2019).</li>
<li>https://www.federalregister.gov/articles/2015/11/18/2015-29294/final-rules-for-grandfathered-plans-preexisting-condition-exclusions-lifetime-and-annual-limits. (Last accessed August 17, 2019).</li>
<li>PHSA §2712.</li>
</ol>

<u>Dependent coverage</u> for children under age twenty-six must be offered, except for adults eligible for coverage through their own employer.[1]
<u>SBC Requirement</u>. The requirement to provide at least a four-page summary of benefits and coverage to plan participants applies to grandfathered plans.[2] This is discussed in more detail in Part VII of this publication.
<u>Medical Loss Ratio (MLR)</u> reporting and rebates, designed to lower health insurance costs apply to grandfathered plans.[3]

237. What health reform coverage mandates apply to new plans or plans that lose grandfathered status?

The following thirteen requirements apply to new plans as well to nongrandfathered plans. The requirements do not apply to grandfathered plans.

<u>Additional Rules Applicable to New and Nongrandfathered Health Plans</u>
<u>Fair health insurance premiums</u>.[4] These are the rules that limit insurers in the individual or small group market as to allowable factors to alter premiums: • Coverage category (e.g., whether the coverage is individual versus family coverage) • Rating area (as established by states) • Age (may not vary by more than 3 to 1 for adults) • Tobacco use (may not vary more than 1.5 to 1)[5]
<u>Guaranteed-Availability Rules Applicable to Small and Large Group Markets</u>.[6] Healthcare reform makes changes to these requirements. Through December 31, 2013, the guaranteed-availability rules applied to health insurance issuers in the small group market, but not to issuers in the large group market. These rules required a health insurance issuer that actively marketed coverage in the small group market to accept every small employer that applied for coverage and to make all products that it actively markets in the small group market available to all small employers. The issuer also was required to accept for enrollment every eligible individual who applied for coverage when first eligible. Insurers were permitted to impose employer contribution and minimum participation requirements (to the extent consistent with applicable state law), within certain limitations. As of January 1, 2014, the guaranteed-availability rules were significantly expanded. The statutory changes amended and restructured the guaranteed-availability provisions, making these rules applicable to health insurance issuers in the large and small group markets and effecting certain other changes.[7]

---

1.   PHSA §2714.
2.   PHSA §2715.
3.   PHSA §2718.
4.   PHSA §2701; 45 CFR 147.102.
5.   PHSA §2701(a)(1)(A); 45 CFR 147.102.
6.   PHSA §2702.
7.   PPACA renumbered PHSA §2711 as PHSA §2731; PPACA §1105 included new PHSA §2702(a); and PPACA §1563(c)(8) made changes to PHSA §2731 and renumbered it as PHSA §2702.

Each health insurance issuer that offers health insurance coverage in the individual or group market (regardless of whether the coverage is offered in the large or small group market) is required to accept every employer and individual in the state that applies for such coverage. Enrollment may, however, be restricted to open or special enrollment periods.[1]

Guaranteed renewability, which means that an insurer must renew coverage if requested by the plan sponsor.[2] Prior to January 1, 2014, these rules applied to both the small and large group market. They required group insurance issuers in both the small and large group market to renew coverage at the option of the plan sponsor subject to specified exceptions and restrictions (such as nonpayment of premiums, fraud, or violation of certain employer contribution or group participation requirements).

Nondiscrimination based on health status. Group health plans and health insurance issuers offering health insurance coverage are prohibited from discriminating against an individual with regard to eligibility or coverage based on a health status factor.[3] Health reform extended these rules, effective January 1, 2014, to health insurance issuers offering individual health insurance coverage.[4]

Nondiscrimination against healthcare providers, beginning in 2014 if they act within the scope of their license or certification.[5]

Comprehensive health insurance coverage. Effective for plan years beginning on or after January 1, 2014, health insurance issuers offering coverage in the individual or small group market must ensure that such coverage includes the "essential health benefits package."[6] A plan must provide essential health benefits,[7] limit cost-sharing,[8] and provide either bronze, silver, gold, or platinum level coverage (benefits that are actuarially equivalent to 60 percent, 70 percent, 80 percent, or 90 percent of the full actuarial benefits provided under the plan), or a catastrophic plan (also known as "young invincibles" coverage).[9] An insurer that offers bronze, silver, gold, or platinum coverage must offer the same level of coverage in a "child-only plan" designed for persons under age twenty-one.[10]

No denial of coverage for individuals participating in approved clinical trials.[11]

No cost-sharing (copayments) for preventive and wellness services.[12]

Transparency in coverage.[13] A health plan seeking Qualified Health Plan (QHP) certification from an exchange must disclose certain information to the exchange, HHS, and the state insurance commissioner, and make the information available to the public as well as cost-sharing disclosures to participants.

---

1.   PHSA §2702(b).
2.   PHSA §2703.
3.   Health status factors are health status; medical condition (including both physical and mental illnesses); claims experience; receipt of health care; medical history; genetic information; evidence of insurability (EOI) (including conditions arising out of acts of domestic violence); disability; and any other health status-related factor determined appropriate by the Secretary of HHS. IRC Sec. 9802(a)(1); ERISA Sec. 702(a)(1); PHSA §2705(a). The last category was added by health reform. PHSA §2705(a).
4.   PHSA §2705.
5.   PHSA §2706.
6.   PHSA §2707(a).
7.   PPACA §1302(b).
8.   PPACA §1302(c).
9.   PPACA §1302(e).
10.   PHSA §2707(c).
11.   PHSA §2709.
12.   PHSA §2713.
13.   PHSA §2715A.

<u>Nondiscrimination is prohibited in favor of highly compensated employees by nongrandfathered insured group plans.</u>[1] Those rules are discussed in detail in Part VII of this book.

<u>Quality of care reporting</u> requires group health plans and health insurance issuers annually to report to HHS about plan or coverage benefits and provider "reimbursement structures" that may affect the quality of care.[2]

<u>Claims appeals</u>[3] <u>and external review</u>[4] <u>rules.</u>[5] These rules apply in addition to the ERISA claims procedures. Insurers will handle this duty for insured plans. Plan documents, Summary Plan Descriptions (SPDs), existing claims procedures, any forms and notices used to communicate benefit determinations, and service contracts with TPAs and insurers will need to be updated. Non-ERISA self-insured plans not previously subject to the ERISA claims procedure requirement must adopt the existing DOL claims procedures and comply with these new requirements, such as governmental and church plans that have not elected to be subject to ERISA. In March 2011, a grace period for some requirements was extended until plan years beginning on or after January 1, 2012, (with one exception).[6]

<u>Patient protections</u>[7] for women to select an OB-GYN and parents to select a pediatrician as their child's primary care provider. Additionally, for group health plans providing for emergency services, the plan:
- may not require preauthorization, including for emergency services provided out-of-network;
- must provide coverage regardless of whether the provider is in- or out-of-network;
- may not impose any administrative requirement or coverage limitation that is more restrictive than would be imposed on in-network emergency services; and
- must comply with cost-sharing requirements.[8]

---

238. How are these coverage mandates enforced?

The health reform requirements discussed in Q 207, i.e., the coverage mandates incorporated into the PHSA, are enforceable by:

- the Internal Revenue Service (IRS) or the Department of Labor (DOL);

- participants, beneficiaries, and plan fiduciaries; and

- the states and HHS, for state and local government plans.

Although the mandates applicable to group health plans and insurers are virtually identical, the consequences of noncompliance differ depending on type of entity and plan because of the different enforcement mechanisms under the Internal Revenue Code (Code), ERISA, the Fair Labor Standards Act (FLSA), and the PHSA.

---

1.   PHSA §2716, IRC Sec. 9815 and ERISA Sec. 715.
2.   PHSA §2717.
3.   DOL Reg. §2590.715-2719(b)(2).
4.   DOL Reg. §2590.715-2719(a).
5.   PHSA §2719.
6.   DOL Technical Release 2011-02.
7.   PHSA §2719A.
8.   Treas. Reg. §54.9815-2719A (b)(3)(i); DOL Reg. §2590.715-2719A(b)(3)(i); HHS Reg. §147.138(b)(3)(i).

The PHSA mandates are directly applicable to (and therefore enforceable against) state and local governmental employer group health plans. Insurers in the group and individual markets are subject to the PHSA.[1] Due to incorporation of the mandates into ERISA, they are also applicable to private-sector employer group health plans. Private-sector group health plans are also subject to the mandates incorporated into the Code. While the group health plans of church employers are generally not subject to ERISA (unless they opt in to ERISA coverage), they are subject to the mandates as incorporated into the Code.

Litigation due to violation of these mandates to enforce them could be brought against employers, plan sponsors, and fiduciaries under the PHSA, ERISA, and the FLSA. In addition, there could be other litigation, for example, when an employer moves employees to part-time status (fewer than thirty hours per week) to eliminate or soften the impact of the employer mandate tax penalty. Any such workforce realignment inherently carries with it risks of litigation under ERISA section 510, which prohibits interference with a participant's benefits or rights under ERISA, as well as potential claims under other antidiscrimination statutes, such as the Age Discrimination in Employment Act and Title VII of the Civil Rights Act.

<u>Internal Revenue Code</u>. The IRS can assess excise taxes upon group health plans that do not comply with the coverage mandates. For group health plans, the penalty tax upon a noncomplying plan sponsor is $100 per day of noncompliance per affected individual,[2] and the violations must be self-reported on IRS Form 8928[3]. The tax may be higher where violations occurred or continued during a period under IRS examination or where the violations are more than *de minimis*. The tax does not apply where the failure was based on reasonable cause and not on willful neglect,[4] and the failure is corrected within thirty days after the person knew or should have known that the failure existed.[5] If the plan (other than a church plan)[6] is audited by the IRS, the minimum excise tax for a compliance failure discovered after a notice of examination generally is $2,500.[7] The minimum excise tax is increased to $15,000 if violations are "more than de minimis."[8] If not corrected and if the failure was due to reasonable cause and not willful neglect (an unintentional failure), the tax imposed may not exceed the lesser of 10 percent of the amount paid to provide medical care during the taxable year or $500,000. In the case of a multiemployer plan, the tax is levied upon the plan.

The PHSA also imposes an additional new penalty of up to $1,000 per day per affected individual for willful violations of the Summary of Benefits and Coverage (SBC) rules for group health plans.[9] For an insured plan, the insurer and plan administrator are potentially subject to this penalty.[10]

---

1.   PHSA §2723.
2.   IRC Sec. 4980D, which does not apply to insurers.
3.   Form 8928, Revised May 2016, https://www.irs.gov/pub/irs-pdf/f8928.pdf.
4.   IRC Sec. 4980D(c)(1).
5.   IRC Sec. 4980D(c)(2). See IRC Sec. 4980D(c)(2)(B)(ii), which gives church plans 270 days after the date of mailing by the Secretary of a notice of default with respect to the plan's failure.
6.   IRC Sec. 4980D(b)(3)(c).
7.   IRC Sec. 4980D(b)(3)(B).
8.   IRC Sec. 4980D(c)(3)(A).
9.   PHSA §2715(f).
10.   PHSA §2715(f); Treas. Regs. §54.9815-2715(e); DOL Regs. §2590.715-2715(e); 45 CFR §147.200(e).

There is an exception for small employers with between two and fifty employees. This exception seems limited to failures by an insurer to comply with the mandates and not because an insured plan violates the rules, for example, the health insurance nondiscrimination rules, discussed at Q 398 to Q 402.

ERISA. Using ERISA's enforcement mechanisms, health reform imposes substantial, complex, and plan-wide coverage mandates on employers. ERISA did this for pension benefits, and health reform has now extended this to the complex world of health benefits. It is quite likely that the plaintiffs' bar, or perhaps even DOL, will test the limits of grandfathered status, as well as of the employers' and plan fiduciaries' good faith efforts to comply with the many coverage mandates.

Health reform allows health plans that were in effect on March 23, 2010, to continue as "grandfathered" plans without having to comply with many of the law's coverage mandates. Under the DOL's regulations, grandfathered plans must include a statement, in any plan materials provided to participants, noting the plan's grandfathered status, describing the plan's benefits, and providing contact information for questions and complaints.[1] When there is more than one grandfathered option or "package," the notice must be given for each grandfathered option.

It is unclear whether technical notice failures, such as being thirty days late, will forfeit grandfathered status, and good faith or substantial compliance on notice and changes in benefits may prevent loss of such status.[2] Because the loss of grandfathered status triggers compliance with certain of the law's coverage mandates on preventative care, it is likely that plaintiffs will often look to challenge grandfathering on a class basis. Plaintiffs also will be expected to contend that the "appropriate equitable relief" section of ERISA allows them to seek recovery of benefits that otherwise would have been provided from the date that such status elapsed.

The DOL may enforce the coverage mandates against group health plans by bringing a civil action to enjoin a noncompliant act or practice or for appropriate equitable relief under Part 7 of ERISA.[3] In addition, participants, beneficiaries, and fiduciaries can sue under ERISA, either individually or through class actions, to enforce the PHSA mandates against private-sector group health plans and their insurers.[4] Such lawsuits might include claims for payment of benefits alleged to be due under the plan, and the affected party could seek damages for unpaid benefits, interest, and attorney's fees.

The coverage mandates result in litigation exposure because of their complexity and the uncertainty that surrounds implementation. In addition, many of these mandates will upset

---

1.   75 Fed. Reg. 34538 (June 17, 2010).
2.   Participant notices are required to "maintain status as a grandfathered health plan." 75 Fed. Reg. 34538, 34541. A representative of the Treasury Department stated in nonbinding remarks that failing to provide the required notices will not automatically revoke a plan's grandfathered status, and that the facts and circumstances surrounding a notice failure will be determinative as to continued grandfathering. See http://www.employersgroup.com/Content.aspx?id=1675. (Last accessed August 17, 2019).
3.   ERISA Sec. 502(a).
4.   ERISA Sec. 502(a).

existing practices (e.g., the potential lifting of annual limits on durable medical equipment or therapy services) and will impose substantial costs on employers. For example, plaintiffs may be expected to test whether limits on doctor visits, mental health sessions, and the like (which are often imposed by plans) are permitted, or instead constitute impermissible forms of annual limits. Finally, if a court later determines that the benefit at issue was required, the employer or plan fiduciary may face plan-wide exposure, with plaintiffs seeking to use ERISA's remedial provisions to acquire these benefits, including payment of money for any lost benefits.

Since 2014, no Essential Health Benefits (EHB) are permitted to have annual or lifetime limits, so plaintiffs may challenge annual or lifetime limits on certain items and services as violating the prohibition on such limits for EHBs. Health plans should be able to show compliance with the "good faith" implementation standard set forth in the regulations[1] until more specific EHB criteria are issued.

ERISA's fee-shifting provision,[2] giving courts the power to award legal fees to plaintiffs who show "some success on the merits"[3] may also increase the likelihood of class litigation. Previous ERISA litigation has resulted in large "common fund" fee awards for class actions,[4] as well as large lodestar fee awards,[5] making ERISA class litigation attractive to plaintiffs.

<u>PHSA</u>. Nonfederal (state and local) governmental plans and health insurance issuers are subject to penalties for violations of the PHSA mandates by HHS (but only if the state takes no enforcement action).[6] The PHSA civil money penalties of up to $100 per day may be assessed against the issuer, the sponsoring employer of a nonfederal governmental plan, and the plan itself if it is sponsored by more than one employer.[7] Like the tax penalty, there are exceptions if the failure was not discovered with the exercise of reasonable diligence.[8] Failures due to reasonable cause that are self-corrected within thirty days of the date the entity knew or should have known of the failure have no penalty.[9] Like the tax penalty, this penalty is capped at 10 percent of the aggregate amount paid or incurred by the employer during the preceding taxable year for the group health plan or $500,000, whichever is less.[10]

<u>FLSA</u>. The Department of Labor and individuals denied their rights may sue to enforce the FLSA. Health reform amended the FLSA to protect employees reporting or otherwise opposing

---

1.   Dep't of Labor's FAQs About the Affordable Care Act Implementation Part IV, available https://www.dol.gov/sites/default/files/ebsa/about-ebsa/our-activities/resource-center/faqs/aca-part-iv.pdf. (Last Accessed August 17, 2019).
2.   ERISA Sec. 502(g), 29 U.S.C. §1132(g).
3.   See *Hardt v. Reliance Std. Life Ins. Co.*, 130 S. Ct. 2149, 2157-58 (2010).
4.   E.g., *IBM Personal Pension Plan v. Cooper*, 2005 WL 1981501 (S.D. Ill. August 16, 2005) (settling cash balance conversion case for $314.3 million, with attorney's fees of 29 percent of first $250 million, and 25 percent of remainder).
5.   *Continental Group v. McClendon*, 872 F. Supp. 142 (D.N.J. 1994) (ERISA 510 claim settled for $415 million, with $33.3 million fee award based on "enhanced" lodestar method).
6.   PHSA §§2723(a) and (b)(1).
7.   PHSA §2723(b)(2).
8.   PHSA §2723(b)(2)(C)(iii)(I).
9.   PHSA §2723(b)(2)(C)(iii)(II).
10.   PHSA §2723(b)(2)(D).

violations of the healthcare reform law. That amendment prohibits an employer from discharging or otherwise discriminating against an employee who:

- has received a premium tax credit or subsidy for a qualified health plan;

- provided information or is about to provide information to the employer, the federal government, or the state attorney general about any violation of significant portions of the PPACA;

- testified or is about to testify in a proceeding concerning such a violation;

- has otherwise participated or is about to assist or participate in such a proceeding; or

- has objected to, or refused to participate in, any activity, policy, practice, or task that the employee reasonably believes to be such a violation.[1]

This amendment adopts the complaint procedures of the already existing whistleblower protection provision of the federal Consumer Product Safety Improvement Act. Under that provision, an employee who believes that he or she has been retaliated against may file a complaint with the U.S. Department of Labor.

The employee may also file suit in federal court within ninety days after receiving a written determination or within 210 days of the filing of the complaint, if the DOL has not issued a final decision.

239. What is the status of transitional policies not compliant with healthcare reform?

They have been allowed to continue since 2014 and have been continuously extended since that time. There is no reason to believe that they will not continue to be extended as they have been again this year.

A component of the basis of the federal healthcare reform was the concept that if individuals are required to acquire health insurance (or pay a penalty up until 2019), the insurance must be worth buying, meaning:

(1)   important benefits must be covered; and

(2)   older and unhealthier people should not be charged amounts dramatically larger than young, healthy individuals.

On November 14, 2013,[2] HHS announced a one-year retreat and allowed policies that did not comply with certain healthcare reform requirements to continue to be sold if the insurance companies wish to do so and if the state insurance regulators allow them to do so. The Obama

---

1.   FLSA §18C.
2.   See HHS, CMS, Center for Consumer Information & Insurance Oversight (CCIIO) letter from CCIIO Director Gary Cohen to state insurance commissioners at http://www.cms.gov/CCIIO/Resources/Letters/Downloads/commissioner-letter-11-14-2013.PDF. Footnote 2 of this letter indicates that the IRS and Department of Labor concur with this program. (Last accessed August 17, 2019).

administration announced through this HHS letter that it would allow insurance companies to renew individual and small group market policies that do not meet health law standards through the end of 2013 and 2014 for policy years starting between January 1 and October 1 if that coverage was in effect for the insured or small group on October 1, 2013. This letter allowed such policies to be renewed for one policy year beginning between January 1, 2014 through October 1, 2014 if insurers decide to do so and if the state insurance regulators permit. Since that time, letters issued by CMS have extended transitional policies. In keeping with that tradition, on March 25, 2019, CMS issued a letter extending transitional policies beginning on or before October 1, 2020 and provided that non-compliant policies end by December 31, 2020.

These actions were in response to the complaints of millions of individuals who received notices that the insurance they had in 2013 would be cancelled, thus meaning that those people would not be able to keep their insurance, even if they liked it. Under the change, a person with a policy that ended in June 2014 would have had the option to renew that same plan for one more year, but only if their insurance company decides to continue the policy and the state allows it to be sold. This change of administration policy was probably aimed at causing those unhappy with the policy cancellations to be upset with insurers who choose not to continue the cancelled policies rather than Congress and the administration. Had the website HealthCare.Gov been working properly, many people getting cancellations could have seen if they could get a better deal in an exchange (better coverage, lower cost due to subsidies, or both).

Insurers who use this option must notify policyholders:

(1)   of the various health law benefits missing from the plan;[1] and

(2)   about the other options they would have on the health law's state exchanges (marketplaces), including the possibility of financial assistance, and outside the exchanges that comply with healthcare reform requirements.

Such notices must be sent as soon as possible to those who have received cancellation notices or when a cancellation notice would have otherwise in the future been sent. The administration's change will only allow people who are already signed up for these pre-Obamacare plans to keep buying them.

Anyone remaining in one of these pre-Affordable Care Act plans will be in a separate risk pool, meaning that their premiums are set based on those in their group. Everyone who buys an Affordable Care Act plan will be in a different risk pool. If many insurers continue these plans, many if not most persons who have them may be willing to have their lesser benefit package. These individuals would tend to be healthier, which would drive up premiums sold on the state exchanges.

---

1.   These could include any or all of the following requirements contained in the following sections of the Public Health Service Act, as amended by healthcare reform: 2701 (relating to fair health insurance premiums); 2702 (relating to guaranteed availability of coverage); 2703 (relating to guaranteed renewability of coverage); 2704 (relating to the prohibition of pre-existing condition exclusions or other discrimination based on health status), with respect to adults, except with respect to group coverage; 2705 (relating to the prohibition of discrimination against individual participants and beneficiaries based on health status), except with respect to group coverage; 2706 (relating to non-discrimination in health care); 2707 (relating to comprehensive health insurance coverage); and 2709 (relating to coverage for individuals participating in approved clinical trials).

Status of Individual Mandate and Penalties

240. Does the hardship exemption which was available under the individual mandate still exist?

Yes, in limited circumstances.

Beginning with the 2019 plan year (for which taxes are filed in April 2020), the individual mandate penalty (Shared Responsibility Payment) no longer applies. Individuals who do not have healthcare coverage during 2019 do not need an exemption to avoid the penalty, since the penalty has been reduced to zero.

Catastrophic Health Plans

For some people wishing to buy a Catastrophic health insurance plan, a hardship exemption is required. Catastrophic health insurance plans have low monthly premiums and very high deductibles. They may be an affordable way for some consumers to protect themselves from worst-case scenarios, like getting seriously sick or injured. However, the policy holder must pay most routine medical expenses themselves. While monthly premiums are generally low, but the premium tax credit is not available to reduce cost. Those that qualify for a premium tax credit based on income, a Bronze or Silver plan is likely to be a better value. In addition, the deductibles are very high. For 2020, the deductible for all Catastrophic plans is $8,150.

Catastrophic plans cover the same essential health benefits (EHBs)[1] as other Marketplace plans. Catastrophic plans cover certain preventive services at no cost. Preventive services vary from those for all adults, those for women, and those for children.[2] In addition, these plans must cover at least three primary care visits per year before meeting deductibles.

People under thirty can purchase a Catastrophic health plan without a hardship exemption. Individuals aged thirty and older that want to purchase a Catastrophic health plan MUST apply for a hardship exemption to qualify. Catastrophic health plans offer lower-priced coverage that mainly protect subscribers from high medical costs if seriously hurt or injured. In order to enroll in a Catastrophic plan it is necessary to submit a hardship or affordability exemption application and obtain an exemption certificate number.

Link for **hardship exemption** form: https://marketplace.cms.gov/applications-and-forms/hardship-exemption.pdf.

Link for **affordability exemptions** for those with residency in Alabama, Alaska, Arizona, Arkansas, Delaware, Florida, Georgia, Hawaii, Illinois, Indiana, Iowa, Kansas, Kentucky, Louisiana, Maine, Michigan, Mississippi, Missouri, Montana, Nebraska, Nevada, New Hampshire, New Jersey, New Mexico, North Carolina, North Dakota, Ohio, Oklahoma, Oregon, Pennsylvania, South Carolina, South Dakota, Tennessee, Texas, Utah, Virginia,

---

1.   https://www.healthcare.gov/glossary/essential-health-benefits/.
2.   https://www.healthcare.gov/coverage/preventive-care-benefits/.

West Virginia, Wisconsin, Wyoming: https://marketplace.cms.gov/applications-and-forms/affordability-ffm-exemption.pdf.

Link for **affordability exemptions** for those with residency in California, Colorado, District of Columbia, Idaho, Maryland, Massachusetts, Minnesota, New York, Rhode Island, Vermont, Washington: https://marketplace.cms.gov/applications-and-forms/affordability-sbm-exemption.pdf.

241. What are the qualifications for the hardship exemption?

As stated in the prior question, beginning with the 2019 plan year, the individual mandate penalty (Shared Responsibility Payment) no longer applies to normal purchases of healthcare insurance from the exchanges. Individuals who do not have healthcare coverage during 2019 do not need an exemption to avoid the penalty, since the penalty has been reduced to zero.

However, for people wishing to buy a Catastrophic health insurance plan, a hardship exemption IS required. See prior question for requirements.

Qualifications for Hardship Exemption for Catastrophic Plans

For 2019, 2020 and subsequent years, in order for someone over thirty to qualify to purchase Catastrophic coverage, the purchaser must meet a hardship requirements. Qualifications include:[1]

- homelessness;

- evicted in the past six months or facing eviction;

- receipt of a shut off notice from the utility company;

- experienced domestic violence;

- death of a close family member;

- substantial damage to property from a fire, flood or other natural or human-caused disaster;

- bankruptcy;

- unpaid medical expenses resulting in substantial debt;

- unexpected increases in necessary expenses in caring for an ill, disabled or aging family member;

- dependent child that has been denied coverage in Medicaid and CHIP;

---

1.   https://www.healthcare.gov/health-coverage-exemptions/hardship-exemptions/ (Last accessed August 18, 2019).

- an eligibility appeals decision has granted qualification for enrollment in a Quali-fied Health Plan (QHP) the Marketplace, lower monthly premiums, or cost-sharing reductions for a time period not enrolled in a QHP through the Marketplace;

- ineligibility for Medicaid because domicile state did not participate in Medicaid expansion;

- grandfathered insurance plan was cancelled and other plans are unaffordable;

- another hardship – needs to be explained on the form.

History of the Hardship Exemption

The Obama administration announced on December 19, 2013, that individuals whose insurance plans have been canceled would be eligible for "hardship exemptions" from the indi-vidual mandate requirement to have coverage in 2014 or pay a penalty. HHS Secretary Kathleen Sebelius outlined the policy in a letter[1] to Sen. Mark Warner and five other senators who had raised concerns about the issue. "I agree with you that these consumers should qualify for this temporary hardship exemption, and I can assure that the exemption will be available to them," Sebelius said. However, she made it clear that the exemption is limited to persons who have difficulty purchasing exchange coverage.

Sebelius also announced that individuals with canceled policies will be allowed to purchase catastrophic coverage. Previously, only individuals under the age of thirty could avoid incurring a financial penalty after March 31, 2014, by purchasing such plans. However, there were no federal subsidies available for those buying catastrophic coverage.

Thus, the application of the hardship exemption to consumers whose plans were can-celed did not appear to be a change in policy. The form[2] for the application for a waiver from the individual mandate included such a category: "You received a notice saying that your current health insurance plan is being canceled, and you consider the other plans available unaffordable."

Thus, the announcement by the administration was largely symbolic and a political response to the criticism that healthcare reform was causing people to lose the policies and physicians they liked and wanted to keep, as they were told generically that they could keep.

In fact, some argued that the hardship definition was so broad that it undermines the indi-vidual mandate.

For the 2017 and 2018 taxable years to claim a hardship exemption, a taxpayer needed to fill out a paper form and return it to the Marketplace. Qualifications included those listed above for catastrophic plans.

---

1.   At http://www.scribd.com/doc/192619675/Sec-Sebelius-Response-to-Senator-Warner?wpisrc=nl_wonk. (Last accessed August 17, 2019).
2.   At https://www.healthcare.gov/health-coverage-exemptions/hardship-exemptions/. (Last accessed August 18, 2019).

No Annual Limits on Essential Health Benefits Beginning in 2014

242. What changes has health reform imposed on annual limits in health plans?

Health reform prohibits health plans from putting an annual dollar limit on essential health benefits for individual insurance and insurance issued in the small group market.[1] Essential health benefits do not include "excepted benefits," which are not subject to health reform provisions. (See Part I, Q 13 to Q 24, for more information on "excepted benefits.") Self-funded, large group market, and grandfathered health plans are not required to offer essential health benefits.

The law initially restricted, then phased out the annual dollar limits a health plan, other than a grandfathered plan, could place on essential health benefits.[2] Annual limits have been prohibited completely from 2014 and thereafter for Essential Health Benefits (EHBs). While grandfathered plans are exempt from the essential health benefit requirement, they are subject to the prohibition on annual limits for any essential health benefit they offer.[3] Since 2014, all insurance coverage available on the exchanges will provide essential health benefits.

Before the healthcare law, many health plans set an annual limit – a dollar limit on their yearly spending for covered benefits. Many plans also set a lifetime limit – a dollar limit on what they would spend for covered benefits during the entire time a participant was enrolled in that plan.

Under the law, lifetime limits on most benefits are prohibited in any health plan or insurance policy issued or renewed on or after September 23, 2010.

The law restricted and phased out the annual dollar limits that all employment-related plans, and individual health insurance plans issued after March 23, 2010, can put on most covered health benefits. Specifically, the law stated that none of these plans could set an annual dollar limit lower than:

- $750,000: for a plan year or policy year starting on or after September 23, 2010, but before September 23, 2011

- $1.25 million: for a plan year or policy year starting on or after September 23, 2011, but before September 23, 2012

- $2 million: for a plan year or policy year starting on or after September 23, 2012, but before January 1, 2014

No annual dollar limits are allowed on most covered benefits beginning on or after January 1, 2014. The ban on lifetime dollar limits for most covered benefits applies to *every* health plan, whether individual or group coverage.

---

1. https://www.federalregister.gov/articles/2015/11/18/2015-29294/final-rules-for-grandfathered-plans-preexisting-condition-exclusions-lifetime-and-annual-limits.
2. PHSA §2711.
3. PHSA §2711.

In the pending lawsuit filed by the Attorneys-General of twenty conservative-leaning states, the constitutionality of the Affordable Care Act as a whole and the elimination of the pre-existing conditions coverage provisions in particular is being challenged and has been found to be unconstitutional by the United States District Court of the Northern District of Texas. The litigation is currently before the U.S. Court of Appeals for the Fifth Circuit, but if successful, it could potentially allow insurers to impose dollar limits on policies in the future.[1]

243. How does the Affordable Care Act apply to self-insured (self-funded) health plans?

The Department of Health and Human Services (HHS) has addressed[2] amendments by the PPACA to the law permitting self-funded nonfederal governmental plans to opt out of compliance with certain federal benefit mandates. Except for a narrow band of requirements, these group health plans will no longer be permitted to opt out of HIPAA rules regarding the preexisting condition exclusion, enrollment periods, and the prohibition on discriminating against persons due to preexisting conditions. Plan sponsors may continue to opt out of requirements under the Newborns' and Mothers' Health Protection Act, Mental Health Parity and Addiction Equity Act, Women's Health and Cancer Rights Act, and Michelle's Law.

Self-funded plans generally are treated the same as insured plans under the PPACA. Analysis of the application of PPACA (the 2010 healthcare reform law) to self-insured plans begins with section 1562, which adds section 715 to ERISA and section 9815 to the Code. These provisions state that all of the provisions of Part A of Title XXVII of the Public Health Service Act (PHSA), as amended by the PPACA, apply to both ERISA group health plans and health insurance issuers that insure group health plans. ERISA group health plans include both self-insured and insured plans.

The section further provides that if anything in ERISA's group plan requirements conflicts with Part A of the PHSA, the PHSA shall govern. The fact that this section refers both to group health plans and to insured group health plans makes it clear that the provision is meant to apply to self-insured plans. This is reinforced by subsection (b) of this section adding new section 715 to ERISA and Code section 9815, both of which state that section 2716 and section 2718 of the PHSA do not apply to self-insured plans, indicating that the remaining provisions do.

The definition of group health plan under PPACA section 1301(b)(3), which incorporates the definition of section 2791 of the PHSA,[3] states that group health plan means an employee welfare benefit plan as defined in ERISA section 3(1).[4] Section 1551 of the PPACA also provides that the definitions of PHSA section 2791 apply to the PPACA.

---

1. See *Texas, et. al. v. United States Department of Health and Human Services, et. al.*, filed February 26, 2018, U.S. District Court, N.D. Texas, Case 4:18-cv-00167-O (Currently before the United States Court of Appeals for the Fifth Circuit in oral argument).
2. See "Self-Funded Non-Federal Governmental Plans" at http://www.cms.gov/CCIIO/Programs-and-Initiatives/Health-Insurance-Market-Reforms/nonfedgovplans.html. (Last accessed August 13, 2018).
3. 42 USC 30gg-91.
4. 29 USC 1002(1).

Several sections of the PPACA refer specifically to self-insured plans:

- Section 2701(a)(5), applying the health status underwriting provisions to large group plans in an exchange, does not apply to self-insured plans. Section 2715 requires a plan sponsor or designated administrator to make disclosures required by that section for self-insured plans.

- Section 2716, discrimination in favor of highly-compensated employees, expressly states that it does not apply to self-insured plans, which already are covered by a similar requirement under Internal Revenue Code section 105(h).

- Self-insured plans expressly are subject to the external review requirements, that is, the appeal requirements, of section 2719 to be established by HHS.

- The reinsurance provisions of section 1341 expressly apply to self-insured plans; the risk-pooling provisions of section 1343 expressly do not.

- Self-insured plans expressly are subject to a per-member fee to fund patient centered outcomes research under recently added Internal Revenue Code section 4376.

These changes are effective beginning on or after September 23, 2010, for noncollectively bargained self-funded nonfederal governmental plans. For example, self-insured nonfederal governmental plans maintained pursuant to a collective bargaining agreement ratified before March 23, 2010, have a different compliance effective date. These have been exempted from any of the relevant HIPAA requirements, limits on preexisting condition exclusions, special enrollment periods, and health status nondiscrimination requirements. They will not have to come into compliance with those requirements until the first day of the first plan year following the expiration of the last plan year governed by a collective bargaining agreement.

244. What are the essential health benefits?

Essential Health Benefits are a set of ten classifications of services that health insurance plans must cover under the Affordable Care Act.

These include doctors' services, inpatient and outpatient hospital care, prescription drug coverage, pregnancy and childbirth, mental health services, and more. Insurance policies must cover these benefits in order to be certified and offered through the exchanges, and all Medicaid state plans needed to cover these services since 2014. A definition and list of essential health benefits is found in Part I, Q 2.

245. What exceptions to the annual limit rules are there?

Excepted Benefits: The annual limit rules do not apply to "excepted benefits." The rules are not specific as to whether there can be nondollar limits, such as limits on certain types of visits to providers. As noted, self-funded, large group market, and grandfathered health plans are not required to offer essential health benefits, but they are not subject to the prohibition on annual limits on the essential health benefits they do offer.[1]

FSAs/MSAs/HSAs/HRAs and QSE-HRAs: The rule does not apply to health flexible spending arrangements, medical savings accounts, or health savings accounts. If a Health Reimbursement Arrangement (HRA) or a Qualified Small Employer Health Reimbursement Arrangement (QSE-HRA) is integrated with other coverage as part of a group health plan, and the other coverage standing alone would comply with this rule, then the HRA will not be subject to the rule.[2] The rule generally does not apply to retiree-only stand-alone HRAs. The tri-agency task force (HHS, DOL, and Treasury) has requested comments regarding the application of the rule to nonretiree-only stand-alone HRAs.

The regulations clarify that the rule does not preclude a plan from excluding all benefits with respect to a particular condition. If the plan provides any benefits for a condition, however, the rule applies.

246. Were any waivers to the annual limit rule available?

Yes. Some plans (typically "mini-med" plans offering restricted benefits) were eligible for a waiver from the rules concerning annual dollar limits, if complying with the limit would mean a significant decrease in benefits coverage or a significant increase in premiums. On June 17, 2011, the Centers for Medicare & Medicaid Services (CMS) introduced a process for plans that have already received waivers and want to renew those waivers for plan or policy years beginning before January 1, 2014. Revised guidance extended the duration of waivers granted through 2013, if applicants submitted annual information about their plan and comply with requirements to ensure that their enrollees understand the limits of their coverage.

As a condition of receiving a waiver, a plan needed to provide a notice explaining to participants that the plan does not meet the annual limit requirements.

Lifetime Limits on Essential Health Benefits Eliminated

247. When did the rules against lifetime limits become effective?

Unlike the rules for annual limits, there is no waiver procedure for the rules against lifetime limits. Effective for plan years beginning on or after September 23, 2010, group health plans and insurers, other than grandfathered plans, could not and cannot impose any lifetime limit on the dollar amount of essential health benefits for any individual.[3] As noted, self-funded, large group market, and grandfathered health plans are not required to offer essential health benefits but are subject to the prohibition on lifetime limits on the essential health benefits they do offer.[4] As noted above in Q 242, plans are not prohibited, however, from placing lifetime dollar

---

1.   Frequently Asked Questions on Essential Health Benefits Bulletin, Q&A-10, at https://www.dol.gov/sites/default/files/ebsa/about-ebsa/
      our-activities/resource-center/faqs/aca-part-i.pdf. (Last accessed August 18, 2019).
2.   Preamble to Interim Final Rules Relating to Preexisting Condition Exclusions, Lifetime and Annual Limits, Rescissions, and Patient Protec-
      tions Under PPACA, 75 Fed. Reg. 37188, 37190. (June 28, 2010).
3.   PHSA §2711(a)(1)(A); https://www.federalregister.gov/articles/2015/11/18/2015-29294/final-rules-for-grandfathered-plans-preexisting-
      condition-exclusions-lifetime-and-annual-limits (Last accessed August 18, 2019) .
4.   https://www.cms.gov/cciio/resources/data-resources/ehb.html (Last Accessed August 13, 2018).

limits on specific covered benefits that are <u>not</u> essential health benefits to the extent such limits are otherwise permitted under applicable federal or state law.[1] The rules against lifetime limits apply to both in-network and out-of-network benefits.[2] All coverages offered on the exchanges will offer essential health benefits.

The applicable essential health benefits benchmark for the state in which the insurance policy is issued would determine the essential health benefits for all participants, regardless of the employee's state of residence or domicile.[3] The preventive services described in section 2713 of the PHSA are part of essential health benefits.[4] Beginning January 1, 2014, all Medicaid benchmark and benchmark-equivalent plans were required to include at least the ten statutory categories of EHBs.[5]

It is uncertain whether this provision would survive under the various versions of "repeal and replace" of the Affordable Care Act which have been or might be considered by Congress or would survive the current legal action being brought by twenty state Attorneys-General in federal court challenging the constitutionality of the Affordable Care Act.

Dependent Coverage Extended to Children until Age Twenty-six

248. What are the rules that require extending coverage to children of the insured until the child reaches age twenty-six?

The adult child coverage until-age-twenty-six requirement consists of the following:

A group health plan and a health insurance issuer offering group or individual health insurance coverage that provides dependent coverage of children shall continue to make such coverage available for an adult child until the child turns twenty-six years of age. Nothing in this section shall require a health plan or a health insurance issuer described in the preceding sentence to make coverage available for a child of a child receiving dependent coverage.[6]

Thus, coverage is available until the day before the child's twenty-sixth birthday. Therefore, unless extended by the plan until the end of the year, coverage terminates at age twenty-six.

Like all of health reform, the age twenty-six rules do not apply to "excepted benefits," but only to major medical coverage.

This provision is considered to be very popular by both Republicans and Democrats and is endorsed by President Trump. This provision is likely to survive in some fashion even if the

---

1. PHSA §2711(b); https://www.federalregister.gov/articles/2015/11/18/2015-29294/final-rules-for-grandfathered-plans-preexisting-condition-exclusions-lifetime-and-annual-limit. (Last accessed August 18, 2019).

2. Nonbinding comments of James Mayhew, Office of Consumer Information and Insurance Oversight, Centers for Medicare & Medicaid Services of HHS, Department of Labor Affordable Care Act Compliance Assistance Webcast Series: Part I (September 7, 2010).

3. https://www.cms.gov/cciio/resources/data-resources/ehb.html. (Last Accessed August 18, 2019).

4. https://www.cms.gov/cciio/resources/data-resources/ehb.html. (Last Accessed August 18, 2019).

5. https://www.cms.gov/cciio/resources/data-resources/ehb.html. (Last Accessed August 18, 2019).

6. PHSA §2714; 29 CFR 2590.715-2714. (Eligibility of children until at least age twenty-six).

Affordable Care Act is replaced by Democratic proposals. If the ACA is found to be unconstitutional, it is uncertain what the future of this clause will be.

249. When was the until age twenty-six coverage requirement effective?

The "until age twenty-six rule" became effective for plan years beginning on or after September 23, 2010.[1] For policies in the individual market, the mandate became applicable for the initial period of coverage beginning on or after September 23, 2010, regardless of what the policy year is.[2] Grandfathered plans only need to cover children not eligible for coverage from their own employer's health plan (other than coverage as a dependent child) until the plan year beginning in 2014.[3]

For income tax purposes, the change was effective March 30, 2010.[4]

250. What about adult children who were previously ineligible for coverage who became eligible for the first plan year beginning on or after September 23, 2010?

The regulations require a notice to these newly eligible adult children and an enrollment period for plans meeting specified conditions.[5]

251. What is the definition of a child for this purpose?

In defining which children under age twenty-six are eligible for coverage, the regulations prohibit a plan from requiring a child to satisfy any conditions other than "a relationship between a child and the participant."[6]

The definition of a child is the definition of a child for purposes of defining a dependent under Internal Revenue Code section 152 and includes natural, adopted, stepchildren, and foster children. The Final Rules on PHSA section 2714,[7] reads:

"PHS Act section 2714 does not require a plan to provide dependent coverage of children but instead provides that if a plan does provide dependent coverage of children it must continue to make such coverage available until the child turns age twenty-six. Neither PHS Act section 2714 nor the interim final regulations defined the term child for purpose of the dependent coverage provision."

---

1.   PPACA §1004(a).
2.   HHS, DOL & TREASURY, FAQs About the Affordable Care Act Implementation Part II, Q&A-9, at http://www.dol.gov/ebsa/faqs/ faq-aca2.html. (Last accessed August 18, 2019).
3.   PPACA, Pub. L. No. 111-148, §1251(a).
4.   IRS Notice 2010-38.
5.   DOL Reg. §2590.715-2714(f); Treas. Reg. §54.9815-2714T(f); HHS Reg. §147.120(f); Final Rules for Grandfathered Plans, Preexisting Condition Exclusions, Lifetime and Annual Limits, Rescissions, Dependent Coverage, Appeals, and Patient Protections Under the Affordable Care Act (replaces Interim Final Rules of May 13, 2010), https://www.federalregister.gov/articles/2015/11/18/2015-29294/final-rules-for-grandfathered-plans-preexisting-condition-exclusions-lifetime-and-annual-limits (November 18, 2015). (Last accessed August 18, 2019).
6.   Final Rules for Grandfathered Plans, Preexisting Condition Exclusions, Lifetime and Annual Limits, Rescissions, Dependent Coverage, Appeals, and Patient Protections Under the Affordable Care Act (replaces Interim Final Rules of May 13, 2010), https://www.federalregister. gov/articles/2015/11/18/2015-29294/final-rules-for-grandfathered-plans-preexisting-condition-exclusions-lifetime-and-annual-limits (November 18, 2015). (Last accessed August 18, 2019).
7.   75 Fed. Reg. 27122, 27131 (May 13, 2010).

Q&A-14 of the Part I FAQs provides:

"A plan or issuer does not fail to satisfy the requirements of PHSA section 2714 or its implementing regulations because the plan limits health coverage for children until the child turns twenty-six to only those children who are described in section 152(f)(1) of the Internal Revenue Code. For an individual not described in Internal Revenue Code section 152(f)(1), such as a grandchild or niece, a plan may impose additional conditions on eligibility for health coverage, such as a condition that the individual be a dependent for income tax purposes."

Internal Revenue Code section 152(f)(1)(A) defines the term "child" means an individual who is:

(i)   a son, daughter, stepson, or stepdaughter of the taxpayer; or

(ii)   an eligible foster child of the taxpayer.

Code section 152(f)(1)(C) provides that the term "eligible foster child" means an individual who is placed with the taxpayer by an authorized placement agency or by judgment, decree, or other order of any court of competent jurisdiction.

Relatives such as grandchildren or nephews and nieces are not required to be covered to age twenty-six, even if the plan grants them eligibility.[1] Thus, it is permissible for a plan that covers them to impose a lower age limit with respect to coverage for them. The plan could also limit coverage to those stepchildren who reside with or are financially dependent on a plan participant.

252. Must all health plans now offer the until age twenty-six coverage?

No. Plans are not required to offer any dependent care (or even spousal) coverage. However, if a group health plan or insurer provides coverage of children, the plan must make such coverage available for a child until age twenty-six. Eligible adult children wishing to take advantage of the coverage up to age twenty-six will be included in the parents' family coverage.

253. If adult child coverage is provided, was it required that prohibitions against preexisting conditions for adult children be eliminated before 2014?

While this is not specifically addressed, it seems that the answer is "no." Section 2704 of the Affordable Care Act prohibits preexisting condition exclusions for children under age nineteen, effective for the first plan year beginning on or after September 23, 2010.[2]

---

1.   HHS, DOL & TREASURY, FAQs About the Affordable Care Act Implementation Part I, Q14, available at https://www.dol.gov/sites/default/files/ebsa/about-ebsa/our-activities/resource-center/faqs/aca-part-i.pdf. (Last accessed August 18, 2019).
2.   PHSA §2704.

254. Does this rule require the elimination of preexisting condition exclusions for all Code section 152(f)(1) children up to age twenty-six?

The IRS has informally indicated that the Department of Health and Human Services, the Department of Labor, and the Department of the Treasury agree that the prohibition on benefit variance does not mandate an elimination of preexisting condition exclusions up to age twenty-six.[1]

255. May a plan exclude, for the up to age twenty-six rule, children based on tax-dependent status, residency, age, income, employment, marital, or tax-filing status?

It depends. If a plan covers dependents, then the answer is NO, at least not for children who are Internal Revenue Code section 152(f) children, i.e., dependents.[2] These factors cannot be used whether the child is a minor or an adult. The statute itself makes clear that marriage is not a disqualification.[3] However, coverage need not be offered to the child's spouse.[4]

Generally, a plan cannot deny eligibility to an Internal Revenue Code section 152(f) child because that child is eligible for other coverage.[5] Thus, if a plan offers dependent coverage to Code section 152(f) children of employees, it must extend coverage even to Internal Revenue Code section 152(f) children who are eligible for coverage through another parent's employer or a spouse's employer. As discussed at Q 249, for a limited time, grandfathered plans need not offer dependent coverage to a child under age twenty-six who is eligible to enroll in another employer-sponsored group health plan, other than that of the other parent's employer.[6]

256. What is the definition of "child" and how should the employer define child in its health plan?

The definition of a child for healthcare reform is the definition of a child for purposes of defining a dependent under Internal Revenue Code section 152 and includes natural, adopted, step, and foster children. Based on the U.S. Supreme Court decision in 2015 in *Obergefell v. Hodges,* these definitions will apply whether the parents are of opposite sex or the same sex.[7]

The preamble to the interim final rules on PHSA section 2714,[8] said: "The Departments . . . concluded, as they have in other regulatory contexts, that plan sponsors and issuers should be free to determine whether to cover children or which children should be covered by their

---

1. Nonbinding comments of Russ Weinheimer, IRS Attorney, Department of Labor Affordable Care Act Compliance Assistance Webcast (September 7, 2010).
2. DOL Reg. §2590.715-2714(b); Treas. Reg. §54.9815-2714 (b); HHS Reg. §147.120(b).
3. PHSA §2714(b) because the phrase "who is not married" was removed.
4. Final Rules for Grandfathered Plans, Preexisting Condition Exclusions, Lifetime and Annual Limits, Rescissions, Dependent Coverage, Appeals, and Patient Protections Under the Affordable Care Act (replaced Interim Final Rules of May 13, 2010), https://www.federalregis-ter.gov/articles/2015/11/18/2015-29294/final-rules-for-grandfathered-plans-preexisting-condition-exclusions-lifetime-and-annual-limits (November 18, 2015). (Last accessed August 18, 2019).
5. DOL Reg. §2590.715-2714(b); Treas. Reg. §54.9815-2714 (b); HHS Reg. §147.120(b).
6. PPACA, Pub. L. No. 111-148, §1001(5).
7. Obergefell v. Hodges, 135 S.Ct. 2675, June 26, 2015.
8. 75 Fed. Reg. 27122, 27131 (May 13, 2010); See Also Final Rules for Grandfathered Plans, Preexisting Condition Exclusions, Lifetime and Annual Limits, Rescissions, Dependent Coverage, Appeals, and Patient Protections Under the Affordable Care Act (replaces Interim Final Rules of May 13, 2010), https://www.federalregister.gov/articles/2015/11/18/2015-29294/final-rules-for-grandfathered-plans-pre-existing-condition-exclusions-lifetime-and-annual-limits (November 18, 2015). (Last accessed August 18, 2019).

plans and policies (although they must comply with other applicable Federal or State law mandating coverage, such as ERISA section 609). Therefore, these interim final regulations have not limited a plan's or policy's flexibility to define who is a child for purposes of the determination of children to whom coverage must be made available."

Q&A-14 of the Part I FAQs provides:

"A plan or issuer does not fail to satisfy the requirements of PHSA section 2714 or its implementing regulations because the plan limits health coverage for children until the child turns 26 to only those children who are described in section 152(f)(1) of the Code. For an individual not described in Internal Revenue Code section 152(f)(1), such as a grandchild or niece, a plan may impose additional conditions on eligibility for health coverage, such as a condition that the individual be a dependent for income tax purposes."

Internal Revenue Code section 152(f)(1)(A) defines the term "child" as an individual who is (i) a son, daughter, stepson, or stepdaughter of the taxpayer, or (ii) an eligible foster child of the taxpayer. Internal Revenue Code section 152(f)(1)(C) provides that the term "eligible foster child" means an individual who is placed with the taxpayer by an authorized placement agency or by judgment, decree, or other order of any court of competent jurisdiction.

Given the potential for litigation and liability for medical care for someone who should have been covered but was not, the plan sponsor should not impose conditions beyond the relationship with the participant on any child within the Internal Revenue Code section 152(f)(1) dependent definition. This means, for example, that a plan should treat all stepchildren and foster children equally. i.e., cover all or none until they turn twenty-six.

257. May a plan allow a choice of coverage as an employee or dependent coverage as a child, but not both?

This provision would seem permissible, since the child could choose whether to enroll for dependent coverage (through an employed parent) or for the child's own employee coverage. Again, absent a clear answer, the prudent course would be not to use this plan provision.

258. What about the children of a person's same-sex partner (stepchildren)?

Stepchildren are the children of an individual's spouse. Given the 2015 decision of the U.S. Supreme Court in *Obergefell v. Hodges* recognizing same sex marriage as a constitutional right, the child of an employee's same-sex spouse should be treated as a stepchild.[1]

259. What if a plan covers grandchildren? Does the until age twenty-six requirement apply to them?

No. The coverage mandate does not require coverage to be offered to a grandchild of an employee.[2] Some plans previously extended eligibility to an employee's grandchild if the

---

1.   *Obergefell v. Hodges*, 135 S.Ct. 2675, June 26, 2015.
2.   DOL Reg. §2590.715-2714(c); Treas. Reg. §54.9815-2714 (c); HHS Reg. §147.120(c).

grandchild was the employee's tax dependent. A plan may place eligibility conditions on grandchildren (e.g., requiring that they be qualifying children or qualifying relatives of the employee), since they are not within the definition of Internal Revenue Code section 152(f) children.[1]

260. Who is a child for income tax purposes and what is the tax treatment of the until age twenty-six coverage?

Health reform revisions to Internal Revenue Code section 105(b) now makes excludable from an employee's income employer and health plan reimbursements for medical care attributable to the employee's child to the extent such child is not yet age twenty-seven during the taxable year. The 2010 law also included numerous conforming changes to the Code regarding Voluntary Employees Beneficiary Associations (VEBAs), Internal Revenue Code section 401(h) transfer accounts, and the deduction for medical insurance for self-employed persons under Internal Revenue Code section 162(l). As discussed in Q 264, health reform inadvertently failed to amend Internal Revenue Code section 106, but the IRS is treating that provision as if it were amended.

IRS Notice 2010-38 addresses these tax changes in connection with the adult child coverage provisions of the PHSA. Employer-provided coverage for an employee's Internal Revenue Code section 152(f) children under age twenty-seven is now nontaxable[2] for the "taxable year" (see discussion in Q 262 for meaning of "taxable year") in addition to coverage for an employee's Internal Revenue Code section 105(b) dependents. For income tax purposes, a "child" is "a son, daughter, stepson, or stepdaughter of the taxpayer, or . . . an eligible foster child of the taxpayer."[3] This definition is used when determining the taxability of employer-provided coverage for children under age twenty-seven.[4] Children who have their twenty-sixth birthday mid-year still enjoy favorable income tax treatment, as does the plan, until the end of the plan year or the policy year for individual policies.

261. Do the Internal Revenue Code's dependency tests apply in determining qualifying adult child status?

No. Notice 2010-38 makes clear that the age, limit, residency, and support tests applicable to Internal Revenue Code section 152 dependents do not apply in determining whether an individual qualifies as an adult child for purposes of tax-free employer-paid coverage.

Therefore, all that is necessary to qualify as an adult child is simply to be younger than twenty-seven for the taxable year at issue as well as being either a legal child, stepchild, or eligible foster child of the employee in order to qualify.

---

1.   HHS, DOL & TREASURY, FAQs About the Affordable Care Act Implementation Part I, Q14, at https://www.dol.gov/sites/default/files/ebsa/about-ebsa/our-activities/resource-center/faqs/aca-part-i.pdf. (Last Access August 18, 2019).
2.   IRS Notice 2010-38.
3.   IRC Sec. 152(f)(1).
4.   IRS Notice 2010-38.

262. What is a "taxable year" for employees?

The law amended Internal Revenue Code section 105(b) to make excludable from an employee's income any employer-paid coverage attributable to the employee's child to the extent such child is not yet age twenty-seven during the "taxable year" at issue. IRS Notice 2010-38 makes clear that "taxable year" means the employee's taxable year and that employers may assume that an employee's taxable year is the calendar year.[1]

263. How does a plan sponsor know the age of adult children?

Employers may rely on employees' representations regarding their children's date of birth.[2] The guidance is silent as to whether such representations must be in writing but requiring a written statement would be prudent for employers.

264. Will the employer's payments to a health plan for adult children also be given favorable tax treatment?

Yes, although health reform inadvertently failed to amend Internal Revenue Code section 106. Nevertheless, the IRS issued regulations for that section that makes excludable the employer-paid coverage itself.[3] "On and after March 30, 2010, both coverage under an employer-provided accident or health plan and amounts paid or reimbursed under such a plan for medical care expenses of ... an employee's [qualifying adult] child ... are excluded from the employee's gross income."[4]

265. Can mid-year election changes be made to cafeteria plans due to the new adult child until age twenty-six rules?

Yes, such changes can be made on March 30, 2010 and after. Although existing rules[5] do not permit mid-year changes to cafeteria plan elections when a coverage change results from an individual either qualifying or no longer qualifying as an adult child (because such election changes may only apply with respect to an employee, spouse, and dependents based on a modified Internal Revenue Code section 152 definition), the IRS will provide relief. Notice 2010-38 expressly states that "IRS and Treasury intend to amend the regulations under section 1.125-4, effective retroactively to March 30, 2010, to include change in status events affecting nondependent children under age twenty-seven, including becoming newly eligible for coverage or eligible for coverage beyond the date on which the child otherwise would have lost coverage."

---

1.   IRS Notice 2010-38.
2.   IRS Notice 2010-38.
3.   Notice 2010-38 addresses this issue and notes that "[t]here is no indication that Congress intended to provide a broader exclusion in Code section 105(b) than in Code section 106," and that, therefore, "IRS and Treasury intend to amend the regulations under Code section 106, retroactively to March 30, 2010, to provide that coverage for an employee's child under age 27 is excluded from gross income."
4.   Notice 2010-38.
5.   Treas. Reg. §1.125-4(c).

266. What other changes were made for HRAs, QSE-HRAs, FICA, FUTA, VEBAs, and Section 401(h) accounts?

IRS Notice 2010-38 states the following:

- Its principles apply to health reimbursement arrangements (HRAs and QSE-HRAs)

- Adult Child coverage is excepted from wages for FICA/FUTA purposes

- Its principles apply to VEBAs,[1] Internal Revenue Code section 401(h) transfer accounts, and deductions for self-employed individuals under Internal Revenue Code section 162(l)

Regarding VEBAs, for purposes of providing for the payment of sick and accident benefits to members of a VEBA and their dependents, the term "dependent" includes any qualifying adult child (i.e., a child who has not attained age twenty-seven by the close of the calendar year).

As amended by the health reform law, Internal Revenue Code section 401(h) "provides that the term dependent includes any individual who is a retired employee's [qualifying adult] child" (i.e., a child who has not attained age twenty-seven by the close of the calendar year).

Internal Revenue Code section 162(l), as amended, covers expenses associated with medical insurance attributable to a qualifying adult child (i.e., a child who has not attained age twenty-seven by the close of the calendar year).

267. Does the "until age twenty-six" adult child rules apply to Health Savings Accounts (HSAs)?

No. Health Savings Accounts (HSAs) are not group health plans. However, the law DOES apply to the underlying High Deductible Health Plan (HDHP) offered in conjunction with the HSA. The HSA rules however, were not amended by healthcare reform to allow medical expenses of nondependent children under age twenty-seven to be reimbursed tax-free from a parent's HSA.[2]

> *Example:* A parent has coverage under her employer's HDHP and enrolls her twenty-four-year-old daughter, in the coverage. The coverage provided by the HDHP is not taxable to the employee, because it is a group health plan. However, distributions from the parent's HSA are not taxed only if they reimburse or pay medical expenses of the HSA account holder, spouse, or dependents. If the daughter incurs medical expenses that are not paid by the HDHP, any distributions that the parent takes from the HSA to cover those expenses will be taxable because the daughter does not qualify as her dependent for HSA purposes. She is not a qualifying child, nor a qualifying relative unless she is disabled or the parent provides more than 50 percent of the daughter's support.[3] However, the daughter could create an HSA and the parent could fund it.

---

1. Voluntary Employees Beneficiary Associations, which are governed by IRC Section 501(c)(9).
2. IRC Sec. 223(d)(2)(A).
3. IRC Sec. 223(d)(2)(A) (for HSA purposes, dependent is as defined in IRC Sec. 152 without regard to subsections (b)(1), (b)(2), and (d)(1)(B).

268. Does the "until age twenty-six" adult child rules apply to Health Reimbursement Arrangements (HRAs) or Qualified Small Employer Health Reimbursement Arrangements (QSE-HRAs)?

No. Health Reimbursement Arrangements (HRA) and Qualified Small Employer Health Reimbursement Arrangements (QSE-HRA) are not group health plans.

269. May employees purchase health care coverage for their adult child using pre-tax dollars through an employer's cafeteria plan?

Yes. In addition to the exclusion from income of any employer contribution towards qualifying adult child coverage, employees may pay the employee portion of the health care coverage for an adult child on a pre-tax basis through the employer's cafeteria plan—a plan that allows employees to choose from a menu of tax-free benefit options and cash or taxable benefits.[1]

270. What options do adults have that "age out" of a parent's plan at age twenty-six?

Once an individual reaches age twenty-six and "ages out" of a parents' coverage, there are several options. If the young adult or their spouse are employed and that employer offers a health plan, there might be eligibility for coverage under that plan. Losing coverage under the parents' plan may qualify the person for special enrollment in any other employer plan for which they are eligible. Special enrollment in another employer plan must be requested within thirty days of loss of coverage.

If the parents' plan is sponsored by an employer with twenty or more employees, the young adult also may be eligible to purchase temporary extended health coverage for up to thirty-six months under the Consolidated Omnibus Budget Reconciliation Act (COBRA). To elect COBRA coverage, it is necessary to notify the parents' employer in writing within sixty days of reaching age twenty-six. In turn, the young adult's plan should notify them of the right to extend health care benefits under COBRA. They will have sixty days from the date the notice was sent to elect COBRA coverage. If they parents' plan is sponsored by an employer with twenty or fewer employees, the young adult may have similar rights under State law, instead of under COBRA. Inquiries can be made of the state insurance department and/or the parents' employer.

In addition, the young adult might be eligible for special enrollment in individual coverage purchased through the Health Insurance Marketplace. To special enroll in Marketplace coverage, one must enroll within sixty days of aging out of the plan.

Civil Rights Discrimination by Health Programs Prohibited

271. What existing antidiscrimination laws were affected by health reform?

Health reform[2] prohibits discrimination by any health program or activity. A plan may not exclude persons from participation in, or deny benefits under, any health program or activity

---

1. IRS Notice 2010-38.
2. PPACA §1557.

for a reason that is discriminatory under the Civil Rights Act (race, color, or national origin), the Education Amendments Act (sex / gender), the Age Discrimination in Employment Act (age), or the Rehabilitation Act (disability).

272. What guidance has been issued on these rules?

Although health programs and activities are subject to these nondiscrimination requirements, the terms are undefined in the statute. In September 2015, HHS issued a Notice of Proposed Rulemaking addressing nondiscrimination rules under healthcare reform that apply to health programs and activities receiving federal financial assistance.[1] On May 18, 2016, the Final Rule was promulgated.[2]

The Office for Civil Rights (OCR) has enforcement authority for health programs and activities that receive federal financial assistance from HHS.[3]

Preventive Health Services Required

273. What does health reform do to encourage preventive care?

To encourage people to be treated as early as possible, health reform added section 2713 of the Public Health Service Act (PHSA). It provides that a group health and a health insurance issuer (as to both group and individual coverage) must provide benefits for and may not impose cost-sharing (with certain out-of-network exceptions) with respect to, preventive care and screening. It has been noted, however, that while preventative care visits are not subject to cost-sharing, if the patient incurs other coverage or treatment, cost-sharing provisions do apply.

This rule is effective for plan years (policy years in the individual market) beginning on or after September 23, 2010, and it affects all health plans that are not grandfathered health plans or that provide "excepted benefits."

Women's preventive service rules were generally effective August 1, 2012, although, as discussed in Q 279, there is an exemption for contraception and sterilization for religious organizations and a one-year delay for social organizations sponsored by religious organizations.

Health plans that violate section 2713 could be subject to the assessment of penalties of $100 per day per affected employee as long as the violation continues.[4]

---

1.   http://www.regulations.gov/document?D=HHS-OCR-2015-0006-0001. (Last Accessed August 18, 2019).
2.   https://www.federalregister.gov/documents/2016/05/18/2016-11458/nondiscrimination-in-health-programs-and-activities. (Last accessed August 18, 2019).
3.   https://www.federalregister.gov/documents/2016/05/18/2016-11458/nondiscrimination-in-health-programs-and-activities. August 18, 2019).
4.   IRC Sec. 4980D, and the penalty must be self-reported on Form 8928.

274. What guidance has been issued by the agencies regarding the preventive care coverage requirements?

The Departments of Health and Human Services (HHS), Treasury and Labor (collectively "the agencies") issued regulations regarding the new preventive care coverage requirements.[1] As discussed in Q 282, they were later amended as to contraceptive services.

275. What preventive services are covered?

Generally, group health plans that are not "grandfathered health plans" must cover and waive all cost-sharing requirements for the following "recommended preventive services":

- Evidence-based items or services with an "A" or "B" rating from the U.S. Preventive Services Task Force (USPSTF)[2]

- Immunizations for routine use in children, adolescents, and adults with a recommendation in effect from the Advisory Committee on Immunization Practices of the Centers for Disease Control and Prevention[3]

- Evidence-informed preventive care screenings for infants, children, and adolescents provided in guidelines supported by the Health Resources and Services Administration (HRSA)[4]

- Evidence-informed preventive care and screening for women provided in guidelines supported by HRSA and not otherwise addressed by the USPSTF[5]

The complete list of recommendations and guidelines that must be covered by plans is at https://www.healthcare.gov/preventive-care-benefits/ and will be continually updated to reflect both new recommendations and guidelines and revised or removed guidelines.

Plans are not required to provide coverage (or waive cost-sharing) for any item or service that ceases to be a recommended preventive service, for example, if the USPSTF downgrades a recommended preventive service from a rating of "B" to a rating of "C" or "D." Likewise, plans may provide coverage for items and services in addition to those included in the recommendations and guidelines (and such services may be subject to cost sharing).

The ratings are summarized as follows:[6]

- Grade A: The USPSTF recommends the service. There is high certainty that the net benefit is substantial.

---

1.   Coverage of Certain Preventive Services Under the Affordable Care Act, July 14, 2015 https://www.federalregister.gov/articles/2015/07/14/2015-17076/coverage-of-certain-preventive-services-under-the-affordable-care-act (80FR 41317).
2.   PHSA §2713(a)(1); Treas. Reg. §54.9815-2713 (a)(1)(i); DOL Reg. §2590.715-2713(a)(1)(i); HHS Reg. §147.130(a)(1)(i).
3.   PHSA §2713(a)(2); Treas. Reg. §54.9815-2713 (a)(1)(ii); DOL Reg. §2590.715-2713(a)(1)(ii); HHS Reg. §147.130(a)(1)(ii).
4.   PHSA §2713(a)(3); Treas. Reg. §54.9815-2713 (a)(1)(iii); DOL Reg. §2590.715-2713(a)(1)(iii); HHS Reg. §147.130(a)(1)(iii).
5.   PHSA §2713(a)(4); Treas. Reg. §54.9815-2713 (a)(1)(iv); DOL Reg. §2590.715-2713(a)(1)(iv); HHS Reg. §147.130(a)(1)(iv). The regulations note that HHS is developing these.
6.   https://www.uspreventiveservicestaskforce.org/Page/Name/grade-definitions.

- Grade B: The USPSTF recommends the service. There is high certainty that the net benefit is moderate or there is moderate certainty that the net benefit is moderate to substantial.

- Grade C: The USPSTF recommends selectively offering or providing this service to individual patients based on professional judgment and patient preferences. There is at least moderate certainty that the net benefit is small.

- Grade D: The USPSTF recommends against the service. There is moderate or high certainty that the service has no net benefit or that the harms outweigh the benefits.

- Grade I: The USPSTF concludes that the current evidence is insufficient to assess the balance of benefits and harms of the service. Evidence is lacking, of poor quality, or conflicting, and the balance of benefits and harms cannot be determined.

276. What specific preventive care is offered for adults under the Affordable Care Act for 2019?

All Marketplace health plans and many other plans must cover the following list of preventive services without charging a copayment or coinsurance. This is the case even if the yearly deductible has not been met. It is important to note that these services are free only if provided by a doctor or other authorized provider within your plan's network.

- Abdominal aortic aneurysm one-time screening for men of specified ages who have ever smoked

- Alcohol misuse screening and counseling

- Aspirin use to prevent cardiovascular disease and colorectal cancer for adults aged fifty to fifty-nine years old with a high cardiovascular risk

- Blood pressure screening

- Cholesterol screening for adults of certain ages or those who are at higher risk

- Colorectal cancer screening for adults aged fifty to seventy-five years old

- Depression screening

- Diabetes (Type 2) screening for adults aged forty to seventy years who are overweight or obese

- Diet counseling for adults at higher risk for chronic disease

- Fall prevention therapy (coupled with exercise or physical therapy and vitamin D use) for adults aged sixty-five years old and over, living in a community setting

- Hepatitis B screening for people at high risk, including:

- o   people from countries with 2 percent or more Hepatitis B prevalence, and

  - o   U.S.-born people not vaccinated as infants and with at least one parent born in a region with 8 percent or more Hepatitis B prevalence.

- Hepatitis C screening for adults at increased risk, and one time for anyone born between1945–1965

- HIV screening for everyone between the age of fifteen to sixty-five, and other ages at considered to be at an increased risk

- Immunization vaccines for adults—doses, recommended ages, and recommended populations vary:

  - o   Diphtheria

  - o   Hepatitis A

  - o   Hepatitis B

  - o   Herpes Zoster

  - o   Human Papillomavirus (HPV)

  - o   Influenza (flu shot)

  - o   Measles

  - o   Meningococcal

  - o   Mumps

  - o   Pertussis

  - o   Pneumococcal

  - o   Rubella

  - o   Tetanus

  - o   Varicella (Chickenpox)

- Lung cancer screening for adults aged fifty-five through eighty at high risk for lung cancer because they're heavy smokers or have quit smoking within the past fifteen years

- Obesity screening and counseling

- Sexually transmitted infection (STI) prevention counseling for adults at higher risk

- Statin preventive medication for adults aged forty to seventy-five years old at high risk

- Syphilis screening for adults at higher risk

- Tobacco use screening for all adults and cessation interventions for tobacco users

- Tuberculosis screening for certain adults without symptoms at high risk

277. What specific preventive care is offered for women under the Affordable Care Act for 2019?

All Marketplace health plans and many other plans must cover the following list of preventive services without charging a copayment or coinsurance. This is the case even if the yearly deductible has not been met. It is important to note that these services are free only if provided by a doctor or other authorized provider within your plan's network.

Services for Pregnant Women or Women Who May Become Pregnant

- Anemia screening on a routine basis

- Breastfeeding comprehensive support and counseling from trained providers, and access to breastfeeding supplies, for pregnant and nursing women

- Contraception:

  - Food and Drug Administration-approved contraceptive methods, sterilization procedures, and patient education and counseling, as prescribed by a health care provider for women with reproductive capacity (not including abortifacient drugs).

  - This section does not apply to health plans sponsored by certain exempt "religious employers."

- Folic acid supplements for women who may become pregnant

- Gestational diabetes screening for women twenty-four to twenty-eight weeks pregnant and those at high risk of developing gestational diabetes

- Gonorrhea screening for all women at higher risk

- Hepatitis B screening for pregnant women at their first prenatal visit

- Preeclampsia prevention and screening for pregnant women with high blood pressure

- Rh incompatibility screening for all pregnant women and follow-up testing for women at higher risk

- Syphilis screening

- Expanded tobacco intervention and counseling for pregnant tobacco users

- Urinary tract or other infection screening

Other Covered Preventive Services for Women in General

- Breast cancer genetic test counseling (BRCA) for women at higher risk

- Breast cancer mammography screenings every one to two years for women over forty

- Breast cancer chemoprevention counseling for women at higher risk

- Cervical cancer screening

  - Pap test/Pap smear every three years for women aged twenty-one to sixty-five

  - Human Papillomavirus (HPV) DNA test with the combination of a Pap smear every five years for women aged thirty to sixty-five who don't want a Pap smear every three years

- Chlamydia infection screening for younger women and other women at higher risk

- Diabetes screening for women with a history of gestational diabetes who aren't currently pregnant and who haven't been diagnosed with type 2 diabetes before

- Domestic and interpersonal violence screening and counseling for all women

- Gonorrhea screening for all women at higher risk

- HIV screening and counseling for sexually active women

- Osteoporosis screening for women over age sixty depending on risk factors

- Rh incompatibility screening follow-up testing for women at higher risk

- Sexually transmitted infections counseling for sexually active women

- Syphilis screening for women at increased risk

- Tobacco use screening and interventions

- Urinary incontinence screening for women yearly

- Well-woman visits to get recommended services for women under sixty-five

278. What specific preventive care is offered for children under the Affordable Care Act for 2019?

All Marketplace health plans and many other plans must cover the following list of preventive services without charging a copayment or coinsurance. This is the case even if the yearly deductible has not been met. It is important to note that these services are free only if provided by a doctor or other authorized provider within your plan's network.

Coverage for Children's Preventive Health Services

- Alcohol, tobacco, and drug use assessments for adolescents

- Autism screening for children at eighteen and twenty-four months

- Behavioral assessments for children aged from birth to eleven months, one to four years of age, five to ten years of age, eleven to fourteen years of age, fifteen to seventeen years of age

- Bilirubin concentration screening for newborns

- Blood pressure screening for children aged from birth to eleven months, one to four years of age, five to ten years of age, eleven to fourteen years of age, fifteen to seventeen years of age

- Blood screening for newborns

- Cervical dysplasia screening for sexually active females

- Depression screening for adolescents beginning routinely at age twelve

- Developmental screening for children under age three

- Dyslipidemia screening for all children once between nine and eleven years of age and once between seventeen and twenty-one years of age, and for children at higher risk of lipid disorders aged one to four years, five to ten years, eleven to fourteen years, fifteen to seventeen years

- Fluoride chemoprevention supplements for children without fluoride in their water source

- Fluoride varnish for all infants and children as soon as teeth are present

- Gonorrhea preventive medication for the eyes of all newborns

- Hearing screening for all newborns; and for children once between eleven and fourteen years of age, once between fifteen and seventeen years of age, and once between eighteen and twenty-one years of age

- Height, weight and body mass index (BMI) measurements for children aged birth to eleven months, one to four years of age, five to ten years of age, eleven to fourteen years of age, fifteen to seventeen years of age

- Hematocrit or hemoglobin screening for all children

- Hemoglobinopathies or sickle cell screening for newborns

- Hepatitis B screening for adolescents at high risk, including adolescents from countries with 2 percent or more Hepatitis B prevalence, and U.S.-born adolescents not vaccinated as infants and with at least one parent born in a region with 8 percent or more Hepatitis B prevalence: eleven–seventeen years of age

- HIV screening for adolescents at higher risk

- Hypothyroidism screening for newborns

- Immunization vaccines for children from birth to age eighteen—doses, recommended ages, and recommended populations vary:

  - Diphtheria, Tetanus, Pertussis (Whooping Cough)

  - Haemophilus influenza type b

  - Hepatitis A

  - Hepatitis B

  - Human Papillomavirus (HPV)

  - Inactivated Poliovirus

  - Influenza (flu shot)

  - Measles

  - Meningococcal

  - Pneumococcal

  - Rotavirus

  - Varicella (Chickenpox)

- Iron supplements for children aged six to twelve months at risk for anemia

- Lead screening for children at risk of exposure

- Maternal depression screening for mothers of infants at age one, two, four, and six-month visits

- Medical history for all children throughout development aged from birth to eleven months, one to four years of age, five to ten years of age, eleven to fourteen years of age, fifteen to seventeen years of age

- Obesity screening and counseling

- Oral health risk assessment for young children ages: zero to eleven months, one to four years of age, five to ten years of age

- Phenylketonuria (PKU) screening for newborns

- Sexually transmitted infection (STI) prevention counseling and screening for adolescents at higher risk

- Tuberculin testing for children at higher risk of tuberculosis aged from birth to eleven months, one to four years of age, five to ten years of age, eleven to fourteen years of age, fifteen to seventeen years of age

- Vision screening for all children

279. Are there any limits on the frequency, method, treatment, or setting for preventive services to prevent patients from abusing this rule?

Yes. Reasonable medical management techniques can be used when the applicable recommendations and guidelines do not specify the frequency, method, treatment, or setting for a particular preventive service. Plans and insurers may use reasonable medical management techniques to determine any coverage limitations.[1]

280. What are the requirements as to the prohibition on patient payment, i.e., cost-sharing requirements?

Generally, cost sharing for network providers with respect to "recommended preventive services" is prohibited. "Cost sharing" for these rules include deductibles, copayments, and coinsurance. Cost sharing is permitted for any item or service that ceases to be a recommended preventive service or for services or treatments in addition to those included in the specified recommendations.

Cost-sharing is permitted for office visits when preventive services are billed or tracked as individual encounter data separately or are not the primary purpose of an office visit. Conversely, cost-sharing cannot be imposed when preventive services are not billed or not tracked as individual encounter data separately and are the primary purpose of an office visit.

> *Example 1:* A child visits an in-network pediatrician for a preventive care screening. As a result of the screening, the pediatrician recommends that the child undergo surgery for a heart disorder. Because the preventive care screening is a recommended preventive service, the plan cannot impose a cost-sharing requirement. However, the plan may impose a cost-sharing requirement for the child's heart surgery, which resulted from the preventive care screening.

---

1.   Treas. Reg. §54.9815-2713 (a)(4); DOL Reg. §2590.715-2713(a)(4); HHS Reg. §147.130(a)(4).

Example 2: A child covered by a group health plan visits an in-network pediatrician to receive an annual physical exam that is a recommended preventive service. During the office visit, the child receives additional services that are not recommended preventive services. The provider bills the plan for the office visit. Because the primary purpose for the office visit was to provide recommended preventive services, and the plan was not billed separately for the additional services, the plan may not impose a cost-sharing requirement with respect to the office visit.

Example 3: A patient is covered by a group health plan and visits an in-network healthcare provider. While visiting the provider, the patient is screened for cholesterol abnormalities with a rating of A or B (which are recommended preventive services). The provider bills the plan separately for the office visit and for the laboratory work of the cholesterol screening test. The plan may not impose any cost-sharing requirements with respect to the separately billed laboratory work of the cholesterol screening test. However, the plan may impose cost-sharing requirements for the office visit since it was billed separately from the recommended preventive service.

Example 4: A patient visits his network provider for abdominal pain. During the visit, he has a blood pressure screening that is a recommended preventive service. The provider bills the plan for the office visit, and there is no separate bill for the blood pressure screening. The plan may impose cost sharing on the office visit because the primary purpose of the office visit was not the delivery of a recommended preventive service.

281. How do these rules deal with in-network and out-of-network providers?

The regulations clarify that a network-based plan is not required to provide coverage for recommended preventive services delivered by an out-of-network provider and may impose cost-sharing requirements for any such out-of-network services that are offered.[1]

Contraception and Sterilization Services

282. How have the ACA rules relating to contraception and sterilization services for employees of religious organizations and social organizations sponsored by religious groups changed under the Trump administration?

On November 15, 2018, the Trump administration issued final regulations that have greatly expanded the number of types or employers and the ability of those employers' to exempt themselves from the Affordable Care Act's contraceptive coverage requirements.

These regulations represent a major change from the Obama administration regulations that exempted only houses of worship. The new regulations allow an employer or college or university with objections to contraception based on religious beliefs to qualify for an exemption. Any employer (except publicly traded corporations) with moral objections to contraception also qualifies for an exemption.

These final regulations are substantially the same as the interim final regulations issued in October 2018. The legality of the interim regulations was challenged as they were issued without opportunity for public notice or comment as is generally required under the Administrative Procedures Act. Four nonprofit advocacy groups and eight states filed lawsuits challenging the

---

1.   Treas. Reg. §54.9815-2713 (a)(3); DOL Reg. §2590.715-2713(a)(3); HHS Reg. §147.130(a)(3).

interim regulations. Federal courts issued preliminary injunctions in December 2017 (which have been appealed to the Third and Ninth Circuit U.S. Courts of Appeal) blocking the enforcement of these regulations pending the outcome of the litigation. These decisions have been appealed to the Third and Ninth Circuit Courts of Appeal. The status of these lawsuits is unclear now that the final regulations have been published. Nonetheless, is it likely that there will be continuing legal challenges to the final regulations.

One of the regulations allows nonprofit or for-profit employers with an objection to contraceptive coverage based on religious beliefs to qualify for an exemption and drop contraceptive coverage from their plans.[1]

The other regulation exempts all but publicly traded employers with moral objections to contraception from rule. These new policies apply to private institutions of higher education that issue student health plans. The new regulations open the door for many more employers to withhold contraceptive coverage from their plans.[2]

The contraceptive coverage provision has always been controversial. While very popular with the public, it has been the focus of litigation brought by religious employers, with two cases (*Zubik v. Burwell* and *Burwell v. Hobby Lobby*) reaching the Supreme Court. See Q 284 and Q 286.

At the state level, ten states and the District of Columbia have expanded the federal contraceptive coverage requirement (CA, IL, ME, MD, MA, NV, NY, OR, VT, WA). An additional nineteen states have contraceptive laws that require plans to cover contraceptives if they also provide coverage for prescription drugs, however, this laws does not require coverage of all FDA-approved contraceptives or eliminate cost-sharing provisions.

Historical Background

Since they were announced in 2011, the contraceptive coverage rules have evolved through litigation and new regulations. Section 2713(a)(4) of the PHSA requires that nongrandfathered group health plans and health insurance issuers offering nongrandfathered group or individual health insurance coverage provide benefits for certain women's preventive health services without cost sharing, as provided by Health Resources and Services Administration (HRSA) guidelines. The August 1, 2011, HRSA Guidelines included all FDA approved contraceptive methods, sterilization procedures, and patient education and counseling for women with reproductive capacity, as prescribed by a health care provider (collectively, contraceptive services). The HRSA guidelines did not cover men.

In July 2013, the agencies (DOL, HHS, and IRS) issued revised final regulations, changing how the previous 2012 regulations applied the contraceptive coverage mandate to not-for-profit religious organizations. Under the 2013 final regulations, a religious employer included

---

1.   https://www.federalregister.gov/documents/2018/11/15/2018-24512/religious-exemptions-and-accommodations-for-coverage-of-certain-preventive-services-under-the.
2.   https://www.federalregister.gov/documents/2018/11/15/2018-24514/moral-exemptions-and-accommodations-for-coverage-of-certain-preventive-services-under-the-affordable.

    (1)   churches, their integrated auxiliaries, and conventions or associations of churches[1] or

    (2)   the exclusively religious activities of any religious order[2]

and was exempt from the mandate.[3] With the exception of the amendments to the religious employer exemption, which apply to group health plans and health insurance issuers for plan years beginning on or after August 1, 2013, the 2013 final regulations applied to group health plans and health insurance issuers for plan years beginning on or after January 1, 2014.

The prior exemption requirements that the organization had to have as its purpose the inculcation of religious values and had to primarily employ and serve persons who share its religious tenets were removed.

Under the 2013 final regulation, an eligible organization was an organization that:

    (1)   opposes providing coverage for some or all of the contraceptive services required to be covered under section 2713 of the PHSA on account of religious objections;

    (2)   is organized and operates as a not-for-profit entity;

    (3)   holds itself out as a religious organization; and

    (4)   certifies that it satisfies the first three criteria. An eligible organization also includes student health insurance coverage arranged by eligible organizations that are institutions of higher learning.

Therefore, group health plans of not-for-profit houses of worship that provided educational, charitable, or social services to their communities qualified for the exemption. An employer that is a not-for-profit entity was not limited to any particular form of entity under state law, and it is not necessary to determine the federal tax-exempt status of a not-for-profit entity in determining whether the religious employer exemption applies.

283. What specific changes have been made under the Trump Administration versus the Obama Administration's contraception rules?

1.   Types of Contraceptives Covered Without Cost-Sharing Provisions

There have been no changes from the Obama Administration. At least one of each of the 18 FDA approved contraceptive methods for women, as prescribed, along with counseling and related services must be covered without cost-sharing.

---

1.   IRC Sec. 6033(a)(3)(A)(i).
2.   IRC Sec. 6033(a)(3)(A)(iii).
3.   The revised religious employer exemption applies to group health plans and health insurers for plan years beginning on or after August 1, 2013. HHS Reg. §147.131(a): Coverage of Certain Preventive Services Under the Affordable Care Act, 26 CFR Part 54; 29 CFR Part 2590; 45 CFR Parts 147, 148, and 156; 78 Fed. Reg. 39869 (July 2, 2013).

2. Employers Exempt From Contraceptive Mandate

Under the Obama Administration, exempt organizations included religious organizations defined as houses of worship and also grandfathered plans.

Under the Trump rules, exempt organizations include

- religious organizations defined as houses of worship,

- grandfathered plans,

- Non-profit or for-profit employers (including publicly traded companies), insurers, and private colleges and universities that issue student insurance plans if they have a religious opposition to contraception

- Non-profit or closely-held for profit employers, insurers, and private colleges and universities that issue student insurance plans if they have a moral opposition to contraception

3. Who Pays for Conceptive Coverage of Employees of Companies With Exemptions?

Female employees and dependents cover the cost. There is no assurance or guarantee that contraceptive coverage is offered to employees of an exempt company or organization. The employer may choose to cover some methods but has no obligation to cover all 18 FDA methods without cost sharing. This has not changed under the Trump rules.

284. How did the *Zubik v. Burwell* case affect the Affordable Care Act?
Background of the Case

Under the Affordable Care Act – employer insurance plans are legally required to cover the costs of contraception without charging co-pays. Facing opposition from groups opposed to use of contraception, the Obama Administration carved out two exceptions:

- Churches and houses of worship are entirely exempt from offering contraceptive coverage.

- Nonprofit religious organizations including hospitals, charitable organizations and institution of higher as well as for-profit organizations with a limited number of shareholders (close corporations) do not want to pay for employees' contraception for religious reasons, there is an option to complete a form explaining why it wants to opt out. When the form is completed, the organization's insurer takes over. It can either work with employees directly to provide no-cost contraception coverage or locate a third-party to do so.

The plaintiffs' argument is based on the Religious Freedom Restoration Act of 1993, arguing that completing the forms places a "substantial burden" on the organization and is an infringement of religious beliefs. The case differs from the Hobby Lobby case in that Hobby Lobby expanded the "opt-out" ability from only religious organization to closely held for-profit corporations as well.

The case is a consolidation of seven similar and related cases with the lead plaintiff being Roman Catholic Bishop David A. Zubik of the Diocese of Pittsburgh. Other plaintiffs include the Little Sisters of the Poor, East Texas Baptist University, Southern Nazarene University and Geneva College. The Little Sisters of the Poor have made the argument that that the government does not need a form from them – that it can provide services to anyone that it wishes. The argument is that the notification itself triggers the contraceptive coverage and this is unacceptable. At the United States Court of Appeals level, five courts had ruled in favor of the contraceptive mandate and one against it.

Decision

With the death of Justice Scalia, the Supreme Court was left essentially with a four to four tie. On May 16, 2016, the remaining eight Justices, in a unanimous Per Curium decision,[1] vacated the and remanded the case back to the four appellate courts and ordered them to attempt to get the sides to arrive at a solution the protects religious freedom while allowing women to have access to contraceptive coverage under the Affordable Care Act. In making the decision, the Court stated that it expresses no view on the merits of the case and is not deciding if the Government has a compelling interest, whether exercise of religion has been substantially burdened or even if the current regulations are the least restrictive means of serving the interest.

285. Are there any other options for religious organizations that object to these rules?

Employers that do not intend to comply with PPACA section 2713 could terminate their group health plan and encourage their employees to obtain individual policies. As of January 1, 2014, such individual policies must be offered on state health insurance exchanges on a guaranteed issue, guaranteed renewability basis. However, employers with at least fifty full-time equivalent employees or with at least thirty-one full-time employees that do not offer health coverage are subject to penalties.[2]

286. How did the Supreme Court Hobby Lobby decision affect the ACA contraception mandate for profit businesses?

The U.S. Supreme Court in *Burwell v. Hobby Lobby Stores, Inc.*[3] created a new exemption to the Affordable Care Act provision requiring that for-profit companies offer birth control coverage to their employees. The Court ruled that closely-held for-profit corporations are entitled to

---

1.   https://www.supremecourt.gov/opinions/15pdf/14-1418_8758.pdf Zubik, et. al,, *Petitioners v. Burwell*, 576 U.S. , No. 14-1418, May 16, 2016.

2.   Employers with at least 50 full-time equivalent employees must offer insurance meeting specified requirements or pay a $2,000 (now $2,320) penalty per full-time worker (in excess of 30 full-time workers) if any of its full-time employees receive a federal premium subsidy through a Health Care Exchange. IRC Sec. 4980H(c)(2)(D). A different penalty applies for employers of at least 50 full-time equivalent employees that offer insurance that does not meet federal requirements. IRC Sec. 4980H(b)(1).

3.   573 U.S. ___ (2014) at http://www.supremecourt.gov/opinions/13pdf/13-354_olp1.pdf (Last accessed August 24, 2019).

statutory religious freedom protections where their owners' sincere religious beliefs are violated, at least as to birth control. Religious nonprofit employers, such as churches, are already exempt from the contraceptive mandate.[1] The Court rules that "persons" protected under the Religious Freedom Restoration Act of 1993 (RFRA) include the owners of closely-held corporations. This decision does not address the free exercise of religion clause under the First Amendment to the Constitution. It also does not affect state law, which as discussed below, may require all forms of contraception to be provided by insured health plans.

The RFRA provides that the federal government shall not "substantially burden a person's exercise of religion" unless that burden is the least restrictive means to further a compelling governmental interest. The Court noted that for the government to prevail, it needed to demonstrate a compelling state interest and to show that its application was the least restrictive means to achieving its objectives. While the Court assumed a compelling governmental interest, it concluded that there were less restrictive alternatives available to the government for achieving its objectives as to the healthcare reform rules regarding contraception. The Court noted that the government could itself simply provide these benefits to all without charge.

The Supreme Court's decision in effect allows for-profit business corporation owners to impose their religious choices about contraception on its employees' health plan, even where those employees follow different religions or no religion. In many cases, closely-held businesses employ many more people than they have owners. As the dissent notes, "the family-owned candy giant Mars, Inc., takes in $33 billion in revenues and has some 72,000 employees, and closely-held Cargill, Inc., takes in more than $136 billion in revenues and employs some 140,000 persons."[2]

The RFRA does not apply to state laws.[3] Therefore, the *Hobby Lobby* decision has no impact on state laws. Twenty-eight states, including California and New York, require insurers to provide coverage of contraceptive drugs and devices.[4] Twenty two states have no contraception mandate. Seventeen states also require coverage of correlated outpatient services.[5]

For example, California's law includes a provision permitting a "religious employer" to opt out of providing such coverage. However, the California law's definition of "religious employer"

---

1. In August, 2011, the HHS's Health Resources and Services Administration ("HRSA") released guidelines that mandated coverage for all FDA-approved contraceptives, but which include a narrow exemption for religious employers. To qualify for this exemption, a religious employer must (i) have the inculcation of religious values as its purpose, (ii) primarily employ persons who share its religious tenets, (iii) primarily serve persons who share its religious tenets, and (iv) be a non-profit organization. Thus, the exemption applied primarily to group health plans established or maintained by churches, synagogues, mosques, and other houses of worship, and religious orders. The religious exemption was subsequently expanded to accommodate religious nonprofit organizations with religious objections to providing coverage for contraceptive services. Under this accommodation, an insurance issuer must exclude contraceptive coverage from the employer's plan and provide plan participants with separate payments for contraceptive services without imposing any cost sharing requirements on the employer, its insurance plan, or its employee beneficiaries.

2. Dissent Slip Op. at 20, fn. 19.

3. *City of Boerne v. Flores*, 521 U.S. 507 (1997).

4. See Guttmacher Institute, State Policies In Brief, Insurance Coverage of Contraceptives (July 1, 2014); and http://www.ncsl.org/research/health/insurance-coverage-for-contraception-state-laws.aspx; (Last accessed August 24, 2019).

5. For example, California Health and Safety Code §1367.25 is part of the state's managed care law. California law requires all individual and group health plans (though not employer self-funded plans) that include prescription drug benefits to cover "a variety of federal Food and Drug Administration approved prescription contraceptive methods designated by the plan." California Insurance Code §10123.196 imposes similar requirements on health insurance.

is narrower than that of the *Hobby Lobby* decision. California's law defines a "religious employer" as a nonprofit entity whose primary purpose is to inculcate religious values, and which primarily serves and employs people who share the entity's religious beliefs.[1] The plaintiffs in *Hobby Lobby*, for-profit retailers specializing in crafts and furniture, do not meet this definition. Thus, in states with law like California's, a closely-held for-profit corporation, such as the retailers in *Hobby Lobby*, would need to comply with state law. Unlike California, a few states have enacted RFRA statutes and there the *Hobby Lobby* rationale could succeed. However, the majority of states mandating contraceptive drug and device coverage appear to be similarly insulated from court challenge.

The majority decision was limited only to four of the twenty contraception mandates (those that work after fertilization) and not to other health care mandates that might violate other religious beliefs. The Court said that there was no proof to the government's claim that vaccinations and blood transfusions violated any religious beliefs. The Court stated: "In any event, our decision in these cases is concerned solely with the contraceptive mandate. Our decision should not be understood to hold that an insurance coverage mandate must necessarily fall if it conflicts with an employer's religious beliefs. Other coverage requirements, such as immunizations, may be supported by different interests (for example, the need to combat the spread of infectious diseases) and may involve different arguments about the least restrictive means of providing them."[2]

In terms of business entity law, the *Hobby Lobby* decision seems seriously flawed. The Court does not (i) define a closely-held business (the corporations in the *Hobby Lobby* case were each owned by members of one family); (ii) recognize that the closely-held concept has varying meanings in different contexts, depending on the purpose the law in that context is supposed to serve (closely-held businesses comprise 50 to 90 percent of US businesses, depending on which definition is used); (iii) mention the entity versus aggregation of owners distinction and that distinction's ramifications, where the law previously sometimes looked, in the case of partnerships, to the partners, not the entity; (iv) recognize that the decision is a type of piercing of the corporate veil, looking through the entity to its owners; which typically is only done where there is some type of fraud, fault, or wrongdoing; and (v) reconcile its holding with its *Citizens United* decision[3], where it held that corporations are themselves persons and have free speech rights to spend money in political campaigns. Had the Court looked to the corporations in *Hobby Lobby* and not their owners, the result seemingly would have been different. As the dissent notes, "the exercise of religion is characteristic of natural persons, not artificial legal entities."[4]

287. How did the Hobby Lobby decision affect disclosure and notice requirements for employers who cease providing contraceptive services?

DOL FAQ Part XX[5] addresses the notice requirements for employers who cease providing contraceptive services in a single Q&A. It states that where a closely held

---

1. Cal. Health & Safety Code §1367.25(b)(1).
2. Slip Op. at 46.
3. *Citizens United v. Federal Election Commission*, 558 U.S. 310 (2010).
4. Dissent Slip Op. at 14.
5. See DOL FAQs about Affordable Care Act Implementation (Part XX) https://www.dol.gov/sites/default/files/ebsa/about-ebsa/our-activities/resource-center/faqs/aca-part-xx.pdf . (Last accessed August 24, 2019).

for-profit corporation's health plan will cease providing coverage for some or all contraceptive services mid-plan year, this reduction in coverage triggers a notice requirement to plan participants and beneficiaries. Remember that the employers in the Supreme Court's *Hobby Lobby*[1] decision were owned by family members, but it is not clear if family ownership is required to be closely held, as the Supreme Court did not define that term and it has many meanings in different contexts, although it is probably unlikely to be as narrowly defined as requiring related owners

The DOL states that ERISA's requirements for welfare benefit plans, such as health plans, require disclosure of information relevant to coverage of preventive services, including contraceptive coverage. DOL regulations provide that the Summary Plan Description (SPD) must include a description of the extent to which preventive services (which includes contraceptive services) are covered under the plan.[2] Accordingly, if an ERISA plan excludes all or a subset of contraceptive services from coverage under its group health plan, the plan's SPD must describe the extent of the limitation or exclusion of coverage.

For plans that reduce or eliminate coverage of contraceptive services after having provided such coverage, expedited disclosure requirements for material reductions in covered services or benefits apply and generally require disclosure at least sixty days after the date of adoption of a modification or change to the plan that is a material reduction in covered services or benefits.[3] The notice of the material modification must be provided no later than sixty days prior to the date on which such change will become effective. Alternatively, plan sponsors may provide an SMM in health plan coverage at regular intervals of not more than ninety days.[4] Other disclosure requirements may apply, for example, under State insurance law applicable to health insurance issuers."

Rescissions Limited

288. How does health reform limit insurers' ability to terminate coverage?

Before enactment of health reform in 2010, the Public Health Service Act (PHSA) included some protections regarding cancellation of coverage. Additional protections were also provided in the HIPAA nondiscrimination rules. This new rescission regulation builds on the existing protections, and sets a federal floor on rescissions.

The restriction limiting rescissions is effective for plan years (for individual policies in the individual market, policy years) beginning on or after September 23, 2010.

States may limit rescissions beyond the limits of the federal health reform law.[5] The federal law prohibiting rescissions does not apply to "excepted benefits."

---

1.   *Burwell v. Hobby Lobby Stores, Inc.*, 573 U.S. 2751 (June 30, 2014), available at http://www.supremecourt.gov/opinions/13pdf/13-354_olp1.pdf. (Last access August 24, 2019).

2.   29 CFR 2520.102-3(j)(3).

3.   See ERISA Sec. 104(b)(1) and 29 CFR §2520.104b-3(d)(1).

4.   *Id.*

5.   Preamble, 75 Fed. Reg. 37188, 37192 (June 28, 2010).

Additional guidance was provided in Frequently Asked Questions (FAQs) issued on April 20, 2016 regarding insurers' ability to terminate coverage.

PHSA section 2712 and its implementing regulations provide that group health plans and health insurance issuers offering group or individual health insurance coverage generally cannot rescind coverage unless the individual (or a person seeking coverage on behalf of the individual) commits fraud or makes an intentional misrepresentation of material fact as prohibited by the terms of the plan or coverage.

In question 2, the FAQ dealt with a situation with a school teacher who was employed in a school district through ten month contract from August 1 through May 31 with a health plan for a plan year from August 1 through July 31. The teacher resigned effective on July 31 but the plan termination her health coverage from May 31. The plan's termination of health coverage retroactive to May 31 was held to be a rescission prohibited under PHSA section 2712 and the implementing regulations, because:

(i)   it is a cancellation or discontinuance of coverage that has retroactive effect;

(ii)   it is not attributable to a failure to timely pay premiums toward coverage;

(iii)   there was no fraud or intentional misrepresentation of material fact; and

(iv)   the other limited circumstance exceptions specified in the implementing regulations do not apply.[1]

The plan may terminate coverage prospectively, subject to other applicable Federal and State laws or collective bargaining agreements.

A rescission is a cancellation or discontinuance of coverage that has a retroactive effect, except to the extent attributable to a failure to pay timely premiums towards coverage (including COBRA premiums) or in certain other limited circumstances specified in the implementing regulations.[2]

Other requirements of Federal or State law may apply in connection with a rescission of coverage.

289. What is a rescission?

A "rescission" is a retroactive cancellation or discontinuance of coverage of an "enrollee," i.e., a person who is covered by the policy. Whether an individual or group policy, the statute indicates that a rescission can only apply to the individual who committed the fraud or intentional misrepresentation of a material fact.[3] However, the regulations contemplate

---

1.   https://www.dol.gov/sites/default/files/ebsa/about-ebsa/our-activities/resource-center/faqs/aca-part-31.pdf (Updated April 20, 2016) (Last accessed August 24, 2019).
2.   26 CFR 54.9815-2712; 29 CFR 2590.715-2712; 45 CFR 147.128.
3.   PHSA §2712.

that a group policy can be rescinded as well.[1] A cancellation or discontinuation of coverage is not a rescission if it:

- has only a prospective effect; or

- is effective retroactively to the extent it is attributable to a failure to timely pay required premiums or contributions toward the cost of coverage.[2]

A rescission is an adverse benefit determination that is subject to the healthcare reform internal claims and appeals and external review requirements discussed at Q 294 to Q 304.

290. When is an insurer allowed to rescind or terminate an individual or group policy retroactively?

An insurer may retroactively terminate a policy for fraud or an intentional misrepresentation of a material fact with notice.[3] Misrepresentations that are inadvertent are not intentional.[4]

The regulations require a group health plan or an issuer offering group coverage to provide at least thirty days' advance written notice to each participant who would be affected before coverage may be rescinded—regardless of whether the coverage is insured or self-insured, or whether the rescission applies to an entire group or only to an individual within the group (same rules apply with respect to a rescission of individual coverage).[5] The purpose of the waiting period is to provide individuals and plan sponsors with an opportunity to explore their rights to contest the rescission, or look for alternative coverage, as appropriate."[6]

291. If an employer with an insured group plan covering employees who work thirty hours or more per week forgets to advise the insurer that a covered employee's hours have been reduced below thirty, can this individual's policy be rescinded?

No, because there is no fraud or intentional material misrepresentation. However, the insurer could cancel the employee's coverage prospectively, subject to requirements of state and federal laws.[7]

292. What should the sponsor of an insured group plan do if the plan wants to be able to rescind coverage retroactively?

If a plan wants to be able to cancel coverage retroactively, the Plan Document and Summary Plan Description (SPD) should define what constitutes fraud and what will be considered an intentional misrepresentation of material fact, consistent with the statute that will trigger the plan's right to rescind coverage.

---

1. Preamble, 75 Fed. Reg. 37188, 37192 (June 28, 2010).
2. Treas. Reg. §54.9815-2712 (a)(2); DOL Reg. §2590.715-2712(a)(2); HHS Reg. §147.128(a)(2).
3. PHSA §2712;
4. Treas. Reg. §54.9815-2712 (a)(3), Example 1; DOL Reg. §2590.715-2712(a)(3), Example 1; HHS Reg. §147.128(a)(3), Example 1.
5. Treas. Reg. §54.9815-2712 (a)(1); DOL Reg. §2590.715-2712(a)(1); HHS Reg. §147.128(a)(1).
6. Preamble, 75 Fed. Reg. 37188, 37193 (June 28, 2010).
7. Treas. Reg. §54.9815-2712 (a)(3), Example 2; DOL Reg. §2590.715-2712(a)(3), Example 2; HHS Reg. §147.128(a)(3), Example 2.

A frequent reason for retroactive cancellation of coverage is the enrollment of an ineligible dependent or adult child. In order to retain the right to rescind coverage of ineligible children and dependents, the SPD should clearly describe who is eligible for coverage and the requirements for documenting eligibility. The SPD should state that intentionally enrolling or continuing coverage for an ineligible individual constitutes fraud and an intentional misrepresentation of a material fact that will trigger rescission. In addition, the SPD should describe the results of rescission, including but not limited to liability for improper benefits paid.

293. Has the government declared any coverage terminations not to be rescissions?

Yes. An FAQ clarified several eligibility matters. For example, some employers' human resource departments may reconcile lists of eligible individuals with their plan or issuer via data feed only once per month. If a plan covers only active employees (subject to the COBRA continuation coverage provisions) and an employee pays no premiums for coverage after termination of employment, the agencies do not consider the retroactive elimination of coverage back to the date of termination of employment, due to delay in administrative record-keeping, to be a rescission.

Similarly, if a plan does not cover ex-spouses (subject to the COBRA continuation coverage provisions), the plan is not notified of a divorce, and the full COBRA premium is not paid by the employee or ex-spouse for coverage, the agencies do not consider a plan's termination of coverage retroactive to the divorce to be a rescission of coverage.[1]

New Claims and Appeals Procedures

294. What are health reform's required claims and appeals procedures?

Nongrandfathered group health plans (excluding those for "excepted benefits") were required to have internal claims and external appeals procedures in place for plan years beginning on and after September 23, 2010.[2] PPACA in the Public Health Service Act (PHSA) section 2719 set forth standards for nongrandfathered group health plans, insured and self-insured, and for internal claims and appeals and external reviews. The Employee Benefits Security Administration (EBSA), IRS, and Department of Health and Human Services (HHS) published the interim final regulations implementing PHSA section 2719 on July 23, 2010[3] and the final regulations on November 18, 2015.[4]

295. Were any of the requirements postponed?

Yes. The DOL's Employee Benefits Security Administration (EBSA) in Technical Release 2010-02 initially provided group health plans and self-funded nonfederal governmental health

---

1.   See FAQs About the Affordable Care Act Implementation Part II, Q&A-7, https://www.dol.gov/sites/default/files/ebsa/about-ebsa/our-activities/resource-center/faqs/aca-part-ii.pdf. (Last accessed August 24, 2019).
2.   Appeals Regulations, 75 Fed. Reg. 43329, 43337–38 (July 23, 2010).
3.   Interim Final Rule on Internal Claims and Appeals and External Review Processes, 75 Fed. Reg. 43329 (July 23, 2010).
4.   80 FR 72192-01.

plans relief until July 1, 2011, from enforcement actions by IRS (including the otherwise applicable excise tax for noncompliance) and by EBSA for plans that work in good faith to implement the new regulatory internal claims and appeals rules. EBSA extended this grace period until January 1, 2012, in Technical Release 2011-01. The original grace period and new extension are, however, only for three minor new standards, less than 1 percent of the entire PPACA Claims Regulations, and have no effect on the PPACA statutory effective date of September 23, 2010, for the bulk of the PPACA Claims Regulations. Specifically, Technical Release 2011-01 extended the enforcement grace period until plan years beginning on or after January 1, 2012, with respect to Standard #2 (regarding the timeframe for making urgent care claims decisions), Standard #5 (regarding providing notices in a culturally and linguistically appropriate manner), and Standard #7 (regarding substantial compliance).

Plans of a private-sector or church employer and those health plans subject to the Internal Revenue Code did not have to report any excise tax liability on Form 8928 for the rules extended by the grace period.[1]

Many state insurance departments offer claims assistance.[2]

296. Which state insurance departments offer claims assistance?

The following states offer Consumer Assistance Programs under PHSA section 2793. This list is current as of January 16, 2019

STATE	CONTACT INFORMATION
Alabama	No program
Alaska	No program
American Samoa	No Program
Arizona	No program
Arkansas	Arkansas Insurance Department, Consumer Services Division 1200 West Third St. Little Rock, AR 72201 (800) 282-9134 https://insurance.arkansas.gov/pages/consumer-services/ (website) Insurance.consumers@arkansas.gov (email)
California	California Department of Insurance 300 Capitol Mall, Suite #1600 Sacramento, CA 95814 (800) 927-4357 http://www.insurance.ca.gov/ (website)
Colorado	No program

---

1.   See DOL Technical Release 2011-01.
2.   See https://www.dol.gov/sites/default/files/ebsa/laws-and-regulations/laws/affordable-care-act/for-employers-and-advisers/consumer-assistance-programs.doc (Current through January 16, 2019) (Last Accessed August 24, 2019).

STATE	CONTACT INFORMATION
Commonwealth of Northern Mariana Islands	No Program
Connecticut	Connecticut Office of the Healthcare Advocate P.O. Box 1543 Hartford, CT 06144 (866) 466-4446 http://www.ct.gov/oha/site/default.asp (website) healthcare.advocate@ct.gov (email)
Delaware	Delaware Department of Insurance 841 Silver Lake Blvd Dover, DE 19904 (302) 674-7310 as the toll free number is only for in-state https://insurance.delaware.gov/ (website) consumer@state.de.us (email)
District of Columbia	DC Office of the Health Care Ombudsman and Bill of Rights One Judiciary Square 441 4th Street, NW, 900 South Washington, DC 20001 (877) 685-6391 http://www.healthcareombudsman.dc.gov (website) healthcareombudsman@dc.gov (email)
Florida	No Program
Georgia	Georgia Office of Insurance and Safety Fire Commissioner Consumer Services Division 2 Martin Luther King, Jr. Drive West Tower, Suite 716 Atlanta, Georgia 30334 (800) 656-2298 http://www.oci.ga.gov/ConsumerService/Home.aspx (website)
Guam	Guam Department of Revenue and Taxation 1240 Army Drive Barrigada, Guam 96921 (671) 635-1846
Hawaii	No program
Idaho	No program
Illinois	Illinois Department of Insurance 320 W. Washington St, 4th Floor Springfield, IL 62767 (866) 445-5364 http://insurance.illinois.gov/ (website) DOI.Director@illinois.gov (email)

STATE	CONTACT INFORMATION
Indiana	No program
Iowa	No program
Kansas	Kansas Insurance Department Consumer Assistance Division 420 SW 9th Street Topeka, KS 66612 (800) 432-2484 (in state) (785) 296-7829 (all others) http://www.ksinsurance.org (website) kid.commissioner@ks.gov(email)
Kentucky	Kentucky Department of Insurance, Consumer Protection Division 215 West Main Street Frankfort, KY 40601 P.O. Box 517 Frankfort, KY 40602-0517 (800) 595-6053 http://insurance.ky.gov (website) consumerservices@ky.gov (email)
Louisiana	No program
Maine	Bureau of Insurance State of Maine Consumer Service Division 76 Northern Avenue Augusta, ME 04333 (800) 300-5000 https://www.maine.gov/consumer (website) insurance.pfr@maine.gov (email)
Maryland	Maryland Office of the Attorney General Health Education and Advocacy Unit 200 St. Paul Place, 16th Floor Baltimore, MD 21202 (410) 576-6300 https://www.oag.state.md.us/Consumer/(website) heau@oag.state.md.us (email)
Massachusetts	Division of Insurance 1000 Washington St. #810 Boston, MA 02118 (517) 563-4467 https://www.mass.gov/health-care (website) doicss.mailbox@state.ma.us (email)

STATE	CONTACT INFORMATION
Michigan	Michigan Health Insurance Consumer Assistance Program (HICAP) Michigan Department of Insurance and Financial Services (DIFS) PO Box 30220 Lansing, MI 48909-7720 (877) 999-6442 http://www.michigan.gov/difs (website) difs-HICAP@michigan.gov(email)
Minnesota	No program
Mississippi	Health Help Mississippi 800 North President St Jackson, MS 39202 (877) 314-3843 http://www.healthhelpms.org (website) healthhelpms@mhap.org (email)
Missouri	Missouri Department of Insurance Truman State Office Building, Room 530 P.O. Box 690 Jefferson City, MO 65102 (800) 726-7390 http://insurance.mo.gov/consumers/ (website) consumeraffairs@insurance.mo.gov (email)
Montana	Office of the Montana State Auditor Commissioner of Securities and Insurance 840 Helena Ave Helena, MT 59601 (800) 332-6148 (in-state only) http://www.montanahealthanswers.com (website)
Nebraska	No program
Nevada	Office of Consumer Health Assistance Governor's Consumer Health Advocate 555 East Washington Ave #4800 Las Vegas, NV 89101 (702) 486-3587 (888) 333-1597 http://www.dhhs.nv.gov (website) cha@govcha.nv.gov (email)
New Hampshire	New Hampshire Department of Insurance 21 South Fruit Street, Suite 14 Concord, NH 03301 (800) 852-3416 http://www.nh.gov/insurance (website) consumerservices@ins.nh.gov (email)

STATE	CONTACT INFORMATION
New Jersey	New Jersey Department of Banking and Insurance 20 West State Street PO Box 471 Trenton, NJ 08625 (800) 446-7467 (609) 292-7272 http://www.state.nj.us/dobi/consumer.htm (website) ombudsman@dobi.state.nj.us (email)
New Mexico	New Mexico Office of Superintendent of Insurance Managed Health Care Bureau Phone: (855) 427-5674 Fax: (505) 427-5674 Online submission http://osi.state.nm.us/consumer-assistance/ forms/managed-healthcare.html
New York	Community Service Society of New York Community Health Advocates 633 Third Avenue, 10th floor New York, NY 10017 (888) 614-5400 http://www.communityhealthadvocates.org/ (website) cha@cssny.org (email)
North Carolina	North Carolina Department of Insurance Health Insurance Smart NC 325 N. Salisbury Street Raleigh, NC 27603 (855) 885-408-1212 http://www.ncdoi.com/Smart/ (website)
North Dakota	No program
Ohio	No program
Oklahoma	Oklahoma Insurance Department Five Corporate Plaza 3625 Northwest 56th Street, Suite 100 Oklahoma City, OK 73112-4511 (800) 522-0071 (in-state only) (405) 521-2828 https://www.ok.gov/oid/Consumers/Consumer_Assistance/ (website)
Oregon	Oregon Health Connect 1435 NE 81st Ave. Suite 500 Portland, OR 97213-6759 (866) 698-6155 http://211info.org/health/ (website) health@211info.org (email)

STATE	CONTACT INFORMATION
Pennsylvania	Pennsylvania Insurance Department 1326 Strawberry Square Harrisburg, PA 17120 (877) 881-6388 http://www.insurance.pa.gov (website)
Puerto Rico	Puerto Rico Oficina de la Procuradora del Paciente Calle Recinto Sur #303 San Juan, PR 00910 (787) 979-0909 http://www.pr.gov/ (website) querellas@opp.gobierno.pr (email)
Rhode Island	Rhode Island Consumer Assistance Program Rhode Island Parent Information Network, Inc. 1210 Pontiac Avenue Cranston, RI 02920 (401) 270-0101 http://rireach.org(website) callcenter@ripin.org (email)
South Carolina	South Carolina Department of Insurance Office of Consumer Services 1207 Main Street, Suite 1000 29202P.O. Box 100105 Columbia, SC 29202 (803) 737-6180 http://www.doi.sc.gov/638/Health-Insurance(website) consumers@doi.sc.gov (email)
South Dakota	No program
Tennessee	Tennessee Department of Commerce & Insurance 500 James Robertson Parkway Davy Crockett Tower, 4th floor Nashville, TN 37243-0565 (615) 741-2218 https://www.tn.gov/commerce/insurance/consumer-resources.html(website)
Texas	Texas Consumer Health Assistance Program Texas Department of Insurance Mail Code 111-1A 333 Guadalupe P.O. Box 149091 Austin, TX 78714-9091 (800) 252-3439 http://www.texashealthoptions.com (website) ConsumerProtection@tdi.texas.gov (email)

STATE	CONTACT INFORMATION
Utah	No program
Vermont	Vermont Legal Aid 264 North Winooski Ave. Burlington, VT 05402 (800) 889-2047 http://www.vtlegalaid.org (website)
Virginia	Virginia State Corporation Commission Life & Health Division, Bureau of Insurance P.O. Box 1157 Richmond, VA 23218 (877) -310-6560 http://www.scc.virginia.gov(website) bureauofinsurance@scc.virginia.gov (email)
Virgin Islands	U.S. Virgin Islands Division of Banking and Insurance 1131 King Street Suite 101 Christiansted St. Croix, VI 00820 (340) 773-6459 http://ltg.gov.vi (website)
Washington	Washington Consumer Assistance Program 5000 Capitol Blvd Tumwater, WA 98501 (800) 562-6900 https://www.insurance.wa.gov/(website) cap@oic.wa.gov (email)
West Virginia	West Virginia Offices of the Insurance Commissioner Consumer Service Division P.O. Box 50540 Charleston, WV 25305-0540 (888) 879-9842 https://www.wvinsurance.gov/consumerservices (website)
Wisconsin	No program
Wyoming	No program

297. Is there a minimum claim (de minimis claim) threshold under these new claim and appeal rules?

No. There is no *de minimis* exception for small claims eligible for external review, including some HRAs and dental and vision plans that do not qualify as excepted benefits. The appeals regulations specifically provide that the "state process may not impose a restriction on the minimum dollar amount of a claim for it to be eligible for external review."[1] Thus, there can be no minimum claims threshold. Although the appeals regulations and guidance are silent on this point for federal standards for external review, plans subject to the federal standards similarly are likely not permitted to impose minimum thresholds for claims.

298. How are health reimbursement account claims handled?

For many HRAs and QSE-HRAs, the claim decision simply is whether the expense meets the definition of "medical expense" under Internal Revenue Code section 213(d). As a result, HRA claims are simpler and less urgent than many other health plan claims. As a practical matter, there are fewer appeals for HRAs or QSE-HRAs than other types of plans.

299. How do these claims and appeal rules relate to the ERISA claims and appeal rules?

The ERISA claims procedure continues to apply.[2] Non-ERISA self-insured plans, such as church plans, while not subject to ERISA (assuming they have not affirmatively made themselves subject to ERISA), are subject to these new health reform rules. The health reform regulations expand on the 2000 DOL claims regulations, add several new requirements, and extend application of the requirements to non-ERISA group plans and to issuers of individual health insurance.

The health law claims and appeal regulations apply to group health plans and group and individual health insurance issuers for plan or policy years beginning after September 23, 2010. For nongrandfathered ERISA plans, these new requirements are in addition to existing claims procedures in the ERISA internal claim procedure rules at 29 CFR 2560.503-1. Where applicable, if an internal appeal is denied, patients may choose to have the claim reviewed by an independent reviewer. The regulations do not require the plan to provide continued coverage during the claim and any internal appeal, other than the coverage for an ongoing course of treatment. Plans are generally prohibited from reducing or terminating an ongoing course of treatment without notice and an opportunity to review. Individuals in urgent care situations and those receiving an ongoing course of treatment may be allowed to proceed with an expedited external review at the same time as the internal appeals process. However, the regulations do not make it clear whether this continued coverage requirement applies to appeals of eligibility claims and rescissions.

300. Can state versus federal standards apply?

Yes. Group health plans must determine whether they are subject to state standards or federal standards. For health insurance coverage (i.e., fully insured group health plans), if a state's external review process is binding on an insurer and includes the consumer protections in the NAIC Uniform Model Act in place as of July 23, 2010, the insurer must comply with the applicable state standards. This requirement is imposed on the insurer and not the plan. If a state's process does not meet such requirements, then the federal process will apply. The federal

---

1. Treas. Reg. §54.9815–2719 (c)(2)(v); DOL Reg. §2590.715–2719(c)(2)(v); HHS Reg. §147.136(c)(2)(v).
2. DOL Reg. §2560.503-1.

external review process generally will apply to ERISA-covered, self-insured plans. However, the preamble to the final regulations also notes that this would not preclude a state from applying its external review process to self-insured group health plans not covered by ERISA or subject to other state insurance law (i.e., nonfederal governmental plans, church plans and multiple employer welfare arrangements).

301. Which external review process (state or federal) applies to plans?

Type of Plan	What Process Applies?	Who Is Liable?
Insured Plan	State process (if state process applies and is binding)	Insurer (not plan)
	Federal process (if no state process applies and is binding)	Insurer or plan **
Self-Insured ERISA Plan	Federal process (unless plan voluntarily complies with an applicable state process, if available)	Plan
Self-Insured Non-ERISA Plan (e.g., nonfederal governmental plans and church plans)	State process (if state process applies and is binding)	Plan
	Federal process (if no state process applies and is binding)	Plan

** Although the federal external review requirement applies by its terms to plans or insurers, as a practical reality, insured plan sponsors will use the process used by their insurers to comply with this requirement.

302. What are the requirements of the new claims and appeals rules?

These regulations amended ERISA claims procedures applicable to group health plans, and made the new standards applicable to both group health plans and health insurance issuers. Specifically, the regulations provide the following new rules for internal claims and appeals processes:

- The appeals process provision under the law imposes obligations owed to health plan "enrollees."[1] The appeals regulations, however, generally use the term "claimant." A claimant is an individual (participant or beneficiary) who makes a claim under the rules for internal claims and appeals and external review procedures, which may include a claimant's authorized representative.[2] This is the same definition as under the DOL claims procedure regulations.[3]

- As part of full and fair review, a claimant must be permitted to review his or her claim file.[4] This is in addition to the right under the DOL claims procedures to

---

1.   PHSA §2719(a).
2.   DOL Reg. §2590.715-2719(a)(2)(iii).
3.   DOL Reg. §2560.503-1(a).
4.   PHSA §2719(a)(1)(C).

have access to and copies of "documents, records, and other information relevant" to the claim.[1] Existing DOL regulations permit claimants to present written comments, records, and information relating to a benefits claim.[2] Claimants also must be permitted to present evidence and testimony;[3] however, the law and regulations do not define testimony. The term "testimony" likely includes personal and written testimony from a witness, for example, by affidavit.[4] It generally is made by oath or affirmation under penalty of perjury.[5] Informally, the DOL has indicated that the appeals regulations were not intended to add a new rule requiring plans to hold hearings and allow claimants to make oral statements.[6]

- An adverse benefit determination eligible for internal claims and appeals was expanded to include a rescission of coverage, whether or not the rescission has an adverse effect on any particular benefit at the time.[7]

- A final internal adverse benefit determination is either an adverse benefit determination that has been upheld by a plan or insurer at completion of the plan's internal appeals procedures or an adverse benefit determination for which the internal appeals procedures have been exhausted.[8] Typically, most plans a claim and one internal appeal.

- A plan or issuer must notify a claimant of a benefit determination, whether or not adverse, for a claim involving urgent care as soon as possible, taking into account the medical exigencies, but not later than seventy-two hours after the receipt of the claim by the plan or issuer. The original standard of twenty-four hours was amended to seventy-two hours.[9]

- The appeals regulations require plans or insurers to provide claimants, free of charge, and without any requirement of a claimant's request, with "any new or additional evidence considered, relied upon, or generated by" the plan or insurer (or at the direction of the plan or insurer) in connection with a claim.[10] This evidence must be provided as soon as possible and soon enough so the claimant can respond.[11] These rules must be followed at each stage of the process.

- Decisions regarding hiring, compensation, termination, promotion, or other similar matters by decision-makers, such as claims adjudicators and medical experts, must

---

1. DOL Reg. §2560.503-1(h)(2)(iii).
2. DOL Reg. §2560.503-1(h)(2)(ii).
3. PHSA §2719(a)(1)(C).
4. Black's Law Dictionary (9th ed. 2009) ("testimony").
5. Black's Law Dictionary Free Online 2nd Ed. at http://thelawdictionary.org/testimony . (Last accessed August 24, 2019).
6. Nonbinding comments, Amy Turner, EBSA, ABA Joint Committee on Employee Benefits teleconference, "Health Plans: Compliance with PPACA's Health Claims and Appeals Process" (November 17, 2010).
7. DOL Reg. §2590.715-2719(b)(2)(ii)(A).
8. DOL Reg. §2590.715-2719(a)(2)(v).
9. Preamble to amended Appeals Regulations, 76 Fed. Reg. 37208, 37212 (June 24, 2011).
10. DOL Reg. §2590.715-2719(b)(2)(ii)(C)(1).
11. DOL Reg. §2560.503-1(i).

avoid any conflict of interest and not be based upon the likelihood that the individual will support the denial of benefits.[1]

- Notices must be provided in a culturally and linguistically appropriate manner,[2] including notices in a non-English language if 25 percent of all participants are literate in the same non-English language. For plans with 100 or more participants, the notices must be provided in a non-English language if the lesser of 500 participants or 10 percent of all participants are literate in the same non-English language.[3]

- Notices to claimants must comply with certain content requirements:

    o Any notice of an adverse benefit determination or a final internal adverse benefit determination must include information sufficient to identify the claim involved, including the date of the service, the healthcare provider, the claim amount (if applicable), the diagnosis code and its corresponding meaning, and the treatment code and its corresponding meaning.

    o The plan or issuer must ensure that the reasons for an adverse benefit determination or final internal adverse benefit determination include the denial code and its corresponding meaning, as well as a description of the plan's or issuer's standard, if any, that was used in denying the claim; and in the case of a final internal adverse benefit determination, this description must also include a discussion of the decision.

    o The plan or issuer must provide a description of the available internal appeals and external review processes, including information regarding how to initiate an appeal.

    o The plan or issuer must disclose the availability of, and contact information for, an applicable office of health insurance consumer assistance or ombudsman established under PHSA section 2793.

303. What if a plan fails to follow these claims and external review rules?

Prior to filing a lawsuit, a claimant must exhaust the appeals process. If a plan or issuer fails to adhere strictly to all requirements of the interim final regulations, the claimant is deemed to have exhausted the plan's or issuer's internal claims and appeals process, regardless of whether the plan or issuer asserts that it has substantially complied. The claimant may initiate any available external review process and remedies available under ERISA and state law.

The claimant may request a written explanation of a violation of the procedures from the plan or insurer, and the plan or insurer must provide such explanation within ten days, including

---

1.   DOL Reg. §§2560.503-1(b) and (h).
2.   PHSA §2719(a)(1)(B); Reg. §54.9815-2719T(e); 2016 Culturally and Linguistically Appropriate Services (CLAS) County Data, at https://www.cms.gov/CCIIO/Resources/Fact-Sheets-and-FAQs/Downloads/CLAS-County-Data_Jan-2016-update-FINAL.pdf (Last accessed August 24, 2019).
3.   HHS Reg. §147.136(e)(3).

a specific description of its bases for asserting that the violation should not cause the internal claims and appeals process to be deemed exhausted.[1]

If an external reviewer or court rejects a claimant's request for immediate review on the basis that the plan met the standards for the exception described above, the claimant has the right to resubmit and pursue the internal appeal of the claim. In such a case, within a reasonable time after the external reviewer or court rejects the claim for immediate review (not to exceed ten days), the plan must provide the claimant with notice of the opportunity to resubmit and pursue the internal appeal of the claim. Time periods for re-filing the claim begin to run when the claimant receives the notice.[2]

304. What are the requirements for Summary Plan Descriptions (SPDs) to incorporate the new claims and appeals rules?

The enhanced internal claims and appeals requirements and external review procedures required that existing SPDs and other plan communications that describe the plan's claims procedures be updated. In March 2011, the agencies modified and extended the enforcement grace period for certain internal claims and appeals requirements.[3] SPDs and plan communications must provide participants and beneficiaries with information relating to internal claims and appeals requirements and external review procedures, as updated in June 2011.[4]

Wellness Program Rules

305. What are wellness programs?

Some wellness programs are stand-alone programs and others are offered as part of or in conjunction with a group health plan. Wellness programs encourage good health and healthy lifestyles. Additionally, some may provide physical examinations, cholesterol screening, flu shots, nutrition counseling and education, and similar benefits. To the extent that a wellness program provides such medical benefits, it will likely be treated as a group health plan subject to the PHSA mandates in ERISA and the Internal Revenue Code for private employers or in the PHSA for state and local government employers.

The 2014 prohibition against discriminating based on a health status-related factor means, among other things, that plans and insurers may not charge individuals different premiums or impose different costs based on the presence or absence of a health status-related factor. However, nondiscrimination provisions were not meant to prevent a group health plan or insurer from establishing premium discounts or reduced copayments or deductibles in return for "adherence to programs of health promotion and disease prevention."[5] Thus, certain programs of health promotion or disease prevention (referred to as "wellness programs") are an exception to the general prohibition on discrimination based on a health status-related factor.

---

1.   DOL Reg. §2590.715-2719(b)(2)(ii)(F)(2). (80 FR 72264, November 18, 2015).
2.   DOL Reg. §2590.715-2719(b)(2)(ii)(F)(2). (80 FR 72264, November 18, 2015).
3.   DOL Technical Release 2011-01 (March 18, 2011).
4.   Amendment to Interim Final Rule on Internal Claims and Appeals and External Review Processes, 76 Fed. Reg. 37208 (June 24, 2011).
5.   IRC Sec. 9802(b)(2); ERISA Sec. 702(b)(2); PHSA §2705(b)(2).

Most employers that offer health benefits today also offer at least some wellness programs designed to promote employee health and productivity and ultimately to reduce health-related expenses. Workplace wellness programs in what they offer and approximately 30 percent of larger employers incent employees' participation.

306. How are stand-alone wellness programs treated?

Stand-alone wellness programs are not subject to the PHSA mandates if they are not group health plans. A wellness plan is not a group health plan if it does not provide or pay for health or medical benefits. Examples of types of stand-alone wellness programs that are not group health plans include programs that pay for health or weight-loss club dues, award prizes to persons who walk a certain number of miles, or provide health information. Even when a wellness plan offers incentives, this does not make it a group health plan if the incentives are unrelated to the group health plan, such as a plan offering extra vacation days or bonuses to those who do not smoke or have a good cholesterol level, for example.

On the other hand, stand-alone wellness programs that provide or pay for medical benefits (such as a physical exam program) are group health plans[1] and are subject to the PHSA mandates unless they qualify for an exception.

307. How are wellness programs that relate to group health plans regulated?

A wellness program that relates to, or is a part of, a larger group health plan is subject to the PHSA mandates, if the group health plan to which it is connected is subject to the mandates and is not an excepted benefit, such as a stand-alone vision or dental plan.

A wellness program is related to a group health plan if it is actually one of the benefits under the larger group health plan or if any of the incentives or rewards that it offers affect the benefits or contributions under the larger group plan. For example, an employer-sponsored wellness program that offers, as an incentive for undergoing certain testing, a discount on the amount that an employee must pay for major medical coverage is subject to the PHSA mandates.

Health-Contingent Wellness Programs: In 2010, the Affordable Care Act amended ERISA to permit group health plans to adopt "health-contingent" wellness programs. These programs provide rewards, such as premium discounts, to people who can meet certain health outcomes, such as normal weight or blood pressure. Some programs identify people with health problems and then provide rewards if they participate in wellness classes or activities. These types of programs can include "activity-based" or "outcome-based" types programs. The activity-based programs include completing an activity such as walking programs, health coaching, etc. Outcome-based is focused more on results such as achieving a particular result such as weight loss or smoking cessation.

---

1.   See, e.g., DOL Information Letter to Joseph S. Dunn (November 17, 1993) http://www.dol.gov/ebsa/pdf/josephdunnletter.pdf. (Last access September 5, 2016).

Final DOL regulations[1] enabled health-contingent wellness programs to modify group health plan premiums or cost-sharing based on health status and are deemed not to discriminate based on health status if they meet the below standards.

- Limitations on Rewards/Avoidance of Penalties: The maximum reward is 30 percent of the total cost the self-only group health plan coverage (or 30 percent of the cost of family coverage if spouses and dependents are eligible to participate in the wellness program).

- Health-contingent wellness programs also must be reasonably designed to promote health or prevent disease.[2]

- Also, reasonably designed health-contingent wellness programs must provide notice to participants, allow waivers and/or alternative ways for participants to earn rewards, and must make the rewards available to participants at least on a yearly basis.

Participatory Wellness Programs: Under the DOL rule, wellness programs that do not base rewards or penalties on health status are called "participatory" wellness programs. Participatory wellness programs are not required to the standards that apply to health-contingent wellness programs and generally are not considered to implicate ERISA nondiscrimination rules. However, the DOL rule notes that other employment discrimination laws, such as the ADA and GINA, also apply, and that being in compliance with the ERISA/ACA wellness program standards does not relieve employers from having to comply with other federal laws. These are types of programs where rewards are based upon participation – examples including health center discounts or medical assessments.

Reasonable alternatives must be offered for health contingent programs:

- Employers must offer a reasonable alternative to any individual who fails to meet the requirements for a reward. Every employee must be given the opportunity to earn the full reward regardless of their personal health status.

  - Activity-only – If it is medically inadvisable for an employee to participate in an activity the activity requirement can be waiver of the employer can offer the employee a reasonable alternative activity to earn the full reward.

  - Outcome-based – An employee who fails to meet the required health standard must be offered an alternative, such as working with a health coach.

The maximum financial incentive is 30 percent of the total cost (employer and employee share) of self-only group health plan coverage. This includes both employee and employer contributions. The maximum for tobacco related programs is fifty percent. This limit applies to both health-contingent and participatory wellness programs. A wellness program will be

---

1.   https://www.govinfo.gov/content/pkg/FR-2013-06-03/pdf/2013-12916.pdf.
2.   71 Federal Register at 75018-75019.

considered voluntary under the ADA if the amount of an incentive offered for participation — alone or in combination with incentives offered for health-contingent wellness programs — does not exceed this maximum. The rule further specifies that incentives need not be conditioned on participating in the group health plan.

308. How does the Genetic Information Nondiscrimination Act (GINA) affect wellness programs?

Federal regulations implementing GINA were first published in October 2009. The regulations generally detailed that GINA forbids employers from requesting, requiring or purchasing genetic information from employees unless an exception applies.

Under these rules, there is an exception that allows employers to offer financial incentives as part of a wellness program that solicits genetic information from the employee, so long as it is made clear that disclosing this information is voluntary.

Additional regulations issued in May 2016 further clarify these rules by providing an exception under which employers can offer financial incentives connected to a spouse's completion of a health assessment that asks about the spouse's health (but not genetic) information.

Differences between GINA and the Affordable Care Act:

- Limit use of genetic health information collected through a wellness program.

- Regulate sharing of health information collected from spouses.

- Prohibit health and genetic information collection from employees' children.

- Prohibit the sale of genetic information provided through a wellness program to other vendors. In combination, it is clear that compliance with one set of regulations does not necessarily ensure compliance with all the others. Employers should review their wellness programs and incentives against all regulations, and consult with legal counsel if their current wellness programs don't align with the final ADA and/or GINA regulations.

309. What effect did the case of *AARP v. EEOC* have on wellness programs?

In July 2016, the EEOC issued a new rule under ADA and GINA relating to wellness plans. The ADA rule stated that, in connection with such plans, employers could implement penalties or rewards of up to only 30 percent of the cost of self-only coverage to encourage employees to disclose ADA-protected information, without causing the disclosure to be involuntary. The GINA rule similarly stated that offering a 30 percent incentive to an employee to disclose certain genetic information would not render the disclosure involuntary. In addition, the EECO implemented several requirements that a plan needed to meet to show that participation was voluntary including showing that the program was reasonably designed, voluntary, limited rewards for participation, offered confidentiality, and was reasonably accommodating to everyone. The ADA and GINA both have prohibitions that impact wellness programs. The ADA forbids discrimination based on disabilities and GINA does not allow healthcare plans to use genetic information to discriminate on coverage. In this regard, a privacy issue is also raised when participants are asked to answer health-related questions or undergo testing.

The new rule took effect on January 1, 2017, to provide employers with enough lead time to design the structure of their wellness plans to meet the rules. More than 85 percent of employers offered some sort of wellness bonus to employees who participate in wellness programs designed to encourage healthier and active lifestyles. In addition, the average amount of the incentive offered to health plan participants steadily increasing during the past four years, according to a recent survey by the National Business Group on Health. With millions of Americans participating in wellness programs, it becomes critical to have well-established rules to ensure that the program complies with the law and is administered consistently.

Compounding this issue was that in October 2016, the AARP filed suit against the EECO seeking a ruling that the new regulations were invalid, arguing that a 30 percent incentive made an employee's disclosure of ADA information and GINA-protected information involuntary an involuntary disclosure and essentially a 30 percent "penalty" because employees who could not afford to pay a 30 percent surcharge would effectively be forced to provide the information.

In *AARP v. EEOC*[1], the US District Court granted the motion by the AARP to vacate the EEOC's wellness regulations, allowing companies to charge employees who decline to participate in wellness questionnaires and exams with penalties. This decision is considered a victory for privacy rights of working regarding medical and genetic information but has confused how the wellness program situation will work.

A wellness program involving medical exams or inquiries must be voluntary in order to comply with the Americans with Disabilities Act (ADA) and the Genetic Information Non-Discrimination Act (GINA). Until the AARP decision, the term "voluntary" was never actually defined. There had been no judicial or legislative guidance, on allowable penalties or incentives that could be tied to screenings or health reimbursement arrangements (HRAs). The only clear guidelines were from the Affordable Care Act's 30 percent-of-total-health-benefit-spending limitation and 50 percent for smoking programs.

The AARP decision means that the Equal Employment Opportunity Commission must rewrite its definition of "voluntary". Additionally, the EEOC must issue rules soon for employers to incorporate the new limits for incentives and penalties into their own wellness programs starting in January 2019. The AARP suit was brought in October 2016 alleging that the EEOC's wellness rules were coercive, forcing workers to pay more for health insurance if they chose not to reveal private medical information.

Under the court's ruling the EEOC wellness program regulations became null and void beginning on January 1, 2019. As a result, there will uncertainty regarding employer wellness programs under the ADA and GINA beginning in 2019.

---

1.   https://benefitslink.com/src/ctop/AARP-v-EEOC_DDC_12202017.pdf.

The main types of employer wellness program features impacted by the court's ruling are:

- Biometric screenings (and any other medical examinations) for employees and spouses;

- Disability-related inquiries directed at employees (which could affect questions on an HRA);

- Family medical history questions relating to diseases and disorders, and

- Other program aspects that that involve genetic information of the employee, employee's spouse, or employee's family members

The Equal Employment Opportunity Commission (EEOC) recently announced that it plans to issue amended regulations related to incentivizing participation in employer-sponsored voluntary wellness programs under the Americans with Disabilities Act (ADA) and the Genetic Information Nondiscrimination Act (GINA) by the end of this year. Until that point it is difficult to advise companies considering or continuing wellness programs on how to act in regard to 2020 planning. There are several options at this point in order of less to most risk:

- Delay implementing a wellness program until 2020 or beyond when the rules might stabilize.

- Discontinue wellness programs that require anyone that participates to provide health-related information or undergo any medical tests to be given the financial incentive.

- Continue wellness programs and continue to follow the EEOC's regulations (even though they are slated to be vacated January 1, 2019). This would include following the incentive limits and meeting the notice requirements.

- Ignore the EEOC's rules and opt to follow the less restrictive HIPAA and Affordable Care Act rules.

Bringing Down the Cost of Coverage

Medical Loss Ratio (MLR) Rules; PHSA, ERISA and Tax Ramifications

310. What are the health reform provisions relating to reducing the cost of health insurance?

Health reform added PHSA section 2718 entitled "Bringing Down the Cost Of Health Care Coverage." The purpose of the law is to limit the amount insurers can spend on administrative costs. If an insurer exceeds the limit, it is required to rebate the excess. The medical loss ratio (MLR) is the cost of claims plus amounts expended on health care quality improvement as a percentage of total premiums, excluding taxes, fees, and adjustments for risk adjustments and risk corridors, as well as reinsurance.[1] The Affordable Care Act requires insurance companies to pay annual rebates if the MLR for groups of health insurance policies issued in a state is less than 85 percent for large employer group policies and 80 percent for most small employer group policies and individual policies.

Health care reform's Medical Loss Ratio (MLR) rules became effective January 1, 2011, and the first rebates were required to be issued on August 1, 2012. These rules apply to individual insurance policies and insured group plans but not self-insured health plans. Insurers must provide rebates (refunds)[2] if their percentage of premiums spent on medical claims (and quality improvement) for policies issued in a state is less than 80 percent in the small group and individual markets or 85 percent in the large group market.[3]

Until 2014, the rebate was calculated using the figures for the reporting year. After January 1, 2014, the calculation to determine rebate amounts is be based on the average ratio over the previous three years.[4] This three-year moving average causes the effect of losses to be lagged. Notices of rebates must be sent to both plan sponsors and participants in the plan to which the rebate relates.

Rebates must be paid by August 1 of the year following the year for which the Medical Loss Ratio (MLR) data are calculated.[5] Insurers must also report how the rebate was calculated. Insurers who fail to comply with the law are subject to civil fines to be assessed by HHS up to $100 per day per individual affected by the violation. During 2015, health insurers were required to pay $469 million in rebates to 5.5 million people – with a total rebate over the four years since 2011 to over $2.4 billion. Total rebates by year have been:

- $1.1 billion in 2012 (for 2011);

- $519 million in 2013 (for 2012);

- $333 million in 2014 (for 2013);

- $469 million in 2015 (for 2014);

- $396 million in 2016 (for 2015);

- $446 million in 2017 (for 2016); and

- $706 million in 2018 (for 2017).

---

1.   PHSA §2718(a) and (b)(1)(A).
2.   PHSA §2718(b)(1)(A).
3.   PHSA §§2718(b)(1)(A)(i) and (ii). This ratio is determined on a state-by-state basis and it is measured in the state in which the policy is issued. States can require higher minimum MLR percentages, but HHS can also adjust state MLR requirements downward where necessary to prevent destabilization of the individual market. State MLR targets tend to be lower than the health reform law targets.
4.   PHSA §2791(e)(4).
5.   45 CFR §158.240(d).

311. When were the final Medical Loss Ratio (MLR) regulations issued?

In December 2011, HHS issued final Medical Loss Ratio (MLR) regulations,[1] and the DOL has issued related guidance on healthcare reform's MLR rules, making changes for employer-sponsored group health plans, including who receives the rebates and how such amounts may be applied.[2] Insurers must provide the rebates for individuals covered by group health plans subject to ERISA or the PHSA to the policyholder, which is generally the employer for a group plan. The effective date of this final regulation was January 3, 2012.

312. How may the insurance company rebates be paid to persons ("enroll-ees") purchasing individual policies in the individual market?

For current individual policy owners, insurers may issue rebates in the form of either a premium credit, a reduction in the premium, or a lump-sum payment.[3] For former individual policy owners, only a lump-sum payment is permitted.[4] If an insurer finds that its Medical Loss Ratio (MLR) is lower than the standard required during an MLR reporting year, it may also institute a premium holiday to avoid paying rebates, but only if permitted under state law.[5] An insurer seeking to suspend or reduce premiums must obtain permission from the governing state agency and do so in a non-discriminatory manner. An "enrollee" for rebate purposes is the policyholder or government entity that paid the premium for healthcare coverage received by an individual during the respective MLR reporting year.[6]

In addition to a premium credit or a lump-sum payment, if the premium is paid using a credit or debit card, an insurer is permitted to return the entire rebate to the account used to pay the premium[7] and no additional fees are charged.[8]

313. How much in rebates have been paid out thus far under the Medical Loss Ratio (MLR)?

The Medical Loss Ratio seems to have had an effect on reduction of administrative expenses. From 2012 through 2014, the amount of rebates dropped by a significant amount. However, by 2015, the amount had gone up from $333 million to $469 million. The average MLR has actually increased since 2011.[9] For 2017, (the latest year figures are available) 5.9 million people

---

1.   On November 22, 2010, the Department of Health and Human Services (HHS) issued its interim final regulations implementing the MLR requirements of section 2718 of the Public Health Services Act (PHSA) entitled "Bringing Down the Cost of Health Care Coverage." The term "medical loss ratio" does not appear in section 2718.
2.   Medical Loss Ratio Requirements under PPACA, 45 CFR Part 158, 76 Fed. Reg. 76574 (December 7, 2011); Medical Loss Ratio Rebate Requirements for Non-Federal Governmental Plans, 45 CFR Part 158, 76 Fed Reg. 76596 (December 7, 2011); DOL Technical Release 2011-04 (December 2, 2011); HHS Fact Sheet: Medical Loss Ratio: Getting Your Money's Worth on Health Insurance (December 2, 2011).
3.   45 CFR §158.241(a).
4.   45 CFR §158.241(b).
5.   CCIIO Technical Guidance (CCIIO 2012-002): Questions and Answers Regarding the Medical Loss Ratio Regulation, Q&A-30, at https://www.cms.gov/CCIIO/Resources/Files/Downloads/mlr-qna-04202012.pdf. (Last accessed August 25, 2019).
6.   45 CFR §158.240(b).
7.   45 CFR §158.241.
8.   CCIIO Technical Guidance (CCIIO 2012-002): Questions and Answers Regarding the Medical Loss Ratio Regulation, Q&A-37, at https://www.cms.gov/CCIIO/Resources/Files/Downloads/mlr-qna-04202012.pdf. (Last accessed August 25, 2019).
9.   https://www.cms.gov/CCIIO/Resources/Forms-Reports-and-Other-Resources/Downloads/2014_Medical_Loss_Ratio_Report.pdf.

(up from 3.9 million in 2016) received rebates. The average family rebate was $119, up from 113 in 2016.[1] The breakdown by state is listed below:

2017 ACA HEALTH INSURANCE PREMIUM REBATES		
Location	**Total Rebates**	**Total Consumers Benefiting from Rebates**	**Average Rebate per Person**
United States	$706,735,126	5,960,498	$119
Alabama	$206,196	5,061	$41
Alaska	$0	0	$0
Arizona	$27,576,292	157,020	$176
Arkansas	$1,944,299	12,870	$151
California	$97,386,263	919,608	$106
Colorado	$7,475,523	70,758	$106
Connecticut	$48,929	1,154	$42
Delaware	$6,551,746	37,324	$176
District of Columbia	$26,601,653	93,420	$285
Florida	$86,231,898	679,522	$127
Georgia	$29,380,080	403,707	$73
Hawaii	$314,241	818	$384
Idaho	$64,430	2,021	$32
Illinois	$14,554,527	118,385	$123
Indiana	$1,499,908	74,991	$20
Iowa	$2,468,147	17,473	$141
Kansas	$3,695,019	23,526	$157
Kentucky	$26,253	923	$28
Louisiana	$314,880	61,158	$5
Maine	$0	0	$0
Maryland	$75,754,059	552,175	$137
Massachusetts	$31,895,756	208,749	$153
Michigan	$55,651,722	392,288	$142
Minnesota	$19,659,847	41,034	$479
Mississippi	$10,466,683	91,084	$115
Missouri	$45,538,433	298,071	$153
Montana	$116,211	1,102	$105
Nebraska	$69,737	1,665	$42
Nevada	$6,451,083	43,778	$147

---

1.   https://www.cms.gov/CCIIO/Resources/Data-Resources/Downloads/2014_MLR_Refunds_by_State.pdf.

2017 ACA HEALTH INSURANCE PREMIUM REBATES			
Location	Total Rebates	Total Consumers Benefiting from Rebates	Average Rebate per Person
New Hampshire	$8,064,209	34,995	$230
New Jersey	$14,368,862	94,341	$152
New Mexico	$4,513,998	32,498	$139
New York	$25,961,536	445,849	$58
North Carolina	$4,355,031	112,738	$39
North Dakota	$64,550	794	$81
Ohio	$4,706,404	26,186	$180
Oklahoma	$2,434,273	33,380	$73
Oregon	$96,757	636	$152
Pennsylvania	$30,734,528	416,910	$74
Rhode Island	$0	0	$0
South Carolina	$453,504	41,437	$11
South Dakota	$0	0	$0
Tennessee	$10,634,459	100,638	$106
Texas	$7,813,406	54,851	$142
Utah	$3,722,184	27,957	$133
Vermont	$0	0	$0
Virginia	$35,342,998	210,094	$168
Washington	$0	0	$0
West Virginia	$1,207,286	6,840	$177
Wisconsin	$317,325	10,671	$30
Wyoming	$0	0	$0
American Samoa	N/A	N/A	N/A
Guam	N/A	N/A	N/A
Northern Mariana Islands	N/A	N/A	N/A
Puerto Rico	N/A	N/A	N/A
U.S. Virgin Islands	N/A	N/A	N/A

314. How are insurers to pay Medical Loss Ratio (MLR) rebates in connection with employer health insurance plans?

If an employer selects the insurer and administers the health insurance plan, it is an employee welfare benefit plan and subject to ERISA. Section 3(l) of ERISA describes an employee welfare plan as "any plan, fund, or program which was heretofore or is hereafter established or maintained by an employer or by an employee organization, or by both, to the extent that such plan, fund, or program was established or is maintained for the purpose of providing for its participants or their beneficiaries, through the purchase of insurance or otherwise, . . . medical, surgical, or hospital care or benefits. . ."[1]

Insurers must provide rebates for group health plans subject to ERISA (private employers) or the PHSA (state and local governments) to the policyholder, which is generally the employer sponsoring the plan.[2] For these plans, the rebates can have both ERISA and income tax ramifications, both of which are discussed in more detail below, in Q 328 and Q 329.

315. What if the plan has been terminated when the Medical Loss Ratio (MLR) rebate is due?

If a group health plan, regardless of whether it is subject to ERISA, has been terminated at the time of rebate payment and the insurer cannot, despite reasonable efforts, locate the policyholder (the employer), the insurer must distribute the entire rebate, including the employer's share, to the participants who were enrolled in the terminated plan during the Medical Loss Ratio (MLR) reporting year on which the rebate was calculated by dividing the rebate equally among the individuals entitled to a rebate.[3] If an insurer is able to locate the policyholder with respect to a terminated ERISA plan, the policyholder would need to comply with ERISA's fiduciary provisions when handling any rebate. Despite the fact that the plan has been terminated, the plan document should be consulted and its terms followed. If the plan document does not provide direction, the employer must pay the employees' portion to them unless it is not cost effective.[4]

316. What if the Medical Loss Ratio (MLR) limits on insurers cause financial problems for insurers?

HHS may "adjust" (but not waive) the Medical Loss Ratio (MLR) target[5] in individual states where enforcement of the 80 percent target would "destabilize" the individual market.[6] HHS must provide detailed, public information as to its conclusions and the public may comment. HHS may elect to hold a hearing and must respond promptly to state requests.

317. Do the Medical Loss Ratio (MLR) rules limit commissions paid to brokers and agents?

Brokers and agents commissions reportedly may account for 5 percent or more of premiums as of this writing. The statute requires that sales commissions be counted as administrative

---

1.   ERISA Sec. 3(1), 29 U.S.C. §1002(1).
2.   45 CFR §158.242(b). ERISA generally applies to private employer plans, while the PHSA applies to non-federal governmental employer plans.
3.   45 CFR §158.242(b)(4).
4.   DOL Technical Release No. 2011-04, Guidance on Rebates for Group Health Plans Paid Pursuant to the Medical Loss Ratio Requirements of the Public Health Service Act (December 2, 2011), at https://www.dol.gov/agencies/ebsa/employers-and-advisers/guidance/technical-releases/11-04. (Last accessed August 25, 2019).
5.   CCIIO Technical Guidance (CCIIO 2011-002): Questions and Answers Regarding the Medical Loss Ratio Interim Final Rule, Q&A-17, at https://www.cms.gov/CCIIO/Resources/Files/Downloads/mlr-qna-04202012.pdf. (Last Accessed August 25, 2019).
6.   OCIIO Technical Guidance (OCIIO 2010-2A): Process for a State to Submit a Request for Adjustment to the Medical Loss Ratio Standard of PHSA section 2718, at https://www.cms.gov/CCIIO/Resources/Files/Downloads/mlr-qna-04202012.pdf. (Last Accessed August 25, 2019).

costs, although HHS could consider such compensation in assessing market destabilization.[1] Insurance companies, as a general rules, have reduced commissions paid to agents and brokers for ACA sales, with some eliminating commissions outright. Since agent and broker commissions are counted as administrative costs, insurance companies are incented to either increase their profits – or reduce their administrative costs (required to be under 20 percent) by cutting broker compensation. Currently bills are before Congress to remove broker/agent fees from the administrative cost compensation.[2] The Trump Administration has announced that it supports proposals to simplify the calculation of the Medical Loss Ratio and also to allow states to regulate insurers.[3]

318. How is the Medical Loss Ratio (MLR) computed?

The numerator of the MLR formula includes reimbursement of claims for clinical services and expenditures for quality improvement activities. Clinical services reimbursement includes direct payments for services and supplies as well as changes in contract reserves (where an issuer holds reserves for later years when claims are expected to rise as experience deteriorates) and reserves for contingent benefits and lawsuits. Payments under capitation contracts with providers may be counted fully as claims, but insurers must count as administrative costs rather than claims costs payments made to third party vendors (such as behavioral health or pharmacy benefit managers) that are attributable to administrative services.

The definition of quality improvement activities found in PPACA section 2717 of the health reform law is used for the MLR rules. Quality improvement activities include activities that:

- improve health care outcomes;

- reduce medical errors;

- improve patient safety;

- encourage wellness and prevention; and

- reduce re-hospitalizations.

MLR quality improvement costs also include:

- related IT expenses;

- the cost of healthcare hotlines;

- the cost of collecting and reporting quality data for accreditation purposes; and

- expenditures for facilitating the "meaningful use" of certified electronic health record technologies.

---

1. 75 Fed. Reg. 74863, 74877 (December 1, 2010).
2. H.R. 2328, H.R. 815, and S. 1661.
3. Patient Protection and Affordable Care Act; HHS Notice of Benefit and Payment Parameters for 2019, 45 CFR Parts 147, 153, 154, 155, 156, 157, and 158.

Prospective utilization review may be considered quality improvement to the extent it is intended to ensure appropriate treatment, but concurrent and retrospective utilization review activities are administrative costs.

The regulations provide that the MLR is calculated as follows:

$$\frac{\text{medical care claims} + \text{quality improvement expenses}}{\text{premiums} - (\text{federal and state taxes} + \text{licensing and regulatory fees})}[1]$$

<u>Fraud Prevention</u>. PPACA does not allow insurers to count fraud prevention costs in the numerator as quality improvement expenses. However, the rule allows insurers to offset their fraud detection and recovery expenses against successful fraud recoveries.

<u>Quality Improvement Expenses Must Be Verifiable and Objective</u>. The HHS rule states that only activities "capable of being objectively measured and of producing verifiable results and achievements" can be counted as quality improvement. The preface to the HHS rule states: "While an issuer does not have to present initial evidence proving the effectiveness of a quality improvement activity, the issuer will have to show measurable results stemming from the executed quality improvement activity."

319. How are Medical Loss Ratios (MLRs) calculated if an insurer has several entities licensed in a state?

Medical Loss Ratios (MLRs) are calculated separately for each licensed entity within a state by market segment (individual, small, or large group). Experience can be aggregated to the state in which the contract is located for employers with employees in multiple states. Affiliated insurers can also aggregate their experience where they combine to offer an employer in- and out-of-network coverage. No national reporting is allowed. Association health plans selling individual coverage must report their experience in the state in which individual certificates of coverage are issued.[2]

320. What are the rules for Medical Loss Ratio (MLR) rebates for state and local government (non-federal) group health plans?

Group health plans maintained by nonfederal governmental employers, including state and local governments, are not subject to ERISA. HHS issued separate interim final regulations for these plans.[3] The plan policyholder is required to use the portion of rebates attributable to the amount of premium paid by plan subscribers for the benefit of subscribers. At the option of the policyholder, this portion of the rebate must be used either to reduce employee premium contributions or to provide cash refunds to employees covered by the group health policy on which the rebate is based. In either case, however, the rebate is to

---

1.   103 45 CFR §158.140, 104 45 CFR §158.150.105, 45 CFR §§158.161 and 158.162, 106 45 CFR §158.240(c); see also http://www.gao.gov/products/GAO-12-90R (Last accessed August 25, 2019).

2.   45 CFR §158.120(a).

3.   Vol. 76 Federal Register No. 235, pp. 76596-76599 (December 7, 2011) at http://www.gpo.gov/fdsys/pkg/FR-2011-12-07/pdf/2011-31291. pdf. (Last accessed August 25, 2019).

be used to reduce premiums for (or pay refunds to) employees enrolled during the year in which the rebate is actually paid (rather than the MLR reporting year, i.e., the prior year, on which the rebate was calculated).

321. What are the rules for group insured health plans sponsored by employers and subject to ERISA?

Most employer-provided health plans are subject to ERISA. The exceptions for state and local governments and church plans are discussed in Q 299.

Where the health plan is funded by a trust, the rebate is paid to that trust. If the plan is not funded by a trust, DOL Technical Release 2011-04, excuses insured group health plans from the obligations to hold participant contributions in trust and to file Form 5500 *IF* the Medical Loss Ratio (MLR) rebates are used within three months of receipt to make employee refunds (the preferred option, as discussed in Q 316 or to pay the employees' share of premiums, in each case to the extent premiums were paid by employees.[1]

322. How does an employer comply with the three-month rule?

To be safe under the three-month rule, Medical Loss Ratio (MLR) rebates belonging to participants must be used to benefit plan participants within three months. An employer that decides to distribute the rebate to plan participants must issue checks, by regular payroll or special check, within three months of the employer's receipt of the rebate. If the employer decides to use the portion of the rebate belonging to employees to reduce required participant contributions, it must adjust payroll deductions for affected participants within three months of the rebate's receipt. Thus, a plan that receives a rebate on August 1 cannot wait until the next plan year begins to reduce employee contributions if the beginning of the next year is more than three months after receipt of the rebate.

323. How does an employer decide whether a Medical Loss Ratio (MLR) belongs to the employer or the employees when the health plan is not funded through a trust?

DOL Technical Release 2011-04[2] discusses MLR payments relating to ERISA health insurance plans and explains the fiduciary and plan asset rules that apply. As noted in Q 321, plans without a trust need to dispose of the rebates belonging to participants within three months of receipt. Plan sponsors should review plan documents to determine if they address how the plan assets portion of a rebate is determined and to verify whether such provisions are consistent with the final regulation.

---

1.   DOL Technical Release No. 2011-04, Guidance on Rebates for Group Health Plans Paid Pursuant to the Medical Loss Ratio Requirements of the Public Health Service Act (December 2, 2011), at https://www.dol.gov/agencies/ebsa/employers-and-advisers/guidance/technical-releases/11-04. (Last accessed August 25, 2019).

2.   DOL Technical Release No. 2011-04, Guidance on Rebates for Group Health Plans Paid Pursuant to the Medical Loss Ratio Requirements of the Public Health Service Act (December 2, 2011), at https://www.dol.gov/agencies/ebsa/employers-and-advisers/guidance/technical-releases/11-04. (Last accessed August 25, 2019).

The DOL states that MLR rebates may be ERISA plan assets in whole or part, depending on various factors, including the terms of the insurance contract and plan documents. Quite often, there will be no specific provisions in either the insurance contract or the employer's health insurance plan. In that case, the 2011 Technical Release offers guidance on how to deal with the MLR refunds.

Assuming the plan documents, the insurance contract, and other extrinsic evidence do not resolve the allocation issue, the DOL says the portion of a rebate that is attributable to employee contributions belongs to the participants. Any portion of a rebate that constitutes ERISA plan assets must be used for the exclusive benefit of plan participants and beneficiaries.

For an ERISA plan, the employer may never retain more than the amount of premiums and plan expenses paid by the employer. Otherwise, this would be a breach of fiduciary duty and a prohibited transaction under ERISA. The DOL guidance directs employers to look to who paid the premiums for the health plan for the year to which the MLR rebate relates to determine whether the rebate is owned by the plan if a trust, the employer, or the employees.

- If the employer paid entire premium, the employer may retain the entire rebate.

- If a trust or the employees paid the entire premium, the entire rebate belongs to the trust or employees.

- If the employer and employees each paid a specified percentage of the premium, they each are entitled to the rebate based on those percentages.

- If the employer was required to pay a fixed amount and participants were responsible for paying any additional costs, then the portion of the rebate under such a policy that does not exceed the participants' total amount of prior contributions during the relevant period would be attributable to participant contributions.

- If participants paid a fixed amount and the employer was responsible for paying any additional costs, then the portion of the rebate under such a policy that did not exceed the employer's total amount of prior contributions during the relevant period would not be attributable to participant contributions.

324. How does an employer decide how amounts belonging to employees are used?

The preferred option for participant rebate funds is to return them to the participants. If that is not cost effective, then the employee's share of the rebate can be used to reduce participant contributions due within the three months after the rebate is received, or to enhance benefits. DOL Technical Release 2011-04[1] states that if a fiduciary finds that the cost of distributing shares

---

1.   DOL Technical Release No. 2011-04, Guidance on Rebates for Group Health Plans Paid Pursuant to the Medical Loss Ratio Requirements of the Public Health Service Act (December 2, 2011), at https://www.dol.gov/agencies/ebsa/employers-and-advisers/guidance/technical-releases/11-04 . (Last accessed August 25, 2019).

of a rebate to former participants (terminated employees who participated in the program during the year for which the rebates are paid), approximates the amount of those proceeds, the fiduciary may properly decide to allocate the proceeds to current participants based upon a reasonable, fair and objective allocation method If there are former participants who cannot be located after use of a locator service, then the plan should be followed. If the plan is silent, it would seem reasonable to add those funds to the amounts being distributed to current and former participants.

Making Payment to Employees Is Fail-Safe. As a practical matter, employers may return 100 percent of the Medical Loss Ratio (MLR) rebate to participants, even when the employers legally could retain all or a portion of the rebate as the employer's share under the rules discussed in Q 323. This approach assures compliance with ERISA's fiduciary requirements and allows the employer to communicate positive news to employees. When there are terminated employees who were participants during the year to which the rebate is attributable, they too are entitled to their share of the rebate unless they cannot be located with reasonable effort (a locator service should be used) or the refund is not cost-effective, as discussed above in Q 315.

325. What are the special considerations when an employer has a plan with several insurance options?

Where an employer has several health insurance plans, such as an HMO, PPO, and high deductible options, those employers must distribute the Medical Loss Ratio (MLR) rebates only to participants that were covered by the specific policy for which the rebate is issued. The DOL states that using rebates to benefit non-participants is a breach of ERISA fiduciary duties.[1]

326. What are the special issues if insurance is paid in part by employee pre-tax cafeteria plan payments?

With respect to an Medical Loss Ratio (MLR) rebate to a cafeteria plan under Internal Revenue Code section 125, refunding part or all of the rebate to participants should not be a violation of the "use it or lose it" rule of the regulations because that rule applies to healthcare and dependent care flexible spending accounts, not to premium conversion amounts that are plan assets. The rebate should not be used to reduce the employees' contribution for the next three months. That would be an impermissible election change unless this is done by virtue of the fact that the employee's share of the premiums are reduced, and the plan allows for changing payroll deductions based on changes in the insurance premiums.

327. How do the Medical Loss Ratio (MLR) rebate rules differ for non-ERISA plans?

Plans of state and local governments and churches are exempt from ERISA unless their plan documents make them subject to ERISA. If not subject to ERISA, they are not bound by the three-month rule and can apply the rebates to reduce the costs for the upcoming plan year.

---

1.   *See, e.g.,* Advisory Opinions 2001-02A (February 15, 2001); 99-08A (May 20, 1999); 94-31A (September 9, 1994); and 92-02A (January 17, 1992).

328. What is the income tax treatment for Medical Loss Ratio (MLR) rebates paid to owners of individual health insurance policies issued in the individual market?

For individual market coverage (non-group individual policies), the rebate is not taxed if the individual did not deduct the premiums for that year to which the MLR rebate relates.[1] If the individual did deduct the premium, the rebate is taxable,[2] including a premium deducted by a sole proprietor or partner.[3]

329. What are the income tax rules for Medical Loss Ratio (MLR) rebates paid to employees in employer-sponsored group health insurance plans?

For those participating in insured group plans, the concepts are the same: the rebates are not taxable if paid with after-tax (no deduction taken) dollars, whether paid directly to the employee by the insurer or by the insurer to the employer and in turn by the employer to the employee.[4] However, if the employee deducted the premium on the employee's personal income tax return, the rebate is taxable income.[5] If a person participates in the plan in the year in which the rebate is paid, but not the prior year, and receives a share of the rebate, the rebate is not taxed.[6]

Where the insurance policy is a group policy, and the employee paid the employee's share of the premium with pretax dollars (amounts not taxed to an employee, such as a salary reduction payment through a cafeteria plan that is not reported as taxable income to the employee) in the plan year to which the rebate relates, the following rules apply:

- If the employer applies the employee's share of the rebate to reduce the employee's share of the premium, this is taxed to the employee.[7]

- The rebate is also taxable in the year paid if it is paid to the employee and is "wages" subject to payroll and employment taxes.[8]

1. IRS Medical Loss Ratio (MLR) FAQs Q&A-2 at https://www.irs.gov/newsroom/medical-loss-ratio-mlr-faqs (Last accessed August 25, 2019).
2. IRS Medical Loss Ratio (MLR) FAQs Q&A-3 at https://www.irs.gov/newsroom/medical-loss-ratio-mlr-faqs (Last accessed August 25, 2019).
3. IRS Medical Loss Ratio (MLR) FAQs Q&A-4 at https://www.irs.gov/newsroom/medical-loss-ratio-mlr-faqs (Last accessed August 25, 2019).
4. IRS Medical Loss Ratio (MLR) FAQs Q&A-5&6 at https://www.irs.gov/newsroom/medical-loss-ratio-mlr-faqs. (Last accessed August 25, 2019).
5. IRS Medical Loss Ratio (MLR) FAQs Q&A-7 at https://www.irs.gov/newsroom/medical-loss-ratio-mlr-faqs. (Last accessed August 25, 2019).
6. IRS Medical Loss Ratio (MLR) FAQs Q&A-8&9 at https://www.irs.gov/newsroom/medical-loss-ratio-mlr-faqs (Last accessed August 25, 2019).
7. IRS Medical Loss Ratio (MLR) FAQs Q&A-10 https://www.irs.gov/newsroom/medical-loss-ratio-mlr-faqs (Last accessed August 25, 2019).
8. IRS Medical Loss Ratio (MLR) FAQs Q&A-11 at https://www.irs.gov/newsroom/medical-loss-ratio-mlr-faqs. (Last accessed August 25, 2019).

Where the insurance policy is a group policy, the rebate is paid to participants regardless of whether they participated in the plan in the year generating the rebate, and the employee pays the employee's share of the premium in the current plan year with pretax dollars:

- If the employee's share of the rebate is allocated to reduce the cost of insurance for the year in which the rebate was received, the rebate is taxable and is wages in the year paid subject to employment taxes.[1]

- If the rebate is paid to the employee, who participated in the plan in the year for which the rebated is paid, the rebate is taxable and is wages in the year paid subject to employment taxes.[2]

If the rebate is paid to the employee, who did not participate in the plan in the year for which the rebated is paid, the rebate is taxable and is wages in the year paid subject to employment taxes.[3]

330. Are self-funded plans subject to the MLR reporting and rebating requirements?

No. Section 2718(a) of the PHSA and the regulation[4] provide that the MLR requirements apply to health insurance issuers offering group or individual health insurance coverage. A self-funded (self-insured) plan is not a health insurance issuer, as defined by section 2791(b)(2), and thus is not subject to the MLR requirements. It does not matter if the self-funded plan is subject to the Employee Retirement Income Security Act of 1974 (ERISA) or if it is a non-ERISA plan.

331. Are health insurance benefits provided through a Medicaid Managed Care Organization (MCO) though a state Medicaid agency subject to the MLR reporting and rebate requirements?

No. Section 2718(a) of the PHSA applies to health insurance issuers offering employer group or individual health insurance coverage. Medicaid coverage offered under a contract with a state Medicaid agency is governed by Title XIX of the Social Security Act and regulations at 42 CFR Part 438, and not by state insurance law. Under these circumstances, issuers are not offering group health insurance coverage as defined under section 2791(b)(4) of the PHSA because the coverage is not offered in connection with a group health plan, nor are they offering individual health insurance coverage as defined under section 2791(b)(5) of the PHSA because the coverage is not offered to individuals in the individual market.

---

1.   IRS Medical Loss Ratio (MLR) FAQs Q&A-12 at https://www.irs.gov/newsroom/medical-loss-ratio-mlr-faqs (Last accessed August 25, 2019).
2.   IRS Medical Loss Ratio (MLR) FAQs Q&A-13 at https://www.irs.gov/newsroom/medical-loss-ratio-mlr-faqs. (Last accessed August 25, 2019).
3.   IRS Medical Loss Ratio (MLR) FAQs Q&A-14 at https://www.irs.gov/newsroom/medical-loss-ratio-mlr-faqs. (Last accessed August 25, 2019).
4.   45 CFR §158.102.

332. Are health insurance benefits provided through CMS through Medicare, such as Medicare Advantage or Medicare Part D prescription coverage subject to the MLR reporting and rebate requirements?

No. Section 2718(a) of the PHSA applies to health insurance issuers offering group or individual health insurance coverage. Medicare Advantage plans and Medicare Part D prescription drug plans are not group health insurance coverage as defined under section 2791(b)(4) of the PHSA (because the coverage is primarily provided under a contract with the Medicare program not an employer group health plan) or individual health insurance coverage as defined under section 2791(b)(5) of the PHSA (because the coverage is not offered to individuals in the individual market). Such coverage is instead subject to a comprehensive regulatory scheme under Parts C and D of Title XVIII of the Social Security Act and regulations at 42 CFR Parts 422 and 423.

Summary of Benefits and Coverage (SBC) Requirement for Insurers and Employers

333. Are insurance companies and health plans required to prepare and distribute to participants/insureds a Summary of Benefits and Coverage (SBC)?

Yes, for those providing essential health benefits, and they also must provide a Uniform Glossary, a list of important defined terms. This health reform requirement[1] applies to essential health benefits and not "excepted benefits." Where a plan is insured, the insurer is required to prepare the SBC, and the employer or other plan sponsor is required to distribute it annually in a timely manner. A self-funded plan must prepare its own SBC. Where an employer has several health benefit package options, this requirement will require coordination. A new SBC has been finalized and is available at the Department of Labor website.[2]

334. What guidance has been provided for the SBC requirement?

The DOL, HHS, and IRS issued on April 23, 2013:

(1)   FAQs, Part XIV,[3] addressing changes to the summary of benefits and coverage (SBC) effective for coverage beginning on or after January 1, 2014, and before January 1, 2015.

(2)   An updated SBC template.[4]

---

1.   PHSA §2715(a), ERISA Sec. 715, and IRC Sec. 9815.

2.   https://www.dol.gov/sites/default/files/ebsa/laws-and-regulations/laws/affordable-care-act/for-employers-and-advisers/sbc-completed-final.pdf.

3.   FAQs at http://www.dol.gov/ebsa/faqs/faq-aca14.html . (Last Accessed August 25, 2019).

4.   SBC Template at https://www.cms.gov/CCIIO/Resources/Forms-Reports-and-Other-Resources/Downloads/SBC-Sample-Completed-MM-508-fixed-4-12-16.pdf (Last Accessed August 25, 2019).

(3)   Sample completed SBC[1] (2018 version).

More information can be found at the DOL website.[2]

335. What is new in the updated SBC template?

The updated sample SBC template (and sample completed SBC) require information about whether the plan or coverage provides "minimum essential coverage" and satisfies the "minimum value" standard. The SBC template for the first year of applicability did not require this information. A copy of a completed updated sample SBC template is located in Appendix A.

To the extent that it would be administratively burdensome for a plan or insurer to modify its SBCs to add this new information, the agencies indicate that no enforcement action will be taken for using the previous template, provided that the necessary minimum essential coverage and minimum value information is set forth in a cover letter or other disclosure furnished with the SBC. Model language is provided for this purpose.

The SBC disclosures of minimum essential coverage and minimum value is important for employees. Enrollment in minimum essential coverage is required to avoid individual mandate penalties. Additionally, information about minimum value is needed for determining potential eligibility for subsidized Exchange coverage. An employee is not eligible for subsidies for health insurance purchased on an Exchange if he or she is offered employer minimum essential coverage that provides minimum value and is affordable.

These 2015 final regulations[3] finalized the December 2014 proposed regulations, with the following minor changes:

- Clarify when and how a plan or issuer must provide an SBC.

- Add to the rules to prevent unnecessary duplication in providing the SBC.

- Streamline the SBC template, but also add certain information that will be useful to consumers.

- Make permanent some of the SBC enforcement safe harbors and transitions.

Additionally, for individual policies sold through the Marketplace, the final regulations also require that health insurance issuers must notify consumers at the time of enrollment if the abortion services available under the policy are the type for which public funding (i.e., subsidies) are prohibited.

---

1.   Sample Completed SBC at https://www.dol.gov/sites/default/files/ebsa/laws-and-regulations/laws/affordable-care-act/for-employers-and-advisers/sbc-completed-final.pdf (Last accessed August 25, 2019).

2.   https://www.dol.gov/agencies/ebsa/laws-and-regulations/laws/affordable-care-act/for-employers-and-advisers/summary-of-benefits. (Last accessed August 25, 2019).

3.   Summary of Benefits and Coverage and Uniform Glossary; Final Rules, 26 CFR Part 54, 29 CFR Part 2590, 45 CFR Part 147, 80 Fed. Reg. 34292 (June 16, 2015).

For group health plans, the final regulations generally apply to coverage that begins on or after September 1, 2015. For individual policies the requirements apply to coverage that begins on or after January 1, 2016.

On April 6, 2016, the Department of Labor, the Department of the Treasury and Department of Health and Human Services finalized a new SBC Template, Uniform Glossary and Instructions.

The new version includes:

- A new question identifying any services that are covered before the deductible is met

- Instructions requiring specific language as to whether the plan has "embedded" or "non-embedded" deductibles or out of pocket maximum.

- Instructions requiring specific language as to whether the plan has a tiered network to notify participants that costs for in-network services can vary based on tier of facility or physician.

- Instructions requiring a list of core limitations such as cost-sharing for in-network services does not apply to out of pocket costs, prior authorization requirements, limits on visits, exclusions such as generic vs. brand name drugs.

- New coverage example of a simple fracture.

- Statement detailing whether the plan meeting Minimum Essential Coverage (MEC) and Minimum Value (MV).

336. Are there any changes to the glossary, instructions, or coverage examples?

Yes, the glossary, instructions and coverage examples have been re-written for 2018. At time of printing no changes had been made for 2020.

A new glossary has been issued and can be found here.[1]

New instructions (last updated April 2017) for completing the Group Coverage can be found here.[2]

New instructions for completing the Individual Health insurance coverage can be found here.[3]

Information regarding Coverage Example is located here.[4]

---

1.   https://www.dol.gov/sites/default/files/ebsa/laws-and-regulations/laws/affordable-care-act/for-employers-and-advisers/sbc-uniform-glossary-of-coverage-and-medical-terms-final.pdf. (Last accessed August 25, 2019).

2.   https://www.dol.gov/sites/default/files/ebsa/laws-and-regulations/laws/affordable-care-act/for-employers-and-advisers/sbc-uniform-glossary-of-coverage-and-medical-terms-final.pdf. (Last accessed August 25, 2019).

3.   https://www.dol.gov/sites/default/files/ebsa/laws-and-regulations/laws/affordable-care-act/for-employers-and-advisers/sbc-instructions-for-completing-the-individual-health-insurance-coverage-final.pdf. (Last accessed August 25, 2019).

4.   https://www.cms.gov/Regulations-and-Guidance/Regulations-and-Guidance.html?redirect=/home/regsguidance.asp. (Last accessed August 25, 2019).

337. What impact do the SBC changes have on annual limits?

While no changes have been made to the SBC template or the sample completed SBC regarding annual limits, there is recognition that, for plan years beginning on or after January 1, 2014, the prohibition on imposing annual limits on the dollar value of essential health benefits will take effect. Thus, the agencies have indicated that no enforcement action will be taken against a plan or insurer that modifies its SBC for the second year of applicability by removing the entire row containing the question "Is there an overall annual limit on what the plan pays?"

338. What if there is more than one benefit package for essential health benefits?

A plan sponsor may offer more than one essential health benefits benefit package, such as a choice among an HMO, a PPO, and a self-insured option, or a high deductible option paired with an HSA. In such a case, for a newly eligible participant, SBCs for each benefit package must be distributed. For those already enrolled, the SBC for the option previously selected must be distributed.[1] In addition, the SBC for any benefit package must be provided within seven days of a participant or insured's request.[2]

339. Does the SBC/Uniform Glossary requirement apply to grandfathered plans?

Yes.[3]

340. What plans are exempt from the SBC and Uniform Glossary requirements? What about HSAs, HRAs, QSE-HRAs, MERPs, health FSAs, EAPs, and wellness programs?

Any plan or policy that is not an essential health benefit need not comply with these rules.[4] Thus, policies and plans that provide "excepted benefits" need not comply. Generally, health savings accounts, health reimbursement accounts (medical expense reimbursement accounts), and health flexible spending accounts are "excepted benefits." Where the employer provides a High Deductible Health Plan (HDHP) that funds HSAs, the role of the HSA is mentioned when discussing the HDHP.[5] When stand-alone HRAs and health FSAs are not excepted benefits, they must comply with the SBC/Uniform Glossary rules.[6] Plans in which HRAs are integrated with other coverage may use one SBC.[7] In this case, the HRA plan administrator is responsible for the SBC's description of the HRA's coverage.[8]

---

1.   Treas. Reg. §54.9815-2715(a)(1)(ii); DOL Reg. §2590.715-2715(a)(1)(ii); HHS Reg. §147.200(a)(1)(ii).
2.   Treas. Reg. §54.9815-2715(a)(1)(ii)(F); DOL Reg. §2590.715-2715(a)(1)(ii)(F); HHS Reg. §147.200(a)(1)(ii)(F).
3.   PPACA, §§1251(a) and 10101(d) (2010).
4.   Preamble to Final Rule: Summary of Benefits and Coverage and the Uniform Glossary, 77 Fed. Reg. 8668, 8670 (February 14, 2012).
5.   Preamble to Final Rule: Summary of Benefits and Coverage and the Uniform Glossary, 77 Fed. Reg. 8668, 8670–8671 (February 14, 2012).
6.   Preamble to Final Rule: Summary of Benefits and Coverage and the Uniform Glossary, 77 Fed. Reg. 8668, 8671 (February 14, 2012).
7.   HHS, DOL & TREASURY, FAQs About the Affordable Care Act Implementation Part VIII, Q&A-6, at https://www.dol.gov/sites/default/files/ebsa/about-ebsa/our-activities/resource-center/faqs/aca-part-viii.pdf. (Last accessed August 14, 2018). (Last accessed August 25, 2019).
8.   HHS, DOL & TREASURY, FAQs About the Affordable Care Act Implementation Part IX, Q&A-10, at https://www.dol.gov/sites/default/files/ebsa/about-ebsa/our-activities/resource-center/faqs/aca-part-ix.pdf (Last accessed August 25, 2019).

The SBC rules do not discuss employee assistance programs (EAPs). Whether the SBC requirements apply depends on whether the EAP is a group health plan. EAPs offer a range of benefits, such as counseling for alcohol and substance abuse, marital, family, and personal problems, stress, anxiety, grief, finances, retirement as well as childcare and elder care. These benefits are not included in the model SBC. Thus, EAPs are governed by the rule that where a plan's terms cannot reasonably be described in a manner consistent with the template and instructions, the plan or insurer must describe the terms using its best efforts to do so in accordance with the instructions and prescribed format.[1] Where an EAP is offered to employees, whether or not they are covered in the plan providing essential health benefits, it should seem that the SBC would not mention the EAP.

A wellness program may or may not be part of a group health plan. The FAQs refer to a wellness program that is an "add on" to major medical coverage that could affect the individual's cost-sharing and other information on the SBC. In such circumstances, the agencies explain that the coverage examples (discussed in Q 346) should note the assumptions used in creating them.[2] The sample SBC provides an example of how to describe a diabetes wellness program.[3]

341. What is the reason for the SBC requirement?

The SBC and a Uniform Glossary[4] of commonly used terms are to be distributed to all persons with essential health benefits in an individual policy or group plan. It applies to grandfathered policies and plans. The purpose is to provide a uniform summary of important provisions to assist individuals in understanding their coverage and provide the ability to compare it to other available options on an "apples to apples" basis.

It is intended to help consumers compare and select coverages that best meet their needs by providing understandable language explanation of health plan benefits.

The SBC must include the following:

1.   Uniform definitions of standard insurance terms and medical terms allowing customers to compare health coverage and understand the terms and exceptions of coverage.

2.   Coverage descriptions for each type of benefit including cost sharing.

3.   Exceptions, reductions and limitations of coverage.

4.   Cost-sharing provisions, including deductibles, co-insurance and co-pay requirements.

---

1.   Preamble: Summary of Benefits and Coverage and the Uniform Glossary, 77 Fed. Reg. 8668, 8674–8675 (February 14, 2012).

2.   HHS, DOL & TREASURY, FAQs About the Affordable Care Act Implementation Part VIII, Q&A-6, at https://www.dol.gov/sites/default/files/ebsa/about-ebsa/our-activities/resource-center/faqs/aca-part-viii.pdf. (Last accessed August 25, 2019).

3.   See https://www.dol.gov/sites/dolgov/files/ebsa/laws-and-regulations/laws/affordable-care-act/for-employers-and-advisers/sbc-completed-final.pdf (Last accessed August 25, 2019).

4.   Final Rule: Summary of Benefits and Coverage and Uniform Glossary, 77 Fed. Reg. 8668 (February 14, 2012); Summary of Benefits and Coverage and Uniform Glossary – Templates, Instructions, and Related Materials; and Guidance for Compliance, 77 Fed. Reg. 8706 (February 14, 2012).

5. Renewability and continuation of coverage provisions.

6. Examples of coverage.

7. A statement detailing if the coverage provides minimum essential coverage and whether the plan's or coverage's share of the total allowed costs of benefits provided under the plan or coverage meets applicable requirements.

8. A statement explaining that the SBC is a summary and that the plan document, policy, certificate or contract of insurance should be read to determine the contractual provisions of coverage.

9. Contact information for questions and for obtaining a copy of the plan document or the insurance policy, certificate or contract of insurance.

10. For plans and issuers that maintain one or more networks of providers, a website address (or similar contact information) for obtaining a list of network providers.

11. For plans and issuers that use a formulary in providing prescription drug coverage, a website address (or similar contact information) for obtaining information on prescription drug coverage.

12. Website address for obtaining the uniform glossary, as well as a contact phone number to obtain a paper copy of the uniform glossary, and a disclosure that paper copies are available.

342. Who must distribute the SBC and Glossary, and what happens if they fail to do so?

For insured plans, the insurer must distribute them to the plan administrator, which is often the employer. The plan administrator must distribute them to the participants. For a self-insured plan, the plan administrator, unless the plan says otherwise, is responsible to prepare and distribute the SBC and glossary.[1] Thus, employers with insured plans should seek contractual protection by requiring the insurer to deliver the SBC with sufficient lead time that the plan's plan administrator can timely deliver the SBC and Glossary to participants. Alternatively, the employer contractually can require the insurer to distribute the SBC to participants, which eliminates the employer and plan administrator for any penalty liability.[2]

Those responsible for preparation and delivery of the SBC and glossary are subject to substantial penalties for failure timely to do so. As discussed earlier in Q 238 as to the enforcement of the health reform coverage mandates, the law imposes a penalty of up to $1,000 per day per affected individual (per participant) for willful violations of the SBC rules for group health plans. For an insured plan, the insurer and plan administrator are each potentially subject to this penalty because the insurer must distribute the SBC to the plan administrator, and the

---

1. Treas. Reg. §54.9815-2715(a)(1)(iii)(A); DOL Reg. §2590.715-2715(a)(1)(iii)(A); HHS Reg. §147.200(a)(1)(iii)(A).
2. Treas. Reg. §54.9815-2715(a)(1)(iii)(A); DOL Reg. §2590.715-2715(a)(1)(iii)(A); HHS Reg. §147.200(a)(1)(iii)(A).

plan administrator must distribute it to the participants. Additionally, the penalty tax upon a noncomplying plan sponsor is $100 per day of noncompliance per affected individual,[1] and the violations must be self-reported on IRS Form 8928. The tax may be higher where violations occurred or continued during a period under IRS examination or where the violations are more than minimal. The tax does not apply where the failure was based on reasonable cause and not on willful neglect,[2] and the failure is corrected within thirty days after the person knew or should have known that the failure existed.[3]

343. When is the SBC required to be distributed?

Open Enrollments, New Enrollments, Special Enrollments and Re-Enrollment. All health plans and insurers will provide an SBC to enrollees at important points in the enrollment process, including application and renewal. The SBC requirements apply to disclosures made to those enrolling or re-enrolling in group health plan coverage through an open enrollment period. For enrollments occurring outside of open enrollment, the requirements apply beginning on the first day of the first plan year.

SBC and Glossary on Demand. Whether shopping for health insurance or already enrolled in coverage, consumers will be able to request the SBC at any time, and health plans will have to provide it within seven business days. Consumers will also be able to request and receive the Uniform Glossary within seven business days.[4]

Material Modification: Mid-Year Change. To the extent a plan or policy implements a mid-year change that is a material modification that affects the content of the SBC, and that occurs other than in connection with a renewal or reissuance of coverage, a notice of modification must be provided sixty days in advance of the effective date of the change.[5]

A group health plan or insurer must provide notice of a plan change if it makes a material modification in any of the terms of the plan that is not reflected in the most recently provided SBC. A material modification[6] is any modification to the coverage offered under a plan that alone or in conjunction with other modifications is an important change in benefits or other terms of coverage to an average plan participant, including diminished or enriched benefits, coverage of previously excluded benefits, changes to cost sharing (copays or deductibles), premiums, or referrals requirements. However, only material modifications that would affect SBC content require plans and insurers to provide this notice. The notice may be provided in paper or electronic form, in accordance with the requirements discussed previously for providing the SBC.[7]

---

1. IRC Sec. 4980D, which does not apply to insurers.
2. IRC Sec. 4980D(c)(1).
3. IRC Sec. 4980D(c)(2). See IRC Sec. 4980D(c)(2)(B)(ii), which gives church plans 270 days after the date of mailing by the Secretary of a notice of default with respect to the plan's failure.
4. Treas. Reg. §54.9815-2715(a)(1)(ii)(F); DOL Reg. §2590.715-2715(a)(1)(ii)(F); HHS Reg. §147.200(a)(1)(ii)(F).
5. Treas. Reg. §54.9815-2715(b); DOL Reg. §2590.715-2715(b); HHS Reg. §147.200(b).
6. ERISA Sec. 102.
7. Treas. Reg. §54.9815-2715(b); DOL Reg. §2590.715-2715(b); HHS Reg. §147.200(b).

This requirement can be satisfied either by a separate notice describing the material modification or an updated SBC containing it. For ERISA-covered group health plans, this will satisfy the requirement to provide a Summary of Material Modification under ERISA.[1]

COBRA Continuation Notice. As discussed in Q 348, the SBC must contain a verbatim statement about state and COBRA continuation options.

344. To whom must an SBC be provided?

The SBC requirement applies to all health insurance plans, individual and group, and all employer sponsored plans, both insured and self-insured, grandfathered, grandmothered and nongrandfathered. Persons in any such plan or arrangement must receive an SBC.

345. May the SBC be distributed electronically?

Yes. The SBC can be distributed electronically to participants in an ERISA welfare benefit plan if the Department of Labor's requirements are met.[2] Rules include:

The DOL provides a safe harbor which gives the employer guidelines for electronic distribution to plan participants who meet the following guidelines:[3]

- ready access to the employer's computer system (ready access does not include mere access to a central computer or kiosk at the job site);

- computer access is in the same area where they are expected to perform job duties (which can include the home, in the case of participants who work from home); and

- regularly access a computer as an integral part of their job duties.

Under the safe harbor, employers may still provide benefit plan documents electronically to employees not meeting the above requirements if:

- de an e-mail address where the documents can be delivered has been provided; and

- a consent form is electronically completed giving permission to receive the documents digitally.

Electronic delivery is not limited to particular media. Methods can include electronic mail, DVD, websites, as well as other more dated options such as diskettes or CD-ROM.

Employers are required to take "appropriate and necessary measures" to ensure actual receipt of the transmitted information (this includes a read-receipt or notification of undelivered email). In addition, employees receive notice prior to electronic distribution

---

1.   Preamble to Final Rule: Summary of Benefits and Coverage and the Uniform Glossary, 77 Fed. Reg. 8668, 8677 (February 14, 2012).
2.   DOL Reg. §2590.715-2715(a)(4)(ii)(A); Treas. Reg. §54.9815-2715(a)(4)(ii)(A). The requirements of the DOL are in DOL Reg. §2520.104b-1(c).
3.   DOL Reg 2520.104b-1(c).

stating that the documents will be delivered digitally. If posting on a website, employers must notify plan participants when documents have been posted on the website or intranet. Posting the plan documents without providing notice to participants of the posting does not satisfy the DOL's electronic delivery rules. Finally, employers must provide an explanation of why the information is important to participants and that the employee can request a paper version without cost.

346. What is the required format for the SBC?

A specified format is required, and detailed instructions for the format are provided.[1] Form language and formatting must be precisely reproduced, unless instructions allow or instruct otherwise. Unless otherwise provided, the plan or insurance company must use twelve-point font, and replicate all symbols, formatting, bolding, and shading on the specimen formats, which are provided later in this question. While the law requires four pages, the agencies (HHS, DOL, and Treasury) have interpreted this to be eight pages because the pages have a front and back side. Surprisingly, the size of the paper that one can use is not specified.

To the extent a plan's terms that are required to be described in the SBC template cannot reasonably be described in a manner consistent with the template and instructions, the plan or insurance company must accurately describe the relevant plan terms while using its best efforts to do so in a manner that is still as consistent with the instructions and template format as reasonably possible. Such situations may occur, for example:

- if a plan provides a different structure for provider network tiers or drug tiers than is represented in the SBC template;

- if a plan provides different benefits based on facility type (such as hospital inpatient versus non-hospital inpatient);

- in a case where a plan is denoting the effects of a related health flexible spending arrangement or a health reimbursement arrangement; or

- if a plan provides different cost sharing based on participation in a wellness program.

Plans and insurance companies must customize all identifiable company information throughout the document, including Web sites and telephone numbers.

The items shown on pages 1 and 2 must always appear on pages 1 and 2, and the rows of the chart must always appear in the same order. However, the chart rows shown on page 2 may extend to page 3 if space requires, and the chart rows on page 3 may extend to the beginning of page 4 if space requires. The Excluded Services and Other Covered Services section may appear on page 3 or page 4, but must always immediately follow the chart starting on page 2. The Excluded Services and Other Covered Services section must be followed by the Your Rights

---

1.   http://www.cms.gov/CCIIO/Programs-and-Initiatives/Consumer-Support-and-Information/Summary-of-Benefits-and-Coverage-and-Uniform-Glossary.html. (Last accessed September 5, 2016).

to Continue Coverage section, the Your Grievance and Appeals Rights section, and the Coverage Examples section, in that order.

A footer must appear at the bottom left of every page with the appropriate telephone number and Web site information.

The language used must be plain language and present the information in a culturally and linguistically appropriate manner, utilizing terminology understandable by the average individual.

Plans and insurance companies with questions about completing the SBC may contact the Department of Health and Human Services at SBC@cms.hhs.gov or the Department of Labor at 866-444-EBSA(3272).

Two coverage examples are required. CMS provides the information necessary to perform the two coverage example calculations for having a baby (normal delivery) and managing type 2 diabetes (routine maintenance of a well-controlled condition).[1]

The SBC for a group health plan need not be a standalone document. Plans or insurance companies may provide the SBC as a separate document or in combination with other summary materials, such as a Summary Plan Description (SPD), so long as the SBC information is "intact and prominently displayed at the beginning of the materials," such as after the Table of Contents in a SPD. However, SBCs issued for a plan in the individual market must be provided as a standalone document.[2]

A model SBC[3] and Uniform Glossary[4] of health coverage and medical terms has also been provided by CMS. These are provided in English, French Creole, German, Gujarti, Hindi, Italian, Japanese, Korean, Polish, Portugese, Russian, Vietnamese, Chinese, Spanish, and Tagalog.[5] An updated model SBC and Uniform Glossary are provided in Appendix A.

347. Can a state impose its own requirements on the SBC or Uniform Glossary?

No. Any state law that requires less information is preempted.[6] However, a state can impose additional disclosure requirements unless the plan is subject to ERISA, which preempts any contrary state law.[7] Private employer plans will be welfare benefit plans governed by ERISA. Government plans, church plans, and insurance policies purchased by individuals without significant employer involvement are not subject to ERISA.

---

1.   https://www.cms.gov/cciio/Resources/forms-reports-and-other-resources/index.html. (Last accessed August 14, 2018).
2.   https://www.cms.gov/cciio/Resources/forms-reports-and-other-resources/index.html. (Last accessed August 14, 2018).
3.   http://cciio.cms.gov/resources/files/sbc-sample.pdf. (Last accessed August 14, 2018).
4.   https://www.dol.gov/sites/default/files/ebsa/laws-and-regulations/laws/affordable-care-act/for-employers-and-advisers/sbc-uniform-glossary-of-coverage-and-medical-terms.pdf. (Last accessed August 14, 2018).
5.   https://www.healthcare.gov/language-resource/. (Last accessed September 5, 2016).
6.   PHSA §2715(e).
7.   Preamble to Final Rule: Summary of Benefits and Coverage and the Uniform Glossary, 77 Fed. Reg. 8668, 8678 (February 14, 2012); ERISA Sec. 514(b)(2)(B).

348. Is the SBC used in connection with COBRA continuation coverage?

Yes. The exact language in the SBC template must be used without change.[1] The SBC template includes a section called "Your Rights to Continue Coverage." The instructions to this section of the template provide different required language for group and for individual coverage. For group coverage, the language provides a general statement about state and federal continuation coverage rights that "must appear without alteration," as follows:

If you lose coverage under the plan, then, depending upon the circumstances, Federal and State laws may provide protections that allow you to keep health coverage. Any such rights may be limited in duration and will require you to pay a premium, which may be significantly higher than the premium you pay while covered under the plan. Other limitations on your rights to continuation coverage may also apply. For more information on your rights to continue coverage, contact the plan at [contact number]. You may also contact your state insurance department, the U.S. Department of Labor, Employee Benefits Security Administration at 1-866-444-3272 or www.dol.gov/ebsa, or the U.S. Department of Health and Human Services at 1-877-267-2323 x61565 or www.cciio.cms.gov.[2]

This section must be placed, as indicated in the template and instructions, after the section entitled "Other Covered Services" and before the section entitled "Your Grievance and Appeals Rights."

Exchange Notice Required

349. What is the Exchange Notice Requirement for employers?

FAQ guidance[3] provides that Exchange notices are required to all employees about the health insurance marketplace exchanges after October 1, 2013, and each year thereafter as well as to new employees on the date of hire.[4] The Department of Labor considers providing notice within 14 days of hire to meet the new employee requirement. Employers of all sizes, whether or not they have health plans, that are subject to the Fair Labor Standards Act must provide all new hires and current employees with a written notice about the health benefit Exchange and some of the consequences if an employee decides to purchase a qualified health plan through the Exchange in lieu of employer-sponsored coverage.[5] (Regulations implementing the Notice of Exchange requirement will be issued by the Secretary of Labor; the FLSA is enforced by the DOL).

---

1. See What This Plan Covers and What it Costs: Instruction Guide for Group Coverage, February 2012, at https://www.cms.gov/CCIIO/Resources/Files/Downloads/instructions-group-final.pdf (Last accessed August 25, 2019).
2. What This Plan Covers and What it Costs: Instruction Guide for Group Coverage, February 2012, at https://www.cms.gov/CCIIO/Resources/Files/Downloads/instructions-group-final.pdf (Last August 25, 2019).
3. See FAQs About the Affordable Care Act Implementation Part V, Q&A-2, at https://www.dol.gov/sites/default/files/ebsa/about-ebsa/our-activities/resource-center/faqs/aca-part-v.pdf. (Last accessed August 25, 2019).
4. https://www.dol.gov/agencies/ebsa/laws-and-regulations/laws/affordable-care-act/for-employers-and-advisers/coverage-options-notice. (Last accessed August 25, 2019).
5. FLSA §18B.

Employers need to provide a Model Notice to Employers who provide a health care plan to some or all employees[1] as well as a Model Notice for Employers who do not provide a health care plan.[2] The Department of Labor has extended this requirement through March 31, 2020. Even if this expiration is not extended, the current version can still be used.

350. When must employers give employees this Exchange Notice?

This disclosure requirement originally was to go into effect for employers beginning on March 1, 2013. In January 2013, however, the DOL announced a delay in the statutorily prescribed March 1, 2013, effective date.[3] The effective date became October 1, 2013, and each year thereafter. See Q 349.

The Exchange Notice must inform the employees about the existence of the health benefit exchange and give a description of the services provided by the exchange. Additionally, it must explain how the employee may be eligible for a premium tax credit or a cost-sharing reduction if the employer's plan does not meet certain requirements. The Exchange Notice must inform employees that if they purchase a qualified health plan through the exchange, then they may lose any employer contribution toward the cost of employer-provided coverage, and that all or a portion of the employer contribution to employer-provided coverage may be excludable for federal income tax purposes. Finally, the Exchange Notice must include contact information for customer service resources within the exchange and an explanation of appeal rights. The notice requirement has been extended through March 31, 2020.

351. Which employers are subject to the Exchange Notice requirement?

The Exchange Notice requirement applies to employers that are subject to the FLSA. Although the FLSA's minimum wage and maximum hour provisions are generally limited to entities that are engaged in interstate commerce and have a gross annual volume of sales that is not less than $500,000[4] it is not clear that the Exchange Notice has this same limitation. As a result, its scope appears to be determined by the FLSA's definition of "employer," which generally includes "any person acting directly or indirectly in the interest of an employer in relation to an employee."[5]

352. Is there a penalty for failing to give the Exchange Notice?

No. The law provides no specific penalty for noncompliance. On September 11, 2013, the Department of Labor posted an FAQ on Notice of Coverage Options stating that an employer SHOULD provide notice of the Exchanges but that there is no penalty under the law.[6] In addition, the Small Business Administration posted a similar message the next day

---

1. https://www.dol.gov/sites/default/files/ebsa/laws-and-regulations/laws/affordable-care-act/for-employers-and-advisers/model-notice-for-employers-who-offer-a-health-plan-to-some-or-all-employees.pdf. (Expires 5/31/2020).
2. https://www.dol.gov/sites/default/files/ebsa/laws-and-regulations/laws/affordable-care-act/for-employers-and-advisers/model-notice-for-employers-who-do-not-offer-a-health-plan.pdf. (Expires 5/31/2020).
3. FAQs About the Affordable Care Act Implementation Part XI, Q&A-1 at https://www.dol.gov/sites/default/files/ebsa/about-ebsa/our-activities/resource-center/faqs/aca-part-xi.pdf ml. (Last accessed August 14, 2018).
4. 29 U.S.C. §§206 and 207.
5. 29 U.S.C. §203(d).
6. https://www.dol.gov/agencies/ebsa/about-ebsa/our-activities/resource-center/faqs/notice-of-coverage-options (Last accessed August 25, 2019).

which is no longer available online.[1] As of August 2019, there is still no penalty for failing to provide the Exchange Notice and the Department of Labor categorically states that there is no fine.[2]

HIPAA Electronic Transactions and Operating Rules

353. How has health reform expanded HIPAA's electronic transaction requirements?

HIPAA's provisions include standards for electronic transactions to reduce healthcare costs by encouraging the use of Electronic Data Interchange (EDI), standardize the electronic processing of health care claims, improve efficiency and effectiveness, and improve overall communication in the health care industry. Health reform[3] includes an expansion of HIPAA's electronic transaction requirements and requires HHS to adopt uniform standards and operating rules governing transactions with health plans.

HHS issued regulations[4] adopting operating rules for two HIPAA electronic transactions:

(1)   eligibility for a health plan and

(2)   healthcare claim status.

Further guidance is provided by CMS by establishing electronic standards for health care transactions.[5]

354. What are the HIPAA's adopted standards and operating rules?

HIPAA's uniform standards and operating rules governing transactions with health plans apply to all HIPAA-covered entities including

- Health plans

- Health Care Clearinghouses

- Health Care Providers who participate in electronic transactions. (This includes transactions beyond simply processing Medicaid and Medicare).

Any provider who accepts payment from any health plan or other insurance company must comply with HIPAA if they conduct the transactions electronically.

---

1.   https://www.sba.gov/blogs/myth-vs-fact-myth-3-business-owners-will-be-fined-if-they-dont-notify-their-employees-about.(This document is no longer available on sba.gov but is mentioned in other websites such as https://www.allbusiness.com/small-business-owners-health-care-marketplaces-opening-october-1st-notify-employees-9795-1.html.

2.   https://www.dol.gov/agencies/ebsa/about-ebsa/our-activities/resource-center/faqs/notice-of-coverage-options. (Last accessed August 25, 2019).

3.   PPACA §1104.

4.   76 Fed. Reg. 40458 (July 8, 2011).

5.   https://www.cms.gov/Regulations-and-Guidance/Administrative-Simplification/HIPAA-ACA/AdoptedStandardsandOperating Rules.html. (Last accessed August 25, 2019).

These providers must also have written agreements in place to ensure those that they do business with (covered entities) comply with HIPAA as well. HIPAA. Examples of business associates include clearinghouses and independent medical transcriptionists.

The following are adopted standards in place as of September 2019:

- ASC X12 Version 5050[1] is the adopted standard for all transactions except retail pharmacies

- Retail Pharmacies – two standards

    - Pharmacy and supplier transactions – NCPDP Version D.)

    - Medicaid subrogation – NCPDP Version 3.0

    - These are adopted from the National Council for Prescription Drug Programs (NCPDP)[2]

355. What is a covered entity under HIPAA?

HIPAA covers both individuals and organizations. Those who are required to be in compliance with HIPAA are referred to as "covered entities". These covered entities include health care plans, health care clearinghouses and some health care providers.

Health Plans: under HIPAA, a classification as a health plan includes:

- Health insurance companies

- HMOs, or health maintenance organizations

- Employer-sponsored health plans

- Medicare, Medicaid, military and veterans' health programs and other government-paid health care plans

Clearinghouses include organizations that process nonstandard health information to conform to standards for data content or format, on behalf of other organizations.

Providers who submit HIPAA transactions electronically are covered. These providers include, but are not limited to doctors, dentists, nursing homes, clinics, pharmacies, etc.

356. What is a business associate under HIPAA?

A business associate is an individual or company by a covered entity to help carry out its health care activities and functions. The covered entity must have a written business associate contract or other arrangement with the business associate that:

---

1.   https://www.cms.gov/Regulations-and-Guidance/Administrative-Simplification/HIPAA-ACA/AdoptedStandardsandOperating Rules.html (Last accessed August 25, 2019).
2.   https://www.ncpdp.org/home. (Last accessed August 25, 2019).

- Establishes specifically the reason that the business associate was hired, and

- Requires the business associate to comply with HIPAA

Examples of business associates include third-party administrators that handle claims processing, consultants preforming utilization reviews, health care clearinghouses that process claims, etc. Covered health care providers can be business associates of another covered entity.

357. What is a transaction under HIPAA?

A transaction is an electronic exchange of information between two parties to carry out financial or administrative activities related to health care. This can include the submission of a claim for payment.

HHS has adopted certain standard transactions for the electronic exchange of health care data. These transactions include:

- Claims and encounter information

- Payment and remittance advice

- Claims status

- Eligibility

- Enrollment and disenrollment

- Referrals and authorizations

- Coordination of benefits

- Premium payments

358. When is compliance required with these expanded requirements?

Compliance was required by January 1, 2013, for:

(1)   eligibility for a health plan; and

(2)   healthcare claim status.[1]

HIPAA required HHS to establish national standards for electronic transactions to improve the efficiency and effectiveness of the nation's health care system.

These standards apply to all HIPAA-covered entities:

- Health plans

- Health care clearinghouses

---

1.   76 Fed. Reg. 40458 (July 8, 2011).

- Health care providers who conduct electronic transactions, not just those who accept Medicare or Medicaid

Any provider who accepts payment from any health plan or other insurance company must comply with HIPAA if they conduct the adopted transactions electronically.

These providers must also have written agreements in place to ensure business associates comply with HIPAA. Examples of business associates include clearinghouses and independent medical transcriptionists.[1]

359. When Must Self-Insured Group Health Plans Certify Compliance with HIPAA's Transaction Standards?

Self-Insured Group health plans had to certify compliance with HIPAA's transaction standard by November 15, 2014, or November 15, 2015, depending on whether annual receipts were over $5 million.

HIPAA required HHS to establish standards for common transactions between covered entities (such as health plans and health care providers) to facilitate the electronic exchange of health information. Healthcare reform required HHS to adopt operating rules for each covered transaction to create uniform electronic standards. Health plans conducting these covered transactions must comply with the standards and the operating rules.

In addition, healthcare reform required health plans to:

(1)   obtain unique Health Plan Identifiers (HPIDs) (by November 15, 2014, for large plans with more than $5 million in annual receipts, while plans under that threshold have until Nov. 15, 2015; and

(2)   certify to HHS that their data and information systems are in compliance with applicable standards and operating rules.[2]

In January 2014, HHS issued proposed regulations[3] regarding the certification requirements for three covered transactions: eligibility for a health plan; health claim status; and healthcare electronic funds transfers and remittance advice. Certification requirements for the other covered transactions will be addressed in other guidance. Under the proposed regulations, health plans would have to provide a submission to HHS that includes the number of covered lives in the plan, and documentation of either of two permissible certifications of compliance. HHS will match the submissions against its list of HPIDs to verify that health plans have complied with this requirement.

The two permissible certifications of compliance, the HIPAA Credential and the Phase III CORE Seal, are administered by an independent Council for Affordable Quality Healthcare

1.   https://www.cms.gov/Regulations-and-Guidance/Administrative-Simplification/HIPAA-ACA/AdoptedStandardsandOperating Rules.html. (Last accessed August 25, 2019).
2.   PPACA §1173(h).
3.   45 CFR §160 AND 162 (Jan. 2, 2014), 79 Fed. Reg. 298 – 324 (Jan. 2, 2014).

Committee on Operating Rules (CAQH CORE). The certifications differ in their details, but both require a health plan to conduct external testing and submit an attestation signed by a senior-level executive indicating that, to the best of the applicant's knowledge, the entity is HIPAA-compliant for security, privacy, and the relevant transaction standards.

Pending finalization of the requirements for the certifications of compliance employers with self-funded health plans should develop a strategy for compliance. If a plan uses a TPA to conduct covered transactions, the employer will want to ensure that the TPA is able to conduct required testing and provide the necessary documentation to enable your plan to obtain a certification of compliance.

360. What should group health plan sponsors do to comply with these expanded requirements?

Most health plans do not process their own electronic transactions but instead engage a third party (called a "business associate") to process them. In this case, plan sponsors should ensure the relevant documents (such as a business associate agreement, a trading partner agreement, and policies and procedures) are consistent with these rules. Plan sponsors' business associate agreements should require that the business associates as well as their agents and contractors comply with the rules.

361. What requirements are there for electronic funds transfer and health claims attachment transactions?

HHS has established standards for electronic funds transfer and health claims attachment transactions. HHS has issued regulations called "Health Care Electronic Funds Transfers (EFT) and remittance advice."[1] These new standards deal with EFT payments made through the Automated Clearing House (ACH) Network, and the remittance advice that explains the payment, the Explanation of Benefits (EOB).[2]

362. What new development has occurred relating to HPIDs and OEIDs?

As required by health reform,[3] HHS issued regulations[4] establishing standards for a national unique Health Plan Identifier (HPID) and implementation of the HPID. The regulations also establish another entity identifier (OEID) for nonhealth plan entities that may need to be identified in standard transactions.[5] The standards are based on recommendations from the National Committee on Vital and Health Statistics (NCVHS).

On October 31, 2014, the HHS announced a delay in the implementation of the regulations concerning use of the HPID. In hearings in front of the NCVHS, on May 3, 2017, a

---

1. 45 CFR 162.1601 – Health care Electronic Fund Transfers (EFT) and remittance advice transaction.
2. 45 CFR 162.1602 – Standards for health care Electronic Fund Transfers (EFT) and remittance advice transaction; 45 CFR 162.1603 – Operating rules for health care electronic funds transters (EFT) and remittance advice transaction.
3. PPACA §1104(c)(1).
4. Administrative Simplification: Adoption of a Standard for a Unique Health Plan Identifier; Addition to the National Provider Identifier Requirements; and a Change to the Compliance Date for ICD-10-CM and ICD-10-PCS Medical Data Code Sets, 77 Fed. Reg. 22950 (April 17, 2012).
5. Prop. HHS Reg. §162.514.

number of health care organizations, including the American Dental Association, the American Hospital Association, the American Medical Association and the Medical Group Management Association testified in favor of changing the rule to eliminate to the use of the HPID in electronic transactions and use the HPID solely for use by CMS in health care plan compliance related activities. NCVHS responded by sending a letter to the Secretary of HHS with three recommendations – each focused on rescinding final rules and educating the industry on what comes next. The recommendations included:

(1)   HHS should rescind the HPID Final Rule adopted on September 5, 2012. This rule requires health plans to obtain and use the HPID

(2)   HHS should communicate its intent to rescind the HPID Final Rule to all affected industry stakeholders as soon as a decision is made. HHS should provide the applicable guidance on the effect a rescission may have on all parties involved.

(3)   HHS should continue with the 2014 HPID Enforcement Discretion until publication of the regulation rescinding the September 5, 2012 HPID Final Rule.

On December 19, 2018, the Department of Health and Human Services (HHS) published a notice of proposed rulemaking (NPRM) - CMS-0054-P - to modify 45 CFR 162.103 and repeal 45 CFR 162.502-514 to rescind the adoption of the Health Plan Identifier (HPID) and Other Entity Identifier (OEID). Following publication of the final rule in September 2012, HHS received feedback from stakeholders and the National Committee on Vital and Health Statistics (NCVHS) regarding provider burden, implementation costs, and inefficiencies. On October 31, 2014, HHS announced an enforcement discretion, meaning covered entities would not be penalized for non-compliance with the HPID final rule. During the comment period, and until a final rule is published, the enforcement discretion remains in effect for all covered entities.

The proposed rule would eliminate the regulatory requirement for health plans to obtain and use an HPID as well as eliminate the voluntary acquisition and use of the OEID. The proposed rule would also simplify the process for terminating the existing identifiers to minimize operational costs for covered entities.

363. What are the HPID rules for a Controlling Health Plan (CHP) and a Subhealth Plan (SHP)?

A Controlling Health Plan (CHP) is a health plan that controls its own business activities, actions, or policies, or is controlled by an entity that is not a health plan. Additionally, a CHP is an entity that directs the business activities, actions, or policies of one or more SHPs. All CHPs must obtain an HPID. A Subhealth Plan (SHP) is defined as a health plan whose business activities, actions, or policies are directed by a CHP. Health plans include group health plans, health insurance issuers, and HMOs.[1]

---

1.   45 CFR §162.103.

A CHP, which includes a self-insured CHP, would be required to obtain an HPID. A SHP would not be required to obtain an HPID but could obtain an HPID at the direction of its CHP or on its own initiative. A CHP also would be able to obtain HPIDs for its SHPs.[1]

If a CHP uses a single data processing center for all of its SHPs, the CHP may use one HPID for itself and its SHPs. Alternatively, if an SHP has its own processing center, the CHP could obtain a separate HPID for such SHPs or ask them to do so.

364. How are HPIDs and OEIDs used?

When and if implemented, a covered entity would be required to use an HPID when it identifies a health plan in a standard transaction. If a covered entity uses one or more business associates to conduct standard transactions, the covered entity would require them to use an HPID to identify the health plan in the standard transactions.[2]

Other uses for the HPID that are permitted, including in internal files, are

- to facilitate processing of healthcare transactions;

- on an enrollee's health insurance card;

- as a cross-reference in healthcare fraud and abuse files and other program integrity files and as an enumeration tool to facilitate health plan certification;

- in patient medical records to identify patients' healthcare benefit packages; and

- for reporting purposes.[3]

The OEID is a voluntary identifier for entities that are not health plans but need to be identified in standard transactions. HHS asked for comments as to whether use of an OEID should be required.[4]

365. What are the penalties for failure to comply with the requirements and operating rules?

Through the Social Security Act (SSA) HHS will conduct audits to ensure that health plans (including third parties, such as business associates) comply with requirements and operating rules.[5]

HHS can assess a penalty against a health plan for failing to meet the certification and documentation requirements.[6] HHS will assess a penalty of $1 per covered life up to a ceiling until the certification is complete.[7] The penalty doubles for any health plan that

---

1.   45 CFR §162.512.
2.   45 CFR §162.510.
3.   77 Fed. Reg. 22950, 22958 (April 17, 2012).
4.   77 Fed. Reg. 22950, 22962-63 (April 17, 2012).
5.   SSA §1173(i).
6.   SSA §1173(j)(1)(A).
7.   SSA §1173(j)(1)(B).

knowingly provides inaccurate or incomplete information in a statement of certification or documentation of compliance.[1] The annual penalty against a health plan may not exceed $20 per covered life and $40 per covered life if the plan knowingly has provided inaccurate or incomplete information.[2]

Automatic Enrollment – Repealed

366. What is the status of the requirement that employers automatically enroll employees in their health benefits plan?

The Affordable Care Act amended the Fair Labor Standards Act (FLSA) by adding a new section – section §18A which required employers with more than 200 full-time employees to automatically enroll new full-time employees into a health benefits plan and continue enrollment of current employees. Notices would have given the employee the option to "opt-out" if they wished.

The section had not yet been implemented because it was awaiting Department of Labor regulations. The pending regulations had not yet been created when on November 2, 2015, President Barack Obama signed the Bipartisan Budget Act of 2015,[3] which as one of its provisions repealed the automatic-enrollment requirement.

Employers may voluntarily decide to utilize automatic enrollment, including default or negative elections, but they have no requirement to do so. A default or negative enrollment is one in which the employee must return a timely written waiver of coverage. This is permitted under IRS Revenue Ruling 2002-20[4] and Internal Revenue Bulletin 2007-39.[5]

For most employers, it is likely this change was met with happiness over the cancellation of an unpopular compliance requirement.

New Health Insurance Nondiscrimination Provisions

367. What are the health insurance income tax nondiscrimination rules?

Prior to the Affordable Care Act, the Internal Revenue Code only imposed nondiscrimination rules on self-insured health plans. No benefits-related nondiscrimination rules applied to an insured health plan. Thus, an insured group health plan could cover management and other highly paid employees under terms that were more favorable than those applicable to other employees, or not even cover the other employees.

Self-insured plans and employers' medical expense reimbursement plans are subject to the nondiscrimination provisions of Internal Revenue Code section 105(h), in effect since 1980. Congress originally believed that insurance underwriting considerations limited abuses favoring

---

1.   SSA §1173(j)(1)(C).
2.   SSA §1173(j)(1)(E).
3.   H.R. 1314, Bipartisan Budget Act of 2015.
4.   Rev. Rule 2002-20.
5.   IRB 2007-39 https://www.irs.gov/irb/2007-39_IRB/ar14.html. (Last accessed August 15, 2018).

the highly paid in insured plans. However, underwriting practices in fact allowed plans to favor the highly compensated.

Health reform imposes similar rules to those that apply to self-insured plans or insured group health plans, other than grandfathered plans. The law does this in a very circular way. Health reform law[1] added new ERISA section 715 and Internal Revenue Code section 9815, respectively. Both ERISA section 715 and Code section 9815 incorporate by reference Public Health Service Act (PHSA) section 2716, which incorporates by reference the concepts of Internal Revenue Code section 105(h). The law leaves the details of the insured plan nondiscrimination rules to the regulations. It merely requires "rules similar to" those in Internal Revenue Code section 105(h), regarding nondiscrimination eligibility, nondiscriminatory benefits, and controlled groups.[2] These rules prohibit discrimination in favor of Highly Compensated Individuals (HCIs), who are generally the highest paid 25 percent of the employer's workforce.

368. How do the health insurance income tax nondiscrimination rules apply to retiree medical coverage?

There is an exception for retirees under the Internal Revenue Code section 105(h) self-insured nondiscrimination rules. It is not clear how the rule applies when the only retirees are highly compensated individuals, although it could be read that the exception to the nondiscrimination rule does apply when all of the retirees are HCIs.

Here is the regulation as relates to applying the nondiscrimination rule for retirees:[3]

(iii) Retired employees. To the extent that an employer provides benefits under a self-insured medical reimbursement plan to a retired employee that would otherwise be excludible from gross income under section 105(b), determined without regard to Internal Revenue Code section 105(h), such benefits shall not be considered a discriminatory benefit under this paragraph (c). The preceding sentence shall not apply to a retired employee who was a highly compensated individual unless the type, and the dollar limitations, of benefits provided retired employees who were highly compensated individuals are the same for all other retired participants. If this subdivision applies to a retired participant, that individual is not considered an employee for purposes of determining the highest paid 25 percent of all employees under paragraph (d) of this section solely by reason of receiving such plan benefits.

Retiree-only plans are excepted from the ACA rules.

---

1.   PPACA §§1001 and 1562(e), (f).
2.   PHSA §2716(a), which imposes such requirements in IRC Sec. 9815, and ERISA Sec. 715. PHSA §2716(a) requires nongrandfathered insured group health plans to satisfy the requirements of Code section 105(h)(2) (relating to prohibition on discrimination in favor of highly compensated individuals). For this purpose, "rules similar to the rules contained in" Code section 105(h)(3) (relating to nondiscriminatory eligibility), (4) (relating to nondiscriminatory benefits) and (8) (apply the rules to controlled groups). Code section 105(h)(5) (relating to which employees are "highly compensated") is not included, which means that the regulations are not bound to the highest paid 25 percent text in defining the group in favor of which a nongrandfathered insured plan cannot discriminate.
3.   Reg. §1.105-11(c)(3)(iii).

369. Will the income tax nondiscrimination rules for nongrandfathered group health insurance plans ever become effective?

The law provides that these nondiscrimination rules[1] were to be effective for nongrandfathered plans for plan years beginning on or after September 23, 2010. However, the IRS postponed the effective date until regulations are issued and the IRS announces a new effective date.[2] This had not yet occurred but it is expected that the nondiscrimination rules will ultimately apply to the nongrandfathered group health insurance plans as well. These rules are virtually the same as the ones that apply to self-insured plans. It appears quite likely that they will never become effective. As of September 2019, no action has yet been taken.

370. What is the consequence of violating the new health insurance non-discrimination rules?

As a result of incorporating the HIPAA penalty, the excise tax that applies in the event of a violation of the HIPAA requirements also applies in the event of a violation of these new nondiscrimination requirements.[3] The health insurance nondiscrimination rules for nongrand-fathered plans have different and potentially much harsher sanctions than for self-insured plans that fall under Internal Revenue Code section 105(h). For discriminatory self-insured plans, the highly compensated employees have taxable income based on the benefits paid by the employer. However, with respect to the new health insurance nondiscrimination requirements, the sanction is a $100 per day excise tax[4] on the "affected employees" and is paid by the employer or the plan in the case of a multiemployer plan. While the IRS has not yet issued any regulations on the penalty, its request for comments indicates that the term "affected employees" means all those who are not highly compensated. Thus, if an employer has an insured health plan that is not grandfathered and violates these new nondiscrimination rules for the plan year beginning on or after September 23, 2010, and if that employer has twenty nonhighly compensated employees, the penalty will be $2,000 per day (twenty employees X $100/day) as a result of having a discriminatory nongrandfathered health insurance plan.

371. What is the small employer exception to the application of the excise tax, and does it apply to avoid the nondiscrimination tax penalty?

Internal Revenue Code section 4980(D)(d)(1) contains an exception to the excise tax for small employers, but the language is somewhat ambiguous. It states:

In the case of a group health plan of a small employer which provides health insurance coverage solely through a contract with a health insurance issuer, no tax shall be imposed by this section on the employer on any failure (other than a failure attributable to section 9811) *which is solely because of the health insurance coverage offered by such issuer.* (Emphasis added.)

---

1.   https://www.irs.gov/pub/irs-irbs/irb11-02.pdf.

2.   IRS Notice 2011-1.

3.   Joint Committee Staff Technical Explanation of the Revenue Provisions of the Reconciliation Act of 2010, as amended, in combination with the Patient Protection and Affordable Care Act. (JCX-18-10) 3/21/10, p. 50.

4.   IRC Sec. 4980D.

It is not clear whether this exception applies to the new nondiscrimination rules or simply to a health insurance policy that does not meet federal requirements. The italicized language may mean that the exception will apply only if the insurance policy is discriminatory as opposed to the employer's plan being discriminatory. In other words, the small business exception may not apply if the plan, rather than the insurance policy, is nondiscriminatory. For the purpose of this exception, a small employer is defined as one with two to fifty employees.[1]

372. What are the issues involved in applying the nondiscrimination excise tax?

Internal Revenue Code section 4980D(a) imposes an excise tax on the failure of a group health plan to meet the requirements of Chapter 100 relating to group health plans. The amount of tax is $100 for each day in the noncompliance period with respect to each individual to whom such failure relates.[2] As noted in Q 369, Notice 2011-1 deferred the effective date of the insured plan nondiscrimination rules and indicates that the penalty will apply to Nonhighly Compensated Individuals ("NHCIs"). Notice 2011-1 states:

> [I]f an insured group health plan fails to comply with Code Sec. 105(h), it is subject to a civil action to compel it to provide nondiscriminatory benefits and the plan or plan sponsor is subject to an excise tax or civil money penalty of $100 per day *per individual discriminated against*. [Emphasis added.][3]

The noncompliance period is the period beginning on the date on which the failure occurs,[4] and ends on the date the failure is corrected.[5] A failure is treated as corrected if it is retroactively undone to the extent possible,[6] and the person to whom the failure relates is placed in a financial position that is as good as the position such person would have been in had the failure not occurred.[7]

373. What are the limits or exceptions to the application of the nondiscrimination excise tax on nongrandfathered insured plans?

There are a number of limitations on the amount of the tax. First, no tax is imposed on any failure during any period for which it is established to the satisfaction of the IRS that the person liable for the tax did not know, and, exercising reasonable diligence, would not have known that such failure existed.[8] For church plans,[9] no tax is imposed if the failure is corrected before the end of the correction period.[10] For most plans, no tax is imposed if the failure was due to reasonable cause and not to willful neglect,[11] and such failure is corrected during the thirty-day

---

1.   IRC Sec. 4980D(d)(1).
2.   IRC Sec. 4980D(b)(1).
3.   See also Notice 2010-63.
4.   IRC Sec. 4980D(b)(2)(A).
5.   IRC Sec. 4980D(b)(2)(B).
6.   IRC Sec. 4980D(f)(3)(A).
7.   IRC Sec. 4980D(f)(3)(B).
8.   IRC Sec. 4980D(c)(1).
9.   Defined in IRC Sec. 414(e).
10. IRC Secs. 414(e)(4)(c) and 4980D(c)(2)(B)(ii).
11. IRC Sec. 4980D(c)(2)(A).

period beginning on the first date the person otherwise liable for such loss knew, or exercising reasonable diligence would have known, that such failure existed.[1]

Notwithstanding these limits on the Internal Revenue Code section 4980D excise tax, in the case of one or more failures for an individual before the date a notice of examination of income tax liability is sent to the employer, and when such failure occurred or continued during the period under examination, there is a minimum tax with respect to such individual of not less than the lesser of $2,500, or the amount of tax that would have been imposed without regard to the limitations on tax.[2] To the extent that the violations are more than *de minimis* (an undefined term), $15,000 is substituted for $2,500.[3]

With respect to unintentional failures (i.e., those due to reasonable cause and not to willful neglect), the tax imposed on single employers for failures during the employer's tax year cannot exceed the lesser of:

- 10 percent of the aggregate amount paid or incurred by the employer (or predecessor employer) during the preceding tax year for group health plans; or

- $500,000.[4]

With respect to specified multiple employer health plans,[5] the excise tax cannot exceed the lesser of:

- 10 percent of the amount paid or incurred by such trust during the tax year to provide medical care directly or through insurance, reimbursement, or otherwise; or

- $500,000.[6]

However, if an employer is assessed a tax by reason of failure with respect to a specified multiple employer health plan, the limit is determined in the same manner as for a single employer plan, rather than for a specified multiple employer health plan.[7] For a failure due to reasonable cause and not to willful neglect, the IRS may waive all or a portion of the tax "to the extent that the payment of such tax would be excessive relative to the failure involved."[8]

---

1. IRC Sec. 4980D(c)(2)(B)(i).
2. IRC Sec. 4980D(b)((3)(A).
3. IRC Sec. 4980D(b)(3)(B).
4. IRC Sec. 4980D(c)(3)(A)(i).
5. A specified multiple employer health plan is a group health plan that is either a multiemployer plan or a multiple employer welfare arrangement (MEWA), as defined in section 3(40) of ERISA , as in effect on March 23, 2010. IRC Sec. 4980D(f)((2). IRC Sec. 4980D(c)(3)(ii) provides that if not all persons who are treated as a single employer for purposes of IRC Sec. 4980D have the same tax year, the tax years taken into account are determined under principles similar to the principles of IRC Sec. 1561. However, IRC Sec. 414(t), which provides for application of controlled group rules to various sections of the Code, references IRC Sec. 4980B, but not IRC Sec. 4980D. IRC Sec. 4980(D)(2)(A), for purposes of determining if an entity is a small employer, references sections 414(b)(c), (m), and (o).
6. IRC Sec. 4980D(c)(3)(B)(i). For purposes of this section, all plans of which the same trust forms a part are treated as one plan.
7. IRC Sec. 4980D(C)(3)(B)(ii).
8. IRC Sec. 4980D(C)(4).

The excise tax does not apply to a group health plan of a small employer[1] that provides health insurance coverage[2] solely through a contract with a health insurance issuer[3] with respect to any failure[4] that is solely because of the health insurance coverage offered by such issuer. The issues about the scope of this exception are discussed previously.

374. Who is liable to pay the excise tax?

Liability for the tax is generally imposed on the employer.[5] However, with respect to a multiemployer plan[6] or a failure under Internal Revenue Code section 9803 relating to guaranteed renewability with respect to a multiple employer welfare arrangement,[7] the tax is imposed on the plan.

375. Who must file to pay the excise tax?

The tax is paid using Form 8928[8] and must be filed by the following.

- Any employer, group health plan, plan administrator, or plan sponsor liable for the tax under section 4980B for failure to provide the required level of pediatric vaccine coverage or to offer continuation coverage to a qualified beneficiary

- Any employer or group health plan liable for the tax under section 4980D for failure to meet portability, access, renewability, and market reform requirements for group health plans under Internal Revenue Code sections 9801, 9802, 9803, 9811, 9812, 9813, and 9815

- Any employer liable for the tax under section 4980E for failure to make comparable Archer MSA contributions for all participating employees

- Any employer liable for the tax under section 4980G for failure to make comparable HSA contributions for all participating employees

376. How is the liability for the excise tax reported?

Employers subject to the excise tax must file Form 8928 Return of Certain Excise Taxes.[9] Under Chapter 43 of the Internal Revenue Code.[10] For single employer plans, the employer

---

1. IRC Sec. 4980D(d)(2)(A) defines a small employer as an employer who, with respect to a calendar year and a plan year, employed an average of at least two but not more than fifty employees on business days during the preceding calendar year and who employed at least two employees on the first day of the plan year. For these purposes, as for tax-qualified plans, all persons treated as a single employer under sections 414(b), (c), (m), and (o) are treated as one employer. With respect to an employer that was not in existence during the preceding calendar year, the determination of whether such employer is a small employer is based on the average number of employees that it is reasonably expected such employer will employ on business days in the current year. IRC Sec. 4980D(d)(2)(B). All references to "employer" include a reference to any predecessor of such employer. IRC Sec. 4980D(d)(2)(C).
2. IRC Sec. 4980D(d)(3) provides that health insurance coverage has the meaning set forth in IRC Sec. 9832.
3. IRC Sec. 4980D(d)(3) provides that health insurance issuer has the meaning set forth in IRC Sec. 9832.
4. The exemption for certain insured small employer plans does not apply to a failure described in IRC Sec. 9811, i.e. standards relating to benefits for mothers and newborns.
5. IRC Sec. 4980D(e)(1).
6. IRC Sec. 4980D(e)(2).
7. IRC Sec. 4980D(e)(3).
8. https://www.irs.gov/pub/irs-pdf/f8928.pdf (IRS Form 8928).
9. https://www.irs.gov/pub/irs-pdf/f8928.pdf.
10. Reg. §§54.6011-2 and 54.4980D-1, A-1(a).

must file the return on or before the due date for filing the employer's income tax return, without any extensions unless a separate extension request is filed properly for Form 8928.[1] It also must reflect the portion of the noncompliance period for each failure that occurs during the employer's tax year.[2] If the person liable for the excise tax is a specified multiple employer health plan, the return must be filed on or before the last day of the seventh month following the end of the plan's plan year.[3] The return is filed at the place specified in Form 8928 and the instructions, and the tax shown on the return is paid to the IRS office with which the return is filed, at the time and place for filing each return.

377. What is the penalty if an insured plan incorrectly believes that it is grandfathered, but it is not?

How should Internal Revenue Code section 4980D be applied if a nongrandfathered health plan fails one of the technical requirements because the employer believes it to be grandfathered? For example, if a nongrandfathered plan provides coverage for obstetrical or gynecological care or both and requires the designation of an in-network primary care provider, the plan may not require authorization or referral by the plan or any person for a female participant who seeks gynecological or obstetrical care provided by an in-network specialist i.e., an obstetrician or a gynecologist. Additionally, the plan must advise each participant that the plan cannot require authorization or referral for gynecological care.

What if the employer believes that the plan is grandfathered but it is not grandfathered because it was unaware of the notice or recordkeeping requirements of the regulations or because it inadvertently failed to satisfy them?

> *Example:* Alice, a plan participant, requests a gynecological exam with Dr. Brady, an in-network OB-GYN, the plan requires prior authorization from Alice's designated primary care provider, Dr. Welby, for the exam. Dr. Welby provides the authorization, and Alice sees Dr. Brady. This prior authorization for a woman to see an OB-GYN is not permitted for a nongrandfathered plan.

In the example in the preceding paragraph, when did the failure occur? A failure cannot occur until the status as a grandfathered health plan is lost, but the regulations do not specify when this occurs. No precise time is provided for the required notice, but presumably, it should have been provided during the open enrollment period, but it was not. Therefore, (1) every female participant and dependent (at least those above a certain age) was affected by the failure to receive the notice and (2) at least all individuals in that category who saw a gynecologist or obstetrician in that period and had requested an authorization from the primary care physician were affected by that failure.

However, the IRS could argue that the latter failure related to all female plan participants and dependents because they may not have sought to obtain authorization from their primary

---

1.   Reg. §54.6151-1. An automatic six-month extension for filing Form 8928 is available for applications filed on or after June 24, 2011, by submitting a Form 7004 on or before the prescribed day for filing the return and remitting the amount of the estimated tax liability. Reg. §54.6081-1(b).

2.   Reg. 54.6071-1(b)(1). An extension for filing the employer's income tax return does not extend the time for filing Form 8928. Reg. 54.4980D-1, A-1(b).

3.   Reg. §§54.6071-1(b)(2) and 54.4980D-1, A-1(c).

care physician for the OB-GYN treatment. It is not clear if, with respect to one individual, there can be multiple failures relating to one Code requirement.

Assuming there was a failure, when would it be corrected, if at all? The first requirement is that the failure be retroactively undone to the extent possible. The second requirement is that the person to whom the failure relates be placed in the same financial position in which he or she would have been had the failure not occurred. However, unless the primary care physician charged the participant for obtaining that authorization/referral, there was no financial detriment to the participant unless the referral process caused a delay in seeing the OB/GYN, and the OB/GYN increased its fees in the interim. If so, the detriment is the difference between those fees. Absent this, the failure arguably is self-correcting but it is unknown whether the IRS will recognize this concept.

378. What if the failure to meet the nondiscrimination rules is due to reasonable cause and not willful neglect?

As to whether the failure was due to reasonable cause and not to willful neglect, the issue in all likelihood will not be whether the plan sponsor had some reasonable basis for a position that it took, but rather a matter of inadvertence (in the example above about a plan that the employer thought was grandfathered but was not), whether a participant failed to receive an SPD or open enrollment material, or whether some documents relating to verification, or clarification of grandfathered health plan status were not maintained. In the context of an inadvertent error, it may not be clear that, by exercising reasonable diligence, the employer would have known if the failure occurred. If a participant fails to receive a summary plan description or a document is improperly discarded, it is unclear if reasonable diligence would have located the errors. The issue of what constitutes "reasonable diligence" is based on all relevant facts and circumstances.

If the failure to provide notice or retain records was due to erroneous advice from a plan's advisor, many cases address what constitutes reasonable cause and not willful neglect.

A failure to give a notice or to maintain records is not as serious as a HIPAA violation, such as discrimination due to health status, which was the type of action that initially resulted in the imposition of this excise tax that was enacted with HIPAA. At a minimum, the amount of excise tax for the violation of the group health plan rules applicable only to non-grandfathered group health plans that do not violate HIPAA should depend on whether the plan administrator believed in good faith, albeit erroneously, that the plan had grandfathered status.

Waiting Period Limits and Eligibility Requirements

379. What is a waiting period?

A waiting period is the time that must pass before coverage for a person who is *otherwise eligible for coverage* under the terms of the plan is effective if the person applies for it.[1] The waiting period for coverage cannot exceed ninety days.

---

1.   DOL Tech. Rel. 2012-01 (February 9, 2012); IRS Notice 2012-17 (February 10, 2012); Fact Sheets and Frequently Asked Questions at
      https://www.cms.gov/CCIIO/Resources/Fact-Sheets-and-FAQs/index.html. (Last accessed August 25, 2019).

380. What is the definition of eligibility or "being otherwise eligible"?

Being "otherwise eligible" for coverage means having met the plan's substantive eligibility conditions other than any waiting period, such as being in a job category that is covered by the plan's terms or completing a valid employment-based orientation period.[1]

381. Are conditions for eligibility permitted?

Conditions for eligibility under a group healthcare plan are ordinarily allowed as long as they are not designed to avoid complying with the limitations of not exceeding the ninety-day waiting period.

There are two specific conditions for eligibility defined under the regulations:[2]

1. **Cumulative Service**: If a group healthcare plan defines eligibility based on an employee having completed a cumulative number of hours of service – this requirement DOES NOT violate the maximum ninety-day waiting period as long as the cumulative hours-of-service do not exceed 1200 hours.

2. **Orientation periods**: Orientation periods that do not exceed ONE MONTH are permissible. In the instance of orientation periods,[3] the ninety-day period must being on the first day after the orientation period.

   a. NOTE: Applicable Large Employers (ALE) may not be able to use a full month of orientation AND the ninety-day waiting period without becoming subject to "Pay or Play" penalties.

   b. CALCULATION OF ORIENTATION PERIOD: A month is calculated by adding one calendar month and subtracting one calendar day. This is measured by starting from the start date of the otherwise eligible employee.

      i. If an employee starts on January 3, the last allowable day of orientation is February 2.

382. What is the maximum waiting period for essential health benefits?

Eligibility conditions based solely on the lapse of time are permissible for ninety days and no more. All calendar days are counted to calculate the ninety-days, including any holidays or weekend days. The calculation begins on the first day of the employee's enrollment.

---

1. DOL Tech. Rel. 2012-01 (February 9, 2012); IRS Notice 2012-17 (February 10, 2012); HHS Bulletin: Frequently Asked Questions from Employers Regarding Automatic Enrollment, Employer Shared Responsibility, and Waiting Periods (February 9, 2012) at http://cciio.cms.gov/resources/files/Files2/02102012/employer_faq_bulletin_2_9_12_final.pdf. (Last Accessed August 25, 2019).

2. https://www.dol.gov/agencies/ebsa/laws-and-regulations/laws/affordable-care-act/for-employers-and-advisers/90-day. (Last accessed August 25, 2019).

3. Orientation periods: https://www.federalregister.gov/documents/2014/06/25/2014-14795/ninety-day-waiting-period-limitation. (Last accessed August 25, 2019).

Other eligibility conditions are permitted unless the condition is designed to avoid compliance with the ninety-day waiting period limitation. If an employee may elect coverage and be covered on a date that does not exceed a ninety-day waiting period, the ninety-day limit is met.

Group health plans and insurers offering group or individual coverage, including grandfathered plans or individual policies, are prohibited from applying a waiting period that exceeds ninety days for plan years beginning on or after January 1, 2014.[1] The prohibition on excessive waiting periods does not apply to "excepted benefits."[2] The prohibition applies regardless of the size of the employer/plan sponsor.

Compliance guidance was issued by the IRS, DOL, and HHS.[3]

383. When does a waiting period begin?

The ninety-day waiting period begins when an employee is *otherwise eligible* for coverage under the terms of the group health plan.[4] If a plan provides that full-time employees are eligible for coverage without satisfying any other condition, and an employee was hired as a full-time employee, the waiting period for that employee would begin on the date of hire. Any eligibility condition based solely on the lapse of a time period is permitted for no more than ninety days.[5]

Employers can decide how long the waiting period can be – as long as it does not exceed ninety days. The waiting period can be changed during the benefits year if desired but cannot be changed for only one employee.

384. Is the ninety-day limit extended if employees take additional time to elect coverage?

No. A plan or insurer does not violate the ninety-day limit if employees take additional time to elect coverage.[6] Thus, if employees are eligible on the first day of the month following completion of enrollment forms, the fact that an employee hired on the first day of the month does not complete the forms that day does not violate the excessive waiting period rule.[7] Thus, if employees are eligible on the first day of the month following completion of enrollment forms, the fact that an employee hired on the first day of

1.   PHSA §2708.

2.   PHSA §2708.

3.   https://www.dol.gov/agencies/ebsa/laws-and-regulations/laws/affordable-care-act/for-employers-and-advisers/90-day. (Last accessed August 25, 2019).

4.   Treas. Reg. §54.9801-3(a)(3)(iii); DOL Reg. §2590.701-3(a)(3)(iii); HHS Reg. §146.111(a)(3)(iii).

5.   DOL Tech. Rel. 2012-01, Q&A-7 (February 9, 2012), available at https://www.dol.gov/agencies/ebsa/employers-and-advisers/guidance/technical-releases/12-01. (Last accessed August 25, 2019).

6.   IRS Notice 2012-59 (August 31, 2012); DOL Tech. Rel. 2012-02 (August 31, 2012); HHS Guidance on 90-Day Waiting Period Limitation PHSA §2708 (August 31, 2012) at https://www.cms.gov/CCIIO/Resources/Files/Downloads/2708-guidance-8-31-2012.pdfl. (Last accessed August 25, 2019).

7.   IRS Notice 2012-59, Q&A-1 (August 31, 2012); DOL Tech. Rel. 2012-02, Q&A-1 (August 31, 2012); HHS Guidance on 90-Day Waiting Period Limitation PHSA §2708, Q&A-1 (August 31, 2012), at https://www.cms.gov/CCIIO/Resources/Files/Downloads/2708-guidance-8-31-2012.pdf. (Last accessed August 25, 2019).

the month does not complete the forms that day does not violate the excessive waiting period rule.[1]

It is not permissible to allow eligibility on the first weekday, the first day of the month, or the beginning of the first pay period after a ninety-day waiting period ends even though the statute provides that a waiting period may not exceed ninety days.

385. What other eligibility requirements can an employer have?

Other eligibility requirements are allowed such as using full-time status as a requirement. In calculating "full-time" status, a plan may use a reasonable measurement period of up to twelve months to determine whether a new employee with variable hours meets the condition. This period will not be considered to be designed to avoid compliance if coverage is available no later than thirteen months from the employee's start date (plus, if applicable, the time between the start date and the first day of the next month). If a plan requires a cumulative number of hours to become eligible, that requirement will not be considered to be designed to avoid compliance if the required hours do not exceed 1,200.[2]

386. What other prohibitions apply to the eligibility requirements?

It is not permissible to allow eligibility on the first weekday, the first day of the month, or the beginning of the first pay period after a ninety-day waiting period ends even though the statute provides that a waiting period may not exceed ninety days.

387. How are permissible eligibility requirements applied to part-time and variable hour employees?

If a plan conditions eligibility on an employee regularly working a specified number of hours per period or working full-time, and the employer cannot determine that a new employee is reasonably expected regularly to work that number of hours or work full-time, the plan may take a reasonable amount of time to determine whether the employee meets the plan's eligibility condition. This may include a measurement period that is consistent with the timeframe used for purposes of the employer shared responsibility (employer mandate or "play or pay" penalty) provision.[3]

A period is reasonable if coverage is effective no later than thirteen months from the employee's start date, plus, if applicable, the time remaining until the first day of the next calendar month. Where cumulative hours of service are required for eligibility, up to 1,200 hours may be required; more than 1,200 hours would be considered designed to avoid compliance with the ninety-day waiting period limitation.

---

1.   IRS Notice 2012-59, Q&A-1 (August 31, 2012); DOL Tech. Rel. 2012-02, Q&A-1 (August 31, 2012); HHS Guidance on 90-Day Waiting Period Limitation PHSA §2708, Q&A-1 (August 31, 2012), https://www.cms.gov/CCIIO/Resources/Files/Downloads/2708-guidance-8-31-2012.pdf. (Last accessed August 25, 2019).

2.   IRC Section 4980H.

3.   IRS Notice 2012-59 (August 31, 2012); DOL Tech. Rel. 2012-02 (August 31, 2012); HHS Guidance on 90-Day Waiting Period Limitation PHSA §2708 (August 31, 2012) at https://www.cms.gov/CCIIO/Resources/Files/Downloads/2708-guidance-8-31-2012.pdf (Last accessed August 25, 2019).

<u>Illustration 1: Going from Part-Time to Full-Time Employment</u>. Employer's plan limits eligibility for coverage to full-time employees. Coverage becomes effective on the first day of the calendar month following the date the employee becomes eligible. Employee begins working full-time on May 15. Prior to this date, employee worked part-time for employer. Employee enrolls in the plan, and coverage is effective June 1. The period while employee was working part-time is not part of the waiting period because employee was not in a class of employees eligible for coverage while working part-time. Full-time employment is a condition that is not designed to avoid compliance with the ninety-day waiting period rule.[1]

<u>Illustration 2: Part-Time Employee Satisfies Cumulative Hours of Service Requirement</u>. Employee begins working twenty-five hours per week for Employer on January 1 as a part-time employee for purposes of employer's plan. Employer sponsors a plan that provides coverage to part-time employees after they have completed a cumulative 1,200 hours of service. Employee satisfies the plan's cumulative hours of service condition on December 15. The cumulative hours of service condition for part-time employees is not designed to avoid compliance with the ninety-day waiting period rule. Accordingly, coverage for employee under the plan must begin no later than the ninety-first day after employee works 1,200 hours. If the plan's cumulative hours of service requirement were more than 1,200 hours, that requirement would be deemed designed to avoid compliance with the ninety-day waiting period limitation.[2]

<u>Illustration 3: Variable Hour Employee to Full-Time Status</u>. Under employer's group health plan, employees who work full-time (defined as regularly working thirty hours per week or more) are eligible for coverage. Employee begins work for employer on May 15 of Year 1. Employee's hours are expected to vary between twenty and forty-five hours per week depending on work and employee's availability. Thus, it cannot be determined at employee's start date that employee is reasonably expected to work full-time. Under the terms of the plan, variable hour employees are eligible to enroll in the plan if they are determined to be full-time after a measurement period of twelve months. Coverage is made effective no later than the first day of the first calendar month after the applicable enrollment forms are received.

The employee's twelve-month measurement period ends May 14 of Year 2. Employee is determined to be full-time and is notified of his plan eligibility. If employee then elects coverage, his first day of coverage will be July 1 of Year 2. Here, the measurement period is permissible and not considered to be designed to avoid compliance with the ninety-day waiting period limitation because the plan may use a reasonable period of time to determine whether a variable hour employee is full time if the period of time is consistent with the timeframe permitted for such determinations under the employer shared responsibility rules. In such circumstances,

---

1.   IRS Notice 2012-59, Q&A-2 (August 31, 2012; DOL Tech. Rel. 2012-02, Q&A-2 (August 31, 2012); HHS Guidance on 90-Day Waiting Period Limitation PHSA §2708, Q&A-2 (August 31, 2012) at https://www.cms.gov/CCIIO/Resources/Files/Downloads/2708-guidance-8-31-2012.pdfl (Last accessed August 25, 2019).

2.   IRS Notice 2012-59, Q&A-4 (August 31, 2012); DOL Tech. Rel. 2012-02, Q&A-4 (August 31, 2012); HHS Guidance on 90-Day Waiting Period Limitation PHSA §2708, Q&A-4 (August 31, 2012) https://www.cms.gov/CCIIO/Resources/Files/Downloads/2708-guidance-8-31-2012.pdf (Last accessed August 25, 2019).

the time period for determining whether an employee is full time will not be considered to avoid the ninety-day waiting period limitation if coverage can become effective no later than thirteen months from employee's start date, plus the time remaining until the first day of the next calendar month.[1]

Guaranteed Coverage

No Preexisting Conditions or Health Status Discrimination for Essential Health Benefits

388. How does health reform affect the ability of a health insurance policy or plan covering essential health conditions not to deny coverage or reimbursement for preexisting condition exclusions (PECs)?

Health reform eliminated the ability of a health insurance policy or plan covering essential health conditions to deny coverage or reimbursement for Preexisting Condition Exclusions (PCEs) for plan years beginning on or after September 23, 2010, for persons under age nineteen.[2] Group health plans and group health insurance companies, as well as individual policies cannot impose PCEs for plan years beginning on or after January 1, 2014.[3] A PCE may still be imposed for excepted benefits.

389. What is a Pre-existing Condition Exclusion (PCE)?

A PCE is "a limitation or exclusion of benefits (including a denial of coverage) based on the fact that the condition was present before the effective date of coverage (or if coverage is denied, the date of the denial)."[4] Thus, the prohibition covers:

(1)   denial of enrollment and

(2)   denial of specific benefits based on a preexisting condition.

A preexisting condition can be a serious medical condition, such as cancer, diabetes, or high blood pressure, or something relatively minor, such as tendonitis.

A PCE includes any limitation or exclusion based on information relating to an individual's health status, "such as a condition identified as a result of a pre-enrollment questionnaire or physical examination given to the individual, or review of medical records relating to the pre-enrollment period."[5]

It should be noted that the pre-existing exclusion rule does not apply to "grandfathered plans" that existed on or before March 23, 2010 and are still in effect.

---

1.   IRS Notice 2012-59, Q&A-3 (August 31, 2012); DOL Tech. Rel. 2012-02, Q&A-3 (August 31, 2012); HHS Guidance on 90-Day Waiting Period Limitation PHSA §2708, Q&A-3 (August 31, 2012) at https://www.cms.gov/CCIIO/Resources/Files/Downloads/2708-guidance-8-31-2012.pdf (Last accessed August 25, 2019).
2.   PPACA §10103(e)(2) (2010).
3.   PHSA §2704(a); IRC Sec. 9815, and ERISA Sec. 715.
4.   Treas. Reg. §54.9801-2; DOL Reg. §2590.701-2; HHS Reg. §144.103.
5.   Treas. Reg. §54.9801-2; DOL Reg. §2590.701-2; HHS Reg. §144.103.

390. Are certificates of creditable coverage still required?

No. A "certificate of creditable" coverage was a document provided by a previous insurer stating that insurance coverage has ended. It includes the name of the person covered and the effective cancellation date. Under HIPAA rules relating to preexisting conditions coverage, group health plans and health plan issuers were required to issue certificates of creditable coverage.

Final regulations, entitled *"Patient Protection and Affordable Care Act; Exchange and Insurance Market Standards for 2015 and Beyond"*[1] issued on May 16, 2014, provided that beginning on or after January 1, 2014, PPACA's prohibition on preexisting condition exclusions applies and a certificate of creditable coverage need no longer be issued. Since people can no longer be excluded because of pre-existing conditions, certificates of creditable coverage are no longer necessary.

Cost-Sharing Limits

391. What are the cost-sharing limits on out-of-pocket expenses and annual deductibles?

For plan years beginning in 2014, except as discussed subsequently, the cost sharing for self-only and coverage other than self-only coverage cannot exceed the maximum out-of-pocket expense limits for self-only and family coverage for HSA-compatible High Deductible Health Plans (HDHPs) for taxable years beginning in 2014,[2] namely $6,350 for individuals ($6,450 in 2015,[3] $6,550 for 2016[4] and for 2017,[5] $6,650 for 2018, $6,750 for 2019) and $12,700 for families ($12,900 in 2015, $13,100 for 2016 and 2017, $13,300 for 2018,[6] and $13,500 for 2019[7]). The HDHP deductible amount is adjusted for increases in the cost of living. This sets the maximum out-of-pocket expense limit, i.e., the plan's annual deductible and other annual out-of-pocket expenses (such as copayments) the insured is required to pay. In the case of a plan using a network of providers, cost sharing paid by, or on behalf of, an individual for benefits provided outside of such network does not count toward the annual limitation on cost sharing or the annual limitation on deductibles.[8]

However, employer plans that have "separately administered" benefits, such as a primary package of health benefits and a different insurer or administrator for other benefits such as prescription drugs, did not need to comply until 2015.[9] Employer plans with separately administered benefits that qualify for the delay must apply some out-of-pocket limits beginning in 2014. These plans must ensure that their primary package of health benefits has an out-of-pocket limit of no more than $6,350 ($6,450 in 2015, $6,550 for 2016 and for 2017, $6,650 for 2018,

---

1.   https://www.cms.gov/CCIIO/Resources/Regulations-and-Guidance/Downloads/508-CMS-9949-F-OFR-Version-5-16-14.pdf. (No longer available on the internet).
2.   PPACA §1302(c)(1)(A) (2010); IRC Sec. 223(c)(2)(A)(ii).
3.   IRS Rev. Proc. 2014-30 https://www.irs.gov/pub/irs-drop/rp-14-30.pdf. (Last accessed August 25, 2019).
4.   IRS Rev. Proc. 2015-30 https://www.irs.gov/pub/irs-drop/rp-15-30.pdf. (Last accessed August 25, 2019).
5.   IRS Rev. Proc. 2016-28 https://www.irs.gov/pub/irs-drop/rp-16-28.pdf. (Last accessed August 25, 2019).
6.   IRS Rev. Proc. 2017-37 https://www.irs.gov/pub/irs-drop/rp-17-37.pdf. (Last accessed August 25, 2019).
7.   IRS Rev. Proc. 2018-30 https://www.irs.gov/pub/irs-drop/rp-18-30.pdf. (Last accessed August 25, 2019).
8.   HHS Reg. §156.130(c).
9.   FAQs About the Affordable Care Act Implementation Part XII, Q&A-2 at https://www.dol.gov/sites/dolgov/files/ebsa/about-ebsa/our-activities/resource-center/faqs/aca-part-xii.pdf (Last accessed August 25, 2019).

and $6,750 for 2019) individuals and $12,700 for families ($12,900 in 2015, $13,100 for 2016 and 2017 $13,300 for 2018, and $13,500 for 2019). A separately administered benefit, such as prescription drugs, that already has an existing limit on out-of-pocket costs must also comply with the limits of $6,350 for individuals $6,450 in 2015, $6,550 for 2016 and for 2017 $6,650 for 2018, and $6,750 for 2019) and $12,700 for families in 2014 ($12,900 in 2015, $13,100 for 2016 and 2017, $13,300for 2018 and $13,500 for 2019).[1]

For a plan year beginning in a calendar year after 2014, the cost-sharing limit for self-only coverage is the amount for self-only coverage for plan years beginning in 2014, increased by an index amount equal to the product of that amount and the "premium adjustment percentage" for the calendar year. For coverage other than self-only coverage, the cost-sharing limit for a plan year beginning in a calendar year after 2014 is twice the amount for self-only coverage.[2] The premium adjustment percentage for a calendar year is determined by HHS and is the percentage by which the average per capita premium for health insurance coverage in the United States for the preceding calendar year exceeds the average per capita premium for 2013.[3]

392. What are the limits for annual deductibles?

There are none. The prior rule that for plans in the small group market, the deductible could not exceed $2,000 for a plan covering one individual and $4,000 for any other plan[4] was repealed. Under the Protecting Access to Medicare Act of 2014,[5] this annual deductible limit was eliminated retroactively. The repeal occurred due to the desire by small businesses to offer high deductible plans paired with HSAs, HRAs, or health FSAs.

Clinical Trials and Coverage

393. What patient protections does the law create for persons participating in clinical trials?

Specifically, a group health plan may not:

- deny any qualified individual the right to participate in a clinical trial as described below;

- deny, limit, or impose additional conditions on the coverage of "routine patient costs" for items and services furnished in connection with participation in the clinical trial;[6] or

- discriminate against any qualified individual who participates in a clinical trial.[7]

---

1.   Id.
2.   PPACA §1302(c)(1)(B) (2010); PPACA §1302(c)(4) (2010).
3.   PPACA §1302(c)(4) (2010).
4.   PPACA §1302(c)(2)(A) (2010).
5.   Section 213, Protecting Access to Medicare Act of 2014, Pub. L. No. 113-93 (Apr. 1, 2014), amending both PPACA §1302(c) and PHSA §2707(b).
6.   PHSA §2709(a)(1)(B).
7.   PHSA §2709(a)(1)(C).

A plan can require a "qualified individual" to use an in-network provider participating in a clinical trial if the provider will accept the individual as a participant. A person participating in an approved clinical trial conducted outside the state of the individual's residence is also protected if the plan otherwise provides out-of-network coverage for routine patient costs.[1]

"Routine patient costs" include items and services provided for a person not enrolled in a clinical trial. However, such items and services do not include:

- the investigational item, device or service itself;

- items and services not included in the direct clinical management of the patient, but rather in connection with data collection and analysis; or

- a service clearly not consistent with widely accepted and established standards of care for the particular diagnosis.[2]

A "qualified individual" is a group health plan participant or beneficiary who is eligible to participate in an approved clinical trial for the treatment of cancer or other life-threatening disease or condition and:

- the referring healthcare professional is a participating provider and has concluded that the participant's or beneficiary's participation in the clinical trial would be appropriate; or

- the participant or beneficiary provides medical and scientific information establishing that the individual's participation in the clinical trial would be appropriate.[3]

An "approved clinical trial" is a Phase I, Phase II, Phase III, or Phase IV clinical trial that:

- is conducted in connection with the prevention, detection, or treatment of cancer or other life-threatening disease or condition[4] and is federally funded through a variety of entities or departments of the federal government, including the National Institutes of Health, the CDC, the Centers for Medicare & Medicaid Services, a cooperative group or center of any of the previous entities or the Department of Defense or the Department of Veterans Affairs, a qualified nongovernmental research entity identified in guidelines issued by the National Institutes of Health for center support grants and, if certain conditions are met, the Department of Veterans Affairs, the Department of Defense, and the Department of Energy;[5]

- is conducted in connection with an investigational new drug application reviewed by the Food and Drug Administration;[6] or

- is exempt from investigational new drug application requirements.[7]

---

1.   PHSA §§2709(a)(3),(4) and 2709(c).
2.   PHSA §2709(a)(2).
3.   PHSA §2709(b).
4.   A "life-threatening condition" is a disease or condition likely to result in death unless the disease or condition is interrupted. PHSA §2709(e).
5.   PHSA §2709(d)(1)(A).
6.   PHSA §2709(d)(1)(B).
7.   PHSA §2709(d)(1)(C).

Fair Insurance Premiums
Health Insurance Rating Rules
394. What are the health insurance rating rules imposed by health reform?

Effective in 2014 and thereafter, health reform has imposed new federal rules on how health insurers may "rate" or price their products. Grandfathered plans, grandmothered plans and plans in the large group and self-insured markets are not subject to these rules. However, if large group market insurance plans are offered on an exchange, they will be subject to these rating rules.[1]

Under the 2014 rules, insurers were allowed to vary premiums for coverage in the individual and small group markets using only four factors:

- Self-only versus family coverage

- Geographic "rating area," established by each state[2]

- Age (was limited for zero to twenty for children and unique age for twenty-one and older)

- Tobacco use

In the cases of age and tobacco use, the new rules also limit the extent of the permitted premium variations.[3]

For tobacco use, the maximum allowed variation is 1.5 to 1, meaning that a plan will not be allowed to charge a tobacco user more than one and a half times (or 50 percent above) the rate charged to a nontobacco user. With respect to age rating, the maximum allowed variation for adults is 3 to 1, meaning that a plan will not be allowed to charge a sixty-four-year-old more than three times the premium charged a twenty-one-year-old for the same coverage. It should be noted that some of the "repeal and replace" plans that were proposed during the early part of 2017 would have changed the maximum age rating variation from 3 to 1 to 5 to 1, which would allow a plan to charge a sixty-four year old FIVE times as much as a twenty-one year old rather than the current THREE times as much.

Under the law, premiums also may vary based only on self-only or family enrollment and rating area, as specified by the state.[4] Factors such as gender and health status are not allowed.[5]

Additionally, health reform[6] prohibits employer-sponsored health plans and commercial health insurers from imposing a pre-existing-condition exclusion on the coverage of any enrollee

---

1.   PHSA §2701(a)(5).
2.   PPACA §1255.
3.   PPACA §1201(4).
4.   PHSA §2701.
5.   PHSA §2701(a)(1)(B).
6.   PPACA §1201(2)(A).

or applicant under any circumstances.[1] This blanket prohibition took effect for children (under age nineteen) on September 23, 2010, and will take effect for adults on or after January 1, 2014.[2] Under prior law, insurers and employer self-insured health plans are required to provide coverage to enrollees in employer-sponsored plans on a guaranteed-issue basis and are prohibited from varying premiums based on individual health status.[3] Sections 1201(2) and (4) of PPACA (the health reform law) extend those requirements to the individual market as well, effective January 1, 2014.[4]

Effective in 2016, the Centers for Medicare & Medicaid Services (CMS) regulations that change the member-rating structure for dependents under the age of twenty-one for plans sold or renewing on January 1, 2018 or thereafter. Under the new rules, carriers may charge one single rate for dependent children ages zero-fourteen, and unique rates by age for dependents ages fifteen, sixteen, seventeen, eighteen, nineteen, and twenty. Under the amended rules, carriers may still only charge for the three oldest dependent children under the age of twenty-one. Effectively, the factors change as follows:

- Self-only versus family coverage

- Geographic "rating area," established by each state[5]

- Age

    o Single band for individuals from age zero through fourteen

    o One-year age bands for individuals fifteen through twenty

    o One-year age bands for individuals from twenty-one through sixty-three (unchanged)

- Tobacco use

These rules will impact policyholders who have family coverage with dependent children aged fifteen to twenty on their policies. While the rates spike that generally occurs from age twenty- to twenty-one will be lessened, it will provide steadily increasing rates for those with dependents aged fifteen or older.

Health Insurance Coverage Transparency Reporting and Cost-Sharing Disclosure

395. What are the "transparency in coverage" reporting and cost-sharing disclosures?

Health reform requires each state to have a health insurance exchange for the purchase of Qualified Health Plans (QHPs).[6] A health plan seeking QHP certification must disclose certain

---

1. PHSA §2701.
2. PPACA §1255.
3. 42 U.S.C. §§300gg, 300gg-1, and 300gg-11.
4. PHSA §§2701 and 2702.
5. PPACA §1255.
6. PPACA §1311(b)(1).

information to the exchange, HHS, and the state insurance commissioner, and make the information available to the public ("transparency in coverage" reporting and cost-sharing disclosures).[1] Both exchange QHPs and health plans and insurers outside an exchange must comply.[2] The requirements for QHPs and plans and insurers outside of the exchange are identical to the requirements for QHPs on an exchange, except that with respect to transparency in coverage reporting, non-exchange plans and insurers are not required to provide the information to the exchange. As of 2017, while some information is being collected and reported, the requirements are of this section are not yet fully implemented (See Q 396).

Grandfathered policies and group plans are not required to comply[3] except for QHPs sold on an exchange.[4]

396. What information must be provided for transparency in coverage reporting and made available to the public?

Health plans and insurers subject to the transparency in coverage reporting requirement must make accurate and timely disclosure of the following information to HHS, the state insurance commissioner, and the public:

- claims payment policies and practices;

- periodic financial disclosures;

- data on enrollment and disenrollment;

- data on the number of claims denied;

- data on rating practices;

- information on cost-sharing and payments regarding any out-of-network coverage;

- information on enrollee and participant rights under Title I of PPACA; and

- other information as determined by HHS.[5]

Additionally, exchange-based QHPs must disclose this information to the exchange.

The information must be disclosed using "plain language" that the intended audience, including individuals with limited English proficiency, can readily understand and use because that language is concise, well-organized, and follows other best practices of plain language writing.[6]

---

1.   PPACA §1311(e)(3)(A).
2.   PHSA §2715A.
3.   PPACA §§1251(a) and 10103(d)(1); Treas. Reg. §54.9815-1251T(c)(1).
4.   PPACA §§1251(a) and 10103(d)(1); Treas. Reg. §54.9815-1251T(c)(1).
5.   PPACA §1311(e)(3)(A).
6.   PPACA §1311(e)(3)(B).

It should be noted that although this "transparency in coverage" has been in effect since 2010 enactment of the Affordable Care Act, CMS has only mandated reporting since 2017 and only for Qualified Health Plans.

Insurers have been required to provide links to websites identifying the applicable policies and reporting numbers on claims, denials of claims, and appeals. In 2016, CMS had indicated that claim denial classifications and mental health parity information reporting would be mandated for 2018, but had decided to delay full implementation of the transparency requirements and collect for 2018 the same information that it had been collected for 2017.

The CMS has now made a great deal of information available on their website to support transparency in coverage. While not yet in plain language, there is a great deal of information available to those who need it.

The CMS Consumer Information and Insurance Oversight (CCIIO) is charged with increasing transparency in the Health Insurance Exchanges. This year, CMS began publishing download-able public use files (PUFs) so that researchers and other stakeholders can more easily access Exchange data. The Health Insurance Exchange Public Use Files (Exchange PUFs) are available for plan years 2014 to 2018 to support benefit and rate analysis. The 2018 Exchange PUFs will be updated regularly to reflect the plan data that consumers will see when shopping for an Exchange Qualified Health Plan (QHP). Data for the 2018 Exchange PUFs were imported to CMS systems by July 27, 2018.

The Exchange PUFs include plan and issuer level information for certified Qualified Health Plans (QHPs) and stand-alone dental plans (SADPs) offered to individuals and small businesses through the Health Insurance Exchange. The Exchange PUFs include data from states participating in the Federally Facilitated Exchanges (FFE), State Partnership Exchanges (SPEs) and states whose State-based Exchanges rely on the federal information technology platform for QHP eligibility and enrollment functionality (SBE-FP). The PUFs also include data on Multi-State Plans (MSPs) and certified off-exchange SADPs. The Exchange PUFs exclude information from SBEs that do not rely on the federal platform for QHP eligibility and enrollment functionality.

The Exchange PUFs consist of ten separate files as described below:[1]

- Benefits and Cost Sharing PUF (BenCS-PUF) – Plan variant-level data on essential health benefits, coverage limits, and cost sharing.

- Rate PUF (Rate-PUF) – Plan-level data on individual rates based on an eligible subscriber's age, tobacco use, and geographic location, and family-tier rates.

- Plan Attributes PUF (Plan-PUF) – Plan-level data on maximum out of pocket payments, deductibles, HSA eligibility, formulary ID, and other plan attributes.

- Business Rules PUF (BR-PUF) – Plan-level data on rating business rules, such as allowed relationships (e.g., spouse, dependents) and tobacco use.

---

1.   https://www.cms.gov/CCIIO/Resources/Data-Resources/marketplace-puf.html#.

- Service Area PUF (SA-PUF) – Issuer-level data on geographic service areas including state, county, and zip code.

- Network (Ntwrk-PUF) – Issuer-level data identifying provider network URLs.

- Plan ID Crosswalk PUF (CW-PUF) – Plan-level data mapping plans offered in the previous plan year to plans offered in the current plan year.

- Machine-readable URL PUF (MR-PUF)—Issuer-level URL locations for machine-readable plan network provider and formulary information.

- Transparency in Coverage PUF (TC-PUF) – Issuer-level claims, appeals, and active URL data. The PY2019 PUF contains data from PY2017 for issuers participating in the Exchange in PY2017.

- Quality PUF (Qual-PUF) –The PY2019 PUF can be accessed at https://www.cms.gov/Medicare/Quality-Initiatives-Patient-Assessment-Instruments/QualityInitiativesGenInfo/Downloads/Plan-Year-2019-Nationwide-Quality-Rating-System-PUF.zip

397. What cost-sharing disclosures to individuals must be made?

Health plans and insurers subject to this requirement must provide certain cost-sharing (including deductibles, copayments, and coinsurance) information in a timely manner on request by an individual.[1] At a minimum, the information must be made available to the individual through an Internet Web site. However, for those individuals who do not have access to the Internet, the information must be provided in some other means.[2]

No Discrimination against Providers

398. How does health reform prohibit discrimination against healthcare providers, such as physicians?

A group health plan and a health insurance issuer offering group or individual health insurance coverage cannot discriminate as to participation under the plan or coverage against any healthcare provider acting within the scope of that provider's license or certification under applicable state law. However, this rule does not require that a group health plan or health insurance issuer contract with any healthcare provider willing to abide by the terms and conditions for participation established by the plan or issuer.[3]

In addition, this law does not prevent HHS, a group health plan, or a health insurance issuer, from establishing varying reimbursement rates based on quality or performance measures.[4]

---

1.   PPACA §1311(e)(3)(C).
2.   PPACA §1311(e)(3)(C).
3.   PHSA §2706(a).
4.   PHSA §2706(a).

This law is the first federal provider nondiscrimination law applicable to nongovernment and to self-insured ERISA plans. "Group health plans" and "health insurance issuers offering group or individual health insurance coverage" include self-insured employee health benefit plans, group health insurance, individual health insurance, and likely the federal employees health benefits program. This nondiscrimination requirement applies to products sold through the new health insurance exchanges starting in 2014.

The provision covers any state licensed or state-certified healthcare provider. This includes any practitioners including such specialties as chiropractors, D.O.'s, M.D.'s, acupuncturists, massage therapists, optometrists, nurse practitioners, midwives and podiatrists, and any others that are licensed by the state.

399. What are some examples of prohibited discrimination against providers?

Possible prohibited activities could include the following:

- Health insurer requires that optometrists seeking to be participating providers in health plan provider network must also contract to be participating providers in free-standing vision plan, but does not impose same requirement on ophthalmologists or other physicians.

- Health insurer maintains "closed" or "limited" network of podiatrists but has "open panel" approach to participation by qualified orthopedic physicians and primary care physicians.

  - Could be vulnerable to charge of discrimination.

  - Could perhaps be defended on ground that law does not impose "any willing provider requirement" and plan has different needs for orthopedic surgeons than for podiatrists or achieves legitimate business objectives by varying contracting approach taking into account services provided by orthopedists compared to podiatrists, and is not discriminating based on license.

- Health insurer includes optometrists or nurse midwives in network only in rural areas but not in urban areas.

- Health insurer has different fee schedule for same CPT code service based on whether service is performed by psychologist or Medical Doctor (M.D.)

- Insurer has limited network for provision of certain eye exams for which it uses an RFP bid process to choose a vendor, but has a separate provider network for a different set of eye care services some of which are not performed in that state by optometrists, such as eye surgery. If optometrists are able to participate in bid activity for the former, but are not able to qualify for the second, is this federal law violated?

- What if insurer imposes new credentialing criteria that are hard for non-MDs to meet, and it grandfathers people in its existing network, which includes a few non-MDs?

400. What is the effective date of the provider nondiscrimination requirements?

This provision was effective on January 1, 2014, or, for group plans, plan years beginning on or after January 1, 2014.[1]

401. How will the nondiscrimination requirement be enforced?

HHS enforces the PHSA for government plans, and the states enforce the law for its private health insurance requirements.[2] Sanction for insurers that violate the law would depend on state law. HHS enforces the PHSA for self-insured group health plans and, if the state does not enforce it, for health insurers.[3]

For HHS enforcement, HHS may impose a civil monetary penalty on insurance issuers that fail to comply with the PHSA requirements. The maximum penalty imposed under the PHSA is $100 per day per individual with respect to which such a failure occurs.[4] Similar to the Internal Revenue Code, certain minimum penalty amounts may apply to a plan or employer if the violation is not corrected within a specified period, or if a violation is considered to be more than *de minimis*. In determining the amount of the penalty, HHS must take into account the entity's previous record of compliance with the PHSA provisions.

In addition, a penalty may not be imposed for a violation if it is established to the Secretary's satisfaction that none of the entities knew (or if exercising reasonable diligence would have known) that the violation existed. If the violation was due to reasonable cause and not willful neglect, a penalty would not be imposed if the violation were corrected within thirty days of discovery.[5] Entities found to violate the PHSA requirements may challenge the penalty in a hearing subject to a decision by an administrative law judge.[6] Following this administrative hearing, entities may file an action for judicial review.[7] There has not been a significant amount of enforcement action, however, in West Virginia, *ex rel. Morrisey v. United States Department of Health and Human Services*, an unsuccessful attempt was made to force the federal government to begin enforcement proceedings, which was ultimately rejected by the United States Supreme Court on April 17, 2017.[8]

---

1. PPACA §1255.
2. 42 U.S.C. §300gg-22(a)(1).
3. 42 U.S.C. §300gg-22(a)(2).
4. 42 U.S.C. §300gg-22(b)(2)(C)(i).
5. 42 U.S.C. §300gg-22(b)(2)(C)(iii).
6. 42 U.S.C. §300gg-22(b)(2)(D).
7. 42 U.S.C. §300gg-22(b)(2)(E).
8. *State of West Virginia, ex rel. Patrick Morrisey v. United States Department of Health and Human Services*, No. 16-721, U.S. Sup. Ct., April 17, 2017, Petition denied, July 1, 2017 Decision rendered.

402. To what products or programs do these provider nondiscrimination rules not apply?

These provider nondiscrimination rules do not apply to Medicare, Medicare Advantage, Medicare Supplement or Medicaid. Medicare Advantage plans already are prohibited from discriminating, in terms of participation, reimbursement, or indemnification, against any healthcare professional who is acting within the scope of his or her license or certification under state law, solely on the basis of the license or certification. Additionally, the requirement does not apply to "excepted benefits," such as stand-alone dental and vision coverage, workers compensation, long-term-care insurance, insurance for a specific disease or illness, or hospital indemnity insurance, for example.

PART VIII: REQUIRED DISCLOSURES AND INFORMATION REPORTING

W-2 Reporting Beginning 2013 and Subsequent Years

403. What is the W-2 reporting requirement and when did it become effective?

Employers, including those with grandfathered plans,[1] must report the "aggregate cost" of "applicable employer sponsored coverage" on an employee's Form W-2.[2] This cost generally consists of employer-sponsored coverage under a group health plan (insured or self-funded) that is excludable from the employee's gross income. Section 6051(a)(14) generally requires the aggregate cost of applicable employer sponsored coverage to be reported on Form W-2.[3] IRS Notice 2012-9 superseded earlier notices[4] that delayed and created exceptions to the PPACA W-2 reporting requirement, which originally was to apply for 2011 W-2s that normally would be issued by employers in January 2012. The W-2 reporting requirement, which was delayed by the IRS, first applied to 2012 W-2s that were issued in January 2013.

The IRS website www.irs.gov provides that the transition relief from the reporting requirement, meaning that small employers need not report, and that certain types of coverage need not yet be reported yet will continue to apply until the IRS publishes guidance giving at least six months advance notice of any change to the transition relief. This transition relief first applied to the 2013 Forms W-2 that were issued in 2014. The relief applies for the 2015 tax year and will continue to apply to future calendar years until the IRS publishes additional guidance. (Note: employers generally are required to provide employees with the 2018 Forms W-2 in January 2018.) Reporting by small employers and for reporting of non-required coverages is permissible on a voluntary basis, even while the transition relief applies and reporting is not required.[5]

404. What is the income tax impact of this requirement to employers and employees?

None. This requirement is merely designed to provide information to the federal government. The provisions of §6051(a)(14) do not affect whether any particular coverage is excludable from gross income under §106 or any other Code provision, and the reporting of any amount on Form W-2 in compliance with the requirements of §6051(a)(14) will not affect the amount includable in income or the amount reported in any other box on Form W-2. The purpose of the reporting is to provide useful and comparable consumer information to employees on the cost of their health care coverage. It does not change any rules regarding the employer's deductions or the taxation to the employee. Failure to properly report will not cause coverage that is excludible from gross income under Internal Revenue Code section 106 or any other provision

---

1.   PPACA §1251(a) lists the requirements for which an employer is exempt and does not include the W-2 requirement.
2.   PPACA §9002.
3.   IRC Sec. 6051(a)(14).
4.   IRS Notices 2010-69 and 2011-28.
5.   https://www.irs.gov/affordable-care-act/form-w-2-reporting-of-employer-sponsored-health-coverage. (Last accessed August 3, 2019)

of the Internal Revenue Code to become taxable or to be reported in any other box on Form W-2.[1] See Question 1 at the IRS website "Employee-Provided Health Coverage Informational Reporting Requirements: Questions and Answers".[2]

405. Which employers must comply with the expanded W-2 reporting?

This requirement includes employers that are federal, state and local government entities (except with respect to plans maintained primarily for members of the military and their families), churches and other religious organizations, and employers that are not subject to the COBRA continuation coverage requirements under Internal Revenue Code section 4980B.[3] This does not include federally recognized Indian tribal governments or, until further guidance, any tribally chartered corporation wholly owned by a federally recognized Indian tribal government. See also the IRS website for further details.[4]

406. Do third-party sick pay providers have to report costs of coverage?

No.

Third-party sick-pay providers that provide the Forms W-2 to the employees of the employers with which they have contracted do not have to report the cost of coverage. However, a Form W-2 provided by the employer to the employee must report the cost of coverage regardless of whether that Form W-2 includes sick pay or whether a third-party sick pay provider is furnishing a separate Form W-2 reporting the sick pay.

407. Is the amount reported on the W-2 the amount for health coverage paid by the employer?

No. The reportable cost generally includes the amounts paid by both the employer and employee, regardless of whether paid through pretax or after-tax contributions. The aggregate reportable cost is reported on Form W-2 in Box 12, using Code DD.[5]

408. Which employers are exempt from the W-2 reporting requirement?

The W-2 reporting requirement does not apply to the following:

- Employers with fewer than 250 W-2s issued for the prior calendar year until further notice.[6] (Note that these could be included, but that the IRS would need to provide at least six months notice).

---

1.   Notice 2012-9, Q&A 2.
2.   https://www.irs.gov/newsroom/employer-provided-health-coverage-informational-reporting-requirements-questions-and-answers. (Last accessed August 3, 2019.
3.   Notice 2012-9, Q&A 3.
4.   Question 3 https://www.irs.gov/newsroom/employer-provided-health-coverage-informational-reporting-requirements-questions-and-answers. (Last accessed August 3, 2019).
5.   Notice 2012-9, Q&A 5.
6.   Notice 2012-9, Q&A 3. Tribally chartered corporations wholly owned by a federally recognized Indian tribal government are also exempt. *Id.*

- An employer that would have filed only 100 Forms W-2 for the previous year had it not used an agent under Code section 3504[1] will not be subject to the reporting requirement for the year, nor will an agent under Code section 3504 with respect to that employer's W-2 Forms for the year. In contrast, if the same employer would have filed 300 Forms W-2 for the previous year had it not used an agent under Internal Revenue Code section 3504, that employer would be subject to the reporting requirement for the year. If an agent under Internal Revenue Code section 3504 is used again, the information will need to be provided to the agent and reported on the Form W-2.[2]

- An employer is not required to report any amount in Box 12 using Code DD for an employee who, pursuant to section 31.6051-1(d)(1)(i), has requested to receive a Form W-2 before the end of the calendar year during which the employee terminated employment.[3]

- Coverage under a flexible spending arrangement if contributions occur only through employee salary reductions.[4]

- "Excepted benefits," which include dental and vision plans offered under a separate policy, certificate, or contract of insurance, or if the participants have the right to elect the dental or vision benefits and, if they do, pay an additional premium or contribution.[5]

- Excess reimbursements that are includible in the income of highly compensated individuals under Internal Revenue Code section 105(h) or payments or reimbursements of health insurance premiums for a 2 percent shareholder-employee of an S corporation.[6]

Example. An employer provides self-insured health coverage with a cost of coverage of $12,000 under which a highly compensated individual receives a $4,000 excess reimbursement. As a result, under §105(h), that individual must include the $4,000 excess reimbursement in gross income. The excess reimbursement is not included in the determination of the aggregate reportable cost, so that the employer must include $8,000 as the cost of coverage under the plan in determining the aggregate reportable cost for that individual.

- The cost of hospital or other fixed indemnity coverage, or coverage only for a specified disease or illness, is not reportable if the coverage is offered as an independent, noncoordinated benefit and is includible in the employee's income or paid for on an after-tax basis. However, the cost of such coverage is reportable when paid for on a

---

1. This agent is not a payroll service that prepares paychecks for the employer's signature. Rather, an agent under IRC Sec. 3504 performs acts such as the withholding, reporting and paying of federal employment taxes with regard to wages paid by the agent for the employer, as well as the agent's own employees. A Section 3504 agent agrees to assume liability along with the employer for the employer's Social Security, Medicare and federal income tax withholding responsibilities. An agent is appointed using IRS Form 2678 and files aggregate returns using the agent's EIN. The Section 3504 designation does not apply to FUTA tax, with a limited exception provided for certain household workers. See IRS Notice 2003-70.
2. Notice 2012-9, Q&A 3.
3. Notice 2012-9, Q&A 6.
4. Notice 2012-9, Q&A 19.
5. Notice 2012-9, Part II and Q&A 20.
6. Notice 2012-9, Q&A 23.

pretax basis under a cafeteria plan or with employer contributions that are excludable from income.

409. What about related employers that each employ and pay the same person?

Related employers that do not use a common paymaster can either provide the full reportable cost to an employee on a single Form W-2 or allocate the cost and reporting among the employers.[1] The notice does not define the term "related employers." Presumably, it means related employers as defined for W-2 purposes.[2] This definition includes the following types of corporations if they satisfy any one of the following four tests at any time during a calendar quarter:

(i)   The corporations are members of a "controlled group of corporations", as defined in IRS Code section 1563, or would be members if Internal Revenue Code section 1563(a)(4) and (b) did not apply and if the phrase "more than 50 percent" were substituted for the phrase "at least 80 percent" wherever it appears in Internal Revenue Code section 1563(a).

(ii)   In the case of a corporation that does not issue stock, either 50 percent or more of the members of one corporation's board of directors (or other governing body) are members of the other corporation's board of directors (or other governing body), or the holders of 50 percent or more of the voting power to select such members are concurrently the holders of more than 50 percent of that power with respect to the other corporation.

(iii)   Fifty percent or more of one corporation's officers are concurrently officers of the other corporation.

(iv)   Thirty percent or more of one corporation's employees are concurrently employees of the other corporation.[3]

410. Is the cost of coverage under a multiemployer plan required to be included in the aggregate reportable cost reported on Form W-2?

No. An employer that contributes to a multiemployer plan is not required to include the cost of coverage provided to an employee under that multiemployer[4] plan in determining the aggregate reportable cost. If the only applicable employer-sponsored coverage provided to an employee is provided under a multiemployer plan, the employer is not required to report any amount under §6051(a)(14) on the Form W-2 for that employee.

---

1.   Notice 2012-9, Q&A 7 provides that if two or more related corporations concurrently employ the same individual and compensate such individual through a common paymaster which is one of such corporations, each such corporation shall be considered to have paid as remuneration to such individual only the amounts actually disbursed by it to such individual and shall not be considered to have paid as remuneration to such individual amounts actually disbursed to such individual by another of such corporations.

2.   Reg. §31.3121(s)-1.

3.   Reg. §31.3121(s)-1.

4.   As defined in §54.4980B-2.

411. In the case of an individual who transfers to a new employer that qualifies as a successor employer must both the predecessor and successor employers report the aggregate reportable cost of coverage each provided?

Yes, each of the predecessor and successor employers must report the aggregate reportable cost of coverage that that employer provided, unless the successor employer follows the optional procedure in Rev. Proc. 2004-53, 2004-2 C.B. 320, and issues one Form W-2 reflecting wages paid to the employee during the calendar year by both the predecessor employer and the successor employer. Consistent with the rules applicable to reporting of wages, the successor employer following the optional procedure must include the aggregate reportable cost of coverage provided by both employers on the Form W-2 that it issues, and the predecessor employer must not report the cost of coverage it provides.[1]

412. How is the amount of reportable cost determined?

Employers that use a composite rate to determine premiums for active employees and another method to determine COBRA premiums may use either rate to determine the reportable cost, but they must use that method consistently when reporting the cost for each applicable group.[2] An employer may also include in the reportable cost of coverage certain amounts that need not be reported, such as the cost of coverage for a Health Reimbursement Account.

The reportable cost of coverage may be based on the information available to the employer on December 31 and need not be adjusted for later elections or notifications, such as a divorce or other change in family status that retroactively affects coverage during the prior year.[3]

413. How do employers with self-insured health plans calculate the aggregate cost of applicable employer-sponsored coverage?

There are rules in COBRA governing how a self-insured plan determines its applicable premium, generally requiring that such plans calculate the applicable premium through the actuarial method or the past cost method.[4] These are the methods that have been used and the IRS notices provide no special guidance.[5]

414. How is the cost for EAPs, wellness programs, and on-site medical clinics reported?

The cost of EAPs (Employee Assistance Programs), wellness programs, and on-site medical clinics is includible in the reported cost of coverage to the extent that the program is a group health plan for IRC section 5000(b)(1). However, such coverage is not reportable if the employer does not charge a premium for that coverage for purposes of COBRA (or other federally required

---

1.   I.R.C. §3121(a)(1).
2.   Notice 2012-9, Q&A 34.
3.   Notice 2012-9, Q&A 35.
4.   ERISA Sec. 604(2); IRC Sec. 4980B(f)(4)(B); PHSA §2204(2).
5.   IRS Notices 2011-28 and 2012-9.

continuation coverage) or if the employer is not subject to COBRA.[1] If an employer charges a premium with respect to that type of coverage provided to a beneficiary qualifying for coverage in accordance with any applicable federal continuation coverage requirements, that employer is required to include the cost of that type of coverage provided. An employer that is not subject to any federal continuation coverage requirements is not required to include the cost of coverage provided under an EAP, wellness program, or on-site medical clinic

415. What is the penalty for failure to follow the W-2 reporting requirements?

There is no specifically enumerated penalty for failure to properly report healthcare costs. Presumably, the normal W-2 penalties will apply.[2]

416. What about health costs paid for retirees not entitled to a W-2?

Employers are not required to issue a W-2 to report health plan costs to persons not otherwise required to receive a W-2.[3]

417. Has the IRS provided a chart summarizing the W-2 health cost reporting requirements?

Yes. It is as follows:[4]

Form W-2 Reporting of Employer-Sponsored Health Coverage			
Coverage Type	Form W-2, Box 12, Code DD		
	Report	Do Not Report	Optional
Major medical	X		
Dental or vision plan not integrated into another medical or health plan			X
Dental or vision plan which gives the choice of declining or electing and paying an additional premium			X
Health Flexible Spending Arrangement (FSA) funded solely by salary-reduction amounts		X	
Health FSA value for the plan year in excess of employee's cafeteria plan salary reductions for all qualified benefits[1]	X		

---

1.   Notice 2012-9, Q&A 32.
2.   IRC Secs. 6721, 6722, and 6674.
3.   Notice 2012-9, Q&A 9.
4.   See https://www.irs.gov/affordable-care-act/form-w-2-reporting-of-employer-sponsored-health-coverage (Last accessed September 16, 2018).

Health Reimbursement Arrangement (HRA) contributions			X
Health Savings Arrangement (HSA) contributions (employer or employee)		X	
Archer Medical Savings Account (Archer MSA) contributions (employer or employee)		X	
Hospital indemnity or specified illness (insured or self-funded), paid on after-tax basis		X	
Hospital indemnity or specified illness (insured or self-funded), paid through salary reduction (pre-tax) or by employer	X		
Employee Assistance Plan (EAP) providing applicable employer-sponsored healthcare coverage	Required if employer charges a COBRA premium		Optional if employer does not charge a COBRA premium
On-site medical clinics providing applicable employer-sponsored healthcare coverage	Required if employer charges a COBRA premium		Optional if employer does not charge a COBRA premium
Wellness programs providing applicable employer-sponsored healthcare coverage	Required if employer charges a COBRA premium		Optional if employer does not charge a COBRA premium
Multi-employer plans			X
Domestic partner coverage included in gross income	X		
Governmental plans providing coverage primarily for members of the military and their families		X	
Federally recognized Indian tribal government plans and plans of tribally charted corporations wholly owned by a federally recognized Indian tribal government		X	
Self-funded plans not subject to Federal COBRA			X
Accident or disability income		X	
Long-term care		X	

Liability insurance		X	
Supplemental liability insurance		X	
Workers' compensation		X	
Automobile medical payment insurance		X	
Credit-only insurance		X	
Excess reimbursement to highly compensated individual, included in gross income		X	
Payment/reimbursement of health insurance premiums for 2 percent shareholder-employee, included in gross income		X	
Other Situations	**Report**	**Do Not Report**	**Optional**
Employers required to file fewer than 250 Forms W-2 for the preceding calendar year (determined without application of any entity aggregation rules for related employers)			X
Forms W-2 furnished to employees who terminate before the end of a calendar year and request, in writing, a Form W-2 before the end of that year			X
Forms W-2 provided by third-party sick-pay provider to employees of other employers			X

The chart was created at the suggestion of and in collaboration with the IRS' Information Reporting Program Advisory Committee (IRPAC). IRPAC's members are representatives of industries responsible for providing information returns, such as Form W-2, to the IRS. IRPAC works with IRS to improve the information reporting process. (Current as of June 20, 2019).

Exchange Notice Required Beginning October 1, 2013

418. What is the Exchange Notice that employers must give and when was the requirement effective?

The health insurance exchanges became operational on January 1, 2014. PPACA requires employers to provide a notice prior to the beginning date of the exchange. Originally required beginning March 1, 2013, this notice had to be provided by all employers, regardless of size, that are subject to the Fair Labor Standards Act (FLSA) (virtually all employers, as discussed below) to employees by October 1, 2013.[1] Notices must be provided by employers, including those without a group health plan, to both active part-time and full-time employees (not spouses or dependents), regardless of whether eligible for the employer's health plan, if any.[2]

New employees hired since October 1, 2013, must receive the notice within fourteen days of hire.

The employer's health plan year is not relevant in regard to the required delivery of this exchange notice. Notice may be sent first class mail or electronically.

There are two model notices.

- For employers with a health plan, see https://www.dol.gov/sites/default/files/ebsa/laws-and-regulations/laws/affordable-care-act/for-employers-and-advisers/model-notice-for-employers-who-offer-a-health-plan-to-some-or-all-employees.pdf.

- For employers with no health plan, see https://www.dol.gov/sites/default/files/ebsa/laws-and-regulations/laws/affordable-care-act/for-employers-and-advisers/model-notice-for-employers-who-do-not-offer-a-health-plan.pdf.

These model notices are reproduced in Appendix B. Part B of the notice for employers with health plans is optional and complicated. Many employers with health plans will not use it, preferring instead to customize the information on the Part B notice for employers with no health plans. The model notices are approved for use through May 31, 2020.

Most firms under $500,000 in annual dollars received from "sales made or business done" are exempt from the FLSA and thus exempt from the notice requirement, other than those specifically included regardless of annual income. Those included regardless are hospitals; institutions primarily engaged in the care of the sick, aged, mentally ill, or disabled who reside on the premises; schools for children who are mentally or physically disabled or gifted; preschools, elementary and secondary schools, and institutions of higher education; and federal, state, and local government agencies.

In addition, only employers with $500,000 or more in annual dollars received from "sales made or business done" who are also engaged in interstate commerce are subject to the FLSA. Examples of engaging in interstate commerce include:

- an employee uses a telephone, facsimile machine, the U.S. mail, or a computer e-mail system to communicate with persons in another state for the business;

- an employee who drives or flies to another state while performing his or her job duties;

---

1. DOL Technical Release No. 2013-02; FAQs about Affordable Care Act Implementation Part XI, Q&A 1, available at https://www.dol.gov/agencies/ebsa/employers-and-advisers/guidance/technical-releases/13-02. (Last accessed August 4, 2019).
2. FLSA §18B.

- the business uses goods from an out-of-state supplier; or

- the business uses an electronic device that authorizes a credit/debit card purchase.

A simplified but acceptable Sample Notice follows.

State Health Insurance Marketplace (Exchange)
Health Insurance Coverage Options & Your Coverage

PART A: General Information. When key parts of the health care reform law take effect in 2014, there will be a new way to buy health insurance – the Health Insurance Marketplace or Exchange that will exist in every state. To assist you evaluate options for you and your family, this notice provides basic information about the new state Marketplaces (Exchanges).

What is the Health Insurance Marketplace (Exchange)? Each state's Marketplace (Exchange) is designed to help you find health insurance that meets your needs and fits your budget. The Marketplace (Exchange) offers "one-stop shopping" to find and compare private health insurance options. You may also be eligible for a new kind of federal tax credit that lowers your monthly premium. Open enrollment for health insurance coverage through the Marketplace (Exchange) begins in October 2013 for coverage starting as early as January 1, 2014.

Can I Save Money on my Health Insurance Premiums in the Marketplace (Exchange)? You may qualify to save money and lower your monthly premium, but only if your employer does not offer coverage, or offers coverage that doesn't meet certain standards. The savings on your premium for which you may be eligible depends on your household income.

Does Employer Health Coverage Affect Eligibility for Premium Savings through the Marketplace (Exchange)? Yes. If you have an offer of health coverage from your employer that meets certain standards, you will not be eligible for a tax credit through the Marketplace (Exchange) and may therefore wish to enroll in your employer's health plan. However, you may be eligible for a federal income tax credit that lowers your monthly health insurance premium if your employer does not offer health plan coverage to you or does not offer coverage that meets affordability and minimum value standards. If the cost of a plan from your employer that would cover you (but not any other members of your family) is more than 9.66 percent of your household income for the year, or if the coverage your employer provides does not meet the "minimum value" standard set by the Affordable Care Act, you may be eligible for a tax credit.

Note: If you purchase a health plan through the Marketplace (Exchange) instead of accepting health coverage offered by your employer, then you may lose the employer contribution (if any) to any employer-offered coverage. Also, this employer contribution -as well as your employee contribution to employer-offered coverage- is generally excluded from income that is taxed for Federal and State purposes. Your payments for coverage through the Marketplace (Exchange) are made on an after-tax basis.

How Can I Get More Information? The Marketplace (Exchange) can help you evaluate your coverage options, including your eligibility for coverage through the Marketplace (Exchange) and its cost. Please visit https://www.healthcare.gov on the internet for more information, including an online application for health insurance coverage and contact information for a Health Insurance Marketplace (Exchange) in your state. There will also be "Navigators" who are person trained to help you use your exchange.

PART B: Information About Your Employer. If you decide to complete an application for health insurance in your state Marketplace (Exchange), you will be asked to provide this information below. This information is numbered to correspond to the Marketplace (Exchange) health insurance application.

3. Employer name _______________________________________

4. Employer Identification Number (EIN) _______________

5. Employer address _____________________________

6. Employer phone number _______________________

7. City _________________________________

8. State _______________________________

9. ZIP code ____________________________

10. Who can we contact at your job about information about the employer's health plan, if any? ____

11. Phone number (if different from above) _______________

12. Email address _______________________________

Here is some basic information about health coverage by this employer:

- As your employer, we offer a health plan to:

    ○   All employees. Eligible employees are:

    ○   Some employees. Eligible employees are:

- With respect to dependents:

    ○   We do offer coverage. Eligible employees are:

    ○   We do not offer coverage. Eligible employees are:

- If checked, this coverage meets the minimum value standard, and the cost of this coverage to you is intended to be affordable, based on employee wages.

    ** Even if your employer intends your coverage to be affordable, you may still be eligible for a premium discount through the Marketplace. The Marketplace will use your household income, along with other factors, to determine whether you may be eligible for a premium discount. If, for example, your wages vary from week to week (perhaps you are an hourly employee or you work on a commission basis), if you are newly employed mid-year, or if you have other income losses, you may still qualify for a premium discount.

    If you decide to shop for coverage in the Marketplace, Healthcare.gov will guide you through the process. Here's the employer information you'll enter when you visit Healthcare.gov to find out find out if you can get a tax credit to lower your monthly premiums.

419. Who is an employer for this purpose?

The notice requirement applies to employers that are subject to the Fair Labor Standards Act (FLSA). The term "employer" is defined in the FLSA as "any person acting directly or indirectly in the interest of an employer in relation to an employee." This broad definition will likely encompass most employers.

420. What is the purpose and content of the Exchange Notice?

The notice is intended to inform the employees about the existence of the health benefit exchange and give a description of the services provided by the exchange. The notice also will explain how the employee may be eligible for a premium tax credit or a cost-sharing reduction if the employer's plan does not meet certain requirements. The notice must inform employees that if they purchase a qualified health plan through the exchange:

- they may lose any employer contribution toward the cost of employer-provided coverage; and

- all or a portion of the employer contribution to employer-provided coverage may be excludable for federal income tax purposes.

Lastly, the notice will include contact information for customer service resources within the exchange and an explanation of appeal rights. The regulations clarified that the notice must meet certain accessibility and readability requirements, as well as be in writing.

421. Which employees must receive the notice?

All employees, not just those eligible for health coverage must receive the notice. The Fair Labor Standards Act (FLSA) broadly defines an employee as "an individual employed by an employer."[1]

422. What are the penalties for failure to give the Exchange Notice to employees?

There is no penalty at this time.[2] If a company is covered by the Fair Labor Standards Act, it should provide a written notice to its employees about the Health Insurance Marketplace, but there is no fine or penalty under the law for failing to provide the notice.

423. What information should the Exchange Notice provide to employees?

The notice should inform employees:

- About the health insurance marketplace;

---

1.   FLSA §3(e)(1), 29 USC §203(e)(1).
2.   See FAQ on Notice of Coverage Options https://www.dol.gov/agencies/ebsa/about-ebsa/our-activities/resource-center/faqs/notice-of-coverage-options. (Last accessed August 4, 2019).

- What coverage may be offered by the employer, depending on income will determine whether they may be able to get lower cost private insurance in the marketplace; and

- If they buy insurance through the marketplace, that they may lose the employer contribution (if any) to their health benefits

Reporting of Health Insurance Coverage (Insurers and Employers that Self-Insure)

424. In addition to the W-2 reporting, what other reporting must employers make to the IRS and covered individuals?

Healthcare reform requires any person who provides "minimum essential coverage"[1] beginning in 2015 or thereafter, to an individual during a calendar year to report certain health insurance coverage information to the IRS.[2] Reporting is required for grandfathered plans.[3] No reporting is required for "excepted benefits."[4] The employer must also provide a written statement to the covered individual, as discussed in Q 451.

425. When did this reporting requirement go into effect?

The requirement for Reporting of Health Insurance Coverage originally was to be effective in 2014. However, IRS Notice 2013-45, issued in July 2013, provided a one-year delay to three reporting requirements under the healthcare reform law.

The reporting requirements that were postponed were:

- the annual obligation under section 6055 of the Internal Revenue Code for insurers, self-insuring employers and other parties that provide "minimum essential coverage" to provide certain information to the IRS;

- the annual obligation under Internal Revenue Code section 6056 for applicable large employers to report to the IRS and to the employer's full-time employees as to whether and what healthcare coverage is offered to such employees;

- the requirement under Internal Revenue Code section 4980H for applicable large employers to offer healthcare coverage to full-time employees or pay penalties, commonly known as the "play-or-pay" penalties (POP).

(See Q 453 through Q 459 for discussions of Internal Revenue Code section 6056 for Applicable Large Employers.)

---

1. IRC Sec. 5000A.
2. IRC Sec. 6055.
3. IRC Sec. 5000A(f)(1)(D).
4. IRC Sec. 5000A(f)(3).

426. Who is required to report under Section 6055?

Anyone that provides insured and self-insured minimum essential coverage plans to an individual must report to the IRS and furnish statements to individuals, including the following:

- health insurance issuers, or carriers, for insured coverage (but see below regarding certain limited exceptions),

- plan sponsors of self-insured group health plan coverage, and

- the executive department or agency of a governmental unit that provides coverage under a government-sponsored program.

427. Is an employer required to report under Section 6055 if it sponsors a health plan that provides coverage by purchasing insurance from a health insurance issuer?

No. An employer that sponsors an insured health plan (a health plan that provides coverage by purchasing insurance from a health insurance issuer) will not report as a provider of health coverage under Section 6055. The health insurance issuer or carrier is responsible for reporting that health coverage. However, if the employer is subject to the employer shared responsibility provisions in Section 4980H, it is responsible for reporting information under Section 6056 about the coverage it offers to its full-time employees.

428. For self-insured group health plan coverage, who is the plan sponsor that must report under Section 6055?

- For a self-insured group health plan maintained by a single employer, the plan sponsor is the employer. For a plan maintained by more than one employer that is not a multiemployer plan (as defined in ERISA) the plan sponsor is each participating employer. For purposes of identifying the employer, the Section 414 employer aggregation rules do not apply.

- For a plan that is a multiemployer plan (as defined in ERISA), the plan sponsor is the association, committee, joint board of trustees, or other similar group of representatives of the parties who establish or maintain the plan.

- For a plan maintained solely by an employee organization, the plan sponsor is the employee organization.

- For any plan for which a plan sponsor is not identified above, the plan sponsor is the person designated by plan terms or, if no person is designated, each entity that maintains the plan is the plan sponsor.

429. How do the reporting requirements under Section 6055 apply to reporting entities that are part of a controlled group?

Plan sponsors in a controlled group that is not an applicable large employer member (ALE Member) under Section 4980H, and coverage providers (such as issuers) that are not reporting as employers, may report under section 6055 as separate entities, or may have one entity report for the controlled group.

430. Must a government employer report under Section 6055 if it maintains a self-insured health plan?

Yes. However, unless prohibited by other law, a government employer that maintains a self-insured group health plan may designate a related governmental unit, or an agency or instrumentality of a governmental unit, as the person to file the returns and furnish the statements for some or all individuals covered under that plan.

431. For a government-sponsored program, who must report under Section 6055?

- For Medicaid and CHIP coverage, the state agency that administers the program must report. For Medicare, TRICARE, benefits administered by the Department of Veterans Affairs, and benefits for Peace Corps volunteers, the executive department or agency of the governmental unit that provides the coverage must report. However, Medicaid and CHIP agencies in U.S. possessions are not required to report their Medicaid or CHIP coverage.

- For health insurance coverage under a government-sponsored program (such as Medicaid, CHIP, or Medicare) obtained through an issuer, the executive department or agency of the governmental unit that provides the coverage and not the issuer must report.

- For the Nonappropriated Fund Health Benefits Program, the Secretary of Defense may designate the Department of Defense components that must report.

432. Should a health insurance issuer report under Section 6055 for coverage in a qualified health plan in the individual market enrolled in through a Marketplace?

No. An issuer should not report on coverage under a qualified health plan in the individual market enrolled in through a marketplace. The marketplaces will separately report information on enrollments in a qualified health plan to the IRS and individuals under Section 36B(f)(3). Under IRS Notice 2017-41, issuers of catastrophic plan coverage may, but are not required to, report on catastrophic plan coverage enrolled in through the marketplace for 2015, 2016, and 2017. The Treasury Department and the IRS encourage issuers to voluntarily report on catastrophic plan coverage enrolled in though the marketplace.

433. Must a health coverage provider report under Section 6055 for arrangements that provide benefits in addition or as a supplement to an arrangement that is minimum essential coverage?

If the additional or supplemental benefits are not minimum essential coverage (for example, if they are excepted benefits like coverage at an on-site medical clinic), no reporting is required for the additional or supplemental benefits. In addition, no reporting is required under Section 6055 for additional or supplemental benefits that are minimum essential coverage if the primary and supplemental coverages have the same plan sponsor or the coverage supplements government-sponsored coverage such as Medicare.

434. Must a health coverage provider report under Section 6055 if some or all of its covered individuals may be exempt from the individual shared responsibility provision?

Yes. A health coverage provider may not have the information necessary to determine whether an individual is exempt from the shared responsibility provision. To ensure complete and accurate reporting, providers must report under Section 6055 for all their covered individuals.

435. What type of information must be reported to the IRS?

The type of information includes:

- the name and address of the primary insured and other individuals covered under an applicable policy

- dates of coverage, and

- whether and by what method Minimum Essential Coverage is provided.[1]

This information is used to determine various employer and individual penalties, when applicable.[2]

436. Did the IRS Notice 2013-45 postpone all elements of the PPACA reporting requirements?

No. The Notice postponed compliance with only the three requirements listed below until 2015. All other requirements went into effect during 2014.

Postponed Requirements:

- the annual obligation under section 6055 of the Internal Revenue Code for insurers, self-insuring employers and other parties that provide "minimum essential coverage" to provide certain information to the IRS;

- the annual obligation under Internal Revenue Code section 6056 for applicable large employers to report to the IRS and to the employer's full-time employees as to whether and what healthcare coverage is offered to such employees;

- the requirement under Internal Revenue Code section 4980H for applicable large employers to offer healthcare coverage to full-time employees or pay penalties, commonly known as the "play-or-pay" penalties (POP).

See PPACA Timeline, Part III, Q 140.[3]

---

1.   IRC Code Section 6055.
2.   IRS Notice 2013-45 https://www.irs.gov/pub/irs-drop/n-13-45.PDF.
3.   IRS Notice 2013-45 https://www.irs.gov/pub/irs-drop/n-13-45.PDF.

437. Did Notice 2016-70 affect the rules under sections 6721(b) and 6722(b) concerning the reduction of penalty amounts for reporting under section 6055 or 6056?

No. Notice 2016-70 did not affect the rules under sections 6721(b) and 6722(b) concerning the reduction of penalty amounts for 2016 reporting under section 6055 or 6056.

438. What were the filing deadlines for Forms 1094-C and 1095-C for 2019?

Deadline to furnish Form 1095-C to employees was Thursday, January 31, 2019, however the IRS issued an extension for employers to furnish employees with Form 1095-C until March 4, 2019 for 2019 only.

The deadline for filing forms 1094-C and 1095-C if filing by paper was February 28, 2019 and April 1, 2019 if filing electronically.

Form 1095-C helps employees complete their individual tax returns by providing important information regarding their health coverage for the previous calendar year. Employees must be able to show whether they or their family members had minimum essential coverage on Line 61 of their individual tax returns.

439. What are the filing deadlines for Forms 1094-C and 1095-C for 2020?

Deadline to furnish Form 1095-C to employees is January 31, 2020, however, based on past years, it is likely that a thirty-day extension will be issued.

The deadline for filing forms 1094-C and 1095-C if filing by paper is February 28, 2020 and March 31, 2020 if filing electronically.

440. What relief is available from penalties for incomplete or incorrect returns either filed with the IRS or for statements furnished to employees for coverage offered or not offered?

Applicable Large Employers (ALE) have been subject to new information reporting requirements starting in 2016 for offers of coverage in 2015.

For these new information reporting requirements, the penalty under section 6721 may apply to an ALE that:

- fails to file timely information returns,

- fails to include all the required information, or

- includes incorrect information on the return.

Similarly, the penalty under section 6722 may apply to an ALE that:

- fails to timely furnish the statement,

- fails to include all the required information, or

- includes incorrect information on the statement.

Short-term relief from reporting penalties has been provided. This relief allowed additional time to develop appropriate procedures for collection of data and compliance with the new reporting requirements. For reporting in 2016 of offers of coverage in 2015 and for reporting in 2017 of offers of coverage in 2016 (Notice 2016-70) and for reporting in 2018 of offers of coverage in 2017 (Notice 2018-06), and for reporting in 2018, (Notice 2018-94) the IRS will not impose penalties under sections 6721 and 6722 on ALE Members that can show that they have made good faith efforts to comply with the information reporting requirements.

Specifically, relief is provided from penalties under sections 6721 and 6722 for returns and statements filed and furnished in 2016 to report offers of coverage in 2015 and in 2017 to report offers of coverage in 2016, and in 2018 to report offers of coverage in 2017 for incorrect or incomplete information reported on the return or statement.

No relief is provided in the case of ALE Members that cannot show a good faith effort to comply with the information reporting requirements or that fail to timely file an information return or furnish a statement.

441. Are nonprofit and government entities required to report under Section 6056?

Yes. Section 6056 applies to all employers that are ALE members, regardless of whether the employer is a nonprofit, tax-exempt or government entity (including federal, state, local, and Indian tribal governments).

442. Why were the reporting requirements postponed until 2015?

The information reporting required by Internal Revenue Code sections 6055 and 6056 must occur in order for the IRS to enforce and administer the employer mandate requirements under Internal Revenue Code section 4980H. The employer mandate penalties are triggered if one or more of an applicable large employer's full-time employees are entitled to premium tax credits for the purchase of insurance on a state exchange marketplace under Internal Revenue Code section 36B and:

(1)   the employer fails to offer 95 percent (70 percent in 2015) of full-time employees and their dependents (unless the employer qualifies for dependent transition relief[1])

---

1.   See Questions and Answers on Employer Shared Responsibility Provisions Under the Affordable Care Act at http://www.irs.gov/Affordable-Care-Act/Employers/Questions-and-Answers-on-Employer-Shared-Responsibility-Provisions-Under-the-Affordable-Care-Act (Last accessed August 5, 2019).

   This extended transition relief applies to employers for the 2015 plan year for plans under which (1) dependent coverage is not offered, (2) dependent coverage that does not constitute minimum essential coverage is offered, or (3) dependent coverage is offered for some, but not all, dependents. The transition relief is not available to the extent the employer had offered dependent coverage during either the plan year that begins in 2013 (2013 plan year), or the 2014 plan year and subsequently dropped that offer of coverage.

   The transition relief, as extended, applies only for dependents who were without an offer of coverage from the employer in both the 2013 and 2014 plan years and if the employer takes steps during the 2014 or 2015 plan year (or both) to extend coverage under the plan to dependents not offered coverage during the 2013 or 2014 plan year (or both).

the opportunity to enroll in minimum essential coverage (the penalty in 2020 is $2,570 for each FTE after thirty); or

(2)   the employer offers full-time employees and dependents the opportunity to enroll in minimum essential coverage but the coverage is not affordable or does not provide minimum value. The second penalty can never exceed the first penalty. The penalty in 2020 is $3,860 per FTE.

An employer typically will not know whether a full-time employee has received such a tax credit, and the employer will not have all the information needed to determine whether it owes an employer mandate penalty. Therefore, applicable large employers did not have to calculate employer mandate penalties or file returns submitting payment for such penalties in 2014.

Instead, the IRS, after receiving the information returns filed by applicable large employers under Internal Revenue Code section 6056 and the information about employees claiming the premium tax credit for any given calendar year, will determine whether any of the employer's full-time employees received the premium tax credit and, if so, whether any employer mandate penalty is due. The IRS will thus contact any applicable large employer if the employer owes a penalty, and the employer will have an opportunity to respond to the information provided by IRS before any penalty is assessed. (See Q 453 through Q 459 for information on the Internal Revenue Code section requirements affecting certain large employers.)

443. Do the employer shared responsibility provisions apply if an employer that is not otherwise an ALE offers coverage through an Association Health Plan (AHP)?

No. Whether an employer member of an association that offers coverage through an AHP is an ALE that is subject to the employer shared responsibility provisions depends on the number of full-time employees (and full-time equivalent employees) the member employer employed in the prior calendar year and is unrelated to whether the employer offers coverage through an AHP. An employer that is not an ALE under the employer shared responsibility provisions does not become an ALE due to participation in an AHP, and an employer that is an ALE under the employer shared responsibility provisions continues to be an ALE subject to the employer shared responsibility provisions regardless of its participation in an AHP.[1]

444. What do the final regulations on employer information reporting require?

Sections 6055 and 6056 of the Internal Revenue Code ("Code") prescribe reporting of healthcare coverage and became effective in 2015, with the first forms to be filed in 2016, an administratively delayed effective date.[2] The employer mandate generally requires employers with fifty or more full-time employees (Applicable Large Employers or "ALEs") to offer coverage to their full-time employees that meets minimum value and affordability standards under

---

1.   See Federal Register, Volume 83, No. 120, Thursday, June 21, 2018. https://www.gpo.gov/fdsys/pkg/FR-2018-06-21/pdf/2018-12992.pdf (Last accessed August 5, 2019).
2.   IRS Notice 2013-45 delayed that law's 2014 effective date until 2015.

the ACA or pay a penalty. Employers that have fewer than fifty full-time and full-time equivalent employees are exempt from the ACA employer shared responsibility provisions and therefore from the employer reporting requirements. The final March 2014 regulations on this reporting provided for a single, combined form for information reporting under both Internal Revenue Code Sections 6055[1] and 6056[2] as well as a simplified option for employer reporting of "qualified offers" of coverage to employees.

For employers that were subject to a delayed employer mandate, i.e., those with at least fifty full-time employees but fewer than 100 full-time employees (including Full-Time Equivalent employees), in transitioning into compliance with Internal Revenue Code section 4980H, the final regulations provided transition relief from section 4980H for 2015 (plus, in the case of any noncalendar plan year that began in 2015, the portion of the 2015 plan year that fell in 2016).[3]

Internal Revenue Code section 6055 describes reporting requirements to the IRS and individuals for self-insuring employers, insurers, government entities, and certain other providers of Minimum Essential Coverage (MEC). Wellness programs that are an element of other minimum essential coverage (such as wellness programs offering reduced premiums or cost sharing under a group health plan) do not require separate section 6055 reporting. Internal Revenue Code section 6056 describes reporting requirements for applicable large employers to provide employees with information so that they can determine whether they can receive a premium tax credit if they purchase insurance from a health care exchange. Internal Revenue Code section 6056 also requires such employers to report to the IRS information concerning health care coverage. Reporting under these new requirements is similar to the reporting of W-2 information where individual statements are provided to each employee on form W-2 and the W-2s are accumulated and summarized on Form W-3. Employers who sponsor self-insured health care plans, and who are therefore required to report under both Internal Revenue Code sections 6055 and 6056, may file a combined report for the IRS and employees. Electronic reporting is required for employers who have more than 250 employees for whom individual reports are required. Large employers that self-insure (employers that pay their employees' medical costs directly, instead of joining a traditional plan) will fill out both sections of the form. Large employers that do not self-insure will only fill out the top half of the form, for reporting under Internal Revenue Code section 6056.

The final regulations under Internal Revenue Code section 6055 require an employer to report information about the employer, the employees insured, and information on the minimum essential coverage provided, including employee and dependent social security numbers or a date of birth if the SSN is not available after reasonable efforts to obtain it. Code 6056 requires applicable large employers to report information about themselves, such as the number of full-time employees for each month during the calendar year, certify whether they offered coverage to their full-time employees, and provide certain information about the plan offered, including the monthly premium for the plan.

---

1.   Treas. Reg. §1.6055-1 and 1.6055-2.
2.   Treas. Reg. §301.6056-1 and -2.
3.   See section XV.D.6 of the preamble to the final regulations under section 4980H for a description of eligibility conditions for transition relief.

The regulations provide that a qualifying offer of coverage is "an offer of minimum value coverage that provides employee-only coverage at a cost to the employee of no more than about $1,100 (9.56 percent of the estimated Federal Poverty Level in 2015 and 9.66 in 2016, 9.69 in 2017, 9.56 percent in 2018, 9.86 percent in 2019, and 9.78 percent into 2020[1]) in 2015" combined with an offer of coverage to the employee's family, which does not need to meet the cost threshold. An employer makes a qualifying offer if it offered the employee coverage that provides 60 percent minimum value at an employee cost for employee-only coverage of no more than 9.78 percent of the Federal Poverty Level, and also offered Minimum Essential Coverage to employees' spouses and dependents. For employees receiving a qualified offer for all twelve months, employers will need to report only the names, addresses, and taxpayer identification numbers of such employees. For employees receiving a qualifying offer in fewer than twelve months in the year, employers will be able to report such employees for each of those months by simply entering a code.

445. Is an employees' ability to receive premium tax credits affected by the reporting requirement delay?

No. The Notice states that the transition relief does not affect an individual's eligibility for a premium tax credit if he or she purchases health insurance through one of the health insurance exchange marketplaces established under the Act. Participants in the exchanges will continue to qualify for premium tax credits if their household income is within the specified range and they are not eligible for other minimum essential coverage. Such other minimum essential coverage includes eligible employer-sponsored group health plans that are affordable and provide Minimum Value (MV).

446. Were any 2014 requirements of the PPACA affected by the extension of the effective date of these reporting requirements?

No. The Notice made clear that the 2014 transition relief was limited solely to the three items and had no effect on the effective date or application of other provisions under the Act, many of which went into effect in 2014. For example, the transition relief has no effect on the provisions which took effect in 2014 as to premium tax credits for those purchasing subsidized health insurance on an exchange marketplace or the individual mandate requirements under Internal Revenue Code section 5000A for individuals to maintain healthcare coverage for themselves or pay penalties.

447. What are the reporting requirements that were not affected by the postponement of these three reporting requirements?

Provisions taking effect for Plan Years beginning on or after January 1, 2014, include the following:

- Group health plans, whether or not "grandfathered" under the Affordable Care Act, may not impose dollar limits on "essential health benefits."

---

1.   Revenue Procedure 2018-34 https://www.irs.gov/pub/irs-drop/rp-18-34.pdf (Issued May 24, 2018).

- Nongrandfathered health insurance plans in the small group market must offer essential health benefits.

- Group health plans and health insurance issuers offering group health insurance coverage may not establish rules for initial or continued eligibility of an individual to enroll in the plan or discriminate as to coverage based on the individual's or dependent's health status-related factors, such as medical condition (both physical and mental illnesses); claims experience; receipt of healthcare; medical history; genetic information; evidence of insurability (including conditions arising out of acts of domestic violence); and disability. Nevertheless, premium or contribution provisions for similarly-situated individuals in connection with a wellness program that satisfies certain requirements are permitted.

- Group health plans and health insurance issuers offering group health insurance coverage, including grandfathered plans and policies, may not impose any preexisting condition exclusion.

- Group health plans, including grandfathered plans, cannot apply waiting periods for coverage that are greater than ninety days.

- Nongrandfathered group health plans may not impose annual cost-sharing that exceeds the maximum out-of-pocket expense limits for health savings account-compatible high-deductible health plans.

(See Part III, Q 140, for a complete PPACA implementation timeline.)

448. What is the "Minimum Essential Coverage" that must be reported?

Most employer-provided group health coverage is "Minimum Essential Coverage (MEC)." The definition includes any "eligible employer-sponsored plan." This includes a group health plan or group health insurance coverage offered by an employer to an employee that is a governmental plan or any other plan or coverage offered in a state's small or large group market.[1]

Minimum essential coverage means health coverage under any of the following programs:

- Eligible employer-sponsored coverage

- Individual market coverage, including qualified health plans offered by the Health Insurance Marketplace, health insurance provided through a student health plan, catastrophic coverage, or coverage under an expatriate health plan for non-employees

- Medicare Part A coverage and Medicare Advantage plans

- Most Medicaid coverage

- Children's Health Insurance Program (CHIP) coverage

---

1.   IRC Sec. 5000A(f)(2).

- Most types of TRICARE coverage

- Comprehensive health care programs offered by the Department of Veterans Affairs

- Health coverage provided to Peace Corps volunteers

- Department of Defense Nonappropriated Fund Health Benefits Program

- Refugee Medical Assistance

- Coverage through a Basic Health Program (BHP) standard health plan

- Certain coverage provided to business owners who aren't employees

- Coverage recognized by HHS as minimum essential coverage

- Grandfathered and grandmothered plans

449. When did the reporting requirement become effective?

The Internal Revenue Code section 6055 reporting requirement is first required for coverage provided on or after January 1, 2014. The first information returns were filed in 2015.

450. What information must be reported to the IRS?

The return is on a form provided by the IRS and must contain the following information:

- the name, address, and Taxpayer Identification Number (TIN) of the primary insured (this term is undefined but most likely refers to employees and not family members), and the name and TIN of each other individual obtaining coverage under the policy;

- the dates during which the individual was covered during the calendar year;

- if the coverage is health insurance coverage, whether the coverage is a Qualified Health Plan (QHP) offered through a health benefit exchange;

- if the coverage is health insurance coverage and that coverage is a QHP, the amount of any advance cost-sharing reduction payment or of any premium tax credit with respect to such coverage; and

- any other information required by the IRS.[1]

In addition, if health insurance coverage is through an employer-provided group health plan, the return must contain the following information:

- the name, address, and Employer Identification Number (EIN) of the employer maintaining the plan;

---

1.   IRC Sec. 6055(b)(1).

- the portion of the premium (if any) required to be paid by the employer; and

- any other information the IRS may require for administering the new tax credit for health insurance for eligible small employers.[1]

451. What statement must be furnished to covered individuals?

The person who is required to report the health insurance coverage to the IRS must also furnish a written statement to each individual whose name must be included in the information return. This statement must include:

- the name, address, and contact information of the reporting person; and

- the information required to be shown on the return with respect to that individual (discussed in Q 450).[2]

This statement must be furnished to the covered individual on or before January 31 of the year following the calendar year for which the information was required to be reported to the IRS for the 2016 year and beyond.[3]

452. What is the sanction for noncompliance with this reporting requirement?

An employer that fails to comply with these reporting requirements is subject to penalties for failure to file an information return and failure to furnish payee statements.[4]

For specific fines, please see

- **26 U.S. Code § 6721.** Failure to furnish correct information returns[5]

  - Penalties currently range from $250 per occurrence to a maximum of $3,000,000 (although rapid correction can reduce penalties from $50 per occurrence to a maximum of $500,000)

- **26 U.S. Code § 6722.** Failure to furnish correct payee statements[6]

  - Penalties currently range from $250 per occurrence to a maximum of $3,000,000 (although rapid correction can reduce penalties from $50 per occurrence to a maximum of $500,000)

- **26 U.S. Code § 6723.** Failure to comply with other information[7]

---

1.   IRC Sec. 6055(b)(2).
2.   IRC Sec. 6055(c)(1).
3.   IRC Sec. 6055(c)(2).
4.   IRC Sec. 6724(d) defines "information return" for the penalty provisions in IRC Secs. 6721, 6722, and 6723.
5.   https://www.law.cornell.edu/uscode/text/26/6721.
6.   https://www.law.cornell.edu/uscode/text/26/6722.
7.   https://www.law.cornell.edu/uscode/text/26/6723.

    o   Penalties currently range from $50 per occurrence to a maximum of $100,000.

Health Insurance Coverage Reporting by Large Employers and Offering Employers for 2015 and Thereafter

453. In addition to the requirements described above in Q 418 to Q 452, for employers to report to the IRS and employees, what other similar reporting requirements exist?

Internal Revenue Code section 6056 contains requirements similar to those described in Q 450 that are imposed by Internal Revenue Code section 6055. Section 6056 requirements apply to "Applicable Large Employers" and "Offering Employers." The IRS may allow for any return or written statement required under this provision (i.e., large employers and "offering employers") to be provided as part of a return or written statement required under Internal Revenue Code section 6055, discussed above in Q 450.[1]

Applicable Large Employers. "Applicable large employers" are employers with fifty or more full-time equivalent employees (on average, during the preceding year) that may be liable for the employer mandate penalty tax under Internal Revenue Code section 4980H if they provide no health coverage or do not provide affordable health coverage to their full-time employees (and their dependents).[2]

Offering Employers. The reporting requirement also applies to "offering employers," which are employers that offer "minimum essential coverage" to employees under an eligible employer-sponsored plan and the employee contribution of any employee exceeds 8 percent of the wages paid to that employee by the employer.[3]

454. Who is required to report under Section 6056?

Employers subject to the employer shared responsibility provisions, called applicable large employers or ALEs, are required to report under Section 6056. An ALE is an employer that employed an average of at least fifty full-time employees (including full-time equivalent employees) on business days during the preceding calendar year.

An ALE may be a single employer or may consist of a group of related employers (such as parent and subsidiary entities or other related/affiliated entities), called an Aggregated ALE Group. An Aggregated ALE Group refers to a group of employers treated as a single employer under section 414(b), (c), (m) or (o). Any employer that is an ALE or a member of an Aggregated ALE Group is called an ALE Member. An ALE Member is a member of the Aggregated ALE Group for a month if it is treated as a single employer with the other members of the group on any day of the calendar month. The reporting requirements under Section 6056 apply to each ALE Member separately.

---

1.   IRC Sec. 6056(d)(2).
2.   IRC Sec. 4980H.
3.   IRC Sec. 6056(f)(1).

455. If two or more related employers together are an Aggregated ALE Group under Section 4980H (so that each related employer is an ALE Member), how do they comply with the information reporting requirements?

For purposes of the information reporting requirements, each ALE Member must file Forms 1094-C and 1095-C with the IRS and furnish Form 1095-C to its full-time employees, using its own EIN. This is the case even if a particular ALE Member does not employ enough employees to meet the fifty-full-time-employee threshold.

For purposes of the information reporting requirements under Section 6056, government entities, churches, and a convention or association of churches should determine whether a person or group of persons is an ALE and whether a particular entity is an ALE Member in the same way they made those determinations for purposes of the employer shared responsibility provisions under section 4980H.

456. Are nonprofit organizations and government entities required to report under Section 6056?

Yes. Section 6056 applies to all employers that are ALE Members, regardless of whether the employer is a nonprofit, tax-exempt or government entity (including federal, state, local, and Indian tribal governments).

457. What information is reported by the Applicable Large Employers and offering employers?

The employer files an information return with the IRS with the following information:

- the employer's name, date, and Employer Identification Number (EIN);

- a certification of whether the employer offers its full-time employees and their dependents the opportunity to enroll in "Minimum Essential Coverage" under an "eligible employer-sponsored plan";[1]

- the number of full-time employees the employer has for each month during the calendar year;

- the name, address, and Taxpayer Identification Number (TIN) of each full-time employee employed by the employer during the calendar year and the months (if any) during which the employee and any dependents were covered under a health benefit plan sponsored by the employer during the calendar year; and

- any other information required by the IRS.[2]

---

1.   Defined in IRC Sec. 5000A(f)(2).
2.   IRC Sec. 6056(b).

Employers that offer the opportunity to enroll in "Minimum Essential Coverage" must also report:

- the months during the calendar year for which coverage under the plan was available;

- the monthly premium for the lowest cost option in each of the enrollment categories under the plan;

- the employer's share of the total allowed costs of benefits provided under the plan;

- in the case of an employer that is an applicable large employer, the length of any waiting period for such coverage;

- for an offering employer, the option for which the employer pays the largest portion of the cost of the plan and the portion of the cost paid by the employer in each of the enrollment categories under such option; and

- any other information required by the IRS.[1]

458. Which statements must be furnished to employees by "applicable large employers" and "offering employers?"

Employers required to submit a report of health insurance coverage to the IRS under Internal Revenue Code section 6056 must also furnish a written statement to each of their full-time employees whose name was required to be included in the report to IRS. This statement includes:

- the name, address, and contact information of the reporting employer; and

- the information required to be shown on the return with respect to the individual.[2]

The written statement must be furnished to full-time employees on or before January 31 of the year following the calendar year for which the information was required to be reported to the IRS.[3]

459. What are the consequences for failure to comply with the Internal Revenue Code section 6056 reporting requirements?

An employer that fails to comply with these reporting requirements is subject to penalties for failure to file an information return and failure to furnish payee statements.[4]

For specific fines, please see

- **26 U.S. Code § 6721.** Failure to furnish correct information returns[5]

---

1.   IRC Sec. 6056(b).
2.   IRC Sec. 6056(c)(1).
3.   IRC Sec. 6056(c)(2).
4.   IRC Sec. 6724(d) defines "information return" for the penalty provisions in IRC Secs. 6721, 6722, and 6723.
5.   https://www.law.cornell.edu/uscode/text/26/6721.

- o Penalties currently range from $250 per occurrence to a maximum of $3,000,000 (although rapid correction can reduce penalties from $50 per occurrence to a maximum of $500,000)

- **26 U.S. Code § 6722.** Failure to furnish correct payee statements[1]

  - o Penalties currently range from $250 per occurrence to a maximum of $3,000,000 (although rapid correction can reduce penalties from $50 per occurrence to a maximum of $500,000)

- **26 U.S. Code § 6723.** Failure to comply with other information[2]

  - o Penalties currently range from $50 per occurrence to a maximum of $100,000.

460. How do ALE Group members under Section 4980H comply with information reporting requirements?

Each ALE Member must file Forms 1094-C and 1095-C with the IRS and furnish Form 1095-C to its full-time employees, using its own EIN. This is the situation even if a particular ALE Member does not employ enough employees to meet the fifty-full-time-employee threshold.

For purposes of the information reporting requirements under section 6056, government entities, churches, and a convention or association of churches need to ascertain whether a person or group of persons is an ALE and whether a particular entity is an ALE Member in the same way they made those determinations for purposes of the employer shared responsibility provisions under section 4980H.

461. Does an Applicable Large Employer under section 6056 if the ALE has no full-time employees?

No. An ALE that does not have any employee who was a full-time employee (at least thirty hours of work per week in any moth of the year) in any month of the year is not required to report under section 6056. An ALE Member must report if it has one or more employees who were full-time employees for any month of the year.[3]

462. Do ALEs that sponsor self-insured health plans need to file Form 1094-C and Form 1095-C if the ALE has no full-time employees?

Generally, yes. While an ALE Member without any full-time employees is not required to report under section 6056, an ALE Member that sponsors a self-insured health plan in which any employee or a spouse or dependent of any employee has enrolled is required

---

1.   https://www.law.cornell.edu/uscode/text/26/6722.

2.   https://www.law.cornell.edu/uscode/text/26/6723.

3.   https://www.irs.gov/affordable-care-act/questions-and-answers-on-information-reporting-by-health-coverage-providers-section-6055. (Last accessed August 5, 2019).

to file Form 1094-C and Form 1095-C, to satisfy the section 6055 information reporting requirements for providers of minimum essential coverage. This is the case for any individual who was an employee (or spouse or dependent of an employee) for any month of the year, whether or not the employer has any full-time employees and whether or not the employee is a full-time employee.

However, for an individual who enrolled in coverage but was not an employee in any month of the year (and whose coverage was not a result of the relationship to the employee, such as a spouse or dependent), the employer may file Forms 1094-B, Transmittal of Health Coverage Information Returns and 1095-B, Health Coverage, or Forms 1094-C and 1095-C for that individual. For more information on reporting of enrollment information for non-employees, see the Instructions for Forms 1094-C and 1095-C.

463. Is an employer that is not an ALE Member required to report under section 6056 or to file Form 1094-C or Form 1095-C?

No. An employer that is not subject to the employer shared responsibility provisions is not required to report under section 6056. Therefore, an employer that employed fewer than fifty full-time employees (including full-time equivalent employees) during the preceding calendar year is not subject to the reporting requirements of section 6056.

464. Is an employer that sponsors a self-insured health care plan but is not an ALE required to report under section 6056 or to file Form 1094-C or Form 1095-C?

No. An employer that is not an ALE Member that sponsors a self-insured health plan in which any individual has enrolled is not subject to the reporting requirements of section 6056 and should not file Form 1094-C or Form 1095-C. However, the employer is subject to the reporting requirements under section 6055 for providers of minimum essential coverage. The employer will generally satisfy its reporting obligations under section 6055 by filing Form 1094-B and Form 1095-B for employees (and spouses and dependents of employees) who enrolled in coverage.

465. Is an ALE required to report under section 6056 for a full-time employee who is not offered coverage during the year?

Yes. An ALE Member is required to report information about the coverage, if any, offered to each of its full-time employees, including whether or not an offer of coverage was made. This requirement applies to all ALE Members with full-time employees, regardless of whether they offered coverage to all, none, or some of their full-time employees. For each of its full-time employees, the ALE Member is required to file Form 1095-C with the IRS and furnish a copy of Form 1095-C to the employee, regardless of whether coverage was or was not offered to the employee. Therefore, even if an ALE Member does not offer coverage to any of its full-time employees, it must file returns with the IRS and furnish statements to each of its full-time employees to report that coverage was not offered.

466. Are different reporting methods available to ALEs for reporting required information statements?

Yes. Section 6056 regulations provide a general method that all ALE Members may use for reporting to the IRS and for furnishing statements to full-time employees, and also provide alternative reporting methods for eligible ALE Members. If an ALE Member is not eligible to use either one of the alternative reporting methods for some or all of its employees, the ALE Member must use the general method for those employees. In any case, the alternative reporting methods are optional, and an ALE Member may choose to report for all of its full-time employees using the general method even if an alternative reporting method is available.

467. What is the general method of reporting?

Under the general method, each Applicable Large Employer must satisfy:

- the requirement to file a section 6056 return with the IRS by filing a Form 1094-C (transmittal) and, for each full-time employee, a Form 1095-C (employee statement); and

- the requirement to furnish a section 6056 statement to a full-time employee by providing each of its full-time employees a Form 1095-C.

An ALE using the general method with employees participating in a self-insured plan also uses Form 1095-C to satisfy the reporting requirements under section 6055 for providers of minimum essential coverage, by filling out a separate section (Part III) of the Form 1095-C. Part III allows ALEs that sponsor self-insured group health plans to combine reporting to satisfy both the section 6055 reporting requirements and the section 6056 reporting requirements, as applicable, on a single return.

The requirement of a Section 6056 return as well as a section 6055 return under the general method also may be satisfied by using a substitute form. The substitute form must include all of the information required on Form 1094-C and Form 1095-C and satisfy all form and content requirements as specified by the IRS.

468. What are the alternative methods of reporting?

There are two alternative methods of reporting under section 6056. These were developed to minimize the cost and administrative burdens for employers. The alternative reporting methods are:

- Reporting based on a certified Qualifying Offer

- Reporting without separate identification of full-time employees if certain conditions related to offers of coverage are satisfied (98 percent offers)

469. How does an ALE report under the Qualifying Offer method?

The Qualifying Offer method allows an employer to complete the Form 1095-C under simplified rules and to furnish to certain full-time employees a document other than the Form

1095-C. To be eligible to use the Qualifying Offer method, the ALE must certify that it made a Qualifying Offer to one or more of its full-time employees for all calendar months during the calendar year in which the employee was a full-time employee for whom an employer shared responsibility payment could apply.

An ALE reporting under the Qualifying Offer method may furnish a simplified statement to an employee that received a Qualifying Offer for all twelve months of the calendar year rather than furnishing a copy of the Form 1095-C that will be filed with the IRS. In general, however, an employer that sponsors a self-insured plan may not use the alternative statement for any employee who has enrolled in that self-insured coverage because the employer is required to report that coverage on Form 1095-C.

470. What is a Qualifying Offer in relation to the Form 1095-C?

A "Qualifying Offer" is an offer that satisfies all of the following criteria:

- It is an offer of coverage that provides minimum value;

- The employee cost for employee-only coverage for each month does not exceed 9.78 percent (as adjusted for 2020) of the mainland single federal poverty line divided by twelve; and

- The offer of coverage is also made to the employee's spouse and dependents (if any).

471. How does an ALE report under the 98 percent Offer Method?

An ALE may qualify for the 98 percent Offer Method of reporting if it:

- Offered affordable coverage providing minimum value to at least 98 percent of its employees for whom it is filing a Form 1095-C

    o Must consider all months during which the individuals were employees and were not in a Limited Non-Assessment Period and

- Offered coverage to those employees' dependents, and

- Certifies to the IRS that it did so.

The ALE is still required to file and furnish Forms 1095-C for all its full-time employees who were full-time employees for one or more months of the calendar year.

472. When must an ALE file the required information return?

An ALE must usually file Form 1094-C and Form 1095-C on or before February 28 (March 31 if filed electronically) of the year immediately following the calendar year for which the offer of coverage information is reported. Filing for reporting for 2020 is April 1, 2020 if filing electronically and February 28, 2020.

473. When must an ALE furnish the statements to full-time employees?

An ALE must generally furnish Form 1095-C on or before January 31 of the year immediately following the calendar year to which the information relates. And under the section 6056 regulations, the IRS may grant extensions of time of up to thirty days to furnish Form 1095-C for good cause shown. The IRS allowed extension of these dates for 2015, 2016, 2017, 2018, and 2019.

474. Must an ALE file returns with the IRS electronically?

The regulations require electronic filing with the IRS of Form 1094-C (transmittal) and Form 1095-C (employee statement) except for an ALE filing fewer than 250 Forms 1095-C during the calendar year. Each Form 1095-C is counted as a separate return, and only Forms 1095-C are counted in applying the 250-return threshold for section 6056 reporting.

475. Must an ALE furnish the employee statements to full-time employees electronically?

No. ALEs are permitted under the regulations but not required to furnish Form 1095-C electronically to full-time employees if notice, consent, and hardware and software requirements are met. The regulations require that, for each full-time employee to whom the information is furnished, the ALE must obtain consent from the employee before Form 1095-C may be furnished electronically.

Statements reporting coverage under an expatriate health plan, however, may be furnished electronically unless the recipient explicitly refuses to consent to receive the statement in an electronic format.

476. May an ALE furnish a Form 1095-C to an employee by hand delivery?

Yes. Form 1095-C may be delivered to employees in any manner permitted for delivery of Form W-2.

477. Must an ALE furnish a Form 1095-C within 30 days of the employee's written request if the employee terminates employment and requests the statement?

No. This requirement applies for Forms W-2 (Wage and Tax Statement) under the provisions of section 6051, but does not apply for a Form 1095-C. Therefore, the employee may provide but is not required to furnish a Form 1095-C upon an employee's request following a termination of employment. However, if the employer furnishes a Form 1095-C to the employee under these circumstances and the relevant information changes the employer will need to furnish an updated Form 1095-C to the employee reflecting the updated information as filed with the IRS.

478. May an ALE file more than one Form 1094-C?

Yes. An ALE may file more than one Form 1094-C, provided that one (and only one) of those transmittals is an Authoritative Transmittal reporting aggregate employer-level data for the ALE.

479. May an ALE satisfy reporting requirements for an employee by filing and furnishing more than one Form 1095-C that together provide the necessary information?

No. There must be only one Form 1095-C for each full-time employee for that full-time employee's employment with the ALE.

480. May an ALE hire a third-party administrator or service provider to file the return with the IRS and furnish the statements to employees required under section 6056?

Yes. ALEs may enter into arrangements with issuers, other ALEs or third parties to have the other party file the return with the IRS, furnish the statements to its employees, or both. However, entering into a reporting arrangement does not transfer the ALE 's potential liability under section 4980H and (except in the case of a related entity properly designated by a governmental unit) does not transfer the potential liability for failure of the ALE to file timely, complete and accurate returns and furnish timely, complete and accurate statements under section 6056. If a person who prepares returns or statements required under section 6056 is a tax return preparer, that person will be subject to the requirements generally applicable to tax return preparers.

481. May an ALE that is a governmental unit designate a third party to file the return and furnish the statements under section 6056 on its behalf?

Yes. Section 6056 and the regulations provide that an ALE that is a governmental unit (defined as the government of the United States, any State or political subdivision thereof, or any Indian tribal government, may report under section 6056 on its own behalf or may designate another person or persons, including another entity, to report on its behalf. A person may be designated to file the return and furnish the statements under section 6056 on behalf of the ALE if the person is part of or related to the same governmental unit as the ALE. A government entity that is appropriately designated to file for another governmental unit is referred to as a Designated Government Entity (DGE).

A separate Form 1094-C must be filed for each ALE for which the DGE is reporting - including the name, address and EIN of both the DGE and the ALE for which it is reporting. There has to be a single Authoritative Transmittal, Form 1094-C, reporting aggregate employer-level data for the ALE and only one Form 1095-C for each full-time employee of the ALE with respect to employment with that ALE.

482. May an ALE that is a governmental unit that sponsors a self-insured health plan designate a third party to file the return and furnish the statements under section 6055 on its behalf?

Yes. An employer that is a governmental unit that sponsors a self-insured health plan may designate a DGE to satisfy its reporting obligations under section 6055.

483. May an ALE that is a governmental unit that sponsors a self-insured health plan designate a DGE for its reporting obligations under section 6055 but not for its reporting obligations under section 6056?

Yes. An employer that is a governmental unit that sponsors a self-insured health plan may designate a DGE for its reporting obligations under section 6055, as discussed in the question above, but decide not to designate a DGE for its reporting obligations under section 6056.

484. How does the delegation of the reporting responsibility to a DGE affect the requirement that one Form 1094-C be designated as the Authoritative Transmittal containing aggregate employer-level data?

Each governmental unit that is an ALE must file a single Authoritative Transmittal, Form 1094-C, containing the aggregate employer-level data for the governmental unit (including the total number of full-time employees and the total number of employees of the governmental unit for each month of the calendar year, regardless of the number of Form 1095-Cs transmitted with that particular Form 1094-C. The governmental unit may delegate to the DGE the requirement to file a Form 1094-C Authoritative Transmittal.

Annual Report by DOL about Self-Insured Plans (Using Form 5500 Information)

485. What information must the DOL report to Congress regarding self-insured health plans?

Healthcare reform requires the DOL to prepare and submit to Congress an aggregate annual report that includes general information collected from Form 5500 filings by self-insured group health plans, including plan type, number of participants, benefits offered, funding arrangements, and benefit arrangements.[1]

The Report to Congress Annual Report on Self-Insured Group Health Plans was filed in March 2017.[2] The 2012, 2013, 2014, 2015, and 2016 Reports are also available online, though it should be noted that revisions made to the algorithm and methodology beginning with the 2013 Report have resulted in the Reports not being comparable over time.

The Annual Report on Self-Insured Group Health Plans for 2018 was filed in March 2018.[3]

The Annual Report on Self-Insured Group Health Plans for 2019 was filed in March 2019.[4]

---

1.   PPACA §1253.
2.   https://www.dol.gov/sites/default/files/ebsa/researchers/statistics/retirement-bulletins/annual-report-on-self-insured-group-health-plans-2017.pdf.
3.   https://www.dol.gov/sites/default/files/ebsa/researchers/statistics/retirement-bulletins/annual-report-on-self-insured-group-health-plans-2018.pdf.
4.   https://www.dol.gov/sites/default/files/ebsa/researchers/statistics/retirement-bulletins/annual-report-on-self-insured-group-health-plans-2019.pdf.

486. What types of self-insured plans exist?

The 2019 DOL report states that:

- approximately 22,700 of the self-insured group health plans filing a 2016 Form 5500 were sponsored by a single employer while 1,000 plans were multiemployer plans.

- About 3,500 of the mixed-insured group health plans filing a 2016 Form 5500 were sponsored by a single employer;

- approximately 600 plans were multiemployer plans.

On average, about 49,900 group health plans filed a Form 5500 in the years 2007–2016. While the number of health plans filing a Form 5500 has increased over this period, the fraction of group health plans that are self-insured or mixed-insured has been relatively stable, slipping from 51 percent in 2007 to 48 percent in 2013, and rebounding to 50 percent in 2016.

487. How many participants are there in self-insured plans?

Overall, the 23,700 self-insured group health plans filing a 2016 Form 5500 covered approximately 34 million participants, 31 million of whom were active participants. The 4,100 mixed-insured group health plans filing a 2016 Form 5500 covered approximately 28 million participants, 23 million of whom were active participants.

In general, plans covering a larger number of participants are more likely to be self-insured than plans with fewer participants. While 51 percent of plans are fully-insured, only 18 percent of participants in plans that file the Form 5500 are covered by these plans.

488. What types of benefits are offered though the self-insured health plans?

The 2019 report details that of the 23,700 self-insured group health plans in 2016, 5,100 offered only health benefits and approximately 18,600 offered other benefits in addition to health benefits. Of the 4,100 mixed-insured group health plans, approximately 200 offered only health benefits and about 3,900 offered other benefits in addition to health benefits.

Insured Health Plan Transparency in Coverage and Cost-Sharing Reporting

489. What are the transparency in coverage and cost-sharing reporting requirements?

The transparency in coverage reporting and the cost-sharing disclosure rules apply to individual policies and group health plans, both Qualified Health Plans (QHPs), and those outside of the exchanges.[1] The requirements are the same except that nonexchange health plans need not

---

1.   PHSA §2715A (plans and insurers outside of the Exchange) and PPACA §1311(e)(3)(A)(requirement for exchange-certified health plans).

report to the exchange. These health plan reports are made to HHS, the state insurance commissioner, and the public.[1] The rules do not apply to grandfathered plans,[2] although if a QHP sold on an exchange were grandfathered, it would need to make a report to the exchange.[3] In addition, a health plan seeking QHP certification on an exchange must provide certain cost-sharing disclosures to participants.[4]

490. What information must be reported under these rules?

Health plans and insurers subject to the transparency in coverage reporting requirement must disclose all of the following information:

- Claims payment policies and practices

- Periodic financial disclosures

- Data on enrollment and disenrollment

- Data on the number of claims denied

- Data on rating practices

- Information on cost-sharing and payments regarding any out-of-network coverage

- Information on enrollee and participant rights under Title I of PPACA

- Other information as determined appropriate by the Secretary of HHS[5]

491. Must any of this information be disclosed to individuals?

Yes. Health plans and insurers subject to this requirement must provide certain cost-sharing information (including deductibles, copayments, and coinsurance) in a timely manner on request by an individual.[6] The information generally may be provided on a Web site, but for individuals who do not have access to the Internet, the information must be provided another way.[7]

SPD Content Requirements for ERISA Group Health Plans

492. What is covered in the Summary Plan Description?

The Summary Plan Description (SBD) is a detailed document that informs plan participants about how the plan operates and is managed. Among other things, the SPD must clearly identify in easily understood language the following items:

---

1.   PHSA §2715A.
2.   PPACA §§1251(a), 10103(d)(1).
3.   PPACA §1311(e)(3)(A).
4.   PPACA §1311(e)(3)(C).
5.   PPACA §1311(e)(3)(A).
6.   PPACA §1311(e)(3)(C).
7.   PPACA §1311(e)(3)(C).

- A description or summary of the benefits

- The plan name, sponsor, and administrator and address, and phone number

- The plan sponsor's EIN

- The type of plan administration, e.g., administered by contract, insurer, or sponsor

- Funding mechanisms

- Designation of any named fiduciaries, if other than the plan administrator, e.g., claim fiduciary

- The plan number for ERISA Form 5500 purposes

- Type of plan or brief description of benefits, e.g., life, medical, dental, disability

- The date of the end of the plan year for maintaining the plan's fiscal records (which may be different from the insurance policy

- Participation and qualification guidelines

- Calculation methods for service and benefits

- Benefit vesting schedules

- Benefit payment procedures and timing

- Claims submission process

- Claims appeal process

- Address for service of legal process

- Circumstances that may result in ineligibility or a denial of benefits

- A statement of participants' ERISA rights and other technical notices

- Each trustee's name, title, and address of principal place of business, if the plan has a trust

- The date of the end of the plan year for maintaining the plan's fiscal records (which may be different from the insurance policy year)

- The name and address of the plan's agent for service of legal process, along with a statement that service may be made on a plan trustee or administrator

- Eligibility terms, e.g., classes of eligible employees, employment waiting period, and hours per week, and the effective date of participation, e.g., next day or first of the month following satisfaction of an eligibility waiting period

- How the insurer refunds (e.g., dividends, demutualization, and medical loss ratio (MLR) refunds) are allocated to participants.

- The plan sponsor's amendment and termination rights and procedures, and what happens to plan assets, if any, in the event of plan termination

- A summary of any plan provisions governing the benefits, rights, and obligations of participants under the plan on termination or amendment of the plan or elimination of benefits

- Claims procedures—may be furnished separately in a Certificate of Coverage, provided that the SPD explains that claims procedures are furnished automatically, without charge, in the separate document (e.g., a Certificate of Coverage), and time limits for lawsuits, if the plan imposes them

- A statement clearly identifying circumstances that may result in loss or denial of benefits (e.g., subrogation, coordination of benefits, and offset provisions)

- The standard of review for benefit decisions (We recommend consideration of granting full discretion for the plan administrator or authorized fiduciary to interpret the plan and make factual determinations.)

- ERISA model statement of participants' rights

- The sources of plan contributions, whether from employer and/or employee contributions, and the method by which they are calculated

- Interim SMMs since the SPD was adopted or last restated

- The fact that the employer is a participating employer or a member of a controlled group

- Whether the plan is maintained pursuant to one or more collective bargaining agreements, and that a copy of the agreement may be obtained upon request

- A prominent offer of assistance in a non-English language (depending on the number of participants who are literate in the same non-English language)

- Identity of the insurer(s), if any

493. When must a Summary Plan Description be provided?

Every plan administrator must provide a copy of the SPD to participants in the following circumstances:

- When a new plan takes effect

- When an employee becomes eligible to participate in a plan

- Upon written request of a plan participant or beneficiary

494. Are there any exceptions to the Summary Plan Description?

Employer-provided daycare and welfare plans for management and highly compensated employees are exempt from the SPD requirement. There are no exemptions from the SPD requirement for small plans covering fewer than 100 participants.

495. How often must a Summary Plan Description be updated?

If a plan is amended or modified within a five-year period, a new SPD must be distributed to participants. If there is no change, the original SPD must be distributed to plan participants every ten years.

A "summary of material modifications" may also be used to notify plan participants of a significant plan change.

496. What are common errors found in Summary Plan Descriptions that can result in litigation under ERISA?

Administration errors or disputes that may result in ERISA litigation include but are not limited to:

- Failure to follow the procedures described in the SPD

- Conflicts between the SPD and any underlying plan document which it describes or summarizes

- Failure to clearly disclose circumstances that may result in benefits reduction, forfeitures, or exclusions Failure to provide plan documents in a timely manner

ERISA provides detailed procedures that must be closely followed by plan sponsors and administrators.

Quality of Care Reporting by Group Health Plans and Insurers

497. What reporting is required by group health plans and insurers that is designed to improve the quality of care?

Group health plans and health insurance companies must submit an annual report to HHS addressing plan or coverage benefits and provider reimbursement structures that may affect the quality of care in certain specified ways. The reporting requirements are to be developed in consultation with health care quality experts and representatives of care providers, care recipients, insurers, and employers. This requirement will be enforced by "appropriate penalties" developed by HHS.[1] Grandfathered plans are not subject to these rules.[2]

---

1.   PHSA §2717(a).
2.   PPACA §§1251(a) and 10103(d)(1).

HHS was required to "develop" the reporting requirements and issue regulations no later than March 23, 2012.[1] HHS missed the deadline.[2] On July 11, 2016 the Employee Benefits Security Administration (EBSA) of the Department of Labor posted a proposed rule on annual reporting and disclosure.[3] In addition the IRS, the PGBC and the DOL (EBSA) posted a revision of annual reporting forms and reports.[4] The new Schedule J provided in this proposal is intended to meet the reporting requirements of PHSA section 2717.

498. What information must be reported and when?

The quality of care reports address whether plan or coverage benefits as well as provider reimbursement structures satisfy several criteria related to the cost and quality of health care. These include whether the plan or coverage:

- improves health outcomes for treatment or services under the plan or coverage through such activities as quality reporting, effective case management, care coordination, chronic disease management, and medication and care compliance initiatives (including the medical homes model);

- implements activities to prevent hospital re-admissions using a comprehensive discharge program and post-discharge reinforcement;

- improves patient safety and reduces medical errors through best clinical practices, evidence-based medicine, and health information technology; and

- implements wellness and health promotion activities.[5]

The NCQA's Health Plan Report Cards list commercial, Medicare, Medicaid and Marketplace health plans based on their combined HEDIS®, CAHPS® and NCQA Accreditation standards scores. NCQA evaluates health plans on the quality of care patients receive, how happy patients are with their care and health plans' efforts to keep improving.[6]

Cadillac Plan Excise Tax Determination

499. What is the "Cadillac Tax" and what reporting is required?

The "Cadillac Tax"[7] is an excise tax originally intended to be effective in 2013. Implementation was delayed several times with the latest delay now being a bill signed by President Trump

---

1.   PHSA §2717.
2.   The Government Accountability Office (GAO) released a report on January 13, 2012 stating that HHS has failed to properly supervise the development of quality measures that are required by PPACA. The report, "Health Care Quality Measurement: HHS Should Address Contractor Performance and Plan for Needed Measures" (GAO-12-136), also criticized the National Quality Forum (NQF), a nonprofit group that has a four-year, $100 million contract with HHS to develop quality measures, for missing deadlines and exceeding contract cost estimates. The seventy-five-page GAO report expresses concern that if HHS does not exert more control over NQF's performance, it "may be unable to ensure that [HHS] receives the quality measures needed to meet PPACA requirements," including deadlines for the implementation of new programs and initiatives to control healthcare costs.
3.   29 CFR Pars 2520 and 2590 https://s3.amazonaws.com/public-inspection.federalregister.gov/2016-14892.pdf (Last accessed August 5, 2019).
4.   https://www.dol.gov/newsroom/releases/ebsa/ebsa20160711., dated July 12, 2016 (Last accessed August 5, 2019).
5.   PHSA §2717(a)(1).
6.   These Report Cards can be found at https://reportcards.ncqa.org/#/health-plans/list.
7.   IRC §4980I.

on January 22, 2018 delaying implementation until 2022. The prior delay was effected through the passage of the 2016 Consolidated Appropriations Act. In addition, during 2017, the United States Senate voted 52-48 along partisan lines to repeal the Cadillac Tax entirely, however the U.S. House of Representatives did not followed suit. Currently there is a bill (Middle Class Health Benefits Tax Repeal Act of 2019) before the U.S. House of Representatives intending to repeal the Cadillac Tax.

The intent of the tax is to discourage expensive health plans that require enrollees to pay little for their own care. It is discussed in more detail in Part IX of this book. The tax is 40 percent of the cost of health coverage that exceeds predetermined threshold amounts. Cost of coverage includes the total contributions paid by both the employer and employees, but not cost-sharing amounts such as deductibles, coinsurance and copays when care is received.

An employer, in 2022, will have to determine whether the following costs for each employee for each year exceed $11,200 (individual) and $30,100 (family). Costs will be adjusted upward for qualified retirees and those in high-risk professions:

- Health care coverage

- Employer health FSA contributions and any reimbursements in excess of the employer contributions

- Employer and employee pretax HSA contributions

- HRA contributions

The tax is calculated on a monthly and per-person basis, where any plan above $850 per month for single coverage and $2,292 per month for family coverage is subject to it.

These dollar thresholds will be updated for 2022 when and if final regulations are issued and thereafter indexed for regular (not medical) inflation in future years. The dollar thresholds will also be increased: if the majority of covered employees are engaged in specified high-risk professions such as law enforcement and construction, and for group demographics including age and gender.

If the cost is above the threshold, the employer is required to determine the excess amount and report it to the Secretary of the Treasury and each third-party administrator or insurer, including the excess amounts attributable to each third-party administrator or insurer. Concerns have risen whether it would affect upwards of 75 percent of employee health plans and diminish the viability of Health Savings Accounts and High Deductible Health Plans. Unpopular with both parties, it is still very possible that it will be repealed before 2022 even if the Affordable Care Act is not repealed or replaced.

Some types of coverage are excluded, such as:

- U.S.-issued expatriate plans for most categories of expatriates

- Coverage for accident only, or disability income insurance, or any combination thereof

- Supplemental liability insurance

- Liability insurance, including general liability insurance and automobile liability insurance

- Worker's compensation or similar insurance

- Automobile medical payment insurance

- Credit-only insurance

- Other insurance coverage as specified in regulations under which benefits for medical care are secondary or incidental to other insurance benefits

- Long Term Care

- Standalone dental and vision

- Coverage for the military sponsored by federal, state or local governments

- Employee Assistance Programs

- Employee After-Tax Contributions to HSAs and MSAs

- Coverage for a specified disease or illness and hospital indemnity or other fixed indemnity insurance if payment is not excluded from gross income

List of Required Disclosures and Notices to Health Plan Participants

500. What are the various notices required to be made to health plan participants?

In addition to the mandates discussed earlier in Part VII of this book that need to be described in the health plan SPD, the following notices must be given and are expanded upon in greater detail in Q 501 through Q 514:

- Grandfather and Grandmother Status

- Rescission Prohibition

- Primary Care Designation Notice

- PPACA Prohibition on Lifetime Dollar Limits; Re-enrollment Right

- Annual Limits

- Adult Child Coverage Opportunity

- Claims and Appeals Process

- Summary of Benefits and Coverage (SBC)

- Explanation of Exchange, the Exchange Notice

- Automatic Enrollment (REPEALED BEFORE IMPLEMENTATION)

- Model Wellness Program

- Model Newborns' Act Disclosure

- Model WHCRA Enrollment Disclosure

- Model Special Enrollment Notice

- Disclosure of Plan Data and Financials

501. What notices are required for Grandfathered plans?

Effective for plan years beginning on and after September 23, 2010. Grandfathered plans must include a statement in any plan material provided to participants and beneficiaries each year describing benefits under the plan that the plan believes it is grandfathered and contact information for questions and complaints. See Q 234. The DOL provided model language which could be used to satisfy this disclosure requirement:[1]

> This [group health plan or health insurance issuer] believes this [plan or coverage] is a "grandfathered health plan" under the Patient Protection and Affordable Care Act (the Affordable Care Act). As permitted by the Affordable Care Act, a grandfathered health plan can preserve certain basic health coverage that was already in effect when that law was enacted. Being a grandfathered health plan means that your [plan or policy] may not include certain consumer protections of the Affordable Care Act that apply to other plans, for example, the requirement for the provision of preventive health services without any cost sharing. However, grandfathered health plans must comply with certain other consumer protections in the Affordable Care Act, for example, the elimination of lifetime limits on benefits.

> Questions regarding which protections apply and which protections do not apply to a grandfathered health plan and what might cause a plan to change from grandfathered health plan status can be directed to the plan administrator at [insert contact information]. [For ERISA plans, insert: You may also contact the Employee Benefits Security Administration, U.S. Department of Labor at 1-866-444-3272 or www.dol.gov/ebsa/healthreform. This website has a table summarizing which protections do and do not apply to grandfathered health plans.] [For individual

---

1.   https://www.dol.gov/sites/dolgov/files/EBSA/laws-and-regulations/laws/affordable-care-act/for-employers-and-advisers/grandfathered-health-plans-model-notice.doc.

market policies and nonfederal governmental plans, insert: You may also contact the U.S. Department of Health and Human Services at www.healthreform.gov.]

502. What notice is required for Rescission Prohibition?

Effective for plan years beginning on and after September 23, 2010). All plans must provide at least thirty days' advance written notice to each participant who would be affected by a rescission, whether the rescission applies to the entire group or to an individual.[1]

503. What notice is required for a Primary Care Designation Notice?

When applicable, it is important that individuals enrolled in a plan or health insurance coverage know of their rights to (1) choose a primary care provider or a pediatrician when a plan or issuer requires designation of a primary care physician; or (2) obtain obstetrical or gynecological care without prior authorization. Accordingly, the interim final regulations regarding patient protections under section 2719A of the Affordable Care Act require plans and issuers to provide notice to participants of these rights when applicable. The notice must be provided whenever the plan or issuer provides a participant with a summary plan description or other similar description of benefits under the plan or health insurance coverage. This notice must be provided no later than the first day of the first plan year beginning on or after September 23, 2010.

The following model language can be used to satisfy the notice requirement:[2]

> For plans and issuers that require or allow for the designation of primary care providers by participants or beneficiaries, insert:
>
> [Name of group health plan or health insurance issuer] generally [requires/allows] the designation of a primary care provider. You have the right to designate any primary care provider who participates in our network and who is available to accept you or your family members. [If the plan or health insurance coverage designates a primary care provider automatically, insert: Until you make this designation, [name of group health plan or health insurance issuer] designates one for you.] For information on how to select a primary care provider, and for a list of the participating primary care providers, contact the [plan administrator or issuer] at [insert contact information].
>
> For plans and issuers that require or allow for the designation of a primary care provider for a child, add:
>
> For children, you may designate a pediatrician as the primary care provider.
>
> For plans and issuers that provide coverage for obstetric or gynecological care and require the designation by a participant or beneficiary of a primary care provider, add:

---

1.   45 CFR Section 147.128 Rules regarding Rescissions https://www.law.cornell.edu/cfr/text/45/147.128.
2.   https://www.dol.gov/sites/default/files/ebsa/laws-and-regulations/laws/affordable-care-act/for-employers-and-advisers/patient-protection-model-notice.doc.

> You do not need prior authorization from [name of group health plan or issuer] or from any other person (including a primary care provider) in order to obtain access to obstetrical or gynecological care from a health care professional in our network who specializes in obstetrics or gynecology. The health care professional, however, may be required to comply with certain procedures, including obtaining prior authorization for certain services, following a pre-approved treatment plan, or procedures for making referrals. For a list of participating health care professionals who specialize in obstetrics or gynecology, contact the [plan administrator or issuer] at [insert contact information].

504. What notice is required for the PPACA Prohibition on Lifetime Dollar Limits and re-enrollment rights?

Plan years beginning on or after September 23, 2010. If an individual was no longer eligible for coverage under the plan because of reaching the lifetime dollar limit, the plan must allow the individual into the plan on the first plan year on and after September 23, 2010. The plan must provide notice of the right to re-enroll to this individual. The following model notice can be used:[1]

> The lifetime limit on the dollar value of benefits under [Insert name of group health plan or health insurance issuer] no longer applies. Individuals whose coverage ended by reason of reaching a lifetime limit under the plan are eligible to enroll in the plan. Individuals have thirty days from the date of this notice to request enrollment. For more information contact the [insert plan administrator or issuer] at [insert contact information].

505. What notice is required for Adult Child Coverage through age twenty-six?

Model Language for Notice of Opportunity to Enroll in Connection with Extension of Dependent Coverage to Age 26

The interim final regulations extending dependent coverage to age twenty-six provide transitional relief for a child whose coverage ended, or who was denied coverage (or was not eligible for coverage) under a group health plan or health insurance coverage because, under the terms of the plan or coverage, the availability of dependent coverage of children ended before the attainment of age twenty-six. The regulations require a plan or issuer to give such a child an opportunity to enroll that continues for at least thirty days (including written notice of the opportunity to enroll), regardless of whether the plan or coverage offers an open enrollment period and regardless of when any open enrollment period might otherwise occur. This enrollment opportunity (including the written notice) must be provided not later than the first day of the first plan year beginning on or after September 23, 2010. The notice may be included with other enrollment materials that a plan distributes,

---

1. https://www.federalregister.gov/documents/2015/11/18/2015-29294/final-rules-for-grandfathered-plans-preexisting-condition-exclusions-lifetime-and-annual-limits.

provided the statement is prominent. Enrollment must be effective as of the first day of the first plan year beginning on or after September 23, 2010.

The following model language can be used to satisfy the notice requirement:[1]

> Individuals whose coverage ended, or who were denied coverage (or were not eligible for coverage), because the availability of dependent coverage of children ended before attainment of age 26 are eligible to enroll in [Insert name of group health plan or health insurance coverage]. Individuals may request enrollment for such children for 30 days from the date of notice. Enrollment will be effective retroactively to [insert date that is the first day of the first plan year beginning on or after September 23, 2010.] For more information contact the [insert plan administrator or issuer] at [insert contact information].

506. What notice is required for Claims and Appeals Processes?

Health reform adds additional requirements for claims and appeals procedures for non-grandfathered plans. These requirements were effective for plan years beginning on and after September 23, 2010, but the DOL provided an enforcement grace period for certain provisions for plan years beginning on and after the date noted below. This notice must:[2]

- be written in a culturally and linguistically appropriate manner (effective January 1, 2012);

- provide the following additional content.

  - Information sufficient to identify the claim involved, including the date of service, the healthcare provider, the claim amount, and a statement that the diagnosis code and its corresponding meaning and the treatment code and its corresponding meaning are available on request.

  - An explanation of the reason for the adverse benefit determination or final adverse benefit determination, including the denial code and its meaning and a description of the plan's standard that was used in denying the claim or making the final adverse determination (effective July 1, 2011).

  - Describe the internal appeals and external review process (effective July 1, 2011).

  - Describe the availability of and contact information for an applicable office of health insurance consumer assistance or ombudsman as established under PPACA (effective July 1, 2011).

---

1.   https://www.dol.gov/sites/default/files/ebsa/laws-and-regulations/laws/affordable-care-act/for-employers-and-advisers/extension-of-coverage-for-adult-children-model-notice.doc.
2.   https://www.dol.gov/agencies/ebsa/laws-and-regulations/laws/affordable-care-act/for-employers-and-advisers/internal-claims-and-appeals.

If a plan does not meet all of the requirements in the regulations, the claimant is deemed to have exhausted the internal claims and appeals process and may initiate any available external review or remedies under ERISA or state law. The strict adherence standard will not apply if the errors were:

- de minimis;

- nonprejudicial or nonharmful;

- for good cause or because of matters beyond the plan's control;

- in the context of an ongoing, good-faith exchange of information; and

- not a pattern or practice of noncompliance.

If a plan asserts the exception, it must provide an explanation in response to a written request from the claimant (effective January 1, 2012).

507. What is the notice required for Summary of Benefits and Coverage (SBC)?

Effective for open enrollments beginning for plan years beginning on and after September 23, 2012 and new enrollments). The SBC must be provided to employees. The SBC must not exceed eight pages (four sheets front and back), be in 12-point font, be presented in "culturally and linguistically" appropriate language, and include the following:

- A Uniform Glossary, i.e., definitions of standard insurance terms and medical terms.

- A description of coverage and any cost sharing (including any deductibles, coinsurance, and copayments, but not premiums).

- Any exceptions, reductions, and limitations on coverage.

- Renewability and continuation coverage provisions.

- Coverage examples (currently only childbirth and diabetes, but up to four more may be added in the future).

- A statement of whether the plan provides minimum essential coverage and has an actuarial value of at least 60 percent (effective for plan years beginning on and after January 1, 2014).

- A contact number to call and an Internet address or website for a copy of the policy or the SPD for self-funded plans).

- If a plan has multiple networks, contact information for obtaining a list of network providers.

- If a plan uses a prescription drug formulary, contact information for obtaining information on prescription drug coverage.

- An Internet address or website for obtaining the Uniform Glossary, a contact number to obtain a paper copy of the Uniform Glossary, and a disclosure that paper copies are available.

A sample SBC and Uniform Glossary are provided in the Appendix A of this book. If any material modification of any of the terms of the plan coverage is made and it is not reflected in the most recent SBC, notice of the modification must be provided no later than sixty days before the modification becomes effective.

W-2 Reporting 2012 CalendarYear Health Care Coverage (reportable by January 31, 2013). See Q 403 to Q 422.

508. What notice is required for the Explanation of the Exchange and the Exchange Notice?

Effective March 1, 2013 and for all new hires thereafter.

Reporting of Health Insurance Coverage Effective for Plan Years beginning on and after January 1, 2014. An employer must file a return with the IRS showing:

- the name, address, and TIN of the participant and the name and TIN of each beneficiary;

- the date of coverage;

- the employer's name, address, and EIN;

- the portion of the premium paid by the employer.

An employer must provide to a participant the following before January 31 of the year following the reporting year:

- the name and address of the employer and a phone number of the contact for the information provided to the participant; and

- the information that is required to be on the return to the IRS.[1]

509. What notice was required for the Automatic Enrollment provision?

On November 2, 2015, the Bipartisan Budget Act of 2015 was enacted which repealed the automatic enrollment requirement. This requirement had been established under Section 18A of the Fair Labor Standards Act and required that an employer with more than 200 employees automatically enroll each new full-time employee and continue such enrollment, unless the employee opts out or changes the coverage. The employer would

---

1.   https://www.dol.gov/agencies/ebsa/laws-and-regulations/laws/affordable-care-act/for-employers-and-advisers/coverage-options-notice.

have been required to provide notice of the automatic enrollment and the procedures for opting out.

Section 18A of the FLSA, as added by Section 1511 of the Affordable Care Act has been repealed.[1]

510. What notice is required for the Model Wellness Program Disclosure?

For group health plans offering a wellness program that requires an individual to satisfy a standard related to a health factor, the following is model language that may be used to satisfy the requirement that the availability of a reasonable alternative standard be disclosed:

> Your health plan is committed to helping you achieve your best health. Rewards for participating in a wellness program are available to all employees. If you think you might be unable to meet a standard for a reward under this wellness program, you might qualify for an opportunity to earn the same reward by different means. Contact us at [insert contact information] and we will work with you (and, if you wish, with your doctor) to find a wellness program with the same reward that is right for you in light of your health status.[2]

511. What notice is required for the Model Newborns' Act Disclosure?

The following is language that group health plans subject to the Newborns' Act may use in their SPDs to describe the Federal requirements relating to hospital lengths of stay in connection with childbirth:

> Group health plans and health insurance issuers generally may not, under Federal law, restrict benefits for any hospital length of stay in connection with childbirth for the mother or newborn child to less than 48 hours following a vaginal delivery, or less than 96 hours following a cesarean section. However, Federal law generally does not prohibit the mother's or newborn's attending provider, after consulting with the mother, from discharging the mother or her newborn earlier than 48 hours (or 96 hours as applicable). In any case, plans and issuers may not, under Federal law, require that a provider obtain authorization from the plan or the insurance issuer for prescribing a length of stay not in excess of 48 hours (or 96 hours).[3]

512. What notice is required for the Model WHCRA Enrollment Disclosure?

The following is language that group health plans may use as a guide when crafting the WHCRA enrollment notice:

> If you have had or are going to have a mastectomy, you may be entitled to certain benefits under the Women's Health and Cancer Rights Act of 1998 (WHCRA).

---

1.   https://www.irs.gov/retirement-plans/faqs-auto-enrollment-when-must-an-employer-provide-notice-of-the-retirement-plans-automatic-contribution-arrangement-to-an-employee.

2.   https://www.eeoc.gov/laws/regulations/ada-wellness-notice.cfm.

3.   https://www.dol.gov/sites/dolgov/files/EBSA/about-ebsa/our-activities/resource-center/publications/compliance-assistance-guide-appendix-c.pdf.

> For individuals receiving mastectomy-related benefits, coverage will be provided in a manner determined in consultation with the attending physician and the patient, for: All stages of reconstruction of the breast on which the mastectomy was performed; Surgery and reconstruction of the other breast to produce a symmetrical appearance; Prostheses; and Treatment of physical complications of the mastectomy, including lymphedema. These benefits will be provided subject to the same deductibles and coinsurance applicable to other medical and surgical benefits provided under this plan. Therefore, the following deductibles and coinsurance apply: [insert deductibles and coinsurance applicable to these benefits]. If you would like more information on WHCRA benefits, call your plan administrator [insert phone number].[1]

513. What notice is required for the Model Special Enrollment Notice?

The following is language that group health plans may use as a guide when crafting the WHCRA enrollment notice:

> If you are declining enrollment for yourself or your dependents (including your spouse) because of other health insurance or group health plan coverage, you may be able to enroll yourself and your dependents in this plan if you or your dependents lose eligibility for that other coverage (or if the employer stops contributing toward your or your dependents' other coverage). However, you must request enrollment within [insert "30 days" or any longer period that applies under the plan] after your or your dependents' other coverage ends (or after the employer stops contributing toward the other coverage). In addition, if you have a new dependent as a result of marriage, birth, adoption, or placement for adoption, you may be able to enroll yourself and your dependents. However, you must request enrollment within [insert "30 days" or any longer period that applies under the plan] after the marriage, birth, adoption, or placement for adoption. To request special enrollment or obtain more information, contact [insert the name, title, telephone number, and any additional contact information of the appropriate plan representative].[2]

514. What notice is required for Disclosure of Plan Data and Financials?

The Secretary of Labor will update the participant and plan disclosure requirements to be consistent with the standards established by the Secretary of HHS for exchange plans, relating to the following:[3]

- Claims payment policies and practices

- Periodic financial disclosures

---

1.   https://www.dol.gov/sites/dolgov/files/EBSA/about-ebsa/our-activities/resource-center/publications/compliance-assistance-guide-appendix-c.pdf.

2.   https://www.dol.gov/sites/dolgov/files/EBSA/about-ebsa/our-activities/resource-center/publications/compliance-assistance-guide-appendix-c.pdf.

3.   https://www.dol.gov/sites/dolgov/files/EBSA/about-ebsa/our-activities/resource-center/publications/reporting-and-disclosure-guide-for-employee-benefit-plans.pdf.

- Data on enrollment

- Data on disenrollment

- Data on the number of claims that are denied

- Data on rating practices

- Information on cost-sharing and payments with respect to any out-of-network coverage

- Information on enrollee and participant rights

- Any other information the Secretary of HHS determines appropriate

PART IX: TAX INCREASES AND REVENUE RAISERS

Additional Requirements for Nonprofit Hospitals

515. When was the Affordable Care Act's additional requirements for Internal Revenue Code section 501(c)(3) hospitals effective?

All of the new requirements, with the exception of the Community Health Needs Assessment (CHNA) requirements (see Q 522), applied to taxable years upon the enactment of the Affordable Care Act on March 23, 2010.[1]

By way of background, in July of 2011, the IRS released Notice 2011-52[2] which provided tax-exempt hospital facilities with guidance to follow in conducting a community health needs assessment (CHNA). This was followed in April 2013 with the IRS issuing proposed regulations to clarify IRS Notice 2011-52 and provide additional guidance on the community health needs assessment requirements and the related excise tax under IRC §4959. Proposed regulations on the requirements of IRC §501(r)(4), §501(r)(5) and §501(r)(6) were published in June 2012. These regulations were proposed to apply for tax years beginning on or after the date the regulations were finalized or issued as temporary regulations, however, in the interim, taxpayers were able to rely on the proposed regulations until final or temporary regulations were issued. In August 2013, the IRS issued temporary and proposed regulations that provided guidance to tax-exempt hospital facilities on how and when to file returns reporting the excise tax under IRC §4959 for failure to meet the CHNA requirements for any tax year. These were finalized in December 2014.

There has been some confusion over effective dates in that there is the belief that Internal Revenue section 501(r) is not effective until the Final Regulations' deadline. Actually, charitable hospitals have been required to be in compliance with the statutory IRC section 501(r) requirements beginning as early as 2010. With the exception of Internal Revenue Code section 501(r)(3), the requirements of IRC section 501(r) applied to taxable years beginning after March 23, 2010. Internal Revenue Code section 501(r)(3) applied to taxable years beginning after March 23, 2012.

Charitable hospitals did have until the taxable year beginning after December 29, 2015 to fully implement the specific provisions of the Final Regulations. The Final Regulations state that hospitals may rely on a "reasonable, good faith interpretation" of Internal Revenue Code section 501(r) to meets its statutory requirements. The Final Regulations state that hospitals that comply with the 2012 and 2013 proposed regulations "will be deemed" to be in full compliance with the statutory requirements of IRC section 501(r) until the Final Regulation's compliance deadline. On December 31, 2014, the IRS issued final regulations under the heading Additional Requirements for Charitable Hospitals; Community Health Needs Assessments for Charitable Hospitals; Requirement of a Section 4959 Excise Tax Return and Time for Filing the Return.[3]

---

1. PPACA §§9007(f), 10903; IRC Sec. 501(r).

2. Notice 2011-52.

3. https://www.federalregister.gov/documents/2014/12/31/2014-30525/additional-requirements-for-charitable-hospitals-community-health-needs-assessments-for-charitable.

Final regulations were released on December 29, 2014. For the requirements under Section 501(r), the regulations apply to tax years beginning after December 29, 2015, and this publication reflects those rules. For tax years beginning on or before December 29, 2015, the final regulations provide that a hospital facility may rely on a reasonable, good faith interpretation of Section 501(r). A hospital will be deemed to have operated in accordance with a reasonable, good faith interpretation of Section 501(r) if it complied with provisions of previously issued proposed regulations or the final regulations.

In general, a hospital organization's failure to meet the requirements of Section 501(r) with respect to one or more hospital facilities it operates may result in revocation of the organization's tax-exempt status as an organization described in Section 501(c)(3).[1]

IRS Notice 2014-2 confirmed that hospital organizations can rely on proposed regulations under section 501(r) of the Internal Revenue Code issued on June 26, 2012 and April 5, 2013, pending the publication of final regulations or other applicable guidance.[2]

On December 30, 2013 the IRS issued Notice 2014-3 which contained a proposed revenue procedure that provides correction and disclosure procedures under which certain failures to meet the requirements of §501(r) of the Internal Revenue Code will be excused for purposes of §501(r)(1) and 501(r)(2)(B). This notice invites comments regarding the procedures set forth in the proposed revenue procedure, including what additional examples, if any, would be helpful and whether hospitals should be required to make additional disclosures.[3]

516. Why were these additional requirements enacted?

Charitable hospital organizations seeking to qualify for federal tax-exempt status must now satisfy not only Internal Revenue Code section 501(c)(3) criteria but also the Affordable Care Act's additional requirements for healthcare reform. The rules established under section 501(r) generally establish how hospitals can bill patients and engage in collection practices.

The operative section, Internal Revenue Code section 501(r) imposed four new requirements on tax-exempt hospitals. These requirements include:

- Section 501(r)(3) – Community Health Needs Assessment

- Section 501(r)(4) – Financial Assistance Policy

- Section 501(r)(5) – Limitations on amounts that can be charged for emergency care or for other medically necessary care to those eligible under the hospital's financial assistance policies

- Section 501(r)(6) – Billing and collections policies and practices

---

1. https://www.federalregister.gov/documents/2014/12/31/2014-30525/additional-requirements-for-charitable-hospitals-community-health-needs-assessments-for-charitable.
2. See IRS Notice 2014-2.
3. See IRS Notice 2014-3.

517. What are the requirements under Section 501(r)(4) for the establishment of a Financial Assistance Policy (FAP) and emergency medical care policies?

A Financial Assistance Policy must apply to all emergency and other medically necessary care provided by the hospital facility, including all such care provided in the hospital facility by a substantially-related entity.

The Affordable Care Act and the final regulations – under Internal Revenue Code section 501(r) imposed additional requirements on charitable hospitals to qualify for Internal Revenue Code section 501(c)(3) tax-exempt status.

Under Internal Revenue Code section 501(r)(4), tax-exempt hospital organizations must establish a written Financial Assistance Policy (FAP), to include:[1]

(a)   Eligibility Criteria: The criteria for eligibility for financial assistance, such as income level, assets, etc. The criteria needs to include a description of the types of assistance provided, such as free services or discounts. See Question XX below

(b)   Methodology for Reduced or Limited Charges: The method for applying for financial assistance and what documentation is needed.

(c)   Sources Used for Making FAP Determination: The basis for calculating amounts charged to patients.

(d)   Actions for Nonpayment: For a hospital facility which does not have a separate billing and collections policy, the actions that may be taken in the event of nonpayment.

(e)   A description of the procedures to publicize the policy.[2] The publicizing of the FAP needs to be done in a manner reasonably calculated to reach those that need the assistance. It needs to be provided for free and in plain language as well as posted in public areas. In addition, there are requirements for translation for non-English speaking populations.

(f)   Policy for Emergency Medical Care: In addition, under Section 501(r)(4), the hospitals must establish a written Emergency Medical Care policy concerning emergency medical care, requiring the organization to provide care for emergency medical conditions regardless of the patient's ability to pay.[3]

(g)   Emergency Care Providers: A listing of all providers of emergency and medically necessary care.

(h)   Adoption by Board of Directors:

---

1.   https://www.irs.gov/charities-non-profits/financial-assistance-policy-and-emergency-medical-care-policy-section-501r4.
2.   PPACA §9007(a)(1)(4)(A); IRC Sec. 501(r)(4).
3.   PPACA §9007(a)(1)(4)(B); IRC Sec. 501(r)(4).

Moreover, the organizations must limit the amounts charged for emergency or nonemergency medical care to patients eligible for financial assistance to not more than the amount generally billed and prohibit the use of gross charges.[1] FAP-eligible patients cannot be charged more for emergency or medically-necessary care than the amounts generally billed to those that have insurance. The definition of "charged" is the amount that the individual is personally required to pay. Regarding the "amount generally billed", the hospital can use one of two methods: the "look-back method" or the "prospective payment method". Changes can be made at any time but require updating the FAP PRIOR to the change.[2] The final regulations establish a "safe harbor" provision if the hospital charges more than AGB.

Finally, under Internal Revenue Code section 501(r)(6), nonprofit hospitals must refrain from engaging in extraordinary billing and collection actions until after reasonable efforts have been made to determine whether a patient is eligible for financial assistance.[3] The final regulations detail specifically what are extraordinary collection actions including:

- selling of debt to another party;

- reporting adverse information to credit bureaus;

- actions requiring legal or judicial process, including but not limited to –

    - filing liens on property (with the exception noted below);

    - foreclosing on real property;

    - attaching or seizing a bank account or any other personal property;

    - commencing a civil action;

    - causing an individual's arrest;

    - subjecting an individual to a writ of body attachment; or

    - garnishing wages;

- deferring or denying care can be an extraordinary collection activity unless the hospital can show that it is not based on nonpayment.

518. What are the specific eligibility criteria for financial assistance and the basis for determining charges?

A FAP must specify the eligibility criteria that an individual must satisfy to receive each discount, free care, or other level of assistance available under the FAP.

---

1. PPACA §§9007(a)(1)(5), 10903(a); IRC Sec. 501(r)(5).
2. Additional Requirements for Charitable Hospitals; Community Needs Assessments for Charitable Hospital; Requirement of a Section 4959 Excise Tax Return and Time for Filing the Return, https://www.federalregister.gov/articles/2014/12/31/2014-30525/additional-requirements-for-charitable-hospitals-community-health-needs-assessments-for-charitable (December 31, 2014).
3. PPACA §9007(a)(1)(6); IRC Sec. 501(r)(6).

A FAP must specify all financial assistance available under the FAP, including all discounts and free care, and, if applicable, the amount(s) (for example, gross charges) to which any discount percentages will be applied. Consistent with the limitation on charges requirement described below, a FAP must indicate that, following a determination of FAP-eligibility, a FAP-eligible individual may not be charged more than Amounts Generally Billed (AGB) for emergency or medically necessary care.

A FAP must also specify the method the hospital facility uses to determine AGB. If it uses the look-back method, the FAP must state the AGB percentage(s) that the hospital facility uses to determine AGB and describe how the percentage(s) were calculated. Alternatively, the FAP may explain how members of the public may readily obtain such percentage(s) and accompanying description of the calculation in writing and free of charge.

Not all discounts a hospital facility might offer its patients are properly viewed as financial assistance. Hospital facilities may offer payment discounts or other discounts outside of their FAPs and may charge discounted amounts greater than AGB to individuals that are not FAP-eligible. Therefore, a FAP is only required to describe discounts "available under the FAP" rather than all discounts offered by the hospital facility.

519. What are the methods to apply for financial assistance?

A hospital facility's FAP must describe how an individual applies for financial assistance under the FAP. In addition, either the FAP or FAP application form (including accompanying instructions) must describe the information or documentation an individual may be required to provide as part of their FAP application and must also provide certain contact information.

Financial assistance may not be denied based on the omission of information or documentation if the information or documentation was not specifically required by the FAP or FAP application form. A hospital facility may grant financial assistance under its FAP despite an applicant's failure to provide information or documentation described in the FAP or FAP application form. For example, a hospital facility may grant financial assistance based on an attestation by the applicant or on other evidence even if it's not described in a FAP or FAP application form.

520. What actions can be taken for non-payment?

Either a hospital facility's FAP or a separate written billing and collections policy established for the hospital facility must describe:

- Any actions that the hospital facility (or other authorized party) may take related to obtaining payment of a bill for medical care, including, but not limited to, any extraordinary collection actions (ECAs) described in Section 501(r)(6)

- The process and time frames the hospital facility (or other authorized party) uses in taking the actions described, including, but not limited to, the reasonable efforts it will make to determine whether an individual is FAP-eligible before engaging in any, and

- The office, department, committee, or other body with the final authority or responsibility for determining that the hospital facility has made reasonable efforts to determine whether an individual is FAP-eligible and may therefore engage in ECAs against the individual.

In the case of a hospital facility that has a separate written billing and collection policy, the hospital facility's FAP must state that the actions the hospital facility may take in the event of nonpayment are described in a separate billing and collections policy and explain how the public may readily obtain a free copy of that separate policy.

521. What procedures must be used to publicize the hospital FAP?

A hospital facility must widely publicize its FAP in the community it serves by:

- Making the FAP, FAP application form, and plain language summary of the FAP (the FAP documents) widely available on a website,

- Making paper copies of the FAP documents available upon request and without charge by mail and in public locations in the hospital facility, including at a minimum in the emergency room (if any) and admissions areas,

- Notifying and informing members of the community served by the hospital facility about the FAP in a manner reasonably calculated to reach those members of the community who are most likely to require financial assistance, and

- Notifying and informing visitors to the hospital facility about the FAP.

522. What are the Community Health Needs Assessment requirements under Section 501 (r)(3)?

In order for a hospital to be treated as a tax-exempt organization, it must comply with Internal Revenue Code section 501(r)(3). This requires that a charitable hospital must conduct a Community Health Needs Assessment (CHNA) at least once every three years as well as adopting an implementation strategy and strategic plan to meet the community health needs identified through the CHNA.[1]

Internal Revenue Service Notice 2011-52 was issued in July 2011 and provides guidance as to how to conduct a Community Health Needs Assessment. Proposed Regulations followed in April 2013 with additional guidance and information regarding the excise tax under Internal Revenue Code section 4959.[2]

The steps required in conducting a CHNA include:

1. Define the "community" that is served by the hospital. The community definition must take into consideration the low income and minority communities in the area. (See Question 523 below)

---

1. PPACA §9007(a)(1)(3); IRC Sec. 501(r).
2. Notice 2011-52.

2. Assess the needs of the community. The regulations include the prevention of illness, the ensuring of nutrition and other factors that affect community health. (See Question 524 below)

3. Solicit input from the community including those with expertise in public health. The regulations specifically require that feedback be considered:

    a. The public health community.

    b. Members of the medically underserved, low income and minority populations.

    c. Comments on the most recent CHNA.

    d. Other input should be solicited from consumers of health care, health care advocates, nonprofit organizations, academics, government officials, health care provides, etc. (See Question 526 below)

4. Document the CHNA in a written report which has been approved by the hospital governing board (Board of Trustees, Board of Directors, or other bodies as recognized by state law). (See Question 527 below)

5. Distribute to the community – this can include distribution on a website and making paper copies available for free.

The CHNA MUST include the following components:

- Definition of the community served and a description of how that definition was determined

- Process and methodology used to conduct the CHNA

- How input was solicited from the community and taken into account

- Prioritized list of significant health needs identified through the CHNA with a description of how and through what criteria were used to decide on significance

- List of available resources potentially to address the health needs

- Evaluation of actions taken since the prior CHNA

- Description of Implementation Strategy – how it addresses health needs, what actions will be taken, what resources are needed, any planned partnerships with other organizations

The CHNA must be adopted before the fifteenth day of the fifth month after the end of the taxable year. The reporting must be on Form 990 on an annual basis. The amount of the excise tax must be reported on the organization's annual tax return.[1] Failure to meet the

---

1. PPACA §9007(c); IRC Sec. 501(r).

CHNA requirement can result in a $50,000 tax[1] for each taxable year in which the requirement is not met.[2] Finally, the organization's community benefit activities will be subject to review by the Department of the Treasury at least once every three years.[3]

523. How does Community Health Needs Assessment define the community served?

A hospital facility may take into account all the relevant facts and circumstances in defining the community it serves. This includes:

- The geographic area served by the hospital facility,

- Target populations served, such as children, women, or the aged, and

- Principal functions, such as a focus on a particular specialty area or targeted disease.

However, a hospital facility may not define its community in a way that excludes medically underserved, low-income, or minority populations who live in the geographic areas from which it draws its patients (unless such populations are not part of the hospital facility's target population or affected by its principal functions) or otherwise should be included based on the method the hospital facility uses to define its community.

Medically underserved populations include populations experiencing health disparities or that are at risk of not receiving adequate medical care because of being uninsured or underinsured, or due to geographic, language, financial, or other barriers. Populations with language barriers include those with limited English proficiency. Medically underserved populations also include those living within a hospital facility's service area but not receiving adequate medical care from the facility because of cost, transportation difficulties, stigma, or other barriers.

Additionally, in determining its patient populations for purposes of defining its community, a hospital facility must take into account all patients without regard to whether (or how much) they or their insurers pay for the care received or whether they are eligible for assistance under the hospital facility's financial assistance policy.

If a hospital facility consists of multiple buildings that operate under a single state license and serve different geographic areas or populations, the community served by the hospital facility is the aggregate of these areas or populations.

524. How does a hospital assess community health needs?

To assess the health needs of its community, a hospital facility must identify the significant health needs of the community. It must also prioritize those health needs, as well as identify

---

1.   IRC Sec. 4959.
2.   PPACA §9007(d); IRC Sec. 501(r).
3.   PPACA §9007(c); IRC Sec. 501(r).

resources potentially available to address them. Resources can include organizations, facilities, and programs in the community, including those of the hospital facility, potentially available to address those health needs.

The health needs of a community include requisites for the improvement or maintenance of health status both in the community at large and in particular parts of the community, such as particular neighborhoods or populations experiencing health disparities. Needs may include, for example, the need to:

- Address financial and other barriers to accessing care,

- Prevent illness,

- Ensure adequate nutrition, or

- Address social, behavioral, and environmental factors that influence health in the community.

A hospital facility may determine whether a health need is significant based on all the facts and circumstances present in the community it serves. Additionally, a hospital facility may use any criteria to prioritize the significant health needs it identifies, including, but not limited to the:

- Burden, scope, severity, or urgency of the health need,

- Estimated feasibility and effectiveness of possible interventions,

- Health disparities associated with the need, or

- Importance the community places on addressing the need.

525. How is community input solicited?

A hospital must both solicit and take into account input received from all of the following sources in identifying and prioritizing significant health needs and in identifying resources potentially available to address those health needs.

1. At least one state, local, tribal, or regional governmental public health department (or equivalent department or agency), or a State Office of Rural Health described in Section 338J of the Public Health Services Act, with knowledge, information, or expertise relevant to the health needs of the community.

2. Members of medically underserved, low-income, and minority populations in the community served by the hospital facility, or individuals or organizations serving or representing the interests of these populations.

3. Written comments received on the hospital facility's most recently conducted CHNA and most recently adopted implementation strategy

526. What other sources of input must be solicited?

In addition to soliciting input from the three required sources, a hospital facility may solicit and take into account input received from a broad range of persons located in or serving its community. This includes, but is not limited to:

- Health care consumers and consumer advocates

- Nonprofit and community-based organizations

- Academic experts

- Local government officials

- Local school districts

- Health care providers and community health centers

- Health insurance and managed care organizations,

- Private businesses, and

- Labor and workforce representatives.

Although a hospital facility is not required to solicit input from additional persons, it must take into account input received from any person in the form of written comments on the most recently conducted CHNA or most recently adopted implementation strategy.

527. How must a CHNA be documented?

A hospital facility must document its CHNA in a report that is adopted by an authorized body of the hospital facility. The CHNA report must include the following items.

- A definition of the community served by the hospital facility and a description of how the community was determined.

- A description of the process and methods used to conduct the CHNA.

- A description of how the hospital facility solicited and took into account input received from persons who represent the broad interests of the community it serves.

- A prioritized description of the significant health needs of the community identified through the CHNA. This includes a description of the process and criteria used in identifying certain health needs as significant and prioritizing those significant health needs.

- A description of resources potentially available to address the significant health needs identified through the CHNA.

- An evaluation of the impact of any actions that were taken to address the significant health needs identified in the immediately preceding CHNA,

A CHNA report will be considered to describe the process and methods used to conduct the CHNA report if it:

- Describes the data and other information used in the assessment,

- Describes the methods of collecting and analyzing this data and information,

- Identifies any parties with whom the hospital facility collaborated or contracted for assistance in conducting the CHNA.

A hospital facility may rely on (and the CHNA report may describe) external source material in conducting its CHNA. In such cases, the hospital facility may simply cite the source material rather than describe the methods of collecting the data.

A hospital facility's CHNA report must describe how the hospital facility took into account input received from persons who represent the broad interests of the community it serves. The CHNA report should:

- Summarize, in general terms, the input provided by such persons,

- Describe how and over what time period such input was provided (for example, whether through meetings, focus groups, interviews, surveys, or written comments and between what approximate dates),

- Provide the names of any organizations providing input and summarizes the nature and extent of the organization's input, and

- Describe the medically underserved, low-income, or minority populations being represented by organizations or individuals that provided input.

However, a CHNA report does not need to name or otherwise individually identify any individuals providing input on the CHNA, including individuals participating in community forums, focus groups, survey samples, or similar groups. If a hospital facility solicits, but cannot obtain, input from a required source representing the broad interests of the community, the hospital facility's CHNA report must describe the hospital facility's efforts to solicit the input from such source.

Penalty for Lack of Economic Substance

528. What is the "economic substance" doctrine?

The term "economic substance doctrine" means the common-law doctrine established by court decisions under which income tax benefits are not allowed if the transaction does not have economic substance or lacks a business purpose.[1] As part of health reform, Congress codified the economic substance doctrine in the Internal Revenue Code[2] and imposed penalties for its violation.[3] The law adopts a two-prong test used by most, though not all, of the federal circuit courts. A transaction has economic substance only if:

> (i) the transaction changes in a meaningful way (apart from federal income tax effects) the taxpayer's economic position; and

> (ii) the taxpayer has a substantial purpose (apart from federal income tax effects) for entering into the transaction.[4]

Additionally, the law adopts a strict liability penalty if the taxpayer violates the doctrine (40 percent if not disclosed; 20 percent if disclosed). This will impose a significant downside risk for those who continue to indulge in tax-shelter transactions because there will be no reasonable cause defense available. However, aggressive positions might be tested in refund actions without risk of the penalty imposed under Internal Revenue Code section 6676 on excessive refund claims.[5]

The IRS has announced that there will be no "angel list" (specific transactions to which the penalty does not apply).[6] By avoiding "bright lines," few rational taxpayers should want to test the "tax lottery" in this area.

It is presumed that if the Affordable Care Act is replaced and/or replaced, this "economic substance" doctrine would not survive. The Congressional Budget Office estimates that the elimination of this doctrine would cost $5.8 billion between 2017 and 2025.[7]

529. When did the economic substance penalties become effective?

The law applies with respect to transactions entered into on or after March 31, 2010.[8]

Tanning Bed Tax

530. What is the tanning bed tax?

The tanning bed tax remains in effect although there have been attempts to repeal it. It was effective July 1, 2010, and is a 10 percent tax on indoor tanning salons' tanning sessions.[9] Recipients of any indoor tanning service became responsible for paying an excise tax equal to 10 percent of the amount paid for the indoor tanning services, whether or not the amounts to

---

1.   IRC Section 7701(o)(5)(A).
2.   IRC Section 7701(o).
3.   IRC Sections 6662, 6662A, 6664, and 6676.
4.   IRC Section7701 (o)(1).
5.   Susswein, "Is There a Disclosure Exception to The Economic Substance Penalty?" 133 Tax Notes 871 (Nov. 14, 2011), which discusses the ability to obtain administrative or judicial review of economic substance issues without risk of penalty via refund claims.
6.   IRS Notice 2010-62.
7.   https://www.cbo.gov/sites/default/files/114th-congress-2015-2016/costestimate/hr3762followingenactmentofconsolidatedappropsactof 2016.pdf. (Last accessed August 7, 2019).
8.   IRS Notice 2010-62.
9.   PPACA §10907.

be paid by insurance.[1] The tax is imposed at the time of payment for any indoor tanning service[2] and is collected by the service provider.[3] The tax is 10 percent of the amount of the services and is not grossed up.[4]

As initially enacted by Section 9017 of PPACA (PPACA Section 9017 Excise Tax on Elective Cosmetic Medical Procedures), the excise tax was aimed at "Elective Cosmetic Procedures" and would have levied a five percent tax on elective surgeries such as breast augmentation, tummy tucks, Botox injections, and other elective surgeries.

However, after a great deal of lobbying from medical and dermatology interests, Section 9017, derisively nicknamed the "Botax" was nullified by Section 10907 (PPACA Section 10907 Excise Tax on Indoor Tanning Services in Lieu of Elective Cosmetic Medical Procedures) which substituted the tax on tanning services.

The tanning bed tax was expected to generate $2.7 billion over ten years, significantly less than the $5.8 billion that the "Botax" was supposed to raise. However, the tanning industry was a weaker target and the "Snooki Tax" (nicknamed after the reality television star) replaced the "Botax."

Individuals connected to the tanning industry were infuriated, feeling singled out by a tax they argued was directed at the middle-class, and at an industry dominated by women owners which were far less able to absorb the tax than the wealthier individuals who would have been impacted by the cosmetic services tax.

Another effort to repeal the 10 percent federal tax on indoor tanning services failed in the United States Senate in January 2019 after passing in the U.S. House of Representatives on December 20, 2018 – failing again for the third time. Attempts to repeal the tanning tax, rare bipartisan legislation introduced in both houses of Congress by U.S. Rep. George Holding (R-NC), Rep. Colin Peterson (D-Minn), U.S. Sen. Rand Paul (R-KY) and Sen. Heidi Heitkamp (D-ND) gained broad support in Congress and the White House. The bills had eighty-five co-sponsors in Congress in 2018.

The House bill passed the U.S. House of Representatives on December 20, 2018 with a 220-183 vote. The Senate bill, sponsored by Paul and supported by Senate Majority Leader Mitch McConnell, was not taken up on the senate's last day of the session. Some believe this was due to the government shut-down becoming the sole focus of the Senate over the holiday period.

---

1.   IRC Section 5000B(a); Reg. §49.5000B-1T(d)(1).
2.   Reg. §49.5000B-1T(b)(1).
3.   "Excise Tax on Indoor Tanning Services Frequently Asked Questions," (Current through April 23, 2018) at https://www.irs.gov/businesses/ small-businesses-self-employed/excise-tax-on-indoor-tanning-services-frequently-asked-questions. (Last accessed August 7, 2019).
4.   IRC Section 5000B(a).

531. Which tanning services are covered and which are exempt from the indoor tanning services tax?

An "indoor tanning service" is a service that uses any electronic product designed to incorporate one or more ultraviolet lamps and intended for the irradiation of an individual by ultraviolet radiation, with wavelengths in air between 200 and 400 nanometers, to induce skin tanning.[1]

The term "indoor tanning service" excludes any phototherapy service performed by a licensed medical professional, on the medical professional's premises.[2] Phototherapy services performed by a licensed medical professional on the medical professional's premises are exempt from the indoor tanning services excise tax. Phototherapy service means a service that exposes an individual to specific wavelengths of light for treatment of:

- dermatological conditions (e.g., acne, psoriasis, or eczema);[3]

- sleep disorders;[4]

- Seasonal Affective Disorder (SAD) or other psychiatric disorder;[5]

- neonatal jaundice;[6]

- wound healing;[7] or

- other medical condition determined by a licensed medical professional to be treatable by exposing the individual to specific wavelengths of light.[8]

There is an exclusion for "Qualified Physical Fitness Facilities" (QPFF)[9] that meet specific criteria and offer tanning as an incidental service to members without a separately identifiable fee.

The membership fee to the facility is not taxable if the facility meets the definition below of a "Qualified Physical Fitness Facility." However, if the facility does NOT qualify as a QPFF, then the membership fee IS taxable, even if the member does not utilize the tanning services.

A "qualified physical fitness facility" is a facility:

1.   in which the predominant business or activity is providing facilities, equipment, and services to its members for purposes of exercise and physical fitness;

---

1.   IRC Sec. 5000B(b)(1); Reg. §49.5000B–1T(c)(1).
2.   IRC Sec. 5000B(b)(1); Reg. §49.5000B–1T(c)(1).
3.   Reg. §49.5000B–1T(c)(3)(i).
4.   Reg. §49.5000B–1T(c)(3)(ii).
5.   Reg. §49.5000B–1T(c)(3)(iii).
6.   Reg. §49.5000B–1T(c)(3)(iv).
7.   Reg. §49.5000B–1T(c)(3)(v).
8.   Reg. §49.5000B–1T(c)(3)(vi).
9.   See 26 C.F.R. 49.5000B–1, Treas. Reg. 49.5000B–1 Indoor Tanning Services.

2.   indoor tanning services is not a substantial part of its business; and

3.   it does not offer tanning services to the public for a fee or offer different pricing options to its members based on indoor tanning services.

To determine the predominant business or activity all facts and circumstances should be considered including, but not limited to, the following:

- The cost of the equipment

- Variety of services offered

- Actual usage of services by customers

- Revenue generated by different services

- How the entity holds itself out to the public through advertising or other means

Indoor tanning services also do not include spray tans or topical creams[1] and tanning lotions.[2] Also, there are no exemptions from the tax for tax-exempt entities such as education institutions or charities. For example, if a tax-exempt university charges an activity fee that gives students access to indoor tanning services, the university would not be exempt.

The tanning service provider must maintain adequate books and records showing the amount of revenue received for indoor tanning services.

Limits on Reimbursement of Nonprescription Over-the-Counter Drugs

532. How have the rules changed on the ability to reimburse for Over-the-Counter (OTC) drugs?

Health reform limits the payment for Over-The-Counter drugs to insulin or those that are prescribed by a physician beginning January 1, 2011.[3] Thus, the cost of OTC medicines cannot be reimbursed with excludable income through a health Flexible Spending Account (FSA), Health Reimbursement Account (HRA), Health Savings Account (HSA), or Archer Medical Savings Account (MSA) unless the medicine is insulin or the nonprescription medicine is, in fact, prescribed by a doctor.

IRS Notice 2011-5 states that health FSA and HRA debit cards may continue to be used after January 15, 2011, to purchase prescribed over-the-counter medicines or drugs at drug

---

1.   "Excise Tax on Indoor Tanning Services Frequently Asked Questions," (Current through May 6, 2019) at https://www.irs.gov/businesses/small-businesses-self-employed/excise-tax-on-indoor-tanning-services-frequently-asked-questions. (Last accessed August 7, 2019).
2.   Reg. §49.5000B-1T(c)(2).
3.   See IRC Secs. 106(f), 220(d)(2)(A), and 223(d)(2)(A), as amended by PPACA §9003.

stores and pharmacies, at nonhealthcare merchants that have pharmacies, and at mail order and Web-based vendors that sell prescription drugs, if:

(1)   prior to purchase:

   o   the prescription for the OTC medicine or drug is presented (in any format) to the pharmacist;

   o   the OTC medicine or drug is dispensed by the pharmacist in accordance with applicable law and regulations; and

   o   a prescription number is assigned.

(2)   the pharmacy or other vendor retains, in a manner that meets IRS's recordkeeping requirements:

   o   the prescription number;

   o   the name of the purchaser or person for whom the prescription applies; and

   o   the date and amount of the purchase.

(3)   all of these records are available to the taxpayer's employer or its agent upon request;

(4)   the debit card system will not accept a charge for an OTC medicine or drug unless a prescription number has been assigned; and

(5)   the additional requirements regarding the use of health FSA or HRA debit cards[1] are met.

<u>Use of Debit Cards</u>. After January 15, 2011, health FSA and HRA debit cards may also continue to be used to purchase OTC medicines or drugs from vendors other than those described previously that have healthcare-related "Merchant IRCs,"[2] including physicians, pharmacies, dentists, vision-care offices, hospitals, and other medical care providers. If all other requirements in the previous list are satisfied, then these debit card transactions will be considered fully substantiated at the time and point-of-sale. Co-pays and deductibles continue to be reimbursable from a health FSA. Similarly, funds from an HRA can continue to be used for these expenses and a distribution from an HSA or Archer MSA for these purposes will be tax-free.

Health FSA and HRA debit cards may also be used to purchase OTC medicines and drugs at "90 percent pharmacies" with at least 90 percent of the store's gross receipts during the prior tax year consisting of qualified medical care expenses.[3] For additional information regarding Over the Counter Drug rules, refer to the IRS website.[4]

---

1.   Reg. §1.125-6, Rev. Rul. 2003-43, Notices 2006-69, 2007-2, and 2008-104.
2.   Described in Rev. Rul. 2003-43.
3.   IRC Sec. 213(d).
4.   https://www.irs.gov/newsroom/affordable-care-act-questions-and-answers-on-over-the-counter-medicines-and-drugs. (Last accessed August 7, 2019), Current though June 28, 2019.

Doubled HSA and MSA Penalty for Spending for Nonhealth Care and Nonprescription Over-the-Counter Items

533. How has health reform changed the penalty for a Health Savings Account (HSA) or an Archer Medical Savings Account (MSA) regarding payment for nonmedical items?

The health reform law revised the rules with respect to HSAs[1] and MSAs[2] to provide that for amounts paid after December 31, 2010, a distribution for a medicine or drug is a tax-free qualified medical expense only if the medicine or drug is a prescribed drug or insulin. Thus, to be reimbursed, Over-The-Counter (OTC) drugs must have a prescription or be insulin. Thus, a distribution from an HSA or an Archer MSA for a medicine or drug is a tax-free qualified medical expense only if the medicine or drug:

- requires a prescription;

- is an OTC medicine or drug and the individual obtains a prescription; or

- is insulin.

If amounts are distributed from an HSA or Archer MSA for any medicine or drug that does not satisfy this requirement, the amounts will be distributions for nonqualified medical expenses, which are includable in gross income and generally are subject to a 20 percent additional tax.

The IRS has stated that items that are not medicines or drugs — including equipment such as crutches, supplies such as bandages, and diagnostic devices such as blood sugar test kits — are not reimbursable[3] unless they qualify for medical care expenses. Such items may qualify if they otherwise meet the definition of medical care, which includes expenses for the diagnosis, cure, mitigation, treatment, or prevention of disease, or for the purpose of affecting any structure or function of the body. Expenses for items that are merely beneficial to the general health of an individual, such as expenditures for a vacation, are not expenses for medical care.[4]

534. When were the new HSA and Archer MSA rules effective?

These new rules are effective for items purchased on or after January 1, 2011.[5] This change does not affect HSA or Archer MSA distributions for medicines or drugs made before January 1, 2011, nor does it affect distributions made after December 31, 2010, for medicines or drugs purchased on or before that date.

535. What is a prescription for purposes of these rules?

For the prescription requirement, a "prescription" for a medicine or drug, including one sold over the counter, is a written or electronic order that satisfies the legal requirements

---

1.   IRC Sec. 223(d)(2)(A).
2.   IRC Sec. 220(d)(2)(A).
3.   IRS Notice 2010-59.
4.   IRC Sec. 213(d)(1); Treas. Reg. §1.213-1(e)(1)(ii).
5.   PPACA §9003(d)(2).

for a prescription in the state in which the expense is incurred, including that it be issued by someone who is legally authorized to issue a prescription in that state.[1] In later guidance, the IRS indicated that a prescription could be presented to the pharmacist "in any format."[2] This modification means that if state law allows oral prescriptions by telephone, then the telephone qualifies as a prescription.

In order to get reimbursement, it would be necessary to provide the prescription (or a copy of the prescription or another item showing that a prescription for the item has been issued) and the customer receipt (or similar third-party documentation showing the date of the sale and the amount of the charge).

536. How are purchases of over-the-counter medical devices and supplies affected by healthcare reform?

This does not apply to items for medical care that are not medicines or drugs. Thus, equipment such as crutches, supplies such as bandages, and diagnostic devices such as blood sugar test kits will still qualify for reimbursement by a health FSA or HRA and a distribution from an HSA or Archer MSA for the cost of such items will still be tax-free, regardless of whether the items are purchased using a prescription.

Annual Fee on Manufacturers and Importers of Branded Drugs

537. What is the annual fee on manufacturers and importers of branded drugs?

The Affordable Care Act[3] imposes an annual aggregate flat fee which began at $2.5 billion in 2011 and increased each year until 2018 on the branded pharmaceutical manufacturing sector, including foreign corporations and importers. This nondeductible fee is allocated across the industry according to market share and does not apply to companies with sales of branded pharmaceuticals of $5 million or less or certain orphan drugs. On July 28, 2014, the IRS issued final regulations on the fee which describe the rules related to the fee and how it is computed and how it is paid.[4] Only July 24, 2017, the IRS issued final regulations that define the term controlled group for purposes of the branded prescription drug fee.[5]

Calculation of Fees

The fee is calculated by determining the ration of a) the covered entity's branded prescription drug sales during the sales year to b) the aggregate branded prescription drug sales taken into account for all covered entities during the same year and applying this ratio to the applicable amount.

---

1. IRS Notice 2010-59.
2. IRS Notice 2011-5.
3. PPACA §9008.
4. 26 CFR Pars 51 and 602.
5. 26 CFR Parts 51 and 602.

The aggregate fee amount for each year is as follows:

Fee Year	Applicable Amount
2011	$2.5 billion
2012	$2.8 billion
2013	$2.8 billion
2014	$3 billion
2015	$3 billion
2016	$3 billion
2017	$4 billion
2018	$4.1 billion
2019 and thereafter	$2.8 billion

For sales of Branded Prescription Drugs between $5 million and $125 million, only 10 percent of such sales are taken into account when determining the applicable fee. For sales between $125 million and $225 million, 40 percent of such sales are taken into account; and for sales between $225 and $400 million, 75 percent of such sales are considered. To the extent that a Covered Entity's sales of branded prescription drugs to a specified government program exceed $400 million, 100 percent of such excess sales are taken into account to compute the entity's market share.[1]

Applicable amount means the aggregate fee amount each year for all covered entities under section 9008(b)(4). The applicable amounts for fee years are:

- *Fee year* means the calendar year in which the fee for a particular sales year must be paid to the government. For example, for the fee year of 2014, the sales year is 2012.

- *Sales taken into account* means BPD sales after the application of the percentage adjustment table in section 9008(b)(2) (relating to annual sales less than $400,000,001), as shown below under Preliminary Fee.

- *Sales year* means the second calendar year preceding the fee year.

This nondeductible excise tax is paid to the Medicare Part B trust fund.[2] The IRS issued guidance on this tax.[3]

538. What is a covered entity?

Covered entity means any manufacturer or importer with gross receipts from BPD sales, including a single-person covered entity or a controlled group.

---

1. PPACA §9008(b).
2. PPACA §9008(c).
3. Notices 2010-71 and 2011-9 and Rev. Proc. 2011-24.

539. What is a designated entity?

Designated entity means the person that acts for a controlled group regarding the fee by:

(1)   filing Form 8947;

(2)   receiving IRS communications about the fee for the group;

(3)   filing an error report for the group, if applicable; and

(4)   paying the fee to the IRS.

540. What is the definition of specified government programs?

Specified government programs (Programs) are the Medicare Part B program, the Medicare Part D program, the Medicaid program, any program under which BPDs are procured by the Department of Veterans Affairs (VA), any program under which BPDs are procured by the Department of Defense (DOD), and the TRICARE retail pharmacy program.

541. What is a Controlled Group?

Controlled Group means a group of two or more persons, including at least one person that is a covered entity that is treated as a single employer under section 52(a), 52(b), 414(m), or 414(o).

542. What are Branded Prescription Drugs and Orphan Drugs?

Branded Prescription Drug (BPD) means any prescription drug:

1.   the application for which was submitted under section 505(b) of the Federal Food, Drug, and Cosmetic Act[1]; or

2.   any biological product the license for which was submitted under section 351(a) of the Public Health Service Act[2].

Orphan drug means any branded prescription drug for which:

1.   any person claimed a credit under Internal Revenue Code section 45C and

2.   that credit was allowed for any taxable year, but does not include

(i) any drug for which there has been a final assessment or court order disallowing the full section 45C credit taken for the drug; or

(ii) any drug for any sales year after the calendar year in which the Federal Drug Administration (FDA) approved the drug for marketing for any indication other than the treatment of a rare disease or condition for which a

---

1.   21 U.S.C. 355(b).
2.   42 U.S.C. 262(a).

section 45C credit was allowed, regardless of whether a section 45C credit was allowed for the drug either before, in the same year as, or after this FDA designation.

543. When is the annual fee on manufacturers and importers of branded drugs effective?

The first calculation period was the calendar year beginning January 1, 2011. The fee for 2011 needed to be paid to the IRS no later than September 30, 2012. For subsequent years, the fee needs to be paid by September 30 and is reported on Form 8947, Report of Branded Prescription Drug Information.[1]

544. How is reporting done for Branded Prescription Drug?

Sales data for the fee is generally provided by the Centers for Medicare and Medicaid Programs of the Department of Health and Human Services (CMS), VA and DOD (Agencies). In addition, each covered entity may provide information relevant to the determination of the fee by annually submitting Form 8947, "Report of Branded Prescription Drug Information." Submission of Form 8947 is voluntary.

Generally, covered entities may report the National Drug Code (NDC) of each BPD that the covered entity sold to the Programs (or pursuant to coverage under those Programs), Medicaid state rebate information, Section 45C orphan drug information, members of controlled groups, and designated entity information on Form 8947.

For each fee year, a covered entity that chooses to submit Form 8947 reporting information for the sales year must file the form by November 1 of the preceding year

Repeal of Employer-Paid Retiree Prescription Drug Rebate Income Tax Exclusion

545. What was the employer-paid retiree prescription drug rebate income tax exclusion?

Before taxable years beginning in 2013, employers providing retiree drug coverage to their former employees could both exclude from income the federal subsidy they received and also deduct all of the costs of the retiree drug coverage, including the costs paid by the subsidy. This rule was enacted in 2003 when the Medicare Part D drug coverage program was enacted. This double benefit was intended to encourage employers to continue coverage for retirees and lessen the number of people switching to Medicare Part D coverage. Many retirees preferred the employer-provided coverage to the Medicare coverage because it is usually more generous than Medicare Part D and does not have "doughnut holes" in coverage. Doughnut holes are the gaps in prescription drug coverage under Medicare after subscribers reach a certain level of expenses and before coverage kicks in again.

---

1.   https://www.irs.gov/pub/irs-dft/f8947--dft.pdf.

For taxable years beginning in 2013 and thereafter, the rule that the exclusion from taxable income for Medicare Part D federal subsidy payments to employers is not taken into account in determining the deduction is allowable for an employer's retiree prescription drug expenses is eliminated.[1] Thus, the amount otherwise allowable as a deduction for an employer's retiree prescription drug expenses will be reduced by the amount of the excludible subsidy payments received from the federal government by that employer. Some employers that are losing this double benefit say they will discontinue the retiree drug coverage benefit.

The elimination of the exclusion resulted in treating the subsidy the same as most items that may be excluded from income. Thus, for example, while medical insurance reimbursements are not included in a taxpayer's income, they also are not deductible as medical expenses under Internal Revenue Code section 213.

> *Example:* A company receives a $28 federal subsidy for $100 of eligible drug expenses. The $28 is excludable from income under Internal Revenue Code section 139A, and the amount otherwise allowable as a deduction will be reduced by the $28. If the company otherwise meets the Internal Revenue Code section 162 requirements for its eligible retiree drug expenses, it is entitled to a $72 ordinary business expense deduction.[2]

Tax on Sale of Medical Devices – Moratorium Extended to 2019

546. What is the new tax on the sale of taxable medical devices?

The healthcare reform law amended Chapter 32 of the Internal Revenue Code by establishing section 4191 of the Code imposing a new excise tax on manufacturers or importers of taxable medical devices.[3] The tax was equal to 2.3 percent of the sale price of medical devices sold after December 31, 2012. Certain medical devices, such as contact lenses and hearing aids purchased by the general public at retail stores, are exempt. On December 5, 2012, the IRS and the Department of the Treasury issued final regulations on the new 2.3 percent medical device excise tax[4] that manufacturers and importers began to pay on their sales of certain medical devices starting in 2013. On December 5, 2012, the IRS and the Department of the Treasury also issued Notice 2012-77, which provides interim guidance on certain issues related to the medical device excise tax.

With the passage of the Protection of Americans from Tax Hikes Act, the PATH Act, a moratorium on the Medical Device Tax was imposed effective during 2016 and 2017.

H.R. 195[5] (Pub. L. 115-120), was signed into law on January 22, 2018 and extended for an additional two years the moratorium on the medical device excise tax imposed by Internal Revenue Code section 4191. Because of the moratorium, the medical device excise tax does

---

1.   IRC Sec.139A as amended by PPACA §9012(a).
2.   Joint Comm. Staff, Tech Explanation of the Revenue Provisions of the Reconciliation Act of 2010, as Amended, in Combination With the Patient Protection and Affordable Care Act (JCX-18-10), p. 95 (3/21/2010). See https://www.jct.gov/publications.html?func=fileinfo&id=3673z (Last accessed August 8, 2019).
3.   IRC Sec. 4191(a).
4.   IRC Section 4191.
5.   Pub. L. 115-120.

not apply to the sale of taxable medical devices by the manufacturer, producer, or importer of the device during the period beginning on January 1, 2016 and ending on December 31, 2019. Further, because the extension of the moratorium is retroactive to January 1, 2018, manufacturers, producers and importers of taxable medical devices should not make deposits of tax or report any medical device excise tax liability on Form 720, Quarterly Federal Excise Tax Return, for sales of taxable medical devices between Jan. 1, 2018, and Jan. 22, 2018. As of time of printing, the moratorium on the medical device excise tax is scheduled to end on December 31, 2019.

547. When is the Form 720 due?

The Form 720 is filed quarterly. The first return to report the medical device excise tax will be due on April 30, 2020, for the quarterly period including January, February and March 2020. Quarterly return due dates are as follows:

- January, February, March - due by April 30

- April, May, June – due by July 31

- July, August, September – due by October 31

- October, November, December – due by January 31

Semi-monthly deposits will generally be required if tax liability exceeds $2,500 for the quarter. The first deposit of the medical device excise tax, covering the first fifteen days of January 2013, will be due on Jan. 29, 2013. IRS Notice 2012-77 provides transition relief from deposit penalties during the first three calendar quarters of 2013.

548. What is a taxable medical device?

A "taxable medical device" means any device[1] intended for humans.[2] Several specific devices are exempted from the tax, including eyeglasses, contact lenses, hearing aids, and any other medical device determined by the Secretary to be of a type that is generally purchased by the general public at retail for individual use.[3]

In addition, the following sales by a manufacturer are exempt:

- For use by the purchaser for further manufacture, or for resale by the purchaser to a second purchaser for use by such second purchaser in further manufacture.

- For export, or for resale by the purchaser to a second purchaser for export.

- For use by the purchaser as supplies for vessels or aircraft.

- To a state or local government for the exclusive use of the state or local government.

---

1. Federal Food, Drug and Cosmetic Act (FFDCA) §201(h).
2. IRC Sec. 4191(b).
3. IRC Sec. 4191(c).

- To a nonprofit educational organization for its exclusive use.

- To a qualified blood collector organization for such organization's exclusive use in the collection, storage, or transportation of blood.[1]

549. Are there any exemptions to the medical device tax?

Yes. There are specific statutory exemptions for eyeglasses, contact lenses, and hearing aids. There is also an exemption for other devices that are of a type that are generally purchased by the general public at retail for individual use (the retail exemption). The regulations help determine whether a type of device meets the retail exemption. The regulations enumerate several factors that are relevant, but there may be relevant factors in addition to those enumerated in the regulations. The determination is based on the overall balance of factors relevant to a particular type of device. No one factor is determinative. See Section 48.4191-2(b)(2) of the regulations for more information about the retail exemption.

The regulations also provide a safe harbor for certain devices that will be considered to be of a type that falls within the retail exemption. The regulations identify certain categories of devices that qualify for the retail exemption so that manufacturers and importers do not have to apply the facts and circumstances test. Those categories are set forth in a safe harbor provision in Section 48.4191-2(b)(2)(iii) of the regulations.

550. Are there instances where medical devices can be sold tax-free?

Yes. A manufacturer or importer of a taxable medical device may, in certain circumstances, sell a taxable medical device tax-free for use by the purchaser for further manufacture (or for resale by the purchaser to a second purchaser for further manufacture), or for export (or for resale for export). To make a tax-free sale for further manufacture or export, both parties to the sale must be registered with the IRS. Form 637, Application for Registration for Certain Excise Tax Activities is used for registration.[2]

551. How is the medical device tax computed and who must report it?

The tax is 2.3 percent of the sale price of the taxable medical device. IRS Publication 510[3] and IRS Notice 2012-77[4] have additional information on the "sale price" will be determined.

Generally, the manufacturer or importer of a taxable medical device will be responsible for filing Quarterly Federal Excise Tax Return (Form 720)[5] and paying the tax to the IRS. Individual consumers do not have any responsibility for reporting or paying the tax because the tax is imposed upon the sale of a taxable medical device by the manufacturer or importer.

---

1.   IRC Sec. 4221.
2.   https://www.irs.gov/forms-pubs/about-form-637.
3.   https://www.irs.gov/pub/irs-pdf/p510.pdf (Chapter 5 – Excise Taxes). Revised March 2018 (Last accessed August 8, 2019).
4.   https://www.irs.gov/pub/irs-drop/n-12-77.pdf. (Last accessed August 8, 2019).
5.   https://www.irs.gov/pub/irs-pdf/f720.pdf.

552. Who constitutes the manufacturer or the importer for purposes of the medical excise tax?

Manufacturers: the manufacturer is generally the person who produces a taxable medical device from scrap, salvage or junk material, or from new or raw material, by processing, manipulating or changing the form of a device or by combining or assembling two or more devices.

Importers: the importer is generally the person who brings the device into the United States from a source outside the United States, or withdraws the device from a customs-bonded warehouse for sale or use in the United States.

553. How are "convenience kits" treated under the terms of the medical excise tax?

There is interim guidance provided by IRS Notice 2012-77[1] on the tax treatment of convenience kits. Under this guidance, a taxable medical device that goes into a domestically-produced convenience kit will be subject to tax upon its sale by the manufacturer or importer, but the sale of the convenience kit by the kit producer will not be subject to tax. Special rules apply to imported kits.

Definitionally, a convenience kit is a set of two or more devices within the meaning of §201(h) of the Federal Food, Drug, and Cosmetic Act that is enclosed in a single package, such as a bag, tray, or box, for the convenience of a health care professional or the end user.

554. When does the moratorium on the medical device excise tax end?

The current moratorium ends on December 31, 2019. It appears that the moratorium will not be extended again, the medical device excise tax will apply to sales of taxable medical devices made after December 31, 2019, and taxpayers will be required to report sales of taxable medical devices made during the first quarter of 2020 on Form 720 by April 30, 2020.

Expanded Medicare Tax on Wages

555. How does the Expanded Medicare Tax on Wages work?

Background of the Tax

An additional 0.9 percent Medicare tax (called the Hospital Insurance Tax) on wages in excess of the $250,000/$125,000/$200,000 thresholds for married taxpayers filing jointly, married taxpayers filing separately, and all other taxpayers, respectively, was imposed on individuals in 2013. There is a corresponding 0.9 percent increase in the self-employment tax for self-employed individuals, except that the $250,000/$125,000/$200,000 thresholds are reduced (but not below zero) by the taxpayer's wages.[2] This additional 0.9 percent tax on wages and self-employment income above the applicable thresholds is not deductible for income tax purposes.[3] In this respect, it is like the "employee" portion of the FICA tax, which generally comes out of

---

1.   https://www.irs.gov/pub/irs-drop/n-12-77.pdf. (Last accessed September 3, 2018).
2.   IRC Sec. 1401(b)(2).
3.   IRC Sec. 164(f).

after-tax wages, as opposed to the "employer" portion of the FICA tax that is deductible by the employer (and not included in the employee's wages).

The net effect of this new 0.9 percent Medicare tax is to put the higher-income wage earner in roughly the same position as the higher-income passive investor who must pay a 3.8 percent Medicare tax on investment income above the same dollar thresholds. They both will effectively now pay an additional 3.8 percent tax above the "high-income" thresholds.

However, a taxpayer subject to this extra 0.9 percent tax is effectively allowed to "deduct" the 1.45 percent "employer" portion of the FICA tax when applying the increased 3.8 percent rate, even above the income thresholds, whereas the investor subject to the 3.8 percent tax on net investment income cannot deduct it. All wages and self-employment income are subject to the existing 2.9 percent Medicare tax (the 1.45 percent "employer" portion, which is "deductible," and the 1.45 percent employee portion, which is not), not just the portion of such income above the thresholds.

The new Medicare tax rate structure, including both the new 3.8 percent Medicare tax on investment income, discussed beginning with Q 564, and the 0.9 percent increased FICA/SECA (Self Employment Contributions Act) rate should not have a big impact on most other closely held business tax planning issues. However, it increases the advantage of wages versus dividends from a C corporation. Ironically, a passive investor in a partnership subject to the self-employment tax actually pays tax at a slightly lower marginal rate (44 percent) than that same investor in a partnership whose activities are not subject to the self-employment tax (44.59 percent), because of the deductibility of the 1.45 percent amount.[1]

Additionally, an S corporation shareholder receiving a dividend distribution from S corporation trade or business income (as opposed to self-employment income) pays even less (40.79 percent) as this dividend is not subject to either the expanded Medicare tax on wages or the new Medicare tax on investment income, discussed in Q 564. The rates above are based on the maximum 2019 income tax rate of 37 percent.

556. When is liability incurred for the Additional Medicare Tax?

An individual is liable for Additional Medicare Tax if the individual's wages, compensation, or self-employment income (together with that of his or her spouse if filing a joint return) exceed the threshold amount for the individual's filing status:

Filing Status	Threshold Amount
Married filing jointly	$250,000
Married filing separate	$125,000
Single	$200,000
Head of household (with qualifying person)	$200,000
Qualifying widow(er) with dependent child	$200,000

---

1.   IRC Sec. 1411(c)(6), Illustration #4.

557. What wages are subject to the Additional Medicare Tax?

Any wages currently subject to the regular Medicare Tax are subject to the Additional Medicare Tax if they are paid in excess of the applicable threshold for an individual's filing status.

558. Is Railroad Retirement Tax Act compensation subject to the Additional Medicare Tax?

Any RRTA compensation currently subject to Medicare Tax is subject to the Additional Medicare Tax if it is paid in excess of the applicable threshold for an individual's filing status.

559. Is income subject to the Additional Medicare Tax subject to the Medicare Tax on Investment Income?

No. The tax imposed by section 1411 on an individual's net investment income is not applicable to wages, RRTA compensation, or self-employment income. Thus, an individual will not owe net investment income tax on these categories of income, regardless of the taxpayer's filing status.

560. Are nonresident aliens and expatriate U.S. citizens subject to the Additional Medicare Tax?

Yes. There are no special rules for nonresident aliens and U.S. citizens living abroad for purposes of this provision. Wages, other compensation, and self-employment income that are subject to Medicare tax will also be subject to Additional Medicare Tax if in excess of the applicable threshold.

561. Are non-cash wages or tips subject to the Additional Medicare Tax?

Yes. The value of taxable wages not paid in cash, such as noncash fringe benefits, are subject to Additional Medicare Tax, if, in combination with other wages, they exceed the individual's applicable threshold. Noncash wages are subject to Additional Medicare Tax withholding, if, in combination with other wages paid by the employer, they exceed the $200,000 withholding threshold. Tips are subject to the Additional Medicare Tax, if, in combination with other wages, they exceed the individual's applicable threshold.

562. How is the Additional Medicare Tax reported?

The Additional Medicare Tax is reported on Form 8959, Additional Medicare Tax.[1]

563. When must an employer withhold Additional Medicare Tax and what are the ramifications for failing to withhold?

Effective Jan. 1, 2013, an employer must withhold Additional Medicare Tax on wages it pays to an employee in excess of $200,000 in a calendar year. An employer has this withholding obligation even though an employee may not be liable for Additional Medicare Tax because, for example, the employee's wages together with that of his or her spouse do not

---

1.   Form 8959 https://www.irs.gov/pub/irs-pdf/f8959.pdf. (Last accessed September 22, 2018).

exceed the $250,000 threshold for joint return filers. Any withheld Additional Medicare Tax will be credited against the total tax liability shown on the individual's income tax return. There is no requirement that an employer notify its employee that it is withholding additional Medicare tax. There is no employer match for Additional Medicare Tax as with the regular Medicare tax.

An employer that does not deduct and withhold Additional Medicare Tax as required is liable for the tax unless the tax that it failed to withhold from the employee's wages is paid by the employee. An employer is not relieved of its liability for payment of any Additional Medicare Tax required to be withheld unless it can show that the tax has been paid by filing Forms 4669 and 4670. Even if not liable for the tax, an employer that does not meet its with-holding, deposit, reporting, and payment responsibilities for Additional Medicare Tax may be subject to all applicable penalties.

Individuals with wages subject to both FICA tax and self-employment income subject to SECA tax use a three-step process to calculate their liabilities for Additional Medicare Tax:

- ONE: Calculate Additional Medicare Tax on any wages in excess of the applicable threshold for the filing status, without regard to whether any tax was withheld

- TWO: Reduce the applicable threshold for the filing status by the total amount of Medicare wages received, but not below zero

- THREE: Calculate Additional Medicare Tax on any self-employment income in excess of the reduced threshold.

Example 1: Connie, a single filer, has $130,000 in wages and $145,000 in self-employment income. Connie's wages are not in excess of the $200,000 threshold for single filers, so Connie is not liable for Additional Medicare Tax.

Before calculating the Additional Medicare Tax on self-employment income, the $200,000 threshold for single filers is reduced by Connie's $130,000 in wages, resulting in a reduced self-employment income threshold of $70,000.

Connie is liable to pay Additional Medicare Tax on $75,000 of self-employment income ($145,000 in self-employment income minus the reduced threshold of $70,000).

Example 2: Mike and Rita are married and file jointly. Mike has $150,000 in wages and Rita has $175,000 in self-employment income.

Mike's wages are not in excess of the $250,000 threshold for joint filers, so Mike and Rita are not liable for Additional Medicare Tax on Mike's wages.

Before calculating the Additional Medicare Tax on Rita's self-employment income, the $250,000 threshold for joint filers is reduced by Mike's $150,000 in wages resulting in a reduced self-employment income threshold of $100,000.

Mike and Rita are liable to pay Additional Medicare Tax on $75,000 of self-employment income ($175,000 in self-employment income minus the reduced threshold of $100,000).

Example 3: Zelda, who is married filing separately, has $175,000 in wages and $50,000 in self-employment income.

Zelda is liable to pay Additional Medicare Tax on $50,000 of his wages ($175,000 minus the $125,000 threshold for married persons who file separate).

Before calculating the Additional Medicare Tax on self-employment income, the $125,000 threshold for married persons who file separate is reduced by Zelda's $175,000 in wages to $0 (reduced, but not below zero).

Zelda is liable to pay Additional Medicare Tax on $50,000 of self-employment income ($50,000 in self-employment income minus the reduced threshold of $0).

In total, Zelda is liable to pay Additional Medicare Tax on $100,000 ($50,000 of his wages and $50,000 of his self-employment income).

Example 4: Caleb who files as Head of Household, has $225,000 in wages and $50,000 in self-employment income. Caleb's employer withheld Additional Medicare Tax on $25,000 ($225,000 minus the $200,000 withholding threshold).

Caleb is liable to pay Additional Medicare Tax on $25,000 of his wages ($225,000 minus the $200,000 threshold for head of household filers).

Before calculating the Additional Medicare Tax on self-employment income, the $200,000 threshold for head of household filers is reduced by G's $225,000 in wages to $0 (reduced, but not below zero).

Caleb is liable to pay Additional Medicare Tax on $50,000 of self-employment income ($50,000 in self-employment income minus the reduced threshold of $0).

In total, Caleb is liable to pay Additional Medicare Tax on $75,000 ($25,000 of her wages and $50,000 of his self-employment income).

The Additional Medicare Tax withheld by Caleb's employer will be applied against all taxes shown on her individual income tax return, including any Additional Medicare Tax liability.

3.8 Percent Medicare Tax on Investment Income (Net Investment Income Tax)

564. What is the 3.8 percent Medicare tax on investment?

For taxable years starting on or after January 1, 2013, Internal Revenue Code section 1411 imposes a new 3.8 percent Medicare tax on "net investment income" (this excludes trade or business income, except from passive activities and trading in financial instruments or commodities) for higher income individuals, estates, and trusts through Internal Revenue Code section 1411. For individuals, such "net investment income" is subject to this new tax to the extent that "modified adjusted gross income" exceeds $250,000 in the case of joint returns, $125,000 in the case of married filing separate returns, and $200,000 in all other cases.[1] Modified adjusted gross income is adjusted gross income increased by the net foreign earned income exclusion.[2] Although the new tax is called a "Medicare" tax in the health reform statute, legislative history, and Internal

---

1.   IRC Sec. 1411(a)(1), (b).
2.   IRC Sec. 1411(d). Unlike the definition of "modified adjusted gross income" for purposes of the individual premium tax credit, this definition makes no adjustment for tax-exempt interest.

Revenue Code, the IRS refers to this new tax as the "net investment income tax." Nonresident aliens are not subject to the new tax.

> *Example 1:* A married couple filing jointly has $300,000 of AGI, $100,000 of which is net investment income. They will pay $1,900 in the new tax – i.e., 3.8 percent of the lesser of the amount of net investment income ($100,000) or $50,000 which is the excess of the $300,000 AGI over the $250,000 threshold amount.

> *Example 2:* Same as Example 1 above, except only $25,000 of the AGI is net investment income. They will pay $950 in the new tax – i.e., 3.8 percent of the lesser of the amount of net investment income ($25,000) or $50,000 which is the excess of the $300,000 AGI over the $250,000 threshold amount.

565. Who is subject to the Net Investment Income Tax?

Individuals who have Net Investment Income and have modified adjusted gross income over the following thresholds:

Filing Status	Threshold Amount
Married filing jointly	$250,000
Married filing separately	$125,000
Single	$200,000
Heal of household (with qualifying person)	$200,000
Qualifying widow(er) with dependent child	$250,000

These threshold amounts are not indexed for inflation.

Definition of "modified adjusted gross income": adjusted gross income increased by the difference between amounts excluded from gross income under section 911(a)(1) and the amount of any deductions (taken into account in computing adjusted gross income) or exclusions disallowed under section 911(d)(6) for amounts described in section 911(a)(1). In the case of taxpayers with income from controlled foreign corporations (CFCs) and passive foreign investment companies (PFICs),[1] they may have additional adjustments to their AGI.

Who is NOT subject to the Net Investment Income Tax?

- Nonresident Aliens (NRAs) are not subject to the Net Investment Income Tax.

  - There are special rules for an NRA married to a U.S. citizen. If an NRA is married to a U.S. citizen or resident and has made, or is planning to make, an election under section 6013(g) or 6013(h) to be treated as a resident alien for purposes of filing as Married Filing Jointly, the final regulations provide these couples special rules and a corresponding section 6013(g)/(h) election for the NIIT.

  - A dual-resident individual within the meaning of regulation §301.7701(b)-7(a)(1) who determines that they are a resident of a foreign country for tax

---

1.   https://www.law.cornell.edu/cfr/text/26/1.1411-10. (Last accessed August 8, 2019).

purposes pursuant to an income tax treaty between the United States and that foreign country AND claims benefits of the treaty as a nonresident of the United States is considered a NRA.[1]

- A dual-status individual, who is a resident of the United States for only part of the year and a NRA for the other part of the year, is subject to the tax only for the portion of the year of which they are a United States resident.

566. Will someone have to pay the 3.8 percent Net Investment Income Tax AND the additional 0.9 percent Medicare Tax?

You may be subject to both taxes, but not on the same type of income.

The 0.9 percent Additional Medicare Tax applies to individuals' wages, compensation and self-employment income over certain thresholds, but it does not apply to income items included in Net Investment Income.

567. How does the Medicare tax on investment income apply to estates and trusts?

Yes. For estates or trusts, this new tax applies to the lesser of

(1)   undistributed net investment income or

(2)   the excess of

(i)   AGI (as defined in Internal Revenue Code section 67(e)) over

(ii) the dollar amount at which the highest trust/estate tax rate begins.[2]

The highest tax bracket in Code section 1(e) for estates and trusts during calendar year 2019 is taxable income over $12,750.[3] When the tax began in 2013, the threshold was $11,650. Additionally, as explained below, "net investment income" for purposes of this new tax is defined to include passive activity income.[4] No tax is imposed on tax-exempt trusts, however, where principal and income goes to charity.[5]

Example 1: For 2019, a trust has $250,000 in AGI and $100,000 in undistributed net investment income. Assume that the top federal rate for trusts starts at $12,750 in 2019. The trust pays $3,800 in this tax, namely, 3.8 percent of the lesser of its undistributed net investment income ($100,000) or $237,250 which is the excess of its $250,000 AGI over $12,750.

Example 2: Same as above, except that the trust's AGI equals $100,000. It would pay $3,315.50 in this tax, namely, 3.8 percent of the lesser of its undistributed net investment income ($100,000) or $87,250 which is the excess of its $100,000 AGI over $11,650.

---

1.   https://www.law.cornell.edu/cfr/text/26/301.7701%28b%29-7. (Last accessed August 8, 2019).
2.   IRC Sec. 1411(c)(6). The tax brackets are in IRC Sec. 1(e) for estates and complex trusts.
3.   IRC Sec. 1(j)(2)(E).
4.   *See* IRC Sec. 469(a)(2)(A); Treas. Reg. §1.469-8.
5.   IRC Sec. 1141(e)(2).

The following trusts are not subject to the Net Investment Income Tax:

1.   Trusts that are exempt from income taxes imposed by Subtitle A of the Internal Revenue Code (e.g., charitable trusts and qualified retirement plan trusts exempt from tax under section 501, and Charitable Remainder Trusts exempt from tax under section 664).

2.   A trust or decedent's estate in which all unexpired interests are devoted to one or more of the purposes described in IRC section 170(c)(2)(B).

3.   Trusts that are classified as "grantor trusts" under IRC sections 671-679.

4.   Trusts that are not classified as "trusts" for federal income tax purposes (e.g., Real Estate Investment Trusts and Common Trust Funds).

5.   Electing Alaska Native Settlement Trusts.

6.   Perpetual Care (Cemetery) Trusts.

568. How does the Medicare tax on investment income apply to S corporations electing small business trusts?

The <u>IRS defines net investment income</u> for the purposes of calculating the Medicare surtax as interest, dividends, capital gains, annuities, royalties, rents, and pass-through income from an passive business such as S Corps and partnerships.

If an S Corporation shareholder materially participate in their S Corp then their income is not included in the net investment income calculation because this would not be considered passive income – and therefore not subject to the Net Investment Income Tax.

The IRS test for "material participation" includes the following criteria:

To materially participate in a business for a particular year, the shareholder must meet ONE of the following seven tests discussed in Temp Regs Section 1.469-5T(a)[1]

- The shareholder participated in the activity for more than 500 hours during the year;

- The shareholder's participation in the activity constituted substantially all the participation of all individuals in the activity;

- The shareholder participated for more than 100 hours in the activity, and the shareholder's hours were not less than those of any other participant in the activity;

- The activity is a significant participation activity for the year, and the shareholder's aggregate participation in all significant participation activities exceeded 500 hours;

---

1.   https://www.law.cornell.edu/cfr/text/26/1.469-5T.

- The shareholder materially participated in the activity for any five of the past ten years;

- The activity is a personal services activity where the shareholder materially participated in the activity for any three years preceding the tax year; or

- Based on all the facts and circumstances, the shareholder participated in the activity on a regular, continuous, and substantial basis.

569. What is "net investment income?"

Net investment income does not include trade or business income except income except from Internal Revenue Code section 469 passive activities and trading in financial instruments or commodities.[1] "Net investment income" means the following items, less deductions "properly allocable"[2] to them:

- <u>Interest, Dividends, Annuities, Royalties and Rents</u>.[3] However, these types of income are not subject to this new tax if they are "derived in the ordinary course of a trade or business," as long as that trade or business does not constitute a passive activity with respect to the taxpayer and does not constitute "trading in financial instruments or commodities."[4] Thus, interest on customer receivables and interest derived in an active lending business should not be subject to this new tax. Moreover, royalties earned in the active conduct of a software business should be exempt. However, net investment income attributable to working capital will be subject to the tax.[5]

- <u>Passive Activity Income</u>.[6] Until 2013, passive activity income was a favorable tax classification because it, unlike non-passive trade or business income, could be offset by passive losses.[7] Thus, taxpayers often preferred this income classification. This new tax may cause taxpayers to attempt to avoid passive activity classification. Net investment income includes trade or business income that is a passive activity under Internal Revenue Code section 469.[8]

  For example, an individual might be engaged in ten separate activities, and actively participate in several of them for less than 500 hours per year. If each of these activities is treated as a separate activity, then those activities in which the taxpayer spends more than 100, but less than 500, hours per year (and which generate an overall net loss), along with those in which the taxpayer

---

1.   IRC Sec. 1411(c)(2).
2.   Taxpayers are entitled to subtract "deductions allowed by this subtitle which are properly allocable to such gross income." For many taxpayers some or all "properly allocable" investment expenses are not "allowed by this subtitle" because they are only deductible to the extent that they exceed 2 percent of adjusted gross income.
3.   IRC Sec. 1411(c)(1)(A)(i).
4.   IRC Sec. 1411(c)(1)(A)(i), (2).
5.   *See* IRC Secs. 1411(c)(3); 469(e)(1)(b).
6.   IRC Sec. 1411(c)(1)(A)(ii), (B); (2)(A).
7.   IRC Sec. 469(d)(1)(B).
8.   IRC Sec. 1411(c)(2)(A).

spends less than 100 hours per year, should be classified as passive activities generating passive activity income.[1] However, treating all of the activities in which the taxpayer participates as one single activity for passive activity purposes could avoid this new tax on all of the income from the activities in which he or she participates (though probably not for his or her outside passive activities), because the taxpayer's aggregate material participation in all of these activities totals more than 500 hours.[2]

Such planning considerations are important because the Internal Revenue Service now requires all taxpayers who form new groups of activities or add new activities to existing groups to disclose how they are aggregating or segregating their activities under the passive activity loss rules.[3] These disclosure requirements apply for taxable years beginning after January 15, 2010.[4]

Incorporation of the passive activity rules into this new Medicare Tax structure also creates a number of open issues. For example, the passive activity regulations provide that gross income from each significant participation activity "equal to a ratable portion of the taxpayer's net passive income from such activity for the taxable year shall be treated as not from a passive activity if the taxpayer experiences net taxable income from such significant participation activities."[5] Does this mean that such income is not subject to this new Medicare Tax on "net investment income"? There are no clear answers yet.

- <u>The Business of Financial Instruments and Commodities</u>. The "trade or business of trading in financial instruments or commodities (as defined in Code section 475(e)(2)) is "net investment income," regardless of whether a taxpayer materially participates.[6] This seemingly would include hedge fund income. Although commodities are defined by reference to a specific Code section, the term "financial instruments" will be defined by regulation. Treasury Regulation section 1.1275-6 (b)(3) defines "financial instrument" as "a spot, forward, or future contract, an option, a notional principal contract, a debt instrument, or a similar instrument, or combination or series of financial instruments," but specifically excludes stock. Similarly, Internal Revenue Code section 475(c)(2)(E) and Treasury Regulation section 1.988-1(a)(2)(iii) describe financial instruments in terms of what are commonly considered to be financial derivatives. On the other hand, Code section 731(c)(2)(C) defines financial instrument more broadly as including stocks and other equity investments, evidences of indebtedness, options, forward or futures contracts, notional principal contracts, and derivatives.

---

1.   Treas. Reg. §1.469-5 (a)(1), (3), (c).
2.   Treas. Reg. §1.469-5 (a)(1).
3.   Rev. Proc. 2010-13.
4.   Rev. Proc. 2010-13. Taxpayers who do not add new activities or alter their existing activity groups are grandfathered in, and do not need to disclose their existing grouping decisions.
5.   Treas. Reg. §1.469-2 (f)(2).
6.   IRC Sec. 1411(c)(1)(A)(ii), (2)(B).

Another issue is what constitutes "trading" in financial instruments or commodities? Does the extensive case law relating to the treatment of "dealers" and "traders" come into play, perhaps with individual investors not subject to this new tax?[1]

- <u>Net Gain from Non-Business Property</u>. "Net gain (to the extent taken into account in computing taxable income) attributable to the disposition of property other than property held in a trade or business," is subject to this tax, unless that trade or business is a passive activity with respect to the taxpayer or involves trading in financial instruments or commodities.[2] In general, this is a broad category. This income includes gain from the disposition of nonbusiness assets, such as houses, boats, and airplanes. However, excluded gain from the sale of a personal residence of $250,000 or $500,000[3] is not subject to this Medicare tax on investment income because it is not "taken into account in computing taxable income."[4] Gain from the disposition of stock in a C corporation should be taxable under this provision unless excluded under Internal Revenue Code section 1202.

  Significantly, "property held in a trade or business" is excluded unless the trade or business does not fall within the disfavored passive activity or trading category.[5] There is also an exception for the disposition of interests in partnerships and S corporations (*i.e.*, pass-through entities), which provides that gain on such dispositions will be taken into account "only to the extent of the net gain which would be so taken into account by the transferor if all property of the partnership or S corporation were sold for fair market value immediately before the disposition of such interest."[6] The Technical Explanation concludes that "[t]hus only net gain or loss attributable to property held by the entity which is not properly attributable to an active trade or business is taken into account."[7]

570. What types of gains are included in Net Investment Income?

To the extent that gains are not otherwise offset by capital losses, the following gains are common examples of items taken into account in computing Net Investment Income:

- Gains from the sale of stocks, bonds, and mutual funds.

- Capital gain distributions from mutual funds.

---

1.   *See, e.g., Holsinger v. Comm'r*, T.C. Memo 2008-191 (married couple not traders due to insubstantial trading activity and lack of profit motive); *George R. Kemon*, 16 T.C. 1026 (1951) (partnership found to be a trader); *United States v. Diamond*, 788 F.2d 1025 (4th Cir. 1986) (recognizing the difference between "dealers" who sell to customers and "traders" who do not).
2.   IRC Sec. 1411(c)(1)(A)(iii).
3.   IRC Sec. 121.
4.   See IRC Sec. 121; Joint Committee On Taxation, Technical Explanation Of The Revenue Provisions Of The Reconciliation Act Of 2010, As Amended In Combination With The Patient Protection And Affordable Care Act, p. 135 n. 285 (Mar. 21, 2010) at http://www.jct.gov/publications.html?func=startdown&id=3673). (Last accessed August 8, 2019).
5.   IRC Sec. 1411(c)(1)(A)(iii).
6.   IRC Sec. 1411(c)(4).
7.   Technical Explanation, at 135.

- Gain from the sale of investment real estate (including gain from the sale of a second home that is not a primary residence).

- Gains from the sale of interests in partnerships and S corporations (to the extent the partner or shareholder was a passive owner).

The Net Investment Income Tax does not apply to any amount of gain that is excluded from gross income for regular income tax purposes. The pre-existing statutory exclusion in Section 121 exempts the first $250,000 ($500,000 in the case of a married couple) of gain recognized on the sale of a principal residence from gross income for regular income tax purposes and, thus, from the NIIT.

571. How does the Medicare tax on investment income apply to pass-through entities?

The tax is not intended to apply at all to non-passive, non-trading businesses conducted by S corporations, partnerships, or sole proprietorships.[1] Thus, for pass-through entities that do not have passive investors and do not engage in any financial instrument or commodity trading business, "net investment income" will include only non-business income from interest, dividends, annuities, royalties, rents, and capital gains, minus the allocable deductions. Therefore, business income earned or distributed by such pass-through entities will not be subject to the new Medicare tax.

An S-corporation shareholder's allocable share of trade or business income is not net earnings from self-employment and will not be subject to the extra 0.9 percent Medicare tax on wages nor to the 3.8 percent on net investment income.[2] One technique that clearly does not work is for a professional to form a partnership or LLC "with himself or herself." or otherwise try to "fractionalize" personal services into a large "passive" component and a small "residual" component, and then claim that the income flowing through the "passive" or limited liability ownership is not subject to SECA.[3]

---

1.   Technical Explanation, at 135.
2.   Rev. Rul. 59-221; see also IRC Sec. 1402(a)(2) (excluding "dividends on shares of stock issued by a corporation" from "net earnings from self-employment); Letter Ruling 871606 (Jan. 21, 1987) (income derived by a shareholder-employee from an "S" corporation did not constitute net earnings from self-employment for self-employment tax purposes and taxpayer was not eligible to adopt a qualified pension plan based on the income derived from "S" corporation since such income did not constitute earned income).
3.   *Robucci v. Comm'r.*, 101 T.C. Memo. (CCH) 1060 (Jan. 24, 2011), a psychiatrist on the advice of his CPA set up a structure whereby he formed an LLC between himself and his wholly-owned professional corporation. The Tax Court held that the professional corporation had no business purpose and should be ignored (meaning that the LLC had only one member (the taxpayer) and therefore that all income passed through was subject to SECA) and further upheld the IRS's imposition of negligence penalties. In *Renkemeyer, Campbell & Weaver LLP v. Comm'r.*, 136 T.C. 137 (2011), three attorneys were partners in an LLP. Initially, 10 percent of the LLP was owned by an "S" corporation owned by an ESOP of which the three attorneys were beneficiaries; later, the "S" corporation was eliminated and, in an apparent attempt to come under the Proposed Section 1402 Regulations, the partners split their interests into de minimis general managing partner interests and the remainder into "investing partner" interests. The bulk of the LLP's income was allocated to the "investing" interests and the partners did not pay SECA tax on the amounts so allocated. The Tax Court agreed with the IRS's contention that all income was subject to SECA and that the partners' active involvement in and performance of legal services for the LLP was inconsistent with what Congress had intended in enacting relief under Code section 1402(a)(13) for limited partners as passive investors.

572. What items are not subject to the Medicare tax on net investment income?

<u>Active Trade or Business Income</u>. Active trade or business income is not subject to the 3.8 percent Medicare net investment income tax. The net investment income tax makes extremely important the distinction between activities that are a trade or business on the one hand and not so characterized on the other hand. Activities entered into for profit are not necessarily trade or business activities.[1]

<u>IRA and Qualified Plan Distributions</u>. "Net investment income" does not include any distribution from a plan or arrangement described in Internal Revenue Code sections 401(a) (pension, profit-sharing, 401(k) and stock bonus plans), 403(a) or 403(b) (employee annuity plans), 408 (IRAs), 408A (Roth IRAs), or 457(b) (state and local government and tax-exempt organization deferred compensation plans).[2] Distributions from such plans also do not constitute "wages" for purposes of FICA taxes and withholding,[3] However, distributions from these plans (except for Roth IRAs) enter into a taxpayer's adjusted gross income (AGI) and, therefore, increase AGI above the applicable threshold amount for purposes of determining tax on net investment income from taxable mutual funds and other nonsheltered sources.

<u>Other Exempt Income</u>. The explanation of the Joint Committee on Taxation states that gross income for purposes of computing net investment income does not include items excluded from gross income for income tax purposes, such as interest on tax-exempt bonds or gain excluded under Internal Revenue Code section 121 from the sale of a principal residence.[4] Similarly, proceeds from a life insurance policy (subject to the "transfer-for-value" rules of Internal Revenue Code section 101), and the "inside buildup" in a life insurance policy, should be exempt from the new tax. In addition, wages, unemployment compensation; operating income from a nonpassive business, Social Security Benefits, alimony, tax-exempt interest, self-employment income, Alaska Permanent Fund Dividends (see Rev. Rul. 90-56, 1990-2 CB 102) and distributions from certain Qualified Plans (those described in sections 401(a), 403(a), 403(b), 408, 408A or 457(b)) are exempt.

573. What are some examples of the calculations of the Net Investment Income Tax?

Example 1: A single taxpayer with income less than the statutory threshold

Taxpayer, a single filer, has wages of $180,000 and $15,000 of dividends and capital gains. Taxpayer's modified adjusted gross income is $195,000, which is less than the $200,000 statutory threshold. Taxpayer is not subject to the Net Investment Income Tax.

---

1. See, e.g. *Estate of Roger Stangeland v. Comm'r.*, T.C. Memo. 2010-185, 100 T.C. Memo. (CCH) 156 (Aug. 16, 2010) (consulting enterprise operated by petitioners to manage petitioner's other business interests was not itself a trade or business; instead, its purpose and the nature of its operations was to increase the investment value of petitioners' other businesses); cf. *Wilbur Langford v. Comm'r.*, T.C. Memo. 1988-300, 55 T.C. Memo. (CCH) 1267 (July 19, 1988) (college professor's royalties from co-authorship of one textbook were "royalties" not subject to SECA tax because petitioner's activities did not rise to the level of a "trade or business"; citing Rev. Rul. 55-385 and Rev. Rul. 68-498.

2. IRC Sec. 1411(c)(5).

3. IRC Sec. 3121(a)(5).

4. Joint Committee On Taxation, Technical Explanation Of The Revenue Provisions Of The Reconciliation Act Of 2010, As Amended In Combination With The Patient Protection And Affordable Care Act, p. 135 n. 285 (Mar. 21, 2010) at http://www.jct.gov/publications. html?func=startdown&id=3673). (Last accessed August 8, 2019.

Example 2: A single taxpayer with income greater than the statutory threshold

Taxpayer, a single filer, has $180,000 of wages. Taxpayer also received $90,000 from a passive partnership interest, which is considered Net Investment Income. Taxpayer's modified adjusted gross income is $270,000.

Taxpayer's modified adjusted gross income exceeds the threshold of $200,000 for single taxpayers by $70,000. Taxpayer's Net Investment Income is $90,000.

The Net Investment Income Tax is based on the lesser of $70,000 (the amount that Taxpayer's modified adjusted gross income exceeds the $200,000 threshold) or $90,000 (Taxpayer's Net Investment Income). Taxpayer owes NIIT of $2,660 ($70,000 × 3.8%).

Cafeteria Plan Changes

$2,700 Cap on Employee FSA Contributions

574. What are the cafeteria plan changes enacted in health reform?

For tax years beginning in 2011, the new SIMPLE cafeteria plan, discussed earlier in Part V (Small Business Provisions) is an option for smaller employers.

In taxable years beginning after 2012, health reform limits annual employee contributions to a health Flexible Spending Account (FSA) offered under a cafeteria plan to $2,500 (adjusted for inflation).[1]

For subsequent years, the cap has been raised as follows:

- For 2015 and 2016, the cap was raised to $2,550.[2]

- For 2017, the cap has was raised to $2,600 by Revenue Procedure 2016-55.[3]

- For 2018, the cap has been raised to $2,650 by Revenue Procedure 2017-58.[4]

- For 2019, to the cap was raised to $2,700[5] by Revenue Procedure 2018-57.

- For 2020, it is projected that the cap will be increased by $50 to $2,750 but the IRS will not officially announce the increase until October or November 2019.

- In addition, effective beginning in 2014, Internal Revenue Code section 125(f)(3) permits a qualified employer to offer employees the opportunity to enroll in a qualified health insurance plan of a health exchange through the employer's cafeteria plan, even though reimbursement of expenses paid to a health exchange-participating qualified health plan otherwise is not a permissible benefit under a cafeteria plan.

---

1.   IRC Sec. 125(i).
2.   Revenue Procedure 2014-61 https://www.shrm.org/ResourcesAndTools/hr-topics/benefits/Documents/rp-14-61.pdf (Issued October 30, 2014).
3.   Revenue Procedure 2016-55 https://www.irs.gov/pub/irs-drop/rp-16-55.pdf. (Issued October 25, 2016).
4.   Revenue Procedure 2017-58 https://www.irs.gov/pub/irs-drop/rp-17-58.pdf, (Issued October 19, 2017).
5.   Revenue Procedure 2018-57 https://www.irs.gov/pub/irs-drop/rp-18-57.pdf. (Issued November 15, 2018)

575. To what does the new FSA limit apply?

The $2,500 cap was for employee contributions to health Flexible Spending Accounts (FSAs) for plan years beginning in 2013 and thereafter.[1] Health FSAs are used to reimburse medical and dental expenses not paid by insurance, whether due to copays, deductibles, or otherwise.

The $2,500 was adjusted to $2,550 for 2015 and remained at that amount for 2016.[2] For 2017, the amount has been raised to $2,600.[3] For 2018, the amount has been raised to $2,650.[4] For 2019, the amount has been raised to $2,700.[5]

The $2,700 health FSA limit does not apply to a cafeteria plan health insurance premium conversion (Premium Only Plans or "POP") option and other various options in a cafeteria plan, such as dependent care FSAs and adoption assistance FSAs. The limit also does not apply to employer contributions ("flex credits") to cafeteria plan health FSAs.

576. What clarifications has the IRS made regarding issues relating to the health FSA employee dollar deferral limit?

IRS Notice 2012-40 provides:

- The dollar limit applies only to salary reduction contributions under a health FSA, and does not apply to certain employer nonelective contributions (flex credits) or to any types of contributions or amounts available for reimbursement under other types of FSAs, Health Savings Accounts, or reimbursement arrangements, including salary reduction contributions used to pay an employee's share of health coverage (insured or self-insured) dependent care, or adoption assistance.

- The cap applies to health FSA plan years that begin on or after January 1, 2013. Thus, the new cap did not apply to noncalendar year plans until the plan year beginning in 2013. However, a plan sponsor cannot change from a calendar year to a noncalendar plan year to postpone the new cap without a *bona fide* business reason for the change.

- For plans that have adopted the optional cafeteria plan two-and-a-half month grace period,[6] amounts carried over during the grace period do not count toward the cap.

- The employer can correct employee deferral contributions that exceed the limit if due to a reasonable mistake and not willful misconduct as long as the cafeteria plan is not under IRS audit. To correct the error, the employer pays the excess amount to the employee, which is reported as wages for income tax withholding and employment taxes on the employee's Form W-2 for the employee's taxable year that ends with or after the cafeteria plan year in which the correction is made.

1.   IRC Sec.125 (i).
2.   Revenue Procedure 2014-61 https://www.shrm.org/ResourcesAndTools/hr-topics/benefits/Documents/rp-14-61.pdf (Issued October 30, 2014).
3   Revenue Procedure 2016-55 https://www.irs.gov/pub/irs-drop/rp-16-55.pdf. (Issued October 25, 2016).
4.   Revenue Procedure 2017-58 https://www.irs.gov/pub/irs-drop/rp-17-58.pdf. (Issued October 19, 2017).
5.   Revenue Procedure 2018-57 https://www.irs.gov/pub/irs-drop/rp-18-57.pdf. (Issued November 15, 2018).
6.   See Notice 2005-42, 2005-1 C.B. 1204, and Treas. Reg. §1.125-1(e).

- The relief provided for erroneous excess contributions is not available for an employer if a federal tax return of the employer is under examination with respect to benefits provided under a cafeteria plan.

- If both spouses have an FSA, whether at the same or different employers, each can fund his/her health FSA to the full amount of the dollar limit.

- An individual employed by separate employers that are not members of the same controlled group or affiliated service group may establish and fund an FSA at each employer up to the dollar[1] limit.

- If a cafeteria plan has a short plan year (fewer than twelve months) that begins after 2012, the $2,700 limit is prorated based on the number of months in that short plan year.

577. What was the deadline to amend a cafeteria plan to limit employee deferrals into health FSAs?

Employers had until the end of 2014 to amend their plan documents to incorporate the $2,500 limit, but this change needed to be effective for the plan year beginning in 2013.[2] A cafeteria plan with a health FSA must be amended to include the ACA's dollar limit, although a lower limit is acceptable. Cafeteria plans cannot be made retroactively as a general rule.

578. What is the penalty if a cafeteria plan is not timely amended or does not comply with the $2,700 employee deferral limit?

A cafeteria plan that fails to comply with Internal Revenue Code section 125(i) for plan years beginning in 2013 and subsequent years is not a valid Internal Revenue Code section 125 cafeteria plan and the value of the taxable benefits that an employee could have elected to receive under the plan during the plan year is includible in employee's gross income, regardless of the benefit elected by the employee.[3]

Health Insurers Executive Compensation

579. How has the Trump tax reform affected taxes on executive compensation for health insurance companies?

The law limits the amount that certain health insurers may deduct for a tax year starting after 2012 for compensation to any employee in excess of $500,000. Congress enacted this limitation as part of the Patient Protection and Affordable Care Act (PPACA) of 2010, which, among many other things, essentially requires every individual to be covered by health insurance. Congress included the $500,000 cap to ensure that companies providing mandatory coverage do not utilize premiums received for this coverage to overcompensate executives.

---

1. Rev. Proc. 2014-61 increased the dollar limit from $2,500 to $2,550 for 2015. Rev. Proc. 2016-55 has subsequently raised the dollar limit to $2,600. Rev. Proc. 2017-58 has raised the limit to $2,650. Revenue Procedure 2018-57 has raised the limit to $2,700.
2. IRS Notice 2012-40. Cafeteria plan amendments generally must be effective only prospectively. See Prop. Treas. Reg. §1.125-1(c).
3. IRS Notice 2012-40. See also Treas. Reg. §1.125-1(b). See also Rev. Proc. 2016-55 which raised the cap to $2,600 and Rev. Proc. 2-17-58 which raised the cap to $2,650.

Although the law only applies to certain healthcare insurers, it otherwise has a broader impact than the general deduction limit under Internal Revenue Code section 162(m). Until 2018, this section limited the amount a publicly held corporation could deduct for compensation paid to a narrow group of executives to $1 million per year per executive, made an exception for performance-based compensation and commissions, and excludes the compensation paid to former covered executives once they are no longer covered. These exceptions have been repealed.

The new tax reform legislation law passed which is effective on January 1, 2018[1] and later, modified these rules as follows:

- Repeals the performance-based compensation and commission exceptions to the Section 162(m) $1 million deduction limitation.

- Expands the definition of an applicable employer to include entities that are issuers required to file reports under Section 15(d) of the Exchange Act.

- Revises the definition of a "covered employee" as follows:

  o The principal financial officer is now included as a covered employee;

  o All individuals who hold the position of either principal executive officer or principal financial officer at any time during the taxable year are now covered employees;

- Covered employees include officers whose total compensation is required to be disclosed to shareholders by reason of them being amongst the three highest paid officers (other than the principal executive officer or principal financial officer.). This is not an operational change but conforms the statute to IRS Notice 2007-49;

- for a "publicly held corporation" that is not required to file a proxy statement, covered employees are determined as if these rules applied. In addition, the definition has been expanded to include foreign corporations; and

- Provides that an individual who is a covered employee for any taxable year beginning after December 31, 2016 will continue to be a covered employee for all subsequent taxable years, including years after the death of the individual.

However, the new health insurance company provision applies regardless of whether the health insurer's stock is publicly traded, limits the deduction to $500,000 per individual, and makes no exception for performance-based compensation or commissions. In addition, the limit applies to compensation, including deferred compensation, paid to all current and former employees and most independent contractors, not just to compensation paid to a narrow group of current top executives.

---

1.   Tax Cuts and Jobs Act of 2017, P.L. 115-97.

580. What is a covered health insurance provider?

The $500,000 cap only applies to an employer for a "disqualified taxable year,"[1] which is a taxable year during which the employer is a "covered health insurance provider."[2] A covered health insurance provider is a "health insurance issuer" that writes "minimum essential coverage" and receives premiums for this coverage that account for at least 25 percent of its gross premiums from providing health insurance coverage.[3] A "health insurance issuer" is an insurance company, service, or organization (including a Health Maintenance Organization (HMO)) that is licensed to engage in the business of insurance in a U.S. state and is subject to state law regulating insurance.[4] "Minimum essential coverage" is coverage satisfying the individual mandate, applicable for years after 2013, that every individual have health insurance coverage.[5] For example, employer-sponsored health insurance satisfies the mandate for covered employees and is therefore minimum essential coverage.[6]

Aggregation Rules for Related Employers. A broad range of related persons are aggregated in applying the definition of "covered health insurance provider" by controlled group and affiliated service group rules.[7] Assume an insurance company writes health insurance through two subsidiaries, one of which issues primarily minimum essential coverage and the other of which only issues health insurance that is not minimum essential coverage. The two subsidiaries (and all other members of the corporate group) are treated as one employer for this purpose. Thus, if premiums for minimum essential coverage are at least 25 percent of the gross health insurance premiums received by the group, the $500,000 cap applies to both of the health insurance subsidiaries, including the subsidiary that writes no minimum essential coverage.

581. What is the applicable individual remuneration for purposes of the $500,000 annual limit?

The $500,000 cap generally applies to an employer's deductions for "applicable individual remuneration" for services performed by an "applicable individual" during a disqualified taxable year beginning after 2012.[8] The term "applicable individual" includes all employees, officers, and directors of a covered health insurance provider, and it also includes any other person "who provides services for or on behalf of such covered health insurance provider."[9] An individual performing services as an independent contractor can therefore be an applicable individual.[10]

---

1. IRC Sec. 162(m)(6)(A).
2. IRC Sec. 162(m)(6)(B).
3. IRC Sec. 162(m)(6)(C)(i)(II). This definition applies for years beginning after 2012. Another definition applies for years beginning during the period 2010 through 2012. IRC Sec. 162(m)(6)(C)(i)(I). "Solely for purposes of determining whether a taxpayer is a 'covered health insurance provider,'…premiums received under an indemnity reinsurance contract are not treated as premiums from providing health insurance coverage." Notice 2011-2, III.D.
4. IRC Sec. 9832(b)(2). A "group health plan" is not a health insurance issuer. For the term HMO, see Code Section 9832(b)(3).
5. IRC Sec. 5000A(f).
6. IRC Sec. 5000A(f)(1)(B).
7. IRC Sec. 162(m)(6)(C)(ii). Specifically, two or more persons are treated as a single employer for this purpose if they are so treated under Code sections 414(b), 414(c), 414(m), or 414(o).
8. IRC Sec. 162(m)(6)(A)(i).
9. IRC Sec. 162(m)(6)(F).
10. An independent contractor is not, however, an applicable individual if he or she provides substantial services to multiple unrelated customers, as described in Reg. §1.409A-1(f)(2). Notice 2011-2, 2011-2 IRB 260, III.C.

"Applicable individual remuneration" includes "the aggregate amount" that would, but for the $500,000 cap, be allowed as a deduction for remuneration for services performed by an applicable individual for a disqualified taxable year, whether or not the services were performed during the taxable year.[1] Remuneration paid on a commission basis and other performance-based compensation may be applicable individual remuneration.

Applicable individual remuneration does not include "deferred deduction remuneration," which is remuneration for services performed during one disqualified taxable year that is deductible for a later disqualified taxable year.[2] Deferred deduction remuneration is taken into account for the year of the deduction (usually the year during which the compensation is paid), not the year during which the services are performed. Deferred deduction remuneration may include remuneration, otherwise deductible for a disqualified taxable year beginning after 2012 that is paid for services performed during any disqualified year beginning after 2009.

582. How is the $500,000 cap applied? Does it make any difference if compensation is earned and paid later as deferred compensation?

The cap applies separately to "deferred deduction remuneration" and applicable individual remuneration. For applicable individual remuneration (compensation that is deductible for the year during which the services are performed), remuneration in excess of $500,000 for any individual is not deductible for the current year or at any other time.[3]

The rule for deferred deduction remuneration applies to any such remuneration that is attributable to services performed by an applicable individual during a disqualified taxable year beginning after 2009, but deductible for a disqualified year after 2012. For such compensation otherwise deductible for a particular year, the maximum deduction is the excess of $500,000 over the sum of (1) the applicable individual remuneration for the year during which the services were performed, and (2) any portion of the deferred deduction remuneration for such services that was taken into account under this rule for a preceding post-2009 taxable year.[4]

In other words, deferred deduction remuneration is taken into account for the year for which it is otherwise deductible, but the deduction is only allowed to the extent of the unused cap for the individual from the year during which the services were performed.

> *Example:* Assume an employee's compensation for disqualified taxable year one is cash compensation of $400,000 plus nonqualified deferred compensation of $300,000, which the employer may only deduct when paid; the deferred compensation is paid to the employee in two installments: $150,000 during disqualified taxable year two and $150,000 during disqualified taxable year three.

> Taxable years one, two, and three all begin after 2012. The cash compensation is fully deductible for year one because it does not exceed $500,000. The deferred compensation would normally be deductible for years two and three in the amounts paid during each of those years. The maximum deduction for the deferred compensation paid during year two is $100,000: the excess of $500,000 over the amount deductible for the year during which the services were performed ($400,000).

---

1.   IRC Sec. 162(m)(6)(D).
2.   IRC Secs. 162(m)(6)(D), 162(m)(6)(E).
3.   IRC Sec. 162(m)(6)(A)(i).
4.   IRC Sec. 162(m)(6)(A)(ii).

The employer is allowed no deduction for the deferred compensation paid during year three because the cap is $500,000, less the amount deductible for the year the services were performed ($400,000) and less amounts deductible before year 3 for compensation deferred from year one ($100,000 deducted for year two).

583. What rules applied to a covered health insurance provider for compensation earned in 2010 through 2012?

The application of Internal Revenue Code section 162(m)(6) to deferred compensation earned prior to 2013 but paid out after 2012 is different because the law defines a "covered health insurance provider" in broader terms for 2010, 2011, and 2012 than for 2013 and later. Starting in 2013, a health insurance provider is "covered" only if 25 percent or more of its gross premiums received from providing health insurance coverage is from "minimum essential coverage," which, as defined in Internal Revenue Code section 5000A(f), generally means group or individual medical coverage needed to satisfy the individual coverage. The pre-2013 definition of covered health insurance provider (receiving any premium) applies to more employers than the post-2012 definition (receiving at least 25 percent of premiums from offering minimum essential coverage).

For a taxable year beginning during the years 2010 through 2012, an employer is a covered health insurance provider, and the year is therefore disqualified, if the employer is a health insurer and receives premiums from providing health insurance coverage.[1] For such a year, in other words, the portion of the gross premiums received from providing minimum essential coverage is not relevant. The cap never applies to compensation that is deductible for a year beginning before 2013. An employer's status as a covered health insurance provider for a year during the period 2010 through 2012 is only relevant for the purpose of tainting remuneration for services performed during those years but is not deductible by the employer (e.g., is not paid) until a year after 2012.

If an employer is a health insurance issuer for all years after 2009, it is a covered health insurance provider for the years 2010 through 2012. If at least 25 percent of its gross premiums from health insurance coverage for years after 2012 is for minimum essential coverage, it is also a covered health insurance provider for post-2012 years. The cap can apply to remuneration for services performed during the years 2010 through 2012, but paid during a post-2012 year.[2] In contrast, if premiums for minimum essential coverage are less than 25 percent of the employer's gross premiums for each post-2012 year, it is not a health insurance issuer for any such year, and the cap cannot apply to any remuneration that it pays, regardless of when the services are performed.[3]

The cap applies to deferred deduction remuneration only if the employer is a covered health insurance provider for both the year during which the services are performed and the year for which the remuneration would normally be deductible (e.g., the year of payment), but

---

1.   IRC Sec. 162(m)(6)(C)(i)(I).
2.   Notice 2011-2, III.A, Ex. 1.
3.   Notice 2011-2, III.A, Ex. 2.

the employer's status for other years is not relevant. An entity that was not a covered health insurance provider after 2012 does not have its deductions limited if compensation deferred from 2010, 2011, or 2012 was paid out after 2012.[1]

> *Example:* An employer is a health insurance issuer for all years after 2009, and premiums for minimum essential coverage are less than 25 percent of the employer's gross premiums for the years 2013 through 2015. These premiums account for at least 25 percent of gross premiums for 2016 and later years.[2] The employer is a covered health insurance provider for 2010 through 2012 and for years after 2015, but not for the years 2013 through 2015. The cap applies to deferred deduction remuneration for services performed during a 2010–2012 year if the remuneration becomes deductible for a year after 2015, but not if the deduction is allowed for a year during the period 2013 through 2015.

<u>De Minimis Rule</u>. The IRS has administratively provided a *de minimis* rule not found in the statute.[3] An employer is deemed not to be a covered health insurance provider for a taxable year beginning during the period 2010 through 2012 if the premiums it receives for providing health insurance coverage are less than 2 percent of its gross revenues for the year.[4] For a taxable year beginning after 2012, an employer is not considered a covered health insurance provider if health insurance premiums received for providing minimum essential coverage are less than 2 percent of its gross revenues for the year.

584. What is the current status of executive physical/executive diagnostic reimbursement plans under the Affordable Care Act?

Diagnostic reimbursement plans for executives have been common for over forty years. They allow an employer to pay for or reimburse such employees these expenses with dollars that are deductible to the employer and not taxed to the executive.[5] This exception to the self-insured health plan nondiscrimination rules is allowed by Reg. 1.105-11(g).

The Affordable Care Act made sweeping and complex changes to healthcare especially in regard to executive medical reimbursement plans that had been structured as healthcare products did not meet the requirements of the ACA. Many issuers of these products elected to discontinue these plans, rather than restructure them to either comply with the ACA or to fall within an exception to full ACA compliance. While the decision of some plans to exit the market has helped create an impression that executive medical reimbursement plans are no longer viable, this is not entirely true. It remains possible for companies to offer a benefit program with a medical reimbursement to executives that can pass muster with the ACA. These plans typically fund the executive's co-insurance obligations under the primary plan.

---

1.   Notice 2011-02.
2.   Notice 2011-2, III.A, Ex. 3.
3.   IRC Sec. 162(m)(6)(H) (Treasury "may prescribe such guidance, rules, or regulations as are necessary to carry out the purposes of this paragraph").
4.   Notice 2011-2, III.B.
5.   So long as the executive is an "employee" and not a self-employed individual, such as a proprietor, partner, or more than 2 percent shareholder of an S corporation.

Key Requirements for Executive Coverage to Meet ACA Requirements

Fully Insured

The primary requirement is that the plan must be **fully insured**. Section 105(h) of the IRS tax code states that reimbursements cannot favor highly compensated employees (HCEs) over the rest of the workforce, unless provided under a contract of insurance. Thus, a plan that is largely self-funded, even if administered independently, will <u>not</u> comply with the ACA. Fully insured plants are by their nature, compliant. Self-insured plans, including cost-plus plans, don't allow coverage to be offered to select employee groups due to longstanding nondiscrimination rules, and having a self-insured reimbursement plan can expose the company and its employees to compliance and tax risks.

Excepted Benefits

Excepted benefits are benefits excepted *from* ACA nondiscrimination and other rules, meaning that these benefits can be offered to select employee classes. To qualify as an excepted benefit, a plan must fit into one or more of four defined categories.

Each of the four categories is separately defined and has different requirements. Multiple categories can be "bundled" and offered in a single contract of insurance. However, the require-ments for a specific category continue to apply to that category alone, not all. Thus, it is important when evaluating an insurance policy that includes multiple categories of excepted benefits to apply the right standards to the right benefits.

The four categories of "excepted benefits" are:

- Incidental Health Benefits: Incidental health benefits that are included in other forms of insurance, like auto insurance.

- Limited in Scope: Benefits that are limited in scope, such as vision, dental or long-term care.

- Specific Coverage: Benefits that cover only a specific disease or that provide fixed indemnity.

- Supplementary Benefits: Benefits that supplement Medicare or TRICARE, or that provide similar supplemental coverage to a private primary plan. This type of cover-age is overlaid on top of the primary plan.

  - This category of excepted benefits is the one that has caused the most confu-sion. Federal regulations issued by the Departments of the Treasury, Labor, and HHS in 2004 describe similar supplemental coverage as *coverage that is specifically designed to fill gaps in primary coverage*, such as coinsurance or deductibles. Reimbursement plans generally fit into the similar supplemental category since they can be layered on top of a primary plan and reimburse out of pocket costs.

Safe Harbors for Supplemental Coverage

In addition, further guidance describes four safe harbor criteria which, if met, will automatically qualify a supplemental health insurance product as an excepted benefit. The safe harbor criteria are not mandated - a product is not disqualified as an excepted benefit because the safe harbor requirements are not met but will require additional analysis to ensure that it is supplemental insurance and filling gaps in the primary coverage.

The four safe harbor criteria established by the Departments are:

- The policy cannot be issued by the same insurer that issued the primary plan.

- The policy must be designed to fill gaps in primary coverage with no coordination of benefits. The Departments have recognized that coverage "gaps" include both cost sharing obligations imposed by the primary plan and additional benefits not included in the primary plan as long as those additional benefits are not considered essential health benefits.

- The value of the supplemental coverage cannot exceed 15percent of the cost of the primary coverage. HHS Memo describes this calculation as an evaluation of whether "the proportion of total benefits that is charged to a policyholder as cost-sharing [is] similar to the proportion of total Medicare benefits that is charged to beneficiaries as cost-sharing." [Emphasis added.] The HHS Memo notes that the Departments will consider "any reasonable method" for calculating the value of total coverage.

- The policy cannot use health factors to differentiate between individuals in terms of benefits, eligibility, or premiums.

Increase Threshold for Personal Deduction for Medical Expenses

585. How does health reform limit individual income tax deductions for health care?

In 2013 and thereafter, individual itemized deductions for unreimbursed medical care expenses, including premiums for health, long-term-care, and dental insurance are only deductible to the extent they exceed 10 percent of adjusted gross income. In 2012 and before, the threshold was 7.5 percent.[1] However, through 2016, taxpayers age sixty-five and older will continue to be able to use the old 7.5 percent threshold.[2] In 2017, the percentage went to 10 percent for everyone effective January 1, 2019.

These taxpayers can claim an itemized deduction to the extent that their unreimbursed medical expenses exceed 10 percent of adjusted gross income. Use of this deduction requires taxpayers to itemize deductions and forgo the standard deduction, and the 10 percent threshold made the deduction of minimal value for most taxpayers.

---

1.   PPACA §9013(d) amended IRC Sec. 213(a).
2.   IRC Sec. 213(f).

The IRS enables one to deduct preventative care, treatment, surgeries and dental and vision care as qualifying medical expenses. Visits to psychologists and psychiatrists are also deductible. Prescription medications and appliances such as glasses, contacts, false teeth and hearing aids are also deductible. In addition, expenses paid to travel to medical care such as mileage, cab and bus fare and parking are deductible.

Any reimbursed medical expenses by insurance or employer, cannot be deducted. The IRS also generally disallows expenses for cosmetic procedures. The cost of non-prescription drugs (except insulin) or other purchases for general health such as toothpaste, health club dues, vitamins or diet food, non-prescription nicotine products or medical expenses paid in a different year are not deductible.

The Joint Committee on Taxation estimated the value of this limited itemized deduction for medical expenses to be only $8.7 billion in 2007, as compared to the combined value of $250.9 billion for the exclusion for employer-provided health insurance and the self-employed health insurance deduction.[1]

Further, many taxpayers will receive a tax subsidy for buying insurance on a health insurance exchange.[2]

The Individual Mandate

586. What is the status of the Individual Mandate?

As discussed in detail in Part I of this book, the Individual Mandate requires individuals, unless excluded, to have Minimum Essential Health coverage through their employer or individually or pay a tax penalty. However the Tax Cuts and Jobs Act of 2017 included what is described as a "repeal" of the Individual Mandate, although it should be noted that the Individual Mandate technically has not been "repealed" but the penalty imposed has been set to $0 for 2019 and subsequent years. In addition, the elimination of the penalty has prompted a lawsuit alleging that the elimination of the Individual Mandate penalty renders the entire Affordable Care Act unconstitutional. At the time of this publication, the U.S. Court of Appeals for the Fifth Circuit is hearing oral arguments, but regardless of their finding, it is certain that this case will go to the U.S. Supreme Court.

The repeal of the Individual Mandate tax penalty did no actually take effect until 2019. For 2017 and 2018, the tax penalty remained the law of the land, and the IRS has been enforcing it. Penalties were levied for tax years 2017 and 2018 and all the reporting requirements for individuals and businesses remained in effect. In addition, the IRS has indicated that it will reject individual tax returns that do not include the penalty payment or offer assertation of coverage (unless one of the exemptions is claimed).

---

1.   Joint Committee on Taxation, Tax Expenditures for Health Care, JCX-66-08, pp. 22-24, (July 30, 2008) at http://www.jct.gov/publications. html?func=startdown&id=1193. (Last accessed August 9, 2019).
2.   IRC Sec. 36B.

The Congressional Budget Office (CBO) believes the mandate repeal will have a material impact on enrollment and premium rates in the non-group market. Specifically, the CBO estimated that the mandate's repeal will have the following effects:

- Enrollment in the non-group health insurance market, including the marketplace, will decrease by 3 million in 2019 and by 5 million in 2025;

- Non-group premium rates in the next ten years will be as much as 10 percent higher than if the mandate continued; and

- Five million fewer people may be able to enroll in Medicaid by 2026.

However, figures released in December 2018 by the federal government show that the number of individuals enrolled in ACA covered fell from 8.8 million to 8.5 million, a far smaller drop than most experts had predicted, suggesting that health care coverage is more popular than some critics implied.

Under the Individual Mandate prior to 2019, if an "applicable individual" did not have "Minimum Essential Coverage" for that individual or dependents who also are an "applicable individual," a tax "penalty"[1] equal to the greater of:

(i) the "applicable dollar amount" for the individual and all such dependents (up to a maximum of three applicable dollar amounts); or

(ii) a specified percentage of the applicable individual's "household income," but in no event more than "the national average premium for qualified health plans which have a bronze level (see Q 86) of coverage with coverage for the applicable family size involved, that are offered through exchanges."[2]

The minimum penalty ranged from $95 in calendar year 2014 up to $695 in calendar year 2016, and was inflation-adjusted thereafter.[3] Moreover, the applicable percentage of income increased from 1 percent in calendar year 2014, to 2 percent in calendar year 2015, and to 2.5 percent for calendar year 2016 and thereafter.[4]

In 2018, it was calculated in one of two ways:

- PERCENTAGE OF INCOME:

  o 2.5 percent of household income

  o Maximum of total yearly premium for the national average price of a Bronze plan sold through the marketplace

---

1. IRC Sec. 5000A(f).
2. IRC Sec. 5000A(b)(1), (c)(1), (2). Use of the national average for bronze coverage means that calculation might not bear much relationship to the actual cost of coverage available in a specific location. However, the premium amounts will not be lower than the penalty.
3. IRC Sec. 5000A(c)(3)(A), (B), (D).
4. IRC Sec. 5000A(c)(2)(B). The net effect of these percentage increases for taxpayers who do not procure minimum essential coverage and whose income is sufficient to be above the minimum penalty is an increase in their marginal tax rate by 1 percent in calendar year 2014 rising to a 2.5 percent marginal tax rate increase for subsequent years.

- PER PERSON

    o $695 per adult

    o $347.50 per minor child

    o   Maximum $2,085 per household

The fee is whichever of the two ways is HIGHER.

For low-income employees, the minimum penalty was small in comparison to the actual cost of coverage, thereby increasing the likelihood that an individual without minimum essential coverage will not purchase health insurance, although the tax credit subsidies will make the insurance less expensive.

<u>Definition of Applicable Individual</u>. The individual mandate tax penalty applied only to "applicable individuals," and the definition of that term excludes designated categories of individuals, including:

- members of certain religious faiths already exempt from self-employment tax;

- members of healthcare-sharing ministries which, among other things, share medical expenses among members and have been in continuous existence since December 31, 1999;

- aliens not legally present; and

- incarcerated individuals after they have been convicted.[1]

<u>Definition of Affordability</u>. Another major exemption is the one for applicable individuals whose "required contribution (determined on an annual basis) for coverage for the month exceeds 8 percent of such individual's household income for the taxable year."[2] For this exemption, the "required contribution" for an individual eligible to participate in an employer-sponsored plan was equal to "the portion of the annual premium which would be paid by the individual (without regard to whether paid through salary reduction or otherwise) for self-only coverage."[3]

Taxpayers whose household income for a taxable year was less than the gross income necessary to trigger an income tax return filing requirement[4] are also not applicable individuals and were not subject to the employee mandate. These gross income levels did not exempt many applicable individuals who were not already exempt under the 8 percent affordability exemption

---

1.   IRC Sec. 5000A(d)(2), (3), (4).
2.   IRC Sec. 5000A(e)(1)(A). It is not clear why the "affordability test "for employers is 9.5 percent whereas this individual "affordability test" is 8 percent.
3.   IRC Sec. 5000A(e)(1)(B)(i). This affordability test based on the premium for "self-only coverage" will be integrated into the penalty calculation under which an individual may also be responsible for providing coverage for a spouse and/or dependents. *See* Preamble to Proposed Regulations for Code section 36B.
4.   IRC Sec. 5000A(e)(2).

discussed above. However, many such individuals are also likely to be eligible for Medicaid and thus exempt from the penalty as long as they apply to procure such coverage.

The Administration has now clarified the 2018 deadline, stating that individuals who sign up for insurance on the Exchange within the open enrollment period won't face a penalty. The Administration, as well as the Department of Health and Human Services (HHS), have emphasized that this "clarification" isn't a substantive modification and that the start date for benefits and overall deadline for enrolling remain unchanged. This clarification is viewed by many as welcome news as it effectively gives individuals more time than originally thought to obtain coverage and not face a penalty.

Another factor not to be forgotten is that some states mandate health care at the state level.

- Massachusetts has had a health care mandate since 2006.

- Massachusetts has achieved coverage rates as high as 97.5 percent since the health care overhaul signed by then-Republican Gov. Mitt Romney. The Massachusetts plan served as a model for the Affordable Care Act. The state mandate requires adults to carry insurance that meets a set of minimum standards and exempts people for whom available insurance options are deemed "unaffordable." The state tax penalty for noncompliance is generally set at half the lowest cost plan available to an individual through the state's health insurance marketplace.

- Most residents in New Jersey and the District of Columbus are required to carry healthcare in 2019 or face steep fines.

    o In New Jersey, approximately 800,000 residents have insurance through the ACA or expanded Medicaid, the 2019 individual mandate carries a penalty of 2.5 percent or $695 per taxpayer, whichever is greater. Democratic Gov. Phil Murphy announced in September that rates for the individual health insurance market would drop by an average 9.3 percent in 2019, attributing the decline to the state›s new coverage mandate.

- Vermont will mandate health care coverage beginning in 2020.

- Washington State has been considering a mandate but since they have no state income tax, enforcement would be difficult.

- In addition, Maryland is considering requiring health care coverage as well.

587. What was the intended purpose of the Individual Mandate?

One purpose was to provide incentives to individuals to have health coverage to reduce the burdens imposed by free medical care. If they do not have minimum essential coverage, unless exempt, they would be required to pay a tax penalty. Additionally, a primary goal of health reform was to fix the problems in the market for individual health insurance policies.

Most critically, the law imposes open enrollment[1] and guaranteed renewal[2] requirements on all health insurance plans offered in the individual and small group markets so that these plans must accept all applicants for health insurance. The law was intended to further limit insurance issuers' ability to charge applicants different prices based on their expected health risks. The law will only allow health insurance issuers to vary their prices based on four factors:

1.   The size of the applicant's family (for applicants seeking family coverage);

2.   The geographic region in which the applicant resides;

3.   The applicant's age;

4.   Whether the applicant uses tobacco.[3]

Even with respect to these factors, insurance issuers will be limited to charging their oldest applicants no more than three times the prices charged to their youngest applicants and to charging tobacco users no more than one and a half times the prices charged to nonsmokers.[4] In effect, the law prevents insurance plans from discriminating against applicants with pre-existing health conditions.

These provisions of the law that will significantly limit insurers' ability to engage in risk classification could undermine the individual market. However, health reform does several things to bolster this market, including penalties and incentives, such as:

• the individual mandate tax penalty;

• state-based health insurance exchanges;

• generous tax subsidies for those lower income individuals purchasing insurance; and

• the expansion of state Medicaid programs (in effect made optional by the U.S. Supreme Court).

If these provisions are effective, insurance policies offered on the exchanges could potentially be of better quality and lower cost than employer-provided offerings. Perhaps more likely, if the provisions are only partially effective, employer-provided insurance might retain its advantages over insurance policies offered on the exchanges, but with the advantages of employer-provided insurance being significantly reduced as compared to the advantages employer-provided insurance previously enjoyed over the insurance policies available on the individual market due to income tax advantages as well as bargaining power.

---

1.   PPACA §1201.
2.   PPACA §1201.
3.   PPACA §1201.
4.   PPACA §1201.

The Employer Mandate

588. How does the employer mandate improve health care?

The details of the employer mandate, which potentially affects employers (including related employers) with fifty or more full-time equivalent employees, are discussed in Part I and in detail in Part XI. It is designed to induce employers to offer affordable coverage for essential health benefits.

Maintaining the previous system of employer-sponsored coverage for lower-income employees was critically important for realizing health reform's financial targets because additional lower-income employees qualifying for the exchange subsidies drive up federal costs. Thus, the employer mandate, coupled with the health insurance nondiscrimination rules and the grandfathered plan rules were designed to induce employers to provide care to employees and their families.

589. What are the incentives created by health reform for employers, including but not limited to the employer mandate?

An employer avoids the Internal Revenue Code section (a) "all employee" $2,320 penalty by offering health insurance to all full-time employees 4980H regardless of how much the employees would be charged for that insurance. The Code section 4980H(b) penalty will be triggered when an employer does offer health insurance, but when that insurance is "unaffordable" or fails the minimum value test, namely, that the employer's share of the total allowed costs of benefits provided under the plan is less than 60 percent of such costs.[1]

An employer with few low- and moderate-income employees could face the full Internal Revenue Code section 4980H(b) penalty of $3,860 annually per employee that qualifies for the exchange subsidies. An employer with many low- and moderate-income employees is more likely to have Internal Revenue Code section 4980H(b) assessable payments limited to the Code section 4980H(a) penalty amount of $2,570 times the total number of full-time employees over thirty.

The Internal Revenue Code section 4980H(a) penalty will not prevent employers from providing health insurance to their higher-income employees while sending their lower-income employees to the exchanges. The employers can avoid the Code section 4980H(a) penalty by offering their lower income employees "unaffordable" health insurance. Only the Code section 4980H(b) penalties will apply to an employer who offers "unaffordable" health insurance to its lower-income employees. Although employers often may not know a family's household income, nevertheless, the law somewhat encourages an employer to offer the tax benefits of employer coverage for high earners and provide unaffordable coverage to lower income employees to allow them to benefit from the exchange subsidies. A critical question is whether the health insurance nondiscrimination rules will result in the additional $100 per day per affected (nonhighly compensated) employee.

---

1.   IRC Sec. 36B(c)(2)(C)(ii).

An offer of "affordable" employer-sponsored health insurance will result in an employee's entire family being ineligible for the premium tax credits, not just the employee.[1] Moreover, whether an employer's offer of family coverage is considered "affordable" is determined based on the cost the employee would need to contribute for self-only coverage.[2] In other words, if an employer offers an insurance policy with an option for family coverage, and if the amount an employee would need to contribute to pay for the portion of the policy covering only the employee (and not also the other members of the employee's family) is less than 9.78 percent of the employee's household income, then the employee's entire family is ineligible for the premium tax credits.

Comparing just the exchange subsidies (tax credits for lower income individuals) to the tax exclusions (employer tax deduction and individual exclusion from income and payroll taxes) based on the Tax Policy Center's estimates for 2018, the breakeven point for an individual is when household income is somewhere between 360 percent and 375 percent of the federal poverty line. Figures for 2019 are not yet available. The breakeven point for a family of four is when household income reaches 400 percent of the federal poverty line.[3]

For household incomes below these breakeven points, the exchange subsidies will generally offer more value than the tax exclusions. Conversely, for household incomes above these breakeven points, the tax exclusions will generally offer more value than the exchange subsidies. These breakeven analyses assume that the health-insurance policies offered on the exchanges will be of equivalent cost and quality to employer-sponsored health insurance policies. If all of the exchange coverage options are inferior to employer-sponsored options, then the breakeven thresholds would need to be adjusted.

These breakeven analyses assume that employers offer their employees subsidized health insurance as a form of employee compensation. When comparing the premiums they must pay for exchange coverage against the premiums they must pay for employer-sponsored coverage, many employees will prefer employer-sponsored coverage to the extent that employers continue to subsidize this coverage. Yet, in effect, these employer subsidies come out of the employees' income.

Health Insurance Premium Tax – Moratorium Status

590. What is the health insurance premium "tax" that began in 2014?

Beginning in 2014, Americans began indirectly paying a new fee on health insurance that will be assessed against health insurers but likely will be paid through increased premium rates. Health reform[4] requires individuals, families, and others to help pay a total of $73 billion over five years. The tax is not deductible.[5] This means that health insurers must pay the tax and then pay federal, state, and local taxes on the taxed amount, which increases the amount by which

---

1.   IRC Sec. 36B(c)(2)(C)(i)(II); Treas. Reg. §36B, 76 Fed. Reg. 50931, 50935 (Aug. 17, 2011).

2.   IRC Sec. 36B(c)(2)(C)(i)(II); Treas. Reg. §36B, 76 Fed. Reg. 50931, 50935 (Aug. 17, 2011).

3.   Stephanie Rennane & C. Eugene Steurle, Health Reform: A Two-Subsidy System, Urban Institute and Brookings Institution: Tax Policy Center S10-001, (2010), (no longer available on the internet).

4.   PPACA §9010.

5.   PPACA §9010(f), providing that the tax is nondeductible under IRC Sec. 275(A)(6).

they must increase premiums to break even. The tax is passed on to the consumer through the health care premiums and generally adds between three and four percent to the costs.

Section 9010 of the Patient Protection and Affordable Care Act (ACA) imposes a fee on each covered entity engaged in the business of providing health insurance for United States health risks. The first filings were due from covered entities by April 15, 2014 and the first fees were due September 30, 2014. However, for 2017, The Consolidated Appropriations Act of 2016, Title II, section 201, Moratorium on Annual Fee on Health Insurance Providers imposed a moratorium on the collection of the tax for 2017 only. The expected $13.9 billion dollars referenced below was not to be collected. This moratorium did **not** affect the filing requirement and payment of the fee for 2016 or 2018. This was enacted on January 22, 2018, along with continuing resolution legislation, H.R. 195, Division D — Suspension of Certain Health-Related Taxes, section 4003, suspends collection of the fee for the 2019 calendar year only. Again, this does not affect the filing requirement and payment of the fee for 2018. The "applicable amount" for fee year 2018 is $14.3 billion.[1]

The Health Insurance (HI) premium tax is an annual fee on insurers which began in 2014. The fee (equivalent to a sales tax) applies to U.S. health insurance providers and is intended to collect roughly $90 billion in revenue through 2020. A predetermined amount of revenue will be collected each year:

- $8 billion in 2014

- $11.3 billion in 2015 and 2016

- $13.9 billion in 2017, and (lost to moratorium)

- $14.3 billion in 2018[2]

- For 2019 and thereafter, the "applicable amount" is the "applicable amount in the preceding fee year increased by the rate of premium growth (within the meaning of section 36B(b)(3)(A)(ii)). However, the moratorium is in effect for 2019. (Essentially increasing 2.5 percent to 3 percent per year if in effect)"

As stated above, after 2018, the HI tax in any particular year will equal the fee levied during the previous year, increased by the rate of premium growth for the preceding calendar year. The aggregate fee is apportioned among the providers based on a ratio designed to reflect relative market share of U.S. health insurance business.

A study by former Congressional Budget Office Director Douglas Holtz-Eakin released in March 2011 found that the HI tax can be expected to raise premiums for employer-sponsored insurance by as much as 3 percent, a price increase that is nearly $475 per family per year and $5,000 per family over the first decade.[3] Additionally, the Joint Committee on Taxation estimated

---

1.   See Treas. Reg. section 57.4(a)(3).
2.   https://www.irs.gov/businesses/corporations/health-insurance-provider-fee-2017-moratorium-questions-and-answers.
3.   Douglas Holtz-Eakin, "Higher Costs and the Affordable Care Act: The Case of the Premium Tax", American Action Forum (March 9, 2011) at http://americanactionforum.org/sites/default/files/Case%20of%20the%20Premium%20Tax.pdf. (Last accessed September 4, 2018).

that repealing the tax would reduce premiums of insurance plans offered by covered entities by 2.0 percent to 2.5 percent.[1]

The new tax is not assessed on self-funded ERISA health plans, nonprofit insurers that meet specific criteria, and certain Voluntary Employee Beneficiaries Associations (VEBAs).

In January and February 2019, a bipartisan group of House and Senate lawmakers introduced bills to suspend the tax through December 2021.

Businesses affected by the HIT include:

- Insured individual and group medical plans

- Stand-alone, insured dental and vision plans

- Stand-alone, insured behavioral health and pharmacy plans

- Medicare Advantage plans

- Retiree-only plans

- Part D prescription benefit plans

- Medicaid (and CHIP) programs

- Taft-Hartley Plans to the extent the plans meet the other criteria for inclusion

Excluded from the tax:

- Self-funded employer sponsored group health plans Note: Some benefits may be covered under an insured plan and therefore subject to this fee as well.

- Non-profit corporations that receive more than 80% of their revenue from government sponsored poverty programs (Medicaid, CHIP)and that comply with certain restrictions on political activity

- Medicare supplemental coverage that meets the requirements of section 1882(g)(1)

- VEBAs sponsored by an entity other than an employer or employers

- Coverage for specific diseases or hospital indemnity coverage

- Accident-only coverage

- ASO/Stop-loss

- U.S.-issued expatriate plans after 2015

---

1.   Thomas A. Barthold, letter to Senator Jon Kyl, Joint Committee on Taxation, Washington, DC, 3 June 3, 2011 at http://www.ahipcoverage. com/wp-content/uploads/2011/11/Premium-Tax-JCT-Letter-to-Kyl-060311-2.pdf. (no longer available on the internet).

Tax on "Cadillac" Policies

591. Why did Congress decide to tax generous high-cost health plans?

Originally slated for 2013, with implementation delayed multiple times first to 2018 and subsequently delayed to 2020, leaving the provision's ultimate survival in doubt, the Affordable Care Act imposes a 40 percent tax on high-cost health plans.

In 2017, the U.S. Senate voted 52-48 to repeal the tax but the House of Representatives never addressed it. On January 22, 2018, Congress passed, and the President signed an additional two-year delay tax on high-cost employer-sponsored health plans. This delay was part of a short-term federal spending bill and changes the effective date from 2020 to 2022. Since that time, there have been subsequent attempts to completely repeal the "Cadillac Tax".

In addition to being a revenue raiser, the reason for this provision is to reduce the demand for high-cost ("Cadillac") coverage where the individual has little out-of-pocket cost to encourage employers, providers, and consumers to control health costs.

In the event this provision of the Affordable Care Act should survive, a number of open questions remain that will need to be addressed either through statute or regulation, including:

1.   what constitutes "applicable coverage"

2.   determination of the actual cost of the applicable coverage

3.   determination of dollar limits

4.   determination of who actually pays the tax

5.   how the tax will be paid

592. What type of plans are intended to be taxed?

For purposes of the excise tax on employer-sponsored health insurance, coverage is health coverage under any group health plan offered by an employer to an employee (plus any former employee, surviving spouse, and any other primary insured individual[1]) without regard to whether the employer provides the coverage (and thus the coverage is excludable from the employee's income) or the employee pays for the coverage with after-tax dollars.[2]

Employer-sponsored health insurance coverage includes coverage under any group health plan established and maintained primarily for the civilian employees of the federal government or any of its agencies or instrumentalities and, generally, of any state government or political subdivision or any state agencies or instrumentalities.[3]

---

1.   IRC Sec. 4980I(d)(3).
2.   IRC Sec. 4980I(d)(1)(A).
3.   IRC Sec. 4980I(d)(1)(E).

Employer-sponsored health insurance coverage includes both fully insured and self-insured health coverage excludable from the employee's gross income, including, in the self-insured context, on-site medical clinics that offer more than a minimal amount of medical care to employees and executive physical programs. In the case of a self-employed individual, employer-sponsored health insurance coverage is coverage for any portion of which a deduction is allowable to the self-employed individual under Internal Revenue Code section 162(l).

The following types of plans are specifically included under the Cadillac tax:

- Insured and self-insured group health plans (including behavioral, and prescription drug coverage) Wellness programs that are group health plans (most wellness programs)

- Health Flexible Spending Accounts (FSAs)

- HSAs, employer and employee pre-tax contributions

- Health Reimbursement Accounts (HRAs)

- Archer MSAs, all pre-tax contributions

- Onsite medical clinics providing more than de minimis care

- Executive physical programs

- Pre-tax coverage for a specified disease or illness

- Hospital indemnity or other fixed indemnity insurance

- Federal/State/Local government-sponsored plans for its employees

- Retiree coverage

- Multi-employer (Taft-Hartley) plans

593. How does the Cadillac tax work on expensive health plans work?

Presuming that that Affordable Care Act survives — or that the Cadillac Tax itself is not delayed again or repealed, beginning in 2022, a 40 percent excise tax is imposed on "coverage providers" that provide high-cost health care coverage to the employer's employees. Initially the Cadillac Tax was nondeductible, but with the legislation changing the effective date to 2022, the tax was made deductible. Coverage providers include:

- health insurers for fully insured plans;

- the employer with respect to self-insured plans, HSA or Archer MSA contributions; and

- in all other cases, the "person that administers the plan."

The tax applies to "applicable employer-sponsored coverage," which is coverage under a group health plan:

- that is made available to an employee by an employer; and

- that either:

  o is actually excludable from gross income under Internal Revenue Code section 106; or

  o would be excludable if it were employer-provided coverage within the meaning of Internal Revenue Code section 106.[1]

The excise tax is imposed on the "excess benefit" provided to the employees.

There is no exception to the tax for grandfathered plans.

Excess benefit is determined by comparing the cost of the actual coverage provided (calculated using rules similar to those for determining COBRA premiums) that exceeds annual limits. For 2022, the annual limit for employee-only coverage is $10,200 per year (as adjusted by a "Health Cost Adjustment Percentage" or HCAP) and $27,500 per year (as adjusted by the HCAP) for coverage other than employee-only.

The HCAP takes into account year-to-year increases in the cost of health care coverage, including increases attributable to age and gender differences.

Again, it must be remembered that the survival of this tax, unpopular with both Democrats and Republicans, is in doubt. Attempts have been made to repeal it as well as other bills introduced to kick the implementation down the road to 2025. No regulations have been issued to date. During 2015, the Internal Revenue Service (IRS) issued notices covering a number of questions concerning the Cadillac Tax, and requested comments on the possible approaches eventually might be incorporated into proposed regulations.

594. What is the effect on the excise tax if the employee pays for all or part of the coverage?

Whether the employer or the employee pays for coverage does not impact the determination of whether it is "applicable employer-sponsored coverage."[2] However, it can affect the cost of that coverage when the amount of an employee's excess benefit is calculated, which affects the amount of excise tax payable.

---

1.   IRC Sec. 4980I(d)(1)(A).
2.   IRC Sec. 4980I(d)(1)(C).

595. What coverage is not subject to the excise tax on high-cost employer-sponsored coverage?

In determining whether the value of health coverage exceeds the threshold amount, the following items are not included.[1]

- The value of employer sponsored coverage for long term care and the following benefits described in Internal Revenue Code section 9832(c)(1) that are excepted benefits and exempt from the portability, access and renewability requirements of the Health Insurance Portability and Accountability Act (HIPAA), namely:

    o U.S.-issued expatriate plans for most categories of expatriates

    o Coverage for accident only, or disability income insurance, or any combination thereof

    o Supplemental liability insurance

    o Liability insurance, including general liability insurance and automobile liability insurance

    o Workers' compensation or similar insurance

    o Automobile medical payment insurance

    o Credit-only insurance

    o Other insurance coverage as specified in regulations under which benefits for medical care are secondary or incidental to other insurance benefits

    o Long-term care

    o Stand-alone dental and vision

    o Coverage for the military, sponsored by federal, state, or local governments

    o Employee Assistance Programs

    o Employee after-tax contributions to HSAs and MSAs

- The value of independent, noncoordinated coverage described in Internal Revenue Code section 9832(c)(3) if that coverage is purchased exclusively by the employee with after-tax dollars (or, in the case of a self-employed individual, for which a deduction under Internal Revenue Code section 162(l) is not allowable). Such Code section 9832(c)(3) coverage includes coverage only for a specified disease or illness, as well as hospital indemnity or other fixed indemnity insurance. Fixed indemnity health coverage pays fixed dollar amounts based on the occurrence of qualifying

---

1.   IRC Sec. 4980I(d)(1).

events, including but not limited to the diagnosis of a specific disease, an accidental injury or a hospitalization, and no coordination with other health coverage. The value of employer-sponsored health insurance coverage does include the value of such coverage if any portion of the coverage is employer-provided or, in the case of a self-employed individual, if a deduction is allowable for any portion of the payment for the coverage.

- Any coverage under a separate policy, certificate, or contract of insurance that provides benefits substantially all of which are for treatment of the mouth (including any organ or structure within the mouth) or for treatment of the eye.

596. Is there any relief in the Cadillac tax rules for people whose health coverage is expensive because their occupation is dangerous?

Yes. The annual limits noted in Q 593 are increased by $1,650 and $3,450 ($11,850 for individual coverage and $30,950 for family coverage), respectively, for employees (under the age of sixty-five) in high-risk professions (e.g., law enforcement, EMT/paramedics, construction, mining, longshoremen, and so forth).

597. How is the excise tax calculated and paid?

Liability for the excise tax would be determined on a monthly basis. Employers are required to calculate the amount of the excess benefit subject to the excise tax for each taxable period and to determine each coverage provider's "applicable share" of the excess benefit. A coverage provider's applicable share of an employee's excess benefit is determined by multiplying the aggregate excess benefit for the employee by the ratio obtained by comparing:

(1)   the cost of the coverage provided to the employee by the coverage provider to;

(2)   the aggregate cost of all applicable coverage.[1]

The amount subject to the excise tax on high-cost employer-sponsored health insurance coverage for each employee is the sum of the aggregate premiums for health insurance coverage, the amount of any salary reduction contributions to a health Flexible Spending Account (FSA) for the tax year, and the dollar amount of employer contributions to a Health Savings Account (HSA) or an Archer Medical Savings Account (MSA), minus the dollar amount of the threshold. The aggregate premiums for health insurance coverage include all employer sponsored health insurance coverage including coverage for any supplementary health insurance coverage. The applicable premium for health coverage provided through Health Reimbursement Account (HRA) is also included in this aggregate amount.[2]

---

1.   IRC Sec. 4980I(d).
2.   IRC Sec. 4980I(d).

The tax is equal to 40 percent of the aggregate value of the health insurance coverage that exceeds:

(1)   the threshold dollar amount;[1]

(2)   multiplied by the health cost adjustment percentage; and

(3)   increased by the age and gender adjusted excess premium amount.[2]

For 2020, the threshold dollar amount is $10,200 for individual coverage and $27,500 for family coverage.[3] However, increased thresholds apply for certain classes of taxpayers. The threshold amounts are increased for an individual who has attained age fifty-five, is not Medicare eligible, and is receiving employer-sponsored retiree health coverage, or is covered by a plan sponsored by an employer, the majority of whose employees covered by the plan are engaged in a high-risk profession[4] or employed to repair or install electrical and telecommunications lines. For these individuals, the threshold amount in 2018 is increased by:

(1) $1,650 ($11,850) for individual coverage or $3,450 ($30,950) for family coverage; and

(2)   the age and gender-adjusted excess premium amount.[5]

The basic thresholds are also adjusted by the health cost adjustment percentage for growth in the cost of U.S. healthcare between 2010 and 2020 that exceeds the projected growth for that period. The health cost adjustment percentage is equal to 100 percent plus the excess, if any, of:

(1)   the percentage by which the per employee cost of coverage under the Blue Cross/ Blue Shield standard benefit option under the Federal Employees Health Benefits Plan (standard FEHBP coverage) for plan year 2020 (as determined using the benefit package for standard FEHBP coverage for plan year 2010) exceeds the per employee cost of standard FEHBP coverage for plan year 2010; over

(2)   55 percent.[6]

In 2021, the threshold amounts, after application of the health cost adjustment percentage in 2020, if any, are indexed to the Consumer Price Index for All Urban Consumers (CPI-U), as determined by the Department of Labor, plus one percentage point, rounded to the nearest $50. In 2020 and thereafter, the threshold amounts are indexed to the CPI-U as determined by the Department of Labor, rounded to the nearest $50. For each employee (other than for

---

1.   IRC Sec. 4980I(b)(3)(C).
2.   IRC Sec. 4980I(b)(3).
3.   IRC Sec. 4980I(b)(3)(C).
4.   Law enforcement officers; those engaged in fire protection activities; providers of out-of-hospital emergency medical care (e.g., emergency medical technicians); those whose primary work is longshore work; and those engaged in the construction, mining, agriculture (not including food processing), forestry, and fishing industries. A retiree with at least twenty years of employment in a high-risk profession is also eligible for the increased threshold. See IRC Sec. 4980I(f).
5.   IRC Sec. 4980I(b)(3)(C)(iii) and (iv).
6.   IRC Sec. 4980I(b)(3)(C)(ii).

certain retirees and employees in high-risk professions, whose thresholds are adjusted under rules described below), the age and gender adjusted excess premium amount is equal to the excess, if any, of:

(1)   the premium cost of standard FEHBP coverage for the type of coverage provided to the individual if priced for the age and gender characteristics of all employees of the individual's employer; over

(2)   the premium cost, determined under procedures proscribed by IRS, for that coverage if priced for the age and gender characteristics of the national workforce[1]

In 2021, the primary threshold amounts and additional $1,650 and $3,450 amounts are indexed to the CPI-U, plus one percentage point, rounded to the nearest $50. In 2021 and thereafter, the additional threshold amounts are indexed to the CPI-U, rounded to the nearest $50.[2]

It should be noted that forms and instructions for paying the tax have not yet been made available, nor have regulations been issued.

598. Who pays the excise tax and how it is allocated?

The excise tax is imposed pro rata on the issuers of the insurance. Presumably, that cost will be passed along to the insureds. For a self-insured group health plan, a health FSA or an HRA, the excise tax is paid by the entity that administers benefits under the plan or arrangement (the "plan administrator"). The excise tax is paid by the employer if it acts as plan administrator to a self-insured group health plan, a health FSA or an HRA. Where an employer contributes to an HSA or an Archer MSA, the employer is responsible for payment of the excise tax, as the insurer.[3]

The excise tax is allocated pro rata among the insurers, with each insurer responsible for payment of the excise tax on an amount equal to the amount subject to the total excise tax multiplied by a fraction, having as the numerator the amount of employer-sponsored health insurance coverage provided by that insurer to the employee and having as the denominator the aggregate value of all employer-sponsored health insurance coverage provided to the employee.[4]

For a self-insured group health plan, a health FSA or an HRA, the excise tax is allocated to the plan administrator.[5]

The employer is responsible for calculating the amount subject to the excise tax allocable to each insurer and plan administrator and for reporting these amounts to each insurer, plan administrator and IRS, in the form and at the time that IRS may set. Each insurer and plan administrator is then responsible for calculating, reporting, and paying the excise tax to IRS on such forms and at such time as IRS may set.[6]

---

1.   IRC Sec. 4980I(b)(3)(C)(iii).
2.   IRC Sec. 4980I(b)(3)(C)(v).
3.   IRC Sec. 4980I(c)(1) and (2).
4.   IRC Sec. 4980I(c)(3).
5.   IRC Sec. 4980I(c)(2)(C).
6.   IRC Sec. 4980I(c)(4).

How the Tax Would Work (note that these amounts will be indexed before the tax takes effect – if ever)

Example 1: In 2022, an employee elects family coverage under a fully insured healthcare policy covering major medical and dental with a value of $32,000. The health cost adjustment percentage for that year is 100 percent, and the age and gender adjusted excess premium amount for the employee is $600. On these facts, the amount subject to the excise tax is $3,900

- *$32,000 less the threshold of $28,100, which is the $27,500 threshold multiplied by 100 percent and increased by $600.) The employer reports $3,900 as taxable to the insurer, which calculates and remits the excise tax of $1,560 (40 percent of $3,900) to the IRS.*

Example 2: An employee with self-only coverage with a $14,000 individual plan. The $14,000 individual plan would pay an excise tax of $1520 per covered employee based on the following:

- *$14,000 – $10,200 = $3,800 above the $10,200 threshold. ($3,800 × 40% = $1520)*

- *Example Three: An employee with family coverage with a $36,000 family plan would pay an excise tax of $3,400 per covered employee based on the following calculation:*

  - *$36,000 – $27,500 = $8,500 above the $27,500 threshold ($8500 × 40% = $3,400)*

The following chart indicates the increase in the tax as the cost of the policy increases

Individual (self) coverage						
Cost	$11,000	$12,000	$13,000	$14,000	$15,000	$16,000
Tax	$320	$720	$1,120	$1,520	$1,920	$2,320
Family Coverage						
Cost	$28,000	$30,000	$32,000	$34,000	$36,000	$38,000
Tax	$200	$1,000	$1,800	$2,600	$3,400	$4,200

599. What is the sanction on the employer for underreporting liability for the tax?

A penalty applies to an employer that reports to insurers, plan administrators and IRS a lower amount of insurance cost subject to the excise tax than required. The penalty is the sum of any additional excise tax that each such insurer and administrator would have owed if the employer had reported correctly plus interest[1] attributable to that additional excise tax from the date that the tax was otherwise due to the date paid by the employer.[2]

The penalty does not apply if it is established to the satisfaction of the Internal Revenue Service that the employer neither knew, nor by exercising reasonable diligence would have known, that the failure existed. In addition, no penalty will be imposed on any failure corrected within the thirty-day period beginning on the first date that the employer knew, or exercising reasonable diligence, would have known, that the failure existed, so long as the failure is due to reasonable cause and not to willful neglect. All or part of the penalty may be waived by IRS

---

1. Calculated under IRC Sec. 6621.
2. IRC Sec. 4980I(e).

in the case of any failure due to reasonable cause and not to willful neglect, to the extent that the payment of the penalty would be excessive or otherwise inequitable relative to the failure involved.[1]

Patient Centered Outcomes Research Institute (PCORI) and PCORI Fees

600. What is the Patient Centered Outcomes Research Institute?

The Affordable Care Act (ACA) established, under authorization by Congress, the Patient-Centered Outcomes Research Institute (PCORI) as a 501(c)(1) non-governmental institute designed to conduct research to provide information about the best available evidence to help patients and their health care providers make more informed decisions. PCORI's research is intended to give patients a better understanding of the prevention, treatment, and care options available, as well as the science that supports those options.

More information about PCORI is available at their website at https://www.pcori.org/. PCORI is funded through the Patient-Centered Outcomes Research Trust Fund (PCORTF), which was authorized by the United States Congress as part of the Patient Protection and Affordable Care Act of 2010. Income is obtained through the general fund of the Treasury as well as the Comparative Effectiveness Research Fee (CERF) assessed on Medicare, private health insurance and self-insured plans. The fee began at $2 and is increased yearly based on inflation.

601. What are PCORI fees?

The ACA imposes a Patient Centered Outcomes Research Institute (PCORI) fee on plan sponsors and issuers of individual and group policies. The "PCORI fee", the CERF fee, or the "Section 4376[2] fee" is an annual fee on insured and self-insured plans and is intended to partially fund the Patient-Centered Outcomes Research Institute created by healthcare reform.

The fee applies to certain "specified health insurance" policies and includes medical policies, retiree-only policies, and any accident or health insurance policy (including a policy under a group health benefit plan) issued to individuals residing in the United States. Specifically included are:

- Fully insured medical plans, including minimum premium plans

- Self-insured group medical plans

- Individual/family plans

- Stand-alone behavioral health plans

---

1.   IRC Sec. 4980I(e).
2.   PPACA §4376.

- Limited medical plans (also known as Voluntary plans)

- Individuals living in the U.S. under a temporary visa

- Medicare Surround and Medicare Expand policies

- Retiree-only plans

- Health Reimbursement Accounts (HRAs)

- Flexible Spending Accounts (FSAs) when employer contribution exceeds $500 and is more than employee contribution

The fee does not apply to:

- "Excepted benefits," as defined under HIPAA, such as stand-alone vision or dental plans;

- Employee Assistance Programs (EAP) or wellness programs;

- FSA plans, when they meet the excepted benefits test;

- Health Savings Accounts (HSAs)

- Health Reimbursement Accounts (HRA), when it meets the excepted benefits test.

    - Expatriate coverage (those working outside the United States and their spouses and dependents)

    - Stop-loss, where the issuer is liable for all losses in excess of a specified amount and where the plan sponsor retains its liability for losses

    - Indemnity reinsurance policies, where the reinsuring company accepts all or part of the risk of loss under the policy and the issuing company retains its liability for covered lives

    - Medicare Part A-D coverage

    - Medicaid

    - CHIP

    - TRICARE

    - Stand-alone dental plans

    - Stand-alone vision plans

    - Noninsurance health programs for members (spouses or dependents) of the Armed Forces or veterans o   Federally recognized Indian Health Services and programs under the Indian Health Care Improvement Act

602. How are PCORI fees to be paid?

IRS Form 720,[1] Part II: Applicable self-insured health plans, line 133, and its voucher are used to report and remit the Patient Centered Outcomes Research Institute Fee (PCORI fee) to the IRS by July 31 for the preceding year. Electronic filing is available but not mandatory.

The fee must be paid by the employer no later than July 31 of the year following the last day of the plan year.[2] The fee is a tax-deductible business expense.[3] Fee continues through September 30, 2019, with the last payment due July 30, 2020 (for those on non-calendar year plans)

PCORI Fees

Plan Year	Fee Amount	Fee Established By
Oct–Dec 2012	$1.00	ACA Section 4376
Jan–Sep 2013	$1.00	ACA Section 4376
Oct–Dec 2013	$2.00	ACA Section 4376
Jan–Sep 2014	$2.00	ACA Section 4376
Oct–Dec 2014	$2.08	IRS Notice 2014-56[4]
Jan–Sep 2015	$2.08	IRS Notice 2014-56
Oct–Dec 2015	$2.17	IRS Notice 2015-60[5]
Jan–Sep 2016	$2.17	IRS Notice 2015-60
Oct–Dec 2016	$2.26	IRS Notice 2016-64[6]
Jan–Sep 2017	$2.26	IRS Notice 2016-64
Oct–Dec 2017	$2.39	IRS Notice 2017-61
Jan–Sep 2018	$2.39	IRS Notice 2017-61[7]
Oct–Dec 2018	$2,45	IRS Notice 2018-85
Jan–Sep 2019	$2.45	IRS Notice 2018-85[8]

603. When are PCORI fees due?

The "PCORI fee" is intended to fund partially the Patient-Centered Outcomes Research Institute created by healthcare reform. The PCORI fee is applicable to plan years ending after

---

1.   https://www.irs.gov/pub/irs-pdf/f720.pdf.
2.   26 CFR §6071(a)-1.
3.   IRS Chief Counsel Memo (June 7, 2013) available at http://www.irs.gov/pub/irs-utl/AM2013-002.pdf . (Last Accessed August 10, 2019).
4.   IRS Notice 2014-56.
5.   IRS Notice 2015-60.
6.   IRS Notice 2016-64.
7.   IRS Notice 2017-61.
8.   IRS Notice 2018-85.

September 30, 2012 and extends through plan years ending before October 1, 2019. The fee must be paid no later than July 31 of the year following the last day of the plan year.[1] Therefore, the first PCORI fees are due for 2012 calendar year self-insured plans and certain fiscal year plans by July 31, 2013. So, for example, if the fiscal year end is March 31, 2017, the calendar year in which that plan year ends is 2017, and the tax and return would be due July 31, 2018.

PCORI fee for the first year for plan years ending on or after October 1, 2012, and before October 1, 2013, was equal to $1.00 multiplied by the average number of covered lives in the group health plan. The PCORI fee for the second year increased to $2.00 times the average number of covered lives in the group health plan and is indexed for increases in national health expenditures for the following years. The PCORI fee which was due July 31, 2015, was $2.08 per covered life.[2] The PCORI fee due July 31, 2016 is $2.17 per covered life, the fee due July 31, 2017, is $2.26 per covered life, the fee due July 31, 2018 is $2.39 per covered life and the fee due July 31 2019 is $2.45[3]

604. Who pays the PCORI fees?

Insurers file and pay the fee for insured plans.[4] The PCORI fee must be paid by employers that sponsor self-insured health plans (including many employer funded Health Reimbursement Accounts (HRAs), Qualified Small Employer Health Reimbursement Arrangement (QSE-HRAs), and Medical Expense Reimbursement Plans (MERPs) by July 31 of each year.[5] The fee paid by insurers applies to certain "specified health insurance" policies and includes medical policies, retiree-only policies, and any accident or health insurance policy (including a policy under a group health benefit plan) issued to individuals residing in the United States.

The self-insured plan that is taxed is the "self-insured health plan." This is not tied to the definition of and exemptions from the term "group health plan." However, the regulations provide an exemption for an employer self-funded plan that provides benefits substantially all of which are excepted benefits."[6] On the other hand, plans that are not ERISA plans (covering only partners, for example) or retiree-only plans are not exempted.

Health Reimbursement Arrangements (HRAs), Qualified Small Employer Health Reimbursement Arrangement (QSE-HRAs), and Medical Expense Reimbursement Plans (MERPs) are self-funded group health plans and are subject to the PCORI fee unless the employer also sponsors a *self-insured* group health plan, and both plans have the same plan year. If the plan sponsor maintains a self-funded medical plan with the same plan year, the medical plan and HRA may be treated as one plan for purposes of the PCORI fee if all participants participate in both plans. As discussed below, for an HRA or health care FSA, you only count employee/participants, not dependents. However, any other medical plan that is self-funded and not an

---

1.   26 CFR §6071(a)-1.
2.   IRS Notice 2014-56.
3.   IRS Notice 2015-60, 2016-64, 2017-61 and IRS Notice 2018-85.
4.   26 CFR §4375-1.
5.   IRC Sec. 4376(b)(1) and Reg §46.4376 provide that the fee imposed by section 4376(a) shall be paid by the plan sponsor.
6.   Reg §46.4376-1(b)(ii).

excepted benefit counts all individuals covered by the plan, whether stand-alone or within a regular or simple cafeteria plan.

However, if the medical plan is fully insured, the medical plan and HRA must be treated as separate plans for purposes of the PCORI fee, with the insurer paying the fee for the medical plan and the employer/plan sponsor paying the fee for the HRA. Treas. Reg. §46.4376-1(b)(1) provides the definition of self-insured plans that are subject to the tax and includes medical expense reimbursement plans. It only excludes only health FSAs that are excepted benefits. A rule allows counting only the covered employees for purposes of determining the number of covered lives.

605. Can plan sponsors delegate the PCORI filing and fee payment to third parties?

No. Plan sponsors[1] of self-insured health plans[2] must make arrangements to complete and file the Form and pay the annual PCORI fees to the IRS, as the PCORI regulations directly prohibit using "third-party reporting" arrangements with respect to IRS Form 720. Plan sponsors are also advised that the fee must be paid by the plan sponsor and cannot be paid by the plan or from plan assets.

606. Are any plans excluded from being subject to the PCORI fees?

Yes, a number of employee benefit plans are excluded.

- "Excepted benefits," as defined under HIPAA, such as stand-alone vision or stand-alone dental plans. If the benefits covered under the FSA are limited to "excepted benefits," that FSA is also exempt from the PCORI payment even if FSA participants have no other health plan or the payments exceed the dollar limits described above.[3] Excepted benefits include but are not limited to:

    - coverage for only accident or disability income insurance;

    - liability insurance and coverage issued as a supplement to liability insurance;

    - workers' compensation or similar insurance;

    - automobile medical payment insurance; and

    - coverage for onsite medical clinics.

- Employee Assistance Programs (EAP) or wellness programs.

- Health Savings Accounts (HSAs)

---

1.   PPACA §4376(b)(2).
2.   26 CFR §4375-2.
3.   Treas. Reg. §46.4376–1(b)(1)(ii); IRS, Patient-Centered Outcomes Research Trust Fund Fee (IRC 4375, 4376 and 4377), Q&A-9 at https://www.irs.gov/affordable-care-act/patient-centered-outcomes-research-trust-fund-fee-questions-and-answers (Last accessed September 11, 2018).

- Health FSA plans, when they meet the excepted benefits test. An excepted benefit FSA provides that the maximum benefit payable by the FSA to the participant for a year does not exceed the greater of:

    - two times the participant's salary reduction election under the FSA for the year; or

    - five hundred dollars ($500) plus the amount of the participant's salary reduction election, meaning a $3,000 benefit from a $2,500 salary reduction election and an employer-paid flex credit of $500 is possible. Most FSAs also meet the second requirement.[1]

- Excepted Benefit FSA. If the benefits covered under the FSA are limited to "excepted benefits," that FSA is also exempt from the PCORI payment even if FSA participants have no other health plan or the payments exceed the dollar limits described above. Excepted benefits include but are not limited to:

    - coverage for only accident or disability income insurance;

    - liability insurance and coverage issued as a supplement to liability insurance;

    - workers' compensation or similar insurance;

    - automobile medical payment insurance; and

    - coverage for onsite medical clinics.

- Employer funded HRA, QSE-HRA, and MERP plans where employer's self-insured group health plan if both plans have the same plan year.

- Expatriate coverage (those working outside the United States and their spouses and dependents).

- Long-term care, home health care, and nursing home care.

- Stop loss, where the issuer is liable for all losses in excess of a specified amount and where the plan sponsor retains its liability for losses.

- Hospital and other indemnity insurance policies.

- Medicare (Parts A-D)

- Medicaid.

- CHIP and TRICARE.

---

1.   DOL Technical Release 2013-03 https://www.dol.gov/agencies/ebsa/employers-and-advisers/guidance/technical-releases/13-03 (Last accessed September 11, 2018).

- Noninsurance health programs for members (spouses or dependents) of the Armed Forces or veterans.

- Federally recognized Indian Health Services and programs under the Indian Health Care Improvement Act.

607. How are the average number of lives determined and the fees calculated?

Fully Insured Plans

There are four optional methods for determining the average number of covered lives. Issuers must use the same method consistently for the duration of any year and the same method for all policies subject to the fee. (The insurance carrier is responsible for paying the required PCORI fee in the case of fully insured coverage.)

<u>Actual Count</u>. Count the total number of covered lives for each day of the policy year and divide by the number of days in a year. The total number of lives covered, including employees and their covered family members are only employees if HRA, QSE-HRA, or FSA on each day of the plan year, divided by the total number of days in the plan year.

<u>Snapshot Method</u>. Count the number of members on a single day (or days if consistent for each quarter) during a quarter and divide the total by the number of dates on which a count was made. The date used for each quarter must be the same (i.e., the first day, the last day).

<u>NAIC Member Months Method</u>. The issuer determines the average number of covered lives based on member months reported to the National Association of Insurance Commissioners (NAIC) on the Supplemental Health Care Exhibit for the calendar year. The average number of lives in effect for the calendar year equals member months divided by twelve.

<u>State Form Method</u>. This method is for issuers that are not required to file the NAIC Exhibit. These issuers may determine the number of covered lives using a form that is filed with the issuer's state of domicile, if the form reports the number of covered lives in the same manner as the NAIC Supplemental Exhibit.

Self-funded Plans

Self-funded plans may determine the average number of covered lives by using any of the following methods. Like fully insured plans, plan sponsors must use the same method consistently for the duration of any year and the same method for all policies subject to the fee.

<u>Actual Count</u>. Count the total covered lives for each day of the plan year and divide by the number of days in the plan year.

<u>Snapshot Dates</u>. Count the total number of covered lives on a single day in a quarter (or more than one day) and divide the total by the number of dates on which a count was made. (The date or dates must be consistent for each quarter.)

<u>Snapshot Factor</u>. In the case of self-only coverage, determine the sum of: (1) the number of participants with self-only coverage, and (2) the number of participants with other than self-only coverage multiplied by 2.35. (Do not use this method for HRA or FSA plans.)

<u>Form 5500 Method</u>. For self-only coverage, determine the average number of participants by combining the total number of participants at the beginning of the plan year with the total number of participants at the end of the plan year as reported on the Form 5500 and divide by two. In the case of plans with self-only and other coverage, the average number of total lives is the sum of total participants covered at the beginning and the end of the plan year, as reported on the Form 5500.

608. How the lives covered under a health insurance policy or self-insured health plan determined?

Generally, all individuals who are covered during the policy year or plan year must be counted in computing the average number of lives covered for that year. Thus, for example, an applicable self-insured health plan must count an employee and his dependent child as two separate covered lives unless the plan is a health reimbursement arrangement (HRA) or flexible spending arrangement (FSA).

609. If an employer provides coverage under COBRA or coverage to retirees, do those employees count as "lives covered" for purposes of PCORI?

Yes. The covered individuals and their beneficiaries must be taken into account in calculating the average number of lives covered.

610. How are multiple self-funded plans counted for purposes of the fee?

Under the final rule, if the plan sponsor of a self-funded plan has more than one self-funded plan (e.g., one for medical, another for pharmacy) it may treat them as a single self-funded plan for purposes of this fee to avoid double counting of the members. This special counting rule only applies to self-funded plans in the proposed rule.

611. How were the number of covered lives determined in the first year?

For the first year of the fee, plan years beginning before July 11, 2012, and ending on or after October 1, 2012, a plan sponsor could determine the average number of covered lives using any reasonable method. In the first year, fully insured plans, for example, may report only 25 percent of the number of lives it reported on the NAIC form in 2012.

612. Are there special rules for health FSAs, QSE-HRAs, and HRAs?

If a plan sponsor only maintains a Flexible Spending Account (FSA), a Qualified Small Employer Health Reimbursement Arrangement (QSE-HRA) or a Health Reimbursement Arrangement (HRA), the plan sponsor may treat each participant's account as covering a single life. (The plan sponsor is not required to count spouses or other dependents.) If the FSA/HRA/QSE-HRA is sponsored by a plan sponsor that also has an applicable self-funded health plan (that is not a FSA, QSE-HRA, or HRA), the two arrangements may be treated as one plan.

613. Are health insurance policies for self-insured plans for tax-exempt organizations or government entities subject to the PCORI fee?

Yes. Unless the health insurance policy or self-insured health plan is an exempt governmental program described above, the policy or plan is a specified health insurance policy or applicable self-insured health plan subject to the PCORI fee and, accordingly, the health insurance issuer or plan sponsor is responsible for the PCORI fee.

PART X: STATE INSURANCE EXCHANGES (MARKETPLACES)

State, State-Federal Partnerships, and Federally Facilitated Exchanges (FFEs)

614. What are the state health insurance exchanges or marketplaces?

A cornerstone of the Affordable Care Act is the online interfaces or state insurance exchanges which the federal government has branded as "marketplaces". States and certain other governmental entities[1] are required to create these competitive marketplaces for individuals and small businesses as a location to purchase insurance. Exchanges, for the calendar year beginning January 1, 2014 and thereafter, serve as the primary method for people to obtain insurance coverage when they do not receive it from their employer. (Initial enrollment began October 1, 2013.) While the exchanges are a major avenue to health insurance, majority of people have continued to obtain coverage from their employers.

As discussed below, there are four types of exchanges:

1.   State-based exchanges: Those created by a state (there are twelve of these).

2.   State-based on federal platform exchanges (there are five of these).

3.   State-federal partnership exchanges (there are six of these).

4.   Federally-Facilitated Exchanges (FFEs) in those states that did not create or operate their own exchange (there are twenty-eight of these).

Exchanges provide individuals and small business owners with a "one stop shopping experience" to compare and buy health insurance. Private health insurance companies list their health plans with the exchange, and people comparison shop on the exchange from among the available health plan listings. The purpose is to provide consumers with more control and greater transparency for making choices about health insurance. People can also enroll in public programs, such as Medicaid and CHIP (for children), through exchanges. Exchanges are intended to use the power of a large insurance pool, made up of individuals and small businesses, to generate competition among insurers to offer better quality plans at a lower cost. The exchanges are the only locations in which consumers can obtain premium subsidies and cost-sharing subsides, which serve to reduce premiums and out of pocket costs for eligible enrollees. All U.S. citizens and legal residents who are not imprisoned and not eligible for premium-free Part A Medicare are eligible to purchase a health plan in the exchange in the state in which they live. Undocumented immigrants cannot enroll in coverage through the exchanges, even without premium subsidies.

---

1.   PPACA §1311(b)(1) (2010). "State" means the 50 states of the U.S., the District of Columbia, Puerto Rico, the U.S. Virgin Islands, Guam, American Samoa, and the Northern Mariana Islands. PPACA §1551; PHSA §2791(d)(14).

Terminology Politicized. Opponents of the federal healthcare reform law tend to refer to the exchanges that were set up by the Department of Health and Services as "federal exchanges" because they were established by the federal government, albeit on a state-by-state basis. Opponents of the federal healthcare reform law contended that no one who lives in a state with a "federal exchange" can receive a premium tax credit or subsidy for their exchange purchased health insurance, even if their income is low enough because of the way the law was written. When this book refers to a state exchange or marketplace, the reference typically includes all four types of exchanges described above. However, this issue was resolved by the Supreme Court in *King v. Burwell* (discussed later in this section).

615. What issues have there been with the marketplaces/exchanges and health insurance coverage?

There is no doubt that the implementation and continued operation of the exchanges has not been without its problems. The situation has become highly politicized and how serious the problem with the exchanges might be depends on which sets of number and statistics that are used. Clearly however, there are problems that need to be addressed by the President and Congress – and decisions will be made at some point.

Two of the most commonly reported problems are:

1. Insurer participation in the Exchanges: Clear problems had existed with participation during 2016, 2017 and 2018 – but 2019 has shown signs of recovery:

    a. In prior years, major companies such as Humana, Aetna and some Blue Cross and Blue Shield companies have left with others such as Molina and Anthem threatening to leave the Exchanges. However, issuer participation is now growing and expanding across the country, making health insurance markets more competitive and driven to deliver better value to consumers. In 2019, both market participation and county coverage are recovering from the drop seen in 2018 as evidenced by:

        o   There are twenty-three more issuers for 2019 than were participating during open enrollment in 2018.

        o   Twenty-nine current issuers are expanding their service area into more counties.

        o   Anthem, Wellmark, Molina, and Cigna have returned to markets they had left

    b. In 2013, there were 395 companies in the markets covering 3,007 counties in the United States. During 2017, that number had dropped to 217 and continued to drop during 2018 to 195. In 2014, there were an average of 5.0 insurers participating in each state's ACA marketplace. In 2015, the average per state had increased to 6.0, but the number fell to 5.6 by 2016. The losses incurred by insurance companies in 2017 led to a number of market withdrawals, lowering the average per state to 4.3. The decline continued in 2018 to an average per state of 3.5 insurers, however, in 2019 the average had increased to 4.0.

The number of enrollees offered more than two insurers had fallen to 58 percent by 2017, down from 85 percent the previous year. This average number of insurers per state continues to drop, with only 48 percent of enrollees being offered more than two choices in 2018. In 2019, 58 percent of enrollees had a choice of three or more insurers, up by 10 percent from 2018. When this number is examined by county, with the number of counties offering three or more choices falling from 85 percent in 2016, to 58 percent in 2017 to an appalling 18 percent of counties in 2018.

    c.   Single-company counties: Numbers vary depending upon who is reporting, but it appears that approximately 39 percent (approximately 1,564 counties) of the counties in the United States have either one insurer servicing them in 2019. This is up from a low of 7 percent in 2016, but shows an improvement from 52 percent in 2018. All US counties had at least one insurance provider in 2018, but the trend has become worrisome. There are a number of areas in the country with just one exchange insurer. In 2018, about 26 percent of enrollees, residing in 52 percent of counties, have access to just one insurer on the exchange. Only five states (AK, DE, NE, MS, WY) had only one issuer during 2019 compared to ten in 2018.

    2.   **Costs of insurance**: The Centers for Medicare and Medicaid services released data showing average premiums rates will drop in 2019 for individual health insurance plans sold on the HealthCare.gov platform. The average premium for the Second Lowest Cost Silver Plan (SLCSP) is expected to drop by 1.5 percent. Average premiums more than doubled between 2013 and 2017 and increased another 27 percent in 2018, therefore the 2019 decrease in cost is a hopeful sign.

The efforts in the United States Congress to "repeal" or to "repeal and replace" the Affordable Care Act ended with the loss in the Senate by one vote cast by the late Senator John McCain, who crossed party lines to keep the ACA alive, illustrating the national divide over healthcare reform. However, *Texas v. Azar* was brought by eighteen state attorneys-general are challenging the very constitutionality of the Affordable Care Act. The case is currently in oral argument before the United States Court of Appeal for the Fifth Circuit and likely to go to the Supreme Court.

616. What is the status of the exchanges and healthcare reform in the five US territories?

By letter dated July 16, 2014,[1] HHS has reversed its position that healthcare reform required insurers in five US territories to comply with the law's major market reforms, i.e., guaranteed

---

1.   See letter from HHS to US territory insurance commissioners at http://www.cms.gov/CCIIO/Resources/Letters/Downloads/letter-to-Ilagan.pdf. (Last accessed September 6, 2016 – appears to no longer be available on the internet).

coverage, mandated benefits, and limits on insurers' profits. U.S. territories can decide whether to create their own Health Insurance Marketplace or expand Medicaid coverage. Residents of a U.S. territory aren't eligible to apply for health coverage using the federal or state Marketplace unless they also qualify as a resident within the service area of a Marketplace. Healthcare reform does not require residents in Puerto Rico, the U.S. Virgin Islands, American Samoa, Guam and the Northern Mariana Islands to get coverage nor does it provide subsidies like those on the states' exchanges to help lower income persons afford coverage. In 2014 HHS determined, contrary to its prior position that the definition of "state" in the Public Health Service Act, which is the law that imposes the insurance mandates, indicates that the ACA market rules do not apply to the territories. The territories are exempt from guaranteed coverage, community rating, single risk pools, rate review, the medical loss ratio, essential health benefits requirements, and the rules limiting the profits of insurers. However, group health plans in the territories must still comply with other requirements, such as the prohibition on lifetime and annual limits ((PHSA section 2711), the prohibition on rescissions ((PHSA section 2712), coverage of preventive health services ((PHSA section 2713), and the internal and external appeals process (PHSA section 2719).

617. What is the status of SHOP exchanges and small business insurance purchases?

The Trump Administration ended the SHOP Exchanges effective January 1, 2018. Insurance is still available to small businesses through agents or brokers or directly contacting insurance companies. (See Q 618). Instead of having small businesses use the exchange to enroll in coverage, HealthCare.gov now directs businesses to seek out a broker or contact an insurance company directly. And although the site still maintains a tool where employers can check to see if there are SHOP plans available in their area (for purchase directly from an insurer or with the help of a broker), the tool no longer shows any available plans.

Although SHOP participation was unsuccessful in most state, SHOP participation in some of the state-run exchanges has been relatively successful (although in most cases, far lower than enrollment in individual market plans).

California's SHOP exchange had 47,000 members as of 2018 and DC's SHOP exchange had more than 77,000 members as of 2018, although that is largely explained by the fact that all small-group plans in DC must be purchased through the exchange, and members of Congress also obtain their coverage through the DC SHOP exchange.

HealthCare.gov no longer maintains an enrollment portal for SHOP plans, but most of the state-run health insurance exchanges still have SHOP platforms for small businesses. Some use a direct-to-carrier enrollment approach, while others still offer a full-service enrollment platform:

- California

- Colorado (the state-run exchange no longer administers SHOP, but Kaiser still offers SHOP-certified plans in Colorado)

- Connecticut

- District of Columbia

- Idaho (enrollments are completed directly with the insurers or via a broker)

- Maryland (enrollments are completed directly with the insurers or via a broker)

- Massachusetts

- New Mexico (uses HealthCare.gov for individual enrollments, but has its own SHOP platform)

- New York (eligibility is determined on the NY exchange site, but as of April 2018, enrollment is directly with insurance companies;

    o This has proven to be successful with participation increasing from four insurers to nine.

- Rhode Island

- Vermont (all small-group plans in Vermont are SHOP plans).

It should be noted that Washington and Minnesota have state-run health insurance exchanges, but are no longer offering SHOP programs.

The history of the SHOP exchanges is provided as background and historical information below:

History of the SHOP Exchange

The Affordable Care Act created two kinds of exchanges: health insurance exchanges for individuals and Small Business Health Options Program (SHOP) exchanges for small business owners. In 2015, employers with less than fifty full-time equivalent workers (FTE) could use the SHOP. In 2016, the SHOP opened for businesses with 100 or less FTE. Small employers using SHOP were required to offer coverage to all full-time employees, i.e., those working thirty or more hours per week on average. In many states, at least seventy percent of a small employer's full-time employees must enroll in the SHOP plan for the employer to be eligible. Self-employed individuals with no full-time employees could only obtain coverage on an exchange and not a SHOP exchange. In some states, an employer could select one of the metal categories (bronze, silver, gold and platinum) and let employees select from available plans in that category. However, there was no guaranty that a particular state will have more than one plan in a metal category or in each category. For instance, a state could offer one plan in the silver category and two plans in the gold category and no plan in the bronze or platinum categories. The fifth category, catastrophic coverage, pays less than 60 percent of the total average cost of care on average. These policies are available only to people who are under thirty years old or who have a hardship exemption and are not sold on the exchanges.

The law delegated primary responsibility for governing and operating the exchanges to the states, with the federal government (primarily HHS) setting minimum standards. States had the option to merge the individual and SHOP exchanges, collaborate with other states to form multistate regional exchanges, or to form multiple exchanges within their state if each one serves a geographically distinct area.

Beginning in 2015, however, purchasing employer-provided health coverage for employees through a SHOP was the only way for qualified employers to obtain a small business health care tax credit.

Employers could apply for SHOP coverage online through www.healthcare.gov. They may use brokers, agents, or others to assist them.

HHS issued guidance allowing a state that has already received conditional approval to operate a state-based exchange for 2014 to request permission to operate a SHOP-only Exchange instead while the individual market operates under an FFE.[1] For years after 2014, HHS provided rules requiring states to request approval to operate a SHOP-only Exchange using a special application. The FAQs also clarify that a SHOP-only Exchange must have a state-run navigator program, but it may be limited to consumer outreach and education activities, while the FFE would operate its own navigator program in the individual market.[2]

As of 2017, HHS reported that there were fewer than 39,000 people enrolled in SHOP coverage across the twenty-six states with fully federally-run SHOP platforms. Hawaii was the first state to obtain approval for a 1332 waiver, and its purpose was to eliminate the state's SHOP exchange as of 2017.

618. What is the status of the SHOP program on Healthcare.gov?

Effective 2018, the SHOP exchanges on healthcare.gov have been eliminated. Currently, the SHOP insurance that started on January 1, 2018, enabled employers have two options for enrolling:

- Through an insurance company; or

- Through the assistance of a SHOP-Registered agent or broker.

SHOP insurance is generally available to employers with one-fifty full-time equivalent employees (FTEs). If a company have fewer than twenty-five employees, it may qualify for the Small Business Health Care Tax Credit, if purchasing SHOP insurance. SHOP purchases don't have to wait until the open enrollment, but can be purchased throughout the year.

The Health and Human Services Department announced in May 2017 that it intended to end the SHOP program in 2018.

SHOP had a slow start. Currently only 223,000 people had purchased insurance through the thirty-three states that offer the program and though the federal offering. HHS is citing this

---

1.   Small Business Health Options Program (SHOP)-Only Marketplace FAQs, Q&A-1 at http://www.cms.gov/CCIIO/Resources/Fact-Sheets-and-FAQs/Downloads/shop-marketplace-5-10-2013.pdf. (Last accessed August 12, 2019).
2.   Small Business Health Options Program (SHOP)-Only Marketplace FAQs, Q&A-4 at http://www.cms.gov/CCIIO/Resources/Fact-Sheets-and-FAQs/Downloads/shop-marketplace-5-10-2013.pdf. (Last accessed September 11, 2018).

low participation, noting that it was expected that four million would participate in SHOP. They have pointed out that there are thirty million small businesses in the United States, but only about 27, 000 have availed themselves of the SHOP program.

Opponents have argued, evidently unsuccessfully, that it is unclear whether the Trump Administration can legally dismantle SHOP, citing their opinion that the small business provisions of the Affordable Care Act must mirror that of the Exchanges where individual purchase their own insurance. The SHOP concept has been troubled with the problem of spreading insurance risk over companies with fifty or fewer employees. These issues were recognized even before the 2016 election, with the Obama Administration in late 2016, quietly removing the requirement that health plans being sold in the individual market had to sell in the small business exchanges.

619. What individuals and employers are eligible to purchase health insurance on an exchange?

To be eligible to enroll in health coverage through the Marketplace the following conditions must be met:[1]

- Must live in the United States.

- Must be a United States citizen or national (or be lawfully present). Illegal/undocumented aliens are not authorized to obtain coverage from the exchange.

- Cannot be incarcerated in a jail or prison

- Must be a resident of the state from which the insurance is purchased from the Exchange

620. May individuals with Medicare enroll for coverage through the exchange?

In general, persons covered by Medicare cannot purchase health insurance on an exchange. CMS has released FAQs that explain when individuals with Medicare may and may not enroll for coverage through the Exchanges.[2] In many of the scenarios addressed in the FAQs, the prohibition on the sale of duplicate coverage to Medicare beneficiaries makes it illegal to sell or issue an individual insurance through an Exchange.[3] However, individuals who are not eligible to get Medicare Part A for free may drop both their Premium Part A and their Part B coverage (or choose not to enroll when first eligible). An individual who does not have Medicare (either Part A or Part B) can enroll in a QHP. Note that individuals who get free Part A cannot drop it without dropping their retiree benefits (social security or railroad retirement) and paying back all retirement benefits received and costs incurred by the Medicare program as well.

---

1.   PPACA §1312(f) (2010).
2.   The Relationship between Medicare and the Health Insurance Marketplace (as visited Dec. 10, 2014).
3.   *Id* at Q/A-A.6. https://www.cms.gov/Medicare/Eligibility-and-Enrollment/Medicare-and-the-Marketplace/Downloads/Medicare-Marketplace_Master_FAQ_4-28-16_v2.pdf (Last accessed August 11, 2019).

Before making this choice, there are two important points for individuals to consider: Individuals who do not enroll in Medicare when first eligible (during their initial enrollment period) may have to pay late enrollment penalties if they later apply for both Premium Part A and Part B. The Part B penalty applies for as long as the individual has Part B coverage. In addition, individuals who enroll in Medicare after their initial enrollment period ends can enroll in Medicare only during the Medicare general enrollment period (from January 1 to March 31) and coverage does not begin until July of that year.[1]

621. How do exchanges determine which individuals are eligible to purchase on an exchange?

Exchanges are required to perform eligibility determinations.

Exchanges establish a system of coordinated eligibility and enrollment so that an individual can simultaneously apply for enrollment in an exchange health insurance policy, a Qualified Health Plan (QHP) and advance payment of the premium tax credit and cost-sharing reductions, as well as other insurance affordability programs.[2] The IRS has published rules concerning the requirements for eligibility, reporting, and claiming the credits.[3] HHS has a tool called the Data Services Hub (see Q 622) to help verify applicant information used to determine eligibility for enrollment, advance payment of the premium tax credit, cost-sharing reductions, and other insurance affordability programs.[4]

Eligibility for the premium tax credit is determined by meeting all of the following requirements:

- Have household income that falls within a certain range (In general, individuals and families may be eligible for the premium tax credit if their household income for the year is at least 100 percent but no more than 400 percent of the federal poverty line for their family size.)

- Not filing a Married Filing Separately tax return ((unless qualifying for a special rule that allows certain victims of domestic abuse and spousal abandonment to claim the premium tax credit using the Married Filing Separately filing status

- Cannot be claimed as a dependent by another person; and

- In the same month, the individual or family member:

    o Enroll in coverage (excluding "catastrophic" coverage) through a Marketplace

    o Are not able to get affordable coverage through an eligible employer-sponsored plan that provides minimum value

---

1.   *Id.*
2.   45 CFR §155.305.
3.   See Questions and Answers on the Premium Tax Credit at https://www.irs.gov/affordable-care-act/individuals-and-families/questions-and-answers-on-the-premium-tax-credit (Last accessed August 11, 2019).
4.   Federal Marketplace Progress Fact Sheet: Progress Continues in Building Marketplaces at https://www.cms.gov/CCIIO/Resources/Fact-Sheets-and-FAQs/Downloads/third-party-qa-11-04-2013.pdf. (Last accessed August 11, 2019).

- ○ Are not eligible for coverage through a government program, like Medicaid, Medicare, CHIP or TRICARE

- ○ Pay the share of premiums not covered by advance credit payments

622. What is the Federal Data Services Hub?

Regardless of how someone signs up for coverage under the Affordable Care Act, all paths lead through the Data Services Hub.

The Department of Health and Human Services (HHS), through the Centers for Medicare and Medicaid Services (CMS), which controls the federal Data Services Hub technology infrastructure, has decreed that "all consumers must have their eligibility verified through the Data Services Hub—regardless of which path they use to enroll."

The HealthCare.gov marketplace was built by fifty-five different government contractors and is maintained by scores of contractors has been described as "one of the most complex pieces of software ever created for the federal government. It communicates in real time with at least 112 different computer systems across the country."[1]

The Data Services Hub is a cloud-based routing tool that enables the state and federal marketplaces to provide accurate and timely eligibility determinations. The Data Services Hub enables verification of data by accessing information contained within state and federal databases. When a individual provides information to their state's health insurance exchange, their personal information is verified against databases at the Internal Revenue Service (IRS), Social Security Administration (SSA), Department of Homeland Security (DHS), Department of Veterans Affairs (VA), Department of Defense (DoD), Peace Corps, and Office of Personnel Management (OPM). In addition, the federal government has contracted with private companies such as Equifax to provide income data and employer-sponsored health insurance status. Equifax and other credit bureaus have information that is more current than federal tax returns.

The federal Data Services Hub includes the following personal information regarding applicants:

- first name, last name, middle initial;

- mailing address or permanent residential address (if different from the mailing address);

- date of birth;

- gender and ethnicity;

- residency, email address, and telephone number;

---

1.   https://www.washingtonpost.com/national/health-science/what-went-wrong-with-healthcaregov/2013/10/24/400e68de-3d07-11e3-b7ba-503fb5822c3e_graphic.html?noredirect=on (Last accessed August 11, 2019).

- Social Security Number (if the applicant has one);

- employer information;

- enrollment in employer-sponsored coverage;

- citizenship or immigration status;

- enrollment in Federally funded minimum essential health coverage;

- incarceration status;

- Indian status;

- requests for and accompanying documentation to justify receipt of individual responsibility exemptions, including membership in a certain type of recognized religious sect or health care sharing ministry;

- veteran status;

- limited health status information (pregnancy status, blindness, disability status); and

- household income, including tax return information from the IRS, income information from the Social Security Administration, and financial information from other third party sources

623. What are the specific standards to determine if an individual is eligible to purchase health insurance on an exchange?

An individual is eligible for enrollment in a QHP through the Exchange if he or she meets basic standards that establish that the individual:

- is a citizen, national, or non-citizen lawfully present, and is reasonably expected to remain so for the entire period for which enrollment is sought;

- is not incarcerated;

- resides in the state that established the Exchange or, if different, the Exchange service area; and

- is not institutionalized, is capable of indicating intent, and is not receiving a state supplementary payment.[1]

The Exchange must accept an application and make an eligibility determination for an applicant at any point in time during a benefit year. The Exchange would be required to accept and process changes reported by enrollees during the benefit year as well. HHS has clarified, however, that this does not supersede the limited enrollment periods described in subsection

---

1.   45 CFR §155.305(a).

After the Exchange determines eligibility, the Exchange must provide the individual with a timely, written notice of his or her eligibility determination.[1] U.S. citizens living in a foreign country for at least 330 days of a twelve-month period are not required to get health insurance coverage for that twelve-month period.

624. How are eligibility determinations for premium tax credit and cost-sharing reductions made?

The Exchange coordinates determinations of eligibility for health insurance, a QHP, with determinations for insurance affordability programs, including premium tax credits and cost-sharing reductions.[2]

HHS regulations contain standards for eligibility for advance payments of the premium tax credit to determine that:

- a taxpayer is expected to have a household income of at least 100 percent (138 percent for those states that have expanded Medicaid) but not more than 400 percent of the Federal Poverty Level (FPL) for the benefit year for which coverage is requested; and

- the applicants for whom the taxpayer expects to claim a personal exemption deduction on his or her tax return for the benefit year meet the standards for eligibility for enrollment in a QHP through the Exchange and are not eligible for minimum essential coverage (with the exception of coverage in the individual market), in accordance with Internal Revenue Code sections 36B(c)(2)(B) and 36B(c)(2)(C).[3]

In terms of income – the following is an illustration of when household income would be within 100 percent but not more than 400 percent of the Federal Poverty Level to compute the tax credit for 2019:[4]

- $12,490 (100 percent) up to $49,960 (400 percent) for one individual

- $16,910 (100 percent) up to $67,640 (400 percent) for a family of two

- $25,750 (100 percent) up to $100,300 (400 percent) for a family of four

- Additional family members over four, add $4,420 per addition at 100 percent.

HHS establishes three poverty guidelines: the forty-eight contiguous states, Alaska, and Hawaii. For Alaska, the above numbers at 100 percent are $15,600/$21,130/$32,190 (additional members $5,530). For Hawaii, the numbers at 100 percent are $14,380/$19,460/$29,620 (additional members $5,080).

---

1.   45 CFR §155.310(g).
2.   45 CFR §155.302(d); 45 CFR §155.300.
3.   45 CFR §155.305(f).
4.   HHS Notice 2018-00814.

625. What rules apply for spouses?

A taxpayer's spouse, including same-sex marriages, is included in determining family size, and household income must include both spouses' incomes. Married couples must file a joint tax return to qualify for premium tax credits.[1]

626. What rules apply for determination of household income for eligibility for Exchange tax credits and subsidies?

HHS regulations provide details on how the Exchanges will verify consumer income as part of the eligibility process for insurance affordability programs, including advance payments of the premium tax credit and cost-sharing reductions.[2] The process begins with the projected annual household income that individuals submit on their applications. The process requires an Exchange to use tax filing and Social Security data to verify household income information provided on an application. If the income cannot be verified using IRS and SSA data, then the information will be compared with wage information from employers provided by Equifax. When Equifax data does not substantiate the income, the Exchange will request an explanation or additional documentation. If documentation is requested, an individual generally will be eligible for affordability programs for ninety days, based on the submitted income and subject to reconciliation. If the requested documentation is not provided, the eligibility determination will be based on the IRS and SSA data (but if IRS data is unavailable, the Exchange must discontinue any advance payments of the premium tax credit and cost-sharing reductions).[3]

If the Exchange determines that a taxpayer is eligible to receive advance payments of the premium tax credit, the Exchange will then calculate the advance payments in accordance with IRS rules.[4] IRS regulations provide rules for determining taxpayer eligibility for the credit.[5]

The IRS is required to reconcile advance payments of the premium tax credit to actual premium tax credit eligibility when individuals file their annual tax returns, and it will recoup overpayments and provide refunds, when appropriate.[6] Penalties can apply when an individual fails to provide correct information based on negligence or disregard of the rules, or knowingly and willfully provides false and fraudulent information.[7]

HHS regulations also set forth the rules for the Exchange to determine that an individual is eligible for cost-sharing reductions. Among other things, these standards include three eligibility

---

1.   IRC §36B(c)(1)(C).
2.   Medicaid and Children's Health Insurance Programs: Essential Health Benefits in Alternative Benefit Plans, Eligibility Notices, Fair Hearing and Appeal Processes, and Premiums and Cost Sharing; Exchanges: Eligibility and Enrollment, 42 CFR Parts 431, 435, 436, 438, 440, 447, and 457; 45 CFR Parts 155 and 156, 78 Fed. Reg. 42159 (July 15, 2013).
3.   Medicaid and Children's Health Insurance Programs: Essential Health Benefits in Alternative Benefit Plans, Eligibility Notices, Fair Hearing and Appeal Processes, and Premiums and Cost Sharing; Exchanges: Eligibility and Enrollment, 42 CFR Parts 431, 435, 436, 438, 440, 447, and 457; 45 CFR Parts 155 and 156, 78 Fed. Reg. 42159 (July 15, 2013).
4.   45 CFR §155.305(f)(5).
5.   Treas. Reg. §1.36B-2.
6.   Treas. Reg. §1.36B-4.
7.   PPACA §1411(h) (2010).

categories for cost-sharing reductions and require the Exchange to determine that an individual is enrolled in a QHP in the silver level of coverage in order to receive the reductions.[1]

627. How does an Exchange obtain IRS Tax Return Information to help verify income?

Internal Revenue Code section 6103(l)(21) permits the disclosure of taxpayer return information to assist Exchanges in performing certain functions for which income verification is required, as well as to state agencies. The IRS discloses income and other specified information about an individual taxpayer to HHS for purposes of making eligibility determinations for advance payments of the premium tax credit or the cost-sharing reductions.[2] HHS could then disclose the information to the Exchange or state agency processing the individual's application (but not to any other entity, including individuals applying for coverage, Navigators, agents and brokers, or others assisting in the application process). The IRS may disclose information on any individual listed (by name and social security number) on a submitted application "whose income may bear upon a determination" of an advance payment of a premium tax credit, a cost-sharing reduction, or eligibility for certain other programs.[3] As a condition for receiving return information, each receiving entity (HHS, the Exchanges, and state agencies as well as their respective contractors) is required to adhere to the privacy standards under Internal Revenue Code section 6103(p)(4).

628. What happens when the Exchange determines an applicant is eligible to receive advance payment of the premium tax credits or cost-sharing reductions based in part on a finding that his or her employer does not provide minimum essential coverage, or provides coverage that is not affordable, or does not meet the minimum value standard?

When the Exchange determines an applicant is eligible to receive advance payment of the premium tax credits or cost-sharing reductions based in part on a finding that his or her employer does not provide minimum essential coverage, or provides coverage that is not affordable, or does not meet the minimum value standard, HHS regulations require the Exchange send a notice to the employer and identify the employee.[4] Due to privacy concerns, the preamble explains that HHS believes that only the minimum-necessary personally identifiable information should be released to an employer in the notice.[5] The notice includes the employee's identity that the employee has been determined eligible for advance payments of the premium tax credit, that the employer may be liable for a shared responsibility (employer mandate) payment, and that there is an opportunity to appeal.[6]

---

1.   45 CFR §§155.305(g) and 155.340.
2.   Treas. Reg. §301.6103(l)(21)-1; IRC §6103(l)(21).
3.   Treas. Reg. §301.6103(l)(21)-1.
4.   45 CFR §155.310(h).
5.   Establishment of Exchanges and Qualified Health Plans; Exchange Standards for Employers, 77 Fed. Reg. 18310, 18356 (Mar. 27, 2012).
6.   45 CFR §155.310(h).

Exchanges can either send the notice to employers on an employee-by-employee basis as eligibility determinations are made or send it for groups of employees.[1] It appears that the notices will be sent to the employer at the address provided by employees as part of the Exchange application process. Acknowledging that employees may provide incorrect contact information, HHS has indicated that it will work with Exchanges and employers to ensure that the notices reach the correct employer.[2]

629. How do Exchanges verify whether an employee is enrolled in employer-sponsored health coverage or are eligible for employer-sponsored health coverage that meets affordability and minimum value standards?

HHS regulations describe the process that Exchanges will use to verify whether individuals who apply for advance payment of premium tax credits are enrolled in employer-sponsored health coverage or are eligible for employer-sponsored health coverage that meets affordability and minimum value standards.[3] An applicant or applicant's authorized representative must submit specified information (attestations) to the Exchange when applying to receive advance payment of the premium tax credit.[4] The Exchange is required to verify the attestations and determine whether the applicant is eligible.

The Exchange can rely on an applicant's attestations unless verification of employment is not possible from the approved sources, or if information regarding employment is not consistent with the applicant's representations, then the Exchange must undertake a manual verification process for a "statistically significant" random sample of applicants.[5]

In addition, HHS has an "Employer Coverage Tool"[6] that enables applicants' employers to provide information about the group health plan coverage for which the applicant is eligible. The information is used to determine whether applicants for subsidized coverage are eligible for employer-sponsored health coverage that meets affordability and minimum value standards.

630. Can employers appeal a determination that an employee is eligible for an Exchange tax credit or subsidy?

Yes. There is a detailed appeals process.[7] The employer can appeal a determination that an employee is eligible for advance payments of the premium tax credit or cost-sharing reductions based on a finding that the employer did not offer qualifying coverage to the employee. If an employee is determined eligible for advance payment of premium tax credits, an appeal is an opportunity for the employer to correct any misinformation about employer-sponsored coverage offered to the employee (e.g., whether an employee should even be entitled to premium tax

1.   Program Integrity: Exchange, SHOP, and Eligibility Appeals, 45 CFR Parts 147, 153, 155, and 156, 78 Fed. Reg. 54069, 54113 (Aug. 30, 2013).

2.   Establishment of Exchanges and Qualified Health Plans; Exchange Standards for Employers, 77 Fed. Reg. 18310, 18356 (Mar. 27, 2012).

3.   Medicaid and Children's Health Insurance Programs: Essential Health Benefits in Alternative Benefit Plans, Eligibility Notices, Fair Hearing and Appeal Processes, and Premiums and Cost Sharing; Exchanges: Eligibility and Enrollment, 42 CFR Parts 431, 435, 436, 438, 440, 447, and 457; 45 CFR Parts 155 and 156, 78 Fed. Reg. 42159 (July 15, 2013).

4.   45 CFR §155.320.

5.   45 CFR §155.320(d)(3).

6.   See https://www.healthcare.gov/downloads/employer-coverage-tool.pdf. (Last accessed August 11, 2019).

7.   45 CFR §155.555.

credits if the employee was offered the opportunity to enroll in minimum essential coverage that was affordable and provided minimum value) and for the Exchange to use such information to confirm (or refute) the employee's eligibility determination. Appealing an incorrect eligibility determination can provide an opportunity to "head off" a potential excise tax under Internal Revenue Code section 4980H. Moreover, since Internal Revenue Code section 4980H excise tax is determined monthly, early action may allow the employer to limit liability prospectively. Additionally, the appeal can minimize the employee's potential liability to repay the advance payment of premium tax credits that the employee may not be eligible to receive and avoid adverse tax consequences at year-end. Employers can develop policies to allow an employee to enroll in employer-sponsored coverage outside an open enrollment period when the employee is determined to be ineligible for advance payment of premium tax credits as a result of an employer appeal decision.[1]

At the healthcare.gov website, the is now an "Employer Appeal Form" with instructions detailing how to complete the form, the timeframe required (ninety days of the Marketplace notice) and instructions for designating a secondary contact and obtaining additional help.[2]

631. What are the procedures for Exchanges to determine eligibility for coverage?

Beginning in 2016, applicants are not eligible if they have not filed an income tax return for the preceding year. Prior to open enrollment, the Exchange will request updated tax return information from the IRS. Where an application includes a request for premium tax credits, the Exchange may not determine the individual eligible if the IRS indicates that premium tax credits were previously provided but the individual failed to comply with the requirement to file an income tax return for the year for which tax credits were provided and reconcile those credits.[3] Enrollees who are re-enrolled by the Exchange will receive an eligibility determination notice and an enrollment confirmation message that explains the results of the annual eligibility redetermination and re-enrollment process.

632. How do Exchanges report information about premium tax credits and subsidies?

Health care reform directs Exchanges to report to the IRS and to taxpayers certain information required to reconcile the premium tax credit with advance credit payments, and to administer the premium tax credit generally.[4] Final IRS regulations specify timing rules and provide details on reportable information and the manner of reporting.[5] These regulations require reporting about coverage obtained through an Exchange by an individual, but did not require information about employer-provided coverage obtained through a SHOP.[6]

---

1. Program Integrity: Exchange, SHOP, and Eligibility Appeals, 45 CFR Parts 147, 153, 155, and 156, 78 Fed. Reg. 54069, 54114 (Aug. 30, 2013).
2. https://www.healthcare.gov/downloads/marketplace-employer-appeal-form.pdf. (Last accessed August 11, 2019).
3. 45 CFR §155.305(f)(4).
4. IRC §36B(f)(3).
5. Information Reporting for Affordable Insurance Exchanges, 26 CFR Part 1, 79 Fed. Reg. 26113 (May 7, 2014).
6. *Id.*

Exchanges must send monthly reports to the IRS and annual reports to the IRS and applicable taxpayers. Cumulative monthly reports are due on or before the fifteenth of the month following the month of coverage; annual reports are due on or before January 31st of the year following the coverage year being reported.[1] These monthly and annual reports provide information regarding the taxpayer and related individuals receiving Exchange coverage, including the monthly amount of any advance premium credit payments; specifics relating to the applicable benchmark plan, including the monthly premium; and identifying information regarding the insurer, plan, and Exchange.[2] In addition, monthly reports provide employment specifics (to the extent provided to the Exchange) for the taxpayer, spouse, and each individual covered by the qualified health plan along with an indication of whether an employer offered minimum essential coverage and, if so, the employee contribution for self-only coverage and the Exchange's determination of whether the employer coverage was affordable and provided minimum value. Monthly reports also indicate whether covered family members are the taxpayer's dependents; provide the taxpayer's unique Exchange account number; and list individuals granted exemptions from coverage under the individual mandate, including the exemption certificate number.[3]

Form 1095-A is an information statement used by Exchanges to report individual Exchange coverage to the IRS, and to individuals for purposes of claiming the premium tax credit. It includes the monthly premium used to compute the taxpayer's advance premium tax credit, the total monthly premium for the coverage of the taxpayer or family member, and the amount of the advance credit payments. The IRS has clarified in FAQs that taxpayers should use the information on Form 1095-A to compute the premium tax credit on their tax return and to reconcile the advance credit payments made on their behalf with the amount of the actual premium tax credit, which is reported on Form 8962.

633. What is the biggest loophole in the law as to exchange purchased health insurance?

This loophole is an intentional attempt to assist those who temporarily cannot afford the exchange health insurance they purchased. The result is that insureds receiving subsidies for their health insurance purchased on an exchange need only pay premiums for nine months for twelve months of health insurance coverage. As a result, providers may inadvertently give uncompensated care for up to two months per year for such insureds. Under the law,[4] families who obtain subsidized health plan coverage through an exchange and fail to pay their premiums have a three-month grace period to pay the premiums[5] due before the policy is cancelled.[6]

Thus, doctors and hospitals who treat patients with such subsidized exchange health insurance could find themselves liable for uncompensated treatment costs due to the healthcare reform law. The three-month grace period was meant to ensure continuity of care for low-income families

---

1.   Information Reporting for Affordable Insurance Exchanges, 26 CFR Part 1, 79 Fed. Reg. 26113, 26115 (May 7, 2014).
2.   Treas. Reg. §§1.36B-5(b) and 1.36B-5(e)(1).
3.   Treas. Reg. §1.36B-5(b)(2).
4.   PPACA §1412(c)(2)(B)(iv)(II).
5.   45 CFR §§156.270(d).
6.   76 Fed. Reg. 41866; 45 CFR §§155.400, 155.430 & 156.270 available at https://www.federalregister.gov/articles/2012/03/27/2012-6125/patient-protection-and-affordable-care-act-establishment-of-exchanges-and-qualified-health-plans#h-165. (Last accessed August 11, 2019).

who might be between jobs and could not afford to pay their premiums for a few weeks. However, it also creates a loophole for insureds who want to game the system. Insurers are responsible only for paying claims during the first month of this three-month grace period. During months two and three, families are asked to pay their hospital and doctor's bills (or their delinquent insurance premium) if they seek health care services. However, if they do not pay either bill, providers will not be paid for the cost of the treatment.[1]

Providers might be unable to avoid treating exchange patients, even if they discover they will not be paid if the delinquent premiums are not paid. Contracts by providers with large health insurers often include an "all-products" clause, which requires that doctors treat any patients covered under the health plan. Doctors have legal and ethical obligations not to abandon their patients during course of treatment.

In a notice published in the Federal Register,[2] HHS acknowledged that nonpayment of premiums for subsidized exchange policies would "increase uncertainty for providers and increase the burden of uncompensated care." HHS officials said that the agency will "monitor this issue moving forward and will continue to work on the development of policies to prevent misuse of the grace period."

Persons who have delinquent exchange insurance premiums would face tax penalties for any advance payment of premium tax credits paid on their behalf when the individual did not pay for coverage, but they would not receive a fine, a premium rate increase, or a repayment order. They could also enroll in another subsidized exchange policy the next year even if they never pay all or a part of the three months of missed premiums.

Here is how this three-month grace period works, according to examples 2 and 3 in the summary of the regulations[3]

> *Example 2:* Individual misses $50 payment that is due February 28 for March coverage and misses $50 payment that is due March 31st for April coverage. Individual pays $150 on April 30 for March, April, and May coverage.

- Issuer adjudicates claims for March.

- Coverage continues for April and May (second and third months of the grace period), but:

  ○ providers are notified of the potential for a denied claim;

  ○ issuer pends claims for services performed in April and May until individual pays outstanding premiums;

  ○ individual has paid full premium for March, April, and May as is eligible for premium tax credit for March, April, and May.

1.　45 CFR §§156.270(d)(3) provides that QHP issuers notify providers who submit claims for services rendered during the second and third months of the premium grace period that any such claims will be pended, and potentially not reimbursed by the QHP issuer if the individual does not settle outstanding premium payments.

2.　Id.

3.　Summary, Establishment of Exchanges and Qualified Health Plans; Exchange Standards for Employers, 77 Fed. Reg. 18310 at 18427 (March 27, 2012) et seq. at https://www.federalregister.gov/articles/2012/03/27/2012-6125/patient-protection-and-affordable-care-act-establishment-of-exchanges-and-qualified-health-plans#h-166. (Last accessed August 11, 2019).

Example 3: Same facts as Example 1 except that individual does not pay enrollee's share of premium for March, April, or May.

- Coverage terminated retroactively to March 3.

- Issuer can deny claims for services rendered during April and May. Providers could then seek payment directly from the individual for any services provided during that time.

- Individual may have additional tax liability attributable to the $450 for the advance payment of the premium tax credit paid on his or her behalf for March's coverage. The exact amount of additional tax liability would be determined in accordance with the rules for tax credit reconciliation under section 36B of the Code.

634. What if a state did not create its own exchange?

If a state decided not to run its own exchange or did not meet minimum federal standards, HHS generally created a federal exchange in that state or could find a not-for-profit entity to run it. Twelve states have their own exchanges. Six states have state-federal partnership exchanges. In the rest of the states, HHS has set up the state marketplaces, which are called Federally Facilitated Exchanges (FFEs).

See Q 59.

635. When can individuals and businesses purchase insurance on the exchanges' open enrollment and special enrollment periods?

Absent an exception, one can only get exchange health insurance during an open enrollment period.

- The annual open enrollment period for 2015 began on November 15, 2014 and extended through February 15, 2015. Coverage was effective January 1, 2015, only for applications received by December 15, 2014.[1]

- For 2016, the open enrollment period ran from November 1, 2015 through January 31, 2016.[2]

- For 2017, the open enrollment period began on November 1, 2016 and ended on January 31, 2017.

- For 2018, originally, the open enrollment period for 2018 was going to be from November 1, 2017 through January 31, 2018. However, this was been changed by the Administration to a window from November 1, 2017 through December 15, 2017.

- In 2019, the enrollment periods was also shorter – running from November 1, 2018 to December 15, 2018. The Exchange will provide advance written notice to each enrollee about the annual open enrollment.[3]

---

1. 45 CFR §155.410(e).
2. 45 CFR §155.410(e)(2).
3. 45 CFR §155.410(d).

- For 2020, the enrollment periods are unchanged – running from November 1, 2019 to December 15, 2019.

But in some cases, one may still be able to get coverage after the end of the open enrollment period. First, Medicaid and the Children's Health Insurance Program, which have no limited enrollment periods and provide coverage to families and individuals with limited income or other reasons.

Second, Exchanges must offer special enrollment periods.[1] Under final Exchange regulations, the Exchanges must allow qualified individuals and enrollees to enroll in a QHP or change from one to another because of the following triggering events:[2]

- A qualified individual or dependent loses minimum essential coverage.[3]

- A qualified individual gains a dependent or becomes a dependent through marriage, birth, adoption, or placement for adoption.

- An individual, who was not previously a citizen, national, or lawfully present individual gains such status.

- A qualified individual's enrollment or non-enrollment in a QHP is unintentional, inadvertent, or erroneous and is the result of the error, misrepresentation, or inaction of the Exchange or HHS.

- An enrollee adequately demonstrates to the Exchange that the QHP in which he or she is enrolled substantially violated a material provision of its contract in relation to the enrollee.

- An individual is determined newly eligible or newly ineligible for advance payments of the premium tax credit or has a change in eligibility for cost-sharing reductions, regardless of whether such individual is already enrolled in a QHP. (The Exchange must permit individuals whose existing coverage through an eligible employer-sponsored plan will no longer be affordable or provide minimum value for his or her employer's upcoming plan year to access this special enrollment period prior to the end of his or her coverage through such eligible employer-sponsored plan).

- A qualified individual or enrollee gains access to new QHPs because of a permanent move.

- An Indian may enroll in a QHP or change from one to another one time per month.

- A qualified individual or enrollee demonstrates to the Exchange that the individual meets other exceptional circumstances (as defined by the Exchange).

---

1.   PPACA §1311(c)(6) (2010). Special enrollment periods include those specified in IRC §9801.
2.   45 CFR §155.420(d).
3.   Loss of minimum essential coverage does not include certain situations allowing for rescission. 45 CFR §155.420(e).

- The Exchange determines that a qualified individual or enrollee (or his or her dependent) was not enrolled in QHP coverage, was not enrolled in the QHP selected by the qualified individual or enrollee, or is eligible for but is not receiving advance payments of the premium tax credit or cost-sharing reductions as a result of misconduct by a "non-Exchange entity" (for example, someone fraudulently claiming to be an Exchange-approved agent or broker).

The special enrollment period generally is sixty days from the date of the triggering event.[1] Coverage must be effective as of the first day of the following month for elections made by the fifteenth of the preceding month and on the first day of the second following month for elections made between the sixteenth and the last day of a month. However, coverage must be effective on the date of birth, adoption, or placement for adoption (or foster care), when that is the special enrollment triggering event (unless the Exchange allows an individual to select the first of the month following one of these events as an effective date).[2] Final regulations provide an advance availability requirement, which allows individuals to select a QHP up to sixty days before and after certain triggering events, including a loss of minimum essential coverage.[3] The advance availability requirement is designed to help avoid any gap in coverage, but there are still scenarios under which a potential gap in coverage could arise.

636. What levels of health insurance are available on the exchanges?

The exchange (a/k/a "marketplace") plans will be health insurance offerings at bronze, silver, gold, or platinum level coverage (benefits that are actuarially equivalent to 60 percent, 70 percent, 80 percent, or 90 percent of the full actuarial benefits provided under the plan.[4] The higher the metal grade, the more the insurance will cost but the more healthcare it will pay for.

Individuals under thirty or who a hardship exemption may purchase a catastrophic plan (also known as "young invincibles" coverage).[5] Catastrophic plans must be purchased from an insurance company and are not available on the exchanges. Hardship exemptions can be applied for on the state exchange. If one receives and exemption, then that person has no liability for the individual mandate penalty.[6] A catastrophic plan generally requires you to pay all of your medical costs up to a certain amount, usually several thousand dollars. This limit is known as a deductible. After you reach your deductible, costs for essential health benefits are generally paid by the catastrophic plan.

Catastrophic plans usually have lower monthly premiums than a comprehensive plan. But they cover your costs only after you've used a lot of care. These plans basically protect you from worst-case scenarios like serious accidents or illnesses.

---

1.   45 CFR §155.420(c).
2.   45 CFR §155.420(b). For special effective dates in the case of birth, adoption, or marriage, see 45 CFR §155.420(b)(2).
3.   45 CFR §§155.420(c) and 155.420(d)(1).
4.   PPACA §1302(d).
5.   PPACA §1302(e).
6.   PPACA §1302(c)(1) and (e).

All marketplace plans have a maximum out-of-pocket cost no more than $8,150 for an individual and $16,300 for a family for 2020 (these dollar amounts are indexed) and must provide at least ten essential benefits as part of their covered benefits.

A catastrophic plan is one that provides coverage for essential health benefits and provides no benefit for any plan year until the individual has incurred cost-sharing expenses equal to the overall cost-sharing limit ($8,150 deductible for single coverage and $16,300 deductible for family coverage) for the plan year.[1] The deductible cannot apply to at least three primary care visits.

637. What subsidies are available for individuals purchasing health insurance on an exchange?

Health coverage is available at reduced or no cost for people with incomes below certain levels.

Examples of subsidized coverage include Medicaid and the Children's Health Insurance Program (CHIP). Marketplace insurance plans with premium tax credits are sometimes known as subsidized coverage too.

- In states that have expanded Medicaid coverage, the applicant's household income must be below 138 percent of the federal poverty level to qualify.

- In all states, household income must be between 100 percent and 400 percent of the federal poverty level to qualify for a premium tax credit that can lower your insurance costs.

The lower a person's income, the greater the subsidy will be.

638. If my spouse receives affordable insurance through his/her workplace, but family coverage is too expensive and my spouse does not elect to have it, can family members access health insurance subsidies through a health insurance exchange?

The answer in most cases is no. Whether an employees' family will be eligible for health premium subsidies is based on affordability of the employer-sponsored coverage provided. The IRS regulations clarify that affordability is based only on the cost of coverage for the individual employee, not on the cost of coverage for the family.

Thus, if the cost of employer-sponsored family coverage is prohibitive for the family, but the employee-only premium portion is affordable, federal subsidies will not be available to help buy insurance for the family through the health insurance marketplace. Reg. §1.36B-2(c)(3)(v)(A)(2) states: "Except as provided in paragraph (c)(3)(v)(A)(3) of this section, an eligible employer-sponsored plan is affordable for a related individual if the portion of the annual premium the employee must pay for self-only coverage does not exceed the required contribution percentage, as described in paragraph (c)(3)(v)(A)(1) of this section." That percentage is 9.86 percent of

---

1.   PPACA §1302(c)(1) and (e); IRC Sec. 223(c)(2)(A)(ii).

family income. In other words, if the employee is eligible for minimum essential coverage that is affordable for the employee, family members also are treated eligible for affordable minimum essential coverage, regardless of its cost for the family.[1]

639. What is the Effect of the Supreme Court Upholding Exchange Health Insurance Subsidies in *King v. Burwell*?

Premium subsidies will continue in all states' health insurance exchanges, including those run by the federal government, the U.S. Supreme Court decided by a vote of six to three in *King v. Burwell*.[2] The Court ruled that the healthcare law allows Americans in all states with household incomes from 133 to 400 percent of federal poverty level, not just those that established their own exchanges, to receive the subsidies. The plaintiffs argued that the statutory language provides that health insurance premium subsidies are available only to those who enroll through an "exchange established by the state." The federal government, however, argued that the law's purpose is to allow Americans in every state to be eligible for exchange subsidies.

Chief Justice John Roberts and Justice Anthony Kennedy were the swing votes in the case, siding with the more liberal justices. The three dissenters were Justices Antonin Scalia, Samuel Alito, and Clarence Thomas.

In 2014, approximately 6.4 million Americans received the subsidies in the thirty-four states that don't have their own exchanges, in many cases relying on them to afford their health insurance, according to HHS. "Congress passed the Affordable Care Act to improve health insurance markets, not to destroy them," Roberts wrote in the opinion. "If at all possible, we must interpret the act in a way that is consistent with the former, and avoids the latter."

The Court's majority did not view the phrase "exchange established by the state" in isolation. Instead, they looked at the broader context and structure of the law. "In this instance, the context and structure of the Act compel us to depart from what would otherwise be the most natural reading of the pertinent statutory phrase," Justice Roberts wrote in the majority opinion. If a state chooses not to follow the directive to establish an Exchange, the Act tells the Secretary of Health and Human Services to establish "such Exchange."[3] By using the words "such Exchange," the Act indicates that State and Federal Exchanges should be the same.

Roberts stated that the subsidies "are necessary for the federal exchanges to function like their state exchange counterparts, and to avoid the type of calamitous result that Congress plainly meant to avoid." The Court stated that "the words of a statute must be read in their context and with a view to their place in the overall statutory scheme." The Court reasoned that eliminating subsidies in states not establishing their own exchange would likely create "death spirals" that Congress designed the Act to avoid because fewer people would purchase exchange insurance, and they would tend to be the unhealthiest, which would drive prices, making the insurance even less affordable. The Court stated:

---

1.   *See* Reg. §1.36B-2(c)(3)(v)(D), Example 2.
2.   No. 14–114 (June 25, 2015).
3.   42 U.S.C §18041.

"It is implausible that Congress meant the Act to operate in this manner. Congress made the guaranteed issue and community rating requirements applicable in every State in the Nation. But those requirements only work when combined with the coverage requirement and the tax credits. So it stands to reason that Congress meant for those provisions to apply in every State as well."

The justices declined to apply the *Chevron* doctrine, which provides that federal agencies' interpretation of the law is given deference when the agency in question has expertise in the subject matter. The Court's majority said that it is extremely unlikely Congress would have delegated interpretation of the law to the IRS because the IRS "has no expertise in crafting health insurance policy." The IRS regulation interprets the statute as making tax credits available on "an Exchange,"[1] "regardless of whether the Exchange is established and operated by a State . . . or by HHS."[2] The Fourth Circuit, reaching the same conclusion as the Supreme Court, had relied on the *Chevron* doctrine to uphold the IRS regulations.

While this issue has been settled, the legal challenges to the Affordable Care Act have not ceased. Currently there is a lawsuit by twenty state attorneys-general challenging the constitutionality of the Affordable Care Act. The plaintiffs of *Texas, et. al. v. HHS* argue that because of the repeal of the Individual Mandate tax penalty, it causes the entire Affordable Care Act to be invalid. The case is currently in the District Court of the Northern District of Texas.

640. What is the current status of lawsuits against the Affordable Care Act – *Texas v. United States*?

Texas v. United States is a lawsuit relating to the the constitutionality of the Individual Mandate and by extension, the constitutionality of the entire Affordable Care Act. Twenty state attorneys general and governors (all Republicans), later joined by two individuals, filed a lawsuit in February 2018 after Congressional action in the tax reform bill brought the Individual Mandate penalty to zero in December 2017. The states bringing the action include: Texas, Wisconsin, Alabama, Arkansas, Arizona, Florida, Georgia, Indiana, Kansas, Louisiana, Mississippi, Missouri, Nebraska, North Dakota, South Carolina, South Dakota, Tennessee, Utah, West Virginia, and Maine (via Governor Paul LePage). The argument is that the penalty-less mandate is no longer enforceable as a tax and therefore is no longer valid. The argument continues that entire ACA relies on the Individual Mandate; therefore, the rest of the Affordable Care Act should also be struck down.

Historically, the constitutionality of the Individual Mandate has been upheld. In June 2012, the Supreme Court released its decision in *National Federation of Independent Businesses (NFIB) v. Sebelius*, the first of a number of Supreme Court decisions on the ACA. In that decision, the Supreme Court upheld the individual mandate but struck down the law's mandatory Medicaid expansion. In upholding the individual mandate by a 5-4 vote, the Court, led by Chief Justice John Roberts, rejected an argument that the mandate was permissible under Congress' power to regulate interstate commerce. Instead, the Court construed the mandate as a tax and decided that is was valid under Congress' authority to tax and spend. The opinion pointed

---

1.   Treas. Reg. §1.36B–2.
2.   45 CFR §155.20.

out that the individual mandate looked and operated like a tax and reached the conclusion that Congress could not force people to purchase health insurance but could tax those who fail to purchase the insurance. The Court did not decide whether the Individual Mandate was legally severable from the rest of the Affordable Care Act. The Eleventh Circuit, however, has held that the individual mandate, while unconstitutional, was severable from the rest of the ACA. The court found that the loss of the individual mandate did not prevent the ACA's remaining provisions from being fully operative and, thus, it was irrelevant that the ACA did not include a severability clause.

In May 2018, 17 Democratic state attorneys general, led by California, were allowed to intervene in the lawsuit to defend the ACA in its entirety. In June 2018, the Department of Justice (DOJ) in a unique turn of events, decided not to defend the constitutionality of the mandate and noted its belief that certain additional provisions of the ACA could not be severed from the mandate.

In December 2018, Judge Reed O'Connor of the Northern District of Texas agreed with the plaintiffs and held the entire Affordable Care Act to be unconstitutional. The case has been appealed to the Fifth Circuit by the Department of Justice and Democratic attorneys general. Since then, Maine was allowed to withdraw as a plaintiff, and four additional attorneys general and the U.S. House of Representatives have been allowed to intervene to defend the ACA.

In late March 2019, the Justice Department filed a statement with the Fifth Circuit changing its position to fully agree with the district court's decision that the entire ACA should be invalidated. The action of the Justice Department caused wonder as to whether there would be a replacement for the Affordable Care Act if it was invalidated by the courts.

On July 9, 2019, the U.S. Court of Appeals for the 5th Circuit began hearing oral arguments in *Texas v. U.S.,* the next round of litigation challenging the Affordable Care Act (ACA).

The 5th Circuit is not bound by the trial court's decision interpreting the law and will consider the case anew on appeal.

There are three key issues that the court may consider:

1.   whether the parties have **standing** to invoke the court's jurisdiction on appeal to challenge the Affordable Care Act

2.   whether the ACA's individual mandate, as amended by the TCJA, is **constitutional** after the penalty was set to zero; and

3.   if the mandate is unconstitutional, **whether it can be severed** from the rest of the ACA, or on the other hand, whether other provisions of the ACA also must be invalidated.

There is no deadline by which the court must issue a decision, but it could come as early as fall 2019. A number of results could occur:

- If the court finds that the individual mandate is unconstitutional and invalidates only that mandate, essentially nothing changes and the Affordable Care Act will continue to exist as it does today as amended by the TCJA (zero penalty), The Individual Mandate would be without an enforceable mandate but the rest of the ACA would remain.

- If the court adopts the position that the federal government took during the trial court proceedings and invalidates the individual mandate as well as the protections for people with pre-existing conditions, then federal funding for premium subsidies and the Medicaid expansion would stand, and it would be up to states whether to reinstate the insurance protections.

- If the court decides that the ENTIRE Affordable Care Act is unconstitutional, this will result in significant consequences, affecting nearly everyone in some fashion. The number individuals under the age of sixty-five who are uninsured decreased by nearly 20 million people from the inception of the ACA in 2010 until today. In addition the Affordable Care Act changed the scope of the individual insurance market by creating protections for pre-existing conditions, extending coverage to dependent children until age twenty-six, providing premium subsidies for those who could not afford insurance, extending Medicaid coverage to millions of people, making insurance available through the exchanges, expanding coverage of preventive service, phasing out the Medicare prescription "donut hole", as well as other provisions. All of these provisions could be eliminated if the District Court's opinion is upheld

There is no deadline by which the court must issue a decision, but it could come as early as fall 2019. It is likely that any decision will be appealed to the U.S. Supreme Court. The decision of the District Court invalidating the Affordable Care Act has not been implemented and the Act is still in effect while the case is pending.

641. Can pharmaceutical companies help pay for copays and deductibles for prescription drugs for exchange-purchased insurance; can hospitals and other healthcare providers make premium payments for individuals with exchange health insurance?

Pharmaceutical companies can help cover the cost of copayments on brand-name drugs for patients who get insurance through qualified health plans sold on the insurance exchanges (marketplaces) through coupons and other methods. While drug companies cannot pay any copayments for drugs paid by Medicare (such payments would be an illegal kickback for benefits paid by a federal program), HHS has determined that health insurance offered on the exchanges is not a "federal health care program," whether state run or federally assisted.

However, HHS says that hospitals, other healthcare providers, and other "commercial entities" should not make premium payments to health insurance issuers for qualified health plans purchased on an exchange. HHS states that this practice could skew the insurance risk pool and create an uneven field in the exchanges (marketplaces). "HHS discourages this practice and encourages issuers to reject such third-party payments. HHS intends to monitor this practice and to take appropriate action, if necessary."[1]

However, despite this CMS this statement, seemingly a hospital could assist an uninsured patient with the purchase of exchange insurance. A tax-exempt hospital should consider the relationship of any premium assistance to its mission and charitable purposes and structure such assistance to avoid private benefit issues. Premium assistance provided to patients may also result in tax liabilities for the patients, and providers may be required to report each patient's premium assistance amounts on a Form 1099-MISC.

642. What consumer-assistance tools must exchanges provide?

Each state health insurance exchange (marketplace) must provide a variety of consumer-assistance tools, including the following:

- <u>Call center</u>

    - Toll-free call centers to address the needs of those seeking assistance

- <u>Internet websites</u> providing a variety of features, including comparative information on available QHPs, certain financial information, and information about the navigator and call center

    - Providing standardized comparative information on each available QHP, which may include differential display of standardized options on consumer-facing plan comparison and shopping tools, and at a minimum includes:

        - Premium and cost-sharing information

        - Summary of benefits and coverage

        - Identification of whether the QHP is a bronze, silver, gold, or platinum level plan as defined by section 1302(d) of the Affordable Care Act , or a catastrophic plan as defined by section 1302(e)

        - Results of enrollee satisfaction survey

        - Quality ratings

        - Information on the certifying, recertifying, and decertifying of qualified health plans (QHPs)

        - Medical loss ratio information

        - Provider directory

---

1. See Third Party Payments of Premiums for Qualified Health Plans in the Marketplaces (Nov. 4, 2013) at http://www.cms.gov/CCIIO/ Resources/Fact-Sheets-and-FAQs/Downloads/third-party-qa-11-04-2013.pdf. However, the IRS permits these payments if made with after tax dollars. (Last accessed August 11, 2019).

- Financial information

    - Average cost of licensing

    - Regulatory fees, payments, administrative costs, and monies lost

- Provides information about navigators

- Makes information available by electronic means a calculator to facilitate the comparison of available QHPs after the application of any advance payment of the premium tax credit and any cost-sharing reductions

- Accessibility

- Consumer assistance function

- Outreach and education activities[1]

643. Which decisions of the healthcare marketplace can be appealed?

The following kinds of decisions made by the Health Insurance Marketplaces can be appeal if an individual disagrees with the decisions:

- Eligibility to by a plan, including Catastrophic coverage

- Ability to enroll in a plan outside of an Open Enrollment period

- Eligibility for lower costs based on income

- Amount of savings entitled to

- Reduction in the savings eligibility

- Eligibility for Medicare or Children's Health Insurance Program (CHIP)

    - Applies only in states where the Federally-Facilitated Marketplace makes Medicaid eligibility decision (Alabama, Alaska, Arkansas, Louisiana, Montana, New Jersey, Tennessee, West Virginia and Wyoming)

- Eligibility for exemption from having health insurance

- Timeliness of Marketplace decision on eligibility

644. Which states do not use the healthcare.gov site?

The following states do not use the federal site and individuals from those states should will use these sites to enroll in health care coverage:

- California's site is "Covered California"

    - https://www.coveredca.com/

---

1.   45 CFR §155.205.

- Colorado's site: "Connect for Health Colorado"
  - http://connectforhealthco.com/
- Connecticut: "Access Health CT"
  - http://www.accesshealthct.com/
- District of Columbia: "DC Health Link"
  - https://dchealthlink.com/
- Idaho: "Your Health Idaho"
  - http://www.yourhealthidaho.org/
- Maryland: Maryland Health Connection
  - http://www.marylandhealthconnection.gov/
- Massachusetts: Health Connector
  - https://www.mahealthconnector.org/
- Minnesota: MNsure
  - http://mn.gov/hix/
- New Mexico
  - https://bewellnm.com/
- New York: New York State of Health
  - http://nystateofhealth.ny.gov/
- Rhode Island: HealthSource RI
  - http://www.healthsourceri.com/
- Vermont: Vermont Health Connect
  - http://healthconnect.vermont.gov/
- Washington: Washington Healthplanfinder
  - http://www.wahealthplanfinder.org/

645. How are health care plans on the exchanges rated?

Healthcare.gov is operating a pilot program to rate policies offered though a star rating program. For the 2019 plan year, HealthCare.gov is continuing a pilot program to present health insurance plan quality ratings (or "star ratings") for some plans.

Plans in Michigan, Montana, New Hampshire, Virginia, and Wisconsin will feature the quality ratings this year.

Each rated health plan has been assigned an "Overall" quality rating of one to five stars, with five being the highest. This accounts for member experience, medical care, and health plan administration. This is intended to be an objective way to quickly compare plans, based on quality.

RATING CRITERIA:

The plans' overall rating is based on three categories, each with its own star rating:

- Member Experience — based on member satisfaction with:

    o   Health care

    o   Doctors

    o   Ease of getting appointments and services

- Medical Care — rating of the network providers on managing care including:

    o   Regular screenings, vaccines, and other general services

    o   Monitoring of health conditions

- Plan Administration — based on

    o   Customer service

    o   Access to necessary information

    o   Network providers ordering appropriate tests and treatment

The ratings are based on plans provided in 2019. Healthcare.gov cautions plans not yet rated is not an indication of poor quality but that they might be new or have low enrollment.

The 2017 pilot was a two-state pilot using Virginia and Wisconsin plans.

646. What changes have been effected on the exchanges for American Indians and Alaska Natives?

American Indians or Alaska Natives have new health coverage benefits and protections in the Health Insurance Marketplace.

Health Coverage for American Indians or Alaska Natives

- Benefits are available to members or federally recognized tribes or Alaska Native Claims Settlement Act (ANCSA) Corporation shareholders.

- ○ As of this writing, the Bureau of Indian Affairs recognizes 573 tribes within the United States. This information can be found here: http://www.ncsl.org/research/state-tribal-institute/list-of-federal-and-state-recognized-tribes.aspx.

- Benefits are also available to those of Indian descent or eligible for services from the Indian Health Service, a tribal program or an urban Indian health program.

- Federally recognized tribe members ANCSA shareholders can enroll in the Marketplace at any time and can change plans as frequently as once per month.

Special Health Coverage for American Indians or Alaska Natives

- Marketplace health insurance plans.

  - ○ Purchase of a marketplace plan with income between 100 percent and 300 percent of the federal poverty level offers eligibility of a "zero cost sharing" plan which eliminates out of pocket costs such as copays, coinsurance and deductibles, regardless of income.

  - ○ Services from Indian Health Care provider also has no copays, coinsurance or deductibles, regardless of income.

  - ○ No open enrollment restrictions – can enroll at any time and change plans monthly.

- Medicaid & CHIP benefits for Tribal members and Alaska natives.

  - ○ No premiums or out of pocket costs for Medicaid.

- Enrollment in a private plan through the Marketplace offers the following benefits.

  - ○ Can continue to get services form Indian Health Service, tribal health plans (tribal 638 programs or clinics) or urban Indian Health Programs.

  - ○ Can also get services from any provider on the plan.

Exchange Navigators

647. What is the role of the exchange navigators?

Healthcare reform requires each state exchange to establish a navigator program, under which it awards grants to public or private entities to carry out certain navigator functions.[1] HHS regulations set forth the eligibility requirements for navigators and the duties they are expected to perform. To be eligible, an entity must demonstrate that it has existing relationships or could readily establish relationships with employers, employees, consumers, or self-employed individuals likely to be eligible for enrollment in a Qualified Health Plan (QHP); must meet

---

1.   PPACA §1311(i).

licensing, certification, or other standards imposed by the state or exchange; and must not have a conflict of interest.

Exchanges are required to include entities from at least two of a variety of categories, including community and consumer-focused not-for-profit groups; unions; trade, industry, and professional associations; and licensed agents and brokers. However, a navigator must not be a health insurer or receive any direct or indirect consideration from a health insurer.[1]

CMS announced on July 10, 2018, that they were reducing funding for the Navigators on the thirty-four exchanges. This is a 60 percent cut from the prior year and an 80 percent cut from the original funding. CMS has stated that the navigators have "failed to enroll a meaningful amount of people". It can be argued, however, that the role of the Navigator is to help individuals find insurance and the correct insurance, rather than merely signing people up. A Georgetown University study found that a Navigator spent one to two hours with each individual for an average of four-six people per day.

The five duties of a navigator are:

(1)   maintain expertise in eligibility, enrollment, and program specifications and conduct public education activities to raise awareness of the exchanges;

(2)   provide information and services in a fair, accurate, and impartial manner;

(3)   facilitate enrollment in QHPs;

(4)   provide referrals to any applicable consumer-assistance program or ombudsman in the case of grievances, complaints, or questions about health plans or coverage; and

(5)   provide information in a culturally and linguistically appropriate manner for the needs of the population being served by the exchange.[2]

648. What standards must navigators and non-navigator assistance personnel meet?

HHS regulations create standards for navigators and non-navigator assistance personnel in Federally Facilitated exchanges (FFEs) (including state-federal partnership exchanges) and for federally funded non-navigator assistance personnel in state-based exchanges.[3] State-based exchanges may, but need not, also establish non-navigator consumer assistance programs, which are funded by exchange establishment grants rather than navigator grants, to help provide outreach, education, and assistance to consumers. FFEs, other than certain state-federal partnership exchanges, likely will not include non-navigator assistance programs.

---

1.   45 CFR §155.210.
2.   45 CFR §155.210(e).
3.   PPACA; exchange Functions: Standards for Navigators and Non-navigator Assistance Personnel, 45 CFR Part 155, 78 Fed. Reg. 20581 (Apr. 5, 2013).

Navigators must have expertise in eligibility and enrollment rules and procedures but may not actually make eligibility determinations and may not select Qualified Health Plans (QHPs) for consumers or enroll applicants into QHPs.[1]

States and exchanges cannot prescribe licensing or certification standards for navigators that would conflict with healthcare reform; e.g., they cannot require navigators to be licensed agents or brokers or obtain errors and omissions insurance.[2] There are detailed conflict of interest standards applicable to navigator and non-navigator personnel.[3] State-based exchanges are not required to adopt these standards for their navigators or for non-navigator assistance personnel that are not federally funded, such as enrollment assisters, Certified Application counselors, and producers (insurance agents and brokers).

Agent and Broker Roles

649. What is the role of health insurance agents and brokers on the exchanges?

States may allow health insurance agents or brokers to:

(1)   enroll individuals and small employers in qualified health plans on an exchange; and

(2)   assist individuals in applying for premium tax credits and cost-sharing reductions in exchanges.[4]

In states where a federally-facilitated or state-federal partnership exchange marketplace is operating, all agents and brokers must register with CMS so that they may assist qualified individuals for individual marketplace coverage.[5]

Although agents and brokers may help qualified individuals enroll in a QHP through the exchange, they cannot perform eligibility determinations. Eligibility determinations must be made through the exchange, and the information collected cannot be accessed by insurers, agents, and brokers.[6] Agents and brokers are also permitted to assist individuals in applying for advance payments of the premium tax credit and cost-sharing reductions.[7]

---

1.   HHS Reg. §155.310(d); PPACA; exchange Functions: Standards for Navigators and Non-navigator Assistance Personnel, 45 CFR Part 155, 78 Fed. Reg. 20581, 20583 (Apr. 5, 2013).
2.   HHS Reg. §155.210(c)(2); PPACA; exchange Functions: Standards for Navigators and Non-navigator Assistance Personnel, 45 CFR Part 155, 78 Fed. Reg. 20581, 20585 (Apr. 5, 2013).
3.   HHS Reg. §155.215.
4.   PPACA §1312; 45 CFR §155.220.
5.   HHS Memo: Role of Agents, Brokers, and Web-Brokers in Health Insurance Marketplaces, I.A (May 1, 2013) at http://www.cms.gov/CCIIO/Resources/Regulations-and-Guidance/Downloads/agent-broker-5-1-2013.pdf. (Last accessed August 11, 2019).
6.   PPACA; Establishment of Exchanges and Qualified Health Plans; Exchange Standards for Employers, 77 Fed. Reg. 18310, 18425 (Mar. 27, 2012).
7.   45 CFR §155.220(a)(3).

650. What assistance is available for agents and brokers on the Exchange?

The number of registered brokers and agents on has declined sharply since 2017. In 2017, there were 65,300 agents/brokers, which declined to 49,100 in 2018. Agents and brokers actually account for 42 percent of all enrollment through the Exchanges. However, the drop in number of agents participating is blamed on the cost of coverage as well as the reduction in the amount of commissions.

For the agents and brokers that remain, the Exchanges offer a surprisingly rich amount of support at a dedicated resource page found at https://www.cms.gov/cciio/programs-and-initiatives/health-insurance-marketplaces/a-b-resources.html.

Depending on what is permitted by states, licensed agents and brokers may assist consumers determine their eligibility for insurance affordability programs, including advance payments of the premium tax credit and cost-sharing reductions, and enroll them in qualified health plans (QHPs). As indicated above, nearly half of enrollments on the Exchanges is done by agents/brokers, therefor it is obvious that the agents and brokers play a crucial role in educating consumers about the Marketplace, both during annual Open Enrollment and throughout the coverage year. Agents and brokers also help employers understand their options for enrolling in SHOP coverage and assist them and their employees through the SHOP application and enrollment process.

Some states have set up their own State-based individual and small business Marketplaces, while the federal government runs the Individual Marketplace through HealthCare.gov and/or SHOP in other states. Agents and brokers can help consumers apply for and choose insurance options in any state in which the agents and brokers have an active state license that is approved for a health-related line of authority, regardless of whether the Marketplace is operated by the state or federal government. Agents and brokers wanted to help people in on HealthCare.gov must complete registration and complete required training on an annual basis—prior to assisting consumers enroll in a plan. For 2019, the registration and training is available at the CMS Enterprise Portal found at https://portal.cms.gov/wps/portal/unauthportal/home/.

Other training for new and returning agents is available at https://www.cms.gov/CCIIO/Programs-and-Initiatives/Health-Insurance-Marketplaces/Plan-Year-2019-Registration-and-Training.html including guides for new and returning agents as well as Help On Demand. In addition, there is CMS Approved Vendor Training which allows agents and brokers to earn Continuing Education Credits. There are also periodic webinars as well as a resource center with notices including Eligibility, Special Enrollment Period Pre-enrollment Verification, Cross-Issuer, Data Matching, and Account Transfer notices. Agents and Brokers can also sign up for a periodic newsletter.

With the recent cut in funding for the Navigator program, the role of the agent and broker will be even more important to the success of the Marketplace.

651. What additional guidance has HHS issued about health insurance agents and brokers as to their role vis-à-vis the exchanges?

HHS has issued a memo focusing on the role of agents and brokers in FFEs and state-federal partnership FFEs. It also addresses certain questions related to state-based Exchanges.[1] It addresses, among others, the following issues.

Registration. In states where a Federally-Facilitated or State-Federal partnership marketplace is operating, all agents and brokers must register with CMS so that they may assist qualified individuals for individual marketplace coverage. Agents and brokers will continue to be appointed by insurers that will check licensure status and verify the agent's or broker's registration with exchanges. In states with an FFE or state-federal partnership FFE, all agents and brokers must register with HHS and complete an online training course to assist with individual coverage.[2] Agents and brokers working exclusively with employers in Federally Facilitated SHOP (FF-SHOP) exchanges (which may be combined with the regular exchange for individuals) are encouraged, but not required, to register and complete the training.

Two Website Pathways. Agents and brokers in FFEs and State-Federal partnership FFEs will be permitted to assist individuals and employers through two internet "pathways": (a) an insurer-based pathway that redirects to an exchange website; or (b) an exchange-based pathway that directly accesses an exchange website. Both pathways will allow agents and brokers to assist individuals and employers to receive eligibility determinations, compare plans, and enroll in coverage, and will transmit agent and broker identifying information to the appropriate insurer to facilitate payment.[3] The individual will create a username and password on the exchange website and should not disclose this information to anyone.

Disclosure of All Available QHPs. HHS does not require agents and brokers to display all QHPs or to facilitate enrollment in all QHPs, but state-based exchanges may require agents and brokers to do so. HHS expects agents or brokers using the FFE insurer-based pathway to inform individuals when they are providing information for QHPs with which they have a business relationship, and that other choices and information can be directly accessed through the exchange website. The FFE exchange-based pathway will display all QHPs.

Broker/Agent Compensation. State-based exchanges may establish their own rules for compensation of agents or brokers, including parameters for direct compensation from an exchange or through insurer-paid commissions. HHS also notes that, if insurers will be paying commissions to agents or broker, it has encouraged state-based exchanges to consider providing information to insurers (agent or broker identifying information) to facilitate these transactions. FFEs and state-federal partnership FFEs will not establish a commission schedule or pay commissions directly to agents or brokers. The amount and terms of commissions will be negotiated by the insurer and the agent or broker. The QHP certification standards require QHP insurers to pay the same agent and broker compensation for enrollment in similar health plans offered

---

1.   HHS Memo: Role of Agents, Brokers, and Web-Brokers in Health Insurance Marketplaces (May 1, 2013) at http://www.cms.gov/CCIIO/ Resources/Regulations-and-Guidance/Downloads/agent-broker-5-1-2013.pdf. (Last accessed September 11, 2018).
2.   Id.
3.   Id. at I and its Appendix.

inside and outside of FFEs and state-partnership FFEs. However, agents and brokers acting as navigators may not receive compensation from insurers.[1]

<u>Web-Brokers</u>. This HHS memo also addresses the role of web-brokers (i.e., agents or brokers who enroll individuals through public websites). State-based exchanges are permitted to work with web-brokers and that, with respect to FFEs, HHS is developing the ability to support integration between a web-broker's website and the FFE website to allow individuals to start shopping on the web-broker's website, connect to the FFE website to complete eligibility applications, and return to the web-broker's site to shop for QHPs. The HHS memo also includes information on how QHPs may be displayed on a web-broker's website and certain other relevant issues.

652. What special rules apply to insurance agents and brokers assisting taxpayers on the Exchanges?

States may permit agents and brokers to assist employers and employees enrolling in QHPs.[2] Although agents and brokers may help qualified individuals enroll in a QHP through the Exchange, they cannot perform eligibility determinations. Eligibility determinations must be made through the Exchange, and information collected must be firewalled from insurers, agents, and brokers.[3] Agents and brokers are permitted to assist individuals in applying for advance payments of the premium tax credit and cost-sharing reductions.[4] CMS has a special webpage with resources for agents and brokers.[5]

Agents and brokers are appointed by insurers that are responsible to check licensure status and verify the agent's or broker's registration with Exchanges.[6] In addition, in states with federally run or assisted Exchanges, all agents and brokers must register with HHS and complete an online training course to assist with individual coverage.[7] Agents and brokers working with employers in a Federally Facilitated SHOP (FF-SHOP) are encouraged, but not required, to register and complete the training.[8]

Agents and brokers in federally assisted exchanges can assist individuals and employers two ways. They can use an insurer-based pathway (initiated through an insurer's website) that redirects to an Exchange website or can use an Exchange-based pathway that directly accesses an Exchange website. Both pathways will allow agents and brokers to assist individuals and employers to receive eligibility determinations, compare plans, and enroll in coverage, and will transmit agent- and broker-identifying information to the appropriate insurer to facilitate

---

1.   *Id.*
2.   45 CFR §155.220.
3.   Establishment of Exchanges and Qualified Health Plans; Exchange Standards for Employers, 77 Fed. Reg. 18310, 18425 (Mar. 27, 2012).
4.   45 CFR §155.220(a)(3).
5.   Resources for Agents and Brokers in the Health Insurance Marketplace at https://www.cms.gov/cciio/programs-and-initiatives/health-insurance-marketplaces/a-b-resources.html. (Last accessed August 11, 2019).
6.   Frequently Asked Questions Regarding Agents and Brokers, https://www.cms.gov/CCIIO/Programs-and-Initiatives/Health-Insurance-Marketplaces/Downloads/Agent-Broker-Compensation-and-Discriminatory-Marketing-Practices.pdf. (Last accessed August 11, 2019).
7.   HHS Memo: Role of Agents, Brokers, and Web-Brokers in Health Insurance Marketplaces at https://www.cms.gov/CCIIO/Programs-and-Initiatives/Health-Insurance-Marketplaces/Downloads/Agent-Broker-Compensation-and-Discriminatory-Marketing-Practices.pdf. (Last accessed August 11, 2019).
8.   See Frequently Asked Questions Regarding Agents and Brokers, at https://www.cms.gov/CCIIO/Programs-and-Initiatives/Health-Insurance-Marketplaces/Downloads/Agent-Broker-Compensation-and-Discriminatory-Marketing-Practices.pdf. (Last accessed August 11, 2019).

payment. Agents and brokers must register with HHS before they may assist qualified individuals in enrolling through an FFE.

In addition to agents and brokers, there are a variety of other assisters that provide help to people researching and enrolling in health care plans.

Navigators

Section 1311(i) of the Affordable Care Act (ACA) requires health insurance marketplaces to establish a navigator program. Navigators are organizations that must have (or can readily build) relationships with employers, employees, uninsured and underinsured consumers, or self-employed individuals who likely qualify to enroll in qualified health plans (QHPs). The navigator program was modeled after other successful outreach efforts for public coverage programs, such as Medicaid, CHIP, and the State Health Insurance Assistance Programs (for Medicare). These are paid by state and federal grants and cannot be compensated by insurance companies. They currently make about $30,000 a year. The navigators are being funded for thirty-four states with federally run or partnership exchanges.

Some of the duties of the navigators include:

- conduct public education activities to raise awareness of the availability of QHPs;

- distribute fair and impartial information concerning enrollment in QHPs and the availability of premium tax credits and cost-sharing reductions;

- facilitate enrollment in QHPs; and

- provide information in a manner that is culturally and linguistically appropriate to the needs of the population being served by the marketplace. Navigators may be organizations such as trade, industry, and professional associations; chambers of commerce; ranching and farming organizations; and community and consumer-focused nonprofit organizations.

CMS intends to fund the navigator program in the thirty-four states with a federally facilitated marketplace for 2020 and 2021 at $10 million per year, for a total of $20 million. The amount of funding for navigators is unchanged from last year's significant cuts. This $10 million in annual funding is down from a high of $63 million from 2017. The Trump Administration has reduced the Navigator program by 84 percent since taking office. For 2019, the number of navigator organizations has declined by about 50 percent from eighty organizations to thirty-nine in 2019. Three states (Iowa, Montana, and New Hampshire) had no navigators at all, and entire areas of some states (such as Cleveland and Dallas) are not served by the navigator program.

- <u>Certified Application Counselor (CAC)</u>. They are similar to Navigators but are not required to perform outreach activities and will not have to engage in post-enrollment assistance, although they can. Generally, they have the role of helping people enroll. The Federally-facilitated Marketplace designates organizations to certify application counselors who perform many of the same functions as Navigators and non-Navigator assistance personnel—including educating consumers and helping them complete an application for coverage. An online application for organizations who want to become Marketplace-designated organizations that can certify application counselors can be found at the link below. These groups might include community health centers or other health care providers, hospitals, or social service agencies.

- <u>Insurance Brokers and Agents</u>. They are also certified by the exchanges but will make recommendations based on an enrollee's specific situation. Agents and brokers will continue to work with clients after the purchase as well.

653. What are the rules regarding insurance broker and agent compensation?

State-run exchanges establish their own rules for compensation of agents or brokers, including parameters for direct compensation from an Exchange or through insurer-paid commissions. If insurers pay commissions to agents or brokers, HHS recommends state-based exchanges provide agent or broker identifying information to insurers to facilitate these transactions. Federally-assisted exchanges do not establish a commission schedule or pay commissions directly to agents or brokers. The amount and terms of commissions will be negotiated by the insurer and the agent or broker. HHS notes that the QHP certification standards require QHP insurers to pay the same agent and broker compensation for enrollment in similar health plans offered inside and outside the federally run or assisted exchanges.[1] Although the SHOPs have been eliminated, in the past insurers were also responsible for paying commissions to brokers selling products in the FF-SHOPs, and insurers were required to pay brokers an amount equal to what the insurer pays in the small group market outside the federally run or assisted SHOPs.

654. Are there special rules for brokers operating on-line, i.e., web-brokers?

Yes. HHS has addressed the role of web-brokers (i.e., agents or brokers who enroll individuals through public-facing websites).[2] Among other things, state-based and federally run and assisted Exchanges are permitted to work with web-brokers. HHS guidance includes information on how QHPs may be displayed on a web-broker's website and certain other relevant issues.[3] HHS regulations provide which qualified health plans (QHPs, and what specific information about them) must be displayed on web-brokers' websites.[4]

---

1. HHS Memo: Role of Agents, Brokers, and Web-Brokers in Health Insurance Marketplaces (May 1, 2013) at https://www.cms.gov/CCIIO/Resources/Regulations-and-Guidance/Downloads/agent-broker-5-1-2013.pdf. (Last accessed August 11, 2019).
2. HHS Reg. §155.220; HHS Memo: Role of Agents, Brokers, and Web-Brokers in Health Insurance Marketplaces (May 1, 2013) at https://www.cms.gov/CCIIO/Resources/Regulations-and-Guidance/Downloads/agent-broker-5-1-2013.pdf. (Last accessed August 11, 2019).
3. HHS Memo: Role of Agents, Brokers, and Web-Brokers in Health Insurance Marketplaces (May 1, 2013) at https://www.cms.gov/CCIIO/Resources/Regulations-and-Guidance/Downloads/agent-broker-5-1-2013.pdf. (Last accessed August 11, 2019).
4. HHS Reg. §155.220(c).

655. What other existing organizations will assist individuals on the exchanges?

State Health Insurance Assistance Programs (often called SHIPs) help Medicare beneficiaries understand their Medicare plan options and enroll. Government agencies, such as those that administer the Medicaid and Children's Health Insurance Programs (CHIP), help people sign up for those benefits, and community-based organizations also assist with Medicaid and CHIP enrollment. These entities will also help applicants who don't qualify for Medicaid or CHIP get coverage and premium assistance through the exchange.

PART XI: THE EMPLOYER MANDATE

(a/k/a Shared Responsibility or Play or Pay Rules)

Overview

656. What are the Shared Responsibility Provisions under the Internal Revenue Code and regulations?

The employer shared responsibility provisions[1] were added under section 4980H of the Internal Revenue Code by the Affordable Care Act and supported by applicable regulations. Under these provisions, certain employers (called applicable large employers or ALEs) must either offer health coverage that is "affordable" and that provides "minimum value" to their full-time employees (and offer coverage to the full-time employees' dependents), or potentially make an employer shared responsibility payment to the IRS, if at least one of their full-time employees receives a premium tax credit for purchasing individual coverage on a Health Insurance Marketplace Exchange.[2]

Whether an employer is an ALE and is therefore subject to the employer shared responsibility provisions depends on the size of its workforce.[3] In general, employers employing at least a certain threshold number of employees (generally fifty full-time employees including full-time equivalent employees, which means a combination of part-time employees that count as one or more full-time employees) are ALEs.[4] The vast majority of employers fall below the ALE size threshold and therefore are not subject to the employer shared responsibility provisions.

657. What topics are covered in the employer mandate regulations?

The employer mandate regulations are organized as follows:

- Definitions[5]

- Status as an applicable large employer and applicable large employer member[6]

- Determining Full-time employees[7]

- Assessable payments under Internal Revenue Code section 4980H(a)[8]

- Whether an employer is subject to assessable payments under Internal Revenue Code section 4980H(b)[9]

---

1. Shared Responsibility for Employers Regarding Health Coverage, 26 CFR Parts 1, 54, and 301, 79 Fed. Reg. 8543, 8577 (Feb. 12, 2014).
2. https://www.irs.gov/affordable-care-act/employers/questions-and-answers-on-employer-shared-responsibility-provisions-under-the-affordable-care-act. (Last accessed August 13, 2019).
3. Treas. Reg. §54.4980H-1(a)(24)(ii)(C).
4. IRS Notice 2013-45.
5. Reg. §54.4980H-1.
6. Reg. §54.4980H-2.
7. Reg. §54.4980H-3.
8. Reg. §54.4980H-4.
9. Reg. §54.4980H-5.

- Rules relating to the administration and assessment of assessable payments under Internal Revenue Code section 4980H.[1]

Definitions

658. What employers are subject to the employer mandate penalty?

For purposes of the mandate, employer includes all related employers, predecessors, and successors.

The controlled and affiliated service group rules apply in counting employees, as all members of such a group are treated as one employer.[2] An employer includes a predecessor and successor employer.[3] The regulations do provide specific rules for identifying a predecessor or successor employer. Rules for identifying successor employers have been developed in the employment tax context for determining when wages paid by a predecessor may be attributed to a successor employer.[4] However, Internal Revenue Code section 4980H does not incorporate the Separate Line of Business (SLOB) rules that allow separate testing for retirement plans. All employers (again including controlled group and affiliated service group members) that employ at least fifty full-time employees or an equivalent combination of full-time and part-time employees are subject to the Employer Shared Responsibility provisions, including for-profit, not-for-profit, and government entity employers.[5] "Disregarded entities" are not disregarded for Internal Revenue Code section 4980H purposes. The tax is imposed on the disregarded entity and not its owner(s).[6]

659. Do the employer shared responsibility rules apply to government units, and non-profit businesses?

Yes. There is no exclusion from the employer shared responsibility provisions for government entities. All employers that are ALEs are subject to the employer shared responsibility provisions, including federal, state, local, and Indian tribal government employers as well as non-profit nonprofit (whether or not a tax-exempt organization) employers.

660. What transition relief existed for the employer mandate penalty during 2014, 2015, and 2016?

As discussed above, the employer mandate was effective by statute in 2014 but the effective date was postponed until 2015. The final regulations provided additional transition relief for 2015 and 2016.[7] The regulations also provided special rules for fiscal year health plans, as discussed below.

---

1. Reg. §54.4980H-6.
2. IRC Sec. 4980H(c)(2)(C)(i); Treas. Reg. §54.4980H-1(a)(15).
3. Treas. Reg. §54.4980H-1(a)(15).
4. Reg. §31.3121(a)(1)-1(b); See also IRC Sec. 3121.
5. https://www.irs.gov/affordable-care-act/employers/questions-and-answers-on-employer-shared-responsibility-provisions-under-the-affordable-care-act (Last accessed August 13, 2019). (Current through March 26, 2019).
6. Reg. §301.7701-2(c)(2)(v)(A)(5).
7. See preamble to Shared Responsibility for Employers Regarding Health Coverage, 26 CFR Parts 1, 54, and 301, 79 Fed. Reg. 8543, 8569–8576 (Feb. 12, 2014).

Generally, if an ALE member fails to offer coverage to a full-time employee for any day of a calendar month, that employee is treated as not having been offered coverage during that entire month.[1] However, solely for purposes of January 2015, if an ALE member offered coverage to a full-time employee no later than the first day of the first payroll period that begins in January 2015, the employee will be treated as having been offered coverage for January 2015.[2]

The Applicable Large Employer (ALE) status (what triggers the potential application of the mandate) for a calendar year is generally based on the number of employees in the preceding calendar year.[3] Transition rules included noncalendar year health plans, the ability to count employees for less than twelve months in 2014 to determine applicable large employer status, initial offers of health coverage in 2015, dependent coverage, employers with at least fifty but less than 100 full-time and Full-Time Equivalent (FTE) employees, and reduction of the 95 percent offer of health coverage requirement to 70 percent for 2015.

To determine if an employer is an ALE for a calendar year, employers generally count employees for the prior year. If an employer was not in existence during the prior calendar year, an employer is a large employer for the current calendar year if it is reasonably expected to employ at least fifty FTEs. Employers who are new ALEs (employers not in existence in 2014) will not be subject to penalties for January through March of their first year of applicability as long as they offer employee coverage that provides minimum value on or before April 1. If an employer's FTEs exceed fifty for 120 days or less and the excess employees are seasonal workers, then the employer is not a large employer.[4]

For purposes of the employer mandate penalty assessments (as opposed to determining whether the employer is an applicable large employer), the law defines full-time as thirty hours of service per week, and the regulations provide that 130 (not 120) hours per month is the monthly equivalent, both determined in the current month/year. To address the calculation difficulty concern, the regulations provide alternatives to a month-by-month determination. For on-going employees, an employer has the option of using a "look-back measurement" method for determining current full-time status. The employer selects a measurement period of three to twelve months and calculates whether the employee on average had thirty hours of service per week (or 130 hours per month) during that period. If so, the employer must treat the employee as full-time during a subsequent "stability period", which must be at least six months but no shorter than the length of the measurement period. Thus, if the employer used a twelve-month look-back measurement period beginning on January 1, 2014, employees who are determined to be full-time must be treated as full-time for all of calendar year 2015. An employer may also utilize an optional administrative period of up to ninety days between the measurement period and the stability period in order to determine which on-going employees are eligible for health insurance coverage during the subsequent stability period. However, the administrative period cannot create a gap in coverage. An employee who was enrolled in coverage must remain enrolled during the administrative period.

---

1.   Treas. Regs. §54 .4980H-4(c) and §54 .4980H-5(c).
2.   Shared Responsibility for Employers Regarding Health Coverage, 26 CFR Parts 1, 54, and 301, 79 Fed. Reg. 8543, 8573 (Feb. 12, 2014).
3.   Treas. Reg. §54 .4980H -2(b)(2).
4.   Treas. Reg. §54 .4980H -2(b)(2).

<u>If an employer had on average fewer than fifty Full-Time (and Full-Time Equivalent) employees in 2014</u>:

- No change. Employer is not subject to the mandate. Employers close to the fifty-employee threshold may count employees during any consecutive six-month period (as chosen by the employer) during 2014.

<u>If employer had on average between fifty and ninety-nine full-time (including full-time equivalents) employees in 2014, the employer would not qualify for the delay if the employer currently offers no plan or had made significant changes to the plan. The rules for determining status as an ALE include application of the rule regarding employers whose workforce exceeds the applicable threshold (ninety-nine for this transition rule) for 120 days or fewer during the calendar year due to the employment of seasonal workers.1 Under this fifty to ninety-nine transition rule</u>:

- An employer had a one-year delay in the employer mandate until January 1, 2016 (and for noncalendar-year plans, any calendar months during the plan year beginning in 2015 that fall in 2016) if:

    - Employer certifies it did not lay off employees during the period beginning on February 9, 2014, and ending on Dec. 31, 2014, to fall below the 100-employee threshold and that employer did not reduce any coverage already offered; and

    - During the period beginning on February 9, 2014 and ending on Dec. 31, 2014, employer does not eliminate or materially reduce the health coverage, if any, offered as of February 9, 2014. An employer will not be treated as eliminating or materially reducing health coverage if, for each employee who is eligible for coverage on February 9, 2014:

        (a) the employer offers to make a contribution toward the cost of employee-only coverage that is either (i) at least 95 percent of the dollar amount of the contribution the employer was making toward the coverage in effect as of February 9, 2014, or (ii) at least the same percentage of the cost of coverage that the employer offered to contribute toward coverage in effect as of February 9, 2014;

        (b) benefits offered as of February 9, 2014 at the employee-only coverage level does not change, or, if it does, the coverage after the change provides minimum value; and

        (c) eligibility under the employer's group health plans is not amended to narrow or reduce the class or classes of employees (or the employees' dependents) to whom coverage under those plans was offered as of February 9, 2014.

- Such employer must still report its coverage of employer's employees for 2015 under the reporting provisions.

---

1.   Treas. Reg. §54 .4980H -2(b)(2).

- For employers eligible for the "smaller employer" transition relief described above, no subsection 4980H(a) or (b) penalty will apply for any calendar month during 2015 or any calendar month during the portion of the 2015 plan year that falls in 2016.

If employer had on average 100 or more full-time (including full-time equivalents) employees in 2014:

- An employer failing to offer coverage to a full-time employee for any day of a calendar month, that employee will be treated as not having been offered coverage during the entire month. For January 2015, if an employer offers coverage to a full-time employee no later than the first day of the first payroll period that begins in January 2015, the employee will be treated as having been offered coverage for January 2015. In addition, for 2015 (and for any calendar months during a noncalendar year plan year beginning in 2015 that fall in 2016), the 95 percent threshold is lowered to 70 percent. Finally, for employers that must make an assessable payment under Internal Revenue Code section 4980H(a), the IRS will reduce the penalty for 2015, plus any calendar months of 2016 that fall within the 2015 plan year. For this period, the assessable payment under Internal Revenue Code section 4980H(a) will be calculated by subtracting eighty from the number of full-time employees, rather than thirty. An employer fails to make an offer of coverage to its full-time employees if it does not offer health coverage at all or offers coverage to fewer than 70 percent of its full-time employees and (unless the employer qualifies for the 2015 dependent coverage transition relief) the dependents of those employees in 2015 and for any calendar months during a noncalendar year plan year beginning in 2015 that fall in 2016.

Employers with Fiscal Year Health Plans. The delayed effective date is available for fiscal year plans in effect on December 27, 2012, provided (1) the plan had not been subsequently amended after December 27, 2012 to postpone the plan year start date (e.g., to change the plan year from an April 1 plan year start date to a December 1 plan year start date) and (2) as of the first day of the 2015 plan year, the employer offers health plan coverage to at least 70 percent of its thirty hour or more a week employees (and, unless the employer qualifies for transition relief, their dependents). For fiscal year plans that qualify for the transition relief, the play or pay penalties will not apply until the first day of the plan year that begins in 2015 with respect to employees in three situations.

Transition Rule #1 (Must be eligible for plan under eligibility provisions as of February 9, 2014). First, the employer will not be subject to a penalty until the first day of the 2015 plan year with respect to any of its employees, whenever hired, if they were (or would have been) eligible for coverage under the eligibility provisions of the plan in effect on February 9, 2014. However, to qualify for this relief, the employer must offer health plan coverage on the first day of the 2015 plan year that is "affordable" and provides "minimum value" (as those terms are defined by the regulators). Note that this is a limited form of relief that applies only to those employees who actually were, or would have been, eligible for the plan as of February 9, 2014 (provided that those employees were not eligible for any calendar year health plan maintained by the employer as of February 9, 2014).

Transition Rule #2 (As of February 9, 2014, must have covered or offered coverage to a minimum percentage of ALL employees). Under the second transition rule, an employer qualifies for relief if it either covered at least 1/4th of all of its employees (whether full or part-time) under the employer's fiscal year health plans (each of which had the same plan year as of December 27, 2012) as of any date during the February 10, 2013 through February 9, 2014 period or the employer offered coverage under those fiscal year health plans to at least 1/3rd of all of its employees (whether full or part-time) during the most recent open enrollment period that ended before February 9, 2014. In that case, the employer will not be subject to a penalty under the pay or play rules until the first day of the 2015 plan year with respect to thirty hour or more a week employees (whenever hired) who both (1) were not eligible for coverage under a health plan maintained by the employer as of February 9, 2014, that had a calendar year plan year and (2) are offered health plan coverage as of the first day of the 2015 plan year that is "affordable" and provides "minimum value".

For employees in that second category, the rule is designed to allow the employer additional employees who were not previously eligible for coverage. For example, if during the most recent open enrollment period ending before February 9, 2014, an employer offered coverage under its medical plan with a July 1 plan year to at least one-third of all of its employees, the employer will not be liable for any penalty for failing to offer coverage from January 2015 through June 2015 for those noneligible employees if, by July 1, 2015, the employer expands the plan to offer employer mandate-compliant coverage to those previously ineligible full-time employees.

<u>Transition Rule #3 (As of February 9, 2014, must have covered or offered coverage to a minimum percentage of thirty hour or more a week employees)</u>. The third transition rule is similar to Transition Rule #2 except that it considers only thirty hour or more a week employees. That is, the third transition rule applies if the employer either covered at least 1/3rd of its thirty hour or more a week employees under the employer's fiscal year health plans (each of which had the same plan year as of December 27, 2012) as of any date during the February 10, 2013 through February 9, 2014 period or the employer offered coverage under those fiscal year health plans to at least half of its thirty hour or more a week employees during the most recent open enrollment period that ended before February 9, 2014. In that case, the employer will not be subject to a penalty under the pay or play rules until the first day of the 2015 plan year with respect to its thirty hour or more a week employees (whenever hired) who both (1) were not eligible for coverage under a health plan maintained by the employer as of February 9, 2014 that had a calendar year plan year and (2) are offered health plan coverage as of the first day of the 2015 plan year that is "affordable" and provides "minimum value".

<u>Internal Revenue Code section 6056 Reporting for 2015 Transition Period for Noncalendar Year Plans</u>. Large employers subject to the ACA's shared responsibility provisions must file a return with the IRS that reports the terms and conditions of the health care coverage provided to the employer's full-time employees for the calendar year. Related statements must also be provided to employees.

Because this reporting is needed by the employee and the IRS for the administration of the premium tax credit, applicable large employers are required to report this information for the entire 2015 calendar year, even if during some calendar months in 2015 employer mandate liability will not apply. The section 6056 return instructions will provide additional information on how to report for 2015.

Dependent Coverage Transition Rule. In order to avoid exposure for the employer mandate penalty, an employer must offer coverage not only to full-time employees but also their dependents (but not spouses). The final regulations provide transition relief to plan years that begin in 2015 if the employer takes steps during the 2015 plan year toward satisfying this requirement in 2016. The transition relief applies to employers for the 2015 plan year for plans under which (i) dependent coverage is not offered, (ii) dependent coverage that does not constitute minimum essential coverage is offered, or (iii) dependent coverage is offered for some, but not all, dependents. This relief is not available, however, if the employer had offered dependent coverage during either the plan year that begins in 2013 or the 2014 plan year and subsequently eliminated that offer of coverage.

See also Q 25, Q 27, Q 672 and Q 673.

661. Which workers qualify as employees?

Internal Revenue Code section 4980H(c)(2) defines an Applicable Large Employer (ALE) with respect to a calendar year as an employer that employed an average of at least fifty full-time employees and Full-Time Equivalent employees or FTEs on business days during the preceding calendar year. The regulations[1] adopt the position outlined in IRS Notice 2011-36,[2] that an employee is an individual who is an employee under the common law standard, and an employer is the person that is the employer under the common law standard, as discussed in the next question.

662. If the employer hires additional employees, including some part-time employees, how is it determined when ALE status is achieved?

An employer determines if it is an ALE for a current calendar year based on its number of full-time employees (including full-time equivalent employees) during the prior calendar year. If an employer hires additional employees, including some part-time employees, during the current calendar year, the employer will take those employees into account when determining if it is an ALE for the next calendar year.

663. How are non-traditional employees such as contingent workers (leased employees and independent contractors), seasonal employees, temporary employee, rehired employees, volunteers, education employees, student workers and adjunct faculty defined under the regulations?

The employer mandate final regulations issued in 2014 contain rules on contingent workers, including temporary employees, individuals hired through temporary staffing firms and independent contractors.[3]

---

1.   Treas. Reg. §31.3401(c)-1(b).

2.   IRS Notice 2011-36, https://www.irs.gov/pub/irs-drop/n-11-36.pdf. (Last accessed August 13, 2019).

3.   See https://www.federalregister.gov/articles/2014/02/12/2014-03082/shared-responsibility-for-employers-regarding-health-coverage. (Last accessed on August 13, 2019).

Under the final regulations, a full-time employee remains defined as one who works an average of at least thirty hours per week or 130 hours each month under both the look-back measurement method and the monthly measurement method. It is important to remember that the look-back measurement method for identifying full-time employees is available only for purposes of determining and computing liability for an employer mandate payment and not for purposes of determining if the employer is an applicable large employer.

The definition of employee and the key provisions of the final regulations' rules for contingent and other types of workers are summarized below. The regulations also do not provide any specific relief for employers in high turnover" industries, such as retail workers hired for the holidays, although the latter will be generally excludable under the regular seasonal employee rules.

Definition of Employee.[1] The IRS uses the common law definition of employee to determine employer-employee status. Generally, an individual is the common law employee of an entity if that entity has the right to control the individual's performance of services. The final regulations exclude from the definition of employee the following: leased employees, sole proprietors, partners in a partnership, more 2 percent S corporation shareholders, and certain direct sellers and real estate agents.[2]

Common Law Employees of the Client Employer. When the client (recipient) employer is the common law employer, an offer of coverage made by the staffing firm on behalf of the client employer is treated as an offer of coverage by the client employer if the client employer pays a higher fee to the staffing firm for those employees who enroll in the staffing firm's plan. Thus, if the contract provides for a flat fee per employee placement irrespective of whether the employee enrolls in the staffing company's coverage, the employer will not be considered to have made an offer of coverage. This could lead to exposure under the pay-or-play mandate's $ 2,570 per full-time employee "no coverage offered" penalty if more than 5 percent of its full-time employees (more than 30 percent in 2020) are employed through the staffing agency.

Contingent Worker Misclassification Issues. Employers are not required to offer coverage to independent contractors. However, an IRS examination finding that common law employees have been misclassified as independent contractors could result in significant penalty exposure to the employer. Employers that engage a significant number of such "1099 employees" run the risk of incurring the pay-or-play mandate's $2,570 per full-time employee "no coverage offered" penalty, even if they offer coverage to all of the employees they categorize as full-time. If the number of 1099 employees who are reclassified as common law employees exceeds 5 percent of the employer's full-time workforce (30 percent in 2015), the "no coverage offered" penalty may be triggered.

Another important issue for employers that hire independent contractors is whether they could rely on the IRS so-called "Section 530" relief for identifying common law employees. The ACA employer mandate final regulations reject the availability of section 530 relief for purposes of the pay-or-play requirements. Thus, employers should carefully review their contractual

---

1.   See Pub.15-A, Employer's Supplemental Tax Guide, for more information on determining who is an employee.
2.   Treas. Reg. §54.4980H-1(a)(15).

arrangements with service providers to ensure that they have been properly classified as independent contractors as opposed to common law employees under the more traditional common law tests.

Short-Term Full-Time Employees. Short-term employees (other than seasonal employees) who are reasonably expected to work full-time (thirty hours or more per week) at date of hire must generally be offered coverage within ninety days. There is no exemption for short-term full-time employees—if employment extends beyond the end of the third full calendar month of employment, the employer must offer coverage regardless of the projected termination date.

Variable Hour and Seasonal Employees from Temporary Staffing Firms. Variable hour employees are employees with no set schedule or seasonal employees (generally those working six months or less on a seasonal basis). An employer (staffing company) can use a determination period of from three to six to twelve months to determine an individual's full-time status for a following so-called "stability period" of six or twelve months. The final regulations provide criteria that a staffing company may consider to determine whether a new employee is "variable hour." This assessment is done at the time of hire based on the staffing company's reasonable expectations. Considerations may include whether other similar employees of the staffing company: retain the right to reject assignments, have periods during which no assignments are available, are offered assignments of differing lengths, and are typically offered assignments that do not extend more than thirteen weeks. No one factor is dispositive.

Seasonal Employees. Those in positions for which the customary annual employment is six months or less generally will not be considered full-time employees. Seasonal workers are workers who perform labor or services on a seasonal basis as defined by the Department of Labor, and retail workers employed exclusively during holiday seasons. For this purpose, employers may apply a reasonable, good faith interpretation of the term "seasonal worker" and a reasonable, good faith interpretation of the Department of Labor's definition of seasonal worker.

Rehired Employees. For all employers other than educational institutions, a returning employee may be treated as a new hire as long as there is a break in service (a period without an hour of service) of at least thirteen weeks. For educational institutions, a rehired employee can be considered a new hire if the break in service is at least twenty-six weeks.[1]

Volunteers. Hours contributed by bona fide volunteers for a government or tax-exempt entity, such as volunteer firefighters and emergency responders, will not cause them to be considered as full-time employees. Thus, employers need not track or count volunteer hours. A bona fide volunteer is defined as an employee of a government entity or nonprofit organized under section 501(c) of the tax code whose only compensation from the employer

---

1.   Treas. Reg. §4980H-3(c)(4)(v).

is in the form of reimbursements or allowances for reasonable expenses incurred while performing volunteer work or reasonable benefits and nominal fees customarily paid to volunteers by organizations similar to the employer.[1] For many educational institutions, this may include any number of volunteers, including coaches and athletic trainers. A question remains regarding the extent to which this exclusion applies to individuals who may receive compensation from the school as regular employees and who also work as volunteers.

Educational Employees. Teachers and other educational employees will not be treated as part-time for the year simply because their school is closed or operating on a limited schedule during the summer.

Student Work-Study Programs. Service performed by students under federal or state-sponsored work-study programs will not be counted in determining whether they are full-time employees. For all other positions, hours worked by students are included for purposes of determining full-time employee status under the mandate. This includes any paid internships or externships. This clarification has significant implications for schools with their own student workers like graduate assistants and for schools with students that participate in cooperative (co-op) programs.

Adjunct Faculty. The regulations continue to allow higher education institutions to use any reasonable method to count adjunct faculty hours. Additionally, employers of adjunct faculty may credit an adjunct faculty member with a total of two and one-quarter hours of service for each hour of teaching or classroom time. If an institution uses this safe harbor, an adjunct faculty member would reach the thirty-hour threshold by teaching in excess of thirteen and one-half hours per week. Educational institutions may also use other reasonable methods for determining the number of hours of service for adjunct faculty. In addition, adjuncts may receive an hour of service per week for each additional hour outside of the classroom the faculty member spends performing duties he or she is required to perform (such as required office hours or required attendance at faculty meetings).[2]

These are just a few of the significant issues employers need to consider as they identify their worker classification arrangements. Employers must also examine their contractual agreements with any temporary staffing agency and other possible legal requirements, such as ERISA section 510 liability for intentional interference with attainment of benefits and the healthcare reform whistleblower protections.

664. Which workers are not considered employees?

Various self-employed individuals are not "employees". These include sole proprietors, partners, or two percent or more S Corporation shareholders. Thus, LLPs, LLCs (taxed as partnerships), and partnerships can design eligibility, coverage, and premium obligations for their members/partners however the LLC/partnership desires. An individual

---

1.   Treas. Reg. §54.4980H-1(a)(7).
2.   Preamble to final regulation at 79 Fed. Reg. p. 8,552.

who provides services as both an employee and a non-employee (such as an individual serving as both an employee and a director) is an employee for hours of service as an employee.

The regulations provide that a leased employee as defined under Internal Revenue Code section 414(n) is not an employee for these rules.[1] However, those rules will seldom be met. Additionally, in many if not most cases, the IRS views leased employees as common law employees of the firm that uses their services (the service recipient), not the business that pays them, if the service recipient has the right to control their working conditions.

Bona fide independent contractors, as opposed to employees that an employer erroneously treats as independent contractors, are not employees for this purpose.

665. Who are dependents for purposes of the employer mandate?

While Internal Revenue Code section 4980H does not define the term "dependent," code section 152(f) defines the term to include:

- biological children

- stepchildren

- adopted children, and

- foster children.

However, the employer mandate regulations define dependent to mean "a child (as defined in section 152(f)(1)) but excluding a stepson, stepdaughter or an eligible foster child (and excluding any individual who is excluded from the definition of dependent under section 152 by operation of section 152(b)(3))) of an employee who has not attained age twenty-six."[2]

Applicable Large Employers

666. Which "Applicable Large Employers" are potentially subject to the employer mandate penalties?

Generally speaking, employers with fifty or more full time and full-time-equivalent U.S. employees in the prior calendar year are subject to the employer mandate penalties.

Employers are not required to provide health coverage but employer mandate penalties, discussed later in this Part, may apply if they do not and the "employer" has fifty or more full-time and full-time equivalent employees on business days during the preceding calendar year.[3] While large employers need not provide health care coverage to part-time employees

---

1.   Treas. Reg. §54.4980H-1(a)(13).
2.   See Question and Answer 44, https://www.irs.gov/affordable-care-act/employers/questions-and-answers-on-employer-shared-responsibility-provisions-under-the-affordable-care-act (Last accessed August 13, 2019) ; Reg. §54.4980H-1.
3.   IRC Sec. 4980H(c)(2)(A); Treas. Reg. §54.4980H-1(a)(4).

working less than thirty hours per week, these part-time employees are included in calculating the threshold number of fifty workers (including full-time equivalents) that would require employers to offer affordable coverage to full-time employees and their dependents (but not spouses) or pay a penalty.

Employees working outside the United States are not counted and are excluded.[1] The reference to business days is not explained or defined. It is not clear whether the threshold must be met on one business day, all business days, or some average. Most employers will use an alternate method, discussed subsequently, which allows a monthly counting of employees in the prior year.

For this purpose, an employer does not take into account employees who have coverage under TRICARE or a VA health program (as described in section 4980H(c)(2)(F)).

667. Are related employers treated as one employer?

Yes. Under section 414 the employer shared responsibility provisions include a rule that also applies for certain other tax and employee benefit purposes. Under this rule, two or more businesses that have a certain level of common or related ownership generally are treated as a single employer, and are combined for purposes of determining whether or not they collectively employ at least 50 full-time employees (including full-time equivalent employees). If the combined total meets the ALE threshold, then each separate business is considered to be part of an ALE and is therefore subject to the employer shared responsibility provisions. This includes any business that does not employ enough employees to meet the ALE threshold on its own. Under this rule, an ALE may be a single employer or a group of related employers treated as an aggregated ALE group, which is a group of employers treated as a single employer under section 414(b), (c), (m) or (o). Each employer that is a member of an aggregated ALE group is referred to as an ALE member.[2] See also Q 658.

668. Does the employer mandate shared responsibility rules apply if an employer that is not an ALE offers coverage through an Association Health Plan?

No. Whether an employer member of an association that offers coverage through an AHP is an ALE that is subject to the employer shared responsibility provisions depends on the number of full-time employees (and full-time equivalent employees) the member employer employed in the prior calendar year and is unrelated to whether the employer offers coverage through an AHP.

An employer that is not an ALE under the employer shared responsibility provisions does not become an ALE due to participation in an AHP, and an employer that is an ALE under the employer shared responsibility provisions continues to be an ALE subject to the employer shared responsibility provisions regardless of its participation in an AHP.

---

1. Shared Responsibility for Employers Regarding Health Coverage, 26 CFR Parts 1, 54, and 301, 78 Fed. Reg. 217, 221 (Jan. 2, 2013).
2. IRC Sec. 414.

669. How is a new employer's status as an ALE determined if they were not in existence during the prior year?

An employer not in existence during an <u>entire</u> preceding calendar year (not in existence on any business day of the prior calendar year) is an Applicable Large Employer (ALE) for the current calendar year if it is reasonably expected to employ an average of at least fifty full-time and full-time employees (taking into account FTEs) on business days during the current calendar year.[1] It is not clear what happens if circumstances change during the current year so that the original determination is no longer reasonable.

Two Alternate Employer Mandate Penalties

670. In general, what are the two alternative employer mandate penalties?

There are two alternative penalties. The annual amounts are $2,570[2] or $3,860,[3] but the actual amount is calculated monthly. Both the $2,570 and $3,860 penalty amounts will be adjusted annually for inflation.[4] Neither penalty is triggered unless an employee receives a tax credit for the purchase of health insurance on a state exchange. See Q 25.

Internal Revenue section 4980H(a) penalty is assessed when an employee does not offer the required Minimum Essential Coverage (MEC). See Q 672. Internal Revenue section 4908H(b) penalty is assessed if the MEC is offered but is unaffordable or does not provide minimum value. See Q 673.

One of the employer mandate penalties applied in 2015 and years thereafter to applicable large employers unless they offer affordable and adequate coverage with essential health benefits for insured plans that are not grandfathered plans. No special rules are provided as to what proof is required for an employer to demonstrate an offer of coverage, but an offer must occur at least once each plan year.[5] An applicable large employer is one with at least fifty full-time equivalent employees. This includes all controlled group and affiliated service group members. The exchanges will police this. Status as an "applicable large employer" is determined based on employees' actual hours of service for the preceding calendar year — full year, no equivalencies. However, the regulations include special transition relief so that employers may use a shorter 2014 look-back period to determine whether the employer was an "applicable large employer" for 2015. The look-back measurement method for identifying full-time employees is available only for purposes of determining and computing liability for an employer mandate payment and not for purposes of determining if the employer is an applicable large employer.

---

1.   IRC Sec. 4980H(c)(2)(C)(ii); Treas. Reg. §54.4980H-2(b)(3).
2.   Internal Revenue section 4908H(a).
3.   [Internal Revenue section 4908H(b).
4.   IRC Sec. 4980H(c)(5).
5.   Treas. Reg. §54.4980H-4(b).

Note that neither penalty is triggered unless at least one full-time employee enrolls in a qualified health plan through an exchange for that month and must receive an applicable premium tax credit for that month's coverage.[1]

OVERVIEW OF THE EMPLOYER MANDATE AND PENALTIES

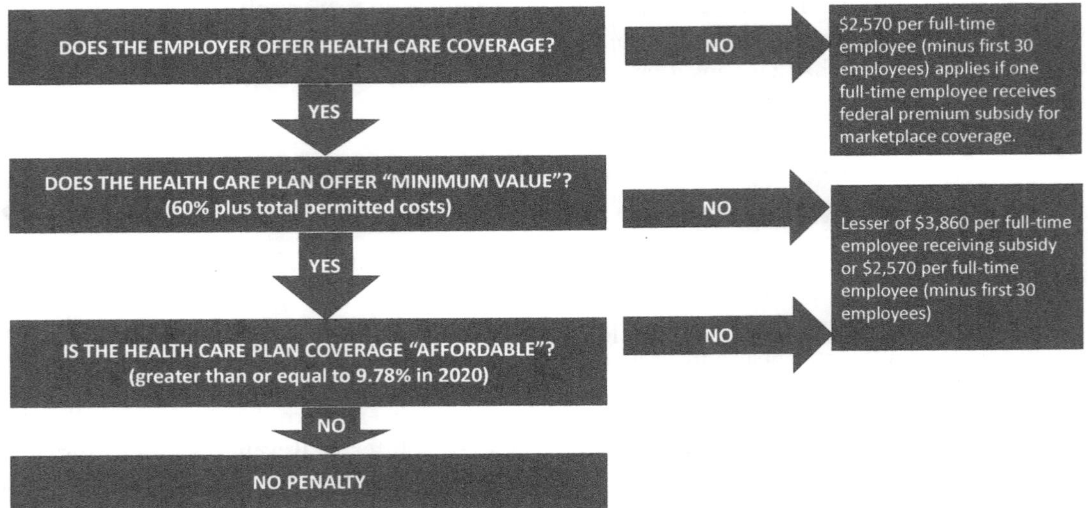

671. What qualifies as an employer offer of health coverage?

If an employee has not been offered an effective opportunity to accept coverage, the employee will not be treated as having been offered the coverage for purposes of the employer mandate. This offer must be made no less than once during each plan year.[2] If the employee does not pay for the employee's share of coverage within thirty days of when payment is due, the employer need not provide coverage.[3]

672. How does the IRC section 4980H(a) penalty work?

The applicable large employer offers at least once during each plan year no Minimum Essential Coverage (MEC)[4] to "substantially all" (all but 5 percent or five employees, if greater)[5] of its full-time employees (and their dependent and adult children up to age twenty-six,[6] but not spouses)[7] and one or more full-time employee is certified to the employer by a state health insurance exchange as having received an applicable premium tax credit or cost-sharing reduction.[8] The penalty is the number of full-times employees less thirty times $2,570 per year.

---

1.   IRC Sec. 4980H(a)(2).
2.   Treas. Reg. §54.4980H-4(b).
3.   Treas. Reg. §54.4980H-3(f).
4.   Minimum essential coverage includes coverage offered by a grandfathered group health plan.
5.   Treas. Reg. §54.4980H-4(a).
6.   "Dependent" is defined as an employee's child under IRC§152(f)(1) who is under 26 years of age. Reg. §54.4980H-1(a)(11).
7.   Reg. §54.4980H-1(a)(11).
8.   Internal Revenue section 4980H(a) liability.

Thus, if an employer has thirty-four full-time employees and does not offer MEC, the penalty is $(34 - 30) = 4 \times \$2,570$ or $\$10,280$ for that year. The penalty is calculated monthly.

Internal Revenue section 4980H(a) employer mandate penalty applies to an employer that fails to offer "minimum essential coverage." Minimum essential coverage does not include excepted benefits, such as stand-alone vision or stand-alone dental benefits. Employers seeking to minimize or avoid the employer penalty must offer minimum essential coverage to 95 percent of their full-time employees and their dependents, including children under age twenty-six. Minimum Essential Coverage is the coverage required to avoid the individual and employer mandates.[1] It is an "eligible employer-sponsored plan," a term that means any group health plan (other than for excepted benefits) offered by an employer to employees, coverage offered in a state's small or large group market, or a self-insured plan[2] meeting only the required Public Health Service Act requirements (discussed in Part VII).[3] It includes grandfathered and grandmothered plans.[4] In other words, any health insurance plan legally sold in a state and self-insured plans meeting PHSA requirements are an "eligible employer-sponsored plan."

673. How does the IRC section 4980H(b) alternative penalty work?

Even if an applicable large employer is not subject to the Internal Revenue section 4980H(a) penalty because the employer offers minimum essential coverage to 95 percent of its employees and their dependents, including children up to age twenty-six, that employer can be subject to the alternative Internal Revenue section 4980H(b) penalty. The 95 percent margin of error rule for the (a) penalty does not apply to the (b) penalty. The (b) penalty applies if the employer offers 95 percent of its full-time employees (and their dependent and adult children up to age twenty-six) the opportunity to enroll in MEC[5] under an employer sponsored plan and one or more full-time employees is certified to the employer as having received an applicable premium tax credit or cost-sharing reduction. The second Internal Revenue section 4980H(b) penalty applies if the coverage offered by the employer is (a) unaffordable under Internal Revenue section 36B(c)(2)(C)(i) or (b) does not provide minimum value under Internal Revenue section 36B(c)(2)(C)(ii).

The Internal Revenue section 4908H(b) penalty applies to employers that offer coverage to at least 95 percent of their full-time employees (or all but five employees if greater) and dependents from 2016 and years thereafter, but that have one or more full-time employee who receives a premium tax credit because the coverage is not affordable or does not offer minimum value. The Internal Revenue section 4980H(b) penalty employer mandate penalty payment is computed separately each month. The amount of the payment for the month equals the number of full-time employees who receive the premium tax credit for that month multiplied by one-twelfth of $3,860 ($321.66). The liability cannot exceed the payment that the employer would owe if it did not offer any minimum essential coverage, i.e., $2,570 times the number of full-time

---

1.   PPACA §1301.
2.   Reg. §1.5000A-2(c)(1)
3.   IRC Sec. 5000A(f)(2)(B); Prop. Reg.§1.5000A-2(a) and (c)(1)(ii).
4.   Reg. §1.5000A-2(a)(c)(1)(iii).
5.   Essential health benefits are subject to the lifetime and annual dollar limits and must include at least the following services: ambulatory patient services, emergency services, hospitalization, maternity and newborn care, mental health benefits and substance use disorder services, prescription drugs, rehabilitative and habilitative services and devices, laboratory services, preventive and wellness services and chronic disease managements, and pediatric services including oral and vision care.

employees less thirty each year. Except in the case of terminated employees, if an employer fails to offer coverage to an eligible full-time employee for any day of a calendar month during which the employee is employed by the employer, the employee is treated as not being offered coverage during that month. However, the employer is not penalized if the employee fails to pay the employee's share of the premium if the employee is afforded the opportunity to do so.

Employer group health plans are not required to provide a particular benefits package to avoid the employer mandate assessable penalties, as long as the plan meets the "affordability" and "minimum value" standards.

674. What does "affordable value" for a plan mean?

Affordable plans are those that cost an employee no more for employee-only coverage than 9.56 percent in 2018, 9.86 percent in 2019, and 9.78 percent in 2020 of the employee's household (or using the safe harbor, the employee's W-2) income.[1]

Employees with household incomes between 100 and 400 percent of the federal poverty level, if not eligible for Medicaid, are eligible for tax credits for exchange coverage if they do not have access to affordable employer-sponsored coverage that is of at least a minimum value. The state health insurance exchange makes the determination as to whether their income is below 400 percent of federal poverty, but the employer can determine if coverage is affordable by using the employee's Box 1, W-2 Income for the current year to determine if the cost to the employee for employee-only coverage exceeds 9.56 percent in 2018, 9.86 percent in 2019, and 9.78 percent in 2020 of the employee's household (or using the safe harbor, the employee's W-2) income. See Q 679.

675. When does an employer health plan provide minimum value?

A plan fails to provide Minimum Value (MV) if the plan's share of the total allowed costs of benefits provided under the plan is less than 60 percent of those costs.[2] Employers will be able to enter information about the plan, such as deductibles and copays, into a calculator being developed to determine whether its plan provides minimum value by covering at least 60 percent of the total allowed cost of benefits expected to be incurred under the plan.[3] Employers may also obtain an actuarial certification to show minimum value by an actuary who is a member of the American Academy of Actuaries.[4]

Employer contributions to an HSA and amounts newly made available under integrated HRAs that may be used only for cost sharing can be taken into account in determining minimum value.[5] For example, a $1,000 HSA employer contribution is treated in the MV calculator as if a plan with a $1,000 deductible is reduced to zero. The $1,000 contribution is counted as the

---

1.   IRS Notice 2012-58. The 9.5 percent can be adjusted after 2014 to reflect rates of premium growth relative to growth in income and after 2018 to reflect rates of premium growth relative to growth in the consumer price index. See Prop. Treas. Regs. §§1.36B-0 through 1.36B-5.
2.   See IRS Notice 2012-31.
3.   https://www.irs.gov/affordable-care-act/employers/questions-and-answers-on-employer-shared-responsibility-provisions-under-the-affordable-care-act. at Q&A 39. (Last accessed August 13, 2019). Current through March 26, 2019.
4.   45 CFR §156.145(b)(1).
5.   45 CFR §156.145(d).

average dollar value it would cost to reduce a $1,000 deductible to zero.[1] Whether other types of integrated HRAs could count toward minimum value is not yet determined. The HRA rules leave important questions unanswered, such as the definition of "integrated" and the meaning of the "used only for cost sharing" condition.

676. Can an inexpensive health plan that fails to cover inpatient hospitalization services provide minimum value and allow employers to avoid employer mandate penalties?

Yes, if it can obtain at least a 60 percent rating on the Minimum Value (MV) Calculator. An employer mandate avoidance strategy called MVP is one that offers major medical but no hospitalization coverage that is marketed as a cheap form of health coverage, often in industries that traditionally did not previously offer coverage to large numbers of workers or offered so-called "mini med" plans. MVP is the acronym for Minimum Value Plan (also called a "skinny plan"), and refers to a health insurance plan with at least 60 percent value, meaning that on average it pays at least 60 percent[2] of the costs of claims submitted by the population covered by self-insured group health plans,[3] including the amount the plan pays and the employee pays.[4]

HHS Minimum Value Calculator

Whether a plan offers minimum value can be determined by using the HHS minimum value calculator[5] at https://www.cms.gov/CCIIO/Resources/Regulations-and-Guidance/Downloads/mv-calculator-final-4-11-2013.xlsm.

Safe Harbors

Alternatively, a plan can use safe harbors developed by the IRS and HHS or, if the plan has nonstandard features not valued by the MV Calculator, an actuary can determine if a plan covers at least 60 percent of the costs of claims.[6] Finally, all plans offered on state health exchanges offer minimum value except the catastrophic coverage available to young adults. Because employers are not likely to know the household income of their employees, there are three safe harbors that an employer may use to determine affordability for purposes of the employer shared responsibility provisions. (These safe harbors do not affect whether an employee's coverage is affordable for purposes of determining the employee's eligibility for the premium tax credit.) In general, under these employer shared responsibility affordability safe harbors, employers are allowed to use Form W-2 wages, an employee's rate of pay, or the federal poverty line, instead of household income in making the affordability determination.

There are three affordability safe harbors employers can take advantage of that are based on information the employer does have available, such as the employee's Form W-2 wages or the employee's rate of pay. If an ALE's offer of coverage is affordable using any of these safe

---

1. Minimum Value Calculator Methodology at http://cciio.cms.gov/resources/regulations/index.html. (Last accessed August 13, 2019).
2. IRC §36B(c)(2)(C)(ii).
3. 45 CFR §156.145(c).
4. 45 CFR §156.145(a).
5. 45 CFR §156.145(a)(1).
6. 45 CFR §156.145(a)(2) and (3).

harbors – that is, the employee's required contribution is no more than 9.5 percent (as adjusted) of the baseline in the applicable safe harbor – then, the offer of coverage is deemed affordable for purposes of the employer shared responsibility provisions regardless of whether it was affordable based on the employee's household income (which is the test that applies for purposes of the premium tax credit).

The three affordability safe harbors are:

(1)   the Form W-2 wages safe harbor

      a.   The Form W-2 wages safe harbor generally is based on the amount of wages paid to the employee that the employer reports in Box 1 of that employee's Form W-2.

(2)   the rate of pay safe harbor, and

      b.   The rate of pay safe harbor generally is based on the employee's rate of pay at the beginning of the coverage period, with adjustments permitted, for an hourly employee, if the rate of pay is decreased (but not if the rate of pay is increased).

(3)   the federal poverty line safe harbor

      c.   The federal poverty line safe harbor generally treats coverage as affordable for a month if the employee required contribution for the month does not exceed 9.5 percent, adjusted annually, of the federal poverty line for a single individual for the applicable calendar year, divided by 12.

An ALE may use one or more of the safe harbors at its option but only if the ALE offers 95 percent of its full-time employees and their dependents the opportunity to enroll in coverage that provides minimum value for the self-only coverage offered to the employee. An ALE may choose to use one safe harbor for all of its employees or to use different safe harbors for employees in different categories, provided that the categories used are reasonable and the employer uses one safe harbor on a uniform and consistent basis for all employees in a particular category. If an ALE offers multiple health care coverage options, the affordability test for a particular employee applies to the lowest-cost self-only coverage option that provides minimum value and that is available to that employee. (See also Q 679)

MVP arrangements need to provide "Minimum Essential Coverage," a "MEC plan."[1] Minimum Essential Coverage may include only preventive care and wellness benefits. To avoid all employer mandate penalties, large employers that do not have grandfathered plans must offer coverage that is not only Minimum Essential Coverage but provides Minimum Value and is Affordable. Applicable Large Employers, those that are subject to the employer mandate, can avoid these tax penalties by offering self-funded, low-cost MEC plans (which may be priced at $50 - $200 per employee per month).

---

1.   IRC §5000A(f)(1).

An MVP plan might be paired with a fixed indemnity hospital plan. A fixed indemnity plan is a plan that pays fixed amounts for specific medical services and care. These plans are "excepted benefits" that are not subject to the insurance market reforms and other requirements. Employees are free to elect or reject this coverage independent of any other coverage they might elect or reject.

One might wonder how an MVP is legal when the law requires health plans to provide ten Essential Health Benefits (EHB), including hospitalization, but this requirement applies only to individual and small group plans.[1] Self-funded groups and large fully insured groups are not required to cover all EHBs. Thus, for these employers, a plan that does not cover Essential Health Benefits can still be considered Minimum Essential Coverage. Whether they provide minimum value is determined by comparing the benefits provided to a benchmark set of the ten EHBs.

The law delegates to HHS the job of establishing rules governing MV.[2] The HHS final regulation[3] provides employers may use one of four methodologies to determine MV, one of which is the MV Calculator. Thus, for an MVP arrangement, minimum value is what HHS says it is, and HHS says that MV is what the calculator says it is.

The MVP strategy is to remove the high-cost inpatient hospital services from the plan while being more generous with other EHB components and by adopting generous cost-sharing features. A November HHS 2011 report[4] concludes that the four categories of benefits and services are the greatest contributors to a health plan's actuarial value are physician and mid-level practitioner care, hospital and emergency room services, pharmacy benefits, and laboratory and imaging services. This HHS report was cited with approval in IRS Notice 2012-31 in which the IRS anticipated that getting to 60 percent minimum value would require coverage of all four major categories. However, the IRS regulations do not require that a plan cover all four categories to reach minimum value.[5] The preamble to that proposed regulation instead explains that the "proposed regulations do not require employer-sponsored self-insured and insured large group plans to cover every EHB category or conform their plans to an EHB benchmark that applies to qualified health plans. The preamble to the HHS regulations[6] notes that employer-sponsored group health plans are not required to offer EHBs unless they are health plans offered in the small group market subject to section 2707(a) of the Public Health Service Act."

---

1. 45 CFR §156.110(a) provides that an EHB-benchmark plan must meet provide coverage of at least the following categories of benefits:

 (1) Ambulatory patient services, (2) Emergency services, (3) Hospitalization, (4) Maternity and newborn care. 5) Mental health and substance use disorder services, including behavioral health treatment, (6) Prescription drugs, (7) Rehabilitative and Habilitative services and devices, (8) Laboratory services, (9) Preventive and wellness services and chronic disease management, and (10) Pediatric services, including oral and vision care.

2. IRS Notice 2012-31, pp. 2-3.
3. 45 CFR §156.145(a).
4. "Actuarial Value and Employer-Sponsored Insurance," ASPE Research Brief, U.S. Department of Health and Human Services, available at http://aspe.hhs.gov/health/reports/2011/av-esi/rb.shtml. (Last accessed August 14, 2019).
5. Treas. Reg. §1.36B-6(c)(1).
6. See 78 Fed. Reg. 12833.

The IRS regulation[1] provides:

- "MV percentage. (1) In general. An eligible employer-sponsored plan's MV percentage is (i) The plan's anticipated covered medical spending for benefits provided under a particular Essential Health Benefits (EHB) benchmark plan described in 45 CFR 156.110 (EHB coverage) for the MV standard population based on the plan's cost-sharing provisions; (ii) Divided by the total anticipated allowed charges for EHB coverage provided to the MV standard population.

- (iii) Expressed as a percentage."

- Clause (i) of the IRS regulation above is not clear. But CMS clarifies on page 6 of its document Minimum Value Calculator Methodology[2] that the numerator begins with all of the ten EHBs in a particular benchmark plan, but then backs out those items that the plan does not cover, such as hospital services not offered by an MVP plan. In the case of an MVP arrangement, that generally includes inpatient hospital services.

677. Does a health plan with no hospitalization option qualify as meeting the Minimum Value standard?

No. The IRS and HHS are ending healthcare reform Minimum Value Health Plans with no hospitalization option. The IRS on November 4, 2014, issued Notice 2014-69 stating that it will not qualify employer-sponsored health plans that fail to cover inpatient hospitalization as meeting the minimum value health plan standard under healthcare reform. This notice states that HHS and Treasury believe that plans that fail to provide substantial coverage for inpatient hospitalization services or physician services (or both) do not provide minimum value as intended by the minimum value requirement, even if they meet the 60 percent threshold under the minimum value calculator[3] or have an actuarial certification of minimum value.

The attraction of these plans to some employers was that they could offer the plans at relatively inexpensive prices and avoid potential employer penalties of both types. The IRS announcement means that while employers offering these plans will still meet the employer mandate rule to offer at least a "Minimum Essential Coverage" plan to 70 percent or more of its full-time employees and their children in 2015 and 95 percent in 2016 and thereafter, they will not satisfy the second requirement to offer plans with a minimum 60 percent actuarial value.

---

1. Treas. Reg. §1.36B-6(c)
2. Available at https://www.cms.gov/CCIIO/Resources/Regulations-and-Guidance/Downloads/mv-calculator-methodology.pdf , stating on page 6: "Because large employer plans are not required to cover the essential health benefits (EHB), the MV Calculator allows the user to indicate that a service listed in the calculator is not covered. In order to account for the shift in the total per member per year (PMPY) average spending distribution when removing carved-out services, the following adjustment is performed. First, the proportion of average spending that the carved out services account for is calculated for every point in the continuance tables. This proportion is then multiplied by the ratio between the total spending level and average per member per year spending for enrollees capped at that spending level, and then subtracted from the total spending level. This creates a new continuance distribution with modified total spending but unmodified utilization rates. The MV calculation proceeds regularly, with carved-out services subject to the deductible, 0% coinsurance, and their MOOP removed from the numerator but not from the denominator of the MV calculation." (Last accessed August 14, 2019).
3. See Minimum Value Calculator at https://www.cms.gov/CCIIO/Resources/Regulations-and-Guidance/Downloads/mv-calculator-final-4-11-2013.xlsm. (Last accessed August 13, 2019).

The new regulation will allow the staff of these employers who want to obtain more comprehensive coverage from a public health exchange to qualify for a subsidy. It also puts the employer at risk of a penalty if the worker chooses to obtain subsidized coverage in an exchange.

For employers that, as of November 3, 2014, had already enrolled or begun to enroll employees in one of these stripped-down health care plans, the IRS will forgive employer mandate penalties through the plan year that begins on or before March 1, 2015.

However, employers offering one of the pre-November 4, 2014, health care plans through the 2015 plan year end are instructed not to state or imply to employees that the offer of coverage precludes the employee from obtaining a premium tax credit in a public exchange. Employers must also "timely correct" any prior disclosures that stated or implied that the offer of coverage precluded an individual from obtaining a subsidy on the exchange.

678. When is employer coverage unaffordable?

An employer-sponsored plan is affordable if the employee's required contribution (within the meaning of Internal Revenue Code section 5000A(e)(1)(B)) for that employee's self-only coverage does not exceed 9.56 in 2018, 9.86 percent in 2019, or 9.78 percent in 2020 of the employee's household income for the taxable year.[1] Household income is the modified adjusted gross income of the employee and any members of the employee's family (including a spouse and dependents) who are required to file income tax returns.[2] Thus, the cost of dependent coverage is irrelevant in measuring affordability.

679. What safe harbors are available for an employer to determine if its health coverage is affordable?

Three safe harbors for affordability (and employer immunity for the penalty) are offered.

(1) **Employer's W-2 Pay for Current Year.** One is the employee's W-2 wages reported in Box 1 safe harbor (this does not count 401(k) and 125 plan elective deferrals) by that employer.

(2) **Rate of Pay Safe Harbor.** The employer (1) takes the hourly rate of pay for each hourly employee who is eligible to participate in the health plan as of the beginning of the plan year, (2) multiplies that rate by 130 hours per month, and (3) determines affordability based on the resulting monthly wage amount. Specifically, the employee's monthly contribution amount (for the self-only premium of the employer's lowest cost coverage that provides minimum value) is affordable if it is equal to or lower than 9.56 percent in 2018, 9.86 in 2019, and 9.78 in 2020 of the computed monthly wages (that is, the employee's applicable hourly rate of pay x 130 hours). For salaried employees, monthly salary would be used instead of hourly salary multiplied by 130. An employer may use this safe harbor only if, with respect to the employees for whom the employer applies the safe harbor, the employer did

---

1.   IRC Sec. 36B(c)(2)(C)(i) and Reg. §1.36B-1(e).
2.   IRC Sec. 36B(d)(2)(A).

not reduce the hourly wages of hourly employees or the monthly wages of salaried employees during the year. The rate of pay safe harbor is a design-based safe harbor that should be easy for employers to apply and allows them prospectively to satisfy affordability without the need to analyze every employee's wages and hours.

(3)   **Federal Poverty Line (FPL) Safe Harbor.** Employer provided coverage offered to an employee is affordable if the employee's cost for self-only coverage under the plan does not exceed 9.56 percent in 2018, 9.86 in 2019, and 9.78 in 2020 of the FPL for that employee, not the family. Employers use the most recently published poverty guidelines as of the first day of the plan year of the health plan.

680. What are the limited nonassessment periods when the employer mandate penalty will not be assessed?

An employer will not be subject to an employer mandate penalty under Internal Revenue Code section 4980H(a), and in certain cases Internal Revenue Code section 4980H(b), during a "limited nonassessment period"[1] with respect to an employee in the following circumstances:

- The transition rule for an employer's first year as an applicable large employer[2]

- The application of Internal Revenue Code section 4980H for the three full calendar month period beginning with the first full calendar month in which an employee is first otherwise eligible for an offer of coverage under the monthly measurement method[3]

- The application of Internal Revenue Code section 4980H during the initial three full calendar months of employment for an employee reasonably expected to be a full-time employee at the start date, under the look-back measurement method[4]

- The application of Internal Revenue Code section 4980H during the initial measurement period to a new variable-hour employee, seasonal employee, or part-time employee determined to be employed on average at least thirty hours of service per week, under the look-back measurement method[5]

- The application of Internal Revenue Code section 4980H following an employee's change in employment status to a full-time employee during the initial measurement period, under the look-back measurement method[6]

- The application of Internal Revenue Code section 4980H to the calendar month in which an employee's start date occurs on a day other than the first day of the calendar month[7]

---

1.   Treas. Reg. §54 .4980H-1(a)(26).
2.   Treas. Reg. §54 .4980H-2(b)(5).
3.   Treas. Reg. §54 .4980H-3(c)(2).
4.   Treas. Reg. §54 .4980H-3(d)(2)(iii).
5.   Treas. Reg. §54 .4980H-3(d)(3)(iii).
6.   Treas. Reg. §54 .4980H-3(d)(3)(vii).
7.   Treas. Reg. §§54 .4980H-4(c) and -5(c).

Relief from the penalty under Internal Revenue Code section 4980H provided by the rules above does not affect an employee's eligibility for a premium tax credit.[1]

HRA Reimbursement Arrangements and the Employer Penalty

681. Can an employer Health Reimbursement Account (HRA) that pays or reimburses employees for exchange or individual health insurance qualify as employer-provided minimum essential coverage to avoid the 4980H(a) penalty?

No. The definition of eligible employer-sponsored plan is that of a "group health plan" and not individual policy arrangements.[2] IRS Notice 2013-54 and FAQ guidance issued in January 2013 indicates that, for purposes of the application of the annual and lifetime limits, employer-sponsored Health Reimbursement Accounts (HRAs) cannot satisfy the exception for integrated arrangements if they are integrated with individual market coverage or with an employer plan that provides coverage through individual policies.[3] Thus, even if an offer of HRA coverage constituted an offer of minimum essential coverage, the offer would violate the rule prohibiting annual and lifetime dollar limits.

Separate Assessment of Shared Responsibility Penalties within Controlled Group

682. Where there is an applicable large employer comprised of related employers, how is the employer mandate penalty, if applicable, calculated?

While determination of large employer status is made on a related group of employers' basis, the assessment of the shared responsibility penalties is determined on a member-by-member basis within the employer group. Therefore, shared responsibility penalties are "computed and assessed separately for each applicable large employer, taking into account that member's offer of coverage and based on that member's number of full-time employees."

Thirty Full-Time Employee Subtraction Prorated. Within an employer group of related employers, only a single thirty full-time employee reduction in determining the penalty is allowed. It must be prorated among the employers in the employer group to prevent smaller members of the group from avoiding the penalty altogether.

683. Will the insured plan nondiscrimination requirements, when effective, impact health insurance offered by related employers?

Yes. While delayed indefinitely until the IRS issues regulations, the nondiscrimination requirements for insured plans (other than for grandfathered plans), when they are effective,

---

1. Preamble to final regulations (Shared Responsibility for Employers Regarding Health Coverage), 26 CFR Parts 1, 54, and 301, 79 Fed. Reg. 8543, 8560 (Feb. 12, 2014).

2. Treas. Reg. §1.5000A-2(c).

3. See FAQs About the Affordable Care Act Implementation Part XI, Q&A-2, available at https://www.dol.gov/sites/default/files/ebsa/about-ebsa/our-activities/resource-center/faqs/aca-part-xi.pdf (Last accessed August 13, 2019).

will also apply to controlled and affiliated service group members. The nondiscrimination rules will limit an employer's ability to offer coverage to some members of an employer group, while not offering coverage to other members, unless done on a nondiscriminatory basis.

Determining Applicable Large Employer Status

684. How are those "applicable large employers" potentially subject to the employer mandate penalty determined?

Internal Revenue Code section 4980H(c)(2) defines an Applicable Large Employer (ALE) on a calendar year basis and as an employer that employed an average of at least fifty full-time and full-time equivalent common law employees on business days during the preceding calendar year. ALE status is determined based on the employer's average number of full-time equivalent employees during the prior calendar year. Full-time employees are those that work on average at least thirty hours a week. For this purpose, the hours of service of part-time employees are taken into account by aggregating the number of hours of service of all part-time employees for each month and dividing by 120 to determine the number of 'full-time equivalent employees' for the month. The determination of whether an employer is an applicable large employer is made by aggregating the hours of service of employees of all members of a controlled group of corporations or businesses under common control. However, penalties are assessed separately against each member of the group.

The look-back measurement method for identifying full-time employees is available only for purposes of determining and computing the Internal Revenue Code section 4980H liability for an employer mandate payment but not for purposes of determining if the employer is an applicable large employer. Note that to calculate the penalty, the monthly number of hours for a full time employee is 130, not 120 for either the look-back method or the monthly method. Special rules apply to employers who wish to measure service based on payroll periods rather than calendar weeks and months. If the employer was not in existence during the preceding calendar year, the employer will qualify as an applicable large employer if the employer is reasonably expected to employ on average at least fifty full-time and full-time equivalent employees and actually employs an average of at least fifty fulltime and full-time equivalent employees. Any fractional full-time equivalent employee total is rounded down. In addition, if the new employer offers minimum value coverage on or before April 1 of the first year it is an applicable large employer, the employer will not be subject to penalties for January through March of that year. A special rule is provided that exempts employers whose workforce exceeds fifty full-time employees for 120 days or fewer during the year if those excess employees are seasonal workers.

685. What if payroll periods begin after the calendar year starts or end after the calendar year ends?

Since payroll periods may not correspond to calendar months, employers using weekly, biweekly, or semimonthly payroll periods can use those periods and exclude the portion of a payroll period otherwise falling within the measurement period, but only if the employer includes the portion of a payroll period otherwise falling outside the measurement period.

For instance, an applicable large employer that uses a calendar-year measurement period can exclude the entire payroll period that includes January 1, Year 1, but only if it includes the entire payroll period that includes, and extends beyond, December 31, Year 1, into January of Year 2. An employer could exclude the payroll period that includes December 31, Year 2, but only if it includes the entire payroll period that includes January 1, Year 2 that includes a portion of December, Year 1.[1]

686. What if the employer only has fifty or more full time and full-time equivalent employees for four or fewer months?

If, in the prior calendar year, the employer only exceeds forty-nine employees for four or less calendar months (not necessarily consecutive) or 120 or fewer days (not necessarily consecutive) and the excess over forty-nine for those four months or 120 days are seasonal employees, then the employer is not an applicable large employer. Seasonal employees are defined by reference to a DOL regulation for seasonal agricultural workers[2] and also include retail workers employed exclusively during holiday seasons.[3] However, seasonal workers are not limited to agricultural or retail workers. The term "seasonal employee" is defined as "an employee who is hired into a position for which the customary annual employment is six months or less."[4] Employers may apply a reasonable, good faith interpretation of the statutory definition of seasonal worker.[5]

Even if an employer is not an applicable large employer, while it is not subject to the employer mandate, it is subject to other healthcare reform rules (other than rules not applicable to grandfathered plans if it has a grandfathered plan), such as the health insurance reforms discussed in Part 7 of this book. For example, such employers are subject to the new wellness program rules and the ninety-day waiting period limitation, both of which go into effect for plan years beginning on or after January 1, 2014.

687. How are total U.S. employees for the preceding calendar year determined using the look-back method?

To determine if the employer is an applicable large employer, the calculation is made as follows:

- Calculate the number of full-time employees (including seasonal employees) for each calendar month in the preceding calendar year.

- Calculate the number of full-time equivalents (including seasonal employees) for each calendar month in the preceding calendar year (using the method described above).

---

1. Treas. Reg. §54.4980H-3(c)(1)(ii).
2. 29 CFR §502.10(b)(3)(ii)(A) provides, "Labor is performed on a seasonal basis where, ordinarily, the employment pertains to or is of the kind exclusively performed at certain seasons or periods of the year and which, from its nature, may not be continuous or carried on throughout the year. A worker who moves from one seasonal activity to another, while employed in agriculture or performing agricultural labor, is employed on a seasonal basis even though he may continue to be employed during a major portion of the year."
3. IRC Sec. 4980H(c)(2)(B)(ii).
4. Treas. Reg. §54.4980H-1(a)(38).
5. 78 Fed. Reg. 217, 222 (Jan. 2, 2013).

- Add the number of full-time employees and full-time equivalents obtained in for each month of the preceding calendar year.

- Add up the twelve monthly numbers from the preceding items and divide the sum by twelve. This is the average number of full-time employees for the preceding calendar year. Fractional amounts are disregarded

If the number obtained is less than fifty, then the employer is not an applicable large employer for the current calendar year. If the number obtained is fifty or greater and the employer included seasonal employees in one or both of the first two steps, the employer may then apply the special rule for seasonal employees to see if they can be excluded, as discussed below.

688. What if an employer's workforce exceeds fifty full-time employees for no more than 120 days?

The statute provides that an employer with fifty or more full-time employees can avoid applicable large employer status if:

- the employer's workforce exceeds fifty full-time employees for no more than 120 days (or four calendar months) during the calendar year; and

- the employees in excess of fifty employed during such 120 day (or four calendar month) period were seasonal workers.[1]

The four-month or 120 day periods need not be consecutive.

Thus, large employer status does not exist where the employer's non-seasonal workforce (including full-time equivalents for part-time employees) is forty nine or fewer.

The 120 day period referred to in Internal Revenue Code section 4980H(c)(2)(B)(ii) is not part of the definition of the term seasonal worker, and an employee would not necessarily be precluded from being treated as a seasonal worker merely because the employee works, for example, on a seasonal basis for five consecutive months. In addition, the 120 day period referred to in Internal Revenue Code section 4980H(c)(2)(B)(ii) is relevant only for applying the seasonal worker exception for determining status as an applicable large employer. It is not relevant for determining whether an employee is a seasonal employee for purposes of the look-back measurement method (meaning that an employee who provides services for more than 120 days per year may nonetheless qualify as a seasonal employee).

An open question exists as to someone hired as a seasonal employee who is converted to a regular employee. Logic indicates that they should be immediately eligible for the employer's health plan if they were hired to work as seasonal help thirty-plus hours a week and remain employed beyond 120 days (or four months).

---

1.   IRC Sec. 4980H(c)(2)(B); Treas. Reg. §54.4980H-2(b)(2).

689. How is an employer with fewer than fifty employees not counting seasonal employees treated?

This question is addressed in the treasury regulation's Example 3:[1]

During 2015, Employer has forty full-time employees for the entire calendar year, none of whom are seasonal workers. In addition, Employer has eighty seasonal full-time workers who work from September through December 2015. Employer has no full-time equivalent employees during 2015.

Before applying the seasonal worker exception, Employer has forty full-time employees during each of eight calendar months of 2015, and 120 full-time employees during each of four calendar months of 2015, resulting in an average of 66.5 employees, namely, (40 × 8) plus (120 × 4) divided by twelve equals 66.66, rounded down to 66. However, Employer can apply the seasonal employees' exception because its workforce exceeded fifty full-time employees for only four calendar months (treated as 120 days) during 2015, and the number of full-time employees would be less than fifty during those months if seasonal workers were disregarded. Thus, Employer is not a large employer for 2016.

Counting U.S. Employees

Full-time and Part-time

690. How are employees' U.S. hours of service counted and determined?

Only hours of service in the United States are counted. The United States is the fifty states and the District of Columbia. "Hours of service" is defined as it is in ERISA, i.e., hours for which an employee is paid or entitled to be paid, including paid time off, such as vacation, holiday, illness, incapacity (including disability paid by a third party insurer), layoff, jury duty, military duty, or leave of absence.[2] This overturns the "hours worked" definition in IRS Notice 2012-58. However, special rules also result in counting unpaid FMLA or USERRA leave. Two options exist.[3] Hours of service worked outside of the U.S. are not counted, regardless of the residency or citizenship of the individual.

Hours of service calculations that result in a fraction are rounded up to the nearest whole number.

---

1. Treas. Reg. §54.4980H-2(d) Example 3.
2. Treas. Reg. §54.4980H-1(a)(21). This definition borrows heavily from existing DOL regulations. 29 CFR §2530.200b-2(a).
3. Reg. §54.4980H-3(e)(4)). Option #1: Determine the average hours of service per week for the employee during the measurement period, excluding the special unpaid leave period, and use that average as the average for the entire measurement period. Option #2: Treat employees as credited with hours of service for special unpaid leave at a rate equal to the average weekly rate at which the employee was credited with hours of service during the weeks in the measurement period that are not special unpaid leave.

691. How are hours of service counted for hourly workers?

For hourly paid employees, the employer is required to calculate actual hours of service from records of hours worked and for non-worked hours for which payment is made or due (vacation, holiday, illness, incapacity, etc., as described in Q 690).[1]

Hours of service are calculated in the following fashion:

- each hour for which an employee is paid, or entitled to payment, for the performance of duties for the employer, and

- each hour for which an employee is paid, or entitled to payment by the employer for a period of time during which no duties are performed due to vacation, holiday, illness, incapacity (including disability), layoff, jury duty, military duty or leave of absence.

Exclusion from the definition of hour of service are met by the definitions below:

- Volunteer employees: Hours of bona fide volunteer service do not count as hours of service.

- Student Work Study: Hours performed by students as part of the federal work study program or a substantially similar program of a state or political subdivision do not count as hours of service.

- Members of religious orders: A religious order is permitted to not count as an hour of service work performed by an individual who is subject to a vow of poverty. The employee must be a member of the religious order and must be performing tasks that are usually required of active members of that order. Caution: further advice may be issued on this topic.

- Non-U.S. source income: Hours of service that is taxed as income from sources outside the United States (generally meaning certain work overseas) does not count.

692. How are salaried employees' hours of service counted?

For salaried employees, an employer has the option to count actual hours or service in each day or two equivalencies, i.e., eight hours per day worked or forty hours per week worked unless the equivalencies understate the hours. Thus, the daily equivalency cannot be used for someone who works three ten-hour days per week.[2] The employer is NOT required to use the same hours of service calculation method for all non-hourly employee as long as the classifications are reasonable and consistently applied.

---

1.   Treas. Reg. §54.4980H-3(b)(1).
2.   Treas. Reg. §54.4980H-3(b)(2).

693. Are there rules for employees with special work patterns?

Certain categories of employees have hours of service that are particularly challenging to identify or track. In other cases, general rules for determining hours of service in the employer shared responsibility regulations may present special difficulties. For these workers, employers are required to use a reasonable method of crediting hours of service that is consistent with the employer shared responsibility provisions. The preamble to the employer shared responsibility regulations provides guidance for the following categories on certain methods of determining hours of service that are reasonable and certain other methods that are unreasonable:

- Commissioned employees

- Adjunct faculty

- Transportation employees (e.g., airline pilots)

- Employees in similar positions

Hours of service for adjunct faculty must be based not only on time spent teaching classes, but also time preparing for classes. The following safe harbor is provided. One (but not the only reasonable) method is to count (1) an additional one and one-quarter hours for each hour of teaching or classroom time (to allow for preparation, grading tests, etc.) plus (2) an hour of service per week for each additional hour outside of the classroom the faculty member spends performing duties he or she is required to perform (such as required office hours or required attendance at faculty meetings).[1]

Hours of service for commissioned employees would also include business travel for a traveling salesperson compensated on a commission basis. An averaging method is provided for employees of education institutions that generally would result in an employee who works full-time during the active portions of the academic year being a full-time employee.

694. Can different counting methods be used by different controlled or affiliated group members?

Yes. An Applicable Large Employer (ALE) member is not required to apply the same methods as other applicable large employer members of the same applicable large employer group for the same or different classifications of non-hourly employees, provided that in each case the classifications are reasonable and consistently applied by the applicable large employer member.[2]

695. What is the definition of a full-time employee under the application of the Affordable Care Act?

The definition is the same for purposes of determining applicable large employer status and calculating the penalty for an applicable large employer. The statute defines full-time employees as those who, with respect to any month, have at least thirty hours of service per week or

---

1. Preamble to final regulations at 79 Fed. Reg. p. 8,552.
2. Treas. Reg. §54.4980H-3(b)(2)(ii).

130 hours of service in a calendar month, provided the employer applies the actual hour or equivalency rules (discussed subsequently) on a reasonable and consistent basis.[1] Hours of service worked outside of the U.S. are not counted, regardless of the residency or citizenship of the individual. Absent use of a look back period, employees must be counted monthly.

The employer mandate penalty must be paid monthly. It is not possible to know for certain whether coverage must be offered to any particular employee because of his or her full-time status until the end of a month because the excise tax payments are determined month-by-month. Since this monthly calculation would make determinations very difficult, the employer can use a look back period to determine if an employer is an "applicable large employer" potentially subject to the employer mandate penalty. If the employer is an applicable large employer during the look back period, then it must offer affordable minimum value coverage during the "stability period" to avoid the penalty.

696. What is the optional method for counting full-time employees in a prior year that eliminates the need to count for the current month?

To calculate the potential penalty for an applicable large, employer, the regulations provide a method for calculating the number of full-time employees during the preceding calendar year, the look-back method that does not differentiate between business days and nonbusiness days.[2] Rather than looking at days, the method focuses on the number of full-time employees during each calendar month and then obtains an average number of full-time employees by dividing by twelve.

Specifically, the method involves the following steps:

(1)   Calculate the number of full-time employees (including seasonal employees) for each calendar month in the preceding calendar year.

(2)   Calculate the number of full-time equivalents (including seasonal employees) for each calendar month in the preceding calendar year (using the method described above).

(3)   Add the number of full-time employees and full-time equivalents obtained in Step 1 and Step 2 for each month of the preceding calendar year.

(4)   Add up the twelve monthly numbers from Step 3 and divide the sum by twelve. This is the average number of full-time employees for the preceding calendar year.[3]

(5)   If the number obtained in Step 4 is less than fifty, then the employer is not an applicable large employer for the current calendar year. If the number obtained in Step 4 is fifty or greater and the employer included seasonal employees in Step 1 and/or Step 2, the employer may then apply the special rule for seasonal employees. This rule is described in Q 697.

---

1.   Treas. Reg. §54.4980H-1(a)(18).
2.   Treas. Reg. §54.4980H-2(b)(1).
3.   Fractional amounts are ignored and the employer rounds down to the next-lowest whole number after dividing by 12 (i.e., 49.9 equals forty-nine full-time employees).

697. What are part-time employees and variable hour employees and how does one determine how part-time employees are converted into full-time equivalent employees?

For applicable large employers (i.e., employers who employed at least fifty full-time and full-time equivalent employees on business days during the preceding calendar year), complying with the employer mandate, i.e., the shared responsibility or play or pay rules, determining an employee's status as is important. The regulations establish two methods to count employees for purposes of calculating the potential penalty:

(1) the current monthly (month-by-month) measurement method and

(2) the look-back measurement method.

The look-back measurement method classifies newly-hired employees as full-time, variable hour, seasonal or part-time. Of these, what constitutes a "new variable hour employee" has proved to be the most confusing.

A new part-time employee is "a new employee who the applicable large employer member reasonably expects to be employed on average less than thirty hours of service per week during the initial measurement period, based on the facts and circumstances at the employee's start date."[1] Part-time employees are tested along with new variable hour and new seasonal employees under the provisions of the look-back measurement method dealing with the initial measurement periods. Once a part-time employee has been employed for a full standard measurement period, he or she is tested as an "ongoing employee."

The number of full-time equivalents the employer employed during the preceding calendar year are taken into account. All employees (including seasonal workers) who were not employed on an average of at least thirty hours of service per week for a calendar month in the preceding calendar year are included in calculating the number of full-time equivalents for that calendar month.[2] Hours of service worked outside of the U.S. are not counted, regardless of the residency or citizenship of the individual.

The approach for converting part-time employees to full-time equivalents is as follows:

- Calculate the aggregate hours of service in a month for employees who are not full-time employees, including seasonal employees, for that month. Do not include more than 120 hours of service for any employee.

- Divide the total hours of service from Step 1 by 120.[3]

Note that for part-time employees, unlike full-time employees, there is no 130 hour per month option. The number is 120 hours for this rule.

---

1.   Treas. Reg. §54.4980H-1(a)(32).
2.   Treas. Reg. §54.4980H-2(c)(1).
3.   Treas. Reg. §54.4980H-2(c)(2).

The result is the number of full-time equivalent employees for the month. This can result in a number and a fraction. The fraction is rounded down. For example, if for a calendar month employees who were not employed on average at least thirty hours of service per week have 1,260 hours of service taken together, there would be 10.5 FTEs for that month. Thus, 49.9 full-time employees (including FTEs) for the preceding calendar year would be rounded down to forty-nine full-time employees.

698. Is there a difference between full-time employees and full-time equivalent employees?

Yes. Full-time equivalent employees are counted by combining the hours of part-time employees, each of whom individually is not a full-time employee, but who in combination count as one or more full-time employees. For purposes of the employer shared responsibility provisions, the number of an employer's full-time equivalent employees is only relevant for purposes of determining whether the employer is an ALE.

An ALE need not offer coverage to its part-time employees to avoid an employer shared responsibility payment, and a part-time employee's receipt of a premium tax credit for purchasing coverage through the Marketplace cannot be the basis for liability for an employer shared responsibility payment.

Calculating the Employer Mandate Penalty

699. How are employees counted in the current year for the "applicable large employer" penalty calculation?

While the determination of whether a company is an applicable large employer is based on prior calendar year employment except for new employers, the shared responsibility penalties are calculated monthly in the current year. If an employer is not an applicable large employer based on the prior calendar year, then it need not worry how to determine if it is liable for any penalty and can ignore the following rules.

There are two ways to calculate the number of full-time employees – the ACTUAL method and the LOOK-BACK method:

ACTUAL METHOD: One method, while difficult and burdensome, is the actual method. Under this method, full-time employee status is determined in the current year to calculate the penalty. There is no counting of full-time equivalent employees for calculating the penalty. The potential liability of a large employer for the "play or pay" penalty for a month is determined by the number of full-time employees it had during a calendar month, while the liability under the "play or pay" penalty is determined by the number of full-time employees who enrolled in Exchange coverage and received a premium tax credit or cost-sharing reduction during the calendar month.

LOOK-BACK METHOD: The IRS acknowledged the difficulties employers may have with making monthly determinations of full-time status. Concerned that monthly determinations could result in employees moving in and out of employer versus exchange coverage, the regulations include an optional look-back measurement method to calculate the penalty that employers can use as an alternative to making a monthly determination. See Q 700.

700. How does the look-back method work?

Rather than using current monthly calculations (month-by-month)[1] for the employer mandate penalty, employers can identify full-time employees by calculating employees' hours during a specified period selected by the employer of three to twelve months (look-back standard measurement period) and then locking in that status (full-time or not) for a subsequent specified period (stability period), which is the same length as the measurement period or six months, whichever is greater. If an employer wants to have an open enrollment during a period that is not part of a measurement or the subsequent stability period, it may do so by using an administrative period not to exceed ninety days between the stability and measurement periods. Thus, the rules require that:

- the measurement and stability periods are no longer than twelve months

- the stability period for ongoing employees who work full-time during the standard measurement period is not shorter than the standard measurement period;

  - For example, if you had a twelve month standard measurement period, the stability period must also be twelve months.

- the stability period for ongoing employees who do not work full-time during the standard measurement period is no longer than the standard measurement period; and

- the administrative period is no longer than ninety days.

A "measurement period" is the look-back period over which hours are calculated to determine whether an employee has averaged at least thirty hours per week. There are two types of measurement periods: standard and initial measurement periods.

These alternative guidelines set out criteria that can help applicable large employers make determinations about the full-time status of employees, including following concepts:

- Initial measurement period. The term initial measurement period means a time period selected by an applicable large employer member of at least three consecutive calendar months but not more than twelve consecutive calendar months.[2] Pay periods including the beginning and end dates of the measurement period may be used.[3] The period begins on the employee's hire date and ends at the end of the three to twelve month initial measurement period.[4]

---

1. Treas. Reg. §54.4980H-3(c).
2. Treas. Reg. §54.4980H-1(a)(22).
3. Treas. Reg. §54.4980H-3(c)(1)(ii).
4. Treas. Reg. §54.4980H-3(c)(1)(ii).

- <u>Standard measurement period</u>. An annual designated period of not less than three months or more than twelve months used to determine whether an ongoing variable or seasonal employee is full-time.

- <u>Optional administrative period</u>. An optional period of up to ninety days for making full-time determinations and offering/implementing full-time employee coverage for the stability period.

- <u>Stability period</u>. An annual designated period of not less than six months (and not less than the corresponding measurement period) during which the employer must offer affordable minimum essential health coverage to all full-time employees, or face financial penalties for not doing so.

- <u>Full-time employees</u>. Employees are full-time if they average thirty hours of service per week or 130 hours (remember is it 120 hours per month for determining if the employer is an applicable large employer that needs to make this current year calculation on a month by month basis) of service per month. If a new employee is reasonably expected to average at least thirty hours per week at the time of hire, the employee must automatically be treated as full-time and offered group health coverage within three months of hire, which must also meet the ninety-day maximum waiting period rule.

- <u>Variable hour and seasonal employees</u>. A variable hour employee is someone whom the employer cannot reasonably determine will average at least thirty hours per week at the time of hire. No definition is provided for a seasonal employee, but presumably it would include anyone who works on a seasonal basis. Employers may use the initial measurement period to determine whether a newly hired variable or seasonal employee actually averages at least thirty hours per week, and the standard measurement period to determine whether an ongoing variable or seasonable employee actually averages at least thirty hours per week. If the employee does average at least thirty hours per week during the initial measurement period or standard measurement period, the employer must offer affordable minimum essential health coverage during the stability period or face financial penalties for not doing so.

- <u>Transition from new to ongoing employee status</u>. Once a new employee has completed an initial measurement period and has been employed for a full standard measurement period, the employee must be tested for full-time status under the ongoing employee rules for that standard measurement period, regardless of whether the employee was full-time during the initial measurement period.

These concepts are discussed in more detail in the following questions and answers.

701. What are the rules for stability periods that are longer than the associated measurement period?

There could be a period of time between the stability period associated with the initial measurement period and the stability period associated with the first full standard measurement period during which a variable hour employee or seasonal employee has been employed. This may occur in cases in which a new employee begins providing services a short period after the beginning of the standard measurement period that would apply to the employee if the employee were an ongoing employee.[1] To prevent this administrative period from creating a period during which coverage is not available, the administrative period must overlap with the prior stability period, so that, during any such administrative period applicable to ongoing employees following a standard measurement period, ongoing employees who are enrolled in coverage because of their status as full-time employees based on a prior measurement period must continue to be covered through the administrative period.[2]

702. How are measurement and stability periods implemented?

Generally, for a new employee who is not reasonably expected (on the date of hire) to work an average of thirty or more hours per week during the first twelve months of employment, the employer must track actual hours during those first twelve months to determine whether the employee must be treated as full-time during the following twelve month stability period. Rather than tracking actual hours during each new employee's (individual) first twelve months of employment, employers may limit the number of initial measurement periods (and initial stability periods) by grouping new hires into twelve groups for purposes of determining initial measurement periods (and initial stability periods). An employer can create such groups by adopting an initial measurement period that begins on the first day of the first calendar month following the employee's start date (or, if later, as of the first day of the first payroll period beginning on or after the employee's start date). For example, an employer that establishes twelve month initial measurement periods that begin on the first day of the first calendar month following the employee's start date will group all variable hour employees and seasonal employees who are hired in the month of May into one group for purposes of determining average hours actually worked during the initial measurement period; each employee in that group will have an initial measurement period that begins on the following June 1st (rather than on the employee's start date).

Many employers will use a twelve-month stability period. i.e., the period during which an employee's status as full-time or not full-time generally is determined for employer mandate purposes. Using a twelve-month stability period dictates that the preceding measurement period also must be twelve months long. However, for the stability period that began in 2019, employers may adopt a transition measurement period that is shorter than twelve months but that is no less than six months. The transition measurement period must begin no later than July 1, 2018, and must end no earlier than ninety days before the first day of the 2019 plan year (ninety days being the maximum permissible administrative period). For example, an employer with a

---

1. 79 Fed. Reg. p. 8,559.
2. Treas. Reg. §54.4980H-3(d)(1)(vi).

calendar year plan (and calendar year stability period) may use a transition measurement period from April 15, 2018 through October 14, 2018 (six months), followed by an administrative period ending on December 31, 2018.

703. How are new nonseasonal full-time employees treated?

If an employee is reasonably expected at his or her start date to be a full-time employee and average thirty hours of service or more per week, and is not a seasonal employee, the look-back and stability period safe harbor rules do not apply.[1] Service to more than one member in the controlled or affiliated service group is aggregated for purpose of determining full-time status.[2] If an applicable large employer does not offer coverage to such employee at or before the end of the employee's initial three full calendar months of employment, the employer may be subject to a penalty for those first three months as well as for any subsequent months of employment for which coverage is not offered.[3] The maximum ninety-calendar-day waiting period rule, which applies to employers of all sizes, must also be met and can require that coverage be offered more quickly than the complete three-month rule when an employee is hired mid-month.[4] Employers are apparently not subject to penalties for failing to offer coverage to such an employee if the employee is hired for less than three months. However, an employee who is hired for a period of less than three months and then later rehired may be a "continuous employee" under the break in service rules. See the following for a more detailed discussion of the break in service rules.

If the employer did not offer coverage to the employee by the end of the employee's initial three full calendar months of employment, the employer may be subject to a section 4980H assessable payment for those months as well as for any subsequent months for which coverage was not offered.[5]

704. How are ongoing employees tested during the safe harbor standard measurement period?

An "ongoing employee" is an employee who has been employed for at least one complete standard measurement period.[6] If an employer's group health plan offers coverage only to full-time employees, the employer may use both a measurement period of between three and twelve consecutive months. The months are not required to be calendar months. Thus, a twelve month measurement period could begin October 15, and end the following October 14, followed by an optional administrative period of up to ninety days for variable-hour and seasonal employees. An employer can choose the months when the standard measurement period starts and ends, such as the calendar year, plan year, or the period ending just before open enrollment begins.

---

1.   Treas. Reg. §54.4980H-3(c)(2).
2.   Treas. Reg. §54.4980H-1(a)(21)(ii).
3.   Treas. Reg. §54.4980H-3(c)(2).
4.   PHSA §2708, added by PPACA §1201 (2010). The 90 days cannot be extended to the first day of the next month or by a weekend. Thus, an employer wanting to enroll people on the first day of a month could use a 60 day wait with enrollment coinciding with or next following end of the 60 days. Treas. Reg. §54.9815-2708(d); Prop. DOL Reg. §2590.715-2708(d); Prop. HHS Reg. §147.116(d).
5.   Treas. Reg. §54.4980H-3(c)(2).
6.   Treas. Reg. §54.4980H-1(a)(27).

Previously determined full-time employees already enrolled in coverage continue to be offered coverage through the administrative period.[1]

705. Can payroll periods be used in lieu of calendar months?

Yes. Since hours are commonly counted during payroll periods and since payroll periods may not correspond to calendar months, a special rule to align calendar month measurement periods with payroll periods for employers using weekly, biweekly, or semi-monthly payroll periods. The employer can exclude the portion of the first, partial payroll period falling in the measurement period if the employer includes the portion of the last payroll period otherwise falling outside the measurement period. For example, if the employer uses a calendar-year measurement period, it can exclude the entire payroll period that starts before the calendar year and includes January 1, Year 1, but only if it includes the entire last payroll period that includes, and extends beyond, December 31, Year 1, into January of Year 2. Similarly, the employer could exclude the entire payroll period that includes December 31 if it includes the entire payroll period that includes January 1, (which will include a portion of the prior calendar year).[2]

706. What happens after an employee has completed an initial measurement period and has been employed for a full standard measurement period?

Once a new employee has completed an initial measurement period and has been employed for a full standard measurement period, the employee must be tested for full-time status under the ongoing employee rules for that standard measurement period, regardless of whether the employee was full-time during the initial measurement period.

The "stability period" is the look-forward period for which an employee's status determined during the measurement period is locked in, regardless of the employee's actual hours during this stability period as long as the employee remains employed. The stability period begins at the end of the measurement period and any administrative period, if the employer elects to have one.[3]

If an employee was employed an average of at least thirty hours of service per week, this stability period must be least six consecutive calendar months and up to twelve months. The stability period can be no shorter than the standard measurement period.[4] Even if employee's position or employment status changes during the stability period, it will not affect the employee's coverage, which must continue to the end of the stability period.[5]

If an employee was not employed an average at least thirty hours of service per week during the standard measurement period, the applicable large employer may treat the employee as not a full-time employee during the stability period that follows, but is not longer than, the standard measurement period. The stability period must begin immediately after the end of the measurement period and any applicable administrative period.[6]

---

1.   Treas. Reg. §54.4980H-3(c)(1)(viii), Example (i).
2.   Treas. Reg. §54.4980H-3(c)(1)(ii).
3.   Treas. Reg. §54.4980H-1(a)(39).
4.   Treas. Reg. §54.4980H-3(c)(1)(iii).
5.   Treas. Reg. §54.4980H-3(c)(1).
6.   Treas. Reg. §54.4980H-3(c)(1)(iv).

Thus, combining these two rules, if there is a measurement period in which some employees are full-time and others are not, the stability period must be the same length as the standard measurement period, and the standard measurement period must be at least six months.

707. How does the optional administrative period work?

The "optional administrative period," if utilized, is a period after the end of a measurement period and before the beginning of the next stability period, not to exceed ninety days, during which the employer can perform administrative tasks, such as calculating the hours for the measurement period, determining eligibility for coverage, providing enrollment materials to eligible employees, and conducting open enrollment.[1] An example would be an employer with a calendar year plan that chooses a measurement period of October 15, 2019 to October 14, 2020, a two and 1½ month administrative period from October 15, 2019 to December 31, 2019 in advance of its 2020 calendar plan year, which is the stability period. The administrative period must overlap with the prior stability period, i.e., full-time employees enrolled in coverage based on a prior measurement period must continue to be covered through the administrative period connected to a more recent measurement period to prevent a gap in health coverage.[2]

Applicable large employer members may use administrative periods that differ in length for the categories of employees. Those categories are discussed in Q 709.

708. Can an employer change its measurement and stability periods?

Yes. An employer may change its standard measurement and stability periods each year but cannot make a change for a given year once the standard measurement period has begun.

709. May different measurement and stability periods be used for different types of employees?

Yes. A ninety-day or less stability period may be used after the measurement period, but any stability period selected by the applicable large employer member must be uniform for all employees. An applicable large employer member may apply different measurement periods, stability periods, and administrative periods for the following categories of employees:

(1)   Each group of collectively bargained employees covered by a separate collective bargaining agreement

(2)   Collectively bargained and noncollectively bargained employees

(3)   Salaried employees and hourly employees

(4)   Employees whose primary places of employment are in different states

(5)   Employees employed by different employers in the related employer group[3]

---

1.   Treas. Reg. §54.4980H-1(c)(1)(vi).
2.   Treas. Reg. §54.4980H-3(c)(1)(vi).
3.   Treas. Reg. §4980H- 3(c)(1)(v).

710. What is the latest update from the IRS regarding changes in employer mandate measurement periods and changes in testing methods?

The IRS is providing additional guidance on changes in employer mandate measurement periods and changes in testing methods, including changes due to mergers and acquisitions.

For purposes of the employer mandate, applicable large employers must identify their "full-time employees." Final regulations issued under Internal Revenue Code section 4980H provide two principle testing methods: the "monthly measurement method" and the "look-back measurement method." IRS Notice 2014-49 explains the approaches that employers may use when addressing changes in and among measurement methods, including:

- a change in the look-back measurement method (e.g., where an employee transfers within an employer from a position for which one measurement period applies to a position for which a different measurement period applies); or

- where the measurement period applicable to an employee changes (e.g., an employer changes the measurement method applicable to employees within a permissible category).

Internal Revenue Code section 4980H final regulations prescribe categories of employees within which an employer may apply a particular measurement period. The categories are

(i)   collectively bargained employees and noncollectively bargained employees,

(ii)   each group of collectively bargained employees covered by a separate bargaining agreement,

(iii)   salaried employees and hourly employees, and

(iv)   employees whose primary places of employment are in different states.

With respect to each of the enumerated categories, an employer may use measurement and stability periods that differ either in length or in their starting and ending dates, or it may apply either the look-back measurement method or the monthly measurement method. But employers are not free, for example, to use the look-back measurement method for employees with variable work schedules and the monthly measurement method for employees with more predictable work schedules.

The final regulations include extensive and complex rules that apply to an employee who experiences a change in employment status from a position for which the look-back measurement method is used to a position for which the monthly measurement method is used (or vice versa). These rules generally require that an employee transferring from a position for which the employer is using the look-back measurement method to a position for which the employer is using the monthly measurement method (and who at the date of transfer is in a stability period during which the employee is treated as a full-time employee) must continue to be treated as a full-time employee during the remainder of the stability period. If the employee is in a stability period for which the employee is not treated as a full-time employee, the employer may continue to treat the employee as not a full-time employee during the remainder of the stability period. The rule extends to the stability period that immediately follows the stability period during which the employee transferred. The intent is to protect the transferring employee by giving him or her the better of the two methods during the handoff to the new measurement method. But the final regulations do not address whether, or under what conditions, an employer that uses a measurement method for a category of employees may subsequently change that measurement method. Instead, the preamble to the final regulations states:[1]

> "The Treasury Department and the IRS anticipate that the rules with respect to a transfer from a position to which one look-back measurement method applies to a position to which another look-back measurement method applies will require complex rules because the methods may differ not only in the length of the applicable measurement and stability periods, but also the starting dates of the measurement periods. . . . To provide for these rules in the most comprehensible format, as well as to ensure flexibility to address situations that arise that have not currently been contemplated, the final regulations provide that with respect to the determination of full-time employee status, the Commissioner may prescribe additional guidance of general applicability, published in the Internal Revenue Bulletin." IRS Notice 2014-49 does that.

Employee transferring from a position for which one measurement period applies to a position for which a different measurement period applies.

This first of the two situations addressed in Notice 2014-49 involves instances in which an employee, who has been employed in one position (the "first position") for which the employer uses the look-back measurement method, transfers to another position (the "second position") for which the employer also uses the look-back measurement method, but with a measurement period that is different from the measurement period applicable to the first position. Under this proposed approach, following a transfer, an employer includes hours of service earned in the first position either by counting the hours of service using the counting method applied to the employee in the first position, or recalculating the hours of service earned in the first position using the hours of service counting method applied to the employee in the second position. The employer must in each case treat all similarly situated employees consistently.

The approach envisioned by the notice varies depending on whether the transferring employee is in a measurement, stability, or administrative period. (The notice reminds us that an initial measurement period does not apply to new employees who are full-time employees, and so are not variable-hour, seasonal, or part-time employees.)

(i) Employees in a stability period or an administrative period.

If an employee is in a stability period or an administrative period applicable to the first position as of the date of transfer, the employee's status as a full-time or nonfull-time employee

---

1.   79 Fed. Reg. 8563 (February 12, 2014).

for the first position remains in effect until the end of that stability period. At the end of the stability period, the employee assumes the full-time employee or nonfull-time employee status that the employee would have under the look-back measurement method applicable to the second position, but including hours of service in the first position when applying that measurement method.

Example: Position 1 and Position 2 are two positions at the same applicable large employer. For Position 1, the employer uses twelve month standard measurement and stability periods beginning January 1. For Position 2, the employer uses twelve month standard measurement and stability periods beginning July 1. There are no administrative periods.

Employee A is an ongoing employee in Position 1 who during the 2018 standard measurement period averages less than thirty hours of service per week (so she is not offered coverage during the 2019 stability period). Employee A does, however, average thirty or more hours of service per week during the period from July 1, 2018, through June 30, 2019. On August 15, 2018, Employee A transfers to Position 2. For the period from August 15, 2018, through December 31, 2018 (the end of the stability period for Position 1 during which the transfer occurs), Employee A retains her status as a non-full-time employee.

As of January 1, 2019, Employee A's status is determined under the look-back measurement method applicable to Position 2. Employee A is a full-time employee starting January 1, 2019, because Employee A averaged thirty or more hours of service per week in the measurement period for Position 2 beginning July 1, 2018 and ending June 30, 2019 (which has a stability period of July 1, 2019 through June 30, 2019). After June 30, 2019, Employee A's status continues to be determined using the applicable measurement period for Position 2.

In sum, the rule requires an employer to run out the employee's status as full-time (or not) for the current Position 1 stability period, then shift to the Position 2 measurement and stability period taking into account all Position 1 hours of service.

(ii) If an employee is not in a stability period or in an administrative period immediately following the end of the initial measurement period, the employee's status as a full-time or nonfull-time employee is determined solely under the look-back measurement method applicable to the second position as of the date of transfer, including all hours of service in the first position.

Example: For Position 1, the employer uses twelve-month standard measurement and stability periods beginning January 1 and a twelve month initial measurement period beginning on each employee's start date. For Position 2, the employer uses six-month standard measurement and stability periods beginning January 1 and July 1 and a six month initial measurement period beginning on an employee's start date. The employer hires Employee B into Position 1 as a new variable-hour employee on January 1, 2019. Employee B averages thirty or more hours of service per week during the period from January 1 through June 30, 2019. On October 1, 2019, at which time Employee B is in the initial measurement period for Position 1, Employee B transfers from Position 1 to Position 2.

At the date of the transfer, Employee B is not in a stability period for Position 1 because Employee B has not been employed for a full initial measurement period or a full standard measurement period. Accordingly, Employee B's status is determined under the measurement method applicable to Position 2 as of the date of transfer, taking into account Employee B's hours of service in Position 1.

Employer change in measurement methods for one or more permissible categories of employees.

The second of the two situations addressed in Notice 2014-49 involves instances in which an employer changes the measurement method applicable to a permissible category of employees. A change in measurement method may include a change from the look-back measurement method to the monthly measurement method (or vice versa), or a change in the duration or start date of any applicable measurement period under the look-back measurement method.

Generally, the status of any employee whose applicable measurement period under the look-back measurement method is changed by the employer is determined as if the employee had transferred from a position for which the original measurement method applies to a position for which the revised measurement method applies as of the effective date of the change, applying the rules described above that govern changes in employment status from a position for which the look-back measurement method is used to a position for which the monthly measurement method is used or vice versa.

The notice provides an example in which an employer determines the full-time employee status of employees covered by a particular Collective Bargaining Agreement (CBA) using six month measurement and stability periods, each starting April 1 and October 1, and determines the status of employees not covered by the CBA using twelve month measurement and stability periods, each starting January 1. On April 1, 2017, the employer changes the look-back measurement method for employees not covered by the CBA to be the same as that used for employees covered by the CBA.

For a transition period following April 1, 2018, the status of employees not covered by the CBA must be made in a manner consistent with this notice, treating each employee who is subject to the measurement method applicable to employees not covered by the CBA as if on April 1, 2018, that employee had transferred from a position subject to the original measurement method to a position subject to the revised measurement method. Accordingly, each employee subject to the measurement method applicable to employees not covered by the CBA who is in a stability period as of April 1, 2018 retains his or her status as a full-time employee or non-full-time employee, as determined under the original measurement method for the remainder of the twelve month stability period applicable to that employee. Each such employee who is not in a stability period as of April 1, 2018, has his or her status determined as of April 1, 2018, in accordance with the six month measurement method.

Impact on mergers and acquisitions.

The notice states that entities involved in corporate transactions may "have different measurement methods for their respective employees in a particular category." Until further guidance is issued, and at least through the end of calendar year 2018, a party to a corporate transaction in which employers use different measurement methods can rely on the approach described in the notice.

In addition, the notice provides transition relief under which a party to the transaction "will not be treated as applying an impermissible categorization of employees" merely because it continues to apply the measurement method in effect immediately before the corporate transaction. The transition period starts on the date of the transaction and ends on the last day of the first stability period following a standard measurement period that would have applied to the new employees and that begins after the date of the transaction or, in the case of an employer that uses the monthly measurement method with respect to a category of employees, the last day of the first calendar year that begins after the date of the transaction.

711. What is a new employee for purposes of the look-back rule?

A "new employee" is an employee who has not been employed for at least one complete standard measurement period.[1]

To determine if the employees meet any minimum hour plan requirements, for determining the full-time employee status of new employees, the methods vary depending upon whether the new employees are

    (1)   reasonably expected to work full-time (and are not seasonal) or

    (2)   are variable hour employees or seasonal employees.[2]

If a new variable-hour or seasonal employee is determined not to be a full-time employee during the initial measurement period, the employer may treat the employee as not a full-time employee during the stability period that follows the initial measurement period.

712. How does the optional lookback method apply to new variable hour, part-time and new seasonal employees?

A benefit of the look-back measurement method is that the employer is not penalized for failing to offer group health plan coverage to newly hired variable hour, seasonal, or part-time employees during their initial measurement period. If the variable hour, seasonal, or part-time employee is determined to work on average thirty hours or more per week during the initial measurement period, he or she must be offered coverage during the corresponding stability period, despite that he or she no longer works on average thirty hours or more per week, so long as he or she remains employed. A similar approach applies to ongoing employees. On the other hand, a new employee who is hired into a position that is full-time, and who does not qualify as part-time, variable hour or seasonal, must be offered coverage within ninety days in order to avoid the prospect of a $100 per day excise tax, and the employer mandate excise tax will apply if the employee is not offered coverage by the earlier of the three-complete-months rule or the ninety day maximum waiting period requirement. Where a person is contracted, for example, to work thirty-five hours a week for two months, they are a full time employee but if they extend beyond the two month period and remain full time, the employer still can make the offer of health coverage in time to avoid any penalty.

---

1.   Treas. Reg. §54.4980H-1(a)(26).
2.   IRS Notice 2012-58.

An employee is a "variable hour employee" if, based on the facts and circumstances at the employee's start date, the employer cannot determine whether the employee is reasonably expected to be employed on average at least thirty hours of service per week during the initial measurement period because the employee's hours are variable or otherwise uncertain. The final regulations prescribe a series of factors to be applied in making this determination and are discussed in a later question.

A "seasonal employee" is an employee who is hired into a position for which the customary annual employment is six months or less.

A "part-time employee" means a new employee who the employer reasonably expects to be employed on average less than thirty hours of service per week during the initial measurement period, "based on the facts and circumstances at the employee's start date." As is the case with variable hour employee determinations, the final regulations prescribe a series of factors to be applied.

For new variable hour employees and new seasonal employees, applicable large employer members are permitted to determine whether the new employee is a full-time employee using an initial measurement period of between three and twelve months selected by that applicable large employer member that begins on any date between the employee's start date and the first day of the first calendar month following the employee's start date.[1] Thus, new non-full-time employees will have initial measurement periods depending on their employment commencement date. The applicable large employer member measures the new employee's hours of service during the initial measurement period and determines whether the employee was employed on average at least thirty hours of service per week during this period.

The stability period for such employees must be the same length as the stability period for ongoing employees.[2] The stability period begins immediately after the end of the initial measurement period and any associated administrative period and is the longer of six consecutive calendar months or the length of the standard measurement period.[3]

If an employer's group health plan offers coverage only to full-time employees, the employer may use both a measurement period of between three and twelve months and an administrative period of up to ninety days. The stability period for such employees cannot be more than one month longer than the initial measurement period and must not exceed the remainder of the standard measurement period plus any associated administrative period in which the initial measurement period ends. Thus, an employer could use an eleven-month initial measurement period and still comply with the general rule that the initial measurement period and administrative period combined may not extend beyond the last day of the first calendar month beginning on or after the one-year anniversary of the employee's start date.

---

1.   Treas. Reg. §54.4980H-3(c)(3)(i).
2.   Treas. Reg. §54.4980H-1(c)(3).
3.   Treas. Reg. §54.4980H-3(c)(3)(ii).

713. How are new variable hour employees treated for an applicable large employer using the look-back method?

An employee is a "variable hour employee" if, based on the facts and circumstances at the employee's start date, the employer cannot determine whether the employee is reasonably expected to be employed on average at least thirty hours of service per week during the initial measurement period because the employee's hours are variable or otherwise uncertain. To prevent abuse, as new variable hour employees need not be offered health coverage, the regulations prescribe a series of factors to be applied in making this determination. The regulations identify a number of factors that ALEs can consider in evaluating whether it is reasonable to determine that a new employee is a variable-hour employee, including whether the employee is replacing an employee who was or was not a full-time employee, the extent to which employees in the same or comparable positions are or are not full-time employees, and whether the job was advertised, or otherwise communicated to the new hire or otherwise documented (for example, through a contract or job description), as requiring hours of service that would average thirty (or more) hours of service per week or less than thirty hours of service per week. No single factor is determinative, and other factors may be considered; however, these factors are only relevant for a particular new employee if the ALE has no reason to anticipate that the facts and circumstances related to that new employee will be different.[1]

Additional factors apply where the employer is a temporary staffing firm (and the temporary staffing firm, not the company where the employee is placed, is considered to be the employer of the employee), including whether other employees in the same position of employment with the temporary staffing firm:

    (1)   retain the right to reject temporary placements that the temporary staffing firm offers the employee;

    (2)   typically have periods during which no offer of temporary placement is made;

    (3)   typically are offered temporary placements for differing periods of time; and

    (4)   typically are offered temporary placements that do not extend beyond thirteen weeks.[2]

If the terms of an employment contract provide for termination before the end of the initial measurement period, can the employer take into account that the employee may terminate employment before the end of the initial measurement period? What if there is some other restriction (such as the expiration of a work visa) that will make it impossible for the employee's employment to continue through the end of the initial measurement period? The IRS informally has said these facts cannot be taken into account in determining if the employee is a variable hour

---

1.   Treas. Reg. §54.4980H–1(a)(49)(ii)(A).
2.   Treas. Reg. §54.4980H–1(a)(49)(ii)(B).

employee.[1] In its answer, the IRS states: "The purpose of the prohibition on taking into account the likelihood of termination of employment is to avoid making assumptions about employees in positions with high turnover, which would penalize employees who are working full-time hours throughout the initial measurement period. This concern is not present when the employment is of a fixed duration, either by agreement or by operation of law."[2] However, the purpose of the variable hour rule is not so limited. Variable hour status is based on the employer's inability at the date-of-hire to reasonably determine whether the employee will work full-time over the initial measurement period. The 1,560 (52 x 30) hour test is applied at the end of the initial measurement period to determine whether the employer must extend an offer of health coverage during the following stability period. Viewed this way, the cap on employee annual hours, whether by contract or otherwise, removes that uncertainty and thus is inconsistent with the premise of variable hour status.

New variable-hour employees must be treated as if they will work the entire initial measurement period.

An employer cannot take into account the likelihood that the employee may terminate employment before the end of the initial measurement period.[3] Therefore, an employer cannot classify an employee as a variable-hour employee based solely on the expectation that the employee will terminate employment at some point before the initial measurement period ends (and therefore will not average thirty hours per week over the entire initial measurement period).

714. What happens if there is a change in status to full-time for new variable hour or seasonal employees?

A new variable hour employee or seasonal employee who has a change in employment status, such that the individual is reasonably expected to work thirty or more hours of service per week during the initial measurement period, must be treated as a full-time employee on the first day of the fourth month following the change in status. However, a change in employment status of an ongoing employee does not change the employee's status as a full-time or non-full-time employee. However, in both of these situations, an employer is always allowed to change the employee's status to full-time.

715. What happens after variable-hour and seasonal employees have been employed for at least one standard measurement period?

Once a new employee has been employed for an entire standard measurement period, the employee must be tested for full-time status, beginning with that standard measurement period, at the same time and under the same conditions as other "ongoing employees." Thus, an employer, for example, with a calendar-year standard measurement period that also uses a one-year initial measurement period beginning on the employee's start date would test a new variable-hour

---

1.   Questions & Answers, American Bar Association's Section of Taxation, Employee Benefits Committee, May 9, 2014 meeting in Washington, D.C., Q&A 25. available at http://www.americanbar.org/content/dam/aba/events/employee_benefits/2014_irs_qa.authcheckdam.pdf. (Last accessed August 14, 2019).
2.   Id.
3.   Treas. Reg. §54.4980H-1(a)(43).

employee whose start date is February 12 for full-time status first based on the initial measurement period (February 12 through February 11 of the following year) and again based on the calendar-year standard measurement period (if the employee continues in employment for that entire standard measurement period) beginning on January 1 of the year after the start date.

An employee determined to be a full-time employee during an initial measurement period or standard measurement period must be treated as a full-time employee for the entire associated stability period. This is the case even if the employee is determined to be a full-time employee during the initial measurement period but determined not to be a full-time employee during the overlapping or immediately following standard measurement period. In that case, the employer may treat the employee as not a full-time employee only after the end of the stability period associated with the initial measurement period. Thereafter, the employee's full-time status would be determined in the same manner as that of the employer's other ongoing employees.

In contrast, if the employee is determined not to be a full-time employee during the initial measurement period, but is determined to be a full-time employee during the overlapping or immediately following standard measurement period, the employee must be treated as a full-time employee for the entire stability period that corresponds to that standard measurement period (even if that stability period begins before the end of the stability period associated with the initial measurement period). Thereafter, the employee's full-time status would be determined in the same manner as that of the employer's other ongoing employees.

716. What are some examples of how these rules work?

Examples – New Variable Hour Employees

The following examples, which are from the IRS regulations,[1] illustrate the look-back measurement methods described in the regulations.[2] In all examples the applicable large employer member offers all of its full-time employees and their dependents the opportunity to enroll in minimum essential coverage under an eligible employer-sponsored plan. The coverage is affordable[3] or is treated as affordable coverage under one of the affordability safe harbors[4] and provides minimum value.[5]

> *Example 1*: Twelve-Month Initial Measurement Period Followed by One-Plus Partial Month Administrative Period. Facts. Employer B uses a twelve-month standard measurement period for ongoing employees of October 15 to October 14 of the following year and a twelve-month stability period associated with that standard measurement period starting the following January 1. During the administrative period from October 15 through December 31 of each calendar year, the employer continues to offer coverage to employees who qualified for coverage for that entire calendar year based upon working on average at least thirty hours per week during the prior standard measurement period.

---

1.   Treas. Reg. §54.4980H-3(c)(5) https://www.govinfo.gov/content/pkg/CFR-2014-title26-vol17/pdf/CFR-2014-title26-vol17-sec54-4980H-3.pdf.

2.   Treas. Reg. §54.4980H-3(c)(2) through (4). https://www.govinfo.gov/content/pkg/CFR-2014-title26-vol17/pdf/CFR-2014-title26-vol17-sec54-4980H-3.pdf.

3.   IRC Sec. 36B(c)(2)(C)(i).

4.   Described in Treas. Reg. §54.4980H-5.

5.   IRC Sec. 36B(c)(2)(C)(ii).

For new variable hour employees, Employer B uses a twelve-month initial measurement period that begins on the start date and applies an administrative period from the end of the initial measurement period through the end of the first calendar month beginning on or after the end of the initial measurement period. Employer B hires Employee Y on May 10, 2018. Employee Y's initial measurement period runs from May 10, 2018, through May 9, 2019. Employee Y has an average of thirty hours of service per week during this initial measurement period ending May 9. The administrative period runs from June 1 to June 30. Employer B offers coverage to Employee Y for a stability period that runs from July 1, 2018, through June 30, 2019.

Conclusion. Employee Y has an average of thirty hours of service per week during his initial measurement period and Employer B uses an initial measurement period that does not exceed twelve months; an administrative period totaling not more than ninety days; and a combined initial measurement period and administrative period that does not last beyond the final day of the first calendar month beginning on or after the one-year anniversary of Employee Y's start date. Accordingly, from Employee Y's start date through June 30, 2018, Employer B is not subject to any employer mandate payment for Employee Y, because Employer B complies with the standards for the initial measurement period and stability periods for a new variable hour employee. Employer B must test Employee Y again based on Employer B's first standard measurement period that begins after Employee Y's start date, i.e., from October 15, 2018, through October 14, 2019.

Example 2: Eleven-Month Initial Measurement Period Followed by Two-Plus Partial Month Administrative Period. Facts. Same as Example 1, except that Employer B uses an eleven-month initial measurement period that begins on the start date and applies an administrative period from the end of the initial measurement period until the end of the second calendar month beginning after the end of the initial measurement period. Employer B hires Employee Y on May 10, 2018. Employee Y's initial measurement period runs from May 10, 2018, through April 9, 2018. Employee Y has an average of thirty hours of service per week during this initial measurement period. The administrative period runs from May 1 to June 30. Employer B offers coverage to Employee Y for a stability period that runs from July 1, 2018, through June 30, 2019.

Conclusion. Same as Example 1.

Example 3: Eleven-Month Initial Measurement Period Preceded by Partial Month Administrative Period Followed by Two-Month Administrative Period. Facts. Same as Example 1, except that Employer B uses an eleven-month initial measurement period that begins on the first day of the first calendar month beginning after the start date and applies an administrative period that runs from the end of the initial measurement period through the end of the second calendar month beginning on or after the end of the initial measurement period. Employer B hires Employee Y on May 10, 2017. Employee Y's initial measurement period runs from June 1, 2017, through April 30, 2018. Employee Y has an average of thirty hours of service per week during this initial measurement period. The administrative period is June 1 to June 30. Employer B offers coverage to Employee Y for a stability period that runs from July 1, 2018, through June 30, 2019.

Conclusion. Same as Example 1.

Example 4: Twelve-Month Initial Measurement Period Preceded by Partial Month Administrative Period and Followed by Two-Month Administrative Period. Facts. For new variable hour employees, Employer B uses a twelve-month initial measurement period that begins on the first day of the first month following the start date and applies an administrative period that runs from the end of the initial measurement period through the end of the second calendar month beginning on or after the end of the initial measurement period. Employer B hires Employee Y on May 10, 2017. Employee Y's initial measurement period runs from June 1, 2017, through May 31, 2018. Employee Y has an average of thirty hours of service per week during this initial measurement period. The stability period is June 1 to July 31. Employer B offers coverage to Employee Y for a stability period that runs from August 1, 2018, through July 31, 2019.

Conclusion. Employer B does not satisfy the standards for the look-back measurement method[1] because the combination of the initial partial month delay, the twelve-month initial measurement period, and the

---

1.   Treas. Reg. §54.4980H-3(c)(4)(v).

two month administrative period means that the coverage offered to Employee Y does not become effective until after the first day of the second calendar month following the first anniversary of Employee Y's start date. Accordingly, Employer B is potentially subject to an employer mandate penalty payment.

<u>Examples for Staffing Firm Employees; Full-Time Employees Can Have Variable Hour Status</u>. The provision barring employer reliance on expected employee tenure in making variable hour decisions does not mean, as some commentators have suggested, newly-hired temporary employees who are offered full-time assignments on their start date cannot be treated as variable hour employees and must be offered health benefits within ninety days. This ignores the specific examples provided in the regulations for determining the variable hour status of temporary employees assigned by staffing firms. The examples make clear that beginning in 2014 and in the years following, staffing firms can use up to a full twelve-month look-back period for temporary employees as long as they are properly classified as variable hour employees based on those examples. The following is a brief summary of the relevant examples:[1]

- In one example, a staffing firm expects, on the employee's start date, that the employee will be offered "short-term" assignments with "several different clients" with "significant gaps" in between, that the assignments will differ in average weekly hours, and that the number and duration of assignments offered and accepted, the gaps between, and the weekly hours, are all uncertain.

- In the other example, an employee is hired on an hourly basis to "fill in for employees who are absent and to provide additional staffing at peak times." In that example, the employer expects the employee to work "full-time for the first few months of employment, while assigned to a specific project, but also reasonably expects that the assignments will be of unpredictable duration, that there will be gaps of unpredictable duration between assignments, that the hours per week required by subsequent assignments will vary, and that [the employee] will not necessarily be available for all assignments."

The examples do not specifically define "short-term" or "few months" but the preamble to the regulations refers to assignment lengths "each generally lasting no more than two or three months"[2] and, at another point, describes short-term as "four or five months."[3]

The examples reflect Treasury and IRS's recognition that temporary employees, when they do work, generally work full-time work weeks. Hence, the mere fact that temporary employee assignments are full-time at the start does not preclude a determination of variable hour status.[4]

Continuous Full-Time Employee

<u>*Example 5*</u>: Continuous Full-Time Employee. Facts. Employer B uses a twelve-month initial measurement period that begins on the start date and applies an administrative period from the end of the initial measurement period through the end of the first calendar month beginning on or after the end of the initial measurement period. Employer B hires Employee Y on May 10, 2017, as a variable hour employee. Employee Y's initial measurement period runs from May 10, 2017, through May 9, 2018. Employee Y has an average of thirty hours of service per week during this initial measurement period. Employer B offers coverage to Employee Y for a stability period that runs from July 1, 2018, through June 30, 2019. Employer B tests Employee Y again based on Employee Y's hours of service from October 15, 2017, through October 14, 2018, Employer B's first standard measurement period that begins after Employee Y's start date and determines that Employee Y has an average of thirty hours of service a week during that period. It offers Employee Y coverage for July 1, 2018, through December 31, 2019. Employee Y also had an offer of coverage for the period of January 1,

---

1.   78 Fed. Reg. at 248. Examples 12 and 13.
2.   78 Fed. Reg. at 230.
3.   78 Fed. Reg. at 229.
4.   78 Fed. Reg. at 227.

2018, through June 30, 2018, because that period is covered by the initial stability period following the initial measurement period, during which Employee Y was determined to be a full-time employee.

Conclusion. Employer B is not subject to any potential employer mandate penalty payment for Employee Y.

Initially Full-Time Employee, Becomes Nonfull-Time Employee

Example 6: Initially Full-Time Employee, Becomes Nonfull-Time Employee. Facts. Same as Example 1; in addition, Employer B tests Employee Y again based on Employee Y's hours of service from October 15, 2017, through October 14, 2018, Employer B's first standard measurement period that begins after Employee Y's start date and determines that Employee Y has an average of twenty-eight hours of service a week during that period. Employer B continues to offer coverage to Employee Y through June 30, 2019, (the end of the stability period based on the initial measurement period during which Employee Y was determined to be a full-time employee) but does not offer coverage to Employee Y for the period of July 1, 2018, through December 31, 2018.

Conclusion. Employer B is not subject to any potential penalty payment for 2018 with respect to Employee Y, provided that it offers coverage to Employee Y from July 1, 2018, through June 30, 2019, the stability period associated with the initial measurement period.

Initially Nonfull-Time Employee

Example 7: Initially Nonfull-Time Employee. Facts. Same as Example 1, except that Employee Y has an average of twenty-eight hours of service per week during the period from May 10, 2017, through May 9, 2018, and Employer B does not offer coverage to Employee Y in 2018.

Conclusion. From Employee Y's start date through the end of 2018, Employer B is not subject to any employer mandate payment under Internal Revenue Code section 4980H because Employer B complies with the standards for the measurement and stability periods for a new variable hour employee with respect to Employee Y.

Example 8: Initially Nonfull-Time Employee, Becomes Full-Time Employee. Facts. Same as Example 7; in addition, Employer B tests Employee Y again based on Employee Y's hours of service from October 15, 2017, through October 14, 2018, Employer B's first standard measurement period that begins after Employee Y's start date, and determines that Employee Y has an average of thirty hours of service per week during this standard measurement period, and offers coverage to Employee Y for calendar year 2019.

Conclusion. Employer B is not subject to any employer mandate payment for 2019 for Employee Y.

Six-Month Measurement and Stability Periods

In Examples 9 and 10, the new employee is a new variable hour employee, and the employer uses a six-month standard measurement period with six-month stability periods associated with those standard measurement periods. The author believes that most employers will use twelve-month measurement and stability periods, but shorter periods are permitted, as shown by the following examples.

Example 9: Initially Full-Time Employee. Facts. For new variable hour employees, Employer C uses a six-month initial measurement period that begins on the start date and applies an administrative period that runs from the end of the initial measurement period through the end of the first full calendar month beginning after the end of the initial measurement period. Employer C hires Employee Z on May 10, 2017. Employee Z's initial measurement period runs from May 10, 2017, through November 9, 2017, during which Employee Z has an average of thirty hours of service per week. The administrative period is November 10 to December 31. Employer C offers coverage to Employee Z for a stability period that runs from January 1, 2018, through June 30, 2018.

Conclusion. Employer C uses an initial measurement period that does not exceed twelve months; an administrative period totaling not more than ninety days; and a combined initial measurement period and administrative period that does not last longer than the final day of the first calendar month beginning on or after the one-year anniversary of Employee Z's start date. From Employee Z's start date through June 30, 2018, the end of the period when coverage was offered, Employer C is not subject to any employer mandate payment because Employer C complies with the standards for the measurement and stability periods for a new variable hour employee with respect to Employee Z. Employer C must test Employee Z again based on Employee Z's hours of service during the period from November 15, 2017, through May 14, 2018, Employer C's first standard measurement period that begins after Employee Z's start date.

Example 10: Initially Full-Time Employee, Becomes Nonfull-Time Employee. Facts. Same as Example 9; in addition, Employer C tests Employee Z again based on Employee Z's hours of service during the period from November 15, 2017, through May 14, 2018, i.e., Employer C's first standard measurement period that begins after Employee Z's start date, during which period Employee Z has an average of twenty-eight hours of service per week. Employer C continues to offer coverage to Employee Z through June 30, 2018, (the end of the initial stability period based on the initial measurement period during which Employee Z has an average of thirty hours of service per week) but does not offer coverage to Employee Z from July 1, 2018, through December 31, 2018.

Conclusion. Employer C is not subject to any employer mandate penalty payment for Employee Z for 2018.

New Seasonal Employee

Example 11: Seasonal Employee, Twelve-Month Initial Measurement Period; One-Plus Partial Month Administrative Period. Facts. Employer D offers health plan coverage only to full-time employees and their dependents. Employer D uses a twelve-month initial measurement period for new variable hour employees and seasonal employees that begins on the start date and applies an administrative period from the end of the initial measurement period through the end of the first calendar month beginning after the end of the initial measurement period. Employer D hires Employee S, a ski instructor, on November 15, 2017, with an anticipated season during which Employee S will work running through March 15, 2018. Employer D determines that Employee S is a seasonal employee based upon a reasonable good faith interpretation of that term. Employee S's initial measurement period runs from November 15, 2017, through November 14, 2018. Employee S is expected to have fifty hours of service per week from November 15, 2017, through March 15, 2018, but is not reasonably expected to average thirty hours of service per week for the twelve-month initial measurement period.

Conclusion. Employer D cannot determine that Employee S is reasonably expected to average at least thirty hours of service per week for the twelve-month initial measurement period. Accordingly, Employer D may treat Employee S as a variable hour employee during the initial measurement period.

New Variable Hour Employee of Staffing Company

Example 12: Variable Hour Employee. Facts. Employer E is in the business of providing temporary workers to numerous clients that are unrelated to Employer E and to one another. Employer E is the common law employer of the temporary workers based on all of the facts and circumstances. Employer E offers health plan coverage only to full-time employees (including temporary workers who are full-time employees) and their dependents. Employer E uses a twelve-month initial measurement period for new variable hour employees and new seasonal employees that begins on the start date and applies an administrative period from the end of the initial measurement period through the end of the first calendar month beginning after the end of the initial measurement period. Employer E hires Employee T on January 1, 2018 and anticipates that it will assign Employee T to provide services for various clients. As of the beginning of the initial measurement period, Employer E reasonably expects that, over the initial measurement period, Employee T is likely to be offered short-term assignments with several different clients, with significant gaps between the assignments and that the assignments will differ in the average hours of service per week (meaning averaging both above and below thirty hours of service per week), all depending on client needs and Employee T's availability. The number of actual assignments that Employee T will be offered, the number that Employee T will accept, the duration of assignments, the length of the gaps between assignments, and whether various assignments will result in Employee T being employed on average at least thirty hours of service per week during the assignment are all uncertain.

Conclusion. Employer E cannot determine whether Employee T is reasonably expected to average at least thirty hours of service per week for the twelve-month initial measurement period. Accordingly, Employer E may treat Employee T as a variable hour employee during the initial measurement period.

New Variable Hour Employee Initially and Temporarily Expected to Work at Least Thirty Hours per Week

Example 13. Variable Hour Employee. Facts. Employee A is hired on an hourly basis by Employer Y to fill in for employees who are absent and to provide additional staffing at peak times. Employer Y expects that Employee A will average thirty hours of service per week or more for A's first few months of employment, while assigned to a specific project, but also reasonably expects that the assignments will be of unpredictable duration, that there will be gaps of unpredictable duration between assignments, that the hours per week required by subsequent assignments will vary, and that A will not necessarily be available for all assignments.

Conclusion. Employer Y cannot determine whether Employee A is reasonably expected to average at least thirty hours of service per week for the initial measurement period. Accordingly, Employer Y may treat Employee A as a variable hour employee.

Anti-abuse Rules and Staffing (Employee Leasing or Professional Employment Organization) Firms

717. Are any anti-abuse rules contemplated for employers who shift employees to staffing companies?

The regulations preamble states that Treasury and IRS are aware of various structures being considered under which employers might use temporary staffing agencies (or other staffing agencies) purporting to be the common law employer to evade application of Internal Revenue Code section 4980H. In one structure, the employer (referred to in this section as the "client") would purport to employ its employees for only part of a week, such as twenty hours, and then to hire those same individuals through a temporary staffing agency (or other staffing agency) for the remaining hours of the week, thereby resulting in neither the "client" employer nor the temporary staffing agency or other staffing agency appearing to employ the individual as a full-time employee.

In another structure, one temporary staffing agency (or other staffing agency) would purport to employ an individual and supply the individual as a worker to a client for only part of a week, such as twenty hours, while a second temporary staffing agency or other staffing agency would purport to employ the same individual and supply that individual as a worker to the same client for the remainder of the week, thereby resulting in neither the temporary staffing agencies or the other staffing agencies, nor the client, appearing to employ the individual as a full-time employee.

The Treasury Department and the IRS anticipate that only in rare circumstances, if ever, would the "client" under these fact patterns not employ the individual under the common law standard as a full-time employee.

The IRS also expects to issue future guidance that includes an anti-abuse rule to prevent employers from using temporary staffing firms to avoid the pay or play rules. Under the anticipated anti-abuse rule, if an individual performs services as an employee of an employer, and also performs the same or similar services for that employer in the individual's purported employment at a temporary staffing firm, then all the hours of service are attributed to the employer for purposes of the pay or play rules. Similarly, to the extent an individual performs the same or similar services for the same client of two or more temporary staffing firms, it is anticipated that: Anti-abuse Rule The IRS also expects to issue future guidance that includes an anti-abuse rule to prevent employers from using temporary staffing firms to avoid the pay or play rules. Under the anticipated anti-abuse rule, if an individual performs services as an employee of an employer, and also performs the same or similar services for that employer in the individual's purported employment at a temporary staffing firm, then all the hours of service are attributed to the employer for purposes of the pay or play rules. Similarly, to the extent an individual performs the same or similar services for the same client of two or more temporary staffing firms, it is anticipated that:

- All hours of service for that client are attributed to the client, if the client is the common law employer; or

- All hours of service are attributed to one of the temporary staffing firms that purports to employ the individual with respect to services performed for that client, if the client is not the common law employer

Planning to Minimize Impact of Employer Mandate Penalties

718. Can an employer reduce or minimize the impact of the employer mandate by reducing employee's hours to less than thirty hours per week to avoid having full-time employees?

This would be a potentially dangerous move until the actions could be legally justified.

Existing Employees: Section 510 of the Employee Retirement Income Security Act (ERISA) bars discrimination for the purpose of interfering with the attainment of any right to employee benefits to which a worker may become entitled. An intentional reduction of hours from thirty or more to under thirty in order to prevent employees from getting benefits raises a potential ERISA section 510 claim. Violation of section 510 can result in court-ordered reinstatement of the worker, restitution, back pay, and the claimant's legal fees. For large companies, there is also the potential for class action lawsuits to be filed. It would be ill-advised for an employer to reduce the hours of existing employees currently receiving health benefits to under thirty hours which would result in a loss of those benefits.

New Employees: However, adopting a policy allowing future workers to work no more than twenty-nine hours per week would likely be a safe move because no action was taken to deprive them of a benefit they otherwise would have received.

Whistleblower Protection: Additionally, healthcare reform under FLSA section 18C provides whistleblower protection, which allows for recovery of damages and attorneys' fees. That section prohibits firing or discriminating against workers in retaliation for complaining to government authorities about noncompliance with healthcare reform's consumer protections or objecting to the employer about noncompliance.[1]

If a company fired workers to avoid the mandate, it might be permitted if it acted due to a legitimate need, such as a corporate restructure or legitimate business need to reduce expenses. However, if it announced its intentions and then fired a worker who objected to the plan, it could be opening the door to a retaliation suit, even if that worker would have been fired regardless of the objections.

719. Is outsourcing work a solution to reduce the employee count?

The use of independent contractors to do work that would otherwise be done by employees is a way to reduce the workforce and the impact of the employer mandate penalties for applicable large employers. However, an employer that reclassifies existing employees as independent contractors takes a large risk in an audit challenging such reclassification. However, if the employees incorporate, with their corporations employing them and their corporation contracting with the employer, case law exists that would support such reclassification.[2]

720. How can an applicable large employer offer low cost health benefits and still avoid or reduce the impact of the employer mandate penalty?

The employer mandate penalty comes in two parts, the Internal Revenue Code section 4980H(a)[3] penalty and the Internal Revenue Code section 4980H(b)[4] penalty. The (b) penalty cannot be greater than the (a) penalty. The (a) penalty is easy to avoid. Whether the (b) penalty is a serious issue for an employer depends on the facts relating to an employer's workforce.

721. How does an employer avoid the section 4980H(a) employer mandate penalty?

There are at least two ways to do so without an employer spending a lot on its health plan.

Employer Pays Nothing: One option to avoid the Internal Revenue Code section 4980H(a) penalty is for an employer to offer its employees health coverage for which the employer pays nothing and employees pay for all of plan. Internal Revenue Code section 4980H(a) merely requires that an employer make an offer of coverage. It does not require the employer to pay for any part of it. The affordability of the coverage is a concept involved in the Internal Revenue Code section 4980H((b) penalty only, as discussed in Q 722. This strategy to avoid the employer mandate would be premised on the employer's belief that most employees who refused the employer's offer of coverage would not purchase health insurance on an exchange, even if they qualified for a subsidy, because even with a subsidy, lower income healthy workers with no

---

1.   FLSA §18C.
2.   *Idaho Ambucare Center Inc. v. U.S.*, 57 F.3d 752 (9th Cir. 1995); *Sargent v. CIR*, 929 F.2d 1252 (8th Cir. 1991).
3.   IRC Sec. 4980H(a).
4.   IRC Sec. 4980H(b).

chronic medical condition would rather save the money and rely on hospital emergency room coverage if they need care.

Bare-Bones "Skinny" Coverage: Another option to enable employers to avoid the Internal Revenue Code section 4980H(a) $2,570 employer mandate penalty (for every full-time employee over thirty) by offering very limited (low benefit, skinny, or bare bones) health care plans that can lack key health benefits, such as hospital coverage. Such policies are low cost because they offer minimal benefits. Unlike the exchange plans, employer plans need not cover the ten categories of services for the healthcare law's essential health benefits. Thus, these low benefit plans are less expensive because they provide much lower benefits than an exchange plan. This technique will not work for employers in the small group insurance market (generally employers with under 100 employees) because healthcare reform requires that insurance to cover all ten essential health benefits.[1]

Prior to healthcare reform, many employers, especially those with predominantly low wage employees, offered so-called "mini-med" health plans, which, as their name implies, had low cost and limited benefits. These low benefit plans may take their place. The law requires employers with fifty or more workers to offer coverage to 95 percent of their full-time employees and dependents or pay a penalty. Many persons understood the rules to require robust major medical insurance, covering a list of "essential" benefits such as mental-health services and a high percentage of workers' overall costs. However, that is not the way the law is written. Articles have reported that federal officials confirmed that this low benefit plan strategy works to avoid the Internal Revenue Code section 4980H(a) penalty.[2]

To comply with the law, the low benefit plan cannot have a lifetime or annual dollar limit on benefits that are provided and must cover preventive services like vaccines and cancer screenings without any cost-sharing, i.e., without any employee deductibles or copays. However, such plans may not cover surgery, imaging, or prenatal care. Alternatively, they could provide a very limited benefit for hospitalizations or surgeries. They might also limit the number of doctor visits or prescriptions available to participants. The cap would be on the number, not the dollar-value of the benefits so they would not have a concern about prohibited annual dollar limits. Anyone wanting better coverage could then opt out and go to an exchange. Such plans could be paired with other limited benefit packages, such as hospital indemnity plans paying specified dollar amounts per day and/or catastrophic coverage, a very high deductible insurance policy.

---

1. Beginning in 2014, a health insurance issuer that offers health insurance coverage in the individual or small group market must include essential health benefits package required under section 1302(a) of the Patient Protection and Affordable Care Act. A small employer is "an employer who employed an average of at least one but not more than 100 employees on business days during the preceding calendar year and who employs at least two employees on the first day of the plan year." For plan years beginning before January 1, 2016, a state may elect to define small employer as an employer who employed an average of at least one but not more than fifty employees on business days during the preceding calendar year, which likely will be appealing for states already using that definition. An employer not in existence throughout the preceding calendar year will determine whether it is a small or large employer "based on the average number of employees that it is reasonably expected such employer will employ on business days in the current calendar year." The control and affiliated service group aggregation rules set forth in IRC Secs. 414(b), (c), (m), and (o) apply to count employees of an "employer."

2. Employers Can Minimize Their Exposure To Obamacare's Penalties By Offering Low-Cost 'Skinny' Coverage, Forbes (June 21, 2013) at http://www.forbes.com/sites/theapothecary/2013/05/21/employers-can-minimize-their-exposure-to-obamacares-health-insurance-mandate-by-offering-low-cost-skinny-coverage/ (Last accessed August 14, 2019) e, Kevin McCurdy, "Skinny" Plans Under PPACA: Are They a Solution?, at http://www.mondaq.com/unitedstates/x/252518/Employee+Benefits+Compensation/Skinny+Plans+Under+PPACA+Are+They+a+Solution&email_access=on (Last accessed August 14, 2019).

The Internal Revenue Code section 4980H(a) employer mandate penalty applies to an employer that fails to offer "minimum essential coverage." Minimum essential coverage does not include excepted benefits, such as stand-alone vision or stand-alone dental benefits. Employers seeking to minimize or avoid the employer penalty must offer minimum essential coverage to 95 percent of their full-time employees and their dependents, including children under age twenty six. Minimum essential coverage is the coverage required to avoid the individual and employer mandates.[1] It is an "eligible employer-sponsored plan," a term that means any group health plan (other than for excepted benefits) offered by an employer to employees or coverage offered in a state's small or large group market or a self-insured plan[2] meeting only the required Public Health Service Act requirements (discussed in Part VII).[3] It includes grandfathered plans.[4] In other words, any health insurance plan legally sold in a state and self-insured plans meeting PHSA requirements are an "eligible employer-sponsored plan." In many states, insurers market inexpensive plans that cover a limited range of services. Further, PHSA requirements only apply if the plan offers the benefit in question. None of the PHSA benefit mandates apply to plans that do not offer a particular benefit. Thus, for example, the protections for mothers and newborns do not apply where a plan does not offer maternity benefits.

Thus, minimum essential coverage includes coverage that need not include the ten types of "essential health benefits." Essential health benefits is the term used by health care reform to describe the benefits that Qualified Health Plans (QHPs) sold on the state exchanges are required to cover.[5] HHS defines essential health benefits with reference to state benchmark plans offered on state exchanges (marketplaces).[6]

Also see Q 670 through Q 672.

722. How does an employer avoid or reduce the 4980H(b) employer mandate penalty?

Applicable large employers offering employee pay all coverage or a low benefit minimum essential coverage plan could still face the Internal Revenue Code section 4980H(b) penalty of $3,860 per year per full-time employee for workers who go to an exchange and qualify for subsidized coverage if the employer's coverage is either:

(1)   not affordable[7] or

(2)   lacks minimum value.[8] See Q 670 and Q 673 through Q 678.

---

1.   PPACA §1301.
2.   Prop Reg. §1.5000A-2(c)(1).
3.   IRC Sec. 5000A(f)(2)(B); Prop. Reg.§1.5000A-2(a) and (c)(1)(ii).
4.   Prop. Reg.§1.5000A-2(a)(c)(1)(iii).
5.   PPACA §1302(b).
6.   45 CFR §156.100.
7.   Coverage is affordable for IRC Sec. 4980H purposes if the cost to the employee of self-only coverage does not exceed 9.86 percent in 2019 (9.56 in 2018) of the employee's "household income." This is true irrespective of whether he or she qualifies for some other level of coverage (e.g., self plus dependents, family). Thus, although family coverage might require a larger employee premium, affordability for IRC Sec. 4980H purposes is determined based on the cost of self-only coverage. The Act defines "household income" to mean "modified adjusted gross income of the employee and any members of the employee's family (including a spouse and dependents) who are required to file an income tax return." Alternatively, employers may use one of three safe harbors as proxies: W-2, rate-of-pay, or Federal Line.
8.   To provide minimum value, a plan must pay for at least 60 percent of plan costs. The remaining 40 percent are paid for by the covered individual in the form of co-pays, deductibles, co-insurance, and other cost sharing features.

Whether this will be a significant penalty depends on how many of an employer's employees qualify for and purchase subsidized health insurance on an exchange when the employer's policy is unaffordable or fails to provide minimum value. In many cases, the result could be much less expensive than the Internal Revenue Code section 4980H(a) penalty because it is likely that many employees, especially those with low incomes, will not go to the exchanges due to the relatively high cost of the coverage after the subsidy and the availability of care at hospital emergency rooms. Additionally, employees can get insurance later if they develop a chronic condition because insurers cannot impose a preexisting condition limit on insureds. Thus, some believe that many if not most of those going to the exchange will likely be only those with existing medical conditions.

Limited benefit policies can cost an employer far less than the employer mandate penalty or the cost of providing benefits that are more comprehensive. Some low benefit plans cost employers $40 - $100 monthly per employee depending on the benefits offered. The low benefit insurance approach is an attractive option for companies with many low wage workers, such as retailers and restaurant operators, especially if workers will not want to pay the cost of the richer exchange coverage. Only full-time employees who qualify for and purchase subsidized exchange coverage trigger the employer $3,860 per full-time employee employer mandate penalty. A full-time worker earning $12 an hour would have to pay approximately $140 a month for a midlevel exchange plan after the subsidies. At $16 an hour, an employee's share of the premium would be approximately $180 per month due to a reduced federal subsidy. Of course, these figures are only examples, as every state exchange will have insurance costs that are based on local conditions.

723. Does this dual option comprehensive insurance or catastrophic insurance employer mandate strategy work?

An employer seeking to minimize impact of employer mandate and offer insurance to employees wants to offer an insured plan with comprehensive coverage that provides minimum value and costs no more than 9.78 in 2020 (9.86 in 2019 and 9.56 percent in 2018) percent of an employee's W-2 compensation. Employer thinks many will decline, so it also wants to offer cheap catastrophic coverage as well. Does this strategy work?

This works under Internal Revenue Code section 4980H for the employer mandate. The obligation is to offer qualifying coverage (affordable, minimum-value MEC), and this would accomplish that result. There are other potential issues, however.

First, the catastrophic plan would be subject to the no annual or lifetime limit rules and would have to offer preventive care without cost to comply with the PHSA mandates. Failure to do so could trigger annual per participant penalty.

Second, is the issue of minimum participation. If the comprehensive plan is subject to an insurance company imposed minimum-participation requirement (meaning that the insurer will not issue policies unless some minimum percentage of employer's workforces subscribes, such as 70 percent of those eligible, the offer of coverage requirement may not be satisfied if a significant number of eligible employees decline the more generous coverage because the insurer will not let the employer offer coverage to this smaller group. Large group insurers should not be allowed to impose minimum participation requirements in light of the guaranteed availability rules under PHSA section 2702, but in practice many still do. Note that the guaranteed availability rule does not apply to self-insured plans, whether large or small.

A third issue is the new insurance nondiscrimination rules, which if and when effective will prevent discrimination in favor of Highly Compensated Individuals (HCIs) for employer sponsored health insurance. There are to date, however, no nondiscrimination rules for insured plans because no regulations have been issued. However, there is speculation that the nondiscrimination rules, when issued, might impose a utilization requirement, which could present a problem if the comprehensive plan is utilized primarily by HCIs, even though it's offered on a nondiscriminatory basis. So the design could require adjustment if and when the insurance company nondiscrimination rules are issued and take effect. If the comprehensive plan is self-insured, then the Internal Revenue Code section 105(h) nondiscrimination rules apply now. It would arguably pass testing using the nondiscriminatory classification test (eligible employees are treated as "benefitting"), which does not, at least at present, require any utilization test.

724. How does an applicable large employer utilize the 95 percent rule in planning for the employer mandate penalties?

Beginning January 1, 2015, employers with fifty or more full-time and full-time equivalent employees have needed to track their workforces' hours of service (usually based on the prior year employee data) to comply with the employer mandate. The 95 percent rule allows an employer to be treated as offering qualifying coverage to all of its full-time employees and their dependents for a calendar month, if the employer offers coverage to all but five percent (or, if greater, five full-time employees) of its full-time employees and their dependents. The preamble to the regulations' states that an employer can utilize the 95 percent rule even if the failure to offer coverage is intentional. The regulations when explaining the 95 percent rule do not condition a full-time employee being included in the calculation on any additional factor besides being a full-time employee (averaging thirty or more hours of service per week during the month).

<u>Full-Time Employees under the Age of Twenty-Six Count</u>. An individual is eligible for a premium tax credit (which is required to trigger the employer mandate penalty) if the individual is not eligible for minimum essential coverage through a different medium other than eligibility through coverage in the individual market. Not all employees under the age of twenty six will be eligible for coverage through their parents or some other means. If such an employee met the other conditions to receive a premium tax credit, the full-time underage twenty six year old employee could trigger an Internal Revenue Code section 4980H penalty unless the 95 percent test is met, taking into account under age twenty-six full-time employees.

<u>Medicare and Medicaid Eligible Employees Count</u>. Employees who are sixty-five years of age or older will not be eligible for a premium tax credit as they will be eligible for Medicare. However, it appears all full-time employees are included when calculating the 95 percent rule. Consequently, if employees eligible for Medicare are not offered the opportunity to enroll in qualifying employer coverage, they will count against the employer when calculating the 95 percent rule. Likewise, if Medicaid employees are not offered the opportunity to enroll in qualifying employer coverage, they will count against the employer when calculating the 95 percent rule.

Employees with Household Income of More than 400 Percent of the Federal Poverty Line Count. While not eligible for a premium subsidy on an Exchange, these employees will count against the employer when calculating the 95 percent rule.

Who Does Not Count When Calculating the 95 Percent Rule?

- Leased Employees, Sole Proprietors, Partners, and 2 Percent S Corporation Shareholders co not count.

- Part-Time Employees. Whether or not a part-time employee is offered qualifying health coverage, the employee is not included when calculating the 95 percent rule.

New Employees – Rules Not Clear. A new nonvariable hour employee who the employer reasonably expects to accumulate more than thirty hours of service per week must be offered coverage by the conclusion of the employee's third full calendar month of employment. If a new employee (who the employer knows will work forty hours a week) is hired on March 15, 2019, that particular employee's initial three full calendar months will be April 2019, May 2019, and June 2019. If the employer does not offer the employee coverage by June 30, 2019, the employee would count as a full-time employee who did not have coverage made available to him/her for April 2019, May 2019, and June 2019 as well as any subsequent month until coverage is offered for the entire calendar month when calculating the 95 percent rule. The partial month of March 2019 would not be included in the calculation of the 95 percent rule.

It is unclear how a new nonvariable hour employee would count for the 95 percent rule if the employer offers coverage to the employee by the three-month deadline. For example, suppose a new employee (who the employer knows will work forty hours a week) is hired on March 15, 2019. The employer makes coverage available to the new employee by June 30, 2019. As in the example in the previous paragraph, it appears the partial month of March 2019 would not be included in the calculation of the 95 percent rule. There are three possibilities for April, May, and June:

1. The first possibility is to include the employee as a full-time employee who was not offered coverage for the calendar months of April 2019, May 2019, and June 2019. The regulations make no exceptions to the rule that 95 percent of full-time employees be offered coverage.

2. A second possibility would include the employee as a full-time employee who was timely offered coverage for the calendar months of April 2019, May 2019, and June 2019 when calculating the 95 percent rule.

3. The third possibility is that the months of April 2019, May 2019, and June 2019 are not considered in the calculation of the 95 percent rule. The employee would begin to be included in the calculation of the 95 percent rule in July 2019.

New Variable Hour Employees. If an employer cannot determine if the employee is reasonably expected to average at least thirty hours of service per week, the regulations allow an employer to use the safe harbor measurement method if an employee can be classified as a variable hour employee. The regulations provide no guidance on how the periods associated with the safe harbor interact with calculating the 95 percent rule.

A reasonable interpretation is that all employees during the initial measurement period are excluded from the calculation of the 95 percent rule. If an employee is determined to be a full-time employee during the initial measurement period, the employee would be included in the calculation of the 95 percent rule during the entire corresponding stability period regardless of whether the employee was offered coverage during that period. However, if an employee is determined not to be a full-time employee during the initial measurement period, the employee would not be included in the calculation of the 95 percent rule during the entire corresponding stability period regardless of whether the employee was offered coverage during that period.

If an employee is determined to be a full-time employee during the standard measurement period, the employee would be included in the calculation of the 95 percent rule during the entire corresponding stability period regardless of whether the employee was offered coverage during that period. However, if an employee is determined not to be a full-time employee during the standard measurement period, the employee would not be included in the calculation of the 95 percent rule during the entire corresponding stability period regardless of whether the employee was offered coverage during that period.

In the case of overlapping stability periods, the employee being included as a full-time employee will always trump the employee not being included as a full-time employee for purposes of calculating the 95 percent rule. Overlapping stability periods should not result in a single employee being included twice when calculating the 95 percent rule.

Employer Mandate Traps for Employers to Avoid

725. What are the traps regarding employer mandate rules that employers should avoid?

<u>Failing Properly to Count All Hours of Service</u>. As discussed earlier in this Part of the book, an hour of service is any hour for which an employee is paid or entitled to be paid. The definition includes hours that the employee is present at work performing services, but also includes other hours that the employee is not at work but is entitled to be paid, like paid vacation days, paid holidays, jury duty days, etc. Employers must count "hours of service" to determine the number of full-time and full-time equivalents necessary to calculate the employer's size. Hours of service must also be counted to determine whether an employee is considered full-time for purposes of offering coverage.

These rules have a direct impact on an employer's liability under Internal Revenue Code section 4980H. Counting hours of service can also be particularly difficult for certain types of employees, like adjunct professors. Special rules exist for certain types of employees that are discussed earlier in this Part. One pitfall to avoid is recording only the hours that employees are physically present at work.

<u>Ignoring Other Employers within Same Controlled or Affiliated Service Group</u>. Splitting up a single corporate entity into multiple entities owned by the same individual(s), holding

company, or group of individuals was one of the initial reactions to avoid the employer mandate and its application to employers with fifty or more full-time and full-time equivalent employees.

As discussed in more detail earlier in this Part, under Internal Revenue Code section 414, a commonly-owned group of entities – also known as a controlled group – may be treated as a single employer in certain circumstances. The employer mandate regulations incorporate the provisions of Internal Revenue Code section 414. This means that all of the employees of each entity within a controlled group must be counted for determining whether or not an employer has fifty or more full-time equivalent employees and is subject to the employer mandate. In addition, all members of an affiliated service group, also defined in Internal Revenue Code section 414, are treated as one employer. These are the same employer aggregation rules that apply under ERISA for retirement and welfare benefit plans and testing for required coverage, nondiscrimination, etc.

Employers who are a subsidiary of a parent company, employers who own subsidiary companies, or employers who are owned by individual owners who have ownership in other companies should consult their attorney regarding whether or not the entity is part of a controlled group. If the answer is yes, the employer mandate may apply even though the employer in question employs less than fifty full-time and full-time equivalent employees within a single entity.

<u>Failing to Identify & Measure Variable Hour Employees</u>. For employers who are not so large as to be aware that they are an applicable large employer (ALE), one of the most difficult items is the Look-back Measurement Method for variable hour and seasonal employees. A variable hour employee is an employee that the employer does not reasonably expect to work an average of thirty hours or more per week when that employee is hired. Many employers have an internal definition of full-time that is something more than thirty hours per week – it could be forty hours, for example. In this scenario, employers often ask if they can measure employees working fewer hours than what their internal definition of full-time requires, or measure employees whose hours vary from week to week but are always above thirty.

For healthcare reform compliance, internal employer definitions of full-time are disregarded. Employees reasonably expected to work an average of thirty hours per week when hired should be counted as full-time employees, regardless of the employer's internal definition of full-time. If an employee is expected to work fewer than thirty hours per week, the employer should be prepared to administer either the Look-back Measurement Method or the Monthly Measurement Method for that employee.

Failing to identify whether an employee is full-time or variable hour may make an employer's size calculation inaccurate, which may impact the availability of transition relief and also the employer mandate penalty calculation. Likewise, a failure to offer coverage to an individual who is considered full-time under the rules can expose an employer to unanticipated penalties.

<u>Classifying Short Term Workers as Seasonal</u>. A seasonal employee is an employee whose customary annual employment is six months or less, and whose position begins about the same time each year. Employers have adopted any variety of internal definitions of seasonal, and not all of these definitions align with the definition in the regulations. Employers in some industries hire

"seasonal" employees to work eight or ten months out of the year. However, an employee who works eight or ten months out of the year is not a seasonal employee under the final employer mandate regulations. Likewise, an employee who works six months or less, but whose position does not begin at a consistent time each year, is not a seasonal employee. These employees are likely considered short-term employees under the rules and should be offered coverage within ninety days of employment if working full-time.

<u>Misclassifying Independent Contractors and/or Temporary Staffers</u>. Employers are required to offer coverage to their "common law" full-time employees. An individual is a common law employee of a company if the company has the right to "control and direct the individual who performs the work, not only as the result to be accomplished by the work but also as to the details and means by which that result is accomplished." Do employers who pay some workers with a Form 1099 have to worry about this issue? Yes, most definitely. If workers paid with a Form 1099 are actually be employees but are classified incorrectly as independent contractors, the employer who thought it had too few employees to be an ALE could be an ALE and need to deal with the employer mandate penalty.

When it comes to temporary staffers, an individual might be issued a Form W-2 by the staffing company, but another company (the "recipient" for whom the worker is providing services) has the right to control and direct that individual as to what job needs to be done and how to do it. The company that has the right to control and direct that individual has the obligation to offer coverage, even though it is not the employer for payroll purposes. There are rules that allow the client employer to take credit for an offer of health coverage made by a staffing agency or employee leasing firm, but the arrangement between the client employer and the staffing agency must meet certain requirements for this to be done.

PART XII: SHORT-TERM LIMITED DURATION HEALTH INSURANCE

(a/k/a "TrumpCare")

Overview

726. What is Short-Term Limited Duration Health Insurance?

Short-Term Limited Duration (STLD) health insurance policies have been around for a long time but with attempts to repeal the Affordable Care Act and the Trump Administration's intent to offer other options for health care, there is increasing focus on these policies. President Trump issued a statement saying that he believes that the new short-term plans could be of help to millions of people that do not want or need comprehensive health care coverage that the ACA requires.[1]

These short-term polices were originally designed to fill a temporary need or cover a gap in coverage. The purchaser might purchase a short-term plan when out of work or cannot unable to get coverage through the Marketplace because of not qualifying for a special enrollment period. As the name obliquely suggests, these policies do not have guaranteed renewability by the policyholder. If the policyholder wants to continue coverage, purchase of a new policy is required with new underwriting.

This type of coverage is exempt from the definition of individual health coverage under the Affordable Care Act.[2]

727. How do short-term plans compare with ACA policies in terms of premiums and coverage?

Short-term health insurance policies are policies that offer lower monthly premiums than ACA-compliant plans mainly because short-term policies offer a lower amount of insurance coverage. These policies are medically underwritten which mean that one must "qualify" for purchase which tends to limit sales to healthy people. A downside is that individuals who purchase short-term limited duration policies and then develop less than purchase health will either lose coverage when the contract ends or if still eligible, will find their policy "rated" and cost more or be provided lesser coverage. Short-term policies typically do not cover essential health benefits, such as prescription drugs, and often apply dollar caps and higher deductibles on coverage that are no longer allowed under ACA-compliant individual market and group health plans. Short-term policy purchasers often take a chance in order to reduce their monthly premiums with the result that if they do need medical care, they could be left with uncovered bills and/or find themselves "uninsurable" under such plans in the future.

There is a worry that healthy individuals will opt for cheaper short-term policies instead of ACA-compliant plans, which might lead to instability and raises the cost of coverage for people

---

1.   "Short-Term" Health Insurance? Up to 3 Years Under New Trump Policy, The New York Times, August 1, 2018, by Robert Pearl.
2.   https://www.federalregister.gov/documents/2018/08/03/2018-16568/short-term-limited-duration-insurance. (Last access August 12, 2019)

who have health issues. Lower-income applicants would be protected by premium subsidies, but middle-income people not eligible for subsidies who buy ACA-compliant plans would likely see premium increases. The elimination of the individual mandate penalty in 2019, which has in the past has offset the cost difference between the STLDs and ACA plans.

Coverage and premiums are considerably different than ACA-compliant policies. For example, monthly premiums for polices (depending on location and region) can be considerably cheaper than ACA policies. On average, policies rang from lows of $35 to $50 per month to a high of $900 per month.

Out of pocket cost-sharing maximums are often considerably higher but range from a low of $250 on some policies to an average for about $30,000 out of pocket. In addition, STLD polices are not subject to the ban on coverage caps and often limit coverage from $250,000 to $2 million.

It should be noted that short-term plans generally do not cover or offer only limited coverage for prescription drugs, emergency services, maternity and newborn care, mental health, and substance abuse and other "essential services".

Implementation

728. What are the limits on covered benefits on STLD policies?

Short-term policies generally cover major-medical benefits, though limits often apply. For example:

- Limits on covered doctor visits – often limited to three covered visits

- Dollar limits on covered benefits – there are often dollar limits on specific covered benefits apply – such as $1,000 per day in the hospital. If a policy applies dollar limits, actual charges above the limit will not be covered. Virtually all short-term policies apply an overall dollar cap to all covered benefits, e.g., ranging from $100,000 to $2 million.

- Limits on prescription drug coverage – Most short-term policies do not cover drugs at all but offer a drug discount card instead. A discount card is not the same as insurance coverage; the patient will have to pay the entire discounted price without any insurance reimbursement.

- Excluded benefits –Short-term policies typically do not cover maternity care; many will not cover substance use treatment or mental health services.

- Pre-existing conditions – short-term policies generally exclude pre-existing conditions. Conditions will be considered pre-existing if the applicant had been treated for them before enrolling in the policy. Depending on the policy and state laws, the insurer might also refuse to cover a condition that existed, even if not-yet diagnosed before purchasing the policy. Some short-term policies offer limited coverage for certain pre-existing conditions, such as allergies, if the applicant is healthy enough to buy the policy.

729. What are the cost-sharing limits for covered benefits?

Most short-term policies have an out-of-pocket limit on cost sharing. In ACA-compliant policies, the out-of-pocket limit caps what consumers pay in a year for all types of cost sharing: deductibles, co-pays, and coinsurance. For 2020, that limit is $8,150 per year for a single person. In a short-term policy, though, the limit might not include the deductible and co-pays. In addition, cost sharing limits reset at the end of the policy term if coverage is renewed or if a new short-term policy is purchased.

730. What notice must Short-Term Limited Duration Health Insurance display for consumers?

All short-term policies must include a prominent notice to consumers to

"check your policy carefully to make sure you are aware of any exclusions or limitations regarding coverage of preexisting conditions or health benefits…"

731. Can eligibility for short-term health insurance be based on health status?

Except in states that prohibit their sale, short term health insurance policies are medically underwritten. That means consumers can, and likely will, be turned down if they have preexisting health conditions. Short-term policy applications will ask questions about health – for example, if the applicant is pregnant or planning to get pregnant, of if the applicant has been diagnosed or treated for cancer, hepatitis, mental health or substance use disorders, HIV/AIDS, or other conditions. Insurers will most likely refuse to sell short-term policies to people who answer "yes" to any of those questions.

732. What rules apply regarding length of coverage and renewability?

Under new regulations, short-term policies are allowed to provide coverage for up to 364 days. Shorter-term policies – for example, which last for 3 or 6 months – are also for sale. At the end of the policy term, coverage ends. Some policies may now include an option to extend or renew coverage at the end of the policy term. However, it is up to the insurer to decide. People who buy a short-term policy and then get sick most likely will not be able to extend or renew coverage.

733. Can STLD policies be sold on the marketplace sites?

Short-term policies cannot be sold on HealthCare.gov or state marketplace websites. Consumers eligible for marketplace subsidies cannot use them to buy short-term policies.

734. Does loss of coverage under a short-term limited duration policy enable you for a special enrollment period (SEP)?

Loss of coverage under a short-term policy during the year does not make people eligible for a special enrollment period (SEP) to switch to an ACA-compliant marketplace policy. They will have to wait until the next Open Enrollment period to buy a plan that cannot turn them down.

735. How does State Regulation impact STLD policies?

States are permitted to regulate STLD coverage and can implement rules that are more restrictive than the federal rule or can even ban STLD policies entirely. If desired, states can require that STLD policies be a shorter initial duration, limit or ban extensions, and require additional language in advertising and on the policies. States can require that short-term policies comply with all ACA requirements, if they choose.

In addition, the federal rule does not override any state rule that prohibits STLD polices.

736. Can Short-Term Limited Duration policies be sold as Student Health Insurance?

No. Student health insurance, is by definition, an individual health insurance policy that is required to comply with most of the Affordable Care Act's rules. Companies can market short-term coverage to students by it cannot be sold in place of student health insurance.

737. Are federal subsidies available for purchase of STLD policies?

No. Since these policies do not comply with the rules of the Affordable Care Act, federal subsidies and tax credits are not available.

738. How do STLD policies compare with the ACA requirement of Minimum Essential Coverage?

The Kaiser Family Foundation conducted a survey of short-term policies and came to the following conclusions:

- On average, the cheapest short-term policy was priced at 20 percent or less than the lowest cost Affordable Care Act Bronze coverage.

- Kaiser examined twenty four different short-term policies being offered in forty five states and the District of Columbia from two different websites and noted the following peculiarities:

    - 43 percent did not offer mental health services

    - 62 percent did not offer substance abuse treatment

    - 71 percent did not offer outpatient prescription drugs

    - NONE offered maternity care

    - In five of the forty five states, none of the coverages above was offered.

- Kaiser noted that of the seven policies that offered prescription drug coverage, six of them cap the coverage at $3,000. Other limitations included $50 maximum for outpatient visits, a thirty one-day maximum for inpatient care.

739. What are the typical characteristics of short-term policies?

Since the STLD policies are not part of the policy pool that are compliant with the Affordable Care Act, they are naturally exempt from the market rules that prohibit medical underwriting, pre-existing condition exclusions, and lifetime and annual limits, and that require minimum coverage standards. Some of the characteristics of short-term policies include:

- Medical underwriting: individuals with less than perfect health can be rejected or issued higher premiums. Applicants can be discriminated against based on health status, gender, and age.

- Pre-existing conditions excluded.

- Essential Health Benefits not required to be covered allowing maternity coverage, prescription drugs, mental health coverage, preventative care, as well as other limitations.

- Lifetime and annual coverage limits. Some limit coverage to $1 million or $2 million.

- No Cost Sharing Limits. Currently the Affordable Care Act limits cost sharing to $7,900 for an individual in 2019 as opposed to much higher for STLD policies.

- Not subject to rate review or minimum medical loss ratios. For example, Federal law requires that the insurance company for ACA-compliant plans spend at least 80 cents of every premium dollar on actual medical bills. Average numbers reported for STLD plans are considerably less averaging 60 to 65 percent.

740. Do any States ban short-term plans?

Yes, currently STLD plans that lack protections for people with pre-existing conditions are banned in the following states:

- California

- Hawaii

- Massachusetts

- New Jersey

- New York completely bans the sale of STLD policies

- Oregon

History

741. How were Short-Term Limited Duration policies managed in the past?

The Affordable Care Act does not reference or define short-term policies. In fact, the ACA incorporated terms found in the Public Service Health Act which defined "individual health insurance coverage" to be coverage offered to individuals but specifically excluding STLD policies. The STLD plans are not subject to the Affordable Care Act.

Short-term healthcare policies have been outside the definition of "individual insurance coverage" since HIPAA was passed in 1996. The final conference committee report established definitions of STLD policies that are now included in the PHS Act, ERISA and the Internal Revenue Code. While STLD plans were not "individual health insurance coverage", they were considered to be "health insurance coverage" for the purposes of establishing creditable coverage.

The HHS interim final rule issued in April of 1997, defined STLD insurance as "health insurance coverage provided pursuant to a contract with an issuer that has an expiration date provided in the contract (taking into account any extensions that may be elected by the policyholder without the issuer's consent) that is twelve months of the date of such contract becomes effective." The final regulations issued in 2004 included the same language.[1]

742. How did the Obama Administration treat Short-Term Limited Duration Coverage?

During the Obama Administration, STLD policies essentially were the same as individual polices before the onset of the Affordable Care Act's reforms to the insurance market. After the implementation of the Affordable Care Act, a number of insurers began selling policies that lasted one day short of a year, this avoiding the requirement to comply with the ACA.

The STLD policies were medically underwritten and often incorporated pre-existing condition rules, annual coverage limits, lifetime coverage maximums, high out of pocket costs and limited benefits. Coverage maximums generally run from $500,000 to $2 million with out of pocket maximums as high as $35,000. These plans, naturally could be offered at a lower price and tended to appeal more to a younger and healthier clientele.

These STLD policies began being the source of misunderstanding for a number of purchasers who thought they were actually major medical coverage and entered into purchase not fully realizing gaps in coverage. This led both state insurance regulators as well as the federal agencies to step in. The state insurance departments began issuing cautionary statements regarding the limitations of these policies as well as identification of dishonest marketing efforts.

On October 31, 2016, the IRS, the HHS, and the Employee Benefits Security Administration issued a regulation limiting short-term plans. The federal regulators decided that STLD coverage was being sold deceptively as primary coverage. The agencies also determined that the sale of these policies was negatively impacting the risk pool for policies that were in accordance with the ACA. The new rule severely limited STLD by:[2]

- Limiting sales of STLD polices to a period of less than three months, and

---

1.   https://www.federalregister.gov/documents/2004/12/30/04-28112/final-regulations-for-health-coverage-portability-for-group-health-plans-and-group-health-insurance (Last accessed August 12, 2019).

2.   https://www.federalregister.gov/documents/2016/10/31/2016-26162/excepted-benefits-lifetime-and-annual-limits-and-short-term-limited-duration-insurance (Last accessed August 12, 2019).

- Limiting any extensions of the policy to three months as well to prevent insurers from indefinitely extending or renewing the coverage, and

- Requiring that the policy clearly state that it does not satisfy the Individual Mandate nor does it meet the ACA requirements of Minimum Essential Coverage.

Proponents cheered this limitation as a reasonable limitation as well as a necessary addressing of a potential problem of creating two risk pools, those with pre-existing conditions and those without. Others objected, arguing that this was an example of federal overuse of authority and that a better effort would be to educate the consumer rather than deny options.

Proposed and Final Rules

743. What changes did the February 2018 proposed rule contain?

On February 21, 2018, the IRS, the EBSA and the HHS issued a proposed rule changing the treatment of short-term coverage.[1] The revisiting of STLD policies was prompted by President Trump who issued an Executive Order in October of 2017 directing the federal government to increase availability of short-term plans, association plans and HRAs, specifically instructing allowing STLD plans to be of longer duration.

The proposed rule noted that purchasers of short-term policies would probably be "relatively young or healthy" and admitted the rule could affect individual market risk pools and even acknowledged that choices in some marketplaces could be further limited. The rule suggested that between 100,000 and 200,000 individuals would be affected by this change in STLD coverage.

After the rule went into discussion period, a number of analyses were issued, notably by the Centers for Medicare and Medicaid Services (CMS) and the Budget Office and Joint Committee on Taxation (CBO/JCT). Both analyses determined that the impact would be far greater than estimated by the three agencies. CMS predicted that enrollment in STLD policies would increase to 1.9 million by 2022 and would increase the cost of average marketplace premiums by $17 per month. Ultimately, extraordinarily little support for the rule was offered, with the media noting that of the 10,000 online comments, nearly 99 percent were not supportive. The NAIC requested that the implementation be delayed until 2020.

744. How has the final rule issued in August 2018 affected length of STLD policies?

On August 1, 2018, the final rule regarding short-term, limited duration policies was issued.[2] The specifics of the rule are discussed below.

---

1.   https://www.federalregister.gov/documents/2018/02/21/2018-03208/short-term-limited-duration-insurance (Last accessed August 12, 2019).

2.   https://s3.amazonaws.com/public-inspection.federalregister.gov/2018-16568.pdf (Last accessed August 12, 2019).

"Short-Term": In some respects, the final rule is identical to the proposed rules in that it allows for short-term coverage up to twelve months. In this regard, the policy must have an expiration date of 364 days or less, based on the effective date of the policy. This does not differ from the 2016 regulation under the Obama Administration.

"Limited Duration": The final rule adds a new wrinkle to the STLD policies in that it allows policies to be extended or renewed up to three years. This extends the maximum coverage from the current three months to as long as thirty six months. The initial maximum has been extended to twelve months.

Under the final rule, the insurance provide is permitted but not required to allow renewals for up to thirty-six months. In addition, there is the option of offering the renewal without new medical underwriting or experience rating. However, the provider could also simply require new underwriting at the renewal. It is presumed that the provider would charge a higher rate for the "guaranteed renewal" option. The justification for the use of a thirty six month renewal option is rooted in COBRA policies, which allow individuals to stay in group coverage for up to thirty-six months.

The three-year maximum duration applies only to one policy. A consumer could engage in "stacking" by enrolling in two or more policies consecutively, jumping from policy to policy as long as they could successfully clear the underwriting requirement.

In summary, the Final Rule allows offering of short-term, limited duration as follows:

- Issued policies are less than twelve months in duration

- Incorporate language which inform the consumer that MEC requirements of the ACA are not met, and

- May be renewed up to thirty six months

745. What are the notice requirements in the final rule?

The final rule requires that short-term polices include a notice in both the contract as well as the application materials detailing specific limitations of the coverage. The notice must be in at least fourteen point type.

In addition, states can impose additional requirements for consumer notice language. The insurance carrier can add more language as long as it is accurate.

Regarding the fact that STLD policies do not meet qualifications as MEC and do not meet the Individual Mandate requirements, there are two different notice options. Both require that the policy stat that it is "not required to comply with certain federal market requirements for health insurance, principally those contained in the Affordable Care Act." In addition, caution is added for the purchases to understand the limitations of the policy as well as pointing out that they might have to wait for another Open Enrollment window to get coverage.

The final rule differs from the proposed rule in that some cautions are actually more pronounced. The final notice states to "make sure you are aware of any exclusions or limitations regarding coverage of preexisting conditions or health benefits (such as hospitalization, emergency services, maternity care, preventive care, prescription drugs, and mental health and substance use disorder services)." In addition, the notice is required to point out that the policy might have lifetime and/or annual dollar limits on benefits but does not require this to be in capital letters.

The final rules do NOT require the policy issuer to provide a Summary of Benefits and Coverage (SBC). In addition, beginning in January 2019, policies will not have to note the Individual Mandate penalty because of the repeal.

746. Does Section 1557, the non-discrimination rule of the Affordable Care Act apply to STLD policies?

It is unclear if Section 1557 applies to STLD policies. Section 1557 applies to providers that receive federal health funding. Any company that markets on the marketplace or participates in Medicaid or Medicare Advantage would generally need to comply with the section. However, since short-term policies do actually discriminate based on gender, age, and disability, this would pose an issue to any insurers are operating in the federally-supported market.

There has been no clarification on this. The rule merely states that Section 1557 is beyond the scope of the rule. However, there is a proposed rule regarding Section 1557 that is expected to be released for review soon.

747. What is the effective date of the regulation on STLD policies?

The final rule was published in the Federal Register on August 1, 2018 with an effective date of sixty days after publication. The effective date of the rule is October 1, 2018.

748. When did the new STLD policies become effective?

The final rule became effective on October 1, 2018, and policies are now available on the market. There are now hundreds of policies offered in nearly all fifty states on various websites including eHealth.com and AgileHealthInsurance.com.

749. What is the final rule's Severability Provision?

A new addition, not contained in the Obama rule or the proposed rule of February 21, 2018 is a provision that the remainder of the rule would stay in place even if the thirty-six month maximum extension was deemed to be unenforceable or invalid. The severability clause would apply if the thirty six month clause is struck down "as applied" or "facially".

PART XIII: "MEDICARE FOR ALL" AND THE FUTURE OF HEALTHCARE REFORM

The Future of Healthcare Reform in the United States

750. What does the future hold for healthcare reform?

One commonality with health care reform is the constancy of change or at least attempted change. It has been nearly a decade since the passage of the Affordable Care Act has been attempts to change or even repeal the provisions of the Act through legislation as well as court action. While the Affordable Care Act has changed over the past decade and some provisions have changed, the law remains in place and has delivered health care to approximately 9 million Americans through the Exchanges as well as additional Medicaid coverage to 11 million through Medicaid expansion.

As we approach 2020, it is impossible to predict the future – other than to realize that the development of healthcare reform in the United States continues. While attempts are made to repeal the ACA, there are continuing efforts to maintain it or even to expand it. An overview of healthcare reform would be incomplete without considering some of the proposals that are being advanced in Congress.

Several bills have been introduced in the 116th Congress that would actually expand the role of public programs in health care. These bills range in scope from proposed legislation to create a new national health insurance program for all residents to more incremental and less ambition approaches that offer a public plan option in addition to current sources of coverage, private or public. The proposals fall into five broad categories as detailed below. This section will explore in detail each of these proposals. The proposals and their sponsors are listed below:

- Single Payer Program (Medicare For All)

    o Sen. Bernie Sanders (I-VT): S 1129, *Medicare for All Act of 2019*

    o Rep. Pramila Jayapal (D-WA): H.R. 1384 *Medicare for All Act of 2019*

- Public Plan with Opt-out Option

    o Rep. Rosa DeLauro (D-CT) and Rep. Jan Schakowsky (D-IL): H.R. 2452, *Medicare for America Act of 2019*

- Four Public Plan Options

    o Sen. Ben Cardin (D-MD), S. 3, Keeping Health Insurance Affordable Act of 2019

    o Sen. Jeff Merkley (D-OR)/Rep. Cedric Richmond(D-LA)/Sen. Chris Murphy (D-CT), S.1261, H.R.2463, *Choose Medicare Act*

- ○ Sen. Michael Bennet (D-CO) and Sen. Tim Kaine (D-VA)/Rep. Antonio Delgado (D-NY), S. 961/H.R. 2000, *Medicare-X Choice Act of 2019*

- ○ Rep. Jan Schakowsky (D-IL)/Sen. Sheldon Whitehouse (D-RI), H.R. 2085/S.1035 *The CHOICE Act*

- Medicare Buy-in for Over fifty Adults

  - ○ Sen. Debbie Stabenow, S.470, Medicare at 50 Act

  - ○ Rep. Brian Higgins (D-NY), John Larson (D-CT), H.R. 1346, *Medicare Buy-In and Health Care Stabilization Act of 2019*

  - ○ Sen. Brian Schatz (D-HI)/Ben Ray Lujan (D-NM), S.489, H.R. 1277, *State Public Option Act*

"Medicare for All" Single Payer Program

751. What does the proposed "Medicare for All" single payer program entail?

The "Medicare for All" programs are exemplified by the plans proposed by Senator Bernie Sanders (I-VT) and Congresswoman Pramila Jayapal (D-WA). These two bills, although containing some differences, are similar – and decidedly the most aggressive of all of the plans intending to expand healthcare and the Medicare program.

The Sanders plan[1] and the Jayapal[2] plan would involve a complete overhaul of the Medicare program from a health care program for those over the age of 65, into a single-payer program providing comprehensive health care coverage (including dental, vision, long-term care) to all Americans. This plan would be phased in over four years. The Sanders and Jayapal plans would eliminate most other federal health care programs, such as Medicaid, Medicare, Tricare, and CHIP. This Medicare for All plan would retain the Indian Health Service as well as the Veterans Health Administration, although it is possible that in time, these organizations would be eliminated as well.

This plan is supported by Senators Cory Booker (D-N.J.), Kirsten Gillibrand (D-N.Y.), Kamala Harris (D-Calif.) and Elizabeth Warren (D-Mass.) and Rep. Tulsi Gabbard (D-Hawaii). In addition, South Bend, Indiana Mayor Pete Buttigieg indicated support for the concept.

752. Would the proposed "Medicare for All" eliminate private health insurance?

Yes. Private insurance plans would end under the Medicare for All plans. Plans offered by employers as well as the plans people can currently buy individually, such as those sold on the Healthcare.gov marketplaces or by private brokers would be eliminated. Under the Sanders and

---

1.   https://www.congress.gov/116/bills/s1129/BILLS-116s1129is.pdf.
2.   https://www.congress.gov/116/bills/hr1384/BILLS-116hr1384ih.pdf.

Jayapal proposals, private insurance companies would actually be banned from selling plans that cover the same services.

While the most comprehensive of the healthcare reform plans, this type of solution is a "third rail" type hot button for most Republicans as well as being objectionable for many Democrats who are leery of implementing a sweeping change eliminating the multibillion-dollar health insurance industry that currently provides services to nearly 70 percent of the population.

753. Who would be eligible to participate in the Medicare for All plan?

All residents of the United States, as defined by the Secretary of Health and Human Services through regulations would be eligible to participate. Employers would no longer have a role in healthcare and would not be participants.

754. How would the enrollment process for Medicare for all work?

The enrollment would occur at birth for newborns. Regulations would be established to enroll currently living individuals, most likely enabling individuals to enroll at the location of health services. Benefits would begin during the fourth year after enrollment in the Sanders plans and the second year in the Jayapal plan. With the Jayapal plan, children under age nineteen and adults aged fifty-five and older would and have option to enroll earlier, beginning one year after date of enactment

755. What benefits are offered under the Medicare for All Proposals?

Under the Sanders plan, medically necessary services are provided in thirteen benefit categories, including home and community-based long-term services and supports (LTSS), dental, hearing, vision, comprehensive reproductive services (The Hyde Amendment is repealed), EPSDT, and transportation to health services for individuals with disabilities and low-income individuals. The Jayapal plan is similar but adds institutional services under the plan, while Sanders proposes institutional and long-term supports (LTSS) covered under Medicaid. HHS will make national coverage determinations for experimental items, services, and drugs. Coverage and services not provided in accordance with practice guidelines will be deemed to be in accordance if the health care provider exercised appropriate professional discretion to deviate from the guideline, however, it is expected that guidelines will be developed over the phase in of the program.

Under both plans, states can add additional coverages at their own expense if desired.

756. What cost-sharing provisions are imposed?

Under the Jayapal program, no cost-sharing provisions at all are planned.

Under Sanders, there is general no cost sharing, cost sharing of up to $200 per year (indexed for inflation) can be imposed for prescription drugs and biologics. The use of generic drugs is encouraged. There is no cost sharing applied to preventive drugs, and cannot be imposed on individuals with household income at or below 200 percent of the Federal Poverty Level.

757. Are there premiums or tax subsidies for Medicare for All?

No. Medicare for All is funded by taxes. During the transition, there may be enhanced tax credits or subsidies.

758. What are the rules for providers to participate in Medicare for All?

All state-licensed and certified providers who meet the defined provider standards and file a participation agreement can participate. Federal standards that apply under the current Medicare program and those pertaining to non-discrimination and quality, and requirements to submit data and other information also apply. Private contracting between institutions or individual providers for covered services is permitted, subject to specified requirements and limitations. The individual states may set additional standards.

Under the Jayapal plan, providers that do not provide items and services directly to individuals cannot participate. The Jayapal plan does not allow states to add additional standards.

759. How will providers be paid under Medicare for All?

The Sanders plan uses a fee schedule similar to the Medicare payment schedule which is updated on a periodic basis.

The Jayapal payment plan is a bit more complicated by establishing a global budget process and engaging in negotiations with providers. Hospitals and other health-care facilities are paid a quarterly lump sum to cover operating expenses and payments are determined by annual negotiation. Physicians and clinicians are paid though a fee-for-service schedule similar to the Medicare fee schedule, as well as by factoring in expertise of providers, and other information sources.

760. How are prescription drug prices set under Medicare for All?

Under the Sanders plan, HHS negotiates drug prices annually, and establishes a formulary for the Medicare for All program. An underlying intent is to discourage the use of ineffective, dangerous or excessively costly medications when better alternatives are available. The program promotes the use of generic drugs. Off-formulary drugs are covered subject to rules established by HHS.

Under Jayapal's plan, HHS negotiates prices with drug manufacturers for covered drugs. If negotiations are not successful, the Secretary shall "authorize the use of any patents, data exclusivity granted by the federal government for the manufacture of the drug", providing reasonable compensation to manufacturer holding the license. HHS is empowered to procure drugs directly. Drug manufacturers are prohibited from engaging in anti-competitive behaviors.

761. How does Medicare for All change the current Medicare program?

The Sanders plan replaces the current Medicare program. Before full implementation of Medicare for All, an annual OOP cost-sharing limit is added to Medicare Parts A and B ($1,500), Parts A and B deductibles are eliminated, and the Part D out-of-pocket threshold is reduced and cost sharing under Medicare Part D above the threshold is eliminated. In addition, vision, hearing aids and exams, and dental benefits are added to Medicare Part B. The twenty-four-month waiting period for Medicare for people receiving SSDI payments is eliminated. Medigap insurers are prohibited from denying or pricing policies based on pre-existing conditions. During the transition period, premiums paid for Medicare buy-in will be deposited into the Medicare Hospital Insurance and Supplementary Medical Insurance Trust Funds.

Under Jayapal, Medicare is eliminated two years after the date of enactment, with provisions for continuation of benefits for persons receiving inpatient and other services. Like Sanders, this program also eliminates the 24-month waiting period for Medicare coverage for individuals with disabilities and receiving SSDI.

762. How does Medicare for All change the current Medigap and Supplemental Insurance?

Both programs offer no restrictions on the sale of health insurance for any non-covered benefits.

763. How does Medicare for All change the current Marketplace plans and private plans?

The Medicare for All plans replace private insurance (marketplace, employer, FEHB, TRICARE) and bar insurers from selling policies and bar employers from providing benefits that duplicate covered benefits

764. How does Medicare for All change existing Medicaid?

The Sanders replaces Medicaid for most services but retains Medicaid coverage for institutional LTSS, and any other benefits furnished by a state Medicaid program as of January 1, 2019 that are not covered by Sander's Medicare For All , with a state maintenance of effort requirement for these services. Jayapal replaces Medicaid entirely.

765. Are there changes to VA and Indian Health Services under Medicare for All?

No, the Veterans Administration and Indian Health Services are retained as is.

766. How would the Sanders Medicare for All plan handle coverage during the four-year transition period?

During the four-year implementation phase in, establishes several transitional programs:

- Children under nineteen have option of enrolling in Medicare for All beginning January 1 of the year following the date of enactment or can retain current coverage.

- Option to buy into Medicare (or enroll in Medicare Advantage) are established for certain adults not yet otherwise eligible for Medicare on a phased in basis:

  - age fifty-five and older: one year after date of enactment;

  - age forty-five to fifty-four: two years after date of enactment;

  - age thirty-five to forty-four: three years after date of enactment)

- Premium rates for Medicare buy-in plan established to cover costs of benefits and administrative costs for Medicare Parts A, B and D benefits:

  o Marketplace subsidies can be applied.

  o Individuals would not be eligible for Medicare cost-sharing assistance provided under Medicaid.

- During transition, a public plan option (the Medicare Transition Plan) will be established and offered in the marketplace. A national premium will be established to cover costs; essential health benefits covered with platinum plan level cost sharing. Enhanced marketplace premium and cost sharing subsidies apply to the Medicare Transition plan, including for poor individuals in states that do not expand Medicaid. Current Medicare providers and payment rates will be used by Medicare Transition plan.

767. How would the Jayapal Medicare for All plan handle coverage during the two-year transition period?

During the two-year transition period, for the year beginning one year after the date of enactment, a transitional Medicare buy-in plan will be offered through the marketplaces with a premium rate set by HHS.

Covered benefits will be the same benefits available under Medicare-for-all; cost sharing for covered benefits will be set to achieve an actuarial value of 90 percent (similar to Platinum marketplace plan)

During the transition, marketplace premium and cost sharing subsidies will be available for transitional Medicare buy-in plan. In addition, the premium tax credits for the transitional buy-in plan would be more generous than otherwise applied in the marketplace and available to individuals with income above 400 percent FPL and to those with income below 100 percent FPL in states that have not expanded Medicaid.

Public Plan Option with Ability to Opt Out

768. What does the proposed "Medicare for America" payer program entail?

The "Medicare for America" program is a plan proposed by

This is a federal program providing a comprehensive benefit plan for all U.S. residents. Individuals can opt out for qualified employer-sponsored health plans as well as other coverage. There are no premiums or cost sharing for people with income below 200 percent of the FPL. Individuals with income above 200 percent of the FPL will have premiums based on their income levels.

The program replaces the marketplace, individual health insurance policies, current Medicare, Medicaid, and CHIP. Employers can either continue to provide qualified group coverage or pay eight percent of pay for their employees to be included in Medicare for America. In addition, individuals that are eligible for qualified coverage can opt in for the Medicare for America coverage. Former Rep. Beto O'Rourke (D-Texas) and Senator Gillibrand have expressed support.

Unlike the Medicare for All plan, private insurance would not be eliminated.

769. Who would be eligible to participate in the Medicare for America plan?

Individuals: All residents of the United States, as defined by the Secretary of Health and Human Services through regulations. This includes all lawfully present immigrants and immigrants eligible for emergency services.

Employers:

- Small employers, defined as fewer than 100 workers or with a payroll under $2 million may participate beginning in 2023;

- Large employers may participate beginning in 2027

- Individuals whose employers offer qualified coverage can choose to enroll in that coverage or in Medicare for America

Standards will be established to prevent employers from inducing sicker individuals to elect Medicare for America. Beginning in 2027, large employers must offer qualified coverage to their full-time employees or pay 8 percent of annual payroll to the Medicare Trust Fund.

Qualified employer coverage defined as:

1. Any plan established by a governmental employer OR

2. Any other employer plan that includes vision, dental and hearing benefits, with an actuarial value equivalent to at least 80 percent of Medicare for America coverage, and for which employer contributes at least 70 percent of the premium.

At this point, it is not clear if qualified employer plans cover benefits identical to or superior to those under Medicare for America.

770. How would the enrollment process work?

Enrollment in Medicare for America would begin 2023 and is for the person's lifetime, except that individuals may opt out for a program year when they have other qualified coverage. In the case of newborns, they would be enrolled at birth. Processes for auto-enrolling others would be established.

Medicare for America participating providers will facilitate enrollment and states shall serve as enrollment organizations. Auto-enrollment process must include ability for individuals to opt out of Medicare for America if they enroll in qualified coverage under an employer-sponsored plan, Veterans health care, Indian Health Service, or FEHBP for a program year. From 2023-2026, ability to opt-out applies, and phases out, for dual-eligibles and those enrolled in CHIP and Medicaid.

771. What benefits are offered under Medicare for America?

The plan covers a comprehensive benefit package including: Essential Health Benefits established by the Affordable Care Act, as well as dental, hearing, vision, abortion (Hyde amendment is eliminated), infertility services, gender-confirming procedures, home and community based LTSS, nursing facility care, EPSDT for children, non-emergency medical transportation, and any other service covered by any state Medicaid program on the date of enactment.

No lifetime or annual limits apply.

Prior authorization and step therapy is prohibited under Medicare for America, Medicare Advantage for America plans, and qualified employer plans.

States may provide additional benefits at state expense.

772. What cost-sharing provisions are imposed?

Cost sharing provisions include:

- Income-related cost sharing generally applies

- No cost sharing applies for people with income below 200 percent of the Federal Poverty Level

- 20 percent coinsurance applies up to annual out-of-pocket (OOP) limit of $3,500/individual or $5,000/family.

  - OOP limit for individuals with household income between 200 percent and 600 percent FPL increases on a linear sliding scale

  - OOP limit indexed annually to CPI-medical

- No cost sharing for preventive services, maternity care, pediatric services, long-term care, or services for individuals who are frail or have special needs

There is no deductible.

773. What are the premiums for the Medicare for All plans?

There will be no premiums for people with income under 200 percent of federal poverty level.

Premiums for individuals with household income between 200 percent and 600 percent FPL increases on a linear sliding scale up to 8 percent of income.

Individuals with income above 600 percent FPL pay lower of 8 percent of income or full premium amount. Full premium amount will be established based on by family size

Current Medicare beneficiaries as of date of enactment pay the lesser of the current Part B premium or the applicable Medicare for America premium

Individuals who opt in to Medicare for America from a qualified employer coverage plan will pay the lesser of the income-related premium, or pay the full Medicare for America premium reduced by the dollar amount their employer would have contributed toward their qualified coverage.

774. What are the rules for providers to participate in Medicare for America?

Medicare and Medicaid participating providers shall be participants in Medicare for America automatically. Process will be established to certify other providers.

A student loan forgiveness program will established for participating providers and new federal minimum nursing staffing requirements will apply to all hospitals. Private contracting between health care providers or institutions and individuals enrolled in Medicare for America for covered services will be prohibited.

775. How will providers be paid under Medicare for All?

Balance billing is prohibited in Medicare for America (including in Medicare Advantage for America plans) and in qualified employer plans that use Medicare for America provider rates. The plan attempts to eliminate surprise medical bills prohibited in all private plans.

Payment rates are based on rates that would have applied under current Medicare or Medicaid (whichever is higher) and are necessary to maintain network adequacy, except:

- Hospital payment rates shall be at least 110 percent of the higher of current Medicare or Medicaid rates and further increased in underserved areas

- Site-neutral payment will be established for services furnished in hospital outpatient and physician offices

- Payment rates for primary care and behavioral health services shall be increased by at least 30 percent

As a condition of participation in Medicare for America, providers must accept Medicare for America payment rates paid by employer plans and by Medicare Advantage for America plans

776. How does Medicare for America change the current Medicare program?

The current Medicare would be replaced by Medicare for America in 2023, except it will continue for individuals dually enrolled in Medicaid until 2025. In addition, the twenty-four-month waiting period for Medicare coverage for individuals with disabilities is eliminated.

Changes would also be made to current Medicare Advantage plans including new network adequacy standards; prohibitions on removing an in-network provider except for cause; prohibitions on broker commissions; requirement to publish annual bid information online; and repeal of bonus payments

777. How does Medicare for America change the current Medigap and Supplemental Insurance?

There are no changes.

778. How does Medicare for America change the current Marketplace plans and private plans?

- Establishes surprise medical bill protections for all private plans, effective January 1, 2020 or when passed:

    - All group health plans will be prohibited from using prior authorization for covered services or step therapy for covered prescription drugs, effective for plan years following date of enactment.

- The Affordable Care Act Marketplaces will expire on January 1, 2023:

    - Beginning in 2023, private insurers and plans, other than qualified employer health plans, are prohibited from selling coverage for Medicare for America benefits. Private insurers can contract with Medicare for America to offer Medicare Advantage for America (MAA) plans to individuals.

- Covered benefits and cost sharing for MAA plans must be identical to Medicare for America:

    - Medicare Advantage for America plans are subject to the following requirements: network adequacy standards, removing participating providers except for cause prohibited, broker commission prohibited, use of prior authorization and step therapy is prohibited.

779. How does Medicare for All change existing Medicaid?

1. Within ninety days of date of enactment, all individuals on State waiting lists for Medicaid home and community-based services must be enrolled. Federal government appropriates such sums as necessary to facilitate enrollment.

2. Medicaid and CHIP are gradually replaced by Medicare for America from 2025-2027

    Federal matching payments for state Medicaid and CHIP programs are increased to pay the difference between Medicare for America provider payment rates and Medicaid and CHIP rates from January 1, 2023 to December 31, 2027.

3. Beginning in 2028, State Maintenance of Effort (MOE) applies and must be satisfied for states to continue receiving other federal health funding, including maternal and child health grants, Ryan White grants, and others.

    MOE payment set to reflect state's Medicaid and CHIP spending for the plan year before the date of enactment. For 2029-2033, a state's MOE amount is indexed annually at rate of:

- GDP per capita growth plus 0.4 percent for states that adopted ACA Medicaid expansion

- GDP growth plus 0.7 percent for non-expansion states

Beginning in 2033, index rate for all state maintenance of effort amounts is equal to GDP per capita growth plus 0.7 percent.

780. Are there changes to VA and Indian Health Services under Medicare for All?

No, the Veterans Administration and Indian Health Services are retained as is.

781. How would the Medicare for America plan handle coverage during the transition period?

For 2021 and 2022, a transitional public plan option will be offered to individuals through the ACA exchange allowing individuals eligible to use the exchange to enroll. The public plan will cover Essential Health Benefits plus abortion and all reproductive health services (state laws prohibiting abortion are preempted and Hyde limits do not apply).

The premiums for public plan are set to fully capitalize the costs and will be adjusted geographically as necessary. The marketplace subsidies continue for other QHPs and are enhanced; benchmark plan that determines tax credit amount will be based on second-lowest-cost Gold plan.

Different premium subsidies apply to the temporary public plan. For public plan enrollees with income below 200 percent of the Federal Poverty Level, no premium is levied. Premium increases on sliding scale until income of 600 percent above Federal Poverty Level. Individuals or households above 600 percent of FPL will pay no more than 8 percent of income for the public plan.

The public plan will be offered at Silver- and Gold-levels; cost-sharing subsidies (CSRs) apply to the Gold-level public plan and to Gold-level QHPs.

CSR subsidies are further enhanced by changing actuarial values as follows:

- 100-200 percent FPL: 95 percent AV

- 200-300 percent FPL: 90 percent AV

- 300-400 percent FPL: 85 percent AV

Medicare and Medicaid participating providers shall participate in transitional public plan and payment rates will be based on Medicare rates.

782. How is the Medicare for America Plan financed?

Medicare for America will be financed by premiums paid by individuals and by an 8 percent payroll tax paid by large employers that do not provide qualified coverage.

Any net increases in federal revenues attributable to enactment of Medicare for America will be transferred to the Medicare for America trust fund on an ongoing basis. The current program receipts for Medicare and Medicaid program will be transferred to the Trust Fund.

In addition, new revenue will be generated from:

- Repeal of 2017 Tax Cut Act;

- 5 percent income tax surcharge on individuals with income above $500,000;

- Estate tax increased;

- Supplemental Medicare tax on high earners increased from 0.9 percent to 4 percent;

- Net investment income tax increased from 3.8 percent to 6.9 percent;

- Health Savings Account tax preference repealed;

- Flexible spending account tax preference limited to benefits not covered by Medicare for America;

- Excise taxes on tobacco products and alcohol increased; new federal excise tax on sugar-sweetened beverages; and

- In addition, the Cadillac Tax will be repealed.

Public Plan Options

783. What does the proposed Public Plan Options entail?

There are *four* public plan healthcare legislative packages being proposed by various Democratic legislators. These plans include the following:

- Keeping Health Care Affordable Act of 2019

- Choose Medicare Act

- Medicare X-Choice Act of 2019 and

- The Choice Act

Each plan shares similar qualities as detailed here

1. All four plans are offered as a federal public plan option for individuals that are eligible to participate in the federal exchanges.

     a. Note: the Choose Medicare Act allows participation by large and small employers.

2.   The Choose Medicare Act and the Medicare-X Choice Act propose expanding the marketplace subsidies, the other plans leave the subsidies unchanged.

3.   All of the plans retain the current sources of private and public coverages.

Senator Amy Klobuchar of Minnesota has expressed support for the Medicare-X plan.

784. What are the rules of participation in the public option plans?

Individuals:

- **Keeping Health Care Affordable Act of 2019**: All individuals are eligible to sign up

- **Choose Medicare Act**: All US residents not eligible for Medicaid or eligible for Medicare or CHIP can enroll in new public plan called "Medicare Part E".

- **Medicare X-Choice Act of 2019**: all individuals eligible to participate in marketplace and not currently eligible for Medicare can sign up

- **The Choice Act**: all individuals eligible to participate in marketplace can sign up.

Employers:

- **Choose Medicare Act:** Employers can offer Medicare Part E to employees. Employees who sign up for Part E can keep the plan after leaving employment.

- **Medicare X-Choice Act of 2019:** Small employers, employees, and dependents have access through SHOP exchanges after 2025.

785. How would the enrollment process work for the public option plans?

- **Keeping Health Care Affordable Act of 2019:** Public health insurance option offered exclusively through the marketplaces using the Affordable Care Act marketplace enrollment procedures and rules.

- **Choose Medicare Act:** Medicare Part E plan is offered in individual and small group and large group markets, through the individual marketplace and SHOP marketplace. Part E follows the Affordable Care Act enrollment procedures and rules.

- **Medicare X-Choice Act of 2019:** The Medicare-X plan is offered through the individual and SHOP marketplaces. It follows the Affordable Care Act marketplace and SHOP enrollment procedures and rules.

- **The Choice Act:** The Choice Act program is offered only through the marketplace and follows Affordable Care Act marketplace enrollment procedures and rules.

786. What benefits are offered under the public option plans?

- **Keeping Health Care Affordable Act of 2019:** Uses the Affordable Care Act 10 essential health benefits.

- **Choose Medicare Act:** Uses the Affordable Care Act 10 essential health benefits as well as Medicare Parts A, B and D benefits. This covers abortions and all other reproductive services and overrules the Hyde Amendment as well as state laws restricting coverage of abortion and reproductive health services under QHPs and Medicare Part E are preempted.

- **Medicare X-Choice Act of 2019:** Uses the Affordable Care Act 10 essential health benefits.

- **The Choice Act:** The Choice Act offers a benefit package that includes the Affordable Care Act 10 essential health benefits State laws prohibiting qualified health plans from covering abortion are preempted for this public health insurance option and declares any provision of law restricting use of Federal funds with respect to any reproductive health service does not apply to the Choice Act.

787. What cost-sharing provisions are imposed on the public option plans?

- **Keeping Health Care Affordable Act of 2019:** Cost sharing follows the ACA marketplace rules. Annual out-of-pocket limit applies ($8,150 in 2020). Public health insurance option will be offered at Bronze, Silver and Gold levels and can be offered at the Platinum level.

- **Choose Medicare Act:** Public plan offered at the Gold level. Annual out-of-pocket limit applies ($8,150 in 2020). It sets a benchmark plan at Gold level for all marketplace participants.

- **Medicare X-Choice Act of 2019:** Cost sharing follows the ACA marketplace rules. Annual out-of-pocket limit applies ($8,150 in 2020). Medicare-X offered at ACA Silver and Gold levels and may also be offered at Bronze and Platinum level HHS can offer up to two Medicare-X options at each metal level.

- **The Choice Act:** Cost sharing follows the ACA marketplace rules. Annual out-of-pocket limit applies ($8,150 in 2020). Public plan offered at the Silver and Gold levels; Secretary may offer at Bronze level.

788. What are the premiums for the public option plans?

- **Keeping Health Care Affordable Act of 2019:**

  - Cost sharing follows the ACA marketplace rules.

  - Annual out-of-pocket limit applies ($8,150 in 2020).

  - Public health insurance option will be offered at Bronze, Silver and Gold levels and can be offered at the Platinum level.

  - Expands premium tax credit eligibility to income 100 percent-600 percent FPL and extends cap on tax credit reconciliation/repayment to all income levels.

- **Choose Medicare Act:**

  - Public plan offered at the Gold level.

  - Annual out-of-pocket limit applies ($8,150 in 2020).

- It sets a benchmark plan at Gold level for all marketplace participants.

- Enhances tax credits for all marketplace plans by changing benchmark plan from second-lowest cost Silver to second lowest cost Gold plan.

- Expands premium tax credit eligibility to income 100 percent -600 percent FPL and increases income threshold for cap on tax credit reconciliation/ repayment to 600 percent FPL.

- **Medicare X-Choice Act of 2019:**

  - Cost sharing follows the ACA marketplace rules.

  - Annual out-of-pocket limit applies ($8,150 in 2020).

  - Medicare-X offered at ACA Silver and Gold levels and may also be offered at Bronze and Platinum level. HHS can offer up to two Medicare-X options at each metal level.

  - Expands premium tax credit eligibility to people with income above 400 percent FPL by capping their required contribution for the benchmark plan to 13 percent of income; also enhances tax credit amount for people at lower income levels.

  - Caps tax credit reconciliation/repayment amount for people with income above 400 percent FPL to no more than $5,000.

- **The Choice Act:**

  - Cost sharing follows the ACA marketplace rules.

  - Annual out-of-pocket limit applies ($8,150 in 2020).

  - Public plan offered at the Silver and Gold levels; Bronze level also may be offered.

789. What are the rules for providers to participate in the public option plans?

- **Keeping Health Care Affordable Act of 2019:** Premium for public health insurance option set to cover 100 percent of benefits and administrative costs plus contingency margin. The premium can vary only by factors allowed by ACA rating rules (age up to 3:1, geography, family size, and tobacco use).

- **Choose Medicare Act:**

  - Premiums for Medicare Part E would be set to cover 100 percent of benefits and administrative costs. The premiums can vary only by factors allowed by ACA rating rules (age up to 3:1, geography, family size, and tobacco use) and whether plan is offered in the individual, small group, or large group market

  - Extends ACA rating rules to large group market

- HHS can deny unreasonable rate increases in states where state regulators do not take action to correct unreasonable rate increases

- Extends ACA rate review to grandfathered health plans

- **Medicare X-Choice Act of 2019:** Premiums for Medicare-X are set to cover 100 percent of benefits and administrative costs. The premiums can vary only by factors allowed by ACA rating rules (age up to 3:1, family size, tobacco use) Single risk pool requirement is specified.

- **The Choice Act:** Premiums for public plan set by Secretary to cover 100 percent of benefits and administrative costs plus a contingency margin Premiums for public plan shall be geographically adjusted and can vary only by factors allowed by ACA rating rules (age up to 3:1, geography, family size, tobacco use); The Choice Act is exempt from state premium taxes.

790. How will providers be paid under the public option plans?

- **Keeping Health Care Affordable Act of 2019:** Medicare participating providers and facilities participate in the Keeping Health Care Affordable Act; Process can be established to allow health care providers to opt out of the public plan and a process can be established to allow additional providers to participate in public health insurance option.

- **Choose Medicare Act:** Medicare participating providers and facilities shall also participate in Medicare Part E. Additional providers can be certified to participate in Medicare Part E.

- **Medicare X-Choice Act of 2019:** Medicare and Medicaid participating providers and facilities also participate in Medicare-X; A process can be created to allow health care providers to opt out of the public plan; however, once fully implemented, a provider who opts out of public plan would not be allowed to participate in Medicare. Additional providers can be certified to participate in Medicare-X.

- **The Choice Act:** Medicare and Medicaid participating providers also participate in public plan unless they opt out. A process for allowing other providers to participate can be developed. Providers must be licensed or certified under state law.

791. How do the public option plans change the current Medicare program?

- **Keeping Health Care Affordable Act of 2019:**

  - Authorizes HHS to negotiate drug prices for Medicare.

  - Establishes a national prescription drug plan under Medicare Part D.

  - Applies Medicaid drug rebates for dual eligible and Medicare Part D low income subsidy recipients.

- **Choose Medicare Act**:

  - HHS negotiates drug prices for Medicare Part D program; if negotiations are not successful in obtaining an appropriate price, a price shall be established that is the lessor of the price paid by the VA or under the Federal supply schedule.

  - Adds annual OOP limit on cost sharing for benefits under Parts A and B at $6,700 in 2021 and indexed thereafter.

- **Medicare X-Choice Act of 2019**:

  - HHS can negotiate drug prices for Medicare. Medicare-X will not affect benefits under the current Medicare program, or impact the Medicare trust funds.

- **The Choice Act**: Establishes a separate account in Treasury for The Choice Act.

792. How do the public option plans change the current Medigap and Supplemental Insurance?

There are no changes with any of the plans.

793. How do the public option plans change the current Marketplace plans and private plans?

- **Keeping Health Care Affordable Act of 2019**: There are no changes.

- **Choose Medicare Act**:

  - Expands premium subsidy eligibility to 600 percent FPL.

  - Enhances premium tax credits by tying to Gold level benchmark plan.

  - Eliminates fail safe provisions of ACA that require reduction of premium tax credits if spending exceeds a threshold.

  - Enhances cost-sharing subsidies for other marketplace plans.

  - Applies ACA rating rules to large group market.

  - Appropriates $30 billion to establish and administer reinsurance and affordability fund for the individual market for three fiscal years (2020-2022) Fund enables states to provide reinsurance to insurers to reduce individual market premiums or to provide other assistance to individuals in the marketplace to reduce out-of-pocket costs.

- **Medicare X-Choice Act of 2019**:

  - Authorizes establishment of reinsurance mechanism to pool costs of highest cost patients on a nationwide basis.

  - Authorizes funding of $10 billion per year for each of fiscal years 2021, 2022, and 2023.

- **The Choice Act**:

    - The Affordable Care Act "level playing field" requirement applies to public plan (must follow market rules applicable to other qualified health plans).

794. How do the public option plans change existing Medicaid?

None of the plans effect changes upon Medicaid.

795. Are there changes to VA and Indian Health Services under the public option plans?

No, the Veterans Administration and Indian Health Services are not changed.

796. How would the public option plan handle coverage during the transition period?

There are no transition provisions needed for any of the plans.

797. How are the public option plans financed?

- **Keeping Health Care Affordable Act of 2019:**

    - Premiums for Keeping Health Care Affordable Act is set to cover benefit and administrative costs.

    - Appropriates $2 billion in start-up costs, to be repaid over ten years.

    - There is no provision for other financing sources.

- **Choose Medicare Act:**

    - Premiums for Medicare Part E plan set to cover benefit and administrative costs.

    - Appropriates $2 billion in start-up funds and such sums necessary to establish initial reserves. Hyde restrictions do not apply to this funding.

    - There is no provision for other financing sources.

- **Medicare X-Choice Act of 2019:**

    - Premium for Medicare-X is set to cover benefit and administrative costs.

    - Appropriates $1 billion in initial claims reserves and authorizes such sums as necessary to establish a Data and Technology Fund.

    - The public option is self-financed and cannot contract with outside organizations to transfer insurance risk, except in case of certain innovative payment models.

    - There is no provision for other financing sources.

- **The Choice Act:**

    - Premium for public plan set to cover benefit and administrative costs.

    - The public option is self-financed and cannot contract with outside entities to transfer insurance risk.

    - Authorizes such sums as necessary to pay for startup costs and initial 90-day claims reserve; startup funds repaid to the Treasury over ten years.

    - Authorizes such sums as necessary to pay for contracting costs for third party to handle administrative functions.

Medicare Buy-In Plans for Over 50 Adults

798. What do the proposed Medicare for Over 50 Adults entail?

There are two proposed plans to extend Medicare to adults between the age of fifty and sixty-five: The Medicare at 50 Act and the Medicare Buy-In and Health Care Stabilization Act of 2019. Their provisions are similar with some differences in approach.

An overview of the plans is as follows:

- Both plans provide an option for individuals fifty and over to buy into Medicare

- Marketplace subsidies unchanged with and comparable subsidies apply to Medicare for the Medicare at 50 Act but the Medicare Buy-In and Health Care Stabilization Act of 2019 offers enhanced marketplace cost sharing subsidies enhanced for all participants as well as with Medicare

- Both plans allow enrollees to buy Medicare Advantage plans

- Current sources of private and public coverage continue

799. What are the rules of participation in the Medicare for Over 50 Adult plans?

Individuals:

- Individuals ages fifty to sixty-four who are U.S. citizens or nationals residing in the U.S. or lawfully admitted for permanent residence in the U.S., and who are not otherwise entitled to/eligible for benefits under Medicare Parts A or B.

- States are prohibited from purchasing Medicare buy-in coverage on behalf of full-benefit Medicaid enrollees ages fifty-sixty-four.

- **Employers:** There are no provisions for employers to participate.

800. How would the enrollment process work for the Over 50 plans?

Enrollment is generally for one year at a time.

The Medicare at 50 Act allows purchase only through the Marketplace and follows Affordable Care Act and SHOP Rules.

The Medicare Buy-In and Health Care Stabilization Act of 2019: Enrollment will be coordinated with marketplace and Medicare enrollment periods. Eligible individuals can enroll in Medicare buy-in option for people fifty-sixty-four (Parts A, B and D, similar to traditional Medicare) or in Medicare Advantage plans. Eligible individuals continue to have option to enroll in private coverage and could do so during the marketplace open enrollment period.

801. What benefits are offered under the public option plans?

Both plans offer Medicare Parts A, B and D benefits.

802. What cost-sharing provisions are imposed on the public option plans?

For both plans, the cost sharing is same as under current Medicare for covered benefits. There is no annual limit on out-of-pocket cost sharing, unless enrolled in a Medicare Advantage plan, or if ACA costs sharing subsidies apply. Individuals who voluntarily enroll in Medigap would have limited out-of-pocket costs for covered benefits.

803. What are the premiums for the public option plans?

Medicare at 50 Act: Establishes a single, national premium set at average annual per capita amount for benefits and administrative costs for the buy-in population, based on average per capita costs for expenses under Parts A, B and D. There is no adjustment for age, geography, family status or tobacco use Buy-in enrollees who select Medicare Advantage or Part D prescription drug plans with premiums above the average would be required to pay additional amount

Medicare Buy-In and Health Care Stabilization Act of 2019: The premium is set to cover 100 percent of benefits and administrative costs for the buy-in population, based on average per capita costs for expenses under Parts A, B and D. There is no adjustment for family status or tobacco use. The premium for buy-in plan shall be adjusted for geography and may be adjusted by age. Buy-in enrollees who select Medicare Advantage or Part D prescription drug plans with premiums above the average would be required to pay additional amount.

804. What are the rules for providers to participate in the public option plans?

Under both plans, the Medicare participating providers and facilities also participate in the buy-in plan

805. How will providers be paid under the public option plans?

Under both plans, Medicare limits on balance billing would apply

806. How do the Over 50 plans change the current Medicare program?

The Medicare at 50 Act: Allows HHS to negotiate drug prices for Medicare. The Medicare buy-in plan will not affect benefits under the current Medicare program or negatively affect the Federal HI and SMI Trust Funds.

The Medicare Buy-In and Health Care Stabilization Act of 2019: HHS can negotiate drug prices for Medicare, with no authorization to establish a formulary. Part D plans permitted to obtain discounts below negotiated price. Nothing in the plan would adversely affect eligibility or benefits for the current Medicare program, or the Medicare HI Trust Fund.

807. How do the Over 50 plans change the current Medigap and Supplemental Insurance?

Eligible individuals can buy Medigap on a guaranteed issue basis each time they enroll in the Medicare buy-in plan.

808. How do the Over 50 plans change the current Marketplace plans and private plans?

The Medicare at 50 Act has no provision for the Marketplace plans or private plans.

The Medicare Buy-In and Health Care Stabilization Act of 2019: Enhances cost-sharing subsidies for marketplace plans. Also establishes reinsurance program for entire individual market. The temporary ACA risk corridor program is reestablished for calendar years 2019- 2021.

809. How do the Over 50 plans change existing Medicaid?

Neither of the plans effect changes upon Medicaid.

810. Are there changes to VA and Indian Health Services under the Over 50 plans?

No, the Veterans Administration and Indian Health Services are not changed.

811. How would the Over 50 plans handle coverage during the transition period?

There are no transition provisions needed for any of the plans.

812. How are the public option plans financed?

For both plans, the premiums are set to cover benefits and administrative costs, and deposited into the Medicare Buy-In Trust Fund. With the Medicare Buy-In and Health Care Stabilization Act of 2019 establishes a new and separate Buy-In Fund.

Medicaid Buy-In Plan

813. What does the State Public Option Act entail?

This plan is a state option to offer healthcare based on Medicaid Marketplace subsidies. The state has flexibility to further reduce premiums and cost sharing for Medicaid buy-in. The current sources of private and public coverage are unchanged.

814. What are the rules of participation in the State Public Option Act plans?

Individuals who are residents of states electing to establish the State Public Option Act who are eligible to participate in the marketplace, and who are not concurrently enrolled in other health coverage.

815. How would the enrollment process work for the State Public Option Act plans?

Enrollment is generally for one year at a time.

Buy-in is offered through the ACA marketplace in states electing the option States may limit enrollment to the ACA marketplace enrollment periods.

816. What benefits are offered under the State Public Option Act?

The plan would offer a Medicaid alternative benefit plan, which would include ACA 10 essential health benefit.

817. What cost-sharing provisions are imposed on the State Public Option Act?

Actuarially fair cost sharing is established by the state. The annual out-of-pocket limit cannot exceed the ACA limit ($8,150 in 2019).

818. What are the premiums for the State Public Option Act?

Premiums are set by states to be actuarially fair. The states may vary the premiums by factors allowed by ACA rating rules (age, up to 3:1, geography, family size, tobacco use). The annual premiums are limited to no more than 9.5 percent of household income.

819. What are the rules for providers to participate in the State Public Option Act?

Medicaid providers, including Medicaid managed care organizations (MCOs), can participate in the program.

820. How will providers be paid under the State Public Option Act?

All states are required to pay primary care providers at least the Medicare rates for the buy-in plan and the current Medicaid rate used for other providers.

821. How does the State Public Option Act change current Medicare, Medigap/Supplemental Insurance, and Marketplace plans?

There are no changes.

822. How does the State Public Option Act change existing Medicaid?

This program creates a new state option to offer Medicaid buy-in. The State Public Option Act requires states to pay at least Medicare rates to primary care providers.

The act requires the development of state level metrics of access to and satisfaction with Medicaid providers and appropriates $200 million to support state implementation of the metrics. The act extends 100 percent federal matching funds for three years to any state that is newly adopting the Medicaid expansion. The act adds a comprehensive reproductive health services plan, including abortion services, as a mandatory Medicaid benefit.

823. Are there changes to VA and Indian Health Services under the State Public Option Act?

No, the Veterans Administration and Indian Health Services are not changed.

824. How would the State Public Option Act handle coverage during the transition period?

There are no transition provisions needed for any of the plans.

825. How is the State Public Option Act financed?

The program costs are partially financed through premiums. The costs for the Medicaid buy-in that are not covered by premiums would be financed with federal matching payments in the same way as the current Medicaid program. All excess revenues would be shared with the federal government at 50 percent matching rate.

Administrative costs for the Medicaid buy-in receive 90 percent federal matching payments.

APPENDIX A

Model SBC and Uniform Glossary

Following are copies of the completed 2018 Summary of Benefits and Coverage (SBC) and the Uniform Glossary, which provides a uniform summary of important provisions to assist individuals in understanding their coverage.

The SBC and a Uniform Glossary of commonly used terms are to be distributed to all persons with essential health benefits in an individual policy or group plan. They provide the information needed to compare it to other available options on an "apples to apples" basis. A self-funded plan must prepare its own SBC.

Form language and formatting must be precisely reproduced, unless instructions allow or instruct otherwise. The SBC and Uniform Glossary that are reproduced here replicate the forms, although for purposes of this publication certain aspects of required formatting—such as the font size—has been altered to fit the page.

The SBC and Uniform Glossary are discussed in detail in Parts VII and VIII of this book.

Source: United States Department of Labor, Employee Benefits Security Administration. The Summary of Benefits and Coverage is available at: https://www.dol.gov/sites/default/files/ebsa/laws-and-regulations/laws/affordable-care-act/for-employers-and-advisers/sbc-completed-final.pdf. (Last accessed August 6, 2019)

The Uniform Glossary is available at: https://www.dol.gov/sites/default/files/ebsa/laws-and-regulations/laws/affordable-care-act/for-employers-and-advisers/sbc-uniform-glossary-of-coverage-and-medical-terms-final.pdf. (Last accessed August 6, 2019)

Summary of Benefits and Coverage: What this Plan Covers & What You Pay For Covered Services

Insurance Company 1: Plan Option 1

Coverage Period: 01/01/2018 – 12/31/2018

Coverage for: Family | **Plan Type:** PPO

⚠ **The Summary of Benefits and Coverage (SBC) document will help you choose a health plan. The SBC shows you how you and the plan would share the cost for covered health care services. NOTE: Information about the cost of this plan (called the premium) will be provided separately. This is only a summary.** For more information about your coverage, or to get a copy of the complete terms of coverage, [insert contact information]. For general definitions of common terms, such as allowed amount, balance billing, coinsurance, copayment, deductible, provider, or other underlined terms see the Glossary. You can view the Glossary at www.[insert].com or call 1-800-[insert] to request a copy.

Important Questions	Answers	Why This Matters:
What is the overall deductible?	$500/Individual or $1,000/family	Generally, you must pay all of the costs from providers up to the deductible amount before this plan begins to pay. If you have other family members on the plan, each family member must meet their own individual deductible until the total amount of deductible expenses paid by all family members meets the overall family deductible.
Are there services covered before you meet your deductible?	Yes. Preventive care and primary care services are covered before you meet your deductible.	This plan covers some items and services even if you haven't yet met the deductible amount. But a copayment or coinsurance may apply. For example, this plan covers certain preventive services without cost-sharing and before you meet your deductible. See a list of covered preventive services at https://www.healthcare.gov/coverage/preventive-care-benefits/.
Are there other deductibles for specific services?	Yes. $300 for prescription drug coverage and $300 for occupational therapy services.	You must pay all of the costs for these services up to the specific deductible amount before this plan begins to pay for these services.
What is the out-of-pocket limit for this plan?	For network providers $2,500 individual / $5,000 family; for out-of-network providers $4,000 individual / $8,000 family	The out-of-pocket limit is the most you could pay in a year for covered services. If you have other family members in this plan, they have to meet their own out-of-pocket limits until the overall family out-of-pocket limit has been met.
What is not included in the out-of-pocket limit?	Copayments for certain services, premiums, balance-billing charges, and health care this plan doesn't cover.	Even though you pay these expenses, they don't count toward the out–of–pocket limit.
Will you pay less if you use a network provider?	Yes. See www.[insert].com or call 1-800-[insert] for a list of network providers.	This plan uses a provider network. You will pay less if you use a provider in the plan's network. You will pay the most if you use an out-of-network provider, and you might receive a bill from a provider for the difference between the provider's charge and what your plan pays (balance billing). Be aware, your network provider might use an out-of-network provider for some services (such as lab work). Check with your provider before you get services.
Do you need a referral to see a specialist?	Yes.	This plan will pay some or all of the costs to see a specialist for covered services but only if you have a referral before you see the specialist.

OMB Control Numbers 1545-2229, 1210-0147, and 0938-1146

Released on April 6. 2016

⚠ All copayment and coinsurance costs shown in this chart are after your deductible has been met, if a deductible applies.

Common Medical Event	Services You May Need	What You Will Pay		Limitations, Exceptions, & Other Important Information
		Network Provider (You will pay the least)	Out-of-Network Provider (You will pay the most)	
If you visit a health care provider's office or clinic	Primary care visit to treat an injury or illness	$35 copay/office visit and 20% coinsurance for other outpatient services; deductible does not apply	40% coinsurance	None
	Specialist visit	$50 copay/visit	40% coinsurance	Preauthorization is required. If you don't get preauthorization, benefits could be reduced by 50% of the total cost of the service.
	Preventive care/screening/ immunization	No charge	40% coinsurance	You may have to pay for services that aren't preventive. Ask your provider if the services you need are preventive. Then check what your plan will pay for.
If you have a test	Diagnostic test (x-ray, blood work)	$10 copay/test	40% coinsurance	None
	Imaging (CT/PET scans, MRIs)	$50 copay/test	40% coinsurance	
If you need drugs to treat your illness or condition More information about prescription drug coverage is available at www.[insert].com	Generic drugs (Tier 1)	$10 copay/prescription (retail & mail order)	40% coinsurance	Covers up to a 30-day supply (retail subscription); 31-90 day supply (mail order prescription).
	Preferred brand drugs (Tier 2)	$30 copay/prescription (retail & mail order)	40% coinsurance	
	Non-preferred brand drugs (Tier 3)	40% coinsurance	60% coinsurance	
	Specialty drugs (Tier 4)	50% coinsurance	70% coinsurance	
If you have outpatient surgery	Facility fee (e.g., ambulatory surgery center)	$100/day copay	40% coinsurance	Preauthorization is required. If you don't get preauthorization, benefits could be reduced by 50% of the total cost of the service.
	Physician/surgeon fees	20% coinsurance	40% coinsurance	50% coinsurance for anesthesia.
If you need immediate medical attention	Emergency room care	20% coinsurance	20% coinsurance	None
	Emergency medical transportation	20% coinsurance	20% coinsurance	
	Urgent care	$30 copay/visit	40% coinsurance	
If you have a hospital stay	Facility fee (e.g., hospital room)	20% coinsurance	40% coinsurance	Preauthorization is required. If you don't get preauthorization, benefits could be reduced by

Common Medical Event	Services You May Need	What You Will Pay		Limitations, Exceptions, & Other Important Information
		Network Provider (You will pay the least)	Out-of-Network Provider (You will pay the most)	
				50% of the total cost of the service.
	Physician/surgeon fees	20% coinsurance	40% coinsurance	50% coinsurance for anesthesia.
If you need mental health, behavioral health, or substance abuse services	Outpatient services	$35 copay/office visit and 20% coinsurance for other outpatient services	40% coinsurance	None
	Inpatient services	20% coinsurance	40% coinsurance	
If you are pregnant	Office visits	20% coinsurance	40% coinsurance	Cost sharing does not apply to certain preventive services. Depending on the type of services, coinsurance may apply. Maternity care may include tests and services described elsewhere in the SBC (i.e. ultrasound).
	Childbirth/delivery professional services	20% coinsurance	40% coinsurance	
	Childbirth/delivery facility services	20% coinsurance	40% coinsurance	
If you need help recovering or have other special health needs	Home health care	20% coinsurance	40% coinsurance	60 visits/year
	Rehabilitation services	20% coinsurance	40% coinsurance	60 visits/year. Includes physical therapy, speech therapy, and occupational therapy.
	Habilitation services	20% coinsurance	40% coinsurance	
	Skilled nursing care	20% coinsurance	40% coinsurance	60 visits/calendar year
	Durable medical equipment	20% coinsurance	40% coinsurance	Excludes vehicle modifications, home modifications, exercise, and bathroom equipment.
	Hospice services	20% coinsurance	40% coinsurance	Preauthorization is required. If you don't get preauthorization, benefits could be reduced by 50% of the total cost of the service.
If your child needs dental or eye care	Children's eye exam	$35 copay/visit	Not covered	Coverage limited to one exam/year.
	Children's glasses	20% coinsurance	Not covered	Coverage limited to one pair of glasses/year.
	Children's dental check-up	No charge	Not covered	None

Excluded Services & Other Covered Services:

Services Your Plan Generally Does NOT Cover (Check your policy or plan document for more information and a list of any other excluded services.)

- Cosmetic Surgery
- Dental Care
- Infertility Treatment
- Long Term Care
- Non-emergency care when traveling outside the U.S.
- Private Duty Nursing
- Routine eye care (Adult)
- Routine Foot Care

Other Covered Services (Limitations may apply to these services. This isn't a complete list. Please see your plan document.)

- Acupuncture (if prescribed for rehabilitation
- Chiropractic Care
- Weight Loss Programs

purposes) • Bariatric Surgery	• Hearing Aids

Your Rights to Continue Coverage: There are agencies that can help if you want to continue your coverage after it ends. The contact information for those agencies is: [insert State, HHS, DOL, and/or other applicable agency contact information]. Other coverage options may be available to you too, including buying individual insurance coverage through the Health Insurance Marketplace. For more information about the Marketplace, visit www.HealthCare.gov or call 1-800-318-2596.

Your Grievance and Appeals Rights: There are agencies that can help if you have a complaint against your plan for a denial of a claim. This complaint is called a grievance or appeal. For more information about your rights, look at the explanation of benefits you will receive for that medical claim. Your plan documents also provide complete information to submit a claim, appeal, or a grievance for any reason to your plan. For more information about your rights, this notice, or assistance, contact: [insert applicable contact information from instructions].

Does this plan provide Minimum Essential Coverage? Yes.
If you don't have Minimum Essential Coverage for a month, you'll have to make a payment when you file your tax return unless you qualify for an exemption from the requirement that you have health coverage for that month.

Does this plan meet Minimum Value Standards? Yes.
If your plan doesn't meet the Minimum Value Standards, you may be eligible for a premium tax credit to help you pay for a plan through the Marketplace.

Language Access Services:
[Spanish (Español): Para obtener asistencia en Español, llame al [insert telephone number].]
[Tagalog (Tagalog): Kung kailangan ninyo ang tulong sa Tagalog tumawag sa [insert telephone number].]
[Chinese (中文): 如果需要中文的帮助，请拨打这个号码 [insert telephone number].]
[Navajo (Dine): Dinek'ehgo shika at'ohwol ninisingo, kwiijigo holne' [insert telephone number].]
————————————*To see examples of how this plan might cover costs for a sample medical situation, see the next section.*————————————

About these Coverage Examples:

This is not a cost estimator. Treatments shown are just examples of how this plan might cover medical care. Your actual costs will be different depending on the actual care you receive, the prices your providers charge, and many other factors. Focus on the cost sharing amounts (deductibles, copayments and coinsurance) and excluded services under the plan. Use this information to compare the portion of costs you might pay under different health plans. Please note these coverage examples are based on self-only coverage.

Peg is Having a Baby
(9 months of in-network pre-natal care and a hospital delivery)

■ The plan's overall deductible	$500
■ Specialist copayment	$50
■ Hospital (facility) coinsurance	20%
■ Other coinsurance	20%

This EXAMPLE event includes services like:
Specialist office visits (*prenatal care*)
Childbirth/Delivery Professional Services
Childbirth/Delivery Facility Services
Diagnostic tests (*ultrasounds and blood work*)
Specialist visit (*anesthesia*)

Total Example Cost	$12,800

In this example, Peg would pay:

Cost Sharing	
Deductibles	$500
Copayments	$300
Coinsurance	$2,300
What isn't covered	
Limits or exclusions	$60
The total Peg would pay is	**$3,160**

Managing Joe's type 2 Diabetes
(a year of routine in-network care of a well-controlled condition)

■ The plan's overall deductible	$500
■ Specialist copayment	$50
■ Hospital (facility) coinsurance	20%
■ Other coinsurance	20%

This EXAMPLE event includes services like:
Primary care physician office visits (*including disease education*)
Diagnostic tests (*blood work*)
Prescription drugs
Durable medical equipment (*glucose meter*)

Total Example Cost	$7,400

In this example, Joe would pay:

Cost Sharing	
Deductibles*	$800
Copayments	$1,200
Coinsurance	$300
What isn't covered	
Limits or exclusions	$60
The total Joe would pay is	**$2,360**

Mia's Simple Fracture
(in-network emergency room visit and follow up care)

■ The plan's overall deductible	$500
■ Specialist copayment	$50
■ Hospital (facility) coinsurance	20%
■ Other coinsurance	20%

This EXAMPLE event includes services like:
Emergency room care (*including medical supplies*)
Diagnostic test (*x-ray*)
Durable medical equipment (*crutches*)
Rehabilitation services (*physical therapy*)

Total Example Cost	$1,900

In this example, Mia would pay:

Cost Sharing	
Deductibles*	$700
Copayments	$50
Coinsurance	$300
What isn't covered	
Limits or exclusions	$0
The total Mia would pay is	**$1,050**

Note: These numbers assume the patient does not participate in the plan's wellness program. If you participate in the plan's wellness program, you may be able to reduce your costs. For more information about the wellness program, please contact: [insert].
*Note: This plan has other deductibles for specific services included in this coverage example. See "Are there other deductibles for specific services?" row above.

The **plan** would be responsible for the other costs of these EXAMPLE covered services.

Glossary of Health Coverage and Medical Terms

- This glossary defines many commonly used terms, but isn't a full list. These glossary terms and definitions are intended to be educational and may be different from the terms and definitions in your <u>plan</u> or <u>health insurance</u> policy. Some of these terms also might not have exactly the same meaning when used in your policy or <u>plan</u>, and in any case, the policy or <u>plan</u> governs. (See your Summary of Benefits and Coverage for information on how to get a copy of your policy or <u>plan</u> document.)
- <u>Underlined</u> text indicates a term defined in this Glossary.
- See page 6 for an example showing how <u>deductibles</u>, <u>coinsurance</u> and <u>out-of-pocket limits</u> work together in a real life situation.

Allowed Amount

This is the maximum payment the <u>plan</u> will pay for a covered health care service. May also be called "eligible expense", "payment allowance", or "negotiated rate".

Appeal

A request that your health insurer or <u>plan</u> review a decision that denies a benefit or payment (either in whole or in part).

Balance Billing

When a <u>provider</u> bills you for the balance remaining on the bill that your <u>plan</u> doesn't cover. This amount is the difference between the actual billed amount and the <u>allowed amount</u>. For example, if the provider's charge is $200 and the allowed amount is $110, the provider may bill you for the remaining $90. This happens most often when you see an <u>out-of-network provider</u> (<u>non-preferred provider</u>). A <u>network provider</u> (<u>preferred provider</u>) may not bill you for covered services.

Claim

A request for a benefit (including reimbursement of a health care expense) made by you or your health care <u>provider</u> to your health insurer or <u>plan</u> for items or services you think are covered.

Coinsurance

Your share of the costs of a covered health care service, calculated as a percentage (for example, 20%) of the <u>allowed amount</u> for the service. You generally pay coinsurance **plus** any <u>deductibles</u> you owe. (For example, if the <u>health insurance</u> or <u>plan's</u> allowed amount for an office visit is $100 and you've met your <u>deductible</u>, your coinsurance payment of 20% would be $20. The health insurance or <u>plan</u> pays the rest of the allowed amount.)

Complications of Pregnancy

Conditions due to pregnancy, labor, and delivery that require medical care to prevent serious harm to the health of the mother or the fetus. Morning sickness and a non-emergency caesarean section generally aren't complications of pregnancy.

Copayment

A fixed amount (for example, $15) you pay for a covered health care service, usually when you receive the service. The amount can vary by the type of covered health care service.

Cost Sharing

Your share of costs for services that a <u>plan</u> covers that you must pay out of your own pocket (sometimes called "out-of-pocket costs"). Some examples of cost sharing are <u>copayments</u>, <u>deductibles</u>, and <u>coinsurance</u>. Family cost sharing is the share of cost for <u>deductibles</u> and <u>out-of-pocket</u> costs you and your spouse and/or child(ren) must pay out of your own pocket. Other costs, including your <u>premiums</u>, penalties you may have to pay, or the cost of care a <u>plan</u> doesn't cover usually aren't considered cost sharing.

Cost-sharing Reductions

Discounts that reduce the amount you pay for certain services covered by an individual <u>plan</u> you buy through the <u>Marketplace</u>. You may get a discount if your income is below a certain level, and you choose a Silver level health plan or if you're a member of a federally-recognized tribe, which includes being a shareholder in an Alaska Native Claims Settlement Act corporation.

Deductible

An amount you could owe during a coverage period (usually one year) for covered health care services before your plan begins to pay. An overall deductible applies to all or almost all covered items and services. A plan with an overall deductible may

also have separate deductibles that apply to specific services or groups of services. A plan may also have only separate deductibles. (For example, if your deductible is $1000, your plan won't pay anything until you've met your $1000 deductible for covered health care services subject to the deductible.)

Diagnostic Test

Tests to figure out what your health problem is. For example, an x-ray can be a diagnostic test to see if you have a broken bone.

Durable Medical Equipment (DME)

Equipment and supplies ordered by a health care provider for everyday or extended use. DME may include: oxygen equipment, wheelchairs, and crutches.

Emergency Medical Condition

An illness, injury, symptom (including severe pain), or condition severe enough to risk serious danger to your health if you didn't get medical attention right away. If you didn't get immediate medical attention you could reasonably expect one of the following: 1) Your health would be put in serious danger; or 2) You would have serious problems with your bodily functions; or 3) You would have serious damage to any part or organ of your body.

Emergency Medical Transportation

Ambulance services for an emergency medical condition. Types of emergency medical transportation may include transportation by air, land, or sea. Your plan may not cover all types of emergency medical transportation, or may pay less for certain types.

Emergency Room Care / Emergency Services

Services to check for an emergency medical condition and treat you to keep an emergency medical condition from getting worse. These services may be provided in a licensed hospital's emergency room or other place that provides care for emergency medical conditions.

Excluded Services

Health care services that your plan doesn't pay for or cover.

Formulary

A list of drugs your plan covers. A formulary may include how much your share of the cost is for each drug. Your plan may put drugs in different cost sharing levels or tiers. For example, a formulary may include generic drug and brand name drug tiers and different cost sharing amounts will apply to each tier.

Grievance

A complaint that you communicate to your health insurer or plan.

Habilitation Services

Health care services that help a person keep, learn or improve skills and functioning for daily living. Examples include therapy for a child who isn't walking or talking at the expected age. These services may include physical and occupational therapy, speech-language pathology, and other services for people with disabilities in a variety of inpatient and/or outpatient settings.

Health Insurance

A contract that requires a health insurer to pay some or all of your health care costs in exchange for a premium. A health insurance contract may also be called a "policy" or "plan".

Home Health Care

Health care services and supplies you get in your home under your doctor's orders. Services may be provided by nurses, therapists, social workers, or other licensed health care providers. Home health care usually doesn't include help with non-medical tasks, such as cooking, cleaning, or driving.

Hospice Services

Services to provide comfort and support for persons in the last stages of a terminal illness and their families.

Hospitalization

Care in a hospital that requires admission as an inpatient and usually requires an overnight stay. Some plans may consider an overnight stay for observation as outpatient care instead of inpatient care.

Hospital Outpatient Care

Care in a hospital that usually doesn't require an overnight stay.

Glossary of Health Coverage and Medical Terms

Individual Responsibility Requirement

Sometimes called the "individual mandate", the duty you may have to be enrolled in health coverage that provides minimum essential coverage. If you don't have minimum essential coverage, you may have to pay a penalty when you file your federal income tax return unless you qualify for a health coverage exemption.

In-network Coinsurance

Your share (for example, 20%) of the allowed amount for covered healthcare services. Your share is usually lower for in-network covered services.

In-network Copayment

A fixed amount (for example, $15) you pay for covered health care services to providers who contract with your health insurance or plan. In-network copayments usually are less than out-of-network copayments.

Marketplace

A marketplace for health insurance where individuals, families and small businesses can learn about their plan options; compare plans based on costs, benefits and other important features; apply for and receive financial help with premiums and cost sharing based on income; and choose a plan and enroll in coverage. Also known as an "Exchange". The Marketplace is run by the state in some states and by the federal government in others. In some states, the Marketplace also helps eligible consumers enroll in other programs, including Medicaid and the Children's Health Insurance Program (CHIP). Available online, by phone, and in-person.

Maximum Out-of-pocket Limit

Yearly amount the federal government sets as the most each individual or family can be required to pay in cost sharing during the plan year for covered, in-network services. Applies to most types of health plans and insurance. This amount may be higher than the out-of-pocket limits stated for your plan.

Medically Necessary

Health care services or supplies needed to prevent, diagnose, or treat an illness, injury, condition, disease, or its symptoms, including habilitation, and that meet accepted standards of medicine.

Minimum Essential Coverage

Health coverage that will meet the individual responsibility requirement. Minimum essential coverage generally includes plans, health insurance available through the Marketplace or other individual market policies, Medicare, Medicaid, CHIP, TRICARE, and certain other coverage.

Minimum Value Standard

A basic standard to measure the percent of permitted costs the plan covers. If you're offered an employer plan that pays for at least 60% of the total allowed costs of benefits, the plan offers minimum value and you may not qualify for premium tax credits and cost sharing reductions to buy a plan from the Marketplace.

Network

The facilities, providers and suppliers your health insurer or plan has contracted with to provide health care services.

Network Provider (Preferred Provider)

A provider who has a contract with your health insurer or plan who has agreed to provide services to members of a plan. You will pay less if you see a provider in the network. Also called "preferred provider" or "participating provider."

Orthotics and Prosthetics

Leg, arm, back and neck braces, artificial legs, arms, and eyes, and external breast prostheses after a mastectomy. These services include: adjustment, repairs, and replacements required because of breakage, wear, loss, or a change in the patient's physical condition.

Out-of-network Coinsurance

Your share (for example, 40%) of the allowed amount for covered health care services to providers who don't contract with your health insurance or plan. Out-of-network coinsurance usually costs you more than in-network coinsurance.

Out-of-network Copayment

A fixed amount (for example, $30) you pay for covered health care services from providers who do **not** contract with your health insurance or plan. Out-of-network copayments usually are more than in-network copayments.

Out-of-network Provider (Non-Preferred Provider)

A provider who doesn't have a contract with your plan to provide services. If your plan covers out-of-network services, you'll usually pay more to see an out-of-network provider than a preferred provider. Your policy will explain what those costs may be. May also be called "non-preferred" or "non-particiapting" instead of "out-of-network provider".

Out-of-pocket Limit

The most you *could* pay during a coverage period (usually one year) for your share of the costs of covered services. After you meet this limit the plan will usually pay 100% of the

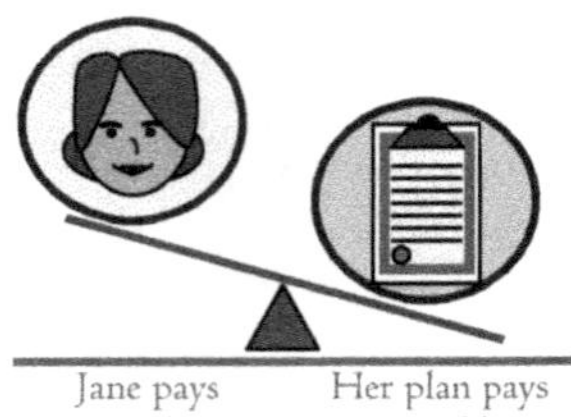

allowed amount. This limit helps you plan for health care costs. This limit never includes your premium, balance-billed charges or health care your plan doesn't cover. Some plans don't count all of your copayments, deductibles, coinsurance payments, out-of-network payments, or other expenses toward this limit.

Physician Services

Health care services a licensed medical physician, including an M.D. (Medical Doctor) or D.O. (Doctor of Osteopathic Medicine), provides or coordinates.

Plan

Health coverage issued to you directly (individual plan) or through an employer, union or other group sponsor (employer group plan) that provides coverage for certain health care costs. Also called "health insurance plan", "policy", "health insurance policy" or "health insurance".

Preauthorization

A decision by your health insurer or plan that a health care service, treatment plan, prescription drug or durable medical equipment (DME) is medically necessary. Sometimes called prior authorization, prior approval or precertification. Your health insurance or plan may require preauthorization for certain services before you receive them, except in an emergency. Preauthorization isn't a promise your health insurance or plan will cover the cost.

Premium

The amount that must be paid for your health insurance or plan. You and/or your employer usually pay it monthly, quarterly, or yearly.

Premium Tax Credits

Financial help that lowers your taxes to help you and your family pay for private health insurance. You can get this help if you get health insurance through the Marketplace and your income is below a certain level. Advance payments of the tax credit can be used right away to lower your monthly premium costs.

Prescription Drug Coverage

Coverage under a plan that helps pay for prescription drugs. If the plan's formulary uses "tiers" (levels), prescription drugs are grouped together by type or cost. The amount you'll pay in cost sharing will be different for each "tier" of covered prescription drugs.

Prescription Drugs

Drugs and medications that by law require a prescription.

Preventive Care (Preventive Service)

Routine health care, including screenings, check-ups, and patient counseling, to prevent or discover illness, disease, or other health problems.

Primary Care Physician

A physician, including an M.D. (Medical Doctor) or D.O. (Doctor of Osteopathic Medicine), who provides or coordinates a range of health care services for you.

Primary Care Provider

A physician, including an M.D. (Medical Doctor) or D.O. (Doctor of Osteopathic Medicine), nurse practitioner, clinical nurse specialist, or physician assistant, as allowed under state law and the terms of the plan, who provides, coordinates, or helps you access a range of health care services.

Provider

An individual or facility that provides health care services. Some examples of a provider include a doctor, nurse, chiropractor, physician assistant, hospital, surgical center, skilled nursing facility, and rehabilitation center. The plan may require the provider to be licensed, certified, or accredited as required by state law.

Reconstructive Surgery

Surgery and follow-up treatment needed to correct or improve a part of the body because of birth defects, accidents, injuries, or medical conditions.

Referral

A written order from your primary care provider for you to see a specialist or get certain health care services. In many health maintenance organizations (HMOs), you need to get a referral before you can get health care services from anyone except your primary care provider. If you don't get a referral first, the plan may not pay for the services.

Rehabilitation Services

Health care services that help a person keep, get back, or improve skills and functioning for daily living that have been lost or impaired because a person was sick, hurt, or disabled. These services may include physical and occupational therapy, speech-language pathology, and psychiatric rehabilitation services in a variety of inpatient and/or outpatient settings.

Screening

A type of preventive care that includes tests or exams to detect the presence of something, usually performed when you have no symptoms, signs, or prevailing medical history of a disease or condition.

Skilled Nursing Care

Services performed or supervised by licensed nurses in your home or in a nursing home. Skilled nursing care is **not** the same as "skilled care services", which are services performed by therapists or technicians (rather than licensed nurses) in your home or in a nursing home.

Specialist

A provider focusing on a specific area of medicine or a group of patients to diagnose, manage, prevent, or treat certain types of symptoms and conditions.

Specialty Drug

A type of prescription drug that, in general, requires special handling or ongoing monitoring and assessment by a health care professional, or is relatively difficult to dispense. Generally, specialty drugs are the most expensive drugs on a formulary.

UCR (Usual, Customary and Reasonable)

The amount paid for a medical service in a geographic area based on what providers in the area usually charge for the same or similar medical service. The UCR amount sometimes is used to determine the allowed amount.

Urgent Care

Care for an illness, injury, or condition serious enough that a reasonable person would seek care right away, but not so severe as to require emergency room care.

How You and Your Insurer Share Costs - Example

Jane's Plan Deductible: $1,500   **Coinsurance:** 20%   **Out-of-Pocket Limit:** $5,000

January 1st
Beginning of Coverage Period

December 31st
End of Coverage Period

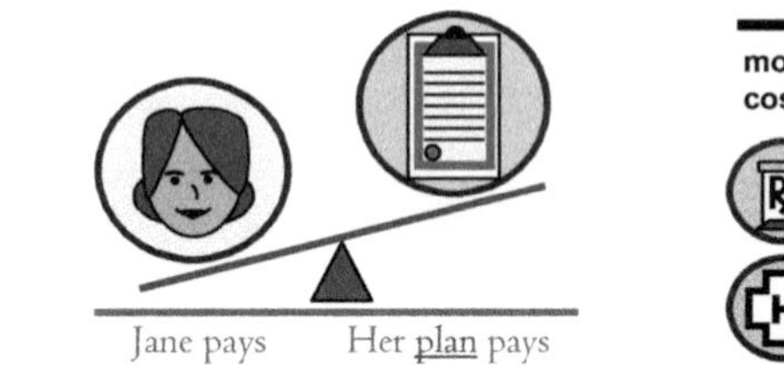

Jane hasn't reached her $1,500 deductible yet

Her plan doesn't pay any of the costs.
Office visit costs: $125
Jane pays: $125
Her plan pays: $0

Jane reaches her $1,500 deductible, coinsurance begins

Jane has seen a doctor several times and paid $1,500 in total, reaching her deductible. So her plan pays some of the costs for her next visit.
Office visit costs: $125
Jane pays: 20% of $125 = $25
Her plan pays: 80% of $125 = $100

Jane reaches her $5,000 out-of-pocket limit

Jane has seen the doctor often and paid $5,000 in total. Her plan pays the full cost of her covered health care services for the rest of the year.
Office visit costs: $125
Jane pays: $0
Her plan pays: $125

APPENDIX B

U.S. Department of Labor Model Notices

Among the PPACA Claims Regulations is a requirement that Notices be provided in a culturally and linguistically appropriate manner and must comply with certain content requirements. Details of the regulations are discussed in this book.

Source: United States Department of Labor.

The links to the three Claims Regulations Model Notices can be found at:

Model Notice of Final Internal Adverse Benefit Determination – Revised as of July 3, 2014: https://www.dol.gov/sites/default/files/ebsa/laws-and-regulations/laws/affordable-care-act/for-employers-and-advisers/revised-model-notice-of-final-internal-adverse-benefit-determination.doc

Model Notice of Adverse Benefit Determination – Revised as of July 3, 2014: https://www.dol.gov/sites/default/files/ebsa/laws-and-regulations/laws/affordable-care-act/for-employers-and-advisers/revised-model-notice-of-final-internal-adverse-benefit-determination.doc

Model Notice of Final External Review Decision – Revised July 3, 2014: https://www.dol.gov/sites/default/files/ebsa/laws-and-regulations/laws/affordable-care-act/for-employers-and-advisers/revised-model-notice-of-final-internal-adverse-benefit-determination.doc

The New Health Insurance Marketplace Coverage Options and Your Health Coverage is found at

Employer Coverage Tool: https://www.healthcare.gov/downloads/employer-coverage-tool.pdf (October 2018) and

Notice for Employers that Do Not Offer a Health Plan: https://www.dol.gov/sites/default/files/ebsa/laws-and-regulations/laws/affordable-care-act/for-employers-and-advisers/model-notice-for-employers-who-do-not-offer-a-health-plan.pdf (Expires 5/31/2020)

Notice for Employers that Offer a Health Plan; https://www.dol.gov/sites/dolgov/files/EBSA/laws-and-regulations/laws/affordable-care-act/for-employers-and-advisers/model-notice-for-employers-who-offer-a-health-plan-to-some-or-all-employees.pdf (Expires 5/31/2020)

(All sites last accessed on September 13, 2018).

Model Notice of Final Internal Adverse Benefit Determination – Revised as of July 3, 2014

Date of Notice
Name of Plan   **Telephone/Fax**
Address   **Website/Email Address**

This document contains important information that you should retain for your records.

This document serves as notice of a final internal adverse benefit determination. We have declined to provide benefits, in whole or in part, for the requested treatment or service described below. If you think this determination was made in error, you may have the right to appeal (see the back of this page for information about your appeal rights).

Internal Appeal Case Details:

Patient Name:				ID Number:				
Address: (street, county, state, zip)								
Claim #:				Date of Service:				
Provider:								
Reason for Upholding Denial (in whole or in part):								
Amt. Charged	Allowed Amt.	Other Insurance	Deductible	Co-pay		Coinsurance	Other Amts. Not Covered	Amt. Paid
YTD Credit toward Deductible:				YTD Credit toward Out-of-Pocket Maximum:				
Description of Service:				Denial Codes:				

[If denial is not related to a specific claim, only name and ID number need to be included in the box. The reason for the denial would need to be clear in the narrative below.]

Background Information: *Describe facts of the case including type of appeal and date appeal filed.*

Final Internal Adverse Benefit Determination: *State that adverse benefit determination has been upheld. List all documents and statements that were reviewed to make this final internal adverse benefit determination.*

Findings: *Discuss the reason or reasons for the final internal adverse benefit determination.*

[Insert language assistance disclosure here, if applicable.

SPANISH (Español): Para obtener asistencia en Español, llame al [insert telephone number].
TAGALOG (Tagalog): Kung kailangan ninyo ang tulong sa Tagalog tumawag sa [insert telephone number].
CHINESE (中文): **如果需要中文的帮助，请拨打这个号码** [insert telephone number]。
NAVAJO (Dine): Dinek'ehgo shika at'ohwol ninisingo, kwiijigo holne' [insert telephone number].]

OMB Control Number 1210-0144 (expires 10/31/2018)

Model Notice of Final Internal Adverse Benefit Determination – Revised as of July 3, 2014

Important Information about Your Rights to External Review

What if I need help understanding this denial?
Contact us [insert contact information] if you need assistance understanding this notice or our decision to deny you a service or coverage.

What if I don't agree with this decision? For certain types of claims, you are entitled to request an independent, external review of our decision. Contact [insert external review contact information] with any questions on your rights to external review. [For insured coverage, insert: If your claim is not eligible for independent external review but you still disagree with the denial, your state insurance regulator may be able to help to resolve the dispute.] See the "Other resources section" of this form for help filing a request for external review.

How do I file a request for external review?
Complete the bottom of this page, make a copy, and send this document to {insert address}.] [or] [insert alternative instructions.] See also the "Other resources to help you" section of this form for assistance filing a request for external review.

What if my situation is urgent? If your situation meets the definition of urgent under the law, the external review of your claim will be conducted as expeditiously as possible. Generally, an urgent situation is one in which your health may be in serious jeopardy or, in the opinion of your physician, you may experience pain that cannot be adequately controlled while you wait for a decision on the external review of your claim. If you believe your situation is urgent, you may request an expedited external review by [insert instructions to begin the process (such as by phone, fax, electronic submission, etc.)].

Who may file a request for external review?
You or someone you name to act for you (your authorized representative) may file a request for external review. [Insert information on how to designate an authorized representative.]

Can I provide additional information about my claim? Yes, once your external review is initiated, you will receive instructions on how to supply additional information.

Can I request copies of information relevant to my claim? Yes, you may request copies (free of charge) by contacting us at [insert contact information].

What happens next? If you request an external review, an independent organization will review our decision and provide you with a written determination. If this organization decides to overturn our decision, we will provide coverage or payment for your health care item or service.

Other resources to help you: For questions about your rights, this notice, or for assistance, you can contact: [if coverage is group health plan coverage, insert: the Employee Benefits Security Administration at 1-866-444-EBSA (3272)] [and/or] [if coverage is insured, insert State Department of Insurance contact information]. [Insert, if applicable in your state: Additionally, a consumer assistance program can help you file your appeal. Contact:[insert contact information].]

<u>**NAME OF PERSON FILING REQUEST FOR EXTERNAL REVIEW:**</u> ______________________

Circle one: Covered person   Patient   Authorized Representative
Contact information of person filing request for external review (if different from patient)
Address:__________________**Daytime phone:**__________________**Email:**______________

If person filing request for external review is other than patient, patient must indicate authorization by signing here:____

Are you requesting an urgent review?   Yes   No

Briefly describe why you disagree with this decision (you may attach additional information, such as a physician's letter, bills, medical records, or other documents to support your claim):

____

____

Send this form and your denial notice to: [Insert name and contact information]
Be certain to keep copies of this form, your denial notice, and all documents and correspondence related to this claim.

Model Notice of Adverse Benefit Determination – Revised as of July 3, 2014

Date of Notice
Name of Plan   **Telephone/Fax**
Address   **Website/Email Address**

<u>This document contains important information that you should retain for your records.</u>
This document serves as notice of an adverse benefit determination. We have declined to provide benefits, in whole or in part, for the requested treatment or service described below. If you think this determination was made in error, you have the right to appeal (see the back of this page for information about your appeal rights).

<u>Case Details:</u>

Patient Name:	**ID Number:**
Address: (street, county, state, zip)	
Claim #:	**Date of Service:**
Provider:	

Reason for Denial (in whole or in part):

Amt. Charged	**Allowed Amt.**	**Other Insurance**	**Deductible**	**Co-pay**	**Coinsurance**	**Other Amts. Not Covered**	**Amt. Paid**
YTD Credit toward Deductible:			**YTD Credit toward Out-of-Pocket Maximum:**				
Description of service:			**Denial Codes:**				

[If denial is not related to a specific claim, only name and ID number need to be included in the box. The reason for the denial would need to be clear in the narrative below.]

<u>Explanation of Basis for Determination:</u>
If the claim is denied (in whole or in part) and there is more explanation for the basis of the denial, such as the definition of a plan or policy term, include that information here.

<u>[Insert language assistance disclosure here, if applicable.</u>
SPANISH (Español): Para obtener asistencia en Español, llame al [insert telephone number].
TAGALOG (Tagalog): Kung kailangan ninyo ang tulong sa Tagalog tumawag sa [insert telephone number].
CHINESE (中文): 如果需要中文的帮助，请拨打这个号码 [insert telephone number]。
NAVAJO (Dine): Dinek'ehgo shika at'ohwol ninisingo, kwiijigo holne' [insert telephone number].]

OMB Control Number 1210-0144 (expires 10/31/2018)

APPENDIX B: U.S. DEPARTMENT OF LABOR MODEL NOTICES

Model Notice of Adverse Benefit Determination – Revised as of July 3, 2014

Important Information about Your Appeal Rights

What if I need help understanding this denial?
Contact us at [insert contact information] if you need assistance understanding this notice or our decision to deny you a service or coverage.

What if I don't agree with this decision? You have a right to appeal any decision not to provide or pay for an item or service (in whole or in part).

How do I file an appeal? [Complete the bottom of this page, make a copy, and send this document to {insert address}.] [or] [insert alternative instructions] See also the "Other resources to help you" section of this form for assistance filing a request for an appeal.

What if my situation is urgent? If your situation meets the definition of urgent under the law, your review will generally be conducted within 72 hours. Generally, an urgent situation is one in which your health may be in serious jeopardy or, in the opinion of your physician, you may experience pain that cannot be adequately controlled while you wait for a decision on your appeal. If you believe your situation is urgent, you may request an expedited appeal by following the instructions above for filing an internal appeal and also [insert instructions for filing request for simultaneous external review)].

Who may file an appeal? You or someone you name to act for you (your authorized representative) may file an appeal. [Insert information on how to designate an authorized representative.]

Can I provide additional information about my claim? Yes, you may supply additional information. [Insert any applicable procedures for submission of additional information.]

Can I request copies of information relevant to my claim? Yes, you may request copies (free of charge). If you think a coding error may have caused this claim to be denied, you have the right to have billing and diagnosis codes sent to you, as well. You can request copies of this information by contacting us at [insert contact information].

What happens next? If you appeal, we will review our decision and provide you with a written determination. If we continue to deny the payment, coverage, or service requested or you do not receive a timely decision, you may be able to request an external review of your claim by an independent third party, who will review the denial and issue a final decision.

Other resources to help you: For questions about your rights, this notice, or for assistance, you can contact: [if coverage is group health plan coverage, insert: the Employee Benefits Security Administration at 1-866-444-EBSA (3272)] [and/or] [if coverage is insured, insert State Department of Insurance contact information]. [Insert, if applicable in your state: Additionally, a consumer assistance program can help you file your appeal. Contact [insert contact information].]

Appeal Filing Form

NAME OF PERSON FILING APPEAL: ___________________________
Circle one: Covered person   Patient   Authorized Representative
Contact information of person filing appeal (if different from patient)
Address:_________________**Daytime phone:**_______________**Email:**_____________

If person filing appeal is other than patient, patient must indicate authorization by signing here:

____

Are you requesting an urgent appeal?   Yes   No

Briefly describe why you disagree with this decision (you may attach additional information, such as a physician's letter, bills, medical records, or other documents to support your claim):

____

____

Send this form and your denial notice to: [Insert name and contact information]
Be certain to keep copies of this form, your denial notice, and all documents and correspondence related to this claim.

Model Notice of Final External Review Decision – Revised July 3, 2014

Date of Notice
Name of Plan   **Telephone/Fax**
Address   **Website/Email Address**

<u>**This document contains important information that you should retain for your records.**</u>
This document serves as notice of a final external review decision. We have
[upheld/overturned/modified] the denial of your request for the provision of, or payment for, a
health care service or course of treatment.

<u>**Historical Case Details:**</u>

Patient Name:	ID Number:						
Address: (street, county, state, zip)							
Claim #:			**Date of Service:**				
Provider:							
Reason for Denial (in whole or in part):							
Amt. Charged	**Allowed Amt.**	**Other Insurance**	**Deductible**	**Co-pay**	**Coinsurance**	**Other Amts. Not Covered**	**Amt. Paid**
YTD Credit toward Deductible:			**YTD Credit toward Out-of-Pocket Maximum:**				
Description of Service:			**Denial Codes:**				

*[If denial is not related to a specific claim, only name and ID number need to be included in the
box. The reason for the denial would need to be clear in the narrative below.]*

Background Information: *Describe facts of the case including type of appeal, date appeal
filed, date appeal was received by IRO and date IRO decision was made.*

Final External Review Decision: *State decision. List all documents and statements that were
reviewed to make this final external review decision.*

Findings: *Discuss the principal reason or reasons for IRO decision, including the rationale and
any evidence-based standards or coverage provisions that were relied on in making this
decision.*

OMB Control Number 1210-0144 (expires 10/31/2018)

Model Notice of Final External Review Decision – Revised July 3, 2014
Important Information about Your Appeal Rights

What if I need help understanding this decision?
Contact us [insert IRO contact information] if you need assistance understanding this notice.

What happens now? If we have overturned the denial, your plan or health insurance issuer will now provide service or payment.

If we have upheld the denial, there is no further review available under the appeals process. However, you may have other remedies available under State or Federal law, such as filing a lawsuit.

Other resources to help you: For questions about your appeal rights, this notice, or for assistance, you can contact [if coverage is group health plan coverage, insert: the Employee Benefits Security Administration at 1-866-444-EBSA (3272)] [and/or] [if coverage is insured, insert State Department of Insurance contact information]. [Insert, if applicable in your state: Additionally, you can contact your consumer assistance program at [insert contact information].]

Health Insurance Marketplace

10/2017

Employer Coverage Tool

Form Approved
OMB No. 0938-1213

Print or download this tool to gather answers about any employer health coverage that you're eligible for (even if it's from another person's job, like from a parent or spouse). You'll need this information to complete your Marketplace application, even if you don't accept the employer insurance you're eligible for. **Write the employee's name and Social Security Number (SSN) in boxes 1 and 2 and ask the employer to fill out the rest of the form. Complete one tool for each employer that offers health coverage that you're eligible for.**

EMPLOYEE information
The **employee** needs to fill out this section.

1. Employee name (First, Middle, Last)

2. Employee SSN

EMPLOYER information
Ask the **employer** for this information.

3. Employer/company name

4. Employer Identification Number (EIN)

5. Employer phone number

Now, enter the information of the person or department who manages employee benefits. We may contact this person if we need more information.

6. Person or department we can contact about employee health coverage

7. Employer address (the Marketplace may send notices to this address)

8. City

9. State

10. ZIP code

11. Phone number (if different from above)

12. Email address

13. Is the employee currently eligible for coverage offered by this employer, or will the employee become eligible in the next 3 months?

○ **YES (Continue)**

    a. If the employee isn't eligible today, including as a result of a waiting or probationary period, when will the employee be eligible for coverage? (mm/dd/yyyy)

    b. Does the employer offer a health plan that covers this employee's spouse or dependent(s)?

    ○ **YES If yes,** which people? ○ Spouse ○ Dependent(s)

    List the names of anyone else in the employee's household who's eligible for coverage from this job.
    Name

    Name

    Name

○ **NO (EMPLOYER** STOP and return this form to the employee. **EMPLOYEE:** Return to your application for Marketplace coverage.)

○ **NO** (Go to question 14.)

continued on the next page

❓ NEED HELP WITH YOUR APPLICATION? Visit **HealthCare.gov** or call us at **1-800-318-2596**. Para obtener una copia de este formulario en Español, llame **1-800-318-2596**. If you need help in a language other than English, call **1-800-318-2596** and tell the customer service representative the language you need. We'll get you help at no cost to you. TTY users can call **1-855-889-4325**.

Tell us about the health coverage offered by this employer.

14. Does the employer offer a health plan that meets the minimum value standard*?

○ **YES** (Go to question 15.)   ○ **NO** (STOP and return this form to employee.)

15. How much would the employee have to pay for the lowest cost plan offered **to the employee only** that meets the minimum value standard*? Don't include family plans. **NOTE:** If the employer offers wellness programs, enter the premium that the employee would pay if the employee got the maximum discount for any tobacco cessation programs and didn't get any other discounts based on wellness programs.

a. Employee would pay this premium: **$**

NOTE: Enter the lowest amount the employee could pay for health coverage.

b. Employee would pay this amount: ○ Weekly   ○ Every 2 weeks   ○ Twice a month   ○ Once a month   ○ Quarterly   ○ Yearly

(Go to next question.)

16. What changes will the employer make for the new plan year?

○ Employer won't offer health coverage as of this date: (mm/dd/yyyy)

○ The premium amount will change for the lowest-cost plan that meets the minimum value standard* and is available to the employee only (Premium should only reflect discounts for tobacco cessation programs. See question 15.)

a. Employee would pay this premium: **$**

b. How often? ○ Weekly   ○ Every 2 weeks   ○ Twice a month   ○ Once a month   ○ Quarterly   ○ Yearly

c. Date of change: (mm/dd/yyyy)

○ I don't know if the employer will make changes.
○ Employer won't make any of these changes.

*A health plan meets the minimum value standard if it pays at least 60% of the total cost of medical services for a standard population and offers substantial coverage of hospital and doctor services. Most job-based plans meet the minimum value standard.

You have the right to get Marketplace information in an accessible format, like large print, Braille, or audio. You also have the right to file a complaint if you feel you've been discriminated against. Visit **CMS.gov/about-cms/agency-information/aboutwebsite/cmsnondiscriminationnotice.html**, or call the Marketplace Call Center at 1-800-318-2596 for more information. TTY users can call 1-855-889-4325.

? NEED HELP WITH YOUR APPLICATION? Visit **HealthCare.gov** or call us at **1-800-318-2596**. Para obtener una copia de este formulario en Español, llame **1-800-318-2596**. If you need help in a language other than English, call **1-800-318-2596** and tell the customer service representative the language you need. We'll get you help at no cost to you. TTY users can call **1-855-889-4325**.

New Health Insurance Marketplace Coverage Options and Your Health Coverage

Form Approved
OMB No. 1210-0149
(expires 5-31-2020)

PART A: General Information

When key parts of the health care law take effect in 2014, there will be a new way to buy health insurance: the Health Insurance Marketplace. To assist you as you evaluate options for you and your family, this notice provides some basic information about the new Marketplace and employment-based health coverage offered by your employer.

What is the Health Insurance Marketplace?

The Marketplace is designed to help you find health insurance that meets your needs and fits your budget. The Marketplace offers "one-stop shopping" to find and compare private health insurance options. You may also be eligible for a new kind of tax credit that lowers your monthly premium right away. Open enrollment for health insurance coverage through the Marketplace begins in October 2013 for coverage starting as early as January 1, 2014.

Can I Save Money on my Health Insurance Premiums in the Marketplace?

You may qualify to save money and lower your monthly premium, but only if your employer does not offer coverage, or offers coverage that doesn't meet certain standards. The savings on your premium that you're eligible for depends on your household income.

Does Employer Health Coverage Affect Eligibility for Premium Savings through the Marketplace?

Yes. If you have an offer of health coverage from your employer that meets certain standards, you will not be eligible for a tax credit through the Marketplace and may wish to enroll in your employer's health plan. However, you may be eligible for a tax credit that lowers your monthly premium, or a reduction in certain cost-sharing if your employer does not offer coverage to you at all or does not offer coverage that meets certain standards. If the cost of a plan from your employer that would cover you (and not any other members of your family) is more than 9.5% of your household income for the year, or if the coverage your employer provides does not meet the "minimum value" standard set by the Affordable Care Act, you may be eligible for a tax credit.[1]

Note: If you purchase a health plan through the Marketplace instead of accepting health coverage offered by your employer, then you may lose the employer contribution (if any) to the employer-offered coverage. Also, this employer contribution —as well as your employee contribution to employer-offered coverage— is often excluded from income for Federal and State income tax purposes. Your payments for coverage through the Marketplace are made on an after-tax basis.

How Can I Get More Information?

For more information about your coverage offered by your employer, please check your summary plan description or contact ____.

The Marketplace can help you evaluate your coverage options, including your eligibility for coverage through the Marketplace and its cost. Please visit **HealthCare.gov** for more information, including an online application for health insurance coverage and contact information for a Health Insurance Marketplace in your area.

---

[1] An employer-sponsored health plan meets the "minimum value standard" if the plan's share of the total allowed benefit costs covered by the plan is no less than 60 percent of such costs.

PART B: Information About Health Coverage Offered by Your Employer

This section contains information about any health coverage offered by your employer. If you decide to complete an application for coverage in the Marketplace, you will be asked to provide this information. This information is numbered to correspond to the Marketplace application.

3. Employer name		4. Employer Identification Number (EIN)	
5. Employer address		6. Employer phone number	
7. City		8. State	9. ZIP code
10. Who can we contact about employee health coverage at this job?			
11. Phone number (if different from above)	12. Email address		

Here is some basic information about health coverage offered by this employer:

- As your employer, we offer a health plan to:

  ☐ All employees. Eligible employees are:

  ☐ Some employees. Eligible employees are:

- With respect to dependents:

  ☐ We do offer coverage. Eligible dependents are:

  ☐ We do not offer coverage.

☐ If checked, this coverage meets the minimum value standard, and the cost of this coverage to you is intended to be affordable, based on employee wages.

** Even if your employer intends your coverage to be affordable, you may still be eligible for a premium discount through the Marketplace. The Marketplace will use your household income, along with other factors, to determine whether you may be eligible for a premium discount. If, for example, your wages vary from week to week (perhaps you are an hourly employee or you work on a commission basis), if you are newly employed mid-year, or if you have other income losses, you may still qualify for a premium discount.

If you decide to shop for coverage in the Marketplace, **HealthCare.gov** will guide you through the process. Here's the employer information you'll enter when you visit **HealthCare.gov** to find out if you can get a tax credit to lower your monthly premiums.

The information below corresponds to the Marketplace Employer Coverage Tool. Completing this section is optional for employers, but will help ensure employees understand their coverage choices.

13. Is the employee currently eligible for coverage offered by this employer, or will the employee be eligible in the next 3 months?

☐ **Yes** (Continue)
13a. If the employee is not eligible today, including as a result of a waiting or probationary period, when is the employee eligible for coverage?_____________________ (mm/dd/yyyy) (Continue)
☐ **No** (STOP and return this form to employee)

14. Does the employer offer a health plan that meets the minimum value standard*?
☐ Yes (Go to question 15) ☐ No (STOP and return form to employee)

15. For the lowest-cost plan that meets the minimum value standard* **offered only to the employee** (don't include family plans): If the employer has wellness programs, provide the premium that the employee would pay if he/ she received the maximum discount for any tobacco cessation programs, and didn't receive any other discounts based on wellness programs.
a. How much would the employee have to pay in premiums for this plan? $__________
b. How often? ☐ Weekly ☐ Every 2 weeks ☐ Twice a month ☐ Monthly ☐ Quarterly ☐ Yearly

If the plan year will end soon and you know that the health plans offered will change, go to question 16. If you don't know, STOP and return form to employee.

16. What change will the employer make for the new plan year?_____________
☐ Employer won't offer health coverage
☐ Employer will start offering health coverage to employees or change the premium for the lowest-cost plan available only to the employee that meets the minimum value standard.* (Premium should reflect the discount for wellness programs. See question 15.)
a. How much would the employee have to pay in premiums for this plan? $__________
b. How often? ☐ Weekly ☐ Every 2 weeks ☐ Twice a month ☐ Monthly ☐ Quarterly ☐ Yearly

---

• An employer–sponsored health plan meets the "minimum value standard" if the plan's share of the total allowed benefit costs covered by the plan is no less than 60 percent of such costs (Section 36B(c)(2)(C)(ii) of the Internal Revenue Code of 1986)

New Health Insurance Marketplace Coverage Options and Your Health Coverage

Form Approved
OMB No. 1210-0149
(expires 5-31-2020)

PART A: General Information

When key parts of the health care law take effect in 2014, there will be a new way to buy health insurance: the Health Insurance Marketplace. To assist you as you evaluate options for you and your family, this notice provides some basic information about the new Marketplace.

What is the Health Insurance Marketplace?

The Marketplace is designed to help you find health insurance that meets your needs and fits your budget. The Marketplace offers "one-stop shopping" to find and compare private health insurance options. You may also be eligible for a new kind of tax credit that lowers your monthly premium right away. Open enrollment for health insurance coverage through the Marketplace begins in October 2013 for coverage starting as early as January 1, 2014.

Can I Save Money on my Health Insurance Premiums in the Marketplace?

You may qualify to save money and lower your monthly premium, but only if your employer does not offer coverage, or offers coverage that doesn't meet certain standards. The savings on your premium that you're eligible for depends on your household income.

Does Employer Health Coverage Affect Eligibility for Premium Savings through the Marketplace?

Yes. If you have an offer of health coverage from your employer that meets certain standards, you will not be eligible for a tax credit through the Marketplace and may wish to enroll in your employer's health plan. However, you may be eligible for a tax credit that lowers your monthly premium, or a reduction in certain cost-sharing if your employer does not offer coverage to you at all or does not offer coverage that meets certain standards. If the cost of a plan from your employer that would cover you (and not any other members of your family) is more than 9.5% of your household income for the year, or if the coverage your employer provides does not meet the "minimum value" standard set by the Affordable Care Act, you may be eligible for a tax credit.[1]

Note: If you purchase a health plan through the Marketplace instead of accepting health coverage offered by your employer, then you may lose the employer contribution (if any) to the employer-offered coverage. Also, this employer contribution —as well as your employee contribution to employer-offered coverage— is often excluded from income for Federal and State income tax purposes. Your payments for coverage through the Marketplace are made on an after-tax basis.

How Can I Get More Information?

The Marketplace can help you evaluate your coverage options, including your eligibility for coverage through the Marketplace and its cost. Please visit HealthCare.gov for more information, including an online application for health insurance coverage and contact information for a Health Insurance Marketplace in your area.

---

[1] An employer-sponsored health plan meets the "minimum value standard" if the plan's share of the total allowed benefit costs covered by the plan is no less than 60 percent of such costs.

PART B: Information About Health Coverage Offered by Your Employer

This section contains information about any health coverage offered by your employer. If you decide to complete an application for coverage in the Marketplace, you will be asked to provide this information. This information is numbered to correspond to the Marketplace application.

3. Employer name	4. Employer Identification Number (EIN)	
5. Employer address	6. Employer phone number	
7. City	8. State	9. ZIP code
10. Who can we contact at this job?		
11. Phone number (if different from above)	12. Email address	

You are not eligible for health insurance coverage through this employer. You and your family may be able to obtain health coverage through the Marketplace, with a new kind of tax credit that lowers your monthly premiums and with assistance for out-of-pocket costs.

EMPLOYER, INC. Health Reimbursement Arrangement

Coverage Period: 01/01/2019 – 12/31/2019

Summary of Benefits and Coverage: What this Plan Covers & What it Costs

Coverage for: Individual | **Plan Type:** HRA

This is a summary. If you want more detail about your coverage and costs, you can get the complete terms in the policy or plan document at www.[insert] or by calling 1-800-[insert].

Important Questions	Answers	Why this Matters:
What is the overall deductible?	$0.	See the chart starting on page 2 for your costs for services this plan covers.
Are there other deductibles for specific services?	No.	You don't have to meet deductibles for specific services, but see the chart starting on page 2 for other costs for services this plan covers.
Is there an out–of–pocket limit on my expenses?	No.	There's no limit on how much you could pay during a coverage period for your share of the cost of covered services.
What is not included in the out–of–pocket limit?	This plan has no out-of-pocket limit.	Not applicable because there's no out-of-pocket limit on your expenses.
Is there an overall annual limit on what the plan pays?	Yes, $1,000.	This plan will pay for covered services only up to this limit during each coverage period, even if your own need is greater. You're responsible for all expenses above this limit. The chart starting on page 2 describes *specific* coverage limits, such as limits on the number of office visits.
Does this plan use a network of providers?	No.	This plan treats providers the same in determining payment for the same services.
Do I need a referral to see a specialist?	No. You don't need a referral to see a specialist.	You can see the specialist you choose without permission from this plan.
Are there services this plan doesn't cover?	Yes.	Some of the services this plan doesn't cover are listed on page 4. See your policy or plan document for additional information about excluded services.

Questions: Call 1-800-[*insert*] or visit us at www.[*insert*].
If you aren't clear about any of the underlined terms used in this form, see the Glossary. You can view the Glossary
at www.[insert] or call 1-800-[*insert*] to request a copy.

EMPLOYER, INC. Health Reimbursement Arrangement

Coverage Period: 01/01/2019 – 12/31/2019

Summary of Benefits and Coverage: What this Plan Covers & What it Costs

Coverage for: Individual | **Plan Type:** HRA

- **Copayments** are fixed dollar amounts (for example, $15) you pay for covered health care, usually when you receive the service.
- **Coinsurance** is *your* share of the costs of a covered service, calculated as a percent of the **allowed amount** for the service. For example, if the plan's **allowed amount** for an overnight hospital stay is $1,000, your **coinsurance** payment of 20% would be $200. This may change if you haven't met your **deductible.**
- The amount the plan pays for covered services is based on the **allowed amount.** If an out-of-network **provider** charges more than the **allowed amount,** you may have to pay the difference. For example, if an out-of-network hospital charges $1,500 for an overnight stay and the **allowed amount** is $1,000, you may have to pay the $500 difference. (This is called **balance billing.**)
- Your cost sharing does not depend on whether a provider is in a network.

Common Medical Event	Services You May Need	Your Cost	Limitations & Exceptions
If you visit a health care provider's office	Primary care visit to treat an injury or illness	Not Applicable	Only expenses for medical care up to available account balance covered
	Specialist visit	Not Applicable	
	Other practitioner office visit	Not Applicable	
or clinic	Preventive care/screening/immunization	Not Applicable	
If you have a test	Diagnostic test (x-ray, blood work)	Not Applicable	Only expenses for medical care up to available account balance covered
	Imaging (CT/PET scans, MRIs)	Not Applicable	
If you need drugs to treat your illness or condition	Generic drugs	Not Applicable	Only expenses for medical care up to available account balance covered
	Preferred brand drugs	Not Applicable	
More information about prescription	Non-preferred brand drugs	Not Applicable	
drug coverage is available at www.	Specialty drugs	Not Applicable	

Questions: Call 1-800-*[insert]* or visit us at www.*[insert]*.
If you aren't clear about any of the underlined terms used in this form, see the Glossary. You can view the Glossary at www.[insert] or call 1-800-*[insert]* to request a copy.

APPENDIX C: HEALTH REIMBURSEMENT ARRANGEMENT

EMPLOYER, INC. Health Reimbursement Arrangement

Coverage Period: 01/01/2019 – 12/31/2019

Summary of Benefits and Coverage: What this Plan Covers & What it Costs

Coverage for: Individual | **Plan Type:** HRA

Common Medical Event	Services You May Need	Your Cost	Limitations & Exceptions
If you have outpatient surgery	Facility fee (e.g., ambulatory surgery center)	Not Applicable	Only expenses for medical care up to available account balance covered
	Physician/surgeon fees	Not Applicable	
If you need immediate medical attention	Emergency room services	Not Applicable	Only expenses for medical care up to available account balance covered
	Emergency medical transportation	Not Applicable	
	Urgent care	Not Applicable	
If you have a hospital stay	Facility fee (e.g., hospital room)	Not Applicable	Only expenses for medical care up to available account balance covered
	Physician/surgeon fee	Not Applicable	
If you have mental health, behavioral health, or substance abuse needs	Mental/Behavioral health outpatient services	Not Applicable	Only expenses for medical care up to available account balance covered
	Mental/Behavioral health inpatient services	Not Applicable	
	Substance use disorder outpatient services	Not Applicable	
	Substance use disorder inpatient services	Not Applicable	
If you are pregnant	Prenatal and postnatal care	Not Applicable	Only expenses for medical care up to available account balance covered
	Delivery and all inpatient services	Not Applicable	
If you need help recovering or have other special health needs	Home health care	Not Applicable	Only expenses for medical care up to available account balance covered
	Rehabilitation services	Not Applicable	
	Habilitation services	Not Applicable	
	Skilled nursing care	Not Applicable	
	Durable medical equipment	Not Applicable	
	Hospice service	Not Applicable	
If your child needs dental or eye care	Eye exam	Not Applicable	Only expenses for medical care up to available account balance covered
	Glasses	Not Applicable	
	Dental check-up	Not Applicable	

Questions: Call 1-800-[*insert*] or visit us at www.[*insert*].
If you aren't clear about any of the underlined terms used in this form, see the Glossary. You can view the Glossary
at www.[insert] or call 1-800-[*insert*] to request a copy.

EMPLOYER, INC. Health Reimbursement Arrangement

Summary of Benefits and Coverage: What this Plan Covers & What it Costs

Coverage Period: 01/01/2019 – 12/31/2019

Coverage for: Individual | **Plan Type:** HRA

Excluded Services & Other Covered Services:

Services Your Plan Does NOT Cover (This isn't a complete list. Check your policy or plan document for other <u>excluded services.</u>)

- *[insert any other benefits not eligible for reimbursement within your HRA]*
- Cosmetic surgery
- Long term care
- Non-emergency care when traveling outside the U.S.

Other Covered Services (This isn't a complete list. Check your policy or plan document for other covered services and your costs for these services.)

- Acupuncture (if prescribed for rehabilitation purposes)
- Bariatric surgery
- Chiropractic care
- Dental care (Adult)
- Hearing aids
- Infertility treatment
- Private-duty nursing
- Routine eye care (Adult)
- Routine foot care
- Weight loss programs

Questions: Call 1-800-[*insert*] or visit us at www.[*insert*].
If you aren't clear about any of the underlined terms used in this form, see the Glossary. You can view the Glossary at www.[insert] or call 1-800-[***insert***] to request a copy.

EMPLOYER, INC. Health Reimbursement Arrangement

Summary of Benefits and Coverage: What this Plan Covers & What it Costs

Coverage Period: 01/01/2019 – 12/31/2019

Coverage for: Individual | **Plan Type:** HRA

Your Rights to Continue Coverage:

If you lose coverage under the plan, then, depending upon the circumstances, Federal and State laws may provide protections that allow you to keep health coverage. Any such rights may be limited in duration and will require you to pay a **premium**, which may be significantly higher than the premium you pay while covered under the plan. Other limitations on your rights to continue coverage may also apply.

For more information on your rights to continue coverage, contact the plan at [contact number]. You may also contact your state insurance department, the U.S. Department of Labor, Employee Benefits Security Administration at 1-866-444-3272 or www.dol.gov/ebsa, or the U.S. Department of Health and Human Services at 1-877-267-2323 x61565 or www.cciio.cms.gov.

Your Grievance and Appeals Rights:

If you have a complaint or are dissatisfied with a denial of coverage for claims under your plan, you may be able to appeal or file a grievance. For questions about your rights, this notice, or assistance, you can contact: [*insert applicable plan contact information*]. You may also contact the Department of Labor's Employee Benefits Security Administration at 1-866-444-EBSA (3272) or www.dol.gov/ebsa/healthreform. [*If coverage is insured, also insert applicable State Department of Insurance contact information.*]

[*If applicable in your state insert: "Additionally, a consumer assistance program can help you file your appeal. Contact [insert contact information]." A list of states with Consumer Assistance Programs is available at www.dol.gov/ebsa/healthreform and http://www.cms.gov/CCIIO/Resources/Consumer-Assistance-Grants/.]*

Does this Coverage Provide Minimum Essential Coverage?

The Affordable Care Act requires most people to have health care coverage that qualifies as "minimum essential coverage." This plan does provide minimum essential coverage.

Does this Coverage Meet the Minimum Value Standard?

The Affordable Care Act establishes a minimum value standard of benefits of a health plan. The minimum value standard is 60% (actuarial value). This health coverage does not meet the minimum value standard for the benefits it provides, but please also refer to the SBC for the [EMPLOYER, INC. Health Plan].

Questions: Call 1-800-[*insert*] or visit us at www.[*insert*].
If you aren't clear about any of the underlined terms used in this form, see the Glossary. You can view the Glossary at www.[insert] or call 1-800-[*insert*] to request a copy.

EMPLOYER, INC. Health Reimbursement Arrangement

Coverage Period: 01/01/2019 – 12/31/2019

Summary of Benefits and Coverage: What this Plan Covers & What it Costs

Coverage for: Individual | **Plan Type:** HRA

Language Access Services:

SPANISH (Español): Para obtener asistencia en Español, llame al [insert telephone number]. TAGALOG (Tagalog): Kung kailangan ninyo ang tulong sa Tagalog tumawag sa [insert telephone number]. CHINESE (中文): 如果需要中文的帮助, 请拨打这个号码 [insert telephone number]. NAVAJO (Dine): Dinek'ehgo shika at'ohwol ninisingo, kwiijigo holne' [insert telephone number].

To see examples of how this plan might cover costs for a sample medical situation, see the next page.

Questions: Call 1-800-[*insert*] or visit us at www.[*insert*].
If you aren't clear about any of the underlined terms used in this form, see the Glossary. You can view the Glossary at www.[insert] or call 1-800-[***insert***] to request a copy.

EMPLOYER, INC. Health Reimbursement Arrangement

Coverage Examples

About these Coverage Examples:

Coverage Period: 01/01/2019 – 12/31/2019

Coverage for: Individual | Plan Type: HRA

These examples show how this plan might cover medical care in given situations. Use these examples to see, in general, how much financial protection a sample patient might get if they are covered under different plans.

This is not a cost estimator.

Don't use these examples to estimate your actual costs under this plan. The actual care you receive will be different from these examples, and the cost of that care will also be different.

See the next page for important information about these examples.

Having a baby
(normal delivery)

- **Amount owed to providers: $7,540**
- **Plan pays** N/A
- **Patient pays** N/A

Sample care costs:

Hospital charges (mother)	$2,700
Routine obstetric care	$2,100
Hospital charges (baby)	$900
Anesthesia	$900
Laboratory tests	$500
Prescriptions	$200
Radiology	$200
Vaccines, other preventive	$40
Total	**$7,540**

Patient pays:

Deductibles	$0
Copays	N/A
Coinsurance	N/A
Limits or exclusions	N/A
Total	**N/A**

Managing type 2 diabetes
(routine maintenance of a well-controlled condition)

- **Amount owed to providers: $5,400**
- **Plan pays** N/A
- **Patient pays** N/A

Sample care costs:

Prescriptions	$2,900
Medical Equipment and Supplies	$1,300
Office Visits and Procedures	$700
Education	$300
Laboratory tests	$100
Vaccines, other preventive	$100
Total	**$5,400**

Patient pays:

Deductibles	$0
Copays	N/A
Coinsurance	N/A
Limits or exclusions	N/A
Total	**N/A**

Note: The amount paid by the plan will be determined by the participant, and is limited by the available balance in the participant's account. No amounts are paid automatically.

Questions: Call 1-800-[*insert*] or visit us at www.[*insert*].
If you aren't clear about any of the underlined terms used in this form, see the Glossary. You can view the Glossary at www.[insert] or call 1-800-[*insert*] to request a copy.

EMPLOYER, INC. Health Reimbursement Arrangement

Coverage Period: 01/01/2019 – 12/31/2019

Coverage Examples

Coverage for: Individual | **Plan Type:** HRA

Questions and answers about the Coverage Examples:

What are some of the assumptions behind the Coverage Examples?

- Costs don't include **premiums.**
- Sample care costs are based on national averages supplied by the U.S. Department of Health and Human Services, and aren't specific to a particular geographic area or health plan.
- The patient's condition was not an excluded or preexisting condition.
- All services and treatments started and ended in the same coverage period.
- There are no other medical expenses for any member covered under this plan.
- Out-of-pocket expenses are based only on treating the condition in the example.
- The patient received all care from in-network **providers.** If the patient had received care from out-of-network **providers,** costs would have been higher.

What does a Coverage Example show?

For each treatment situation, the Coverage Example helps you see how **deductibles, copayments,** and **coinsurance** can add up. It also helps you see what expenses might be left up to you to pay because the service or treatment isn't covered or payment is limited.

Does the Coverage Example predict my own care needs?

X **No.** Treatments shown are just examples. The care you would receive for this condition could be different based on your doctor's advice, your age, how serious your condition is, and many other factors.

Does the Coverage Example predict my future expenses?

X **No.** Coverage Examples are **not** cost estimators. You can't use the examples to estimate costs for an actual condition. They are for comparative purposes only. Your own costs will be different depending on the care you receive, the prices your **providers** charge, and the reimbursement your health plan allows.

Can I use Coverage Examples to compare plans?

1/Yes. When you look at the Summary of Benefits and Coverage for other plans, you'll find the same Coverage Examples. When you compare plans, check the "Patient Pays" box in each example. The smaller that number, the more coverage the plan provides.

Are there other costs I should consider when comparing plans?

1/Yes. An important cost is the **premium** you pay. Generally, the lower your **premium,** the more you'll pay in out-of-pocket costs, such as **copayments, deductibles,** and **coinsurance.** You should also consider contributions to accounts such as health savings accounts (HSAs), flexible spending arrangements (FSAs) or health reimbursement accounts (HRAs) that help you pay out-of-pocket expenses.

Questions: Call 1-800-[*insert*] or visit us at www.[*insert*].
If you aren't clear about any of the underlined terms used in this form, see the Glossary. You can view the Glossary at www.[insert] or call 1-800-[***insert***] to request a copy.

INDEX

References are to question numbers.

A

AARP v. EEOC... 309
Actual method 699
Addiction Equity Act of 2008 80
Adjunct faculty 663
Administrative period 700, 704, 707, 716
   optional 700, 704, 707
Administrative simplification 140
Adult dependent coverage 140
Affiliated group members 694
Affiliated service group 43-49
   rules 153
Affordability 56, 59-65, 69
   safe harbor 56
   waiver 25
Affordable Care Act (ACA) 1
Affordable value plans 674
Age Discrimination in Employment Act 238, 271
Age of adult children 263
Aggregate value of health insurance
   coverage 596
Aggregation rules 181
ALE member 656, 660
   transition relief 660
Alternative minimum contribution
   requirements 182
Alternative penalties 25
American Health Benefit Exchanges 86
Amounts belonging to employees 324
Annual or lifetime limits 140, 238
Annual limits in health plans 242
   exceptions to rules 245
   waivers to limit rules 246
Annual or lifetime limits on benefits 233
   overall 233
   regulations prohibiting 233
Annual report by DOL about self-insured
   plans 485, 486, 487, 488
   aggregate annual report 485
   form 5500 filing 485
Anti-abuse rules 717
   temporary staffing 717
Anti-abuse rules and staffing firms (PEOs) 717
Anti-discrimination laws 271
Anti-Injunction Act 119
Applicable employer-sponsored coverage 593
Applicable individual 70, 581
Applicable large employer 2, 25, 43, 656, 660-661
   and employer mandate 25, 666-669

Applicable large employer (cont'd)
   counting U.S. employees 690-716
   determining status as 684-716
   information reporting 25, 36, 37
   4980H(a) penalty work 672
   4980H(b) alternative penalty work 673
   notice 2013-45 delay 37
Approved clinical trial
   qualified individual 393
   routine patient costs 393
Assessable payment 25
At least 25 percent 580
Automatic enrollment 140, 366
   exclusion 191
Average annual wage 169

B

Benchmark plan options 79
   plan types for 2014 and 2015 79
Benefit nondiscrimination requirement 185
Benefits for mothers and newborns 6
Bona fide employment-based reason 215

C

Cadillac health plan tax 140
Cadillac plan excise tax determination 499
   Cadillac tax 499
   Cadillac tax reporting requirements 499
Cadillac tax 18, 593
   rules 596
Cafeteria plan 67, 124, 171
   amendments 140
   election changes to 137, 265
   ERISA 112
   existing plans 171
   interaction with 89
   new SIMPLE plans 125, 172
   nondiscrimination requirement 125
   regular plan tax rules 172
Cafeteria plan changes 574-578
   cafeteria plan 577
   cafeteria plan penalties 578
   health insurance premium conversion 575
   premium only plans (POP) 575
   $2500 cap on employee FSA
      contributions 574-578
   $2500 FSA 575

References are to question numbers.

Calculating the employer mandate

   penalty 699-716

     actual method.. 699

     administrative period...............................707, 716

     affordability safe harbors.................................. 716

     applicable large employer 699, 703, 707, 709, 712, 713

     calendar year standard measurement period 715

     continuous employee.. 703

     employer mandate excise tax 712

     employer mandate payment 716

     full-time employees 700, 703, 714, 715

     full-time equivalent employees......................... 699

     initial measurement 700-702, 706, 711-716

     look-back method.............................700, 712, 713

     look-back standard measurement period 700

     measurement period 708, 709

     minimum essential coverage 716

     new employee... 711

     ongoing employee 704

     optional administrative period..............700, 704, 707

     optional lookback method................................. 712

     part-time employee 712

     payroll periods 705

     "play or pay" penalty 699

     safe harbor rules.....................................703, 704

     seasonal employee 700-701, 711-712, 714, 716

     stability period 700-703, 706-712, 716

     staffing firm employees 716

     standard measurement period 701, 704, 706,
                          708, 715, 716

       calendar year 715

     temporary employees 716

     temporary staffing firm 713

     transition measurement period........................ 702

     variable hour employee.......... 700-701, 711-714, 716

Centers for medicare & medicaid

   services (CMS).. 246

Certificates of creditable coverage 390

Change calculations

     exchanges and individual tax subsidies 51

Changing insurance companies 207

Chief Justice Roberts.................................... 119

Child

     definition of...251, 665

     for income tax purposes 260

     grandchildren.. 259

     of a same-sex partnership................................ 258

     other categories 251

Children's health insurance program (CHIP) ... 122

Choice of coverage as an employee or

   dependent coverage as a child 256

Church employers.. 238

Civil Rights Act.. 271

Civil rights discrimination by health

   programs prohibited...........................267-271

Claims and appeals procedures...................... 140

Clinical trials 392

     coverage for.. 140

COBRA

     continuation coverage..................................... 348

     continuation notice 343

     provisions 293

     rate of coverage 226

     requirements 405

Code...2

Code section 152(f) children....................255, 259

Code section 4980H 680

Code section 4980H(a) penalty 672, 681

     applicable large employer 672

     minimal essential coverage 672, 681

Code section 4980H(b) alternative penalty

   work 673

     applicable large employer 673

Code section 5000A. *See* Individual Mandate

Code section 6055. *See* Minimum Essential Coverage

Code section 6056. *See* Applicable Large Employers,
   Information Reporting.

Coinsurance 220

     increase in fixed amount.................................. 221

Collectively bargained plans 212, 232

     agreements... 212

     plan rules 212

Common law employees 663

Community living assistance services and

   support (CLASS) act................................. 150

Comparative clinical effectiveness research fee 140

Compensation earned in 2010 through 2012 583

Composite rate to determine premiums 412

Comprehensive 1099 Taxpayer Protection

   Act of 2011 146

Congressional budget office (CBO)................... 51

Constitution's Commerce Clause 119

Consumer price index for all urban

   consumers (CPI-U) 221

Consumer product safety improvement act 238

Contingent workers 663

     adjunct faculty.. 663

     common law employees 663

     definition of employee 663

     educational employees 663

     independent contractors.................................. 663

     look-back measurement 663, 684

     rehired employees 663

     seasonal employee 663, 686

     short-term full-time employees 663

     stability period 663

     student work-study programs 663

References are to question numbers.

Contingent workers (cont'd)
temporary employees 663
temporary staffing firms 663
variable hour employees................................ 663
Continuous employee................................... 703
Contraception and sterilization services.... 282, 285
Controlled group 43-49
members 694
rules... 153
Controlling health plan (CHP) 363
Cost of coverage....................................307-310
Cost reduction 4
Cost-sharing 56, 280
disclosures to individuals 397
features 79
reduction 29, 39, 56, 66
Cost-sharing limits 140, 391
annual deductibles 391
out-of-pocket expenses 391
Counting U.S. employees 690-697
affiliated group members 694
applicable large employers (ALE)..................... 697
controlled group members.............................. 694
full-time employee
definition of 695
optional method for counting 696
stability period 695
full-time equivalents..................................... 697
hourly workers 691
hours of service..................................690, 691, 693
look-back method.. 696
part-time employees 697
salaried employees... 692
variable hour employees................................. 697
Coverage mandates 76-77, 236-237, 240
enforcement of... 238
Coverage terminations................................. 293
Covered health insurance provider........... 580, 583
aggregation rules for related employers 580
Covered services 79
Criminal prosecution 76
Current employees.. 19

D

De minimis rule 583
Deferred compensation 583
Definition of employee 663
Delivery of SBC and glossary 342
Dependent coverage transition rule............... 660
Dependents 30
coverage extended............................247, 269, 270
employer mandate... 665
students...6

Determining unaffordable coverage 25
Disclosure requirement 234
Discrimination...6
Distributing shares of a rebate...................... 324
Distribution of SBC and uniform glossary........ 342
DOL notices... App. B
DOL safe harbor on ERISA plan status............. 112
DOL tools, grandfathered status 200, 201
Double HSA and MSA penalty..................533-535

E

**Early retiree reinsurance program
(ERRP)** 24, 140
expiration of 148-149
reimbursements... 149
Economic substance doctrine 528
"angel list"... 528
excessive refund claims 528
tax-shelter transactions 528
two-pronged test... 528
Economic substance penalties 529
Education Amendments Act......................... 271
Educational employees 663
Effective date of lifetime limit rules...........246-247
EHB
mandate, implementation 77
requirements by market segment 77
8 percent affordability factor 70
Electronic funds transfer............................. 361
Eligibility
adult children... 250
and consumer assistance 97
determinations 29
permissible requirements...........................385-387
Eligible employer-sponsored plan 681
Emergency care................................... 4, 48, 140
Employee
calculating... 32, 34
contribution schedule 66
counting U.S. employees...........................690-716
different types of....................................690-716
in high-risk professions.................................. 596
outsourcing to reduce count 719
premium tax credits.................................40, 59-65
premium tax credits in 2014.............................. 38
pre-tax cafeteria plan payments 326
related individuals 64
whistleblower protections................................ 140
Employee assistance program (EAP)...127, 129, 285,
340, 405, 414, 417
and PCORI... 601
**Employee Retirement Income Act of 1974
(ERISA)** 236, 238, 299

References are to question numbers.

Employee tax credit 25
   calculation of 166

Employer(s)
   and exchanges 87
   appeal 42
   below 50 full time employee limit 43
   counting U.S. employees 690-716
   eligibility requirements for employee
      coverage 385-387
   exchange notice requirement.....110, 349-352, 418-422
   minimum contribution requirement 186
   minimum essential coverage reporting................ 140
   PCORI fees 604
   predecessors 25
   qualification for employer mandate.............. 661, 664
   rebates 314
   reporting 36
   termination of health plans 51
   unaffordable coverage 678
   W-2 reporting postponed 140

Employer free choice vouchers,
   repealing of 140-142
Employer health.. 675
   minimum value... 675
Employer health insurance exchange
   notice.. 140
Employer health insurance tax credit............. 170
   changes for small business 170
Employer incentives.................................588-589
   minimum value test 589
Employer mandate 2, 25, 49, 588-589, 656-724
   "affordable" employer-sponsored
      affordability test 56, 674
   anti-abuse rules... 717
   applicable large employers (ALE).........656, 660, 661,
      666, 672, 684, 686, 697
   avoiding..721, 722
   calculating the employer mandate penalty.......699-716
   contingent workers...................................... 663
   counting U.S. employees.........................690-697
   delay in reporting deadlines........................ 25, 27
   dependents, for purpose of............................. 665
   employer offer of health coverage 671
   exchange subsidies 589
   excise tax 712
   excise tax deductibility................................... 31
   for small employers 191
   4980H(a) penalty 672
   4980H(b) penalty.. 673
   full-time employee, definition of...................... 695
   health insurance 589
   hourly workers... 691
   hours of service................................690, 691, 693
   independent contractors 31

Employer mandate (cont'd)
   information reporting requirements.................... 37
   Medicaid expansion, and 41
   minimizing impact of mandate penalties.........718-724
   minimum value... 675
   new employers 669
   95 percent threshold and property
      health insurance offering 31, 32, 724
   no hospitalization coverage............. 54, 77, 676, 677
   outsourcing to reduce employee count 719
   part-time employees 697
   payment 716
   penalties 11, 34, 52-54, 67, 658, 680
   penalties for certain employers........................... 11
   planning to minimize impact of 718
   related employers... 667
   safe harbors for affordability 679
   salaried employees....................................... 692
   student health satisfying........................... 130, 282
   tax exclusions... 589
   tax penalties,
      examples of....................................... 35, 43
      play or pay......................................25, 140
   temporary staffing 717
   transition relief... 658
   traps for employers to avoid 725
   two alternate employer mandate penalties 670
   two-employer mandate penalties 30, 670-679
   2014 transition relief (Notice 2013-45) 27
   U.S. territories 8
   unaffordable health insurance 589, 678
   variable hour employees..........................663, 697

Employer mandate penalty
   disregarded entities...................................... 658
   health reimbursement arrangements (HRA) 681
   limited non-assessment period 680
   planning to minimize impact of employer
      mandate penalty 718-725
   related employers....................................667, 682
   successor employers...................................... 658
   traps for employers to avoid 725
   two alternate employer mandate penalties 670
Employer shared responsibility payment...... 39, 40
Employer sponsored health insurance.............. 67
Employer tax credit.........................158, 162, 163
   eligibility requirements 153
   for health insurance..................................151-153
Employer-paid retiree prescription
   drug rebate income tax exclusion 545
   "doughnut holes".. 545
   Medicare part D drug coverage program 545
Employer-provided health insurance
   ERISA implications 112-118, 718
   exchange notice 140

References are to question numbers.

Employer-sponsored programs 30
Employers with fiscal year health plans 660
EMTALA 4, 48
Enroll employees automatically 366
Enrollment and re-enrollment 343
ERISA claims and appeal rules 299
ERISA group health plans 112-118
   employer financial involvement 118
   SPD content requirements 492-496
   three-part test to determine 115
ERISA welfare plan 20
   tax ramifications 310
Essential coverage not meeting federal
   guidelines 30
Essential health benefits
   (EHB) 2, 77, 79, 238, 244, 338
   annual limits 242
   benchmark 247
   benchmark plan types 79, 80
   elimination 242
   enrollment determination 79
   lifetime dollar limit 242
   maximum waiting period 379
   package 338
   requirements to be state-selected EHB
     benchmark plan 80
   "typical employer plan" 77
Essential health conditions 388
Excepted benefits 7, 13-14, 236, 242, 245, 408
   and PCORI 601
Excess benefit 593
Exchange *See also* State Health Insurance Exchange,
   Federally facilitated exchange (FFE) 2
Exchange health insurance, private
   distribution of 111
Exchange notice 418, 423
   cost-sharing reduction 420
   customer service resources 420
   employer, definition of 418
   employer distribution of 418
   employers subject to the fair labor
     standards act (FLSA) 419
   model notice 420
   penalties 420
   penalty for failing to give 352
   premium tax credit 420
   purpose and content of 420
   required 349-352, 418-422
Exchange plan, premium credit in 30
Exchange-based OHPs 396
Excise tax 6, 374, 598
   liability for reporting 376
   underreporting liability 599
Excise tax and HIPAA requirement violations 370

Excise tax on high-cost on employer-sponsored
   coverage 595
   accident or disability income 595
   AD&D supplements 595
   automobile medical payment insurance 595
   credit-only insurance 595
   excepted benefits 595
   HIPAA 595
   liability insurance 595
   supplement to liability insurance 595
   treatment of the mouth and eye 595
   value of independent, noncoordinated coverage 595
   value of LTC 595
   worker's compensation 595
Excludable employees 184
Excluding up to age twenty-six 255
Executive order minimizing the economic
   burden
   Patient protection and affordable care act
     pending repeal 46
Expanded coverage 11
Expanded Medicare tax on wages 555-562
   expatriate U.S. Citizens 560
   hospital insurance tax 555
   liability incurred 556
   Medicare tax on investment income 555
   non-cash wages or tips 561
   nonresident aliens 560
   Railroad retirement tax act compensation 558
   reporting of 562, 563
   self-employment tax 555
   wages subject to 557
External review, state or federal 301

F

Factors to allow varying premiums 394
Failure to meet nondiscrimination rules 378
Failure to pay health insurance premiums 91
Fair insurance premiums 394
Fair labor standards act (FLSA) 110, 238, 349
Federal income tax credit, exclusive
   market for 111
Federal long-term care 140
   benefit not implemented 150
Federal poverty level 56, 59-65
Federal SHOP (FFSHOPS) exchanges 106
Federally facilitated exchange (FFE). *See also*
   State Health Insurance Exchanges 111
   fee-shifting provision 238
   fiduciary provisions 315
   generally 614-651
   initial open enrollment period 635
   Section 510 238

References are to question numbers.

Federally facilitated exchange (FFE) (cont'd)
    security act of 1974 (ERISA) 2, 238
    SHOP (FF-SHOP) 634
FFSHOPS (Federal SHOP exchanges) 106
First federal provider nondiscrimination
    law 398
Fixed-amount cost-sharing limitations 222
Flexible Spending Accounts (FSA) 67, 140, 598
Form 8928 376
4980H(a) penalty 672, 681
    applicable large employer 672
    minimal essential coverage 672, 681
4980H(b) alternative penalty work 673
    applicable large employer 673
Four benchmark plan types 79
$500,000 cap
    applicable individual remuneration 581
    deferred deduction remuneration 581
    disqualified taxable year 580
Fraud prevention 318
Fringe benefit tax planning 124-137
FSA. *See* health FSA
FSA/HSA debit cards 532
    qualified medical care expenses 532
Full-time employee 49, 695-697, 700-702,
                                706, 711-716
    changing status of 43
    counting 32
    definition of 34, 695
    95 percent threshold 32, 33
    optional method for counting 696
    stability period 695
Full-time equivalents 697
Future of Health Care Reform 750-825

G

Gay marriage 58, 135, 258, 625
"Good faith" implementation standard 238
Government plans 20
Government-sponsored programs 30
Government-subsidized employer drug benefit,
    elimination of employer deduction 140
Grace period, policies purchased on state
    health insurance exchanges 91
Grandfather provision 140
Grandfathered health plan 2, 11, 21, 30, 77, 79,
         159, 193, 194-197, 208, 238, 247, 275, 339
    checklist 201
    collective bargaining 212
    design changes 218
    DOL tools to determine status 200, 201
    effective date 218
    enhancements or additions 211

Grandfathered health plan (cont'd)
    errors in plan status 377
    health reform requirements of 202
    insured group plan 209
    new enrollees 213
    notice requirements 234
    recordkeeping requirements 235
    retaining 124
    self-compliance tool for part 7 of ERISA:
        affordable care act provisions 200
    self-insured plan 210
    transferring employee plans 215
    transferring of plans 214
Grandfathered health plan status 21-22, 124,
                        194, 195, 197, 282
    losing status of 30, 193, 203, 215, 218
    maintaining status of 199
    preserving status of 199
Grandfathered plan interim final regulations 22
Grandmothered plans 81, 83-84, 205, 206,
                                501-514
Group health plan wellness program,
    regulation of 307
Group health plans 2, 6, 95, 207, 320
    definitions of 127
    requirements on 6
Group insured health plans 321
Guaranteed
    coverage 384
    renewability 6
Guaranteed-issue basis 394

H

Hardship exemptions 71-75
Health claims
    attachment transactions 361
Health FSA 2, 126, 127, 177
    and PCORI 601, 612
Health insurance
    benefit-specific nondiscrimination rules 174
    brokers/agents, role in state health insurance
        exchanges 111
    coverage 95
    exchange 2
    issuer 580
    nondiscrimination requirements 140
    nondiscrimination rules 124, 174
    plans 314
    premium tax 590
    rating rules 394
Health insurance exchanges. *See* State Health
    Insurance Exchange and federally facilitated
    exchange (FFE)

References are to question numbers.

Health Insurance Portability and Accountability Act of 1996 (HIPPA) 6
   electronic transactions 352
   electronic transaction requirements 353
   HSAs 127
   operating rules 352
   regulations 19

Health insurance reform impact on employer fringe benefits 124-137

Health insurance reporting by large employers 453
   applicable large employers 458
   compliance failure consequences 459
   eligible employer-sponsored plan 457
   information required 457
   minimum essential coverage 457
   minimum value.. 675
   noncompliance consequences........................... 459
   notification of reporting to individuals 458
   offering employers....................................... 458
   requirements for applicable large employers... 453, 454
   requirements for "offering employers"................ 453

Health insurance reporting requirements 424-452
   health benefit exchange 450
   minimum essential coverage 448
   notification of reporting to individuals 451
   qualified health plan (QHP) 450
   reporting noncompliance sanctions 452
   required reporting to IRS 424-452
   sanction for noncompliance 452
   who is required to report................................. 424

Health insurers executive compensation 579-583

Health insurers and PCORI fees...................... 604

Health plan fees 140

Health plan identifier (HPID)....................... 362

Health reform...2
   rules that apply to all plans 236

Health reform requirements
   grandfathered plans...................................... 81
   new and nongrandfathered plans 82

Health reimbursement account claims 298

Health reimbursement arrangements (HRA) 222, 681
   eligible employer-sponsored plan 681
   4980H(a) penalty 681
   minimum essential coverage 681

Health savings account (HSA) 67, 127, 132, 133, 135, 139, 159, 233, 257, 325, 399, 499, 532, 534, 593, 596, 597, 598, 669, 672

Healthcare reform...2
   grandfathered plans...................................... 202
   new plans... 203

Healthcare reform (cont'd)
   requirements 202-203
   rules applying to all plans.............................. 202

HHS..2

High deductible health plan (HDHP)...........................222, 267, 391
   deductible amount.. 391

Highly compensated employees (HCE).......186-187

Hourly workers 691

Hours of service................................690, 691, 693
   salaried employees'...................................... 692

Household income
   definition 56, 70
   information 56
   test 56

HRA 67, 112, 127, 129, 133, 140, 141, 222, 297, 298, 340, 392, 417, 499, 532, 533, 584, 597, 598, 601, 604, 606, 612, 675, 681
   and PCORI..601, 612

HSA and annual/lifetime dollar limits............. 127

HSA/MSA excise tax 140

I

Impermissible elimination of benefits 219

Implementation of provisions, timeline........... 140

Inadequate health plan................................. 30

Income below filing threshold........................ 70

Income tax nondiscrimination rules 367
   for grandfathered group health insurance plans...... 369

Increase in percentage cost sharing (coinsurance).. 220

Independent contractors 663

Independent contractors reclassification.......... 43

Individual deduction threshold increase......... 140

Individual health insurance policies
   and ERISA...112-111
   requirements on...6

Individual health insurance premium tax credits..55-56

Individual mandate. *See also* employee mandate 2, 11, 45, 56-65, 69, 586-587
   affordability 56-65, 586
   applicable individual..................................... 586
   as a tax on individuals 119
   dependents.. 70
   effect of repeal.............. 4, 11, 12, 45-48, 54, 55, 70, 76, 120, 137, 140, 639, 742, 745
   effective in 2014 45
   enforcement 70
   executive order for repeal............................... 46
   expansion of state Medicaid programs 587
   inducing individuals to purchase health insurance..... 48
   individuals not subject to 69

References are to question numbers.

Individual mandate (cont'd)
minimum essential coverage 45, 586
minimum penalty 586
open enrollment and guaranteed renewal 587
penalty tax 48
purpose of...48, 587
spouses.. 70
state-based insurance exchanges...................... 587
tax penalty 4, 45, 69, 76, 587
tax penalties.. 140
tax subsidies.. 587

**Individual mandate on employer
decision making, impact of**.....................51-55
Individual market..30
Individual tax credit 30, 42, 56-65
Information reporting requirements.
See also Employer Mandate
delay in requirement 25, 27, 28
interaction with employer mandate
penalties.. 37
Initial open enrollment 97
**In-network, out-of-network providers and
cost sharing** 281
Insurance company rebates......................... 312
Insurance market reforms................................ 17
Insured health plan transparency 489
cost-sharing disclosure rules 489
reporting disclosure rules 490
reporting requirements 490
transparency in coverage disclosure rules 489
transparency in coverage reporting................... 489
Insured plans.. 16
Insurer's ability to terminate coverage............ 288
**Insurer's reporting of health insurance
coverage**..424-452
**Integration of HRA/MERP/QSE-HRA
into other major medical coverage**............. 127
Internal revenue code (Code).......................... 238
dependency tests 261
Section 36B 56-65, 673
Section 162(l) self-employed
persons.. 260
Section 401(h) transfer accounts 260
Section 4980H.............. 8, 10, 25, 28, 29-35, 37, 54,
55, 56, 70, 106, 425, 656-724
Section 5000A(e) 61
Section 6055 .... 425, 426, 427, 428, 429, 449,
451, 457, 459
Section 6056..................425, 430, 431, 432, 433,
434, 442, 453-459, 490
Section 9815 236
IRS
collection tools 76
form 8928 238

K

Key employees... 182, 187
King v. Hodges 58, 60, 140, 286, 639

L

Lack of economic substance 528-529
Large employer..30
**Large employer health information
reporting**.. 140
Liability for excise tax 596
Lifetime limit rules, effective date of.............. 247
Limited non-assessment period 680
Limits for annual deductibles 392
Look-back measurement............. 660, 663, 684, 700
Look-back method
calculating the employer mandate 700, 712, 713
counting U.S. employees.............................. 696
full-time employees 700
initial measurement 700
lookback standard measurement period 700
optional... 712
optional administrative period...................... 700
seasonal employee 700
stability period 700
variable hour employee 700

M

Mandatory coverage 579
**Manufacturers and importers of branded
drugs**...537-542
annual flat fee.. 537
branded pharmaceutical manufacturing
sector 537
branded pharmaceuticals 537
branded prescription drug.............................. 542
controlled group 541
covered entity 538, 539
medicare part B trust fund 537
nondeductible excise tax 537
orphan drugs.. 537
specified government programs 540
Marketplaces. *See also* State Health
Insurance Exchanges
Matching contribution method...................... 187
Material modification.................................. 343
summary of 343
Measurement period 708, 709
Medicaid................................30, 56, 121-122
eligibility 122
expansion..41, 119, 123, 140
expansion not fully implemented 121

References are to question numbers.

Medical Device Tax
Medical loss ratio (MLR) 2, 307-310, 323,
330, 331, 332
    commissions paid to brokers and agents 317
    final regulations 311
    limits 316
    MLR calculation.. 318
    MLR computation 318
    rebates 140
    reports and rebates 140
    requirements 140
    rules 307-310, 316, 323
Medicare Part A premium.................................... 70
Medicare tax increases 140
Medicare tax on investment income 564-568
    electing small-business trust shareholder 568
    estates trust 568
    "Medicare" tax... 564
    net investment income tax 564-565, 566
    passive activity income....................................... 567
    S Corporations 568
    tax-exempt status... 567
    tax-exempt trusts 567
Medicare tax on investment income and
pass-through entities 571
Medicare tax on net investment income
exemption 572, 573
    active trade or business income 572
    gain excluded under Code Section 121 572
    "inside buildup" in life insurance policy 572
    interest on tax-exempt bonds............................. 572
    IRA and qualified plan distributions 572
    other exempt income 572
    proceeds from a life insurance policy.................. 572
Mental health benefits parity..........................6, 80
Merchant IRCs.. 532
Merger or acquisition....................................... 216
MERP.. 127
Mid-year enrollment.................. 47, 54, 89, 97, 109,
140, 213, 282, 343, 377, 378, 418, 586, 587,
617, 630, 631, 635, 660, 700, 704, 707
Mini-med plan... 246
Minimum claim threshold.............................. 297
Minimum essential coverage (MEC).... 2, 25, 30, 39,
42, 45, 55, 56, 66, 77, 580, 583, 681, 716
    STLD.. 738
    unaffordable and affordable 25, 49
Minimum penalty 45, 70
Minimum value... 675
Minimum wage employees.............................. 55
MLR 2
Model disclosure language............................. 234
Model disclosure notice 234
Model DOL notices .... App. B

Model SBC (updated) and Uniform
Glossary.....................................346, App. A
More than 5 percent reduction test................. 227
Multi-employer welfare arrangement
(MEWA) 95
Multiple health packages............................... 227
    offered by plan sponsor 227

N

NAIC Uniform Model Act 300
National average premium 45
National committee on vital and health
statistics (NCVHS)................................. 362
Navigator program......................97, 100-105
Navigators...97
Necessary and Proper Clause 119
Nephews and nieces 251
Net investment income,
    business of financial instruments and
        commodities 569, 570
    definition of 569
    interest, dividends, annuities, royalties and rents... 569
    net gain from nonbusiness property 569
    passive activity income....................................... 569
    property held in a trade or business 569
Network providers... 280
New and nongrandfathered plans,
    additional rules.. 237
New claims and appeals procedures,
    postponement of 295
New employee 711
New employers 669
New plans.. 237
NFIB v. Sebelius **(June 28, 2012)** 119
Ninety-day maximum waiting period............. 140
No discrimination against providers 397
Nondeductible excise tax...................................49
Nondiscrimination excise tax 372
    on grandfathered insured plans 373
Nondiscrimination requirements for
    employer health insurance postponed........ 140
Nondiscrimination requirements for
    insured plans 683
Nondiscrimination rules for health
    program or activity...................................... 140
Non-ERISA 20
Nongranfathered plans 77
    additional rules 203
Nonhighly compensated employees
    (NHCE) 124
Nonhighly compensated individuals (NHCI) ... 372
Nonpayment of premium for Exchange
    insurance...91, 633

References are to question numbers.

Nonprofit hospitals
   additional requirements 515
   adequate charity care 516
   Code Section 501(c)(3) hospitals 515
   community health needs assessment
     (CHNA) 515, 522, 523
   extraordinary billing/collection actions 517
   gross charges 517
   IRS form 990 522
   qualifying for tax-exempt status 516
   written financial assistance policy 517, 523
Notice 2013-45 27

O

Obergefell v. Hodges 256, 258
Ongoing employee 704
On-site medical clinics 414
Open enrollment 47, 54, 89, 97, 109, 140, 213,
        282, 343, 377, 378, 418, 586, 587,
       617, 630, 631, 635, 660, 700, 704, 707
Other eligibility requirements 384
Other entity identifier 362
Overall medical care component (OMCC) 221
Overcompensated employees 579
Over-the-counter drugs 532
   reimbursement for 532

P

Part-time employees 697, 712
Patient centered outcomes research
   institute (PCORI) 140, 600-612
   excluded plans 606
   fee calculation 607, 610, 608
   special rules for FSAs, HRAs and
     QSE-HRAs 612, 613
Patient payment
   prohibition of 280
Patient Protection and Affordable Care Act
   (PPACA) 1, 10, 579
   agencies administering 10
   claims regulations 295
   mandates 17
   Section 4376 fees (PCORI) 140, 601-612
Payroll periods 705
PCORI 140, 600-612
   excluded plans 606
   fee calculation 607, 610
   special rules for FSAs and HSAs 612
PEOs. *See* Professional Employer Organizations
Penalties for spending for nonqualified
   OTC items 533
   Archer medical savings account (MSA) 533, 596

Penalties for spending for nonqualified
   OTC items (cont'd)
   HSA 533
   nonmedical items 533
   tax-free medical expenses 533
Penalty, employer mandate 658, 680
   disregarded entities 658
   health reimbursement arrangements (HRA) 681
   limited nonassessment period 680
   successor employers 658
   two alternate employer mandate penalties 670
Penalty triggers 25
   eligible employer-sponsored plan 25
Percentage of compensation 223
Personal deduction for medical
   expenses 583
PHS Act 2, 14, 127
   prohibition on annual and lifetime dollar limits 127
Plain language 396
Plan communications with providers 140
Plan sponsor contributions 226
   decrease in rate 226, 231
   fixed-dollar amounts 230
   percentage point rules 229
   reduction test 231
Plan values, levels of 79
   bronze 45, 70, 79
   gold 79
   platinum 79
   silver 79
Plan with several insurance options 325
Planning to minimize impact of employer
   mandate penalty 718-725
   applicable large employers 719, 720, 722, 724
   eligible employer-sponsored plan 721
   employer mandate penalties ... 719, 720, 721, 722, 724
   full-time employees 724
   independent contractors 719
   low benefit plan 721
   minimum essential coverage 721, 724
   pre-existing condition 722
   premium tax credit 724
   safe harbor 724
   stability period 724
   standard measurement period 724
"Play or pay" penalty (POP) 25, 699
Policy rescission limited 140
Poverty level tests 56
Poverty-line income levels 56
Pre-existing condition exclusion 140, 254, 394
   for children under age 19 140
Pre-existing conditions (PCEs) 4, 6, 48, 384-388
   definition of 389
   denial of coverage 388

References are to question numbers.

Pre-existing conditions (PCEs) (cont'd)
exclusion, practices eliminated 140
for adult children 253
Premium conversion cafeteria plan (PCCP) 177
Premium conversion plan, special rules 177
Premium tax credit 29, 56, 66, 70
advance payments of 39
Prescription, definition of 535, 536
Preventative care 140
coverage requirements 274, 282, 285, 283
services for women 140, 282, 285
Preventative health services required 272-273
Preventative services 275
recommended 275
Primary care physicians 140
for children and women 140
Privacy safeguards 29
Professional employer organizations (PEO) ... 52-54
anti-abuse rules and staffing firms 717
compliance with employer mandate 52, 54
employer mandate penalties 52, 54
minimum value coverage 54
nature of PEO clients and employer mandate 53
nonminimum value group health plans 54
recipient employers 54
specific issues in regard to employer mandate 54
temporary employees desire for health insurance 54
Provider nondiscrimination requirements
application of 402
effective date of 400
enforcement of 401
Public Health Service Act (PHSA) 2, 236, 238,
260, 310
mandates 238, 306
Section 2713 273

Q

Qualified employees 182
Qualified health plan (QHP) 2, 79, 95, 97, 106,
111, 395
certification 97
options 111
**Qualified small employer health
reimbursement arrangement** 2, 222, 245, 268,
298, 340, 604, 606, 607, 612
cost-sharing restrictions 222
PCORI 531, 534, 537
Qualifying adult child status 261
Quality improvement expenses 318
Quality of care reporting 497
annual report 140
appropriate penalties 497
grandfathered plans 497

Quality of care reporting (cont'd)
improving quality of care 497
quality of care report 498

R

Reasonable break time for nursing mothers 140
**Reasonable medical management
techniques** 279
Rebates 327-329
on terminated plan 315
Reducing the cost of health insurance 310
**Regulation of group health plan wellness
programs** 307
effect of *AARP vs. EEOC* 309
Rehabilitation act 271
Rehired employees 663
Reimbursement for over the counter drugs 140
Reinsurance 97
Related employers 667, 682
nondiscrimination requirements for insured
plans, impact 683
Religious organizations 282
employer, definition of 282
Religious social services organizations 282
**Repayment Exchange Subsidy Overpayment
Act of 2011** 146
Reportable cost 412
Reporting requirements. *See* Required
notices and disclosures and Notice 2013-45
Required disclosures 402-403
Required notices and disclosures 500
adult child coverage opportunity 500
annual limits 500
automatic enrollment (after January 1, 2014) 500
claims and appeals process 500
disclosure of plan data and financials 500
exchange notice 500
explanation of exchange 500
grandfathered and grandmothered plans 500
PPACA prohibition on lifetime dollar limits;
re-enrollment right 500
primary care designation notice 500
re-enrollment rights 504
reporting of health insurance coverage
beginning on January 1, 2015 .... 25, 27, 500
rescission prohibition 500
summary of benefits and coverage 500
uniform glossary 500
W-2 reporting calendar year health care
coverage 500
**Requirements for SPDs to incorporate new
claims and appeals rules** 304
Rescission regulation 288

References are to question numbers.

Rescissions 285-289
   ability to cancel policy retroactively................... 292
Retiree drug subsidy program (RDS) 24
Retiree-only
   exemption.. 16
   plans... 13-24
   stand-alone HRAs.. 245
Retirees
   reporting of healthcare costs............................ 416
Retroactive cancellation or discontinuance of
   coverage... 289
Retroactively terminate a policy for fraud....... 290
Revised rule on contraceptive services............ 282
Risk adjustment..97
Risk corridor..98, 310
Routine patient costs.................................... 393

S

Safe harbor 125
Safe harbor rules 600, 623, 624
Salaried employees' hours of service 692
Same-sex marriage 58, 135, 258, 625
SBC. *See also* Summary of Benefits and
   Coverage (updated) 2
SBC disclosures.. 140
Seasonal employee 663, 686, 700-701, 711-712,
                      714, 716
Self-employed individuals............................ 664
Self-employment Contributions Act
   (SECA).. 555
Self-funded plans 16
Self-insured
   group health plans 95
   health plans 413
Self-only coverage.. 70
Shared responsibility payment 39
Shared responsibility penalties,
   controlled group................................ 682, 683
SHOPs.................... 97, 106, 614, 617, 618, 634, 651
Short-term full-time employees..................... 663
Short-term limited duration health insurance
   (STLD)...646-661
   final.. 744
   minimum essential coverage (MEC)................... 738
   notice requirements 745
   proposed rule.. 743
   state regulation 735
SIMPLE cafeteria plan............................ 180, 182
   benefits of 124, 125, 140, 174, 175, 176
   eligible employer 179
   employer participation in............................... 178
   for small businesses 125
   new 2011 plan.. 172

SIMPLE cafeteria plan (cont'd)
   provisions 188
   workforces over 200 180
Single carrier exchange 111
Single employer 153
Small business health options program.
   See SHOPs
Small employer exception and excise tax 371
Small employer health insurance
   tax credit... 170
   changes for small business 170
"Smaller employer" transition relief.............. 660
Social organizations sponsored by religious
   groups.. 282
Stability period............. 663, 700-703, 706-712, 716
Staffing industry. *See* Professional Employer
   Organizations
Standard measurement period...........701, 704, 706,
                     708, 715, 716
   calendar year... 715
State benefit mandates....................................79
State health insurance exchange....... 2, 29, 56, 122,
                   140, 614-655
   agent and broker roles and compensation 651
   agent and broker training................................ 651
   "Affordable Insurance Exchanges"....................... 63
   consumer-assistance tools 642, 648, 655
   employer notice... 140
   final regulation 97
   functions of 92
   HHS responsibility...93
   initial open enrollment period.......................... 635
   levels of insurance offered.............................. 636
   minimum standards..97
   navigators 647, 648
   nonpayment of premium loophole.................91, 633
   primary federal requirements............................ 94
   regulation of 96
   related individuals 63
   standards for qualified coverage 86
   state health insurance assistance programs 655
   tax subsidies... 140
State health insurance mandates......................77
State partnership health insurance exchanges.
   See state health insurance exchange.
State versus federal claims standards.............. 300
STLD insurance. *See* Short-Term Limited
   Duration Insurance
Student health insurance 736
Student work-study programs....................... 663
Subhealth plan (SHP) 363
Subsidized source of insurance........................ 51
Summaries of material modifications.............. 234

INDEX

References are to question numbers.

Summary of benefits and coverage (updated) (SBC) ... 2, 234, 333-320, 340, 341, App. A
  and exempt plans ... 340
  and glossary on demand ... 336, 343, App. A
  distribution of ... 343
  electronic distribution ... 345
  required format ... 346
  requirement ... 341
  willful violations ... 238
Summary plan descriptions (SPDs) ... 234

T

Tanning bed tax ... 530
  indoor tanning service ... 531
  indoor tanning service excise tax ... 531
  phototherapy services ... 531
Tax credit, general ... 56-65, 140
  calculations (2010 and 2014) ... 166
Tax credit subsidies ... 45
Tax generous health plans ... 591
Tax on Cadillac policies ... 591-599
Tax on sale of medical devices ... 546,554
  computing ... 551
  convenience kits ... 553
  manufacturers ... 552
  moratorium ... 554
  importers ... 552
  taxable medical devices, exempted devices ... 548
Tax penalty ... 45
Tax penalty for individuals ... 11
Tax treatment ... 327-329
Taxable year ... 262
Taxes on executive compensation ... 579
Taxpayer return information, disclosure of ... 29
Technical notice failures ... 238
Temporary employees. *See also* Professional Employer Organizations ... 663, 716
Temporary staffing firms ... 663, 713
1099 reporting failures, expanded penalties for ... 147
1099 requirements, repealing of expansion ... 144
Texas, et. al. vs. HHS ... 76, 120, 242, 639, 640
Three-month rule ... 322
Three-year risk corridor program ... 97
Threshold issue ... 119
Tiers of coverage ... 228
Title VII of civil rights act ... 238
Tobacco use ... 394
Transition measurement period ... 702

Transition relief ... 660
  ALE member ... 660
  applicable large employers (ALE) ... 660
  dependent coverage transition rule ... 660
  employer mandate ... 660
  employers with fiscal year health plans ... 660
  look-back measurement ... 660
  "smaller employer" ... 660
  2015 transition period ... 660
Transparency in coverage reporting ... 396
  and cost-sharing disclosures ... 395
Traps for employers to avoid ... 725
  applicable large employer (ALE) ... 725
  controlled group ... 725
  full-time employees ... 725
  hours of service ... 725
  independent contractors ... 725
  look-back measurement method ... 725
  monthly measurement method ... 725
  seasonal employee ... 725
  variable hour employee ... 725
TrumpCare ... 523, 726-739
Two alternate employer mandate penalties ... 670
2010 Small Business Jobs Act ... 146
2012 Supreme Court decision on health reform ... 111-119
2013 limits on health FSAs ... 124, 125
2015 transition period ... 660
Typical employer plan ... 79

U

Uniform glossary ... 333, 339, 341, App. A
  and exempt plans ... 340
Uniformity rule ... 252
Until age twenty-six adult children
  application to HSAs ... 267
  coverage requirement ... 248, 252
  effective date of ... 249
  rule ... 249
  tax treatment of ... 260
U.S. Territories and healthcare reform ... 8

V

Value-based insurance design plan (VBID) ... 225
  special rules ... 225
Variable hour employees ... 663, 697, 700-701, 711-714, 716
Voluntary employees beneficiary association (VEBAs) ... 260

References are to question numbers.

W

W-2 reporting................ 140, 402-403, 406, 410, 411

    additional rules 408

    aggregate cost for self-insured plans 413

    composite rate to determine premiums............... 412

    controlled group of corporations 409

    determination of reportable cost...................... 412

    EAPS 414

    employee income tax impact 404

    excepted benefits 408

    excess reimbursements 408

    exempt employers 408

    fixed indemnity coverage 408

    flexible spending arrangement......................... 408

    form reporting of employer-sponsored
        health coverage 417

    Health reimbursement account (HRA) ...412, 596, 598

    onsite medical clinics.................................... 414

    penalties 415

    related employers... 409

    reportable cost 407, 412

W-2 reporting (cont'd)

    requirement.. 192, 403

    retirees, reporting of healthcare costs................. 416

    self-insured health plans 413

    wellness programs 414

W-2 safe harbor 56

Waiting period 379-384

    conditions for eligibility 381

    eligibility 380

    limits 382

    otherwise eligible 380

    start of 383

Wellness program 229, 307, 413, 308

    effect of *AARC vs. EEOC* 309

    health plan discount 140

    rules 304-305, 317

    stand-alone programs 306

Women's preventative service 266

    rules 273

Z

Zubik v. Burwell 282-284